THE MEANING OF
"DEMOCRACY"

UNIVERSITETET I OSLO

INSTITUTT FOR STATSVITENSKAP

<u>Skrifter</u>:

Nr. 1. Thomas Chr. Wyller: Nyordning og motstand. Organisa-
sjonenes politiske rolle under ok-
kupasjonen (1958)

Nr. 2. Tertit Aasland: Fra arbeiderorganisasjon til mel-
lomparti. Det Radikale folkepartis
(Arbeiderdemokratenes) forhold til
Venstre og sosialistene (1961)

Nr. 3. Kaare Frøland: Krise og kamp. Bygdefolkets Kri-
sehjelp. En kriseorganisasjon i
norsk mellomkrigspolitikk (1962)

Nr. 4. Thomas Chr. Wyller: Frigjøringspolitikk. Regjerings-
skiftet sommeren 1945 (1963)

Nr. 5. Jens A. Christophersen: The Meaning of "Democracy" as
used in European Ideologies from
the French to the Russian Revolution (1966)

THE MEANING OF "DEMOCRACY"

*as used in European ideologies
from the French
to the Russian Revolution*

AN HISTORICAL STUDY
IN POLITICAL LANGUAGE

BY

JENS A. CHRISTOPHERSEN

UNIVERSITETSFORLAGET

UNIVERSITETSFORLAGETS TRYKNINGSSENTRAL

OSLO

But the most noble and profitable invention of all other, was that of SPEECH, consisting of names and appellations, and their connexion; whereby men register their thoughts; recall them when they are past; and also declare them one to another for mutual utility and conversation; without which there had been amongst men neither commonwealth, nor society, nor contract, nor peace, no more than amongst lions, bears, and wolves.

Hobbes, Leviathan, 1651, Part I, Chap. 4

Words in their primary and immediate signification stand for nothing but the ideas in the mind of him that uses them, how imperfectly soever or carelessly those ideas are collected from the things they are supposed to represent. When a man speaks to another, it is that he may be understood ...

Locke, Essay concerning Human Understanding, 1689, Book III, Chap. 4

PREFACE

The idea for this work and its aim is explained generally in the Introduction. Here I only want to mention that the hero of this somewhat strange dissertation is not a man or an idea or a certain set of happenings, but simply a political word, but a word which is frequently applied in human intercourse. Even at this early stage I feel obliged to say that people eager to know the correct or true connotation of the term "democracy" will seek in vain in this work. Neither may I give a satisfactory answer if people ask more limited questions like what socialists have meant by "democracy", or what Marx meant by the same term, or even what Marx meant by "democracy" before the February Revolution; at least not if short and definite answers are expected. I also want to emphasize that my intention has not been to present ambitious theories concerning political language in general, although I hope that the material presented in this work, or parts of it, may be useful in future research. In this connection it may also be mentioned that my personal approach to research was probably more purely descriptive five or six years ago when the greater part of this book was worked out.

Norges almenvitenskapelige forskningsråd defrayed the cost of publishing and also provided money for research purposes. Mrs. Elizabeth Rokkan and Mr. Alastair Hannay improved my English; and at Oslo University Press, I received very generous assistance from Mr. Trevor Chadwick and from Mr. Thomas Sheahan. I also should like to mention Mrs. Bang who typed the final version of the manuscript. I have further profited from discussions with professors Arne Næss and Jens Arup Seip. I wish to express my gratitude to them all. Most of all, however, I want to thank my wife, Aslaug, for an endless number of unpaid hours in typewriting and proof-reading, and especially for the stimulating and patient support without which this work would hardly have been completed.

Oslo, May 1966   Jens A. Christophersen

CONTENTS

PART B. SYSTEMATIC APPROACH

Related Works

INTRODUCTION

The idea for this work originated as far back as the second session of the General Conference of the United Nations Educational, Scientific and Cultural Organization in 1947. Here a resolution was adopted:

> To arrange for the preparation, by a philosopher of a plan for an inquiry concerning the fundamental concepts of liberty, democracy, law and equality, and concerning the influence of current ideological controversies on different views of such concepts and the actual or apparent conflicts which result therefrom.

This very pretentious project proved impossible to carry out, partly on account of the lack of funds and the shortage of time, but probably also because of the extremely wide character of this scheme. A much more concrete and limited inquiry was planned, and an invitation was sent to about five hundred professional students of ideologies to answer a number of questions relating to concepts of democracy. A collection of answers, together with a preliminary analysis, was published in 1951 in a 540-page UNESCO publication entitled Democracy in a World of Tensions, edited by Richard McKeon and Stein Rokkan. The analytical survey was written by Arne Næss and Stein Rokkan. While a student, I worked as assistant to Arne Næss.

In Democracy in a World of Tensions a section on the historical development of the use of the term "democracy" was originally planned. Our hope had been that contributions from a large number of scholars from different parts of the world and representing different political views would bring forth sufficient factual material for a diachronic survey. This hope, however, proved to be vain. Although we received valuable information on some historical usages, it was barely enough to compose a single chapter. Therefore, no historical survey was written before the more systematic elaboration of problems for which the questionnaire answers partly offered a basis. This work was carried out in Oslo, and in 1956 the book entitled Democracy, Ideology and Objectivity, Studies in the Semantics and Cognitive Analysis of Ideological Controversy by Arne Næss with Jens A. Christophersen and Kjell Kvaløø appeared (345 pp.). In this book I was responsible for writing the chapter "An historical outlook on the different usages of the term "democracy"" (pp. 77-138).

Since the questionnaire answers contained fairly little factual information on the different uses of "democracy", the first thing to do in order to trace its historical development was to try to obtain fairly extensive material for an historical survey. It soon proved, however, to be very difficult to do justice to the high degree of terminological variation which has characterized the use of "democracy" since the French Revolution; though for earlier periods it might be possible to work out somewhat comprehensive surveys, since the term was used infrequently and also since, apart from antiquity, it was not used as a slogan. A similar project would not be possible within a rather limited space with relation to the nineteenth century, when, in several cases, this term was the catch-word of very different political groupings. The sections in question therefore were of somewhat sketchy character, and were entitled "Outlook on European uses etc. " To do justice to the kind of terminological trends mentioned, new research had therefore to be carried out, the results of which are presented in this dissertation.

Chronologically this work is limited to the period between the French and the Russian Revolution; it is also limited to European political thought. The selection of material for this research has been restricted predominantly to persons who have produced written political texts on a certain general level. Exceptions from this rule are Robespierre and Saint-Just, and probably also Cabet, Jaurès, Lagardelle, and Kuusinen. The former two have been included because they were the first central politicians after the ancients to use "democracy" as a positive slogan. In spite of having produced very little of general interest in political thought the four last-mentioned authors have been included because in certain cases they have formulated somewhat important statements containing the term "democracy".

Partly as a reminiscence from the aforementioned works, the word "ideology" has possibly obtained a little too central a position in this book. To avoid possible misunderstanding it should perhaps be added that I do not mean thereby that in political thoughts and political theory we are confronted with a fairly small number of approximately coherent and logical systems. Far from this being the case, we have here a large number of opinions, views, and doctrines. Without doubt it is possible to discover trends, but it is very difficult to construct whole systems when we consider what the authors in question actually wrote. That the word "ideology" has nevertheless not been replaced by another word may be partly because "political theory" would be a little pretentious in this connection, and "politics" a little too wide; in the latter case one would probably also have in mind active politicians like Bismarck and Gladstone.

No method of carrying out this inquiry was regarded as the sole correct one. In my opinion, had the whole work been arranged in the same way as in Part B, "Systematic Approach", it would have been more coherent and also more perspicuous. However, an elaboration of the kind that appears in the "Historical Approach" was nevertheless preferred for a larger part of the work; the reason for this was partly that within this field very little had been written earlier. Obviously a systematic approach could not be based upon material brought forth in earlier research. A second important reason was that a purely systematic approach could hardly give a correct picture of the highly varied terminology as it developed in the language of men like Tocqueville, or Marx, or Proudhon and others, and where its degree of variation in several cases was fairly large. A drawback to this method was the possibility of there being too little coherence between the different chapters. In order to minimize this disadvantage, the "Systematic Approach" was made a little more comprehensive than originally planned.

Concerning the kind of occurrences of "democracy", the attempt to find defining statements has been stressed less here than in Democracy, Ideology and Objectivity. In my opinion such a view was greatly overemphasized in the previous work. Without doubt definitions indicate much about how an author intends to use an expression, but nevertheless they do not tell us much about his actual terminology. And even comprehensive lists of definitions can in no way replace research into occurrences of a more or less inadvertent kind. From a certain point of view, from that of pedagogics, for example, definitions have the advantage that they clarify and organize. But in relation to politics at least, it is a dangerous illusion to regard definitions as necessarily representative of how terms are actually used. On this point there may sometimes seem to be a desire for simplicity analogous to the desire to construct fairly watertight systems in political theory. For teachers as well as for students it is no doubt easier to refer to definitions and systems than to investigate the sources, and as temporary remedies these systems and definitions may be useful. A different situation arises, however, when these tools are regarded as correct condensed characterizations without reservations, for example, when people claim to know much about Marx merely from their version of Marxism, or regard definitions as very representative of actual language. In both cases the texts in question are apt to revolt.

On the wider plane this dissertation does not pretend to bring forward any general description of political language as such, nor does it seek to be regarded as a <u>Tractatus semantico-politicus</u>. Before such a work could be written, similar or, preferably, better research would have to be carried out in the use of other political catch-words, such as "freedom", "socialism", "rule of law", etc. The situation here is almost contrary to that of international politics, where historical research has in many cases brought forward empirical material which forms an adequate basis for further general treatment in political science. Within the study of political language, however, the present demand is primarily for empirical research. To be sure, several books have been written about political language, some of them of significant value, as for example, <u>Language of Politics</u>, 1949, Lasswell, Leites and associates, and <u>The Vocabulary of Politics</u>, Weldon, 1953; the former contains <u>inter alia</u> an inquiry into changes in Comintern political argument. I feel, however, that in several cases problems of an empirical kind are discussed without any serious attempt to carry out empirical research. There are, therefore, within the study of political language, problems that are in part similar to problems within modern philosophy. In contemporary philosophy, and especially in modern logic, analysis of language has played a prominent role during the recent decades. Strangely enough this analysis has only been followed up to a very small degree by research into the actual usage of central terms. In his foreword to <u>Interpretation and Preciseness</u> (1953) Arne Næss says:

> Philosophers disagree abundantly among themselves concerning so-called "ordinary" or "conventional" or "common sense" uses of expressions in conversational languages, e. g. G. E. Moore and C. L. Stevenson on "good", N. Malcolm and Bertrand Russell on "know", and R. Carnap and G. H. von Wright on "probable" ... I do not contend that these philosophers in all cases <u>should</u> have investigated usage by other means than intuition. I merely suggest that empirical procedure should be applied to empirical questions. (pp. vi-vii)

The main intention of this research is not limited to presenting empirical material for possible projects in the future. In addition to the general conclusions drawn in "Systematic Approach", the narrow scope of view which characterizes this inquiry has, I believe, elucidated somewhat important and somewhat neglected aspects of political thought. For similar reasons the treatment of a fairly large number of political thinkers has been preferred to a limited inquiry into a few texts, as is fairly usual in semantic analysis. In other words, the intention has not been to base a certain method of analysis on fairly few occurrences but to attempt to find out how a very central political term has actually been used during an historical period. Furthermore, the high degree of terminological variations in relevant texts makes it very difficult to find shorter texts which contain occurrences of "democracy" of a kind which can be regarded as representative of the general application of the term by a certain political thinker.

I am aware that the method used in this work may invite criticism. Its very empirical, perhaps over-empirical, character may be considered tedious, irksome, and unimaginative; and from an over-all point of view, in relation to methods in social science in general, I would agree with such opinions. In many fields in social science the main question is perhaps not so much to find empirical material as to make reasonable use of empirical material already available. But the contrary applies here, where empirical research has not been sufficiently relied upon, and it is this type of research that is necessary to evaluate the various opinions that have arisen.

PART A

HISTORICAL APPROACH

> Le chaos se cache aujourd'hui sous un
> mot: <u>Démocratie.</u> C'est le mot souverain,
> universel. Tous les partis l'invoquent
> et veulent se l'approprier comme un
> talisman ... Tel est l'empire du mot
> <u>démocratie</u> ...
>
> Guizot, <u>De la Démocratie en France</u>,
> 1849, pp. 9-10

> You asked me about Democracy. You
> say you want to know what it means.
> Shall I try to answer you by merely
> guessing, by expressing an offhand
> opinion growing out of my emotions or
> derived from reading the last edition
> of the newspaper, or from listening to
> the latest blast over the radio? Even
> the best of dictionaries, I have found by
> experience, are unsatisfactory for the
> meaning of the leading words used in the
> humanities. I know only one way to
> attempt to answer. That is to search
> for the origin of the word and explore
> its usage by persons of some intelligence
> up to our time.
>
> Charles A. Beard, <u>The Republic. Con-
> versations on Fundamentals</u>, N.Y. 1946,
> p. 28

CHAPTER I

REVOLUTIONARY IDEOLOGIES

1. Robespierre

From a quantitative point of view, "democracy" does not occupy a central position in the terminology of Robespierre. In contrast to later political leaders, many of whom use "democracy" frequently, the application of this term by Robespierre is almost exclusively limited to a single speech. This does not imply, however, that the term is unconnected with important areas of his political thinking, or that its application does not reveal central elements in his ideology, especially since the speech in question is very probably his most important from the point of view of political theory.

On 5 February 1794, or 18 pluviôse year II, Robespierre made the speech entitled "Rapport sur les principes qui doivent guider la convention." Solemnly he called upon the French people to realize the destiny of mankind in order that France, already illustrious among enslaved countries, should exceed the glory of any free people of any time, and further, become the model of nations, the fear of oppressors, the consolation of the suppressed, and the ornament of the universe. Robespierre then asked:

> Quelle nature de gouvernement peut réaliser ces prodiges? Le seul gouvernement démocratique ou républicain: ces deux mots sont synonymes, malgré les abus du langage vulgaire: car l'aristocratie n'est pas plus la république que la monarchie. [1]

In this initial statement we are evidently faced with meta-occurrences of the terms "republican" and "democratic". And it is also clear that Robespierre put forward this relation of synonymity between "democratic" and "republican" in spite of his awareness that other people used the terms with different significations. This kind of application was further declared to represent a terminological misuse, and we may here suppose that Robespierre had in mind people who used "republic" with a rather wide signification, as the designation of a broader concept of which both 'democracy' and 'aristocracy' were species. It is a little difficult to decide how widespread Robespierre held this alleged misuse to have been in the vernacular. According to one point of view, we may suppose that Robespierre used "langage vulgaire" almost synonymously with the English expression "popular language", [2] and in this way intended to mark out his own terminology against a predominant trend among his contemporaries. But we may also suppose that mainly, or even exclusively, he wished to express his dislike of a certain kind of terminology. Thus "vulgaire" would have been used dyslogistically, or with a negative value-judgement implicit in its signification. The latter alternative seems to be the more probable, especially since "people" and "popular" are terms nearly always treated with great reverence by Robespierre, and since it is generally easier to express a dislike of terminology which differs from that of the sender than to present this alleged misuse as predominant in the vernacular; though Robespierre might with good reason have put forward the proposition that a relationship of non-synonymity between "democratic" and "republican" was equally predominant in existing language.

The use of the terms "democratic" and "republican" to characterize that form of government which was to make France the ornament of the universe and the model of nations is most evidently honorific. At the same time this use was accompanied by accusations of misuse. This tendency to accuse other people of misusing terms used in honorific fashion by oneself is rather widespread in political language. The trend is very common today, and it is scarcely an accident that these two phenomena operate together in the above quotation. Here, however, the charges of misuse seem mainly to have been directed against the application of "republican" and not so much against that of "democratic".

Robespierre proceeded:

> La démocratie n'est pas un état où le peuple, continuellement assemblé, règle par lui-même toutes les affaires publiques, encore moins celui où cent mille fractions du peuple, par des mesures isolées, précipitées et contradictoires, décideraient du sort de la société entière: un tel gouvernement n'a jamais existé, et il ne pourrait exister que pour ramener le peuple au despotisme.

This declaration is one of the most important in the history of the semantics of "democracy". As far as I know, it was the first time that it was positively stated that democracy is not a direct or non-representative rule by the whole people. From a broader point of view it may be said that the tendency to restrict "democracy" to connote a direct form of popular participation in governmental affairs and the making of laws was not merely the sole application of this term in antiquity, when representation was unknown, but was also the practically exclusive usage of "democracy" before Robespierre made this speech. In the language of Hobbes, Spinoza, and Montesquieu, [3] for example, we shall find very clear proof of the restriction of the signification of "democracy" to cover exclusively the area of direct popular rule. Thus Spinoza explicitly held aristocracy, in contrast to democracy, to be rule by elected representatives. [4] Montesquieu also seems to have held rule by any form of elected representatives to be entirely incompatible with what he regarded as democracy. Of the system of representation, he said:

> Le grand avantage des représentants c'est qui'ils sont capables de discuter des affaires. Le peuple n'y est point du tout propre: ce que forme un des inconvénients de la démocratie.

This way of using "democracy" is an essential characteristic of American political vocabulary both before and during the American Revolution. [5] This was probably an important factor explaining why "democracy" was not used as a slogan in America up to that time. The only signs of any new way of using the term are to be found in a letter from Alexander Hamilton to Gouverneur Morris, written in May 1777, where he used a more complex designation, "representative democracy", but where, at the same time, unqualified "democracy" most probably signified a direct and unstable kind of rule. [6] A more differentiated verbal use is found in Rights of Man by Thomas Paine (1792) and in Political Justice by Godwin (1793). These works will be treated in a separate chapter, but we wish to point out that the use of "democracy" by Godwin is somewhat similar to that of Robespierre, particularly since Godwin did not hold rule by representatives to be incompatible with what he considered to be democracy. In neither of these works, however, are we told that democracy is not a form of direct rule.

At an earlier date even Robespierre himself had probably used "absolute democracy" in the sense of non-representative government. In "Discours sur la constitution" (10 May 1793) Robespierre declared that the people themselves were good and sound, but that their delegates might be corruptible. To preserve the virtue of the people in governmental affairs he proposed that all popularly elected magistrates and public functionaries should hold revocable office. Every section of the French republic would in this way come under an influence similar to that of the popular tribunes in Rome.

> C'est à chaque section de la République française que je renvoi la puissance tribunicienne; et il est facile de l'organiser d'une manière également éloignée des tempêtes de la démocratie absolue et de la perfide tranquillité du despotisme représentatif. [7]

What Robespierre held to be absolute democracy on the one hand and representative despotism on the other seem to have been two contrasting phenomena, both of them extremes between which a middle course was to be found. This indicates that representative government was the opposite, or nearly the opposite, of absolute democracy; this probably implies that Robespierre at that time used "absolute democracy" with a signification excluding any kind of representation.

In "Rapport sur les principes..." after giving a negative definition of democracy, Robespierre continued with a positive one:

> La démocratie est un état où le people souverain, guidé par des lois qui sont son ouvrage, fait par lui-même tout ce qu'il peut bien faire, et par des délégués tout ce qui'il ne peut faire lui-même. [8]

"Democracy" is here scarcely used as the designation of a concept in which any kind of direct popular action was excluded. The people themselves could do what they were capable of doing, but it was probably also a necessary condition that they should act through delegates or representatives in questions they could not handle themselves.

The ethical properties of the revolutionary regime provide another aspect of Robespierre's use of "democracy". He frequently emphasized virtue as the fundamental principle of this new kind of rule. And according to him, virtue first of all meant an ardent and enduring love of one's native country and its laws; this implied a love of equality as well as the giving of preference to all public interests before private ones.

> Non seulement la vertu est l'âme de la démocratie; mais elle ne peut exister que dans ce gouvernement. [9]

According to this statement it would seem that virtue was not only a necessary but also a sufficient condition of a form of rule deserving the label "democracy". This implies that a form of rule was a democracy if, and only if, it was marked by what Robespierre held to be virtue. Thus "democracy" would have been synonymous, or almost synonymous, with "virtuous rule", or some related expression.

The relationship between popular rule and virtue, and between virtue and terror, receives further attention when Robespierre states later:

> Si le ressort du gouvernement populaire dans la paix est la vertu, le ressort du gouvernement populaire en révolution est à la fois la vertu et la terreur; la vertu, sans laquelle la terreur est funeste; la terreur, sans laquelle la vertu est impuissante. La terreur n'est autre chose que la justice prompte, sévère, inflexible; elle est donc une émanation de la vertu. [10]

According to the first part of this quotation terror was restricted to times of revolution. Here it may be objected that the claim that virtue without terror is powerless does not refer to times of revolution only; Robespierre would hardly have been in favour of powerless virtue even in times of peace. On the other hand, his statements concerning terror and virtue were made after he had described terror as the resort of popular rule in times of revolution, and it may therefore be inferred that Robespierre held virtue, in times of revolution only, to be powerless when not connected with terror. It is in any case beyond doubt that Robespierre considered his own time to be a revolutionary one, and that therefore any attempt to give society a virtuous stamp would represent a utopian kind of policy if the use of terror were renounced. Since virtue, and a virtuous form of rule, occupies a most central, if not exclusive, part of the signification attributed to "democracy", these statements about terror and virtue are indirectly of high importance to our inquiry. According to these statements it seems that while it is hardly possible to link democracy to terror, when considered from a general point of view, Robespierre would not regard a form of rule as democratic that made no use of terror during times of revolution. The relationship between terror and democracy is directly treated when Robespierre continues:

> ... elle [la terreur] est moins un principe particulier qu'une conséquence du principe général de la démocratie appliqué aux plus pressants besoins de la patrie. [11]

Here again, terror is predominantly associated with democracy as a means in times of emergency, although this statement may also suggest that terror, from a general point of view, was a part of what he held to be democracy. Robespierre did not say, for example, that terror was not a peculiar principle of democracy, only that it was less a principle than a consequence of the general principles of democracy when applied in times of emergency. It may be suggested that this somewhat ambiguous attitude towards the question of democracy and terror may reflect Robespierre's similarly ambiguous attitude in his defence of the principle of terror.

With regard to the designation of contemporary government in France, Robespierre stated several times that France was a democracy and even that she represented the first true democracy in the world:

> ... les Français sont le premier peuple du monde qui ait établi la véritable démocratie... [12]

This rule is not without exceptions, however. A little earlier Robespierre had held,

> ... pour fonder et consolider parmi nous la démocratie, pour arriver au règne paisible des lois constitutionelles, il faut terminer la guerre

de la liberté contre la tyrannie, et traverser heureusement les orages
de la révolution. [13]

Here, "democracy" was most probably used synonymously with "peaceful
reign of constitutional laws", signifying something which was not yet established in France, but which was to be obtained when wars and revolutions
were in the past. This latter statement clearly contradicts the former.
We might perhaps have accepted that France was a democracy -- not yet
a true democracy, but not the contrary version presented here.

As we found in our discussion of Robespierre's views on the relationship between democracy and terror, this ambiguity seems to mean that
Robespierre identified virtuous rule partly with existing Jacobin dictatorship and partly with something which was to be obtained when strict and
merciless dictatorship would no longer be held necessary. This tendency
to idealize the kind of rule which is held to be the final aim of a revolutionary government and, at the same time, the kind of emergency rule which
is considered as the only means for attaining that aim, is a rather common
tendency among members of revolutionary governments, as is also their
way of mingling these two phenomena, using thin lines of demarcation or
none at all. It may therefore be regarded as fairly typical that this tendency
appears in Robespierre's use of "democracy".

The occurrences in this speech of the terms "democracy" and "democratic" which we have not quoted here seem to be of small or no importance
as regards the signification attributed to this term. The essential aspects
are without doubt the ways of including representative forms of governing
and of identifying this signification with what Robespierre held to be virtuous
rule -- something which is confirmed by all the occurrences in this speech.
From a quantitative point of view, these terms were not very frequently
used. They occur about fifteen times, and nearly all of them are in the
first half. His way of linking "democracy" intimately with the central
topics in his speech may nevertheless allow us to consider this word as a
key term in his main presentation of public ethics, which Robespierre almost exclusively limited to the problem of Virtue and Terror. In spite of
this relative importance, we find, as we have stated, almost no continuation
of this terminological trend. On 7 May 1794, or 18 floréal year II, Robespierre said in the National Convention:

Vous pouvez montrer au monde le spectacle nouveau de la démocratie
affermie dans une vaste empire. [14]

But except for this rather sporadic occurrence, I have not been able
to find any use of the term after February 1794. It does not occur in his
last speech, 8 thermidor, or 26 July, in spite of his broad treatment of
questions concerning public virtue. Thus "democracy" leaves Robespierre's
vocabulary almost as suddenly as it enters it. I am not able to explain why
the honorific application from February did not continue.

As far as the period before February 1794 is concerned we have only
been able to find the occurrence of "absolute democracy" quoted above,
where this expression signified something of which Robespierre did not
approve. If we inquire why Robespierre introduced a new term in his
speech on the principle of public morals, we may mention that "republic",
always a most central term in his political vocabulary, had been used in
honorific fashion by his political antagonists, and had thus perhaps become
less adequate as a key term. In the spring of 1792 Robespierre charged

Brissot, Condorcet, and their associates of conspiring with Lafayette, and also of being in favour of great moderation. Making a direct appeal he continued:

> Vous fîtes tout à coup retentir le mot de _république,_ Condorcet publie un traité sur la _république,_ dont les principes, il est vrai, etaient moins populaires que ceux de notre Constitution actuelle; Brissot répand un journal intitulé _Le Republicain,_ et qui n'avait de populaire que le titre.[15]

This formulation was possibly quite forgotten two years later. We may nevertheless presume that similar thoughts may have contributed to his wish to introduce a new term in his vocabulary, especially when emphasizing the most central principles in his political thinking. The charge that others misuse the term "republic" is also rather evident in the first quotation from Robespierre in this section. Charges of misuse did not imply that Robespierre ceased the honorific application of "republic". We have seen that he declared "republican" to be synonymous with "democratic", and in contrast to the absence of "democracy", "republic" also figures in his last speech where he coined the famous sentence,

> ... elle existe, cette ambition généreuse de fonder sur la terre la première République du monde. [16]

We may therefore assume that Robespierre's main intention in introducing "democracy" and "democratic" in his terminology was to delineate the kind of republic which, according to him, was the only one to deserve its name.

Broadly speaking, the relative importance of Robespierre's use of "democracy" is greatly increased by the fact that it represents the first honorific use of this term by any leading politician of any country since antiquity. As far as I know, the sole honorific occurrences during this extremely long period are found among a few early settlers in the New England colonies. [17] Such honorific application of the term "democracy" did not continue in American terminology, however, nor has it been found in the European. This absence was presumably caused by the habit referred to above of letting this term exclusively signify a direct kind of government. As regards the contemporaries of Robespierre, a fairly frequent appreciative usage of "democracy" is evident in _Political Justice,_ by William Godwin. This work was printed in 1793, but his use of the term does not alter the fact that the great Jacobin was the first leading statesman to use "democracy" as a laudatory designation of his own country since the Funeral Oration of Pericles in 431 B.C. [18] Robespierre can thus be considered to have revived a terminological trend which is almost universal today, but which at the time had been in abeyance for more than two thousand years.

2. Saint-Just

Robespierre used "democracy" rather infrequently, but nevertheless in such a way as to allow us to regard this word as a key term in a most central speech. Saint-Just also made very little use of the term, and the occurrences in his terminology are of a somewhat sporadic and arbitrary kind, making it difficult to see what signification, or significations, he attributed to this and related words.

In contrast to Robespierre's language, the term "democracy" does occur in the earlier writings of Saint-Just. These earlier writings, however, cannot be regarded as symptomatic of the unconditional revolutionary spirit of Saint-Just after 1792. He seems, for example, to have been in favour of some kind of balanced constitution, of not identifying himself with what received the label "democracy", and of not using terms like "monarchy" and "aristocracy" in a derogatory way. With regard to the signification of "democracy", it is hardly possible to say much more than that Saint-Just seems to have identified it rather vaguely with popular power. [19]

The first occasion on which he introduced "democracy" in his vocabulary as a slogan was probably 13 March 1794 or 24 ventôse year II, when he attacked the French factions which he held to be inspired and organized by foreign countries, and especially by England. Concerning the political aim of these groups, he held that

... aux effets de la corruption, un coup audacieux, combiné par tous les gouvernements, devait succéder et renverser la démocratie. [20]

With regard to the alleged moderation of certain members of the National Convention, he later said:

Seriez-vous les amis des rois, ô vous qui les avez tous fait pâlir sur le trône, vous qui avez constitué la démocratie. [21]

From these statements it can be inferred that Saint-Just considered contemporary revolutionary rule in France to be what he regarded as democracy, and that he identified himself to a fairly high degree with that kind of rule. This naturally implies an honorific application of "democracy". But apart from this, and given that democracy is something very different from monarchy, it is hard to see with what signification he used "democracy". From a comparative point of view it may be indicative of the influence of Robespierre that the honorific use of "democracy" by Saint-Just appears fairly shortly after Robespierre had introduced this term in his political vocabulary.

The very few later occurrences of this term in the language of Saint-Just are fairly similar to those quoted above. In an important speech directed against the factions, 15 April 1794 or 26 germinal year II, Saint-Just declared these groups to be criminal on account of their alleged destruction of popular unity and public virtue by promoting their particular interests at the expense of the general public. To the adherents of the factions he said:

Insensés, qui voudriez troubler la démocratie pour accomplir vos

desseins coupables, vous vous trompez bien: l'infamie et l'inquiétude
environnent le but où vous tendez. [22]

To the members of the National Convention he continued to declaim
that these counterrevolutionaries must perish from the earth, since they
had no place in a society where public safety was the supreme law. Evidently as a climax, he cried:

Purgez donc la patrie de ses ennemis déclarés. La modestie républicaine
les indigne, il leur faut la puissance, qui n'appartient ici qu'à la
démocratie.

As in earlier quotations, democracy is here spoken of as something
that existed in contemporary France, and it is also evaluated in a most
positive way. The last quotation might indicate that he includes revolutionary power and even a merciless and sanguinary power in the signification of "democracy". But this is unlikely. The last sentence can more
probably be interpreted as referring to democracy as the only form of rule
capable of carrying out, or of sufficient merit to carry out, the necessary
kind of violent suppression. Such power cannot therefore be regarded as
a conceptual characteristic of his concept 'democracy' or as being implicit
in the signification of "democracy", although such sanguinary power was
quite compatible with what received the label "democracy". By contrasting
republican modesty with democratic measures, Saint-Just deviates from
Robespierre's opinion that "democratic" and "republican" were synonymous.
On this point it must also be mentioned that by associating modesty with
"republican", Saint-Just abandons an earlier trend in his own terminology.
About one month earlier he had maintained,

... ce qui constitue une République, c'est la destruction totale de ce qui
lui est opposé. [23]

This statement can scarcely be regarded as compatible with a formulation
like "republican modesty", even though it may be that Saint-Just, in April
1794, had regarded the earlier terror as modest when compared with those
measures he held necessary for the preservation and the salvation of revolutionary rule.

"Democracy" as the label for that political form which was exclusively
capable of the necessary terroristic activities, or which had the exclusive
right to commit such acts, can temporarily be regarded as a central term.
But as with Robespierre, a terminological continuation is not to be found
during the dramatic months up to 8 thermidor, and as far as we can see,
the quoted occurrence was his last use of this term. Thus, neither a large
quantity of occurrences nor occurrences of a kind which enable us to find
out what signification he attributed to this term were at hand in his
application of "democracy". Even if the quoted statement about democracy
and terroristic power is very important, especially in relation to the
increase in terror which in fact took place, it is hardly possible to say that
this term was a key term in his vocabulary. His use of it can fairly reasonably be regarded as being a kind of appendix to that of Robespierre.

3. Babeuf

The execution of Robespierre and Saint-Just on 9 thermidor year II [24]
marks the end of the honorific use of "democracy" by central political
leaders in the first French Republic.   This way of identifying political
or social ideals with what was called "democracy", however, did not
cease.   The main French application of this term is without doubt found
in different writings in connection with the Babeuvist doctrines of equality.
Babeuf and Buonarotti referred to themselves as democrats and used
"democracy" in an honorific way;   and in contrast to the language of Robespierre and Saint-Just, they used "democracy" with some frequency.

This relative frequency does not mean a usage of very long duration,
however;   and according to our material, Babeuf's first use of "democracy"
or some nearly related word occurs as late as 14 vendemaire year III, or
4 October 1794, when Babeuf informed his readers that he would change
his first name as well as the title of his journal.   During the revolution
Babeuf had replaced his original first names Francois Noël with the classical name Camille.   When, later on, he learned that the original Camille
had built a temple to Concord and concluded an agreement between patricians and plebeians, he solemnly declared that he would assume the name
Gracchus and abandon that of Camille, while the paper Journal de la
Liberté de la Presse was to appear as Tribun de Peuple.   In justification
he said:

> Je déclare même je quitte, pour mes nouveaux apôtres, Camille, avec
> lequel je m'étois impatronisé au commencement de la révolution; parce
> que, depuis mon démocratisme c'est épuré, est devenu plus austère. [25]

This democratism, which he held to have been purified and to have
become more austere, was without doubt the main, if not exclusive, reason
for the change of name. It can therefore be inferred that here "democratism"
was used with a signification which was incompatible with class reconciliation, and which, from a more concrete point of view, primarily implied
an uncompromising attitude on behalf of the poor in their struggle against
the rich.   This manner of using "democratism" in an honorific way cannot
be considered as directly inspired by Robespierre's use of "democracy".
While a political aspect, or political ethical aspect, was predominant in
Robespierre's usage, a social, or social-ethical aspect seems to mould
this usage of Babeuf.   While Babeuf was later to become almost unreserved
in his admiration of Robespierre, such an attitude cannot be found at this
time.   When starting his career as editor of Journal de la Liberté de la
Presse, a paper which appeared shortly after the fall of Robespierre, his
tendency was very anti-Robespierrist.   During the autumn a kind of ideological new orientation appears, when this very negative attitude was replaced by a typical ambiguity.   One month earlier, on 17 fructidor year II,
or 4 September 1794, Babeuf had said:

> ... nous distinguerons dans Robespierre deux hommes, Robespierre
> apôtre de la liberté, et Robespierre le plus infâme des tyrans. [26]

As a general characteristic of Babeuf's application of "democracy" and related terms, these words can without doubt be said to have been used in considerable conformity with the quoted occurrence of "democratism". Here too, a very high degree of social and economic equality is an essential, if not an exclusive, part of the signification of these words. On I nivôse year III, or 21 December 1794, Babeuf stated that two extremely different parties existed in contemporary France. He admitted that both wanted a republic, but both would form the republic in their own way:

L'un la désire bourgeoise et aristocratique, l'autre entend l'avoir faite et qu'elle demeure toute populaire et démocratique.

According to Babeuf, the first one was in favour of a republic of one million people who were to dominate and suppress the other twenty-four toiling and sweating millions, while

... l'autre parti veut la république pour ces vingt-quatre derniers millions qui en ont fondé les bases, les ont cimentées de leur sang, nourissent, soutiennent, pourvoient la patrie de tours ses besoins, la défendent et meurent pour sa sûréte et sa gloire. [27]

He went on to say that the first party wanted a republic which consisted of patricians and plebeians, while the other was claiming for all people not only the formal equality of civil rights, but a real economic and social equality.

A somewhat similar way of preferring "democracy" to "republic" can be observed one year later; this implies that Babeuf was strongly opposed to the synonymity between "democratic" and "republican" which had been put forth by Robespierre. On 9 frimaire year IV, or 29 November 1795, Babeuf rejected an appeal to all republicans to join in a common front against royalism. He gave his main reason:

Vous ne paroissez réunir autour de vous que de républicains, titre bannal et fort équivoque: donc vous ne prêchez que la république quelqonque. Nous, nous rassemblons tous les démocrates et les plebeïens, denominations qui, sans doute, présentent un sens plus positif: nos dogmes sont la démocratie pu(re), l'égalité sans tâche et sans réserve.[28]

The last sentence is probably a definition of pure democracy. Babeuf did not say that their dogmas were pure democracy and equality of the most complete kind. The comma after "pu(re)" may therefore be interpreted as an abbreviation for "which is" or "which means". A possible or even a probable interpretation of the last sentence may therefore be: "Nos dogmes sont la démocratie pure, cela signifie l'égalité sans tâche et sans réserve. "

A very distinct emphasis concerning the need to define democracy is observed the same day, the point of departure being Babeuf's demand that the people proclaim their common will to destroy misery. Their manifesto would also contain a definition of democracy:

Que le peuple proclame son Manifeste. Qu'il y definisse la démocratie comme il entend l'avoir, et telle que, d'après les principes purs, elle doit exister. Qu'il prouve que la démocratie est l'obligation de remplir, par ceux qui ont trop, tout ce qui manque à ceux qui n'ont point assez! que tout le déficit qui ce trouve dans la fortune des derniers ne procède que de ce que les autres les ont volé. [29]

Babeuf's idea of how the people ought to define democracy was evidently identical with how he thought democracy ought to exist according to pure principles; this was also identical with his manner of proving democracy to be the obligation to fulfil the needs of those who had too little at the expense of those who had too much, and that the poverty of the poor was nothing else than theft by the rich. This kind of argumentation is a very persuasive way of inducing the people to define democracy in a certain fashion.

The last three quotations, all from <u>Tribun du Peuple</u>, do not need much comment. All of them illustrate a use of "democracy" where the term signifies a highly equalitarian social system. And there is hardly any reason to think that social equality was held to be merely a consequence of a democratic system; such equality was even equivalent to what Babeuf considered to be democracy. In relation to his political thinking, his application of "democracy" was not only very honorific, the term can even with good reason be regarded as the key term in his political terminology. [30]

An application somewhat different from the ones discussed above is found in a letter to Joseph Bodson 9 ventôse year IV, or 28 February 1796. Here again Babeuf obviously used "democracy" in a most honorific way. But in contrast to earlier occurrences, "democracy" seems here to signify more a political than a social system. Babeuf's main intention was to convince his friend Bodson of the necessity of revolutionary emergency rule. Babeuf deplored Bodson's continued adherence to the principles of Hébert, while he himself had become an unconditional admirer of Robespierre and Saint-Just. He believed that a tendency similar to his own was a very widespread trend in large parts of the population.

Le robespierrisme est dans toute la République, dans toute la classe judicieuse et clairvoyante, et naturellement dans tout le peuple. La raison en est simple, c'est que le robespierrisme est la démocratie, et ces deux mots sont parfaitement identiques: donc en relevant le robespierrisme, vous êtes sûrs de relever la démocratie. [31]

Bodson also evidently used "democracy" in an honorific way, and Babeuf's intention was without doubt to make Bodson accept Robespierre's measures by declaring, or by persuasively declaring, "Robespierrisme" and "democracy" to be perfectly identical; this obviously means that Babeuf held these two terms to be synonymous, or to have perfectly identical significations.

The clearest proofs of what Babeuf meant by "Robespierrisme" are to be found somewhat earlier in this letter. Babeuf emphasized here that now, in contrast to his earlier views, he considered Robespierre, Saint-Just, and others, each to be of greater value than all other revolutionaries taken together. He also declared their dictatorship to have been diabolically well devised. Nor would he agree with Bodson that these men had committed crimes when executing Hébert and Chaumette:

Je n'entre pas dans l'examen si Hébert et Chaumette étoient innocents. Quand cela seroit, je justifie encore Robespierre. Ce dernier avoit à bon droit l'orgueil d'être le seul capable de conduire à son <u>vrai but</u> le char de la révolution.

Elaborating this point of view, he went on to say:

Le salut de 25 millions d'hommes ne doit point être balancé contre le ménagement de quelques individus équivoques. Un régénérateur doit voir en grand. Il doit faucher tout ce qui le gêne, tout ce qui obstrue son passage, tout ce qui peut nuire à sa prompte arrivée au terme qu'il s'est prescrit.

According to these quotations, "Robespierrism" can with good reason be said to signify a revolutionary and merciless dictatorship which alone was able to crush and destroy all that obstructed the course of the revolution. It is also evident that Robespierrism, according to Babeuf, might include the execution of innocent people, but there is hardly reason to think that such factors were necessarily included in the signification of "Robespierrism", even if they were quite compatible with what he designated by this term. Since, in addition, it seems certain that "Robespierrism" was used here with a signification identical to that in the statement when this term was declared as being perfectly identical with "democracy", the latter term also signified a dictatorial rule of the same kind. Nothing is mentioned here which directly makes social equality a part of the connotation of "democracy"; this implies a certain difference in relation to earlier applications of the term, although this dictatorship was exclusively thought of as that temporary rule through which, and only through which, complete social equality was to be achieved.

This letter marks an essential part of Babeuf's political thinking during his later phase. About fifteen months later, Babeuf frankly told the judges who were to pass his death sentence:

Je dépose mon opinion dans cette lettre sur le gouvernement révolutionnaire et ses fondateurs et ses régulateurs. [32]

This admiration for Robespierre forms the last link in the development of Babeuf's political thinking, the earlier stages of which had been characterized by open hostility, which in its turn had been replaced by an ambiguous attitude;

... nous distinguerons dans Robespierre deux hommes.

The revolutionary defeats of Germinal and Prairial seem to have convinced him that mere popular uprisings were insufficient and that a dictatorship was needed to lead the revolution to its true end. Here is an important amalgamation of the ideas of Robespierre and Babeuf, and it is here especially important that this amalgamation, or fusion, is clearly revealed in one of his ways of using "democracy".

4. Buonarroti

Apart from Babeuf, Philippe Buonarroti was the only one who left important written evidence of the Conspiracy for Equality. And like Babeuf, Buonarroti also used "democracy" with some frequency. His history of the conspiracy however, was written many years later, and was not published until 1828. This may tempt us to regard his use of the term as typical of his terminology in the eighteen-twenties rather than of his political language at the time of the conspiracy. But it is not possible to find any changes in ideological outlook; this may indicate a terminological stability.

Like Babeuf, Buonarroti used "democracy" and "democrats" in an honorific way, even if the degree is more tempered than that of Babeuf. But it is somewhat difficult to see with what significations he intended to use these terms. Probably his only definition of democracy is to be found when he pointed out that the French revolutionaries had devised a new interpretation of "democracy".

Il ne faut pas croire que les révolutionnaires français aient attaché à la démocratie qu'ils demandaient le sens qu'y attachaient les anciens. Personne ne s'avise en France d'appeler le peuple entier à délibérer sur les actes de gouvernement. Pour eux la démocratie est l'ordre public dans lequel l'égalité et les bonnes mœurs mettent le peuple à même d'exercer utilement la puissance législative. [33]

Buonarroti here presents two different concepts of "democracy"; 'ancient democracy' which was marked inter alia by wide popular deliberation of the acts of government, and 'democracy according to French revolutionaries' which most probably was characterized by the absence of such a kind of deliberation, and where equality and bonnes mœurs were regarded as essential conditions if the people were to exercise legislative power in a useful way. Thus equality and bonnes mœurs were not likely to be the results of popular legislation, but were to be created by some other authority; possibly by a small body of convinced revolutionaries. Further, it was a necessary condition of useful popular legislation that a State should be a democracy according to this version. Buonarroti did not enter upon the question of who should decide whether legislation was useful or not, but it seems almost certain that this question was not to be settled by the people or by a popular assembly. His definition naturally marks a concept 'democracy' in which the role of the people and especially public discussions were rather restricted phenomena. It does not, however, directly follow that Buonarroti himself necessarily adhered to such a concept, or that he used "democracy" with a signification identical with the one he attributed to French revolutionaries. In the context it can be seen that by French revolutionaries Buonarroti had in mind Marat, Robespierre, and Saint-Just, and did not directly include either Babeuf or himself. However, in the Table of Contents, this quotation is referred to as "Démocratie en France ce que C'est". And since this extremely detailed Table of Contents was most probably worked out by Buonarroti himself, it is fairly reasonable to assume that he here identified his own signification of "democracy" with that which he generally attributed to French revolutionaries.

Yet Buonarroti several times mentioned a kind of popular activity and also a popular deliberation of the arts of government which directly gainsay the essential part of this signification of "democracy". In one place, Buonarroti pointed to the popular assemblies, for example, as being the places where the people were to exercise their sovereignty in the future society. As concrete tasks he mentioned

Pour discuter, admettre ou rejeter les lois proposées au peuple par ses mandataires; pour délibérer sur les lois demandées par un certain nombre de citoyens ou par d'autres sections du souverain; pour connaître et publier les lois approuvées par le peuple entier. [34]

This view, which favours a broad popular activity in the future society, does not, however, necessarily contradict the usage of "democracy" with a signfication identical with the one in question, if "democracy" is not used as label of that future form of broad popular activity. "Democracy" does not seem to have been used in this way, although this does not eliminate the possibility of other ambiguities in Buonarroti's language. The definition of democracy referred to on page 19 seems to have been introduced as representing that kind of emergency power which was to function until the population at large had reached a certain level of political maturity. Buonarroti's emphasis on the need for a temporary emergency rule is most evident when he maintained that the experience of the French Revolution had adequately demonstrated that a people whose opinions had been formed in a regime of inequality and despotism were incapable of ruling by themselves during the first stages after the Revolution. According to him, the difficult task of leading the revolution was to be entrusted exclusively to the wise and the brave few who were seeking their immortality in the victory of equality. He concluded:

> Peut-être faut-il, à la naissance d'une révolution politique, même par respect pour la souveraineté réelle du peuple, s'occuper moins de recueillir les suffrages de la nation, que de faire tomber, le moins arbitrairement que possible, l'autorité suprême en des mains sagement et fortement révolutionnaires. [35]

Such a kind of revolutionary emergency rule, or temporary dictatorship, is quite different from what he outlined with regard to future political life in general; on the other hand, it is fairly similar to his definition of democracy as it was understood by French revolutionaries. Whether or not this can be regarded as furnishing a sufficient proof that by democracy Buonarroti primarily had a kind of emergency rule in mind is a question which cannot be answered satisfactorily. And it is not possible to mark out any absolute rules by studying the occurrences of "democracy" and "democrat" in his usage. "Democrats", for example, is somewhat frequently used to denote the adherents of Babeuf and Buonarroti, [36] but in a way which makes it difficult to see what signification he attributed to this term. With regard to "democracy", it may look as if Buonarroti used the term partly to signify social equality, [37] which may indicate that he alternated between the use of "democracy" as signifying (1) social equality, (2) that kind of emergency rule by which, and only by which, this equality was to be achieved. Such an ambiguity is fairly distinct in the terminology of Babeuf, whose tendency to let "democracy" connote an equalitarian communistic system was by far the predominant one, but who also used this term to signify in one case a very strict and merciless kind of dictatorship which was regarded as the only political means by which such a system could be established. This ambiguity may have influenced Buonarroti's terminology.

The problem of emergency rule is among those central to the political thinking of Babeuf and Buonarroti, and it is significant that it was connected with their use of "democracy". Like most revolutionaries, these two men were faced with a dilemma: on the one hand, a distinct rejection of existing forms of rule on account of their having a small or no popular base, and also their intention to have a very broad popular activity as an essential part of future political life; and on the other hand, a more or less developed distrust in the capacity of the people at large to carry out those political measures which were considered to be necessary for the establishment of full popular freedom. This distrust generally leads up to some theory of temporary rule by the enlightened vanguard, or emergency rule, which was to govern according to the interest of the people, but hardly meant government by the people. It may be regarded as a way of justifying the

alleged popular basis of such a dictatorship that "democracy" was introduced as signifying such a political rule. This process can be discerned in
different ways in the terminology of Babeuf and Buonarroti, and similar
ways of arguing are also to be found in the writings of Marx and Lenin. A
similar kind of ambiguity has been noted in the political language of Robespierre, where, in general, existing revolutionary Jacobin Dictatorship was
held to be a democracy, even the first true democracy in the world, but
where in the same speech, in one case, he regarded democracy as something which could not be established until wars and revolutions were a thing
of the past.

Though the political and social ideals, aspirations and viewpoints of the
leading French revolutionaries can hardly be viewed without taking into account the predominant influence of Rousseau's political philosophy, this
does not mean that Rousseau initiated the use of "democracy" by these men.
While their political thinking cannot be understood without inquiring into
volonté générale, their honorific use of "democracy" stands out as an independent phenomenon. Rousseau seldom used "democracy", and he did not
identify the ideal state of society with what he designated as "democracy".
In Du contrat social he said, for example:

S'il y avait un peuple de dieux, il se gouvernerait démocratiquement. Un
gouvernement si parfait ne convient pas à des hommes.

In the same work Rousseau also stated:

A prendre le terme dans la rigueur de l'acception, il n'a jamais existé
de véritable démocratie, et il n'en existera jamais. [38]

CHAPTER II

EARLY RADICALISM

1. Thomas Paine

In spite of the fact that Paine has rather frequently been regarded as a democratic thinker, his own use of "democracy" and related terms is far from frequent. His only use of these terms seems to have been restricted to a few pages in Rights of Man, and this application was mainly caused by what he held to be a provocation by Edmund Burke.

This work is Paine's direct answer to Burke's Reflections on the Revolution in France. One of the things which angered Paine was Burke's use of the term "democracy". We are here at once involved in the common problem whether "democracy" signifies direct or representative rule. Paine seems, at least here, to deny that "democracy" might connote any kind of representative rule.

> Mr. Burke is so little acquainted with constituent principles of government, that he confounds democracy and representation together. Representation was a thing unknown in the ancient democracies. In those the mass of the people met and enacted laws (grammatically speaking) in the first person. [1]

The way he accuses Burke of confusing democracy and representation is good proof of Paine himself being in favour of a fairly sharp dividing line between these two phenomena. His argument in favour of this separation is somewhat weak, however. His assertion that representation was unknown in what he labelled "ancient democracies" does not necessarily imply that representation was incompatible with what he describes with the unqualified term "democracy".

The qualifying terms "ancient", "simple", and "original simple" are sometimes used by Paine in connection with "democracy", and the qualified expression then always signifies direct popular rule. This use of such qualifying terms might indicate that Paine perhaps wanted to define something called "ancient democracy" or "simple democracy" in relation to what was called only "democracy" to avoid confusion. While the former signified direct popular rule, the latter, unqualified "democracy", might be used as a conceptual designation of one broader concept 'democracy' of which the narrower concepts, 'direct democracy' and 'representative democracy' were sub-concepts or species. Such an hypothesis is hardly a probable one, however. In the first quotation we have seen that unqualified "democracy" was probably conceived as signifying something different from representation, and there were other occasions on which the term was used in a similar way.

With regard to the term "republicanism", Paine declared that it had been misused by courtiers and court-governments, and that they had never tried to find out what it really meant. Paine stressed that a republic was no particular form of government, but that, on the contrary, it represented the characteristic of the purport, matter, or object of which any government ought to be constituted. According to Paine, the reason for this relationship was that "the only forms of government are the democratical, the aristocratical, the monarchical, and what is now called the representative. "[2]

In this passage he seems to have intended to classify all forms of government into four mutually exclusive and collectively comprehensive groups. In that case, the term "democracy" would have been exclusively reserved to connote a form of government which clearly differed from the monarchic and aristocratic ones, as well as from the representative.

Later on, however, we are faced with a use of the term which presents some new aspects in its application, although there is no definite change. Up to this point, Paine had been discussing different forms of government without showing any important personal preference. Asking himself which was the best form of government for conducting the public business of the nation after it had become too extensive and populous for what he called "simple democratical forms", Paine rejected both monarchy and aristocracy as being corrupt systems. His first answer to the question was that the best form was to be found in an assembly of practical knowledge, and he went on to say:

> The monarchical form is as much limited, in useful practice, from the incompetence of knowledge as was the democratical form, from the multiplying of population. [3]

"Democratical form" is here most probably used synonymously with "simple democratical form" a few lines earlier, and both phrases evidently signified direct popular rule which was suitable in very small societies only. It can further be noted that the term "democratical" was rarely used in an honorific way by Paine in this context, since he used it to characterize a political form which, in his opinion, was as much limited in useful practice as the monarchical one. [4]

A somewhat different kind of terminological application, however, is to be found in the continuation of this statement. Paine here maintained that

> ... referring, then to the original simple democracy, it affords the true data from which the government on a large scale can begin. It is incapable of extension, not from its principle, but from the inconvenience of its form; - Retaining then, democracy as the ground, and rejecting the corrupt systems of monarchy and aristocracy, the representative system naturally represents itself; - Simple democracy was society governing itself without the aid of secondary means. By ingrafting representation upon democracy, we arrive at a system of confederating all the various interests and every extent of territory and population. [5]

This ingrafting of representation upon democracy was further, according to Paine, what marked the American form of government.

> It is on this system that the American government is founded. It is representation ingrafted upon democracy. It has fixed the form by a scale parallel in all cases to the extent of the principle. What Athens was in miniature, America will be in magnitude. [6]

In these statements Paine used "original simple democracy" and "simple democracy" to signify something which he refers to, and unqualified "democracy" as signifying something which he retains, and on which representation can be ingrafted. Unqualified "democracy" here seems also to connote something which constitutes a part of what was termed "simple democracy". Since

Paine said simple democracy was incapable of extension, "not from its principle, but from the inconvenience of its form", it was probably this principle that he wished to retain. Thus he seems to have said that he referred to simple democracy of which the democratic principle was retained, and by ingrafting representation upon this principle, he arrived at a system of government capable of embracing every territory and population. Thus his concept 'democratical principle' was compatible with representation, but this concept can scarcely have included representation. The process of ingrafting seems to have been conceived as an amalgamation of the concept with something which was compatible with, but different from, itself. This may be taken to imply that the result of this process of ingrafting would not receive the label "democracy". Paine apparently operated with two, and only two, concepts: 'direct democracy' and 'democratic principle', of which the former is incompatible with representation and the latter compatible with, but different from, a representative form of rule, and where "ancient democracy", "simple democracy", "original simple democracy", and unqualified "democracy" were used as conceptual designations of the former, and unqualified "democracy" of the latter concept.

Unqualified "democracy" was thus used as a conceptual designation of two different concepts, and generally speaking the political language of Paine is somewhat vague on this point. Compared with that of Robespierre, for example, in which it was very clearly said that democracy was not direct government, Paine's verbal usage is somewhat ambiguous. We can also see that while Robespierre, Saint-Just, Babeuf, and Buonarroti used the term in at least some different places, Paine's use of the term was probably limited to these few pages. It must be remembered, however, that Paine's usage is at least two years earlier than Robespierre's, a far from unimportant matter at the time. Paine's applications can therefore be considered as interesting symptoms of the early stages of new developments in the semantics of "democracy".

2. Godwin

Thomas Paine's Rights of Man caused a great political sensation in England, and the author was on the point on being arrested before he escaped to France. The following year, 1793, William Godwin's Enquiry concerning Political Justice appeared. It was also regarded as dangerously radical, and it would probably have been sequestrated if it had not been for the high price of the copies.

In describing the form of government which he labelled "democracy", Godwin started by saying that he was about to "examine that democracy of which so alarming a picture has uniformly been exhibited."[7] He referred first of all to the arguments of those who, when driven from every other pretence, always referred to the mischievous nature of democracy, and who considered the imperfect institutions of aristocracy and monarchy to be necessary as accommodations to the imperfection of human nature.

Against this view, Godwin argued that

Democracy is a system of government according to which every member of society is considered a man and nothing more. So far as positive regulation is concerned, if indeed that can with any propriety be termed regulation which is the mere recognition of the simplest of all principles, every man is regarded as equal.

This statement implies that in his opinion democracy was conceptually a form of government that excluded all forms of political and social privilege, and where citizens were regarded as equals. How far equality was to characterize the social and political institutions of what he termed "democracy" is not quite clear, nor is what he strictly meant by "equal" in this connection. But he shortly afterwards stated that talents and wealth, wherever they existed, would not fail to obtain a certain degree of influence in a democracy, but that they could not require any institution of society to give them special support. This indicates that equality, as understood by Godwin, did not include economic levelling, or at least not complete economic levelling, and that the wealth of a few people was not incompatible with democracy as he understood it. Neither was it contrary to democracy that wealth and talent should have a certain degree of influence, as long as such influence was very limited and not based upon any kind of privilege.

A similar kind of association between democracy and equality is also to be found in an attack made by Godwin against surnames, especially aristocratic ones:

> In a state of equality it will be a question of no importance, to know who is the parent of each individual child. It is aristocracy, selflove and family pride that teach us to set a value upon it at present.

He went on to say that no one ought to prefer anybody simply because he was his father, wife, or son. He concluded:

> One among the measures which will successively be dictated by the spirit of democracy, and that probably at no great distance, is the abolition of surnames. [8]

Since Godwin's dislike of surnames is rather closely connected with his systematic dislike of the family as a social phenomenon, [9] we may also infer that ordinary family relations were contrary to the spirit of democracy as understood by Godwin, and were to be abolished as soon as possible in consequence of that spirit.

From a conceptual point of view, these statements about surnames do not convey much in addition to the previous quotation. Abolition of these names seemed to Godwin to be an inevitable consequence of democracy and civil equality, but hardly a conceptual characteristic. There is, therefore, at least on this point, good reason to believe that Godwin operated with a concept 'democracy' of which the fact of its being a governmental system where all citizens were regarded as equals was the sole conceptual characteristic.

With regard to the supposed evils of democracy, Godwin initially referred to what were generally regarded to be the dangers and disadvantages of that form of government. One supposed danger was that the welfare of society would be at the mercy of the ignorance and folly of the multitude, and another, that while all kinds of society needed some steady and uniform principles, democracy was wavering and inconstant. Democracy was further said to be defenceless against ambitious politicians who would wish to deceive the multitude and to achieve absolute power for themselves, while the multitude, conscious of their own weakness, would be perpetually suspicious and uneasy. Godwin concluded:

If this picture must inevitably be realized wherever democratical principles are established, the state of human nature would be peculiarly unfortunate. [10]

Against these views, Godwin firstly emphasized that democracy could not be judged by the existing political maturity of the masses, since mankind had for ages been taught by different forms of governments blind submission to authority, and timid fear and distrust of its own powers.

In the estimate that is usually made of democracy, one of the most flagrant sources of error lies in our taking mankind such as monarchy and aristocracy have made them, and from hence judging how fit they are to legislate for themselves. [11]

Godwin went on to say that the chief obstacles to human improvement, in addition to authority, were fear and distrust of one's own powers, implicit faith and inattention to one's own importance and to the good purposes people were able to effect. These obstacles to human improvement, however, were to be removed by what Godwin held to be democracy.

Democracy restores to man a consciousness of his value, teaches him by the removal of authority and oppression to listen only to the dictates of reason, gives him confidence to treat all other men as his fellow beings, and induces him to regard them no longer as enemies against whom to be upon his guard, but as brethren whom it becomes him to assist. [12]

Especially does this last statement place "democracy" in a most central and laudable position in the terminology of Godwin. In accordance with earlier conclusions, I am here inclined to regard removal of authority and fear not as new conceptual characteristics of 'democracy', but rather as the consequences of characteristics already attributed to this concept. Godwin himself probably did not disagree, conceptually, at any rate not strongly, with his opponents concerning the characteristics of 'democracy'; the disagreement was caused by extremely divergent views concerning the possibilities of human improvement.

With regard to other characteristics of democracy, and probably other non-conceptual characteristics, Godwin admitted democracy in some respect to be less fit for the affairs of war than other forms of government. But when aggressive wars were concerned he felt that this was an advantage instead of a drawback -- and that in any case internal virtues and justice might nevertheless make democrats into confident defenders. [13] This seems to imply that Godwin did agree with those who considered democracy unfit for the making of aggressive wars, and that the difference on this point was not a difference concerning the concrete consequences of democracy, but a difference concerning the value judgements associated with these consequences; in other words, that this difference was of a normative and not of a descriptive or factual kind. It must further be noted that Godwin probably thought democracy was fitted for the making of defensive wars, and that the disagreement on that point, therefore, can very probably be said to have been of a descriptive kind.

A rather normative kind of disagreement, and perhaps, a purely normative one, is present in connection with the relationship between democracy and diplomatic secrecy. Godwin admitted that democracy might not keep secrets; ordinary diplomacy would thus be rendered impossible. According to him, however, this was not at all a disadvantage of democracy. On the contrary, he held,

It happens in this instance, that that which the objection attacks as the vice of democracy, is one of its most essential excellencies. The trick of a mysterious carriage is the prolific parent of every vice; and it is an eminent advantage incident to democracy, that, though the proclivity of mind has hitherto reconciled this species of administration in some degrees to the keeping of secrets, yet its inherent tendency is to annihilate them. [14]

Godwin dealt with the objection that democracy was incapable of those rapid and decisive proceedings,which, according to many people, tended to ensure success in some situations. In his answer to this objection, Godwin touched on the earlier problem whether or not "democracy" exclusively signified a direct form of governing. Concerning speed in governmental affairs, Godwin said:

Democracy is by no means of a phlegmatic character, or obliged to take every proposition that is made to it, ad referendum, for the consideration of certain primary assemblies. [15]

And he continued by asserting that in all kinds of governments, it was necessary, at least under the existing imperfection of mankind, to have some man or body to act on behalf on the whole. Godwin added that it did not therefore "seem unreasonable for a representative national assembly to exercise in certain cases a discretionary power. " [16] Godwin's attitude towards representation is not without reservations, reservations which are repeated frequently later on; but it is also fairly clear that he referred to some kind of representation as evidence that democracy was not necessarily incapable of rapid and decisive action. This statement provides no evidence that Godwin used "democracy" with a signification which necessarily included some sort of representative rule; representation was limited to certain cases, but it shows anyhow that Godwin did not regard some kind of representation to be incompatible with what he designated as "democracy", even when the term was used in an unqualified way.

This line of political language developed no further in Godwin's writings, and it has received rather scant attention compared to the same line in the terminology of Paine. Godwin, however, had far fewer reservations than Paine in labelling a representative kind of government as "democracy".

Godwin's use of "democracy", and the general trend in his political philosophy, are less related to particular political events of the day than those of any other ideologists discussed in the foregoing chapter. By comparison with those of Robespierre, Saint-Just, Babeuf, Buonarroti, and even of Paine, Godwin's terminology as well as his thoughts are more marked by general considerations. For example, although his main work appeared in 1793, there are only a very few references to the existing political storm in France. When comparisons are made with revolutionary terminology in France, it is also highly important that there existed almost contemporaneously a central as well as a very honorific use of "democracy" by a radical thinker whose political philosophy was founded upon the individualism and rationalism of the Enlightenment and not at all upon the collectivism, even perhaps the totalitarian collectivism, of Rousseau. As the philosophical successor of Condorcet, Godwin was the declared enemy of terror and violence and also of centralization. By his exposition of the ills created by strict public government and private property, things which he held mutually to sustain each other, Godwin was to certain extent a forerunner of non-violent anarchism. Central parts of his political philosophy were revealed in his use of "democracy". By presenting this application of the term as early as 1793, Godwin even used "democracy" in a very honorific way at a time when neither unqualified occurrences nor honorific ones were present in Robespierre's language.

CHAPTER III

EARLY CONSERVATISM

An honorific application of "democracy" has been a common mark of all the
ideologists discussed so far. A derogatory kind of application is probably
to be expected, however, where early conservatives are concerned. Yet we
in no way encounter a stable and uniform kind of derogatory use of "democracy" among early conservatives. There were several important differences
between Babeuf and Paine, with regard to the degree of honorific application,
and between Saint-Just and Godwin concerning the premises for such a use,
and similar aspects are also to be found in this chapter. A very derogatory
use of "democracy", possibly even a dyslogistic one, can be seen, as well
as a more moderate use. In contrast to the former chapter, however, there
are more explicit differences here in the attitude towards what was designated as "democracy"; in addition to different degrees of derogatory usage,
a fairly neutral one can also be seen, and in Hegel's terminology one may
perhaps even catch a glimpse of an honorific use of the word.

1. Burke

Of a leading political thinker like Burke, it can be said initially that the
most important uses of "democracy" in his terminology are to be found in
Reflections on the Revolution in France. This work, which is in the form of
a letter intended to have been sent to a gentleman in Paris in 1790, can be
regarded as the strongest ideological attack that was made upon the French
Revolution. The work has also served as model of conservative thought for
many decades. As a very important general rule in political life, Burke
maintained that when popular power was absolute and unrestrained, the
people were to only a very small degree responsible to their sense of fame
and estimation, a factor which Burke held to be one of the strongest controlling powers on earth. He considered the people's approbation of their own
acts in such a government to be public judgement in their own favour, and
he concluded:

A perfect democracy is therefore the most shameless thing in the world,
... as it is the most shameless, it is also the most fearless. No man
apprehends in his person that he can be made subject to punishment. [1]

If we consider the signification of "perfect democracy" it is clear that
absolute and unrestrained popular power was an essential characteristic of
the concept designated by this expression. It is somewhat doubtful, however,
whether the absence of fame and estimation as well as the presence of shamelessness and fearlessness can be regarded as properties implicit in the signification of "perfect democracy". If they are regarded as properties of this
kind, the statement that democracy is the most shameless thing in the world
is an analytic statement or a tautology. It is also certain that this expression
then would have been used in a dyslogistic and not only in a derogatory way,

or to connote something which per definitionem was of negative value. I am more inclined to believe, however, that Burke held the high degree of shamelessness as well as fearlessness to have been inevitable consequences, but hardly conceptual characteristics, of 'perfect democracy'. In that way the statement mentioned would have been of a synthetic and not of an analytic kind.

Later in this work Burke stated that he did not know how to class the existing ruling authority in France.

It affects to be a pure democracy, though I think it in direct train of becoming shortly a mischievous and ignoble oligarchy. 2

In high conformity with his general way of treating political matters, Burke added that he did not reprobate any form of government upon abstract principles. He admitted:

... there may be situations in which the purely democratic form will become necessary. There may be some (very few, and very particularly circumstanced) where it would be clearly desirable.3

But he added that this was not the case with France, or with any other greater country.

This use of "purely democratic form" seems to indicate that Burke either used this expression with a somewhat different signification from that of "perfect democracy", or that he here did not regard shamelessness as an inevitable consequence of unrestrained popular power. It is thus scarcely possible that Burke would have held something which was almost necessarily to result in shamelessness to be desirable even in a very few and particular circumstances. Concerning the reference to France, it is a little difficult to agree with Burke that France, as early as 1790, affected to be what Burke called "a pure democracy", even if he held it as his own opinion that France had developed in the direction of oligarchy. Any arguments in favour of his statement about France, however, were not advanced.

Burke was not in favour of democracies in France or in any great country, and he added:

... until now we have seen no examples of considerable democracies. The ancients were better acquainted with them. 4

This may be taken as proof that Burke considered that democracy, as he understood it, could not work in a large society, and that it was better fitted to the smaller States of antiquity. This may imply that, at least in his context, Burke used "democracy" to signify direct and not representative rule. But nothing definite can be found in this text.

Burke continued by saying that he agreed with the authors who held that neither absolute monarchy nor absolute democracy was to be counted among the legitimate forms of government, and he added:

If I recollect rightly, Aristotle observes, that a democracy has many striking points of resemblance with a tyranny. 5

In a footnote Burke says that in writing this, he had referred to Aristotle's statement from memory. A learned friend, however, had later found the text and made it available to Burke. 6 But this text does not contain the word "democracy", which occurs a few lines later, when Aristotle, referring to the popular State partly governed by demagogues, declares:

... any one, therefore, may with great justice blame such a government as being a democracy and not a free state. [7]

In addition to the quotation from Aristotle, Burke stated that he was certain

... that in a democracy, the majority of the citizens is capable of exercising the most cruel oppressions upon the minority, whenever strong divisions prevail in that kind of polity, as they often must, and that oppression of the minority will extend to far greater numbers, and will be carried on with much greater fury, than can almost ever be apprehended from the dominion of a single sceptre. [8]

Both the reference to Aristotle as well as the last quotation show fairly clearly that Burke held democracy to have certain important properties in common with tyranny, and that oppression might even be worse in a democracy than in a tyranny. What he designated as "democracy" was thus quite compatible with cruel oppression. This implies that absence of oppression, or the freedom of minorities, might definitely not be a property implicit in the signification of this term, but it does not imply that oppression was necessarily attributed to this signification.

The relationship between tyranny and democracy had been discussed in another of Burke's works nearly thirty-five years earlier. In describing different kinds of government, Burke then declared that what was "known by political writers under the name democracy" was a society where the people had transacted all public business in their own persons. He admitted that, on the face of it, they had secured by this method the advantages of order and good government. But no sooner is this political vessel launched from the stocks, than it oversets. Burke concluded:

A tyranny immediately supervened, not by a foreign conquest, not by accident, but by the very nature and constitution of a democracy. [9]

It is hardly possible to know whether this statement was forgotten so many years later. But at least it shows that the revolutionary events in France were not the single factors which led Burke to make associations between tyranny and what he termed "democracy".

In one of his later works, An Appeal from the New to the Old Whigs, Burke also pointed out that a democratic government might create very good opportunities for ambitious politicians.

The democratic commonwealth is the foodful nurse of ambition. Under the other forms it meets with many restraints. [10]

He admitted that through ostracism democracies had tried to save themselves from ambitious men, but generally in vain. And he concluded by referring to ambition as being "one of the natural inbred, insurable distempers of a powerful democracy. "

In the three last quotations we have seen "democracy" and "powerful democracy" to mean something which was capable of cruelly oppressing minorities, "the foodful nurse of ambition", and which by its nature and constitution could easily be replaced by a tyranny. Again I am more inclined to conclude that these properties are not implicit in the signification of "democracy". Thus the statements concerning oppression of minorities, ambition, and tyranny are to be regarded as synthetic statements, or as statements which tell us something about democracy but which do not belong to the con-

ceptual characteristic of the concept 'democracy'. In all the above occurrences the term was used derogatorily. Earlier it had been used in a very
derogatory way when it was used with some qualifications to label something
which Burke held to be the most shameless thing in the world, but we have
also seen that even what was called "pure democracy" might, according to
Burke, have been useful in a very few and particular situations. This last
usage is an application which is not exclusively derogatory, and in one case
he even used the term, with some qualifications, to describe an element of
the British constitution. Burke emphasized that the English wished to conserve the established and traditional constitution of England which had existed time out of mind, and not to make any sudden changes.

> We are resolved to keep an established church, an established monarchy,
> an established aristocracy, and an established democracy, each in the
> degree it exists, and in no greater. [11]

"Established democracy" has here been used to describe something
which ought not to expand, but which nevertheless constituted a part of the
British constitution, a constitution which always was treated with great
reverence by Burke. It is therefore obvious that this expression was not
used in a derogatory way, and that the evil consequences which have generally been associated with what he termed "democracy" were not attributed
to the denotatum of this expression. It seems, then, that he either used "established democracy" with a signification different from that of unqualified
"democracy", or that he had partly changed his mind concerning the inevita-
bility of these consequences. Which part of the British constitution Burke
had in mind when he used the expression "established democracy" is not
mentioned, but it may well have been the House of Commons. [12]

The political language of Burke possibly displays somewhat different,
but not very different, trends with regard to "democracy" and related terms.
His attitude is mainly, but not always, derogatory. It may also be of some
importance to note that Burke, most probably, never used the term "democrats", only the somewhat strange word "democratists". [13] As far as I can
see, this word is found solely in the writings of Burke. It is thus possible
that this term was invented by Burke for want of an adequate term to denote
the adherents of democracy, since the English counterpart of the French
word démocrates had possibly not yet been introduced into the vernacular.

2. De Maistre

Somewhat similar to that of Burke, the use of "democracy" by the prominent
anti-revolutionary ideologist Joseph de Maistre was also to a large degree
inspired, or rather provoked, by the French Revolution. This does not
imply, however, that his use of the term was directly connected with concrete events in contemporary political life. Like Burke, de Maistre discussed general problems, even if the revolution figured more or less clearly
as a background.

In Considérations sur la France, written in 1797, de Maistre asked
himself whether the French Republic was to continue to exist. Of the republican form of government, he declared that the world had seen many monarchies, but only a few republics, and he added that these two were the only

forms of government. He admitted, however, that if anybody wanted sub-
divisions, other terms were needed.

> Si l'on veut ensuite se jeter dans les sous-divisions, on peut appeler
> démocratie le gouvernement où la masse exerce la souveraineté, et
> aristocratie celui où la souveraineté appartient à un nombre plus ou
> moins restraint de familles privilégiées. Et tout est dit. [14]

With regard to the signification of "democracy" this meta-occurrence
does not convey much. We are only told that one may call "democracy" a
republican kind of government where the masses are in possession of sovereignty, but we do not hear whether, for example, this sovereignty was to be
exercised directly or through representatives. I can hardly agree with de
Maistre that everything concerning what he held as democracy and aristocracy was contained in this very short definition. There are more differentiated contributions to the semantics of "democracy" in other parts of his
writings, though he did not use the word frequently.

Later in the same work de Maistre held monarchy to be that form of
government which, without doubt, brought distinction to the greatest number
of persons. His main argument was that the sovereign in a monarchy possessed sufficient splendour to be able to distribute it among its adherents,
while the functionaries in a republic were ordinary men who remained ordinary men. Another reason was that a republic, by its very nature, was the
government which gave the greatest amount of rights to the smallest number
of persons.

> Car la république, par sa nature, est le gouvernement qui donne le plus
> de droits au plus petit nombre d'hommes qu'on appelle le souverain, et
> qui en ôte le plus à tous les autres qu'on appelle les sujets. Plus la
> république approchera de la démocratie pure, et plus l'observation sera
> frappante. [15]

This statement clearly emphasized the allegation that sovereign rights
in a republic were limited to a very few sovereign persons, while the majority, the subjects, had almost nothing. It is a rather important characteristic of his terminology that he used "pure democracy" as signifying something
in which this tendency was most evident. Perhaps de Maistre here had in
mind the emergency powers of the Committee of Public Safety, where the
members of that committee had enormous power and ordinary citizens but
little, even if nothing is directly mentioned which can support an hypothesis
of such a kind.

The last quotation was not in conformity with the previous one, in which
he said that one might call a form of government a "democracy" in which
sovereignty was exercised by the masses. In another work, de Maistre
stated that mankind was generally ruled by kings, but added that it sometimes happened that sovereignty was vested in several persons.

> On voit cependant des nations où la souveraineté appartient à plusieurs,
> et ces gouvernements peuvent s'appeler aristocratie ou démocratie,
> suivant le nombre des personnes qui forment le souverain. [16]

And according to the context he seems to claim that the sovereignty of
the greater number was the characteristic of what could be called "democracy".

The relationship between democracy and sovereignty are not restricted
to these occurrences, however. In a later chapter de Maistre first referred

to Aristotle's central saying that democracy was a corruption of constitution [17], and he went on to mention that Rousseau had declared that a real
democracy had never existed and would never exist. [18] De Maistre was of
the opinion that absolute democracy did not exist any more than absolute
despotism, since both were abstractions. But this did not hinder anyone
from regarding them as theoretical extremes between which all other kinds
of governments were to be classified. Further he said:

> Dans ce sens strict, je crois pouvoir définir la démocratie: une associ-
> ation d'hommes sans souveraineté.[19]

De Maistre's arguments in favour of this manner of defining democracy
seem exclusively to have been that he here regarded sovereignty as something which was above and outside the subject, and since no people could be
in possession of a coercive power over itself, it was obvious that there
would be no kind of sovereignty in a democracy:

> ... car il est impossible d'entendre par ce mot [souveraineté] autre chose
> qu'un pouvoir réprimant qui agit sur le sujet et qui, lui, est placé hors
> de lui. [20]

His reasons for saying in one place that democracy was a State where
sovereignty belonged to the masses or the greatest number, in another that
sovereignty only belonged to a very small number of persons in a democracy,
and in yet another place that democracy lacked sovereignty completely are
not easy to explain. Perhaps he used "sovereignty" with somewhat different
significations. When declaring sovereignty to belong to the masses in a
democracy, did de Maistre regard sovereignty as being a coercive power
which was above and outside the subject. Or by "democracy" in the strict
sense did he have in mind something which was different from what he regarded as the ordinary sense. It is difficult to say which alternative is the
more probable. And there is still the problem of what de Maistre meant
by "democracy" and "sovereignty" when he maintained that sovereignty belonged to a very small number in a democracy. The only way of avoiding
contradictory significations of "democracy" as used in these occurrences
is therefore probably to attribute to "sovereignty" three mutually different
connotations. As regards his political thought in general it can be added
that the theory of the coercive as well as divine [21] origin of sovereignty
seems to have been a fairly consistent feature of de Maistre's political
philosophy. Once he even considered every sovereign to be despotic,

> ... on trouvera d'abord que tout souverain est despotique, et qu'il n'y a
> que deux partis à prendre à son égard: l'obéissance ou l'insurrection.[22]

His opinion of democracy as completely lacking sovereignty is the statement which is in greatest harmony with the general trend in his political
thought, though de Maistre is very far from consistent on this point.

Concerning other aspects of de Maistre's use of "democracy", it is of
importance to note that he used the term at least once to signify a representative form of rule. In treating the aristocratic form of government, de
Maistre declared:

> ... on peut dire en général que tous les gouvernements non monarchiques
> sont aristocratiques, car la démocratie n'est qu'une aristocratie élective.[22a]

This probably implies that he held democracy to be a form of government ruled by a small number of elected representatives. The signification

of "democracy" would therefore be restricted to the fields of rule by elected representatives; this is fairly important in a manuscript that dates from 1795. I have no other examples of de Maistre's limitation of the significa- tion of "democracy" in this way; but I cannot see that he tried at any time to make this term connote explicitly a direct form of government only.

De Maistre's references to what he termed "democracy" are mostly some- what derogatory, though never, as far as I can see, extremely so which, from a certain point of view, might have been expected. The following quo- tation is fairly typical. When discussing the moral reconstruction of France after the revolution, de Maistre stated:

En France, où sont les éléments de la prétendue régéneration? La démocratie ne porte sur rien: il faut qu'elle tombe. [23]

Except for its negative attitude, and except for the statement that democracy was something which de Maistre held to exist in contemporary France, this quotation is of small importance as regards what signification he attributed to "democracy".

3. Bonald

Whereas de Maistre used "democracy" in a way which cannot be said to have been honorific, but which nevertheless cannot be regarded as very deroga- tory, an extremely derogatory kind of application is to be found in the writ- ings of Bonald. In 1796, with regard to revolutionary rule in France, Bonald said in his very voluminous Théorie de pouvoir politique et religieux:

La France, s'érige en démocratie, et s'élève en un instant au plus haut période des désorganisations auquel une société puisse atteindre. [24]

For Bonald, democracy was the converse, or near converse, of mon- archy, and he went on to say:

Le despotisme et la démocratie sont, au fond, le même gouvernement.

In his opinion, the reason for this alleged identity was not only that the power of both kinds of government was exclusively restricted by military force or popular insurrections, nor was it the fact that neither of them had any fixed rules of competence, since despots made ministers of garden- ers and the sovereign people made legislators of dancing-masters, but

... le trait le plus marqué de leur identité, parce qu'il est dans la nature même de l'un et de l'autre, est l'acharnement avec lequel le peuple dans ces révolutions, et le despote dans ses conquêtes, cherchent á anéantir les distinctions héréditaires, par la mort ou l'exil de ceux qui en soit revêtus.

Bonald added that it was not, as was generally believed, on account of either popular vengeance or the suspicious jealousy of a despot that these illustrious victims were butchered,

mais au despotisme et à la démocratie mémes, c'est-á-dire aux principes des ces gouvernements, qui s'empressent de substituer leur nivellement caractéristique aux distinctions propres à la monarchie. [25]

This statement illustrates primarily a very derogatory use of "democ- racy" since the term was used to connote a form of government which in a very cruel way tried to destroy hereditary and monarchical distinctions, even when judged by its nature and principles. Here Bonald also emphasized the similarity, and even identity, between what he designated as "democracy" and "despotism": At this stage it looks as if cruel and consistent levelling of all hereditary distinctions, exclusively by way of violent popular revolution, was not only a consequence of the existence of popular rule, but was even an essential property of the signification he attributed to "democracy". This kind of cruel and consistent levelling was regarded by Bonald as a property which was necessarily associated with democracy as well as with despotism, and it is also very probable that Bonald considered that this common property furnished sufficient support for the alleged relation of identity. Yet it seems improbable that this common property furnishes evidence of such a relationship, at least if "identity" is used with a somewhat strict signification. In Bonald's argument it is also fairly clear that, in spite of a high degree of similarity between democracy and despotism, there were also some differences. Despotism was thus said to destroy hereditary distinctions by means of military conquests, while democracy did the same thing by way of popular revolutions. These last factors are not compatible with a relation of identity, even if they are without doubt compatible with a high degree of similarity.

It can be seen that Bonald regarded monarchy as the only form of government in which man was treated and considered as a social being, while democracy consisted merely of individuals.

Dans la monarchie, tout est social, religion, pouvoir, distinctions. Dans l'État populaire, tout est individuel; ... chacun veut se distinguer ou dominer par ses talents ou par sa force. Dans la monarchie, parce que le pouvoir est social, sa limite est dans les institutions sociales. Dans la démocratie, parce que le pouvoir est individuel, sa limite est dans l'homme. La monarchie considere l'homme dans la société,... ou l'homme social.[26]

The expressions "popular State" and "democracy" are most probably used as synonyms. It appears to be fairly certain that an extremely high degree of individualism was not only regarded as a consequence of a democratic form of rule, but was even included in the signification of "democracy." From a political, as well as from a terminological point of view, such an argument reveals an important element in Bonald's ideology, and we may also presume that the alleged social view of man and society was dependent on hereditary institutions; this he also held as essential for monarchy. From an historical point of view, however, an objection must be raised. If Bonald regarded the Jacobin rule, for example, as being subsumable under what he designated as "democracy" -- and there is very good reason for his being in favour of such a point of view -- his thesis that democracy is individualistic must be rejected. Yet such an objection has little relevance as regards the signification attributed by Bonald to "democracy".

In this work Bonald also dealt with the relationship between religion and politics, and especially that between Calvinism and democracy. He referred initially to a strong affinity between democracy and despotism. On this point we are faced with an alleged relationship of identity. Bonald went on to assert that despotism was nothing but the most absolute military authority, and that democracy had a natural tendency to make alliances with military authority. He also considered Calvinism to favour democracy, while Calvinism was also the ally of military authority of the most absolute kind. The military despotisms in Brandenburg and Hessen, and especially that of

Cromwell were also mentioned as furnishing support for this theory. [27]

Bonald stated that while Calvinism tended to establish democracy, and democracy to establish Calvinism, a State which at the same time was both Calvinistic and democratic ought to be very stable. This view, however, was misguided. There was at that time only one State in Europe, Geneva, where pure Calvinism was united with what he held to be pure democracy. He also maintained that while all aristocracies in Europe were reformed, all other democracies were Catholic, and he even declared the Roman Catholic religion to be more convenient for a democracy than any other religion. It is somewhat strange that an ardent defender of the Catholic religion should regard that religion as being the most suitable for a kind of government whose designation he used very derogatorily. He advanced no arguments in favour of this point of view, however. Nor did he elaborate upon the problem of why Calvinism tended to establish democracy, but did not generally work well with such a form or rule.

He later drew attention to a related problem. In dealing with the relationship between democracy and atheism, he marked out one central property as common to both systems:

> La démocratie proprement dite rejette avec fureur, de la société politique, toute unité visible et fixe du pouvoir, et elle ne voit le souverain que dans les sujets, ou le peuple: comme l'athéisme rejette la cause unique et première de l'univers, et ne la voit que dans les effets ou la matière. Dans le système de ceux-ci, la matière a tout fait; dans le système de ceux-là, le peuple a droit de tout faire; en sorte qu'on pourrait appeler les démocrates, les athées de la politique; et les athées, les enragés ou les jacobins de la religion. [28]

As in earlier statements "democracy" is here used to signify a political system which firmly rejected any kind of visible unity based upon power, and which exclusively regarded its subjects, or the people, as being sovereign. It also looks as if Bonald here used "democrats" as synonymous with "Jacobins" as well as with "enragés". It is evident that he held democracy to represent a theory as false as that of atheism, since both rejected the main and unique principle in their respective fields. Denial of temporal authority is definitely regarded here as a mistake as fundamental as the denial of the existence of God. Even if we are not directly told that democracy was atheistic, the important methodological similarity between democracy and atheism may probably be taken to imply that Bonald at that time would not have declared the Catholic religion to be the most convenient for a democracy.

A relationship of incompatibility between democracy and religion, or a way of declaring without reservations democracy to be atheistic, is probably to be found elsewhere in his works, however. Bonald here declared:

> De religion? la démocratie n'en veut pas; elle a proclamé la loi athée, mot affreux qui a été entendu dans le sanctuaire de la justice. [29]

And he went on to say that everything, even reason, judgement, and literature was to disappear under the unfortunate influence of democracy.

In general, Bonald's resentment, even fury, makes an analysis of his use of "democracy" a little difficult. Thus it seems that a detailed discussion concerning conceptual and non-conceptual characteristics of the concept, or concepts, 'democracy' made use of by Bonald will not be very fruitful. Although it is hardly possible to make any definite statements, there are fairly strong indications that Bonald used "democracy" not only derogatorily, but

dyslogistically, or with a negative value judgement implicit in its signification. Some of his statements may indicate a different view, but there are
also several according to which disorder, violence, and excesses of different
kinds seem to have been directly included in the signification of the term.

Very derogatory if not dyslogistic applications of "democracy" are
somewhat frequent in Bonald's writings, and as far as I can see, there is
no exception. The following quotation is fairly typical:

> ... la démocratie dans le gouvernement est le principe des révolutions,
> les désordres, les violences, les proscriptions, les excès de tout genre
> en sont les conséquences. 30

Bonald also used "military democracy" to denote the rule of Bonaparte.

> Sous Bonaparte, l'administration était aussi despotique que le gouverne-
> ment; mais ce gouvernement même était aussi une démocratie militaire,
> car le despotisme est la démocratie dans le camp, comme la démocratie
> civile est le despotisme dans la cité. 31

In this last statement there is a clearer example of an alleged identity
between democracy and despotism than in the first quotation from Bonald.
Here, too, elimination of hereditary distinctions was, in Bonald's view,
probably an essential property of democracy as well as of despotism, even
if nothing was directly mentioned here concerning that point.

4. Fichte

A negative attitude towards what he designated "democracy" was also a
characteristic of Fichte's terminology, which was somewhat similar to that
of Bonald. Fichte's use of "democracy" is more differentiated than Bonald's,
however, in that although Fichte's negative attitude is evident in several
cases, there are also occurrences of a fairly neutral kind. A most important
factor of Fichte's negative attitude was that he generally held democracy to
be an illegal constitution, or eine rechtswidrige Verfassung. And it is just
such generalities, with no direct references to revolutionary events in contemporary France, which primarily characterize Fichte's use of "democracy".

In 1796 he maintained that, according to Kant's political philosophy, all
kinds of States must be founded upon an original contract; and he went on to
say:

> ferner, dass das Volk die exekutive Gewalt nicht selbst ausüben, sondern
> sie übertragen müsse, dass sonach die Demokratie, in der eigentlichen
> Bedeutung des Wortes, eine völlig rechtswidrige Verfassung sei. 32

It is most probable that Fichte was not just referring to Kant's opinions,
but that he himself accepted this argument. Thus Fichte probably held
democracy, and even what he declared represented the real signification of
"democracy", to be contrary to all laws, or to be an illegal constitution.
The criterion, or one of the criteria, of the illegality of a constitution was
that the people should not in any way delegate executive power to a certain
body. This quotation indicates clearly that Fichte, as well as Kant, was in
favour of a certain kind of separation of powers in accordance with the main
ideas of Montesquieu.

As regards the making and maintenance of laws, and especially penal laws, Fichte said later in this work -- his view is reminiscent of Plato -- that when the common people were in possession of legislative power, and were in addition judges of their own affairs, they would at first let everything go its own way, mainly out of laziness. But later on, when crime had increased immensely, they would behave cruelly and fanatically and terrorize the community. Afterwards they would once more favour mildness, and then again, for the same reasons, revert to cruelty, and so on. Fichte continued:

> Eine solche Verfassung, die <u>demokratische</u> in der eigentlichsten Bedeu-
> tung des Wortes, wäre die allerunsicherste, die es geben könnte, indem
> man nicht nur, wie ausser dem Staate, immerfort die Gewalttätigkeiten
> aller, sondern von Zeit zu Zeit auch die blinde Wut eines gereizten
> Haufens, der im Namen des Gesetzes ungerecht verfüre, zu fürchten
> hätte. [33]

Fichte here alleged the absence of any separation of power in what he held to be a democratic constitution. But while in the former quotation he considered a lack of separation between the legislative and the executive powers to be the essential characteristic of democracy, in the latter he considered lack of separation between the legislative and the judicial powers to be the main characteristic of democratic government. Since here he employs an expression like "the most real sense of the word" while in the first statement he had used "in the real sense of the word", it may, strictly speaking, be assumed that absence of separation between legislative and judicial powers was the most essential characteristic of what Fichte here held to be democracy. From a somewhat broader point of view, it can with very good reason be inferred that Fichte held that no kind of separation of power, whether between the legislative, executive, or judicial branches of government, could represent a conceptual characteristic of this concept 'democracy', or could be implicit in what he held to be the real, or even most real, signification of "democracy". Evidently, this kind of rule might not be of a representative kind, but the people at large would directly exert legislative, executive, and judicial power; this Fichte considered to be an illegal constitution. These latter factors can reasonably be classified as conceptual characteristics of 'democracy', while, for example, behaviour alternating continually between cruelty and mildness can more reasonably be regarded as the alleged consequence of such a form of rule, or as a non-conceptual characteristic.

In relation to the last quotation, Fichte added:

> ... dass die Demokratie in dem oben erklärten Sinne des Worts nicht etwa
> nur eine unpolitische, sondern eine schlechthin rechtswidrige Verfassung
> ist. [34]

What Fichte meant by "unpolitical" is not elaborated upon here. In the second part of this work, Fichte defined what he understood by the term "politics":

> Diejenige Wissenschaft, welche es mit einem besonderen, durch zu-
> fällige Markmale (empirisch) bestimmten Staate zu tun hat, und betrachtet,
> wie das Rechtgesetz in ihm sich am füglichsten realisieren lasse heisst
> Politik. [35]

In using the term "unpolitical" one year earlier Fichte possibly meant something which was in opposition to, or at least not in accordance with, this later definition.

A use of "democracy" very different from the above, however, can be observed somewhat later in the same work. Fichte said here that the wielders of the executive power might be elected or not. He added that if they were elected, either all would be elected, or only a few.

> Im ersten Falle [im Falle wo die Verwalter der exekutiven Gewalt für ihre Person gewählt werden] werden entweder alle, oder nur einige gewählt. Sie werden gewählt, unmittelbar durch die Gemeine, in der Demokratie, im engeren Sinne des Worts, d. h. in der, die eine Repräsentation hat und darum eine rechtmässige Verfassung ist. Wenn alle obrichkeitlichen Personen unmittelbar durch die Gemeine gewählt werden, ist es eine reine, wo nicht, eine gemischte Demokratie. 36

Most probably because this form of government would have some kind of representation, Fichte declared it to be a legal one. This is in good harmony with his earlier criteria on this point. With regard to his terminology, however, it is somewhat strange to see that he used "democracy in the narrower sense of the word" as signifying a kind of representative and legal form of government, while "democracy in the real sense of the word", in the same work, had been used to connote a non-representative and illegal one. In that way 'narrower democracy' could not be a species of 'real democracy'.

With regard to other designations, it is fairly clear that "pure democracy" was used to connote a form of government where all holders of executive power were elected, and "mixed democracy" to connote a form where some, but not all, of these holders were elected. It is also certain that "pure democracy" and "mixed democracy" were conceptual designations of the broader concept or genus 'narrower democracy'. This implies that none of these would be subsumable under what he designated as "democracy in the real sense of the word".

5. Schleiermacher

The most important occurrences of "democracy" in the writings of Schleiermacher are without doubt to be found in his treatise Ueber die Begriffe der verschiedenen Staatsformen from 1814. In the introduction Schleiermacher declared that the discussion of forms of government had for a very long time been marked by the old Greek classifications. According to these, there existed three main classes which covered all forms of rule:

> ... welche nemlich drei Hauptgattungen annimmt unter welche alle Staatsformen gebracht werden können, die Demokratie, die Aristokratie und die Monarchie, je nachdem die ganze Masse des Volks oder eine bestimmte Klasse, deswegen die vornehmere, an der Regierung theilnimmt, oder diese sich in den Händen eines Einzelnen befindet. 37

Schleiermacher added, however, that these classifications were not fit for existing forms of government, since contemporary forms of rule were far too varied and differentiated to be pressed into this simple classical formula. He was also of the opinion that the use of the terms "democratic", "aristocratic", and "monarchical" had therefore caused much misunderstanding and misuse. But this did not imply that he regarded the concepts 'democracy', 'aristocracy', and 'monarchy' as empty concepts.

> Dennoch aber können diese Begriffe, demokratisch, aristokratisch und monarchisch nicht leer seyn, denn sie sind nicht erfunden oder gemacht, gleichen also keinesweges jenen künstlichen Klassen und Ordnungen in der Naturbeschreibung, denen kein lebendiger Typus des ganzen Daseyns zum Grunde liegt, sondern im Gegensatz mit jenen gleichen sie vielmehr den natürlichen Familien und Geschlechtern. [38]

Schleiermacher claimed that these terms have grown in the living Greek language, and that they therefore also must have firm significations.

It is a little difficult to know what Schleiermacher intended to convey here by "artificial classes" and "natural families", and to which system of biological classification, for example, that of Linnaeus, he would have regarded them as belonging. As regards language, however, it seems that Schleiermacher held the following to be sufficient criteria of something belonging to natural families, that (1) the words were not invented by special persons at fixed dates, as, for example, terms like "gas", which was invented by the Dutch chemist van Helmont, or "idéologie", which was invented by Destutt de Tracy, and (2) that the words had some extension in the vernacular. We can agree with Schleiermacher that the terms "democratic", "aristocratic", and "monarchical" belonged to the natural families according to these criteria, but it is a little difficult to accept his view that these terms therefore have firm significations. On the contrary, it is more probable that invented and artificial terms might have more firm significations than the natural ones.

Schleiermacher began to discuss what he called "Begriffe, demokratisch, aristokratisch, u. s. w. ", but later said

> ... diese Ausdrücke sind in der hellenischen Sprache lebendig gewachsen und als leitende Begriffe darin fixirt:

which indicates that these concepts had directly been regarded as expressions. A probable interpretation of this statement is that Schleiermacher intended to say that the concepts 'democracy', 'aristocracy', etc. , of which "democracy", "aristocracy", etc. were conceptual designations, were not empty concepts because these conceptual designations had evolved in the living Greek language and were used to designate central concepts. But he is not very clear on this point.

With regard to the signification of "democracy", the central statement occurs without doubt when Schleiermacher, using fairly difficult terminology, declared that democracy was a State dominated by and at the same time representative of the political consciousness of the uniform and unanimous masses:

> ... dies ist die Demokratie, der durch gleichförmiges Uebergehen einer in sich gleichartigen Volksmasse in das politische Bewusstseyn entstandene und diese Gleichförmigkeit darstellende Staat. [39]

This statement can probably be regarded as containing a condensed characteristic of all denotata of "democracy". The manner of involving, and also of conserving, the unanimity and conformity of the masses was thus an essential property of the signification of the term as used by him. On this point there is a rather high degree of similarity between his terminology and that of Robespierre and Saint-Just. Probably as an implication of this unanimity, Schleiermacher held in addition that there would be a very small difference between private and common interests in this form of State:

> ... weil aber in diesem Staat Gemeingeist und Privatinteresse sich in jedes Einzelnen Bewusstseyn unmittelbar und immer berühren.

From a certain point of view, this statement may be said to be somewhat similar to later statements of Hegel. It must be mentioned, however, that while Hegel considered the general interest to dominate greatly over the particular, Schleiermacher regarded the close intercourse between private and collective interests to be essential to democracy. On this point he even held that the citizen should not forget his workshop when in the popular assembly, and that he should keep this assembly in mind when in the workshop.

Concerning the territorial extension of a form which he held to be a democracy, Schleiermacher was quite certain that democracy, as understood by him, was impossible in larger States. He stated, firstly, that common meetings of all citizens would be quite unthinkable in a large territory; and secondly, that any form of representative rule was incompatible with the essentials of democracy. On the latter point, Schleiermacher said:

> Denn wollte man auch die äussere Bestimmung dahin erweitern, es solle noch für Demokratie gelten, wenn die vom Volk gewählten Repräsentanten oder deren Afterrepräsentanten am Ende in eine Versammlung zusammengedrängt würden; so könnte doch dabei auch das Wesen der Sache nicht bestehn: denn solche Repräsentanten für die ganze Zeit ihres Zusammenseyns ganz von ihrem Privatleben abgetrennt und auf ihre politische Function beschränkt, können jenes freilich verwirrende aber auch leichte und sich bald wieder frölich entwirrende Spiel zwischen Privatinteresse und Gemeingeist, welches der wahre Charakter der Demokratie ist, nicht entwickeln; wie man denn auch die repräsentativen Verfassungen von den Demokratien immer getrennt hat. [40]

In this way, by once more declaring an intimate relationship between private and collective interests to be essential for a democracy, and thereby also holding the system of representatives to be incompatible with this intimate relationship, Schleiermacher can with very good reason be said to have regarded any system of representatives and what he termed "democracy" as being mutually incompatible phenomena in political life.

Concerning the allegation that a dividing line had always been drawn between democracies and representative forms of government, this statement may be interpreted as a way of saying that representative forms had always been separated from what other people had designated as "democracies". This viewpoint is only partly acceptable, since there were at least some persons, for example Robespierre and Godwin, who at that time had used "democracy" with a signification which included some kind of representative rule. Schleiermacher may be said to have been generally right; but he possibly did not intend to introduce a meta-occurrence in this case.

I shall discuss a few occurrences from other parts of his writings. In his first draft of Ethik we find the expressions "Aristokratisch = orthodox, demokratisch = heterodox",[41] and he referred to England and Rome and the difference between the Roman Catholic and Protestant clergy. Further comments were not given, however, and this statement does not seem to have occurred in his printed work Ethik.

In his main pedagogical work, Schleiermacher asked himself if every man was capable of entering the State, the Church, etc. as the equal of others. He went on to say:

Dies läuft auf den schwierigen Gegensatz der aristokratischen und demo-kratischen Ansicht hinaus. [42]

And in discussing whether the differences between human beings were of a social or of a natural, in the sense of a biological, kind, one of his conclusions was:

Man kann sich auch ein gänzliches Verschwinden der angeborenen Diffe-renz denken, aber nur zugleich mit einer vollkommenen Demokratie [43]

-- a statement which marks a high association, if not identification, between complete equality and what he designated as "perfect democracy".
Although Schleiermacher maintained earlier that any form of represen-tation was incompatible with democracy, he once described one kind of feder-ation as what may possibly be summed up as "mainly democratical".

Die grosse Form [des zusammengesetzten Staates] wird dann wesentlich demokratisch, wobei die kleine teils demokratisch, teils monarchisch, teils sogar aristokratisch sein kann. [44]

On this point Schleiermacher referred to Switzerland, the United States, and the German Federation. Schleiermacher probably regarded these federa-tions as having fairly representative kinds of rule. Thus, the signification attributed to "democratic" can at least be said partly to contradict that ear-lier attributed to "democracy".
Such a way of using "democratic" to characterize a probably represen-tative form of government seems to have been restricted to this case, how-ever. One of his political aphorisms was:

Die reine Demokratie beschränkt sich ihrer Natur nach auf die Grösse einer übersehbaren Versammlung. [45]

It may be objected that the use of the qualification "pure" may be taken to indicate that unqualified "democracy" might connote a form of rule compat-ible with some kind of representation. Nothing to support an indication of this kind, however, except what has already been said about his use of "mainly democratical", has been found in Schleiermacher's writings.

6. Hegel

Hegel's approach to democracy, like Schleiermacher's, was a general point of view. Both, for example, make very few or no references to democracy as a contemporary problem. On this point there is an important difference between Burke, de Maistre, and Bonald, on the one hand, and Schleiermacher and Hegel, on the other, which may partly be explained by the fact that the occurrences in Hegel's terminology date from politically fairly quiet years and not from the years of the French Revolution. Another factor, without doubt, is Hegel's tendency to treat every problem in a general, and also in a systematic, way. And we find in his discussion about democracy a degree of systematization which is seldom to be found in the works of most other political thinkers. Of his political and philosophical works, his lectures on the philosophy of history are the most important for this research. These lectures were given at the University of Berlin in 1822-23 and in 1826-27, and were later printed as <u>Vorlesungen über die Philosophie der Weltgeschichte</u>. In the introductory part of this work, <u>Die Vernunft in der Geschichte</u>, Hegel declared that any form of State needed a small group of men with a certain authority. He added:

> Beschliesst z. B. auch in den Demokratien das Volk den Krieg, so muss doch ein General an die Spitze gestellt werden, welcher denselben kommandiert. [46]

This seems to indicate that Hegel held that the people were to decide matters of war and peace in a democracy, but that also here, or maybe even here, the military leadership was to be delegated to a general. In a more general way, we may say that Hegel held democracy, for the most part, and in relation to the most important questions, to be the direct rule of the people, but that this was not incompatible with some delegation of power in special situations.

A little later Hegel stated that the first and most important elements in the classifying of forms of government were the differences between governing bodies and those governed:

> Die allererste Bestimmung ist überhaupt der Unterschied von Regierenden und Regierten; und mit Recht hat man die Verfassung in allgemeinen in Monarchie, Aristokratie und Demokratie eingeteilt. [47]

A few pages later, however, he added

> ... wenn wir von Verfassung reden, wir uns nicht bei abstrakten Unterschiedens aufhalten, wie die bekannten, schon erwähnter von Demokratie, Aristokratie und Monarchie sind. Man gibt ohnehin zu, dass es nicht leicht eine ungemischte Demokratie gebe, ganz ohne ein aristokratisches Prinzip. [48]

Hegel here seems to have regarded the differences between what he called "monarchy", "aristocracy", and "democracy" as differences in the respective relationships between governing bodies and those governed, although these differences were not elaborated upon. He did add, however, that these differences were of an abstract kind, and would not receive any further attention. This probably does not imply that the above differences between monarchy, aristocracy, and democracy, as understood by him, were abstract in relation to some other and more concrete differences, but that the differences as such were abstract ones, and therefore partly outside the scope of his inquiry. Probably in support of this alleged abstraction he said that it would not be easy fo find what he called an "unmixed democracy" quite without any aristocratic principle. If "aristocratic principle" is used here as signifying any kind of delegated power, Hegel here used "unmixed democracy" with a signification somewhat different from "democracy" in our first quotation, where the term signified a kind of rule which was not incompatible with any kind of delegation of power.

The fact that Hegel considered the differences between what he called "monarchy", "aristocracy", and "democracy" to be of an abstract nature may explain why these terms occur somewhat infrequently, but it does not prevent him from sometimes using "democracy", especially in his discussion of the policy in antiquity. Hegel seems to have declared without reservations that democracy, as understood by him, was the main feature in Greek political life. "In Griechenland sehen wir die Demokratie, in ihrer schönsten Ausbildung." And he went on to say that just as despotism was the central point in Oriental political life, so aristocracy was the political form of the Roman world, and monarchy the destiny of the Teutonic, Christian world; "die Demokratie aber ist die Bestimmung der politischen Verfassung für Griechenland gewesen. "[49]

With regard to the principles of democracy, Hegel started by agreeing with Montesquieu's opinion of virtue as the principle of democracy. Hegel made it an absolute condition for a democratic State that there should be unity between the special and the general interests in the State, and that subjectivity should not be developed.

> Die innere absolute Bedingung der Demokratie ist Einheit der Besonderheit mit dem allgemeinen Interesse des Staates; die Subjektivitet muss noch nicht sich selbst erfasst haben, noch nicht zu ihrer Reife zukommen sein. [50]

What Hegel meant by "subjectivity" is not quite clear, but he evidently intended to say that the existence of democracy depended upon there being little or no difference between the personal interest of each citizen, which he probably regarded as subjective, and the general or collective interest of the society as a whole, or that interest which he held to be objective. This seems to imply that democracy, according to Hegel, would be conditional upon its citizens having the welfare of society and not their individual interest in view when taking part in political life. For Hegel, real political leadership and any legitimate claim to share in governing affairs were conditional on the objective spirit by which the respective persons were characterized. And since democracy was necessarily characterized by the political leadership of all, it must in consequence also be characterized by the suppression of all particular and private interests. [51]

Hegel held that the constitution in a democracy was of necessity characterized by all citizens taking part in political affairs. This property he not only regarded as a necessary one, but also a sufficient one for a constitution to be democratic. He was even of the opinion that any constitutional amendments other than this were not compatible with a democracy.

> Es kann keine Beratungen und Beschlüsse über die Verfassung geben. Sondern die Verfassung ist eben dies, dass die Bürger beraten und beschliessen; sonst ist nichts fest. Dies ist allein das Feste.

In my opinion this implies that, in Hegel's view, democracy was not compatible with any fundamental laws, or any constitution in the stricter signification of "constitution".

With regard to the extent of the territory in a democracy, Hegel declared, "Dass nur kleine Staaten diese Verfassung fähig sind. " [53] He admitted that from an abstract point of view it would be possible to bring together many citizens for discussion and decision-making; he emphasized, however, that large meetings would lose the personal intimacy of small ones, in which, and only in which, the people would be under the influence of the objective spirit. As we have seen, he held this to be essential to any democracy. This way of argument can be taken to furnish more proof that Hegel used "democracy" with a connotation which would definitely not include any kind of representative rule, although, in accordance with our first quotation in this section, we cannot regard a certain delegation of power in special situations to have been absolutely incompatible with what Hegel held to be democracy.

With few exceptions, he declared slavery to be connected with democracy. On this point he held;

> ... dass mit der demokratischen Verfassung und der schönen Weise ihrer Freiheit die Sklaverei verbunden ist und verbunden sein muss, wenn es nicht eine Demokratie sein soll zwischen ackerbauenden und Hirtenvölkern wie in der Schweiz von so weniger partikulärer Bildung. [54]

The reasons for this relationship, according to Hegel, were that though the Greeks were adherents of personal freedom, they had not reached that level in the development towards the absolute spirit which was characterized by the freedom of men as such. This latter kind of freedom, according to him, was only to be found in monarchies of the Prussian kind.

In addition, Hegel said that a democracy must be marked by equality; this probably meant that differences in fortune and education among citizens should be quite small. He was also of the opinion that the existence of a democracy was connected with that of the oracle. His argumentation on this point touches earlier problems concerning subjectivity and democracy, and he seems to have been of the opinion that the citizens in a democracy had no absolute faith in their own decisions, on account of their necessary lack of subjectivity.

> Die Menschen wagten es nicht, aus sich den letzten Entschluss zu fassen; es musste eine fremde Autorität dazukommen. [55]

From a broader point of view, Hegel can probably be considered to hold the properties we have discussed above to be necessary as well as sufficient in his attempt to mark out what he designated as "democracy". Thus he would have considered a State to be a democracy if, and only if, the fundamental law were restricted to stressing the direct political activity of all citizens, if collective interests always strongly prevailed over the individual ones, and if the territory were fairly small. Equality and generally, but not necessarily, slavery were also held to be conditions for the existence of such a form of State. Except for slavery, these properties may be reckoned as conceptual characteristics of Hegel's concept 'democracy'; it is somewhat doubtful whether the existence of an oracle can be included among these characteristics, since this seems to have been regarded as being a result and not a condition of democracy.

The denotata of "democracy" as used in Hegel's language are without doubt predominantly restricted to the Greek city-states. However, Hegel also considered Switzerland to be a democracy. On the other hand, he refused the label "democracy" for the revolutionary government of France. As earlier, Hegel declared democracy to be impossible in larger territories, and he went on to state:

> In der französischen Revolution ist deshalb niemals die republikanische Verfassung als eine Demokratie zustande gekommen. [56]

As to Hegel's attitude towards what he labelled with this term, he cannot be regarded as having used "democracy" in a derogatory way. On this point there is a marked difference between Burke, de Maistre, and Bonald, on one hand, and Hegel, on the other. What he designated as "democracy" was for him hardly the ideal constitution, or the political realization of the absolute spirit; that phenomenon was exclusively restricted to a Christian and Teutonic constitution like the Prussian monarchy. But it can also be seen that he considered democracy to be the most beautiful constitution which had ever existed and that it represented the purest form of liberty.

Sie [die Demokratie] ist die schönste Verfassung, die reinste Freiheit, die je existiert hat, und sie kann leicht als die für die Vernunft notwendigste, dem Begriff angemessenste erscheinen.

Hegel added, however,

... dass das Schönste nicht das Tiefste, nicht die wahrhafte Form des geistigen Begriffs ist. [57]

I have only used material from the lectures on the philosophy of history, [58] which contain his most important uses of "democracy". The other few occurrences that exist do not seem to convey anything of additional importance to what can be found in these lectures.

CHAPTER IV

EARLY CONSTITUTIONALISM

In this chapter I shall discuss the use of "democracy" in works written
during or shortly after the French Revolution. Somewhat similar to Burke,
de Maistre, and Bonald, the authors concerned were also characterized by
a negative attitude towards central aspects of French revolutionary rule,
although there is a fairly important difference between the unreserved negative attitude of Burke and Bonald on the one hand, and the differentiated
attitude of Benjamin Constant and Madame de Staël on the other. But here,
too, a derogatory kind of application of the term is a general characteristic.
In Kant's terminology there is even a very derogatory, if not dyslogistic
kind of application. This chapter also presents a different approach in discussing political forms of rule. There is what we may call the German
way, very evident in Kant's arguing, which is of a very general kind, where
there are no references to contemporary events in France, although the
work was written in 1795; and on the other hand, there is the use of "democracy" by Constant, Madame de Staël, and Châteaubriand, which is mostly
to be found in connection with concrete points of view, but also in statements
which are less elaborated.

1. Kant

In his work <u>Zum Ewigen Frieden,</u> published in 1795, Kant opened his description of different forms of governments by saying,

> ... damit man die republikanische Verfassung nicht (wie gemeiniglich
> geschieht) mit der demokratischen verwechsele, muss folgendes bemerkt
> werden. [1]

As background for his investigations into political forms Kant obviously
wished to draw a line of demarcation between the forms of government he
considered to be respectively the democratic and the republican. He also
referred to a common confusion on that point. This may be taken to imply
that Kant held "democratic" and "republican" to have been used as synonyms,
or near synonyms, in the existing vernacular in Prussia, and perhaps in
other countries also, though it has been impossible to check Kant's reference to the vernacular. I only find an approximate relationship of synonymity
in Robespierre's terminology, although I think that his terminology may
possibly have influenced common usage of political terms in Prussia, and,
perhaps particularly, the usage of those people who sympathized with the
revolution in France.

Kant further said that forms of government were to be classified either
(1) according to the number of persons in possession of supreme power in
the State, or (2) according to the ways in which the supreme power was executed. According to the first form of classification, the <u>forma imperii,</u> there

existed three forms, in which one person, or few persons, or all people were in possession of supreme power. These forms were designated by Kant as "autocracy", "aristocracy", and "democracy", and he added the German counterparts of these terms, "Fürstengewalt", "Adelsgewalt", and "Volksgewalt". According to the second form of classification, the forma regiminis, there existed two forms of government which were said to be either republican or despotic.

He went on to say:

> Der Republikanism ist das Staatsprinzip der Absonderung der aus-
> führenden Gewalt (der Regierung) von der gesetzgebenden; der Despotism
> ist das der eigenmächtigen Vollziehung des Staats von Gesetzen, die er
> selbst gegeben hat... [2]

Like Montesquieu, Kant held a separation of power between the legis-lative and executive organs to be essential to freedom. It is also fairly clear that he held absence or presence of this kind of separation to be a necessary as well as a sufficient condition for States being respectively despotisms or republics.

Hitherto we have only seen "democracy" used by Kant as signifying a kind of government in which supreme power was said to be in the hands of all; it has also been said to be synonymous with "Volkherrschaft". Kant, in accordance with the second kind of classification, considered democracy to be a despotic kind of government. In a difficult passage he stated:

> Unter den drei Staatsformen ist die der Demokratie im eigentlichen Ver-
> stande des Worts notwendig ein Despotism, weil sie eine exekutive Ge-
> walt gründet, da alle über und allenfalls auch wider Einen (der also nicht
> miteinstimt), mithin alle, die doch nicht alle sind beschliessen; welches
> ein Widerspruch des allgemeinen Willens mit sich selbst und mit der
> Freiheit ist. [3]

In thus emphasizing that democracy is of necessity despotic, Kant definitely excludes the possibility that anything labelled as "democracy" might be subsumable under what he designated as "republic", since what he held to be republic and despotism evidently mutually excluded each other.

On the basis of his earlier arguments, one might expect him to draw attention primarily to an alleged absence of separation between the legis-lative and executive power in a democracy, when classifying this form of government as a kind of despotism. One might also surmise that Kant con-sidered the executive and legislative power to have been identical in what he regarded as a democracy, even if this was not mentioned explicitly. His main argument, perhaps even his sole argument claiming that democracy, even democracy according to the real signification of "democracy", must necessarily be despotism, was focused on the executive power in such a form of rule. If I interpret his very difficult language correctly, all ruled all in a democracy, and still ruled with the pretension of representing all, even if one person disagreed with the rest. This apparently means that Kant considered that the majority in a democracy behaved as if their stand-points had been unanimously accepted. This would also happen in cases where a smaller or greater minority dissented from the views of the major-ity, and when the minority had no influence upon governmental affairs, but had to obey the majority in everything. According to Kant, such a form of government was contrary to what he held to be liberty, and to the common will.

A somewhat related kind of argumentation is found in Kant's statement:

Alle Regierungsformen nämlich, die nicht repräsentativ ist, ist eigentlich eine Unform. [4]

It can be seen that his sole argument in favour of this rejection of non-representative forms of rule, was his way of holding that executive and legislative powers must be separated. This separation of power, which he considered necessary if a government were to avoid despotism, was most probably dependent on the presence of a representative kind of body. Kant added that it was difficult for monarchies and for aristocracies to adopt a representative system, but he admitted,

... dass sie eine dem Geiste eines repräsentativen Systems gemässe Regierungsart annehmen.

With regard to democracy, he added,

... dahingegen die demokratische es unmöglich macht, weil alles da Herr sein will.

Thus any kind of representation was incompatible with what he designated as "democracy", which implies that his signification of "democracy" was exclusively restricted to cover direct forms of rule.

Kant held what he designated as "democracy" to be conceptually a kind of despotism executed by the masses where there was hardly any possibility of any kind of political minority, and further, that separation of powers as well as any kind of rule by elected representatives were definitely not compatible with the connotation attributed to this term. In spite of Kant's description of a very close relationship between democracy and despotism, he presents no evidence of relationship of identity between those political phenomena. Any democracy was thus subsumable under what he held to be despotism, but hardly vice versa.

Concerning the occurrences of the term "democracy" other than those I have already discussed, I have only been able to find one instance in this and other of Kant's works. Somewhat later in <u>Zum ewigen Frieden</u>, he mentioned different kinds of badly organized governments, referring to their political systems as "z. B. von Demokratien ohne Repräsentationssystem. " [5] The explicit mention of democracies without representative systems may indicate that Kant here did not hold democracy to be necessarily non-representative, or that he might conceive of democracies with representation. Thus the signification would clearly differ from that earlier attributed to "democracy". Kant may also have used the term with a signification identical with the earlier one, however. In this case, the quotation would have been a pleonasm, though this does not exclude the possibility of the latter alternative.

From a somewhat broader point of view, Kant's reason for holding democracy to be necessarily a kind of despotism may be found in the existing usage of "democracy" by leading revolutionaries in France. In their concepts of 'democracy' there is hardly any place for the exertion of influence by minorities. On the other hand, it must also be mentioned that the definition of democracy as a despotic form of government characterized by the absolute rule of the majority cannot be restricted to the time of the French revolution. In 1650, for example, Hobbes had said in <u>De Corpore Politico</u>, that "where the Votes of the major part involve the Votes of the rest, there is actually a democracy. " [6] And almost twenty years later, Spinoza, in <u>Tractatus Theo-</u>

<u>logico-politicus</u>, described a society where all the citizens had conferred upon the society all moral and political power, which was therefore alone in possession of supreme political authority and unrestricted sovereignty, and where all members of society were forced into obedience. Spinoza went on to say that such a constitution was called a "democracy", and that this was to be defined as a public assembly which collectively had the supreme right to carry out everything of which it was capable. This implied that the highest authority could not be restricted by any law, and that everyone had to obey this assembly in everything. [7]

On several important points there is great similarity between these formulations of Hobbes and Spinoza and Kant's definition of democracy. Spinoza and Hobbes similarly rejected the possibility that a democracy might be a rule by elected representatives. [8] On this point we have seen that Robespierre tried to restrict the signification of "democracy" to the area of a representative kind of rule. Both factors may be taken to indicate that the background of Kant's application of "democracy" is to be found to a greater degree in the use of this term by earlier philosophers than in the terminology of leading French revolutionaries. But questions of this kind are rather apt to remain hypothetical, and the possibility of one kind of influence does not necessarily exclude another.

2. Benjamin Constant

Like Kant, Constant also used "democracy" very infrequently, and we have no reason to regard the few occurrences as revealing the most central aspects of his political philosophy. Nevertheless, these occurrences do not lack importance in an inquiry into his political thinking. A key example is found in <u>Principes de Politique</u>, where Constant treated the political philosophy of Hobbes. Constant maintained that, for Hobbes,

... la démocratie est une souveraineté absolue entre les mains de tous. [9]

Against this view Constant held that no sovereignty should be absolute or arbitrary, because when sovereignty was unrestricted, the citizens were left to the mercy of the government. In accordance with this view he said:

La démocratie est l'autorité deposée entre les mains de tous, mais seulement la somme d'autorité nécessaire à la sûreté de l'association. [10]

Similar limitations of authority are also present in what he called "aristocracies" and "monarchies", the only difference being that the restricted authority of the first was vested in a smaller number, and in the latter in a single person.

This statement, however, does not seem to have implied that absolutely everyone, or every man, had a share in such authority. When discussing economic conditions for the execution of political rights, Constant declared that property alone made men capable of exercising political rights, and also that no State should consider all individuals who resided in its territory to be members of that State (<u>membres de l'État</u>). His definition of democracy or even the most absolute democracy was no exception to this rule.

La démocratie la plus absolue établit deux classes: dans l'une sont relégués les étrangers et ceux qui n'ont pas atteint l'âge prescrit par la loi pour exercer les droits de cité: l'autre est composée des hommes parvenus à

cet âge, et nés dans le pays. Il existe donc un principe d'après lequel,
entre des individus rassemblés sur un territoire, il en est qui sont
membres de l'État, et il en est qui ne le sont pas. [11]

This statement reveals that even in a most absolute democracy, political
rights were not granted to all persons present on a certain territory. On
the other hand, this formulation may also be taken to indicate that no property qualifications should be necessary in order to possess such rights in
such a form of government, even if this was not explicitly formulated by
Constant.

Concerning the fairly central problem of whether what was designated
as "democracy" was compatible with a representative form of government,
Constant was most certainly in favour of an absolute line of demarcation
between democracy on the one hand and any rule by representatives on the
other. On another occasion he said:

La démocratie est bien differente du gouvernement représentatif; dans
ce dernier, quel que soit le nombre des représentantes de la nation, il
ne rapprochera jamais de celui des citoyens. [12]

I agree with Constant that in any State governed by elected representatives, the number of representatives will be far less than that of the citizens.
It also seems that an approximate similarity in number was held to be a
necessary condition for granting the label "democracy". From a practical
point of view this implies that "democracy" could be used exlusively to connote direct rule.

Constant also made a brief remark on the conception of democracy
among the revolutionary leaders in France.

Lorsque le flot des événements eut porté à la tête de l'État, durant la
révolution française, des hommes qui avaient adopté la philosophie comme
un préjugé, et la démocratie comme un fanatisme, ces hommes furent
saisis pour Rousseau, pour Mably, ... [13]

This statement shows evidence of his dislike of the revolutionary
leaders who had "adopté la philosophie comme un préjugé, et la démocratie
comme un fanatisme". This probably indicates that Constant himself did
not hold what he called "democracy" to be fanaticism, perhaps to the same
degree as he did not regard what he called "philosophy" as being prejudice.

It can hardly be said that these few occurrences of "democracy" reflect
very much of Constant's political philosophy. The first quotation is the
most important one from an ideological point of view, since it clearly shows
Constant's systematic dislike of absolute power of any kind. The fact that
he did not consider democracy to represent any kind of absolute power and
the fact that he did not consider democracy to be fanaticism do not imply,
however, that Constant used "democracy" in a somewhat honorific way.
Some degree of property qualification was for him a necessary condition for
the execution of political rights, and it is probable that he did not regard
these qualifications to be compatible with what he called "democracy". Furthermore, Constant was an ardent supporter of some kind of representation,
and it is certain that democracy, in his sense, was incompatible with any
kind of representative rule.

3. Madame de Staël

Like Kant and Constant, Madame de Staël makes a very infrequent use of
"democracy". She was in agreement with the other political thinkers discussed in this chapter in that she disapproved of what she labelled "democracy" and related terms. The occurrences in her terminology are generally
somewhat accidental, not likely to reveal anything of importance in her
political thinking.

In her main political work, __Considérations sur la Révolution Françoise__
(1814), she refers to the constitution of 1793 as having been "une constitution
scrupuleusement démocratique". [14] We are not, however, given any further
information concerning her attitude towards this constitution, or the signification she attached to "democracy". The term "scrupuleusement" may indicate that she disliked the constitution, an attitude which is fairly certain
according to other parts of the work; but this does not say much about the
signification attributed to "democratic" in this connection.

A somewhat similar occurrence is present in her account of a conversation with Robespierre at the home of her father, M. Necker, in 1789. She
adds that Robespierre was at that time only known as a solicitor from Artois,
"très-exagéré dans ses principes démocratiques". [15] What she intended
to mean by "Robespierre's democratic principles" is not clear, however.
Perhaps she meant something akin to what is stated a few pages later in relation to the doctrines of Robespierre and other revolutionaries.

L'arbitraire sans bornes étoit leur doctrine; il leur suffisoit de donner
pour prétexte à toutes les violences le nom propre de leur gouvernement,
le salut public; funeste expression, qui renferme le sacrifice de la morale
à ce qu'on est convenu d'appeler l'intérêt de l'état, c'est-à-dire, aux
passions de ceux qui gouvernent. [16]

In this case, she definitely disapproved of democratic principles.

As another point in this work she declared Talleyrand to have been the
most amiable man l'ancien régime had fostered, when he wished to be, and
she continued:

C'est le hasard qui l'a placé dans les dissensions populaires, il y a porté
les manières des cours; et cette grâce, qui devoit être suspecte à
l'ésprit de démocratie, a séduit souvent des hommes d'une grossière
nature. [17]

Why court manners should have been alien to what she held to be the
spirit of democracy is not mentioned, however. But it seems that she considered very plain manners, perhaps even impolite behaviour, to have been
best suited to that spirit.

In discussing the British constitution, she would not accept the generally
held version that the party in opposition was a democratic one.

Toutefois ce seroit bien à tort qu'on se persuaderoit sur le continent que
le parti de l'opposition est démocratique. [18]

She added that the Duke of Devonshire, the Duke of Bedford, and the
Marquess of Stafford were what she ironically designated as "démocrates

singuliers", and that in England, the aristocracy provided a barrier against royal authority. She maintained that the opposition was more liberal in its principles than the ministers, but added,

> ... mais comment pourroit-on craindre un bouleversement révolutionnaire de la part des individus qui possèdent tous les genres de propriété que l'ordre fait respecter, la fortune, le rang, et surtout les lumières? [19]

How far "democrats" and "revolutionary men" were intended to have been used synonymously is hardly clear. But it is quite certain that she envisaged at least a fairly close association between persons who are democrats and persons who are in favour of a revolutionary uprising. Indeed, to her, disapproving of such an uprising was probably sufficient evidence that such persons were not democrats; this probably implies that being in favour of a revolutionary uprising was a necessary condition for acquiring the label "democrats". She most probably also considered possession of property, rank, and talent to be imcompatible with revolutionary sentiment, and thus also probably incompatible with democratic sentiment, according to her definition of "democratic".

4. Châteaubriand

Châteaubriand, too, used "democracy" very infrequently, and as with Madame de Staël, his usage cannot be said to reveal very important aspects of his political thought. In 1814, Châteaubriand referred to the Chamber of Deputies as providing the democratic element in the French constitution of 1814.

> ... dans une monarchie mixte, les corps constitués tenant à parti republicain de gouvernement, l'un (la chambre des pairs) à l'aristocratie, l'autre (la chambre des députés) à la démocratie. [20]

As was fairly usual, 'aristocracy' and 'democracy' were here used as sub-concepts, or species, of a greater concept, or genus 'republic'. Châteaubriand also referred to the existing Chamber of Deputies as the democracy in the government, in spite of the fact that the Chamber was elected on a very narrow basis, only by and from among the fairly rich.

In a much earlier work, Châteaubriand had expressed the opinion that special forms of governments existed which were particular or natural to each historical period in the life of a nation.

> Il me semble qu'il existe un gouvernement particulier, pour ainsi dire naturel à chaque âge d'une nation: la liberté entière aux sauvages, la république royale aux pasteurs, la démocratie dans l'âge des vertus sociales, l'aristocratie dans le relâchement des mœurs, la monarchie dans l'âge du luxe, le despotisme dans la corruption. [21]

Châteaubriand did not mention, however, which social virtues marked the time which was natural for what he held as democracy, but it probably implied a plain style of living, a rather high degree of equality, and the absence, or near absence, of luxury. In associating democracy with social virtue, Châteaubriand touched on central problems in the political philosophies of Montesquieu and Hegel.

An occurrence of "democracy" more important than this one occurs in

1824, in a statement by Châteaubriand in defence of the constitutional monarchy in France. Here he attacked what he considered to be the popular yoke as well as arbitrary despotism.

Toutes les fois qu'on voudra nous conduire à la démocratie ou au despotisme, on trouvera une résistance nationale qui ramènera au gouvernement mixte, parce que nous sommes arrivés à cet état tempéré dans l'ordre social, qui nous rend le joug populaire et le pouvoir arbitraire d'un seul également insupportables.[22]

In this statement, constitutional or mixed government is clearly represented as the favourite form of rule of the French nation and, probably, of Châteaubriand himself. He also declared democracy as well as despotism to be extreme forms of rule which were insupportable in existing France on account of its new and tempered social climate, and it seems as if he used "democracy" synonymously, or almost synonymously, with "popular yoke", probably to the same degree as "despotism" was used synonymously, or almost synonymously, with "arbitrary power of one single person". This marks a near association, if not identification, with what he designated as "democracy" and the political omnipotence of the numerical majority. The fear of such a kind of power, like that of a despotic ruler, occupies an important place in the ideological writings of Châteaubriand, but as far as can be seen, these political ideas were not connected with the use of "democracy" in other places. The signification attached to "democracy" in this case is probably somewhat different from that attributed to this term when, ten years earlier, he associated the Chamber of Deputies with what he held was the democratic element in the French constitution.

CHAPTER V

MID-CENTURY CONSERVATISM

1. Disraeli

While earlier conservative ideologists have made use of an application of "democracy" which, apart from Hegel's, was derogatory, we find in early writings of Disraeli an application of this term which is honorific, and which may even be said to cover very central areas of his political thought. This tendency is found in his first use of this and closely related terms. In one of his earliest political writings, the pamphlet What is he?, Disraeli's intention was to make known his political views in connection with his candidature for Marylebone. He was of the opinion that until the recent change in 1832 the government had been based upon an aristocratic principle. By this change, however, English political life had deserted the old principle without adopting a new one, and he stated in conclusion:

> We must either revert to the aristocratic principle, or we must advance to the democratic. [1]

Disraeli held as his own opinion that

> I feel it absolutely necessary to advance to the new or the democratic principle. [2]

His argument was that the moment the Lords passed the Reform Bill, out of fear, or because of the threat to create new peers, instead of conviction, the aristocratic principle of government had expired forever. [3] He went on to say:

> From that moment it became the duty of every person of property, talent and education, -- to use his utmost exertions to advance the democratic principle in order that the country should not fall into that situation in which, -- it will speedily find itself -- absolutely without any Government whatever. [4]

The signification of "democratic" is rather difficult to grasp in these quotations. "Democratic" first characterizes the alternative to what he called "aristocratic", but "democratic" hardly signifies the methods which, according to him, had destroyed the aristocratic principle in England forever. It also characterizes the kind of principle which he felt absolutely necessary, and to the advance of which every man of property, talents, and education was to use his utmost exertions. The latter factor indicates that Disraeli used the term in a somewhat honorific way, to denote something which he wished to be realized; but further information on this point is difficult to obtain.

Two years later, Disraeli contributed leading articles to the Morning Post. In one of these, he declared that the Lords Spiritual and the Life

Peerage must in general be admired for their talents, their learning, and their piety. These men often sprang from the humbler classes of the people. Disraeli concluded:

> There is not a more democratic institution in the country than the Church, and this is the institution the Radicals are ever menacing and decrying. [5]

If we limited ourselves to this quotation, we can say that Disraeli considered the Church to be the most democratic institution in England because the Lords Spiritual often came from the humbler classes of the people, and possibly also because these men had distinguished themselves by their talents, learning, and piety. Thus, "democratic" probably signified something according to which it was possible for people of humble origin to reach the highest social levels by means of talent and character. But possibly the so-called democratic character of the Church lay not only in this phenomenon, he thought, and perhaps he also had in mind the representative function of the Lords Spiritual.

In the same year, 1835, Disraeli discussed the principle of representation in <u>Vindication of the English Constitution.</u> He said that there was much talk about this principle, but that it was very little understood. An assembly might very well be representative <u>without</u> being elected, and as proof he maintained:

> ...no one can deny that the Church of England is at this day not only virtually, but absolutely, faithfully, and efficiently represented in the House of Lords by the Bishops; yet these Lords of Parliament are not elected by their clergy. [6]

It is difficult, or impossible, to say definitely if, or how far, this view of the representative function of the bishops influences Disraeli's opinion that the Church was the most democratic institution in the country, but a similar view might have influenced this statement, although the term "democratic" did not occur in the last quotation.

A somewhat similar formulation occurs in the same work:

> Of the many popular elements in the House of Lords, I have always considered the bench of Bishops the most democratic. [7]

It is not clear, however, which other elements in the House of Lords he regarded as being popular, or why he characterized the bishops thus.

A most important feature of Disraeli's political philosophy was his conviction that the Tories defended the rights of the British people to a much stronger degree than the Whigs. He once declared:

> The Tory party in this country is the national party; it is the really democratic party in England. It supports the institutions of the country because they have been established for the common good, and because they secure the equality of civil rights, without which, whatever may be its name, no government can be free, and based upon which principle every government, however it may be styled, is in fact a Democracy. [8]

According to this statement it is fairly probable that Disraeli would have labelled any political body "really democratic" if it supported national institutions established for the common good, and if it secured the equality of civil rights. It looks as if Disraeli regarded his own political terminology, and especially his use of "democracy", as somewhat different from the vernacular. Formulations like "whatever be its name" and "however it may be styled" may be taken to indicate this. What Disraeli meant by "equality" is hardly clear at this point, but it can possibly be explained in connection with other occurrences of the term a little later on.

Concerning the nature of the English Constitution, Disraeli said that if one took a superficial view of the question, one would perceive that the government of the country was carried on by a King and two limited orders of his subjects. If one inquired in a more profound and comprehensive way, however, and examined not only the political constitution, but the political condition of the country, Disraeli maintained:

> We shall in truth discover that the state of our society is that of a complete democracy, headed by an hereditary chief, the executive and legislative functions performed by two privileged classes of the community, but the whole body of the nation entitled, if duly qualified, to participate in the exercise of those functions, and constantly participating in them. [9]

We see here that Disraeli considered the English society to be what he called a "complete democracy" if viewed other than superficially. And "complete" may possibly signify something which implies that neither the English nor any other society could ever be more democratic, in his sense of "democratic", than English society in 1835. It is clear that he considered it was no hindrance to a complete democracy to be headed by an hereditary monarch, and for the legislative and executive functions to be carried out by two privileged classes.

Disraeli held that not only the Peers but also the Commons were a privileged section of the people, and were not the people itself. He emphasized several times that the Commons were only the constituency of England which amounted to three hundred thousand, and once he even declared:

> The member of the House of Commons who talks of 'the People's House' is either a gross blockhead or an insolent usurper. [10]

What function he left to the people in his allegedly complete democracy is not clear here. He stated that the body of the whole nation should be entitled, if duly qualified, to participate in the exercise of the executive and legislative functions, but how they were entitled to participate in these functions, and what he meant by "duly qualified", is not explained.

Somewhat later in the same year Disraeli stated that the English nation had established a popular throne in order to retain the convenience of monarchy, and it had invested certain orders of their fellow-subjects with legislative functions in order to enjoy the security of aristocracy. He went on to say that these estates, however highly privileged, were not exclusive ones, and could be constitutionally obtained by every English subject. He also considered the Peers and the Commons of England to be what he called "the trustees of the nation, not its masters. " He added:

> ...the country where the legislative and even executive office may be constitutionally obtained by every subject of the land is a democracy, and a democracy of the noblest character. [11]

The criteria, probably sufficient as well as necessary ones, of a State being what he designated as a "democracy" and also as a "democracy of the noblest character" seem here to be that legislative and executive offices might constitutionally be obtained by every subject. He probably had this factor in mind when saying that the whole body of the nation, if duly qualified, should participate in the exercise of the executive and legislative functions.

Further to his assertion that the English society was a complete democracy, Disraeli went on to state that equality was the basis of English society.
He emphasized, however, that one must always distinguish between two different kinds of equality. There was the equality which levelled and destroyed,
and the equality which elevated and created. According to Disraeli, it was
"this last, this sublime, this celestial equality that animates the laws of
England", [12] while the principle of the first kind of equality was "base,
terrestrial, Gallic and grovelling. " He added however,

... as Equality is the basis, so Gradation is the superstructure; and the
English nation is essentially a nation of classes, but not of castes. [13]

The expression "not of castes" probably signifies that social classes in England were not exclusive, due to their habit of absorbing persons from other
levels of society; this was an essential characteristic of the English kind of
equality, and therefore of what he held to be democracy.

From a somewhat broader point of view, the essential, if not the exclusive, properties of Disraeli's signification of "democracy" when he declared England to be a complete democracy and a democracy of the noblest
kind were this sublime and celestial equality as well as the habit of supporting institutions which had been established for the common good. From a
comparative point of view, this use of "democracy" during 1835 may be said
to differ to a certain extent from his way of using "democratic" two years
earlier. In 1833, by "democratic" he meant something towards which the
English society was advancing, and it is therefore hardly possible that at
this time he would have said that either the English society or its form of
rule constituted a complete democracy. Since Disraeli did not refer to any
institutional or constitutional changes during these two years, there is some
degree of terminological difference here. Disraeli would have declared
England to be a complete democracy in 1833 if "democracy" had been used
with a signification identical to the one attributed to this term two years
later. As regards the background of Disraeli's terminology on this point,
perhaps this was conditioned by his fear that the English society would develop in a more radical direction. His opinion that English society was already a complete democracy might therefore have been consciously or un-
consciously formulated with the intention of conserving the existing state of
affairs.

Other occurrences of the term in Disraeli's political philosophy when a
young man are fairly similar to those of 1835. One year later he said in
Spirit of Whiggism:

It may be as well to remind the English nation that a revolutionary party
is not necessarily a liberal one, and that a republic is not indispensably
a democracy. [14]

And:

The monarchy of the Tories is more democratic than the Republic of
Whigs. It appeals with a keener sympathy to the passions of the millions;
it studies their interests with a more comprehensive solicitude. [15]

With regard to the English Constitution, he believed it to be just and true

... that there is no probability of ever establishing a more democratic
form of government than the present English constitution. [16]

In general, in these ideological works Disraeli used "democracy" and related terms in a way which makes them fairly central in his political terminology. This is most evident in various assertions that England was a democracy, and even a complete democracy, and also in his opinion that the Tory party was the most democratic party in England. As regards the significations of the term "democracy", the best indication is probably his manner of associating what he held to be democracy with the welfare of the people at large and the possibility for every gifted person to obtain the highest social rank. Neither government by the people at large, nor universal suffrage, nor the elimination of social classes, and certainly not a revolutionary policy, were necessary properties of the signification of "democracy". These are probably the main reasons for the absence of any use of these terms in a derogatory way. This absence of derogatory use, and even of the use of these terms in an honorific way, is a unique phenomenon among nineteenth-century conservative ideologists, and can very well be regarded as a peculiarity of young Disraeli's language.

Such an honorific way of using this term, however, was scarcely a terminological characteristic of the later Disraeli, when he was a leading politician. As Chancellor of the Exchequer, Disraeli spoke emphatically in Parliament on 31 March 1859 against the attempts to lower the borough franchise. In his opinion this meant an advance towards democracy, which at this time presented a political danger. "If you establish a democracy you must in due season reap the fruits of a democracy", and these he enumerated as including great impatience with public burdens combined with great increase in public expenditure, and besides, wars, prompted by passion rather than reason, which would be followed by humiliating treaties. He concluded:

> You will, in due season, with a democracy find that your property is less valuable and that your freedom is less complete. [17]

Contrary to the predominant terminological trend in Disraeli's earlier ideological works, democracy is here spoken of as something towards which England might possibly move, but which was not yet established. While unnecessary wars and humiliating treaties as well as less complete freedom are evidently non-conceptual characteristics only of the concept 'democracy' presented in this statement, a fairly extensive suffrage was most probably necessarily included in what he designated as "democracy". At this point, there is a marked difference in relation to his earlier use of this term; this may explain, inter alia, why this time he used the term in a derogatory way.

How far such a use of "democracy" can be regarded as characteristic of Disraeli's political language in his later years is a question which can scarcely be answered since I have not been able to find any other occurrences of the term. It can perhaps be said that his way of using the term in the occurrence under discussion, and especially his somewhat elaborate manner, may be taken to indicate that this represents something more than mere accidental terminology.

2. Carlyle

Carlyle's passionate, individual, and unsystematic manner of argument complicates an inquiry into his terminology. A descriptive analysis becomes somewhat inadequate. It may even seem irreverent to apply the present methods of discussing the language of typical thinkers like Bentham and Lenin to a terminological study of great prose writers such as Carlyle and Nietzsche; but such scruples cannot debar research into Carlyle's use of "democracy", especially since this term occupies a key position in his terminology.

Carlyle's application of "democracy" is predominantly derogatory, but apart from generally valuing in a negative way what he labelled with this term, it is somewhat difficult in several places to see, more concretely, what factual significations he attributed to "democracy". This way of using "democracy" clearly occurs in what can perhaps be regarded as his first application of the word. In typically eloquent language Carlyle stated:

> The age of Chivalry is gone, and that of Bankruptcy is come. A dull, deep, presaging movement rocks all thrones: Bankruptcy is beating down the gate, and no Chancellor can longer barricade her out. She will enter, and the shoreless fire-lava of DEMOCRACY is at her back! [18]

In this statement "democracy" is used to designate a new and probably inevitable element in social life. His associating this new element with bankruptcy and his way of contrasting these two phenomena with the glorious chivalry of earlier times show a dislike of what the term designates. Otherwise, it is difficult to say anything about the signification of the term.

More factual information can be found in Chartism, of 1839. In this work Carlyle held inter alia that

> ... democracy is, by the nature of it, a selfcancelling business, and gives in the long-run a net result of zero. [19]

He admitted that democracy might subsist where no government was wanted, save the parish constable, as in America with its boundless soil, but not elsewhere, except as a swift transition to something different. In this connection Carlyle definitely seems to have refused to assign the label "democracy" to Athens and Rome, since governing there was done

> ... not by loud voting and debating of many but by wise insight and ordering of the few. [20]

According to these statements, we can probably infer that democracy, to Carlyle, was a kind of political rule dominated by the many and that it had very little or almost no authority to regulate the life of its citizens. Since "government" was probably used here as a designation of something of which a certain amount of authority was a necessary property, this term would not denote any democratic system. It also looks as if America was regarded as the only possible denotatum of "democracy", and that all attempts to establish democracies in Europe were bound to result in forms of rule which were not democracies. To support this last hypothesis, Carlyle drew at-

tention to revolutionary rules in England and France in relation to the existing situation in Europe:

> Democracy ... is found but as a regulated method of rebellion and abroga-
> tion. ... It [democracy] is the consummation of No-government and
> Laissez-faire. [21]

The last quotation probably sums up what he considered to be the
general signification of "democracy", while a regulated method of rebellion
and abrogation seems to have been a more special or more narrow signification conditioned by the existing state of Europe. His way of defining
democracy as the consummation of no-government and laissez-faire is very
derogatory. It is thus most likely that no-government, according to Carlyle,
implied the absence of all kinds of gifted leadership as well as absence of
hero-worship, two phenomena he believed essential for any decent social
life. For him, laissez-faire was without reservation a system which to the
highest degree was typified by what he held to be the mean and selfish ethics
of utilitarianism, the worship of wealth, which were primarily responsible
for having eliminated such noble conceptions as reverence, responsibility,
obedience, and fidelity in social matters, and having made cash payment the
only bond between human beings.

A similar application of "democracy" occurs in his somewhat later work
Past and Present. Through one of his characters, Herr Teufelsdrökh from
the Wahngasse of Weissnichtwo, Carlyle declares:

> Democracy, which means despair of finding Heroes to govern you, and
> contented putting-up with the want of them, -- alas -- thou too, mein
> Lieber, seest well how close it is of kin to Atheism, and other Isms:
> he who discovers no God whatever, how shall he discover Heroes, the
> visible Temples of God? [22]

Herr Teufelsdrökh can definitely be regarded as the mouthpiece of Carlyle
himself. Here it is unlikely that new properties were attributed to the signification of "democracy", since in Chartism Carlyle would very probably
also have considered despair of finding heroes as well as closeness to atheism to be essential to democracy, and since both these were regarded as
necessary consequences of something which was the consummation of no-
government and laissez-faire. More broadly, these early uses of "democracy" show evidence of fairly central topics in Carlyle's social and political thinking. The term was used to characterize phenomena which this stern,
ascetic, and very authoritarian prophet classified among the worst in an age
marked by moral and political decline. Thus, although not frequently used
before the February revolution, "democracy" may therefore be said to have
occupied an important place in his vocabulary before 1848.

In accordance with trends in the terminologies of various other ideologists, Carlyle also greatly increased his use of "democracy" during and
shortly after the events of 1848. The Latter-Day Pamphlets were written
during the first half of 1850, and are clearly the work of a man who was
greatly impressed by the February revolution. In his opinion, the revolutionary year of 1848 was one of the most singular, disastrous, amazing, and,
on the whole, humiliating years in European history. And he seems to some
extent to have used "democracy" almost synonymously with "comprehensive
revolutionary events".

> Everywhere immeasurable Democracy rose, monstrous, loud, blatant,
> inarticulate as the voice of Chaos. [23]

At this point the meaning of "democracy" is almost identical with that of the term in <u>Chartism</u> when he declared democracy to be found but as a regulated method of rebellion and abrogation. Thus we find continuity from what he held to be the more narrow signification conditioned by the existing state of affairs in Europe, while his general way of defining democracy as the consummation of no-government and <u>laissez-faire</u> is more remote in this case.

A somewhat similar, but also somewhat different way of using the term occurs shortly afterwards:

> For universal <u>Democracy</u>, whatever we may think of it, has declared itself as an inevitable fact of the days in which we live; and who has any chance to instruct, or lead, in his days, must begin by admitting that: new street-barricades, and new anarchies, still more scandalous if still less sanguinary, must return and again return, till governing persons everywhere, know and admit that. Democracy, it may be said everywhere, is here. [24]

It can hardly be said that what Carlyle here understood to be democracy was permanently associated with street-barricades and new anarchies; those phenomena were only to exist as long as governing persons did not admit that what Carlyle called "democracy" was an inevitable fact. Until then, barricades and anarchy seemed to be almost unavoidable.

After these introductory remarks, Carlyle considers the main question -- what democracy was. To him, this was the most important question of the day.

> What <u>is</u> Democracy: this huge inevitable Product of Destinies, which is everywhere the portion of our Europe in these latter days? [25]

He went on to say that it must have a meaning, or it would not be there, and also stressed that if they could find the right meaning they might still hope to live in the midst of democracy, either wisely submitting to it, or wisely resisting and controlling it. But if they could not find the right meaning, or if they found no meaning, it would be impossible to live. It is unlikely that Carlyle, when asking "what is democracy"? and "what is the meaning of it?", intended to formulate a kind of meta-occurrence; he was therefore probably speaking about democracy and not "democracy", or asking for the meaning of the concept 'democracy' with the conceptual designation "democracy" and not directly for the meaning, or signification of the term "democracy".

A somewhat similar statement, although not formulated as a question, is to be found on the next page, where Carlyle states that the whole wisdom of existing time was summoned to make clear to itself

> ... what the meaning of this universal revolt of the European Populations, which calls itself Democracy, and decides to continue permanently, may be. [26]

Here he probably means that the adherents of the universal revolt in Europe used "democracy" as self-denomination of their movements. Both these statements show what a high degree of importance Carlyle attributed to these questions, which again indicates that his initial manner of declaring democracy to be only a revolt was not sufficient for him.

In attempting to answer his question what democracy was, Carlyle first stated that it certainly was a drama full of action, event fast following event, in which there were enough interests at stake, enough to rivet the attention of all men. Secondly he admitted that it had been welcomed in 1848 with high shouts of exaltation in every dialect and by every vehicle of speech and writing. He added, however;

> ... and yet, to wise minds, the first aspect it presents seem rather to be one of boundless misery and sorrow. [27]

Carlyle believed this to be the first aspect of democracy on account of the fact that nothing could be more miserable than this universal hunting-out of high dignitaries, solemn functionaries, and potent, grave, and reverend "signiors" of the world, and also the stormful rising-up of the inarticulate dumb masses. Carlyle added, however, that these reverend dignitaries of the period prior to 1848, who sat amid their far-shining symbols and long-sounding and long-admitted professions, were impostors, who had merely acquired the attributes and clothing of rulers, and were drawing wages while the work remained undone. Carlyle then declared:

> It is probably the hugest disclosure of falsity in human things that was ever at one time made. [28]

Shortly afterwards he defined democracy as

> ...a Universal Bankruptcy of Imposture; that may be the brief definition of it. [29]

This definition can be regarded as an example of Carlyle's way of using "democracy" as synonymous with "comprehensive revolutionary event". Carlyle also said of democracy: "There is a joy in it, to the wise man too. " He added, however, that it was

> ... but a joy full of awe, and as it were sadder than sorrow, like the vision of immortality, unattainable except through death and grave. [30]

But he also went on to say that no one would "in his heart of hearts, not feel pious that imposture had fallen bankrupt. " These and other statements are good examples of his political attitude towards the February revolution; on the one hand, he had no sympathy with the fallen dignitaries of the past, even looking upon the revolutionary process with conditional sympathy; on the other hand, he was uneasy for what the future might bring. Even his way of regarding democracy with very conditional sympathy was without doubt dependent on his way of defining democracy as something which made imposture bankrupt. It is thus quite certain that he would have treated with contempt something which he had declared to be consummation of no-government and laissez-faire.

Another way of using the term occurs a few pages later on in this pamphlet, however, where Carlyle states:

> Historically speaking, I believe there was no nation that could subsist upon democracy.

His argumentation here was that the ancient republics were based on slavery, which meant that the privileged voters were born to be rulers, or as he put it, "intrinsically a kind of kings". This he probably held to be incompatible with a democratic State. He admitted, however, that the United States was a modern and nearly perfect example of democracy, and asked in conclusion:

> Why should not all nations subsist and flourish on Democracy, as America does?

In the latter statement Carlyle probably used "democracy" with a different signification from the one he used when defining democracy as a universal bankruptcy of imposture, since it is hardly possible that he would have accepted the notion that America subsisted and flourished on bankruptcy. On the contrary, Carlyle here allows a return to his earlier practice of declaring democracy to be the consummation of no-government and laissez-faire, We may therefore say that in his Latter-Day Pamphlets as well as in Chartism Carlyle alternated between one signification of "democracy" in relation to Europe and another one when America was in question.

In support of his arguments that none save the American nation could subsist and flourish on democracy, Carlyle drew attention in the first place to the waste lands which did not exist in Europe. In the second place he emphasized that people should not yet brag of their American cousins, because in spite of their quantity of cotton, dollars, and resources,

> What great human soul, what great thought, what great noble thing that one could worship, or loyally admire, has yet been produced there? None. [31]

And the success of democracy on this side of the Atlantic could not be predicted from the American example.

Carlyle continued:

> Alas, on this side of the Atlantic and on that, Democracy, we apprehend, is forever impossible! [32]

This seems to contradict his statement that America subsisted and flourished upon democracy. But with the alleged absence of any great American thoughts in mind, Carlyle may have meant by "impossible" something practically synonymous with "impossible from a cultural point of view". If so these statements do not necessarily contradict each other. Carlyle admitted that his view would be greeted with loud and astonished contradiction from all kinds of men, but added that it might be asserted once again with an appeal to what he designated as the "Law of Nature". This law of nature meant primarily that the universe itself was a monarchy and a hierarchy, and that it was the will of the Almighty Creator in all times and all countries that the noble should be in high places and the ignoble in lower ones. [33] "Democracy", as presented in my last quotation, must therefore signify something which was very different from, and perhaps contrary to, this alleged law of nature.

This sense of holding democracy as something which definitely ignored the different intellectual and moral capacities of men can be said to agree with the bulk of his political language. An extremely different way of using "democracy" is evident in another of these pamphlets, however. Two months later, Carlyle stated that many gifted persons were born in the lowest and broadest stratum of society -- Robert Burns, for example -- and that one of the great tasks of society was to choose able and gifted men in spite of their birth.

> Is not this Proposal the very essence of whatever truth there is in 'Democracy'; this, that the able man be chosen, in whatever rank he is found? That he be searched for as hidden treasure is; be trained, supervised, set to the work which he alone is fit for. All Democracy lies in this. [34]

He added that this was worth all contemporary movement in favour of ballot-boxes and the suffrage. Carlyle believed the methods by which able men from every rank were to be gathered, like diamond-grains from the general mass of sand, to be what he called, "the question of the question", and concluded:

All that Democracy ever meant lies there; the attainment of a truer and truer <u>Aristocracy,</u> or Government again by the <u>Best.</u> [35]

When compared with his frequent statements that democracy meant despair of finding heroes and the neglect of all intellectual differences, these last statements are proof of one of the most obvious changes in the signification of the term "democracy". While Carlyle used the term in an extremely derogatory way when it connoted such immoral phenomena and only treated it with very conditional sympathy when it signified bankruptcy of imposture, we are here most certainly faced with a very honorific application. Carlyle's desire for a true and new aristocracy of able and gifted men whatever their descent is a permanent factor in his political thinking. It was primarily such men, potential heroes, whom he thought competent for real leadership in a world severely infected by the selfishness of commercial civilization; this naturally places what he designated as "democracy" in an important as well as a very laudatory position.

What Carlyle meant by saying, "all that Democracy ever meant" is not quite clear. Possibly something like: "The term "democracy" has always been used to connote the attainment of a truer and truer aristocracy". In that case, this statement would certainly directly contradict all his earlier usages of that term. Such an interpretation is possible, but not probable. Carlyle at first probably believed democracy to be something which, <u>inter alia,</u> was characterized by properties which would make the attainment of a truer aristocracy possible. The formulations "all democracy lies in this" and "all that democracy ever meant" can perhaps be regarded as persuasive, and possibly also self-persuasive, defining statements about what was of value in what he designated as "democracy". In that case, these statements can hardly be said directly to contradict <u>all</u> his earlier applications of the term. But even his usage of the term to signify something of which the attainment of a truer aristocracy was an essential property cannot be said to be compatible with his earlier application of the term.

"Democracy" and related terms occur very seldom in the later writings of Carlyle. Frequency of usage in the language of Carlyle and other ideologists seems thus to be limited to the years of revolutionary uprisings on the Continent. It can be observed that any later application of the term seems to be derogatory, and the honorific usage may therefore be exclusively regarded as a terminological peculiarity in the pamphlet under discussion. There is very little evidence of later application. In 1867, in "Shooting Niagara: and after?", Carlyle said there were three things on which all Englishmen were in agreement, and the first was, "<u>Democracy</u> to complete itself". This implied what he ironically called "complete liberty" to all persons, a counting of heads to be the divine court of appeal on every question, and a counting of heads to choose Parliaments; the latter would trifle with legislation and administration, while everyone would increasingly follow his own nose in an intricate world. [36] This indicates clearly a derogatory use of the term "democracy" whose signification is here fairly close to no-government and anarchy.

Even later, concluding his work on the early Norwegian kings, Carlyle declared:

The History of these Haarfagrs has awakened in me many thoughts: Of Despotism and Democracy, arbitrary government by one and self-government (which means no-government, or anarchy) by all; of Dictatorship with many faults, and Universal Suffrage with little possibility of any virtue. [37]

The contrast between Olaf Trygvason and a universal suffrage Parliament had grown to be very great in those nine centuries.

Here "democracy" was probably used synonymously with "self-government by all", perhaps to the same degree as "despotism" was used synonymously with "arbitrary rule by one". A derogatory use of the term is evident in that Carlyle considers self-government to mean no-government and anarchy, and also allows this form of rule a very small possibility of virtue. Thus Carlyle's final usage of "democracy" attributed properties to the signification of the term which he thought essential for the ethical disintegration of human social life; a trend which can be regarded as predominant, but not exclusive, in his terminology. It is characteristic that Carlyle's last use of the term was to emphasize the contrast between democracy and a young king whom he held to be a hero of the most noble kind.

3. Stahl

Turning from the vivid but unsystematic thinking of Carlyle to the systematic but dry argumentation of Friedrich Stahl, one notes that according to Stahl the main difference between various forms of constitution depended on what he called "Dem Subjekte der Souveränität (der höchsten Obrichkeit)". He added:

Dies ist entweder ein Mensch bez. eine Familie (Dynastie) -- Monarchie; oder ein bestimmter Stand -- Aristokratie; oder die Gesammtheit des Volkes -- Demokratie.

Stahl maintained that aristocracy as well as democracy needed some kind of artificial assembly, the members of which would simultaneously be governing persons in their assemblies and obedient in their function as citizens:

... dadurch bilden Aristokratie und Demokratie zusammen einen Gegensatz gegen die Monarchie -- die Republik. [38]

This statement reveals that what he designated as "democracy" was a form of State where sovereignty belonged to the whole body of the people, and that 'democracy' as well as 'aristocracy' were species of the genus 'republic'. This implies that everything he called "democracy" was subsumable under what he called "republic", but not vice versa.

Stahl went on to say:

Die Demokratie ist Herrschaft des Volkes unter gleichmässiger Theilnahme aller Stände und Klassen, doch auch immer nur in geordneter Versammlung. [39]

The last part of this statement probably indicates that, as he understood it, democracy was not the decision of an arbitrary joining together of all people, but the participation of all different estates and classes of the people in an ordered assembly. Where the first part is concerned, Stahl was prob-

ably aware of the fact that in saying "aller Stände und Klassen" he differed
from what he held to have been the Greek signification of "democracy",
since he mentioned in a footnote that this meant the rule of the poor class
as distinct from that of the rich. [40] Stahl probably had in mind a statement
of Aristotle, according to which any State was a democracy, if and only if,
the government was in the hands of the poorer classes, and that it did not
matter whether the poor were in the majority or the minority in such a
society. [41] This Aristotelian usage, however, of "democracy" is not identical with the Greek. There are other Greek usages of "democracy" which
clearly differ from this Aristotelian one, and therefore Stahl's reference to
the Greek signification of "democracy" is a little oversimplified. [42]

Stahl further said that there were two different kinds of democracies.

> Sie[die Demokratie] ist unmittelbare Demokratie, wie in den griechischen
> Staaten, dass alle einzelnen Bürger in Einer Versammlung verbunden die
> obersten Regierungsrechte, namentlich die Gesetzgebung und die Bestel-
> lung der Magistraturen, üben, oder repräsentative Demokratie, dass sie
> nur Repräsentanten wählen, die an ihrer Statt diese Rechte üben. [43]

The North-American constitutions belonged to the latter kind. Thus he
operated with the usual triangle of concepts: Two sub-concepts or species,
'direct democracy' and 'representative democracy' of which 'democracy'
was the genus.

Later in this work, Stahl repeated that supreme power or sovereignty,
in republics and even in democracies, rested in some kind of ordered assembly, and he went on to say:

> Auch die Republik, die Demokratie beruht also nicht auf der "Volksouve-
> ränetät". Auch in ihr ist der Staat über dem Volke, nicht das Volk über
> dem Staat. Nur hierdurch ist die Republik eine mögliche Staatsform. [44]

Stahl seems here to consider it to be a necessary condition of any form of
State to be above the people, and not vice versa: republics and democracies,
being forms of State, must be subject to the same rule. It is likely that
"Volkssouveränetät" was used by him to connote an order in which the people
were above the State, thus making any form of State impossible. His way of
writing "Volkssouveränetät" with quotation marks may indicate irony, perhaps to show that he considered the term to be a contradictio in adjecto.

Stahl believed the problem of whether a pure democracy represented a
possible form of rule to be one of the most important problems of the day.

> Es ist eine Grundfrage der Zeit, ob reine Demokratie möglich ist, d. h.
> eine Verfassung, in welcher die Staatsgenossen von selbst, kraft ihrer
> Persönlichkeit, ohne alle Erdfordernisse von Geburt, Stand, Grundbesitz,
> Vermögen, und deshalb auch alle gleich an der gesetzgebenden Versamm-
> lung betheiligt sind. [45]

For Stahl, outward phenomena like fortune, descent, class, etc. , were natural
guarantees, or natürliche Bürgschaften, in political life. "Pure democracy"
seems here necessarily to signify something marked by absence of such
natural guarantees.

A more narrow signification of "pure democracy" occurs shortly, however. Stahl maintained that when a form of government was destitute of
natural guarantees, some kind of ethical guarantees were needed. As proof
of what he regarded as ethical guarantees, Stahl referred to public education
in Sparta and the censorship in Rome. To him the highest form of ethical

guarantee was the Christian faith together with Church discipline, on which, for example, the early American democracy had been founded. By ethical guarantees Stahl evidently had in mind a certain set of moral or religious norms, according to which political life was to be framed, and to which political leaders of all kinds were to submit. It is fairly certain that he did not regard ethical guarantees such as Christian faith to be incompatible with a particular kind of democracy; on the other hand, he regarded pure democracy, at least once, as something in which both kinds of guarantees were absent. In addition to the need for some kind of guarantees, Stahl declared:

> Dagegen die reine Demokratie im üblichen Sinne, dass die Menschen ohne Beides, ohne natürliche und ohne sittliche Bürgschaften, bloss kraft ihres menschlichen Antlitzes an der souveränen Volksversammlung alle gleich betheiligt seyen -- diese reine Demokratie ist für die Dauer schlechtin unmöglich. [46]

According to this statement, "pure democracy" signified a political form most probably marked by absence of natural as well as ethical guarantees, and Stahl also held this signification to be the usual one. At this point there is some difference in relation to the former quotation, in which natural guarantees, but not ethical ones, were regarded as necessarily absent in what he designated as "pure democracy". Thus he gave "pure democracy" two somewhat different connotations. Stahl evidently considered the last concept, 'pure democracy', to represent a political impossibility over a long period. According to both statements, what he held to be pure democracy seems to have been restricted to the field of direct government. On this point, as well as with regard to different kinds of guarantees, the connotations attributed to "pure democracy" and unqualified "democracy" vary.

CHAPTER VI

MODERATE LIBERALISM

Grouping together different political thinkers in one chapter usually raises
some problems, since such groups hardly ever present a homogeneous picture. I have here chosen to treat a man like Sismondi, an adherent of rule
by the political elite, together with a liberal like Macaulay and a fairly conservative oligarch like Guizot. Guizot can hardly be regarded as exclusively
conservative, since he served a monarchy which came into power through
such a political upheaval as the July Revolution. But it is most difficult to
put a man like Tocqueville into any one category. Here we have one of the
most original political thinkers in the last century, a man who approaches
almost every political problem with a remarkable absence of formulas and
a priori theories. This absence of a clear system may partly explain why
several historians of ideas neglected to draw attention to Tocqueville. De-
spite this we have chosen to treat these four thinkers in one chapter under
the rather vague label of "moderate liberalism". A property common to
greater parts of their political thought was more or less negative valuation
of what they termed "democracy", clearly negative in the terminology of
Sismondi and Guizot, much more neutral in that of Macaulay, while a very
varied picture is presented by Tocqueville. A fairly general trend was to
regard what they termed "democracy" as dangerous, that is, as potentially
dangerous for freedom. Here there is continuity with the application of
"democracy" by Kant, Madame de Staël, and Benjamin Constant. The same
trend was also in different degrees to mould later liberal theorists, such as
John Stuart Mill and especially Lord Acton. This relationship between liberalism, in the sense of freedom of speech, and democracy can even be said
to be an important general trait of nineteenth-century political thought.

1. Sismondi

Whereas Tocqueville, as indicated, used "democracy" with different connotations, and alternated between derogatory and honorific applications,
such variety does not typify the use of "democracy" by the Swiss social and
political scientist Sismondi, in whose work absence of any honorific application as well as of ambiguous usage is a dominant characteristic.

In his main political work Études sur les constitutions des peuples
libres, published in 1836, Sismondi claimed that two political groupings
were the main antagonists in contemporary political life. One of these was
in favour of pure royalism, and, according to Sismondi, used the political
catchword, "all for the people, nothing by the people". Sismondi objected
that it was contrary to social science that anything which was not by the
people could be for the people. He added that this war-cry was answered by
another war-cry from the opposite political grouping.

Mais à ce cri de guerre, un autre parti, celui de la démocratie, a répondu par un autre cri de guerre. Tout pour le peuple et par le peuple; et celui-là aussi a perdue de vue un des buts de la science sociale. [1]

This slogan was also contrary to social science, according to Sismondi. He could not accept the point of view that the people alone were capable of anything. Society was in need of the educated and virtuous few in its attempt to secure the greatest happiness of the greatest number, and he doubted whether the masses would ever acquire sufficient learning for the complicated tasks of political government.

These introductory statements can be taken to indicate that Sismondi considered democracy to be a form of government in which the whole body of the people were wrongly regarded as being competent of securing their own welfare.

With regard to more concrete aspects of what he regarded as democracy, Sismondi declared that Switzerland generally had tried to found its form of liberty in a kind of balanced constitution by rendering possible the formation of public opinion and by elevating able men to the leadership of the State. He added, however, that there were also republics or cantons where the democratic principle dominated vigorously.

Mais la Suisse compte aussi plusieurs républiques où le principe démocratique a prévalu dans toute sa vigueur, où toutes les intelligences de même que toutes les volontés ont été tenues pour égales, et où le suffrage universel a étouffé l'opinion publique. [2]

Making able men the leaders of the State and finding liberty in a kind of balanced constitution are here evidently contrasted with the democratic principle. And it further looks as if an expression like "the democratic principle dominated in all its vigour" was used as being synonymous or nearly synonymous with "all intelligence as well as all wills were considered equals", as well as with "public opinion was stifled by universal suffrage". This implies a use of "democracy" with a signification including primarily properties like those characterized in the last two expressions. This can most certainly be regarded as implying a derogatory kind of application.

The three small cantons in the centre of Switzerland, Ury, Schwitz, and Unterwald, were, said Sismondi, pure democracies. In discussing these three small cantons, Sismondi attacked some Swiss publicist who had given the name "aristocrats" to what Sismondi held to be the democratic party in Switzerland. He maintained:

Il n'y a jamais eu d'example au monde de démocratie plus absolue que celle des trois anciens petits cantons.

He admitted that these democracies included demagogues as well as leaders, but added that this was a necessary consequence of the kind of government he held to be democratic.

Sans doute ces démocraties ont des démagogues, des meneurs: c'est la consequence nécessaire d'un tel gouvernement. [3]

When people speak about consequences of certain kinds of rule, I am generally inclined to regard these as non-conceptual characteristics of a certain political concept. In this case, however, it seems more apt to class the presence of demagogues and leaders as conceptual characteristics of Sismondi's concept 'democracy', since he probably could not have imagined a democracy that was not characterized by the political activity of such people.

Sismondi added that the demagogues and leaders generally belonged to
the clergy and the nobility, and one might therefore expect to find these persons in the leadership of a democracy where they would conserve the prejudices of their own orders.   Sismondi also declared that they had continually
tried to strengthen the illiberal sentiments and prejudices of the people. He
was even of the opinion that

> ... les petits cantons ne seraient pas des démocraties, si les ambitieux
> n'y cherchaient pas à élever au pouvoir en séduisant et corrompant le
> peuple. [4]

This last sentence in particular is a fairly clear proof that he considered
democracy to be typified of necessity by ambitious people who tried to obtain
power by corrupting and deceiving the people.   This he hardly regarded as
an almost inevitable result of democracy, but more probably, as with the
activity of demagogues, he included among the conceptual characteristics of
his concept 'democracy'.   His opinions of democracy as characterized by
demagogues or by ambitious people can therefore most probably be regarded
as analytic statements and not as synthetic ones.

There are clear examples of Sismondi's opinions on democracy and
liberty.   He stated that democratic leaders continually strengthen the illiberal sentiments of the people; he has also contrasted liberty in a mixed
constitution with the democratic principle.   He said later, in fairly high
conformity with these points of view, that the adherents of progress had tried
to introduce some degree of liberty and religious tolerance into the different
Swiss constitutions.   This progress, however, was opposed by what he described as

> ... l'esprit démocratique, ou le suprématie accordée par le suffrage
> universel à ceux qui ne savent rien et qui n'entendent point ce qu'ils
> décident, sur ceux qui veulent l'avancement de la vraie liberté. [5]

"Democratic spirit" is here most probably used synonymously with "supremacy throught universal suffrage accorded to those who know nothing and
understood none of their own decisions, over those who desire the advancement of true liberty".   True liberty was thus regarded as very different
from, perhaps incompatible with, the spirit of democracy.   Incompatibility
between democracy and true liberty may be said to be in great harmony with
the properties Sismondi attributed in other places in this work to the signification of "democracy" since he probably believed true liberty to be incompatible with something which was necessarily characterized by the activity
of demagogues, and also by the permanent attempts of ambitious men to gain
power by corrupting and deceiving the people.

Sismondi further gave it as his opinion that a representative democracy
was no better a government than what he called "pure democracy".   Since
the masses were ignorant and retrogressive, they could not transfer the
desire for progressiveness to their representatives.   He concluded:

> Si la démocratie pure est un mauvais gouvernement, la démocratie
> représentative ne peut pas valoir davantage. [6]

Here Sismondi seems to have used "representative democracy" and "pure
democracy" to designate two concepts which probably can be regarded as
species of a broader concept 'democracy'.   It is difficult to see, however,
whether the unqualified term "democracy" alone was used as a conceptual
designation of this last concept, or whether it was used to designate one of

the species directly. Sismondi's terminology in general gives us no evidence in favour of any definite conclusion on this point.

Occurrences of this term very similar to these quoted can be found in several places in this work. [7] I have found no occurrences of "democracy" in which the signification of the term can be said to contradict the trend revealed by the above quotations. We therefore have good reason to infer that Sismondi operated with one, and only one, concept, 'democracy', according to which questions concerning direct government or representation were conceptually irrelevant, and in which the activities of demagogues and corruption of popular opinion by ambitious politicians were among the most central conceptual characteristics.

How far the application of "democracy" in this work can be regarded as being representative of all his usage is a question which cannot be answered definitely, since we have not been able to find any occurrences in his other works. But the work in question was without doubt his most important in the field of politics, and it was most certainly the one in which different forms of government received systematic treatment. The predominant part of his literary production belongs to the fields of economics and social science, although I disagree with those authors who consider these fields to be exclusive in his writings and who maintain that Sismondi scarcely ever dealt with constitutional matters in a comprehensive fashion. [8]

2. Macaulay

Among the rare occurrences of "democracy" in the writings of Macaulay, we find a very few in a review of Mitford's History of Greece. Here Macaulay said that some political writers tended to imagine that popular government was always a blessing, while others, like Milford, omitted no opportunity of asserting that it was always a curse. Macaulay himself held that the errors of both sides arose from ignorance or neglect of the fundamental principles of political science, and he declared that a good government, like a good coat, was the one that fitted the body for which it was designed. A man who, basing his judgement upon abstract principles, pronounced a constitution to be good without exact knowledge of the people who were to be governed by it judged as absurdly as a tailor who measured the Belvedere Apollo for the clothes of all his customers. According to Macaulay, that government was best which desired to make the people happy and knew how to make them happy. He added that neither inclination nor knowledge would suffice alone, and that it was difficult to find them together. He concluded:

Pure democracy, and pure democracy alone, satisfies the former condition of this great problem. [9]

It was necessary, continued Macaulay, that the interest of the governors and the governed should be identical ones. If the governors were to be solicitors for the interests of the governed only, this could not often be the case where power was entrusted to one or to a few. The privileged part of the community would thus doubtless derive a certain degree of advantage from the general prosperity of the state. He admitted that this evil was to be diminished as the number of the governors increased, as the dividend which each could obtain of the public plunder became less and less tempting. He concluded, however:

The interests of the subjects and the rulers never absolutely coincide till the subjects themselves become rulers, that is, till the government be either immediately or mediately, democratical. [10]

What was designated as "pure democracy" in the first quotation seems quite clearly to have been the only form of government which desired to make the people happy; this is probably connected with his use of "democratic" to characterize the kind of government in which, and only in which, the interests of the governing persons were identical with those of the governed. Thus we find two related conditions, which were held to be sufficient and probably necessary conditions for a pure democracy or democratic government. His use of "mediately" and "immediately" in connection with "democratic" may further indicate that a democracy might be of a direct as well as of a representative kind, and that these questions were rather irrelevant in relation to the above-mentioned criteria for pure democracy or democratic government.

Such factors as a desire to make the people happy and identity of interests between rulers and subjects indicate a somewhat sympathetic attitude. But even if Macaulay admitted that the democratic form of rule had certain advantages, he considered them to be far from sufficient. According to him, the people would always desire to promote their own interests, but he doubted whether any community would ever be educated sufficiently to understand what their interests were. At this point he referred to free trade as the greatest blessing which a government could confer on a people, but which nevertheless was unpopular almost everywhere among the people at large. In general he seems to have agreed that the people should in most cases be governed for their own good.

Macaulay admitted that it might be concluded that the happiest state of society was that in which supreme power resided in the whole body of a well-informed people. But this was an imaginary and, perhaps, even unattainable state of affairs. They might approximate it in some measure, however, in the meantime it was dangerous to praise or condemn constitutions in the abstract, since,

... from the despotism of St. Petersburg to the democracy of Washington, there is scarcely a form of government which might not, at least in some hypothetical case, be the best possible. [11]

In accordance with these statements it is evident that Macaulay did not regard what he considered to be democratic government to be the ideal. A main factor was without doubt that things like knowing how to make the people happy, or being able to realize its intentions, were not among the properties included in his signification of "democratical government". From a practical point of view, these factors may even be regarded as rather incompatible with such a form of rule. The American form of government was mentioned as being a denotatum of "democracy", and Macaulay probably considered that form of government to be the most typical among the denotata of that term.

Some years later, when criticizing the utilitarian theory of government, Macaulay disagreed with James Mill, who said the English Constitution was purely aristocratic. Macaulay frequently declared this Constitution to be a mixed one, stating that:

Wherever a king or an oligarchy refrain from the last extremity of rapacity and tyranny through fear of resistance of the people, there the constitution, whatever it may be called, is in some measure democratical. [12]

"In some measure democratical" is here used to characterize any constitution under which the people were not deprived of every kind of hypothetical influence. But according to this criterion it could be difficult, if not impossible, to find any constitution which Macaulay would not consider to be in some measure democratic.

3. Guizot

Guizot used the term "democracy" more often than Macaulay. As in the works of Carlyle, a somewhat sparse application in the eighteen-thirties increased during the February Revolution. And while neither a derogatory nor an honorific application was obvious in Macaulay's usage, a derogatory application is a distinct mark of Guizot's use of "democracy". As in the case of Sismondi, Guizot's derogatory use is not connected with that kind of resentment which sometimes makes it extremely difficult to find the concrete signification of "democracy". Guizot is among the fairly few to combine a negative attitude with a fairly clear terminology.

The first time "democracy" occurs with some frequency in Guizot's writings is an essay entitled "De la démocratie dans les sociétes modernes." This essay, written in 1837, is a review of two books whose titles each contains the term "democracy".[13] According to Guizot, the authors, Alletz and Billiard, had declared existing French society to be democratic, and that the political institutions of France, its laws, its government, and its administration should be framed and adapted accordingly. This seems to imply that both authors used the term "democratic" to characterize the existing French society, but that neither of them would have regarded the reign of Louis Philippe as democratic.

Their political wishes and intentions differed, however. According to Guizot, Alletz desired to build upon the constitutional monarchy and the Charter of 1830, while Billiard was an adherent of a republic and of universal suffrage. Guizot concluded by asking:

Qu'est-ce donc cette démocratie, ce fait souverain qui pousse à des conclusions si contraires deux hommes éclairés et de bonne fois, qui l'admettent également?

And continued:

Ni l'un ni l'autre ne l'a dit. Ni l'un ni l'autre ne parait même se l'être demandé. L'état démocratique de la société est pour eux un fait accompli, convenu, légitime. Il ne s'agit que de régler. [14]

These statements demonstrated the great importance Guizot attached to the questions of what democracy was. It is also evident that he was not at all satisfied with the different views of Alletz and Billiard on this point.

Apparently as a kind of semantic methodology Guizot believed that

...les mots ont leur étoile. Ils naissent au milieu de certaines circonstances qui déterminent, pour des siècles, leur sens et le charactère des faits qu'ils expriment. ... Demandez à la science ce qu'est la démocratie. Elles a des belles réponses. C'est le gouvernement du peuple, c'est-à-dire de la société elle-même c'est-à-dire de tous, c'est-à-dire le droit commun pour tous. [15]

When writers present what they declare to be the scientific definition of a certain phenomenon, their intention is nearly always to use such a definition in support of their own personal view. This does not occur in Guizot's essay, however. Instead of presenting his own definition of democracy in accordance with the authority of science, his purpose was to show that scientific definitions of central political concepts were far from sufficient, and thus to indicate what he himself did not consider to be the correct one. In his opinion science was without doubt of great importance, but science had not made the world, and the world together with human life were much older than science. Life was marked by struggle, and primarily by a struggle between good and evil. It was out of this struggle, and not out of science, that democracy was born.

De cette lutte est née la démocratie. C'est un cri de guerre; c'est le drapeau du grand nombre placé en bas, contre le petit nombre placé en haut. Drapeau levé tantôt au nom des droits les plus saints, tantôt au nom des passions les plus grossières et les plus insensées; levé tantot contre les usurpations les plus iniques, tantôt contre les supériorités les plus legitimes. [16]

Guizot thus disagreed strongly with science concerning the definition of democracy. He admitted that science had what he called beautiful answers on this point, but his general statements about science seem to exclude the possibility that he accepted the definition that democracy was the government of all people. His definition of democracy as a war-cry, and the banner of great numbers from the lowest levels of society raised against the few from the highest, can therefore very probably be regarded as exclusive to him.

It is difficult to say how far this contained a meta-occurrence. His quoted declaration of democracy as a banner and even a war-cry may be taken to indicate a verbal symbol, although the statement can probably not be interpreted in such a literal way.

A very similar formulation appears shortly afterwards in this essay:

Dans tout son cours, aux époques les plus diverses, au sein des triomphes comme des revers, le caractère primitif, essentiel, du mouvement démocratique n'a point changé. Il a été, comme je l'ai dit d'abord, une guerre, la guerre du grand nombre placé en bas, contre le petit nombre placé en haut. [17]

Here Guizot used the expression "democratic movement" instead of "democracy", but there is hardly any difference between holding democracy to be a battle-cry or a banner in the struggle between the many poor and the few rich and declaring that the democratic movement always had been and still was a struggle of that kind. There is association between social revolution and democracy by various political thinkers other than Guizot. But the labels "democracy" and "democratic movement" have seldom been conceptually restricted to the field of violent class-struggle outside Guizot's terminology. The fact that Guizot chose to oppose his own use of "democracy" and related terms to that of other political authors, and especially to what he held to be the scientific definition of democracy, is an evident proof of his marked preference on this point.

In De la Démocratie en France, which was written shortly after the February Revolution, the terminological tendency was almost the same as in

the essay we have been discussing. Referring to the existing political uprising and unrest, Guizot declared:

> ... le chaos se cache aujourd'hui sous un mot: <u>Démocratie</u>. ... C'est
> le mot souverain, universel. Tous les partis l'invoquent et veulent se
> l'approprier comme un talisman. [18]

Guizot further held that the monarchists declared their monarchy to be
democratic, the republicans declared the republic to be the only form of
government in harmony with the interests of the democratic society, and the
socialists and communists had parallel political claims. He even talked
about "l'empire du mot <u>démocratie</u>" [19] and asserted that no party dared to
exist without that word ingrafted upon their banner.

Here we are clearly told that the term "democracy" had a nearly universal honorific application in France in those days, and that different political groupings used the term in various ways. Guizot did not say, however, which of these applications of the term he accepted as the correct one.
It is also a little difficult to know what he meant by saying that the chaos of
existing time was hidden in the word "democracy"; did he mean that there
existed semantic confusion owing to the fact that one single term was used
eulogistically, but with mutually different significations by different groups,
or did he himself, to a large degree, associate political and social confusion
and unrest with the term? His earlier terminology on this point can be said
to make the latter alternative the more probable one, although one alternative does not necessarily exclude the other one.

A little later on, Guizot declared:

> Je ne veux parler qu'avec respect du gouvernement républicain. En soi,
> c'est un noble form de gouvernement. [20]

Three pages later, concerning the official self-denomination of the French
Republic he said:

> Un fait me frappe et m'inquiète beaucoup: c'est l'ardeur que la République
> a mise à se nommer expréssement et officiellement démocratique. [21]

These statements can probably be taken to imply that while using the term
"republic" in a way which was by no means derogatory when used alone,
Guizot had a rather different attitude to what was designated "republic" when
that designation was qualified with "democratic".

This attitude towards what was designated by "democratic republic" and
the intended meaning of that expression are explained a little later when he
asked:

> Que veulent dire aujourd'hui, parmi nous, ces mots <u>République démo-
> cratique</u> invoqués, adoptés comme le nom officiel, comme le symbol du
> gouvernement? C'est l'echo d'un ancien cri de guerre sociale: cri
> qui s'élève et se répète, de nos jours, à tous les étages de la société;
> prononcé avec colère contre certaines classes par d'autres classes qui,
> à leur tour, l'intendent avec affroi retenir contre elles-mêmes. [22]

We have here a use of "democratic" very similar to that we have found
in his essay from 1837. If we take his other statements into account, and
especially the somewhat honorific use of "republic" when not used in a qualified way, it becomes rather obvious that Guizot's very close association if
not identification of "democratic republic" with "revolutionary cry" is condi-

tioned by, and probably exclusively conditioned by, the existence of the qualification "democratic".

Guizot had the United States in mind when saying that a republic, as such, was a noble kind of government. Guizot also asked:

Ont-ils [les Etats-Unis d'Amérique] jamais songé à s'intituler: République démocratique? Je ne'm étonne point qu'ils n'y aient pas songé.

The reason for this verbal omission was, according to Guizot, that in America the leaders of the revolution as well as of the republican form of government were a natural aristocracy. The attainment of independence and the foundation of the republican form of government had been, not the victory of certain classes over others, but the common task of all classes under the guidance of those who were most elevated and most educated. With regard to the American terminology, it is my opinion that Guizot was right in holding that "democracy" did not figure as self-domination during the first decades after the Declaration of Independence. Save a few rather obscure groups, no one used "democracy" in an honorific way in the days of Washington. But Jefferson, in spite of never having used "democracy" in public papers, stated in a private letter, dated April 1816: "We of the United States, you know, are constitutionally and conscientiously democrats. " And in February 1828, The Ohio State Journal wrote:

There are now but two parties to wit, one which support the present administration, and one which support General Jackson, each of these parties names and denominates itself "The Democratic Republican Party of the Nation. "[23]

Thus Guizot's statement was somewhat oversimplified. This does not, however, affect the signification he attributed to "democratic". For him, the alleged absence of "democratic" in official American terminology was a natural consequence of the lack of class-struggle in the American republic. Thus we are again faced with a very close association, or even identification, of what he characterized as "democratic" with the permanent struggle between rich and poor; a trend which without doubt is the most predominant, and may be even exclusive, in his application of "democracy" and related terms in these two works.

Broadly speaking it is difficult to say how far this terminological tendency is representative of the political language in his historical works, his speeches, or his memoirs. I have tried to find occurrences in those of his works which are available, but without success, and the question must therefore be left open. The two works we have discussed are the only ones having the word "democracy" in their titles. In addition, they are works in which Guizot's political attitude and political intention are very much in evidence. These points, and the fact that there was a 12-year interval between the essays, indicate that the terms used therein were representative of Guizot's terminological application.

4. Tocqueville

a. Before 1848

Macaulay used "democracy" very infrequently, and Sismondi and Guizot, on
the other hand, although they used it in a way which can be said to reveal
some important aspects of their political thinking, nevertheless did not use
the term very frequently. In the case of Tocqueville's terminology, quite
a different picture will be found. Here we first of all encounter a very high
degree of frequency. More important is the fact that "democracy" nearly
always occurs in central statements in Tocqueville's political writings; he
nearly always used the term when he intended to say something important.
Accordingly "democracy" can, with very good reason, be regarded as the
key word in his terminology. "Democracy" probably occupies a more central position in Tocqueville's political thinking than in that of any other
thinker in the field. It is possible to discuss the views of Marx, Proudhon,
and Lenin, and maybe even John Stuart Mill without bringing in their attitudes or viewpoints towards what they designated "democracy", or to quote
representative statements which do not contain "democracy", something
that would be impossible in connection with Tocqueville.
  Alexis de Tocqueville's great treatise, De la Démocratie en Amérique,
is the first comprehensive work with something designated "democracy" as
its subject. The first part of this work appeared in the year 1835, and is
probably the most important source for an inquiry into the meaning of "democracy" in the first half of the nineteenth century. There are not many definitions of democracy in this work, or in other parts of his writings, although
the terms "democracy" and "democratic" are very frequently used. The
signification, or significations, of "democracy" and "democratic" will therefore be found by studying the concrete application of the words.
  Tocqueville frequently emphasized that the gradual development towards
social equality was the main historical trend of his time. He held this trend
to be universal and lasting and, from a broader point of view, irresistible.
Although this trend was clearly discernible in France as well as in other
European countries, equality was above all the characteristic of social conditions in America. This social equality included economic equality;Tocque-
ville pointed out that in America there were very few rich people, and that
the greater part of these had started life as poor persons; hence there was
scarcely any possibility of the social stabilization of an hereditary class of
men of property. Social equality was not limited to the fields of economics,
however, but included even education and intellectual capacity. There was
thus no country in the world with a proportionately smaller number of illiter-
ates, but at the same time there was no other country which counted so few
learned people in relation to the population. This last factor was the result
of the fact that the few rich people generally had been obliged to start working
at an early age when they had leanings for more education: then, when they
had time and opportunity later they no longer desired it.
  Our task here is not to prove whether Tocqueville was right in indicating
a general trend towards equality, or whether it was correct that American

social conditions were marked by an extreme equality. Considerations of that kind belong to a more purely historical work, although the social conditions of America would naturally exhibit a marked equality to a European visitor in the eighteen-thirties. But Tocqueville seems to have freely used "democratic" as synonymous with "marked by an extreme equality". Concluding his description of the social condition in America he said:

> L'Amérique présente donc, dans son état social, le plus étrange phéno-
> mène. Les hommes s'y montrent plus égaux par leur fortune et par leur
> intelligence, ou, en d'autre termes, plus également forts, qu'ils né le
> sont dans aucune pays du monde et qu'ils né l'ont été dans aucune siècle
> dont l'histoire garde le souvenir. [24]

A few pages earlier Tocqueville had commented on the same theme:

> On pourrait faire plusieurs remarques importantes sur l'état social des
> Anglo-Américains, mais il y en a une qui domine toutes les autres.
> L'état social des Américains est éminemment démocratique. [25]

It is certain that by using the latter expression Tocqueville wished to formulate something which was almost identical with the former and we may therefore infer that "éminemment démocratique" was used here synonymously with "le plus étrange phénomène. Les hommes s'y montrent plus égaux par leur fortune et par leur intelligence" etc.

Occurrences of a similar kind are very frequent in this work, and it is scarcely possible to see any difference between, for example, his statements:

> Le dévelopement graduel de l'égalité des conditions est donc un fait
> providentiel, il en a les principaux caractères: il est universel, il est
> durable, [26]

and,

> une grande révolution démocratique s'opère parmi nous. [27]

These statements can be taken as not only referring to phenomena in American social and political life. Another statement of a similar general kind is that in which Tocqueville held democracy to be a social movement or a popular force of a fairly revolutionary kind. After having declared the gradual trend towards equality to be the general tendency of the time, Tocqueville asked:

> Serait-il sage de croire qu'un movement social qui vient de si loin, pourra
> être suspendu par les effort d'une génération? Pense-t-on qu'après avoir
> détruit la féodalité et vaincu les rois, la démocratie reculera devant les
> bourgeois et les riches. S'arrêtere-t-elle maintenant qu'elle est devenue
> si forte et ses adversaires si faibles? [28]

"Democracy" is here used in a way which is fairly similar to, but also somewhat different from, the way in which "democratic" was used in the first quotation. Here too, there is a very strong association between democracy and social equality, but while "democratic" had thus signified that something was marked by an extreme equality, "democracy" connotes here a popular and social movement, probably even a revolutionary force, struggling for social equality.

The term "democracy" used to name something which had destroyed feudalism and the monarchies and would not give way to the wealthy classes

would have a very central and also a very honorific application in the terminology of any socialist. In the mouth of Tocqueville, however, this statement takes on a different meaning. This does not imply, however, that
Tocqueville used "democracy" in a clearly derogatory way, and generally it
is his way of alternating between conditioned fear, less conditioned fear,
and also a conditioned sympathy which is typical, although a somewhat negative attitude without doubt predominated. [29]

According to Tocqueville, social equality could certainly have its advantages, but it might also be dangerous, especially for personal liberty and
the independence of the individual. Concerning the consequences of social
equality, Tocqueville was of the opinion that the passion for equality tended
to elevate the humble to the same level as the great. However, this passion
also grafted a depraved taste for equality onto human hearts, which made
the weak try to pull the strong down to their level, thus further reducing men
to prefer equality in servitude to inequality in liberty. According to Tocqueville,

Ce n'est pas que le peuple dont l'état social est démocratique méprisent
naturellement la liberté; ils ont au contraire un goût instinctif pour elle.
Mais la liberté n'est pas l'object principal et continu de leur desir; ce
qu'ils aiment d'un amour éternel, c'est l'égalité. [30]

It is evident that he did not use "democratic" to characterize something
of which liberty was a necessary characteristic, and there is no reason
to believe that he did attribute absence of liberty to the signification of
"democratic". Tocqueville's statements concerning liberty and democratic
conditions are here obviously of a synthetic and not of an analytic kind. A
somewhat different relationship is found in at least one occurrence of "democratic government", however. Tocqueville greatly feared the omnipotence
of the majority and the tyranny of the masses, and on this point his opinions
were somewhat similar to those of Sismondi. He further declared that it
was the essence of democratic government that the power of the majority
was absolute.

Il est de l'essence même des gouvernements démocratiques que l'empire
de la majorité y soit absolue; car, en dehors de la majorité, dans les
démocraties il n'y a rien qui résiste. [31]

This statement is most probably intended to be a general one in which
Tocqueville wanted to characterize something common to all kinds of democratic government and not only the American type. The absolute power of
the majority seems at this point not only to have been associated with such
a kind of government, but can even be regarded as an essential, and maybe
even the sole, conceptual characteristic of his concept 'democratic government'. Since Tocqueville probably considered liberty to be incompatible
with the absolute power of the majority, this statement can be taken to reveal that on this occasion he used "democratic government" to designate not
merely a kind of rule which might be dangerous to liberty but something
which per se was dangerous to, or even incompatible with, political freedom.

Concerning American democracy, Tocqueville further asserted:

Je connais pas de pays où il regne, en général, moins d'indépendence
d'esprit et de véritable liberté de discussion qu'en Amérique. [32]

He also held that the omnipotence of the majority in America might be worse
for the freedom of discussion than a royal despotism. In this connection he
pointed out that in earlier times it had been possible for authors living under
various kinds of governments to describe the vices and follies of their contemporaries. La Bruyère had lived in the palace of Louis XIV, and Molière
had criticized the court in plays performed in the presence of the courtiers.
The popular power which dominated in America, however, was haunted by
the slightest reproach and frightened by the smallest piquant truth. And no
author, regardless of his fame, could escape the obligation to flatter his
fellow-citizens. The majority therefore lived in perpetual self-applause.
Tocqueville concluded:

> Si l'Amérique n'a pas encore eu des grands écrivains, nous ne devons
> pas en chercher ailleurs les raisons: il n'existe pas de génie litteraire
> sans liberté d'esprit et il n'y a pas de liberté d'esprit en Amérique. [33]

In proof he stated that even the Inquisition in Spain could never completely
prevent the circulation of literature contrary to the religion of the majority.
The rule of majority in America, however, had better success; it had even
eliminated the very idea of publishing a public journal of disbelief, in spite
of the fact there were without doubt unbelievers in America. [34]

No occurrences of "democracy" and "democratic" are present in these
statements concerning America and the alleged absence of freedom there.
It is nevertheless somewhat significant that Tocqueville obviously did not
cease to consider America to be a democracy, although he declared it generally to have less real freedom of discussion than any other country known to
him. This is hardly evidence of use of "democracy" where absence of liberty
is necessarily implicit in the signification of the term, but it is good evidence
that freedom of discussion is not included among the properties of his connotation of "democracy".

Yet a different view of liberty in America is to be found on the last page
in this volume. Russia and America are here held forth as the two antagonistic giants of the future. Both had developed unnoticed, but would soon
take their places as leading nations. But while the Americans gained their
conquests with the plowshare, those of the Russians were gained by the sword.
While the former relied upon the individual effort, the Russians centred all
social authority in a single man. He concluded:

> L'un a pour principal moyen d'action la liberté; l'autre la servitude. [35]

This prognosis modified his earlier statements concerning the absence of
freedom of discussion in America, but it does not effect my comment that a
State does not cease to be a democracy even when it permits less freedom
of opinion than any other country.

Broadly speaking, Tocqueville considered it to be his primary duty to
point out the perils of the development of democracy, since he considered
that this development was almost inevitable and that these perils might be
avoided if sufficiently strong warnings were given. His descriptions might
therefore sometimes be gloomier than he intended. A more moderate picture can be seen in a letter to Eugène Stoffels. Here Tocqueville described
the political aims of the first part of his work: he had tried to show those
who had fashioned an ideal democracy, or a brilliant dream which they believed it would be easy to realize, that democratic government did not possess the elevated properties they had given to it in their imagination. On
the other hand,

... aux hommes pour lesquels le mot de démocratie est le synonyme de bouleversement, d'anarchie, de spoliation, de meurtre,

he had tried to show that a society might be democratically governed with respect for private property, recognition of rights, and religious tolerance, and that even if democratic government to a lesser degree than other kinds of government developed the beauty of the human soul, it also had great and attractive aspects. He concluded that the question did not lie between aristocracy and democracy

... mais si l'on aurait une société démocratique marchant sans poésie et sans grandeur, mais avec ordre et moralité, ou une société démocratique désordonné et dépravée, livrée à des fureurs frénétiques ou courbée sous un joug plus lourd que tous ceux qui ont pesé sur les hommes depuis la chute de l'empire romain. [36]

Thus, what was held as democratic government was not necessarily hostile towards property, religion, freedom, and civil rights, and a democratic society might have order and morality. On the other hand, a democratic society probably necessarily lacked poetry and greatness, and might also be undisciplined and depraved, subject to sudden frenzies or to extreme oppression. According to Tocqueville, it was between these, and only these, eventualities that the future had to choose.

In an article in London and Westminster Review, 1836, Tocqueville maintained that current tendencies towards social equality and centralization were traits that had already been clearly inherent in the French society before the Revolution. He was also of the opinion that the revolutionary government had to a large extent made use of these traits in their social and political planning. In the terminology of this essay, a meaning almost identical with that of the foregoing statement is to be found in a formulation like: "En France ... tout marchait depuis longtemps vers la démocratie." [37] "Towards democracy" is probably used synonymously with "towards social equality and centralization". Similar occurrences are found in this essay, and as in his earlier writings, democracy is probably regarded as a possible danger to liberty.

We find yet another aspect of Tocqueville's use of "democratic", however. In his opinion liberty might take two different forms in human thought. What he held to be the aristocratic notion of liberty favoured an exalted sentiment of individual values, which might yield a singular energy and power to egoism. He continued:

D'après la notion moderne, la notion démocratique, et j'ose le dire la notion juste de la liberté, chaque homme, étant présumé avoir reçu de la nature les lumières nécessaires pour se conduire, apporte en naissant un droit égal et imprescriptible à vivre indépendant de ses semblables, en tout ce qui n'a rapport qu'à lui-même, et à régler comme il l'entend sa propre destinée. [38]

Here "democratic" has been used to characterize that notion of liberty which he declared to be a modern as well as a just one. This can be taken to imply that Tocqueville greatly favoured this kind of liberty. It may seem somewhat strange that "democratic" should have been used in this way, while "democracy" was generally used to designate something that might be dangerous to liberty. Verbal applications of this sort cannot necessarily be said to be self-contradictory, however, since to say that something might be dangerous to liberty need not imply a relation of mutual incompatibility. Although his declaration that absolute power of the majority was the essential mark of democratic government may well be taken to imply a relationship of incompatibility between democracy and liberty, thus making self-contradictory an expression such as "democratic notion of liberty". In any case, democratic liberty could not be a necessary property of what in other contexts he held to be democracy. Here, possibly, are the first signs of the close association or even identification of liberty with what he labelled "democracy" which was to typify his terminology during the February Revolution. This trend is not to be found in the second part of De la Démocratie en Amérique, however.

In this second part, which appeared five years after the first, the terminological tendencies are rather similar to those in the first part. Here too, the term "democracy" was generally used as signifying social and economic equality. In the introduction, for example, he stated that he was no adherent of the narrow point of view

... que je considère l'égalité comme la cause unique de tout ce qui arrive de nos jours.

In explanation, he discussed the American precedent:

Je prouverais aisément que la nature du pays, l'origine de ses habitants, la religion des premiers fondateurs, leur lumières acquises, leur habitudes antérieures, ont exercé et exercent encore, indépéndamment de la démocratie, une immense influence sur leur manière de penser et de sentir. 39

Here Tocqueville held that the fact that something was influenced independently of what he called "democracy" was sufficient to prove that equality was not the single cause behind everything that happened in his day. Tocqueville might have used the terms "democracy" and "equality" in an inverted succession without having caused any difference in the significations of these statements. Or, he might have said he was no adherent of the view that "je considère la démocratie comme la cause unique" etc. , and then have stated in explanation that many factors such as religion and customs had very greatly influenced the American way of thinking and feeling "indépendamment de l'égalité". In that case, the terms "démocratie" and "égalité" would have been used synonymously. A closely related application of "democratic" is present when he most certainly used the expression "les siècles démocratiques" 40 synonymously with "les siècles d'égalité. " 41

On the political omnipotence of the majority Tocqueville said:

Il est à croire que l'empire intellectuel du plus grand nombre serait moins absolu chez un peuple démocratique soumis à un roi, qu'au sein d'une pure démocratie; mais il sera toujours très absolu, et, quelles que soient les lois politique qui régissent les hommes dans les siècles d'égalité, l'on peut prévoir qui la foi dans l'opinion commune y deviendra une sorte de religion dont la majorité sera le prophète. 42

"Democratic people" here seems to signify any people living in equal conditions, regardless of form of government. It is clear that he considered intellectual power of the majority to be "très absolu" among any people of that kind, and even stronger in the kind of government he labelled "pure democracy". As with an earlier occurrence of "democratic government", this statement is one of the very few occasions when Tocqueville not only held democracy to be a possible or potential danger to liberty, but also used "democracy", or at least "pure democracy", to signify something which he probably considered to be incompatible with freedom of opinion. Thus Tocqueville probably believed that liberty, as he understood it, was not possible where the absolute intellectual power of the majority had become a kind of religion.

A more moderate view concerning the relationship between a democratic people and liberty is present in Tocqueville's statement that democratic peoples had a natural taste for liberty. He added, however, that above all they had an ardent, eternal, and invincible passion for equality. They desired equality in liberty, but if it were not obtainable, they would prefer equality in servitude. [43]

In conclusion, Tocqueville stated that he had observed during his stay in the United States that a social estate which he held to be democratic might offer singular possibilities for the establishment of despotism. He added that at that time this observation had led him to believe that the Christian nations would perhaps finally have to submit to an oppression similar to that which tyrannized many of the peoples of antiquity. [44] A more detailed examination and five years of new meditation had not diminished his fears, but he nevertheless regarded the problem of democratic suppression somewhat differently. On the one hand, he asserted that he believed

... qu'il est plus facile d'établir un gouvernement absolu et despotique chez un peuple où les conditions sont égales que chez un autre,

and therefore that

... le despotisme me paraît donc particulièrement à redouter dans les âges démocratiques. [45]

On the other hand, however, he emphasized that if despotism were to establish itself among democratic nations, it would possess a character other than that of earlier kinds of tyranny. It would be simultaneously more comprehensive and milder, and it would degrade men without tormenting them. He added,

... cette même égalité, qui facilite le despotisme, le tempère. [46]

Finally, Tocqueville thought the kind of suppression which threatened the the democratic peoples was not similar to any other kind of suppression. He had tried in vain to find an expression that could exactly signify what he wanted to explain, since the ancient terms "despotism" and "tyranny" were inadequate.

I have only quoted and commented on a small proportion of the frequent occurrences of "democracy" and "democratic" in this work, and in general only those occurrences which seem to be characteristic of more important trends in his terminology.

Tocqueville's intention was not only to treat what he held to be American democracy, but rather to develop a broader perspective on the different problems which he generally associated with democracy. In a letter to John Stuart Mill, he declared:

Quand je parlais uniquement de la société démocratique des États-Unis, cela se comprenait aussi. Si j'avais parlé de notre société démocratique de France, telle qu'elle se produit de nos jours, cela se serait encore bien compris. Mais en partant des notions que me fournissait la société

américaine et française, j'ai voulu peindre les traits généraux des
sociétés démocratiques, dont aucun complet modèle n'existe encore. [47]

In another letter to Stuart Mill, almost one year earlier, Tocqueville
said that he had travelled to Paris to get the work printed which he had
written during the last four years, and which was to be the conclusion of an
earlier treatise. He continued: "C'est l'Influence de l'égalité sur les idées
et les sentiments des hommes. "[48] This work was without doubt the second
part of De la Démocratie en Amérique, since he had been writing no other
work for the last four years and which was going to be printed in December
1839. Why Tocqueville labelled the work in this way is unclear. Perhaps
at that time he had intended to use L'influence de l'égalité as the title of the
work, but had changed his mind later. This is not very probable, however;
Tocqueville did not even use the expression as the sub-title of his treatise.
He also clearly said that this volume was to be the conclusion of his earlier
book which had already become famous under the title De la Démocratie en
Amérique, This expression was therefore possibly used with the intention
of letting Stuart Mill know that the content of the work was the influence of
equality on human ideas and sentiments. I have not studied the original of
this letter, and therefore do not know what marks in the handwritten document may have caused the use of italic in the printed work.

We can nevertheless agree with Tocqueville that the content of this
treatise was the influence of equality, and that this expression concerning
equality is rather characteristic of his use of "democracy" and "democratic"
in both parts. His earlier terminology shows that no one signification of
"democracy" and its related terms can be said to have been exclusive, and
it is evident that these terms have been used with somewhat different significations. But the predominant part of the occurrences show a rather strong
association and even identification of social equality with what was called
"democracy" and "democratic", and democracy was also regarded, at least
generally, as something which might be and even was a danger to liberty and
personal independence. However, on one occasion, and not in his main
work, Tocqueville used "democratic" to characterize that notion of liberty
which, in his opinion, was just.

b. During and after 1848

Apart from his main treatise, Tocqueville's speech on the right to work
during the February Revolution can very probably be said to contain the best
known occurrence of "democracy" in his political terminology. In the Constituent Assembly in September 1848, Tocqueville emphasized that he believed socialism to be a profound defiance of liberty as well as of human
reason. Socialism was not to be considered as the perfection of the principles of the French revolution, since that Revolution had always respected
and honoured individual property. Socialism claimed to be the legitimate
development of democracy, but he would not try to find the true etymology
of the word "democracy", as many of his colleagues had. On the contrary,

... je chercherai la démocratie où je l'ai vue, vivante, active,
triomphante, dans le seul pays du monde où elle existe. [49]

He continued comparing equality in France unfavourably with that in America:

...où l'état social, les mœurs, les lois, tout est démocratique, où tout
emane du peuple et y rentre, et où cependant chaque individu jouit d'une
indépendance plus entière, d'une liberté plus grande que dans aucun autre
temps et dans aucune autre contrée de la terre [là, vous verrez] un pays
essentiellement démocratique. [50]

The fact that each individual possessed entire independence and a liberty
greater than that of any earlier time and any other place here seems to
have been regarded as a central criterion for characterizing a country as
"essentially democratic". As in an earlier statement, Tocqueville also
mentioned equality as a condition of democracy. Earlier trends in his ideology as well as in his terminology, however, make it a little difficult to
accept that he considered there was greater liberty in America than in any
other place on earth and in any earlier period, and that this property was
among the most important criteria for American democracy. He declared
on at least one occasion that America had less independence of mind and
less real liberty of opinion than any other country within his knowledge. [51]
And he generally conceived democracy to be a possible danger to liberty and
personal independence. Thus his opinion that the greatest degree of liberty
was indispensable to a country characterized as "essentially democratic"
represents a new element in his terminology.

An intimate association between liberty and what he designated as
"democracy", or even a use of the term which made personal liberty a
necessary property of its signification, is evident when Tocqueville went on
to say that America was the only democracy in existence at that time, the
only truly democratic republic in history, and at the same time the country
where it would be most difficult to present socialistic doctrines. Concerning
the relationship between socialism and democracy, he said:

La démocratie et le socialism ne sont pas solidaires l'un de l'autre: Ce
sont choses non-seulement différentes mais contraires. ... La démocratie
étend la sphère de l'indépendence individuelle, le socialisme la reserre.
La démocratie donne toute sa valeur possible à chaque homme, le socialisme fait de chaque homme un agent, un instrument, un chiffre.   La
démocratie et le socialisme ne se tiennent que par un mot, l'égalité; mais
remarquez la différence: la démocratie veut l'égalité dans la liberté, et le
socialisme veut l'égalité dans la gêne et dans la servitude. [52]

This passage is one of the most outspoken ever uttered concerning an
alleged relationship of incompatibility between what was held to be socialism
and democracy. It is obvious that liberty was not only more or less an inevitable consequence, or a non-conceptual characteristic, but that it can
even be regarded as a central conceptual characteristic of the concept
'democracy', or as being directly implicit in the connotation of "democracy"
as used here. Where the relationship between socialism and democracy is
concerned I must admit that Tocqueville did not use "democracy" synonymously with "socialism" in De la Démocratie en Amérique, The terms
"democracy" and "democratic" signified social and economic equality to a
large degree, but this kind of equality did not imply that the means of production were common property. However, when Tocqueville asked:

Pense-t-on qu'après avoir détruit la féodalité et vaincu les rois, la
démocratie reculera devant les bourgois et les riches?

the signification of "democracy" may be regarded as somewhat similar in

part to what Tocqueville would have attributed to "socialism", though he
would scarcely have used "socialism" to designate the power that destroyed
feudalism.

A use of "democratic" that is almost synonymous with "socialist" occurs
in a manuscript dated 1847, however. In a short draft of a manifesto which
Tocqueville and some of his friends had planned to publish in the autumn of
1847, it was maintained that between 1789 and 1830 France had watched
class struggles between the ancient feudal aristocracy and the middle classes. The great political controversy of the day, however, was between
those who were in possession of property and those who were not. The political problem of private property was therefore by far the most important.
According to Tocqueville, the French Revolution had abolished all privileges
and exclusive rights, save one, the right to property. And now, the right
to own property represented the last remnant of a shattered world, an isolated privilege in a levelled society. He continued:

> C'est à lui seul, maintenant, à soutenir chaque jour le choc direct et
> incessant des opinions démocratiques. [53]

A little later on Tocqueville declared that it was not by chance that special
doctrines bearing different names were being spread, all of them having the
denial of the right to own property as their principal feature. He asked in
conclusion:

> Qui ne reconnaît la le symptôme de cette vieille maladie démocratique
> du temps dont peut-être la crise approche? [54]

The denial of the right to own, or even the destruction of private property,
here seems to be the essential part of the signification Tocqueville attributed
in this context to "democratic". Tocqueville could possibly have replaced
"democratic" with "socialist" without having changed the significations of
these two statements. In that case, "democratic" would have been used
synonymously with "socialist". It is certain that liberty was not one of the
properties included in the signification of "democratic" in these two occurrences, and we may even say that what was characterized by "democratic"
was held to be contrary to liberty as understood by Tocqueville. Thus the
use of "democratic" and "democracy" in Tocqueville's important speech
does not merely differ from his general application of these terms in his main
work, but is also in direct contrast to his use of "democratic" about ten
months earlier.

In seeking to discover why Tocqueville used "democracy" with this new
signification, we turn to a statement in his <u>Souvenirs</u>. These memoirs were
written in 1850, but were not published during his lifetime. In the spring of
1848, Tocqueville stated on entering the Constituent Assembly that he had no
monarchical faith, no affection for any prince, no cause to defend save liberty
and human dignity. To do this he desired to protect the ancient laws of society against the onslaughts of the revolutionaries by making use of the republican principles, thus allowing the will of the French people to triumph
over the passions of the workers in Paris. This meant: "Vaincre ainsi la
démagogie par la démocratie. " [55] From an ideological point of view, we
can assume that Tocqueville had universal suffrage in mind when indicating
the republican principles by which the will of the French nation was to triumph over the passions of the Parisian workers. And it is probable that this
new appraisal of universal suffrage as a proper means in the struggle against
socialism was caused by the result of the general election in April, in which

the non-socialist parties obtained a large majority of the votes. With regard to the signification of "democracy", in the light of this quotation it is probably only possible to say that the term was used here to express a concept having universal suffrage as an essential characteristic. That democracy in this concrete situation was something by which liberty and human dignity were to be conserved, and which well might be used as a barrier against socialism, is here evidently a non-conceptual characteristic only. If we consider this occurrence only, we might therefore think that Tocqueville did not introduce a new concept 'democracy' in 1848, and that we are faced with a change in conceptions of democracy while the connotation of the term "democracy" remains fairly constant. But his general application of "democracy" made in 1848 does not confirm such a view. As used in his main speech, liberty was not only to be conserved by democracy in the existing situation but was most likely even a conceptual characteristic of what he designated as "democracy". On this point there is a marked difference in relation to his earlier use of this term, and we can therefore probably be permitted to speak of a conceptual change, as well as a change in conceptions.

As regards his later application of "democracy" and related terms, other than the one under discussion, I have only been able to find a few occurrences of "democratic" in Souvenirs. And with regard to the signification of this word, his application can generally be regarded as fairly different from that attributed to "democracy" in September 1848.

A peculiar usage occurs when, as proof of his preoccupation in the beginning of 1848, Tocqueville quoted his earlier statement concerning private property:

C'est à lui seul maintenant à soutenir chaque jour le choc direct et incessant des opinions démocratiques. [56]

Here he probably used "democratic" almost synonymously with "socialist". This quotation probably indicates that in 1850 Tocqueville confirmed the terminology he had used in October 1847. In a later passage in these memoirs Tocqueville maintained that the economic and political theories which persuaded workers that human misery was the result of laws and not of Providence were some of the general causes without which the February Revolution had not been possible. He added that these general causes also included the growing desire for material goods among the masses and what he described as "le malaise démocratique de l'envie qui la travaillait sourdement. "[57] Here too he might have replaced "democratic" with "socialist" possibly without changing the signification of the statement. A similar use of "democratic" occurs when, describing the February Revolution, he declared:

Le socialisme restera le caractère essentiel et le souvenir de plus redoutable de la révolution de Fevrier; [58]

and later on the same theme:

... je sentais que nous étions tous au milieu d'une de ces grandes inondations démocratiques. [59]

The way in which he used "democratic" in these three quotations contradicts the previous occurrence of "democracy" when the term was used to label a form of government which was to serve as a barrier against socialism. It is also evident that any degree of liberty was not a necessary condition for characterizing something as "democratic" according to its application in these statements. On these points there is a marked difference between this application and his way of using "democracy" and "democratic" two years earlier, when his political ideas were almost identified with what he designated as "democracy". On the contrary, his use of "democratic" in 1850 is in many ways similar to the trend before 1848, implying that his way of using "democracy" in his great speech cannot be regarded as representing a terminological turning point.

Tocqueville used "democracy" and "democratic" infrequently after 1850, especially when compared with the frequency before 1848. In this he was similar to most political thinkers. On one occasion he applied these terms in a manner similar to his usage in the speech of September 1848; but there are also trends of a different kind, which without doubt predominated.

In L'Ancien Régime et la Révolution, 1856, Tocqueville admitted that

... les sociétés démocratiques qui ne sont pas libres peuvent être riches, raffinées, ornées, magnifiques même,

and that one might find private virtues, good family fathers, but never great citizens or a great people "tant que l'égalité et le despotisme y seront joints. " 60

This statement probably contains rather bold criticism of the contemporary imperial rule. "Democratic" might here characterize a kind of society which was not free, and which was a combination of equality and despotism. This use of the term is in accord with the predominant trends in his terminology before 1848, but not with the verbal usage in his speech on the right to work.

Later on Tocqueville pointed out that the ancient French nobility formed a very exclusive, closed estate compared with that of England. In England the daughter of a nobleman might without shame marry a self-made man. A similar phenomenon was rather rare, however, "même de nos jours, en France, après soixante ans de démocratie. " 61 "Democracy" is evidently used here with a very wide signification, or to cover what had existed in France from the time of the Revolution up to middle of the eighteen-fifties, regardless of different forms of government such as revolutionary dictatorship, various kinds of republics, and monarchies and the imperial rules of both Napoleons. More concretely, by "democracy" Tocqueville primarily intended to mean a kind of society without fixed privileges for any social estate; it can also be inferred that some degree of liberty was probably not a necessary condition to label a society as "democracy".

Again, Tocqueville declared that the so-called "economists" in French political thought, Morelly, Mably, Quesnay, and others, were familiar with what was called "democratic despotism. "

Cette forme particulière de la tyrannie qu'on nomme le despotisme démocratique, dont le moyen âge n'avait pas eu l'idée, leur est déjà familière.62

Probably as a hint to contemporary imperial rule, he said that this democratic despotism meant absence of hierarchy and fixed social estates, and a people composed of individuals almost similar and entirely equal; the masses were considered as the legitimate sovereign, but were absolutely deprived of any opportunity to influence the decisions of the government.

It is difficult to know how far Tocqueville intended to refer in this meta-occurrence to a current trend in the vernacular, or whether the expression "democratic despotism" was generally used at that time to signify a particu-

lar kind of tyranny. But Tocqueville himself seems to have accepted the
expression as adequate. Similarly there is also an occurrence of "democratic" where no degree of liberty at all was necessary for the characterization of a form of rule by that term.

An entirely different application occurs in some preliminary notes to a
work on the Revolution and Napoleon -- a work which was never written.
Under the heading "Démocratie. - Institutions démocratiques. - Principes
de 1789. - Divers sens de ces mots. - Confusion qui en resulte" Tocqueville
declared:

> Ce qui jette le plus de confusion dans l'esprit, c'est l'emploi qu'on fait
> de ces mots: démocratie, gouvernement démocratique.[63]

As long as these terms were not clearly defined, one would live in an inex-
tricable confusion of ideas which would benefit despots and demagogues. A
country governed by an absolute prince would sometimes be said to be a
democracy because the prince governed in a manner favourable to the
people. His government was thus described as democratic government or
a democratic monarchy. Against this view and this terminology Tocqueville
maintained:

> Les mots démocratie, gouvernement démocratique, ne peuvent vouloir
> dire qu'une chose, suivant la vraie signification des mots: un gouverne-
> ment auquel le peuple prend une part plus ou moins grande. Son sens est
> intimement lié à l'idée de la liberté politique. Appeler démocratique un
> gouvernement où la liberté politique ne se trouve pas, c'est dire une ab-
> surdité palpable, suivant le véritable sens du mot.[64]

Here there is a distinct continuation of the terminological trend in
Tocqueville's great speech of September 1848. He even uses an expression
like "the true sense of the word" to mark out the signification of "democracy"
and "democratic government" of which liberty was an essential property. All
other applications of this term were consequently declared to represent an
evident misuse, or to be a palpable absurdity. This statement of Tocqueville
is one of the strongest charges of misuse of "democracy" ever formulated
in the previous century. It might be objected that these were preliminary
notes not intended for publication, and that the importance of this statement
is therefore reduced. But the degree to which the notes are elaborated excludes the possibility of regarding them as merely arbitrary remarks.

With regard to the background of this alleged misuse of "democracy"
and "democratic government", Tocqueville continued by saying that false and
more or less obscure expressions were adopted, firstly on account of the
desire to deceive the multitude, since the words "democratic government"
always had a certain success; and secondly, on account of the real confusion
of a person who wished to explain in a few words an idea as complicated as
the following: an absolute government where the people took no part in political life, but where the classes above the people were in possession of no
privileges, and where the laws were made to favour, as far as possible, the
well-being of the people. The latter statement was certainly intended as a
description of contemporary imperial rule, whose propagandists he therefore charged of misusing "democracy" and "democratic government" with
the intention of deceiving the multitude.

Though he restricted the significations of "democracy" and "democratic
government" exclusively to cover kinds of rules where the presence of freedom was an essential property, there are also occurrences of "democratic"

in a letter of 1857, where this term was used to characterize contemporary
French society, and where it was also clearly stated that this society lacked
liberty. In a personal letter to Freslon, Tocqueville lamented the existing
state of affairs in France. He emphasized that what he deplored was not that
l'ancien régime had been destroyed, but the way in which the destruction
had been carried out. He continued:

> ... je ne suis pas l'adversaire des sociétés démocratiques; ces sociétés
> sont grandes aussi, et n'ont rien que de conforme aux vues de Dieu quand
> la liberté n'en est pas absent.

He added that what depressed him was not that the society was democratic,
but that it should be so difficult to introduce permanent liberty in France.
He concluded:

> Or, je le confesse, je ne connais rien de plus misérable qu'une société
> démocratique sans la liberté. [65]

This use of "democratic" does not necessarily contradict his terminology in the preliminary notes. If by the expression "democratic society",
of which liberty was not necessarily an attribute, Tocqueville meant something which might exist independently of what he called "democratic government", then these two statements are not incompatible. In a few places in
his political writings he tends to hold democratic society to be a possible
social form regardless of its kind of government. Nevertheless in De la
Démocratie en Amérique Tocqueville believed the omnipotence of the majority to be more absolute in a democratic government and in a pure democracy than in a democratic kind of society with another form of rule. On the
whole, reservations of this kind do not eliminate other incompatibilities in
Tocqueville's terminology.

If, for example, it was a palpable absurdity to use "democracy" and
"democratic government" as labels of a form of government marked by absence of liberty, then Tocqueville committed many similar absurdities in
his writings, several of them after 1848. His attitude to democracy as being
something that might well exist without liberty, that might be a danger to
liberty, and that might even be incompatible with liberty, prevailed in the
years before 1848. But we have also seen that, after having declared liberty
to be essential to democracy in 1848, he several times used "democracy"
and "democratic" without making liberty or individual independence possible
properties of their significations. A similar relationship also occurs when
he declared democracy and socialism to be opposed and incompatible phenomena in political life, and then, earlier as well as later, used "democratic"
almost synonymously with "socialist". It is such practices that inter alia
make research into the Tocqueville's political terminology so interesting.
Essential parts of Tocqueville's important ideological thought are probably
revealed in his use of "democracy". For Tocqueville, the conservation of
liberty and human dignity as well as the defence of private property were the
main problems in the new society which succeeded l'ancien régime, and these
factors especially were involved in the different significations he attributed
to "democracy". This somewhat strange aspect, however, cannot be regarded as a peculiarity of his language. Very similar relationships also
occur in the application of "democracy" by Proudhon, Lenin, Thomas Mann,
and others.

CHAPTER VII

RADICALISM

1. Bentham

Chronologically it might have been expected that Bentham would be discussed
earlier in this work. I have found, however, that the dates of the majority
of the occurrences of "democracy" in his writings make it impossible to
discuss him together with Paine and Godwin, and that the nature of his political philosophy makes it most difficult to place him in company with Constant
or Châteaubriand, or with Guizot or Tocqueville.   I have therefore deferred
discussion of Bentham's terminology to this chapter.

As early as 1776, in <u>Fragment of Government</u>, Bentham referred
frequently to Blackstone's use of "democracy" and other political terms with
disapproval. It is nevertheless difficult to discover how Bentham himself
used, or intended to use, the term. [1]

Some other early occurrences are to be found in an unprinted treatise
on Irish affairs, in which Bentham stated that the Irish volunteer associations were self-formed, and that their commanding officers were elected by
the privates. The physical force of the country was manifestly in the hands
of the people, in other words, "democratic ascendency was fully established."[2]
"Democratic ascendency" seems here to signify that the physical force of
the country was manifestly in the hands of the people. With regard to "democracy", however, Bentham added that that kind of political situation was

> ...democratic ascendency -- not democracy; for neither by the armed
> citizens themselves, nor by any man of their choice, was an act of au-
> thority ever exercised. [2]

The difference between what he designated as "democratic ascendency"
and "democracy" here seems to be that it was a necessary condition for
something to be labelled with the latter term that acts of authority should be
exercised; this may be taken to imply that "democracy" exclusively signified a regular kind of political authority, possibly in the form of a government. On the other hand, it seems to have been a sufficient condition for
something to be designated as a "democratic ascendency" that the physical
force of the country was manifestly in the hands of the people.

In 1793, Bentham used "democrats" in an appeal to the French republicans to emancipate their colonies. He referred to the fact that two colonies,
Martinique and Guadalupe, had announced their separation from France.
This fact, however, had irritated rather than satisfied the French republicans, who had decreed armaments to fasten a yoke which they themselves
had shaken off. In a direct appeal, Bentham said:

> You are playing over again our old game. Democrats in Europe, you are
> aristocrats in America. [3]

What was meant more directly by "democrats" is unclear. Bentham did not refuse the French republicans the designation "democrats in Europe", even in 1793, when their rule was one of blood and terror. In addition, we might imagine that working for the emancipation of colonies would be a necessary condition for receiving the unqualified title "democrats", and not only "democrats in Europe". His statement that the French were playing over again "our old game" may tempt us to believe that Bentham considered the English generally to have been what he called "democrats", or even England to have been what he called a "democracy" at the time of the American War of Independence. Other and later trends in his terminology, however, make this conclusion far from probable.

Save for the last sporadic occurrences, an honorific use of "democracy" does not characterize Bentham's terminology up to 1809. Nor is a frequent application to be found. Bentham's first comprehensive use of "democracy" is to be found in Plan of Parliamentary Reform, written in 1809, but not printed before 1817. This happens fairly late in Bentham's life. In 1809 he was more than sixty years old, but from this time a frequent as well as honorific use is an outstanding characteristic of his terminology. It is significant that this trend started when Bentham's belief in rule by enlightened persons was combined with an unlimited confidence in popular rule, partly on account of the influence of James Mill. Earlier, too, Bentham believed in rule by enlightened persons, i. e. persons who knew the interests of the people, and for him this knowledge was always the principal criterion of good government. This belief could also include belief in enlightened despotism. Yet many of the conceptions of government which he originally applied to enlightened despotism, he also applied to popular rule. He had, for example, no misgivings about the possible tyranny of the majority. Before as well as after 1809 he entertained no devices for limitations on sovereignty, such as separation of power, or checks and balances.

In Plan of Parliamentary Reform he maintained:

> Propose anything that would put any power into the hands of those whose obedience all power is composed: you propose democracy. [4]

It is not clear why the term should be stressed. Bentham can hardly have meant the term "democracy", and we can therefore believe that his probable intention was to emphasize the word as an important one. This tendency is rather frequent in his writings. "Democracy" here, primarily or even exclusively, seems to signify that all power should be in the hands of all citizens. Bentham was clearly aware of the fact that the term "democracy" was widely associated in English circles with something dangerous and terrible. Shortly afterwards he asked if

> ... by this bugbear word democracy, are the people of this country to be frightened out of their senses? [5]

Why it was possible to frighten a great part of the English people by this bugbear word, or why "democracy" was considered by many to be a bugbear word, is not explained. But we may presume it was on account of an alleged relation of synonymity between "democracy" and "anarchy" to which Bentham drew attention ten pages later.

In arguing against this way of using "democracy" derogatorily, and possibly even with a dyslogistic signification, Bentham emphasized that one should look to positive experience of it. This, he maintained, could be found in the United States.

> There you have -- not merely democratic ascendancy -- democratic ascendancy in a mixed government -- but democracy -- pure democracy, and nothing else. ... In the language of legitimacy and tyranny, and of the venal slavery that crawls under them, democracy and anarchy are synonymous terms. 6

There was scarcely anywhere on the whole surface of the globe from which this abuse of words could receive support. He referred once more to the United States, and asked if there existed anywhere so regular and so well-regulated a government.

Thus Bentham completely rejected the kind of terminology according to which "democracy" and "anarchy" were synonymous terms -- a terminological relation which might have been partially approved of by Godwin about fifteen years earlier. Bentham's reason for rejecting what he judged to be misuse of the words was the fact that he considered the United States to be what he called a "pure democracy" and at the same time probably the most regular and well-regulated government in the world. Bentham does not seem to have approved of everything that received the label "democracy" when used in some qualified way. But with regard to these negative experiences he declared:

> Look not to Greece or Italy: look not to ancient or middle ages: look not to any self-acting democracy.... Compared with the democracy here in question -- compared with a representative democracy -- a democracy in which the sole power exercised by the people is that of choosing their deputies, and in those deputies their rulers, -- whatever else has been called democracy, has had nothing of democracy but the name. 7

This somewhat paradoxical statement may probably be taken to indicate that by "democracy" Bentham wished exclusively to designate a representative kind of government where the electing of representatives was the sole political function of the people. But Bentham clearly included the direct form of government of ancient Greece and in Italy in the Middle Ages in what he himself termed "self-acting democracy". His declaration that these kinds of direct rule have nothing in common with what he labelled as unqualified "democracy" is a rather clear sign that a democracy was, according to Bentham, exclusively a representative kind of government. And the last part of the quotation may even be taken to indicate that any other use of "democracy" represented a verbal misuse. At this point Bentham cannot be said to have been entirely consistent; remnants of other terminological traditions are discernible, but the principal factor is without doubt his desire to restrict the signification of "democracy" in the way described above.

This desire to restrict the signification of "democracy" to the fields of representative government is still more evident a few pages further on. In praise of Simon de Montfort, Earl of Leicester, who summoned representative knights from each shire in 1254, Bentham maintained:

> Father of the representative system! O rare Simon de Montfort! -- thou who, in giving birth to it -- without perhaps intending good to human being, save one -- didst to mankind more good than ever was done by any one mortal man! -- in giving birth to that most beneficent system, thou gavest birth to the only practicable democracy -- to the only democracy, of which extent beyond a nutshell, or duration beyond a day, are attainable attri-

butes ... But for the English constitution, democracy, the only democracy worth the name, never could have been known. [8]

The last part of this quotation may be taken to imply that all use of "democracy" with a signification other than rule by representatives was a misuse of the word. From a more general point of view, we can say that this application of "democracy" marks an important phase in the development of the connotation of this term. Apart from Robespierre, Bentham was probably the first to attempt to restrict the connotation of the term in this manner. This use of the term in the sense of a representative kind of rule can very probably be regarded as a necessary condition of the very honorific application of "democracy" by persons otherwise so different as Bentham and Robespierre.

Concerning the consequences which Bentham attributed to democracy, perhaps in contrast to those holding "democracy" to be a bugbear word, Bentham said:

-- Forasmuch as in a democracy, standing by itself without support from anything but itself, there be no such thing as danger -- no diminution of security for person, property, reputation, condition in life, religious worship -- in a word, for anything on which man sets value. [9]

This statement definitely indicates appreciative use of "democracy", and also exemplifies an application of the term that was unusual at that time in Europe. What he called "democracy" was not regarded as dangerous to property, person, and religious worship. The relation between the security of private property and what he called "democracy" is not thoroughly elaborated, but apart from the use here, it is an important indicator of his terminology that the same person who consistently used "democracy" in a very honorific way was simultaneously an ardent defender of the capitalistic system and antagonistic to economic levelling.

A few years later Bentham clearly associated what he called "representative democracy" with his main political slogan -- "the greatest happiness of the greatest number. " He stated that the principal cause of misgovernment and consequent misery in England was the corruption of the system of national representation. In every other country, however, the cause of misgovernment was

... the want of a system of adequate national representation, or rather the want of a representative democracy, in place of a more or less mitigated despotism: the want of the only form of government in which the greatest happiness of the greatest number is the end in view. [10]

This formulation may be taken to indicate that representative democracy was already in existence in England. Other statements of Bentham, however, do not confirm such an inference. Why he used the expression "representative democracy" and not unqualified "democracy" here is not quite clear. Perhaps it was his personal opinion that "democracy" exclusively signified a representative kind of government; he nevertheless used the qualification "representative" to avoid possible misunderstanding by his readers. The use of such a qualification in connection with something considered to be a kind of representative government must be regarded as a pleonasm. Pleonasms of this kind are sometimes to be found in political language, however. Unqualified "democracy", partly in contrast to his earlier terminology, might have been used here to describe a form of government which was not representative.

Whereas government by the people, and generally also by elected representatives, can be regarded as belonging to the conceptual characteristics of 'democracy', security of property and religious worship should more probably be classed as consequences, or non-conceptual characteristics of Bentham's concept 'democracy'. It is more doubtful, however, whether the greatest happiness of the greatest number can be regarded as a non-conceptual characteristic of 'representative democracy'. If Bentham had chosen to include that kind of happiness in his definition of this concept, it would have been a conceptual characteristic, and the statement under discussion would then have been of an analytic kind. Hypothetically, the greatest happiness of the greatest number is an almost inevitable consequence of this concept, but hardly a conceptual characteristic. In this case the statement concerning representative democracy and the greatest happiness is of a synthetic kind.

A rather similar relationship also occurs in The Constitutional Code, Bentham's main political work. Here he states that

...under a representative democracy, the constitutional brand of law has, for its actual end, the greatest happiness for the greatest number. [11]

At almost at the same place he maintained that

...in a representative democracy, the exercise of this designative power [the constitutional branch of law] is performed by human judgement; under a monarchy it is performed by fortune or providence.

Concerning other characteristics, Bentham declared the administration of this form of government to be the cheapest one, as frugality was one of its aims. [12] He also held that

...in a representative democracy, unnecessary wars against foreign adversaries can scarcely have existence, [13]

because wars on account of profit or irritation were impossible when the people indirectly formed the supreme ruling body. The latter characteristics are probably non-conceptual, and therefore do not say anything directly about the connotation of "democracy". From an ideological point of view, it is probably on this point of confidence in the people at large that we find the most important differences between Bentham and the later Utilitarians, such as John Stuart Mill and John Austin, who both used "democracy" in a somewhat different way from that of Bentham.

As a general characteristic Bentham stated:

The only species of government which has or can have for its object and effect the greatest happiness of the greatest number, is, as has been a democracy, ... The only species of democracy which can have place in a community numerous enough to defend itself against aggression at the hands of external adversaries, is a representative democracy. [14]

This terminology can in some aspects be said to differ from what we have seen in his Plan of Parliamentary Reform. While he there tried to restrict the signification on the term to cover the fields of representative rule exclusively, Bentham here used the concept 'representative democracy' as one of the species of a genus 'democracy' with "democracy" as conceptual designation. The connotation of "democracy" was therefore wider than that of "representative democracy", and it therefore looks as if a direct kind of popular government might here be subsumable under what received unquali-

fied "democracy" as a conceptual designation. On this point there is quite
an important difference in relation to his earlier terminology, where several
explicit attempts to restrict the connotation of "democracy" in this mentioned
way were very central characteristics of his terminology, though Bentham
earlier had not been absolutely consistent on this point. This naturally indicates some degree of caution in classifying Bentham among those political
thinkers who used "democracy" to signify exclusively a representative kind
of government.

Bentham said here that the greatest happiness of the greatest number
was not only the object of representative democracy but also of what he held
here to be democracy. Since it is hardly probable that Bentham would have
attributed this maxim to a direct form of rule at any earlier time, we are
here not only faced with some kind of terminological difference in relation
to earlier verbal applications, but also some degree of ideological difference
in relation to earlier points of view. But the reservation concerning numerous communities and representative rule is in high conformity with earlier
statements.

In a political appeal made by Bentham to Lafayette and his fellow-citizens
soon after the July Revolution, Bentham made serious objections to any form
of Second Chamber. In a section with the heading "Let not democracy be a
Bugbear", Bentham declared:

> Fellow-Citizens! Anarchy is one Bugbear, Democracy another. Sepa-
> rately, or like dogs coupled, they are sent forth by periodicals -- ministe-
> rial and absolutistic -- to strike terror into weak minds, on both sides
> of the water. [15]

Formulations like "Democracy and anarchy are synonymous terms" were
mentioned as typical of such periodicals. Bentham protested strongly against
these kinds of argumentation and terminology, which he denounced as
"twaddle" and "anility". Anyone who believed in any such connection between
democracy and anarchy must have been blind or deaf, or he must have wished
not to see and hear. In such a man one might see a patient, labouring under
a sort of monomania, and if a charitable practitioner disposed to attempt
relief wanted to cure him, he might say:

> Two words. -- Democracy and Anarchy -- produced the disease: one other
> word -- America -- may take the lead in the cure. [16]

The essence of the somewhat ironic argument that follows consists of
the two premises that America was a democracy and that America was
not an anarchy--arguments very similar to his earlier ones. In the form of
a question directed to his fellow-citizens of France, England, and the whole
civilized world, and also of future ages, Bentham asked:

> If democracy, instead of being the same thing as anarchy, is really a
> better form of government than any which is not democracy -- better than
> an absolute monarchy, an absolute aristocracy, or an aristocracy-ridden
> monarchy, -- what reason is there, why I should not hold the difference
> up to view? [17]

These statements probably contain the final uses as well as mentions of
"democracy" in his terminology. They reveal clearly that, at the age of
eighty-four, Bentham clearly held what he designated as "democracy" to be
the best form of government, and that in accordance with his earlier statements, he also rejected any kind of synonymity between "democracy" and

"anarchy". Here too, America was mentioned as furnishing sufficient proof of the complete falsity of such synonymity, and in similarity with statements he made in 1809 he also declared that an extended application of "democracy" in contemporary English vernacular was a misuse of the term. Thus in Bentham's writings we also find the familiar phenomenon of accusing others of misusing a term which he himself uses in a very honorific way.

2. James Mill

In spite of Bentham's honorific use of "democracy" and in spite of his several attempts to restrict the signification of this term to cover exclusively a representative kind of governing, we shall probably only find "democracy" as signifying a direct form of rule in Mill's terminology, a kind of rule which Mill by no means regarded as an ideal political form.

In his Essay on Government which appeared in the supplement to the fifth edition of the Encyclopaedia Britannica in 1824, Mill puts toward a political theory in favour of representative form of government. This theory is very similar to certain of Bentham's ideas, but unlike Bentham, Mill did not use "democracy" to signify the kind of constitution which he held to be the best one for England and other civilized countries. In discussing what he held to be the simple forms of government Mill rejected the democratic, the aristocratic, and the monarchical, nor could he agree with those who maintained that securities for good government were to be found in a union of these three simple forms. In his section on democratic government which he headed "THE DEMOCRATICAL" Mill began:

It is obviously impossible that the community in a body can present to afford protection to each of its members. [18]

He went on to say that single individuals should be chosen for different political purposes. As regards the absence of such individuals under this form of rule, he continued:

This circumstance alone seems to form a conclusive objection against the democratical form. [19]

Mill further asserted that to assemble the whole of the community as often as the business of government required would almost preclude the existence of labour and hence the existence of community itself. He was also of the opinion that all large assemblies were essentially incapable of any business.

Thus Mill obviously rejected direct rule by the people, and it is also certain that his 'democratical form of government' was conceptually limited to a direct form of rule. This naturally excludes honorific application of "democratical" as used in these two statements, and any other usages of this term, as well as of "democracy", in this work are in high conformity with these two occurrences of "democratical". [20] There is no reason to believe that Mill used these terms here to signify a non-direct or representative form of government. How far this rule can be said to be general in Mill's terminology is a question which cannot be answered here, since the work is the only political one which has been available. The central theme of this essay may be fairly representative of his political terminology in general.

Mill's use of "democratical" and "democracy" naturally makes for a somewhat differentiated use of these terms among early Utilitarians. It is rather strange that Mill, who had been in constant and personal intercourse with Bentham for more than a dozen years before writing this essay, should use these terms in a way which Bentham had tried to eliminate. But Bentham was not absolutely consistent in his attempts to attribute to "democracy" a signification exclusively restricted to the field of governing by elected representatives.

3. Michelet

Let us turn from the terminology of the early Utilitarians to that of French radical republicanism. The historian and ideologist Jules Michelet is frequently called a "democrat".[21] It is nevertheless difficult to find occurrences of the terms "democracy", "democratic", and "democrat" in his writings, and it is difficult to discover the significations with which he intended to use these terms.

Le Peuple is probably his most important political work. In its dedication to Edgar Quinet appear the words: "Ce livre est plus qu'un livre; c'est moi-même."[22] Among the extremely few occurrences of "democracy" and "democratic" it can be seen that Michelet considered the existence and use of machinery in modern industry to be an aristocratic force on account of the financial centralization on which it was dependent. He added, however:

[Qu'elle] n'est pas moins, par le bon marché et la vulgarisation de ses produits, un très-puissant agent du progrès démocratique.[23]

The application of "democratic" in this statement does not convey much. Its use in connection with the term "progress" may be taken as proof of an honorific application, though this is far from certain. It looks as if he regarded the production of cheap commodities as an important factor in what he believed to be democratic progress. This implies that progress, inter alia, consisted in the fact that different articles, which had earlier been available to the rich only, could now be used by a wider section of the population. Michelet especially mentioned articles made of silk, flax, and cotton. "Democratic" may have been used to signify something of which a high degree of equality was one of the necessary properties. The term "vulgarisation" hardly has the dyslogistic connotation general in English, German, or Norwegian counterparts of this word.

Michelet later said of the social character of the church:

l'Église, démocratique par son principe d'élection, fut éminemment aristocratique par la difficulté de son enseignement et le très-petit nombre d'hommes qui y purent vraiment atteindre.[24]

Michelet therefore probably considered election to be a necessary property for the characterization of something as "democratic" and exclusiveness was contrary to characterization by that term.

Elsewhere in this work Michelet stated that he agreed with Aristotle when he declared society to have been made not by similar but by different men, and disagreed with Plato. He added, however, that initially men were different; but harmonized by love and mutual friendship, they became more and more similar. He concluded:

La démocratie, c'est l'amour dans la Cité, et l'initiation.[25]

This statement probably contains the most significant occurrence of "democracy" in his writings. "Democracy" here seems to connote not a kind of government, nor a kind of social or economic estate, but a kind of social attitude of mutual love and friendliness within a society, according to which citizenship involved solemn obligations. This use of "democracy" is without doubt an honorific application of the term. It occurs in one of the few places where it may be possible to see the way in which he intended to use the term. The first occurrence in this work conveys almost nothing. Contrasting the Latin culture with the English and German, Michelet stated:

> L'Allemagne et l'Angleterre, comme race, comme langue et comme instinct, sont étrangères à la grande tradition du monde, romano-chrétienne et démocratique. [26]

He did not describe this great tradition, however, nor did he explain why the Germans and the English were strangers to it. Presumably Michelet, patriot as he was, considered the French to be most familiar with this tradition, but he does not tell us much about what he meant by "democratic" in this connection.

In his Histoire de la Révolution Française there are also a very few rather unimportant occurrences of "democracy" and "democratic". "Democratic" is thus used to characterize the constitution of 1793. On one occasion he described it as "la constitution Jacobine, toute démocratique qu'elle est",[27] and elsewhere in relation to the establishment of the dictatorship:

> On essaya de la faire sortir de la constitution même, et de la plus démocratique qui fut jamais. [28]

Why the constitution should have been characterized thus is not clear.

Michelet was by no means an unreserved admirer of Robespierre, [29] but he admitted that Robespierre bore the ideal of democracy in his heart.

> Robespierre avait au cœur l'idéal de la démocratie; il voulait moins le pouvoir que l'autorité morale, au profit de l'égalité... Ce qu'il ambitionna réellement toute sa vie, ce fut d'être le dictateur des âmes et le roi des esprits par une triumphante formule qui résumerait la foi jacobine, et devant laquelle Girondins, Cordeliers, La France, le monde, tomberaient à genoux. [30]

This latter statement seems to claim that Robespierre preferred moral authority to power for the benefit of equality. Since the first statement may be taken to imply that such a preference for moral authority rather than power was a sufficient condition for a man to have the ideal of what he held to be democracy in his heart, it can firstly be inferred that this ideal was of an equalitarian kind, secondly, that people ought to be convinced instead of forced, and thirdly, that this ideal was not incompatible with the ambition of becoming a kind of spiritual dictator, which would make France as well as the world fall upon their knees. On the contrary, this kind of spiritual ambition seems to be proof that Robespierre was in possession of this ideal; this may be taken to reveal that public opinion in a democracy, according to Michelet, ought not to be pluralistic or diversified.

4. Quinet

Edgar Quinet was one of Michelet's most intimate friends; his ideological
ally as well as his colleague as a professor at the Collège de France. Just
as Michelet's main political work was dedicated to Quinet, one of Quinet's
most important historical and political works, Le Christianisme et la Révolution française, was dedicated to Michelet.

In a chapter headed "Idéal de la Démocratie", Quinet asserted:

L'avénement de la démocratie ne peut être qu'un nouveau progrès de
l'esprit, de la civilisation, de l'ordre universel. [31]

Of what this new spiritual progress was to consist is not mentioned, however, and at this stage he seems to have used "democracy" to signify some
kind of new spiritual principle which would be the mark of all civilized
countries.

Shortly afterwards, Quinet employed a very honorific application of
"democracy".

Je ne veux pas seulement que la démocratie ait son pain quotidien; avec
l'esprit de mon siècle, je veux encore qu'elle règne; voila pourquoi je
demande d'elle des vertues souveraines. [32]

"Democracy" was obviously used to denote something of which he approved,
and the term here more probably connotes a kind of government than in
the first quotation. Democracy was also something intimately connected
with what he held to be the spirit of the century, but it is still difficult to
draw any important conclusion.

Again Quinet declared that democracy had been marching in the skies
during the three days of July. Here he most certainly meant July 1830. He
also asserted that the spirit of the volunteers of 1792, the heroism of Latour
d'Auvergne, the constancy of Carnot, the Spartan Christianity of Madame
Roland, the enthusiasm concerning the oath taken in the Jeu de Paume and
the firm behaviour of the Old Guard; all these things were, according to
him,

... la couronne idéale qui doit flotter sur son front [33] [le front de la
démocratie] ... C'est le diadème que Dieu a preparé pour le sacre de
la démocratie moderne.

This declaration, or this revelation, is among the most eulogistic ever
made in favour of something designated as "democracy". The enumeration
of moral, political, and military glories of the revolutionary history of
France is probably not meant to be complete, but only indicates which properties he hoped would glorify the modern democracy which was to come. It
is seldom so difficult to see what the term was intended to mean. In the
last quotation, we may replace it by "a kind of government", or by "a new
way of human common life", and it is hard to decide which is the more probable. The latter interpretation, if compared with his earlier statements, is
perhaps more plausible. Quinet continued by saying that someone would
probably accuse him of exaggeration:

Que j'élève jusqu'au ciel l'idéal de la démocratie; cela est vrai; mais songez qu'il faut le placer haut, puisqu'il doit être vu, comme un phare, du Globe entier. [34]

This statement can be taken as a continued confirmation of Quinet's extremely positive evaluation of what he designated as "democracy", but it conveys little concerning the meaning he attributed to the term. With regard to his earlier assertion, it is of some importance to note that he not only included the faith of the volunteers of 1792, but also the firm behaviour of Napoleon's Old Guard among the jewels of the crown which God had prepared for the sanctification of modern democracy. This points to an association between what he held to be modern democracy and military glory, even that of Napoleon. From a broader point of view such an association was somewhat typical of the nationalistic and militaristic trends in contemporary radical thought in France. According to these trends the aristocracy had betrayed la patrie by fighting against France during the revolutionary years, the Church was international and its organization dominated by the Holy See, and the higher middle classes tended to be anglophile; it was only the people at large who were the legitimate heirs to the national and military honours of France. Similar ideas occur in several places in the writings of both Michelet and Quinet. Both of them were very proud of French military victories and French military traditions of different kinds, [35] and Quinet even associated the military victories of Napoleon with what he termed "democracy".

In an earlier chapter on Napoleon, Quinet stated that Napoleon did not recognize any difference between the middle class and the people, between rich and poor:

Appliquant à la société son principe de tactique, il fit de tous les enfants de la France une seule masse, la grande Nation, la grande armée, qui respirait, il est vrai, sous la mitraille, mais qui n'avait qu'un foyer, un drapeau, une âme.

He added:

En dépit de tous les déguisement, le principe de la démocratie éclatait, étincelait à la veille des batailles. [36]

The abolition of the social distinctions of l'ancien régime in the army as well as in society, and the introduction of the carrière ouverte aux talents were considered by Quinet to be essential for the principle of democracy. It is also very probable that he did not regard civil rights, the freedom of the press, and the right to dissent in political matters to be necessary properties of his principle. On the contrary, he may even have believed that unity of opinion was essential to the principle of democracy. His very positive reference to Napoleon as the creator of the great nation with one home, one banner, and one soul makes such a conclusion probable. Here, perhaps, is some degree of similarity between the conception of democracy held by Quinet and Michelet and that of Robespierre and Saint-Just.

A strong association between Napoleon and what Quinet held to be democracy is also evident in his references to Napoleon's famous proclamations.

C'est dans ces paroles de feu qu'est toute l'âme de l'Empire; et il faut avouer qu'on ne vit jamais rien de semblable, ni la démocratie plus ouvertement triomphante. [37]

Bonaparte represented the French democracy of the future, but in foreign eyes the Emperor had also been the precursor of what Quinet termed "universal democracy".

> Si le générale d'Italie se fût arrêté a Marengo, il eût représenté dans l'avenir la démocratie française; mais aux yeux des étrangers, celui qui est allé au Cairo, à Vienne, à Madrid, à Berlin, à Varsovie, à Moscou, est le précurseur de la démocratie universelle. [38]

Quinet's terminology does not indicate that he held imperial militarism to be a necessary property of the signification of "democracy"; central aspects of this militarism are probably mentioned only as examples of what he labelled with this term. But he doubtless considered important parts of this imperial militarism to be quite compatible with what he held to be democracy. Indeed, this extreme reverence for Napoleon and this association between what was called "democracy" and imperial policy may well have been among the factors which made the Napoleonic legend a living one as late as 1845, thus indirectly assisting Napoleon III later in his political strategy. Quinet himself was forced to live in exile after 1852, however.

5. Lamartine

Lamartine, like Michelet and Quinet, used "democracy" in an honorific way, in spite of the difference between their radical republicanism and his own Christian pacifistic ideology. In his Histoire des Girondins, Lamartine asserted that the French Revolution had presented one of the greatest of all gifts to the world, which was:

> ... l'avènement d'une idée nouvelle dans le genre humain, l'idée démocratique, et plus tard le gouvernement démocratique. ... Cette idée etait un ecoulement du christianisme. [39]

Christianity had found men enslaved and degraded everywhere on the earth and had grown up like a sort of vengeance on the ruins of the Roman empire; but in the form of resignation, Christianity had nevertheless proclaimed the three words "liberty", "equality", "fraternity", and these were repeated nearly two thousand years later by French philosophy. Christianity had hidden this dogma for some time beneath its faith; feeling too weak to attack civil laws, it had confined itself to the fields of morality. The day would come, however, when the Christian doctrine would escape from the temple, and the world would be renewed.

On this point it is somewhat doubtful whether Lamartine believed the democratic idea to be Christian, or whether he intended to point out a strong degree of similarity between Christianity and democratic ideas. "Écoulement du Christianisme" may be interpreted in favour of both versions, but the former can possibly be regarded as the more probable. It is evident in any case that he considered certain central properties to be common to Christianity and the democratic idea, and from a broader point of view, he may be said to have introduced the kind of terminology predominant in the much later works of Henri Bergson and Jacques Maritain. [40]

A little later, Lamartine declared the French Revolution to have been understood by almost nobody. This included the King as well as the Duke of Orléans, Mirabeau, Lafayette, the Jacobins, and even the people. The only

possible exceptions were Robespierre and those whom he called "les démocrates purs. "[41] He did not mention the persons he had in mind when using
this expression. He was probably, but not certainly, referring to the Giron-
dists, since the Jacobins were among those who did not understand the
Revolution. It is most unlikely that Lamartine regarded Robespierre as a
pure democrat.

Among the other scattered occurrences of "democracy" and related
terms in this somewhat poetical work of history the following occurs in the
second volume:

> La république démocratique est le seul gouvernement selon la raison...
> L'Evangile est démocratique, le christianisme est républicaine, [42]

which reminds us of our first quotation above.

Later in this work, Lamartine stated that the Girondins feared that the
republic which had been established by the French revolution would fall into
the hands of a furious and insane demagogy. He went on to say:

> Hommes imbus des idées républicaines de l'antiquité, où la liberté des
> citoyens supposait l'esclavage des masses et où les républiques n'étaient
> que le nombreuses aristocraties, ils comprenaient mal le génie Chrétien
> des républiques démocratiques de l'avenir.[43]

This statement indicates that Lamartine used one broader concept 'republic'
of which 'aristocratic republic' and 'democratic republic' were sub-concepts
or species. The signification of "republic" was therefore wider than that of
"democratic republic" and it also looks as if the genius of Christianity was
held to be a necessary characteristic of what he described by the latter expression.

I have been unable to study further occurrences of "democracy" in the
political language of Lamartine, except in a later edition of his political
speeches, from which quotations follow.

In the Chamber of Deputies in 1839, Lamartine asserted that the government was born of the people, or the masses, and it ought to govern in accordance with the interests of the greatest number. Lamartine further held
that the political reform of 1789 [45] was accomplished having regard to the
question of political power. The reform within society itself, however, the
reform of the organization, morals, civil rights, interests, and work within
the most numerous class, ought to have been accomplished in 1830. Lamartine considered it to be the mission of a new government in the nineteenth
century to accomplish this reform in a non-revolutionary manner.

> L'accomplir non pas révolutionnairement, mais législativement, par
> l'application graduelle, raisonné, toute religieuse, toute politique, des
> grands principes de démocratie et de fraternité descendus du christian-
> isme dans les mœurs. Qui, voila, selon moi, au dedans la mission
> d'un gouvernement neuf au XIXe siècle.[46]

Here is an application of "democracy" rather similar to that which we
found in his later work, Histoire des Girondins. Here, too, the principles
of what he held to be democracy were descended from Christianity. Although
Christianity is here only referred to with regard to morals, this is probably
a factor which also makes little or no difference. Lamartine also used the
term in an honorific way here, and we can even say that it occupies a prominent place in one of his main political declarations. It is somewhat difficult,
however, to see what he intended to convey by "principles of democracy".

Presumably their realization mainly consisted in the work for the political and economic interests of the working class. It was essential, claimed Lamartine, that this work should be carried on in a peaceful, or non-revolutionary way, but we cannot see, at least not in accordance with this saying, that he believed that a non-revolutionary character was a necessary condition of the principles of democracy.

The honorific use of "democracy" was typical of Lamartine's terminology during and after the February Revolution. The term did not occur in his famous speech in favour of keeping the Tricolore instead of replacing it with the Red Flag. In June, Lamartine opposed those who wanted a revolutionary war in favour of the other European peoples, asserting that republican France would be able to exercise a much greater influence through what he called, "la puissance des principes d'amitié démocratique".[47] In the same speech he also referred to

... les hommes qui ont été comme nous les premiers à proclamer la République populaire, morale et pacifique au nom du peuple, la République démocratique dans le grand et bon sens du mot. [48]

It is most probable that "popular, moral and peaceable republic in the name of the people" was used synonymously with "democratic republic in the great and good sense of the word". Lamartine probably intended to contrast this alleged great and good meaning of "democratic republic" with other usages of that expression, according to which a moral and especially a peaceable character was not a necessary condition of designating a form of rule by that expression. According to this statement, it cannot be assumed that any democratic republic was necessarily to be of a peaceable kind, but a peaceable character was nevertheless most certainly needed in order that a form of rule might be labelled "democratic republic in the great and good sense of the word".

With regard to the political character of the February Revolution, Lamartine asserted:

Elle a proclamé le plus grand fait des temps modernes; elle a changé en un seul jour une oligarchie en démocratie complète. [49]

This indicates rather clearly that Lamartine considered contemporary France to be subsumable under what he designated as "complete democracy". We may assume that the introduction of male and universal suffrage was a sufficient as well as a necessary condition for this label.

In Lamartine's opinion -- and here he agrees with Bentham -- the existence of a second chamber, or a federal chamber,[50] was alien to what he called "democracy". A federal chamber stood for feudal, aristocratic, and even anarchical interests and a lack of national unity. Against those who referred to the American constitution, Lamartine argued:

Vous savez comme moi, ou vous le saurez en y réfléchissant un instant, que le Sénat en Amérique ne représente pas telle ou telle partie, telle ou telle catégorie de cette grande démocratie unitaire.

He emphasized that the Senate represented federal interests exclusively and this was also the only reason of its existence. He concluded:

Ce n'est pas la démocratie, c'est la fédération qu'il [le Sénat] représente; ce n'est pas la perfection de l'unité démocratique, c'est le défaut d'unité nationale, c'est une espèce d'anarchie prolongée encore après une formation si récente. [51]

Lamartine did here not refuse America, or rather the United States, the label "great and unitarian democracy", and thus the existence of a federal chamber was not incompatible with what he called "democracy", although he certainly would not have characterized a federal assembly and the federal principles as "democratic". It is also fairly certain that he would have considered America to have been more democratic if the Congress had consisted of the House of Representatives only. Lamartine probably believed that political and national unity were very important factors for a democracy; and here he exemplifies a central trend in French political radicalism.

Although this discussion of the terminology in Lamartine's political writing is incomplete, his usage of the term "democracy" here may be regarded as characteristic of his application of the term in other works. In L'Idée de l'Etat, by Henri Michel, there are a few occurrences of "democracy" from other of Lamartine's works. Keeping these in mind as well, it can be stated with some confidence that Lamartine always used "democracy" in an honorific way, and that the strong association between Christianity and the signification of "democracy" is a consistent as well as a predominant characteristic of his political terminology. [52]

6. Mazzini

One would reasonably expect a very honorific as well as a very central use of "democracy" by Guiseppe Mazzini, the tireless prophet of Italian unity and independence, a passionate adherent of a republican form of rule. This cannot be found in his terminology, however, although occurrences of an honorific kind do exist. The reason was probably that he associated what he held to be democracy with individualistic and materialistic trends in the philosophy of the eighteenth century, which contrasted strongly with his own romantic conception of a national and Christian collectivism. According to Mazzini, the ideology of Young Italy ought to be based upon religious worship with the slogan "God and the people" as its holy motto. Scepticism was to be replaced by a new faith, and individualism and egotism by a new kind of social solidarity.

This ideological tendency is fairly evident in his essay "Faith and Future" of 1835 in which he asserted that several Italian republicans were still influenced by a creed which did not go beyond the limits laid down nearly half a century earlier in the French Declaration of Rights. They mistrusted all kinds of authority and were only in favour of individual rights.

Their republic is the turbulent, intolerant democracy of Athens: their war-cry is a cry of vengeance: their symbol, Spartacus. [53]

This occurrence of "democracy" does not have much significance for this research. In the notes appended to this quotation, however, there is a very important statement containing several meta-occurrences of "democracy".

The word democracy, although when endowed with historical precision it may express vigorously enough the ideal of a world, at least of the ancient world, is, like all the political phrases of antiquity, unequal to conception of the future Age which we republicans are called to initiate. The expression social government would be preferable as indicating the conception of association, which is the life of the Age. The word democracy was inspired by an idea of rebellion, sacred indeed, but still rebellion. Now, every such conception is evidently imperfect and inferior to the idea of Unity which will be the doctrine of the future. There is a note of strife in the word democracy; it is the cry of Spartacus, the expression of a people in its first attempt to rise.[54]

This points to a very close relationship between violent revolution and the term "democracy". In different writers we have found more or less strong associations between revolution and what has been designated as "democracy" (for example, statements such as: democracy is something which well might be achieved by revolutionary means); here we have one of the rare examples of a direct mention of "democracy" where a revolutionary upheaval is an essential part of the signification of the term. On this point there is great terminological similarity between this statement of Mazzini's and the general use of "democracy" by Guizot. Mazzini greatly preferred the expression "social government" to "democracy" since the former was much more fitted to express the kind of association and national unity which was an essential part of his political ideals.

Mazzini explained what he primarily intended to mean by the expression "social government". The terms "social government" and "social institutions" represent a people organizing itself after victory. He may have considered this constructive character of social government as highly preferable to the destructive character of what he held to be democracy. He concluded by saying, "The extinction of aristocracy will efface the name democracy."

Mazzini's somewhat negative attitude towards what was to be termed "democracy" and even towards the word "democracy" had no connection with any negative attitude towards universal suffrage. On the contrary, Mazzini said:

Our principle of the People, which is simply the application of the doctrine of Humanity to every nation, is the direct and sufficient cause of the principle of universal suffrage, which is the manifestation of the people, and of the exclusion of all authority that is not delegated by the people, or is exercised by one caste or individual. [55]

Mazzini also seems to have rejected using "democracy" to signify the system of universal suffrage. It was probably the replacement of "democracy" with "social government" that Mazzini had in mind when he said:

We place in the very stamp of the age, a new title to universal suffrage.[56]

These statements cannot be regarded as furnishing general proof of a clearly negative attitude towards popular uprisings by this revolutionary leader. This essay was written soon after the disasters of the revolutionaries in Northern Italy in 1832-33, and is primarily taken up with the thought that rebellions, as such, were not sufficient to serve as a kind of fundament in a revolutionary Italian ideology. "We fell down as a political party: we must rise again as a religious party." [59] This does not imply that he rejected rebellions and insurrections, but that something more constructive was needed for the building of a new society than the destruction of the old one. It was on this point that what he designated as "democracy" far from satisfied his claim for a new brotherhood, Christian unity, and national as well as human solidarity.

Several years later, in 1852, there occur an ideology as well as a termi-

nology somewhat similar to the one under discussion. Speaking of France
and the French Revolution, Mazzini said that that country had done much for
the political emancipation of mankind. He added, however, that France had
not given humanity the word of the future.

> Here the great formula, which the imitative mind of democracy has
> rendered European -- liberty, equality, fraternity -- is only a historical
> formula, indicating the stages of progress already attained by the human
> mind. [58]

"Democracy" has been used here as a label of a political grouping, or party,
whose ideology Mazzini held to be of an old-fashioned and even of an imita-
tive kind: this implies that he would not have used "democracy" at that time
as denomination of himself and his adherents. He concluded by saying that
the slogan of the Italian revolution,"God and the People", was much more
advanced and more complete than that of the French republicans.

Compared with the first quotation, the attitude towards what Mazzini
termed "democracy" is here more negative. On the other hand, there is no
reason to believe that a violent revolution was necessarily included in the
signification of this term. This probably implies some degree of terminological change, and reveals that Mazzini was less consistent than Guizot in
including a revolutionary upheaval in the signification of "democracy".

An attitude towards what he characterized as "democratic", which is
fairly different from the one we have noted in relation to "democracy",
appears in 1860. In an appeal to the Italian working class, Mazzini related
that the republican instincts of his mother had taught him to seek the man
among his fellows, not the merely rich and powerful individual. Later on,
he learned that the true life of Italy was the life of the people, and he went
on saying that the slow work of centuries, amid the shocks of foreign conquests, had tended

> ...to prepare the great democratic National Unity. And then, thirty
> years ago, I gave myself to you. [59]

Here "democratic" is evidently used in an honorific way, and it even looks
as if the word connotes something very similar to what he had designated in
1835 as "social government". This indicates a fairly different kind of terminology.

An attitude similar to this is to be found in 1870. Commenting on an
ecclesiastical meeting, Mazzini said:

> Three hundred and twenty bishops who met at Nice did lawfully represent
> the multitude of believers: they were the issue of a democratic inspira-
> tion, which is the soul of every rising faith: they were the elect of the
> clergy and the people. [60]

Election here seems to be a sufficient, perhaps also a necessary, condition
for something to be characterized by "democratic". It is very important
that Mazzini should have indicated what he held to be democratic inspiration
as being the soul of every rising faith; this evidently implies an honorific
kind of application. When compared with the first quotation, it does not
seem that any kind of violent rebellion is implicit in the signification of
"democratic". On the contrary, it may even be that "democratic" was used
with a connotation which included properties like Christian unity and national
and human solidarity, thus pointing out a terminology very similar to the one

he used ten years earlier, but very different from his earlier use of "democracy".

A more differentiated attitude towards what he termed "democracy" occurs the following year, however, concerning the ideological influence of materialism:

It is these and other errors brought to our Democracy from foreign schools of thought that made the Italian intellect stray from the right path. [61]

Here what he designated as "democracy" was possibly something with which he partly identified himself; the formulation "our Democracy" may indicate an interpretation in that direction. But we also see that the denotata of "Democracy" might be infected with materialism -- one of the worst ideological trends, according to Mazzini.

A possible association between materialism and what he designated as "democracy" is discernible in his last writings, although here he primarily asserted that democracy was something which might be purified. Mazzini argued against the political theories of Renan that one should not try to revive the worship of the past, since,

... the ascending movement of democracy is as evident to those who dread it as to those who hail it with applause.

He admitted that "the field of democracy is furrowed by error", but he also asked:

Why not unite with other thinkers to form an apostolate which shall purify it from its errors, and render it all that it ought to be and is capable of becoming? [62]

This clearly implies that Mazzini regarded himself as one of those who tried to purify what he called "democracy", but this political or social phenomenon would probably still be termed "democracy" when purified and made all that it ought to be. This indicates a somewhat honorific application, at least in the case of an expression like "democracy per se", although Mazzini was not in favour of what he would have termed "actual democracy". He continued:

All the actual errors of democracy spring from one common source, from one primary error of direction given to the democratic idea; from the imperfect view taken of human life and of the world. [63]

Here Mazzini was most probably referring to materialism, which does not seem necessarily to be a property of what he held as democracy, even if the materialism was without doubt compatible with that social and political system. This is probably one of the factors that made Mazzini in his older days regard what he called "democracy" more favourably than he had done thirty-five years earlier.

On the whole, there is a marked tendency towards the elimination of violent revolution as implicit in his signification of this term and, at the same time, a new tendency towards the belief that Christian solidarity and human and national unity were compatible with, or that they even could be included in, this signification. This naturally tends towards some degree of honorific application, although there are scarcely any examples of the use of "democracy" as a key political term in Mazzini's language.

CHAPTER VIII

EARLIER SOCIALISM

Generally, "democracy" occupies a key position in different trends in socialist thought. We have seen earlier a very honorific use by a revolutionary
socialist in the case of Babeuf. Later this word was to play a prominent
role in Marx's as well as in Proudhon's terminology. It will also be found
in the more important statements by persons as different as Kautsky, Bernstein, Sorel, and Cole, and it will also headline declarations from divergent
groups during the Russian Revolution. Those eager to find the meaning, in
the sense of sole meaning such as has been attributed to "democracy" by
socialist thinkers, will seek in vain. Here, probably to a larger degree than
elsewhere, there is a tendency to attribute very different significations to
"democracy". In certain cases it meant violent revolution, in other cases
rule by the proletariat, while there also are occurrences where the same
word signifies such contrary things as rule by the capitalists, for example,
or something incompatible with any kind of revolution. On this point there
are not only differences between several socialist thinkers, but also in certain cases there are important differences within the terminology of one
socialist, for example, Proudhon or Marx.

Such a diversity of use was not to characterize the writings of earlier
socialists, however. With regard to Saint-Simon, I have not even found
sufficient material to work out any analysis, and very little has been discovered concerning Fourier and Owen. Some degree of frequency can be
seen in Cabet's writings and especially in the later writings of Considérant,
while a high degree of frequency is not to be found before we come upon
Proudhon's use of the word.

1. Fourier and Considérant

"Democracy" and related terms occur extremely rarely in Fourier's political and economic writings. The occurrences I have found are rather unimportant. Once, describing liberalism, Fourier declared:

> ... que le libéralisme ne présente que le sens d'intrigue démocratique,
> tendance à envahir les fonctions administratives, sous l'apparence d'un
> beau zèle pour le peuple. [1]

This does not convey much for our research, however. Fourier's negative
attitude towards what he called "liberalism" is quite evident, but it is impossible to see from the quotation, or from the context, in what way he intended
to use "democratic". But "democratic" could not have been used here honorifically, since Fourier used "democratic" to characterize a kind of intrigue,
and since this intrigue was obviously something of which he disapproved.

A somewhat similar use of "democratic" is in evidence in his discussion of the ideological effect of the principles of associations:

> Ces principes une fois établis, l'opinion serait intervenue pour rappeler à l'ordre le monde sophistique, lui représenter qu'on est suffisamment repu des vaines subtilités de la métaphysique, des controverses mercantiles et démocratiques. [2]

Here, the terms "mercantile" and "democratic" are used to characterize those controversies which, according to Fourier, were vain subtleties of metaphysics. Almost the same kind of comments which were made on the previous quotation can be applied to this one, so that here too he could not have used "democratic" in an honorific way.

A little more exact material exists in the earlier writings of Considérant, Fourier's most important pupil. In his most important work, Destinée sociale (1834), Considérant stated that human civilization consisted of three different periods: its infancy, which was feudalism; its adolescence, which was marked by the rise of the third estate; and finally its decline, which was marked by anarchical commerce and economic illusions. According to Considérant:

> Il est facile de voir que l'état actuel de la France est une Civilisation de troisième phase, fortement eramponée encore aux illusions et disputes démocratiques de deuxième phase, ce qui complique la position et augmente le danger de la crise. [3]

"Democratic" is used here to characterize those illusions and disputes which were still typical of French civilization. Indirectly we can see that those illusions and disputes must in some way be connected with the rise of the third estate, since they belong to the second period. Therefore, what Considérant held to be democratic must in some way be connected with this social growth. His usage of "democratic" to characterize something which increased the danger of the crisis and especially the relationship between "democratic" and "illusion" indicate that "democratic" here, as with the occurrences in Fourier's writings, was not used in an honorific way.

A different kind of application of "democratic" is found, however, in Considérant's discussion of the different kinds of human intercourse in the ideal society of the future, a kind of society he generally labelled with the term "Harmony". In this Harmony,

> ... vous faites sur les autres la justice que les autres font sur vous. C'est la justice mutuelle, démocratique, sociétaire. Les faux jugements sont inconnus. [4]

"Democratic", together with two other terms, is used here to designate a kind of justice of which Considérant absolutely approved. This indicates an honorific use of the term. It is difficult, however, to see what signification he attached to "democratic" here; characterized by mutual love and friendship is a probable interpretation. But it is difficult, if not impossible, to say anything with certainty, as it is somewhat doubtful whether Considérant would have used "democratic" to characterize that kind of justice if the other two terms had been dropped.

Somewhat more factual knowledge concerning his use of the terms "democracy" and "democratic" is available in his work De la politique générale et du rôle de la France en Europe,

He said of liberal doctrines:

Les doctrines de L'École libérale, -- étaient plus funestes à la Société et plus fausses que celles de la Démocratie proprement dite. [5]

As with Fourier, so Considérant frequently displayed an ideological dislike of liberal doctrines, especially of the doctrine of _Laissez faire_. This statement also shows his dislike of what he designated "democracy, properly called", since to state that something was more fatal to society and more false than another factor can probably be taken to imply that the latter factor is also, to a lesser degree, false and fatal to society.

He goes on to give his arguments in favour of this view:

La Démocratie n'est pas anti-gouvernementale en principe, au contraire; et c'est, au fond, parce qu'elle crôit le Suffrage universel capable de constituer le Pouvoir le plus légitime, le plus solide, le plus fort, qu'elle veut le Suffrage universel. ... La logique démocratique aboutit directement à l'idée d'un Gouvernement très fort, très respectable. C'est la, sans doute, une utopie politique dangereuse, parce qu'elle est irréalisable dans les conditions sociales existantes; mais ce n'est peut-être pas aussi dangereuse en soi, et ce n'est à coup sur pas aussi faux en principe que le niais Laissez faire. [6]

What he designated as "democracy" is here most probably regarded as a political creed, or an ideology in favour of a strong government founded upon universal suffrage. Considérant obviously preferred this kind of strong government to the principles of _laissez faire_. Here too, he implied that what he held to be democratic logic was dangerous and false, and that there was a dangerous utopian element in it. The only argument given in support of this latter point of view was that this democratic logic was unrealizable under present social conditions. This may be taken to indicate that what he designated as "democracy" and "democratic logic" were not false and dangerous _per_ se, but represented something false and dangerous when presented in a society where social conditions made them unrealizable. This hypothesis could modify his generally derogatory usage of these terms.

He does not explain why democratic logic should be unrealizable under existing social conditions. Perhaps he had somewhat similar arguments in mind as in _Destinée sociale_ when he asserted that universal suffrage would be no more legitimate than the existing electoral monopoly, since nineteen out of twenty persons, in contemporary society

... serait incapables de donner le moindre mandat en connaissance de cause; elles ne comprendraient seulement pas la valeur de leur droit. [7]

The infrequency of these terms in Fourier and in earlier writings of Considérant may be attributed to these authors' general indifference towards governmental systems. Their socialist ideology with its extremely detailed planning of the ideal future life in the _phalanstère_ was not associated with any revolutionary, or even republican, principles. Considérant's main work _Destinée sociale_ was thus dedicated to Louis-Philippe,

... étant, à titre de chef du Gouvernement et de premier propriétaire de France, le plus intéressé à l'ordre, à la prospérité publique et particulière, au bonheur des individus et des nations. [8]

To explain the infrequency of "democracy" by referring to the absence of revolutionary or the presence of somewhat conservative or paternalistic trends in political outlook would, however, be to oversimplify matters dealing with Considérant's terminology. In sharp contrast to his earlier writings, a fairly high degree of frequency of "democracy" exists in <u>Principes du Socialisme, Manifeste de la Démocratie au XIX siècle</u> (1843). In this manifesto Considérant drew attention <u>inter alia</u> to his periodical's recent change of name. Previously it had appeared as <u>La Phalange</u>, but it was to continue as <u>La Démocratie pacifique.</u> Considérant argued that the name "Phalange" appealed only to narrow sections of the population, while "Democracy" was an extremely popular slogan. On this point he even said:

> Le mot de <u>Démocratie</u> est le mot à-la-fois le plus profond, le plus général et le plus puissant qui reste aujourd'hui dans le courant de l'actualité, le seul qui ait un avenir de forte vie dans la publicité active. [9]

This is a distinct indication of a most extensive and honorific application of "democracy" in the vernacular, and it reminds one of Guizot's formulation some years later, when he spoke of the empire of the word "democracy". [10] While Guizot definitely rejected what he labelled with this term, however, Considérant desired it as a slogan for his own group. He admitted that it represented a great difficulty that "democracy" was used in different ways by different political sections, and he also referred to the great danger which this most powerful word might represent. Concerning this last point, Considérant held:

> Les parties révolutionnaires font aujourd'hui du mot de <u>Démocratie</u> un drapeau de révolution et de guerre, une arme redoutable, les uns contre l'ordre politique et le gouvernement, les autres contre la propriété et la base de l'ordre sociale. [11]

He went on to say that this weapon, this banner, must be snatched out of their hands, and instead of a banner of war, "democracy" must be made into a banner of peace, organization, and work. How "democracy" was to be stripped of this revolutionary status is not directly explained, but it would seem that an extensive and honorific application of this term by non-revolutionary groups, such as Considérant and his adherents, was regarded as an adequate course of action.

Concerning the signification which Considérant wished to attribute to "democracy" here, the clearest evidence occurs a few pages earlier when he initially spoke very appreciatively about the social theory in favour of peaceful and mutual co-operation between work, capital, and talent. He continued:

> D'après le sens attaché au mot Démocratie par cette opinion nouvelle, ce mot ne signifie point "Gouvernement de la Société par les classes inferieures"; il signifie "Gouvernement et organisation de la société <u>dans l'intérêt de tous,</u> par l'intervention <u>hierarchique</u> dans chaque fonction d'un nombre des citoyens croissant avec les degrés du dévelopement sociale. " [12]

Considérant further asserted that the people differed from a single class, and that government was not the blind, disorganized action of incompetent persons, but on the contrary, intelligent, united action of the competent.

In these key statements we primarily find a definition of the signification of "democracy" which suits Considérant's hierarchical and paternalistic views extremely well. Government <u>not</u> by the people at large, or by the lower classes, but <u>by</u> the competent few <u>for</u> the welfare of all is a permanent trend in his political thinking, and with this definition, "democracy" can with very good reason even be regarded as the key term in his vocabulary. "Democracy" is used frequently in this manifesto, and always honorifically and with a signification in high conformity with the definition quoted above. This is an arresting terminological change compared with his earlier use of this term. Considérant thereby abandoned a somewhat derogatory, or at least neutral, application for a clearly honorific one without changing his political outlook.

I have come across similar phenomena in political language several times, when the signification of a popular term has been changed with the intention of adopting it as a key term in a writer's vocabulary. But seldom, if ever, has the need for a new term, followed by explicit choice of the most popular one, and the definition of its signification in a special and a very personal way been undertaken so openly. Considérant does not admit having used "democracy" earlier with a different signification; this would have been unique in a political manifesto. We must add that in a very few instances Considérant used expressions such as "le vraie démocratie" to designate his own ideals and "la fausse démocratie" in relation to the revolutionary spirit. This indicates a claim of monopoly of this word and also a charge of misuse against those who used "democracy" in a way different from him. Although such an interpretation might be fairly reasonable in certain cases, such a trend cannot be said to be generally correct. On the whole, revolutionaries are not charged with misusing this term, and there are very few, if any, authoritarian claims upon the word "democracy". On the contrary, his formulation "D'après le sens attaché au mot Démocratie par cette opinion nouvelle, ce mot signifie ... " marks a kind of modesty which is rare in political argumentation.

Where Considérant's hierarchical views are concerned, it should be mentioned that he did not consider government by the few to be an eternal political principle. When larger sections of the population acquired the necessary skill and education, these groups would also acquire political influence, but not before. His main argument on this point is in the form of an analogy: no one would deny orphans with a fortune their right to their money, but no one would allow the children to spend their money as they wanted before their reaching a certain age. [13] This role of the gifted and educated few as being the temporary, or perhaps a long-lasting, but never permanent guardians of the people is also clearly implicit in his definition of the signification of "democracy".

2. Owen

Similar to Fourier, Robert Owen's use of "democracy" and related terms is also very infrequent. I have only been able to find one occurrence of "democrat" and no related terms in his writings. In this single occurrence, "democrat" is used in a derogatory way. In The New Existence of Man upon Earth Owen asserted that the new existence of man must be founded upon universal justice and equality. On the question of how the population of the world was to be converted to this great and glorious change, he asked

Who shall convince the Despot, Aristocrat, and Democrat, of their errors, and thus terminate tyranny and slavery, physical and mental? [14]

The signification he attributed to the term, and the kind of persons the word "Democrat" was used to denote, is not made clear. The derogatory character of the application is evident, since it was used together with the words "Despot" and "Aristocrat" to label political persons who ought to be

convinced of their errors, and whose common errors most probably had
resulted in tyranny and slavery.

This statement displays a dislike of politicians from various camps.
Warnings occur in several other places in his writings against the tendency
to use political measures to advance social justice. For Owen, the absolute acknowledgement of the new moral principle of union and co-operation
was a <u>conditio sine qua non</u> for the establishing of a new social order. Any
political attempt made without adopting this principle would therefore be
useless. In proof of this assertion he generally referred to

> ... the vain attempt of the more advanced population of the American
> United States to be governed by an elective republic. [15]

The predominance of moral over the political factors is common to the
ideologies of Owen, Fourier, and Considérant. On this point there is a
considerable difference between their political points of view and those of
Babeuf and Buonarroti, since the latter went far towards acceptance of the
Jacobin conception of politics to realize their kind of socialism. Here we
probably have the main reason for the rare and generally derogatory use of
"democracy" by Owen and Fourier and in the earlier writings of Considérant,
on the one hand, and the highly honorific and quite frequent use of the term
by Babeuf and Buonarroti, on the other. The latter even identified to a high
degree what they designated as "democracy" with their communistic aims.

3. Cabet

In <u>Le catalysme sociale</u>, of 1845, Étienne Cabet declared:

> Nous, Communistes, nous avons toujours invoqué et nous invoquerons
> toujours l'union de tous les Démocrates.

Cabet admitted that there were a few democrats who were in opposition to
communism, but such opposition was merely founded upon political prejudice.
He continued:

> Nous avons toujours dit qu'à leur tour les vrais Démocrates étaient
> Communistes sans le savoir. [16]

This statement implies that any person who was to qualify for the label "true
democrat" bestowed by Cabet and his political adherents must necessarily be
at least an unconscious adherent to their communistic principles. On the
other hand, it does not seem to be a necessary condition to denote oneself a
"communist" in order to be regarded as a true democrat. Cabet concluded:

> Nous le répétons, tous les Démocrates sont Communistes; et s'ils
> faisaient la folie de condamner les Communistes, ce serait de leur part
> un suicide. [17]

In isolation this last statement may be taken to indicate a relation of synonymity between "democrats" and "communists". With the previous quotation
in mind, it is scarcely probable that Cabet would have accepted that such a
kind of synonymity existed. On the other hand, it is fairly certain that he
was of the opinion that such a relation ought to have existed between"democrats" and "communists".

A very intimate relationship, if not a relationship of identity, between what he held to be democracy and communism occurs in another work written in the same year:

> Pour nous, le Communisme n'était autre chose que la réalisation de la Démocratie. [18]

He then pointed out that one section of the middle class was popular and communistic, while another was opposed to communism. Concerning the latter he declared:

> Si la Bourgeoisie veut toujours tenir le Peuple dans l'esclavage et la misère, le titre de Démocratie qu'elle affecte de prendre n'est qu'un mensonge, et elle ne vaut pas mieux que l'Aristocratie, même moins. [19]

Here is one of the few occasions when someone is charged with misusing the term "democracy" during this period, and it is rather significant that this charge of misuse, similar to that made by Robespierre and Bentham, is delivered by one who himself used the term in a very honorific way.

In addition it should be mentioned that in pointing out what he held as the equalitarian and even communistic character of Christianity, Cabet asserted:

> C'est Jesus, c'est un Dieu qui prescrit ainsi la DÉMOCRATIE parmi tous les Chrétiens et dans l'Humanité tout entière !! [20]

I must further draw attention to Cabet's use of two different concepts 'democracy' in his main work, Voyage en Icarie. The designation of the one concept occupies a fairly important place in contemporary political language. In describing the various political groupings during the French Revolution, Cabet said:

> La Convention elle-même se divise en trois partis, la Démocratie populaire (ou les Montagnards), qui veut le progrès et l'égalité réelle; la Démocratie bourgeoise (ou les Girondins), qui veut la résistance et une demi-Égalité, ... et l'Aristocratie. [21]

As far as we know, this application of "démocratie populaire" is the first time this expression was used. Today, with its counterparts such as "People's Democracy", "Volksdemokratie", "Narodnaya Demokratiya", it has a very extensive application, especially in the Soviet Union and Eastern Europe. The difference between what Cabet considered to be people's democracy and bourgeois democracy was that between real equality and semi-equality. It was exclusively what he called "people's democracy" that accorded with his communist principles. This formulation may thus be said to mark some degree of moderation when compared with his earlier statements on the extremely intimate relationship, almost amounting to identity, between what he called "communism" and what he labelled as unqualified "democracy".

4. Proudhon

a. Before and during the February Revolution

Apart from some degree of frequency in Cabet's language and in Considérant's later terminology the ideologists so far discussed in this chapter
very infrequently apply "democracy". The situation is quite otherwise in
the extensive writings of Proudhon, who, like Tocqueville, used this term
very freely. Again like Tocqueville, Proudhon used "democracy" with very
different significations, and attributed properties which he held to be among
the most important ones to mutually different significations of the term. But
this frequency of usage is not typical of his terminology prior to 1848 when
"democracy" and "democrats" were evidently used as designations of phenomena to which Proudhon attached small importance.

Chronologically, the first application probably occurs in Qu'est-ce que
la Propriété, of 1840, where Proudhon let the reader ask which form of
government he preferred. After having answered in the negative to questions whether he was a republican, constitutionalist, or aristocrat, his only
answer was "non" to the question, "eh, bien! vous êtes démocrate?" [22]
The reason for his negative answer, and what he understood by the term
"democrat", is not clear, however. His only affirmative answer was that
he was an anarchist, and we can therefore conclude that "democrat", as
understood by him, was used to designate someone different from what he
held to be an anarchist, even if that conclusion does not convey much.

We find more occurrences in a somewhat later work. In De la création
de l'ordre dans l'humanité, of 1843, Proudhon declared:

> Les communistes, pour exprimer l'objet de leurs voeux, emploient in-
> différemment les termes de communauté, d'association, d'organisation,
> d'égalité: comme moyen de réalisation, ils demandent la réforme électo-
> rale et le gouvernement du peuple par le peuple: ce qui les range entière-
> ment parmi les démocrates les plus avancés. [23]

To claim electoral reform as well as government of the people and by the
people seems here to be a sufficient condition for classing a group of men
among those Proudhon designated as "the most advanced democrats". In
this case, the communists were classed as belonging to such a group; this
implies that, according to Proudhon, any communist was a most advanced
democrat, but not that any advanced democrat was necessarily a communist.
Proudhon possibly applied the term "communists" here to Cabet's adherents,
with whom he most certainly did not identify himself.

Somewhat later in the same work, Proudhon wrote:

> La liberté individuelle nous est apparue dans la démocratie, marchant
> par l'égalité politique et la concurrance industrielle au nivellement des
> fonctions. [24]

Concerning the difference between monarchy and democracy, he went on to
say:

> Dans la monarchie, tout est inféodation et redevance; dans la démocratie,

tout est libre;   le salaire n'existe que pour les magistrats et les manouvriers;   de plus, les emplois sont essentiellement révocables.

Proudhon held, however, that the inconveniences of the two systems were equal, the principle of monarchy leading to insubordination and alienation, while

> ...la tendence démocratique produit l'incoherence et la rivalité;   ce qui est contraire au but de toute société. [25]

This does not seem to imply that he considered insubordination to be identical with incoherence and rivalry. The statement probably only means that "la tendence" of what he held to be democracy was no better than that of monarchy, or that insubordination and alienation were as bad as incoherence and rivalry. For the rest, we can say that individual liberty, political equality, and industrial competition were probably regarded as marks of the social and political system which Proudhon here designated as "democracy", also, that employment was to be revocable and that only magistrates and day labourers were to be salaried persons. Proudhon may have primarily had countries like Switzerland and the United States in mind. His somewhat negative attitude towards what he held as democracy is fairly evident in these quotations, and it even looks as if he considered incoherence and rivalry to be inevitable consequences of this political and social system.

It is thus obvious that "democracy" and related terms did not yet occupy a key position in his terminology, and there is reason to discern a slightly derogatory kind of application. Both factors were changed after February 1848, when frequency of usage and initially a very derogatory application of the term became typical of his political language. In March 1848 Proudhon declared that he had proved that

> ...la démocratie, loin d'être le plus perfait des gouvernements, est la négation de la souveraineté du peuple, est le principe de sa ruine, il sera démontré, en fait et en droit, que la démocratie n'est rien de plus qu'un arbitraire constitutionnel succedant à un autre arbitraire constitutionnel. [26]

The reason why he considered democracy to be the negation of popular sovereignty is given a few pages later on. Adopting the famous dictum of Thiers, "Le roi règne et ne gouverne pas, " Proudhon asserted: "La démocratie dit: Le Peuple règne et ne gouverne pas", [27] the main cause being that democracy, as he understood it, was a rule of chosen representatives, a rule which had nothing to do with popular sovereignty. He asserted:

> Suivant l'idéologie des démocrates, le peuple ne peut se gouverner lui-même, et qu'il est forcé de se donner des représentantes qui le gouvernent par délégation et sous bénéfice de révision. [28]

Proudhon wanted a government of the people by the people, however:

> Nous aurons le Gouvernement du Peuple par le Peuple, et non par une représentation du Peuple; nous aurons, dis-je, la République, ou nous périrons une seconde fois par la démocratie. [29]

According to these statements, it looks as if Proudhon operated with a concept 'democracy' the central conceptual characteristic of which was government by chosen representatives, and in which the political function of the people was definitely limited to the election of representatives. In accordance with his view, such a kind of government was the ruin or even negation of popular sovereignty. This last factor, however, may more probably be reckoned among the inevitable consequences of such a form of government and not among the conceptual characteristics of what he designated with "democracy". In his use of other political terms it can be seen that "republic" was evidently used to designate a form of government characterized by direct popular rule. This indicates a most important difference between the significations of "democracy" and "republic", and both terms are used here in ways contrary to the usage of several other ideologists such as Kant, Montesquieu, and Madison. This way of using "democracy" may in addition be regarded as incompatible with the terminology in our first quotation from De la création de l'ordre dans l'humanité, when the favouring of government by the people of the people was probably held to be a sufficient condition for a man to be a democrat.

An argument rather similar to that quoted above occurs when Proudhon stated that the ballot was the criterion of democracy, and continued:

Avec l'urne électorale, elle [la démocratie] élimine les hommes; avec l'urne législative, elle élimine les idées. [30]

Another very derogatory usage of the term is found in his assertions that democracy was a form of absolutism,[31] that democracy was impotent to solve social questions, [32] and in frequent other occurrences. Proudhon also emphasized once again that the republic, in contrast to democracy, represented the sovereignty of the people.

In this work, written in March 1848, it is impossible to find a single occurrence of "democracy" where the term is not used in a very derogatory way, partly because of Proudhon's extreme dislike of the policy of the provisional government of Lamartine, Ledru-Rollin, and others, who, according to him, betrayed the cause of the revolution with their centralization and State workshops. The honorific usage of "democracy" by these men is without doubt one factor that led Proudhon to adopt his derogatory usage. This way of letting "democracy" signify a phenomenon of which he greatly disapproved is rather unusual in political terminology in France in the spring of 1848, at a time when, for example, Guizot referred to a universal honorific application within different political camps, and even to "l'empire du mot démocratie". [33]

A derogatory use of "democracy" is also evident in various newspaper articles which Proudhon wrote during the first half of 1848. [34] During the autumn of that year, however, two new and very important trends in his terminology were also revealed in the press. In October Proudhon referred to the fact that he and his political adherents used the term "démocrates-socialistes" as political self-denomination. In reply to some political reproaches, Proudhon wrote:

Quand nos amis de la République démocratique inquiets de nos idées et de nos tendances, se récrient contre la qualification de socialistes que nous ajoutons à celle de démocrates ...[35]

This kind of self-denomination may be taken to indicate a kind of co-operation between his few adherents and those of Raspail. The latter, it seems, had also used "socialistes-démocrates" as self-denomination some time before 1848.

How far this positive application of "socialistes-démocrates" might have influenced his use of unqualified "democrat" and "democracy" is somewhat doubtful. A few days later "democrats" was probably used to indicate those who had not grasped the idea that the February Revolution was primarily a social and economic and not a political revolution, [36] an idea which predominates in his ideology, and which probably excludes the possibility of honorific application in this case. His first honorific use of "democracy" and "democrats" occurs in an electoral manifesto in which he heavily supported Raspail's candidature. This manifesto was written some time during the first half of November. Up to that time, Proudhon had favoured abstention from the presidential election, but now he declared:

> Pour nous, qui avons adhéré d'esprit et de cœur à cette candidature; qui, dans cette circonstance, avons jugé nécessaire, pour la dignité de nos opinions, de nous séparer des autres fractions moins avancées de la démocratie... [37]

His claim that this manifesto was necessary on account of the need to separate Proudhon's group from other, less advanced groups of what was here designated as "democracy" can most probably be taken to imply that Proudhon considered his group to be an advanced democratic group. "Democracy" seems to have been used here as a common designation of different political fractions of which some were less and some more advanced. It is the first time Proudhon approved of something which was labelled with unqualified "democracy".

Honorific application is also evident shortly afterwards in the same manifesto. Proudhon declared pure socialism to be their fundamental dogma, a socialism aimed at the enfranchisement of the proletariat and the extinction of misery; something which implied effective equality of conditions. He continued:

> Le socialisme, égalitaire avant tout, est donc la formule démocratique par excellence. Si les politiques moins sincères éprouvent quelque répugnance à l'avouer, nous respectons leur réserve; mais, il faut qu'ils le sachent, à nos yeux ils ne sont point démocrates. [38]

Socialism here was not only definitely considered to be the democratic formulation, but the admission of this fact and agreement with this formulation were most probably also a necessary condition of receiving the label "democrat" according to Proudhon's terminology.

His use of "democracy" half a year earlier reveals a striking change in his attitude towards what he held to be democracy. This, however, does not by itself prove that Proudhon also used "democracy" with a signification which was different from that attributed to this term in the spring. It might thus have been possible that in November Proudhon operated with a concept 'democracy' identical with the one used in March, and that he only differed concerning non-conceptual characteristics, for example, that he no longer regarded negation of popular sovereignty as an inevitable consequence of such a form of government. If so we find a difference in conceptions, but not a conceptual change. Such an hypothesis is not confirmed by later occurrences in this manifesto, however. Here Proudhon greatly recommended a combination of universal suffrage and imperative mandates, implying that representatives should be bound beforehand to act and to vote in a certain way. Against those who opposed this view he asserted:

> Ce qui veut dire qu'à leurs yeux le peuple, en élisant des représentantes,

ne se donne point des mandataires, il aliène sa souveraineté! A coup
sûr, ce n'est pas là du socialisme, ce n'est pas même de la démocratie.[39]

According to this, imperative mandates, in addition to the election of
representatives, were necessary properties, not only of socialism, but also
of democracy. These properties can obviously be regarded as conceptual
characteristics. In March, the political function of the people in a democracy had conceptually been limited to the election of representatives, thus
excluding the possibility of any kind of imperative mandate. The change
from a very derogatory to a very honorific use of "democracy" cannot be
regarded merely as a change in conceptions, or as a new way of estimating
the consequences of a certain political concept under the influence of Proudhon's attitude towards the presidential election, but must also be viewed as
a conceptual change, or as a way of introducing a concept 'democracy' differing from that which caused his aversion during the spring of the same
year.

A very honorific as well as a key application of "democracy" also
characterized his terminology during the first months after the electoral
success of Louis Bonaparte in December 1848. Of his favourite plan to
create a popular bank with free credit, Proudhon declared in April 1849:

> On a pu déjà l'entrevoir, la Banque du Peuple, par le seul fait de son
> rayonnement, est l'organisation de la démocratie, la révolution sociale.[40]

This places his opinion of the organization of democracy in a key position in
his political and social philosophy, and it is also possible that here he may
have used "organization of democracy" synonymously with "social revolution".

Two days later Proudhon answered those who said that there were only
two parties in France, the party of order and stability and that of anarchy,
by agreeing that there were two parties only. In his opinion, however, they
were the monarchical and republican parties in political life, corresponding
to the parties of capital and work in social life. He continued:

> République, démocratie, socialisme, c'est tout un, ce sont termes
> synonymes. République démocratiques et sociale est un pléonasme, qui
> a pour but d'exprimer cette inévitable synonymie. Quiconque la rejette
> n'est ni socialiste, ni démocrate, ni républicain; il ne s'entend pas avec
> lui-même, c'est un menteur ou un sot ignorant. [41]

This declaration probably indicates an attempt to unite some of the
political groupings opposed to the policies of Louis Bonaparte. It is also
evident that Proudhon would refuse the labels "socialist", "democrat", or
"republican" to any who rejected the alleged relation of synonymity between
"socialism", "democracy", and "republic", and that he regarded all other
use of these terms as terminological misuse. The pointing out of this
alleged synonymity marks the zenith of the laudatory use of "democracy"
during the February Revolution. "Socialism", for example, is a term which
probably was always used in a very honorific way by Proudhon, and an
alleged relation of synonymity between that term and "democracy" is therefore per se a proof of honorific application of the latter. With regard to
the alleged synonymity between "democracy" and "republic" there is clear
evidence of a change in the relationship between these two words when we
compare this statement with the one made in March in the previous year
when "republic" and "democracy" were used to designate two contrasting

phenomena in political life, and where only the former was used to label
government of and by the people.

A certain kind of honorific use of "democracy" also occurs in an introductory declaration in <u>Les confessions d'un révolutionnaire,</u> of 1849. Here
Proudhon said:

> Je dirai, sans rien dissimuler, quelles idées ont dirigé ma conduite,
> quelles espérances ont souteni mon courage. En faisant ma confession,
> je ferai celle de toute la démocratie. [42]

"Democracy" here seems to be used to designate a political party, a movement, or perhaps an idea of which Proudhon absolutely approved. We find
in the same work, however, qualified expressions like "la démocratie
gouvernementale" [43] and "les jacobins, démocrates-gouvernementa-
listes", [44] the denotata of which Proudhon did not approve at all. This
indicates that he used "democracy" with a signification differing from that
of "governmental democracy", or that "democracy" did not signify something of which a kind of government was a possible property when the term
was used in an unqualified way.

The use of "democracy" with a non-governmental signification in any
case does not occur in <u>Idée générale de la révolution au XXe siecle,</u> of 1851.
This work is influenced by the political reflections he had made during the
three years he spent in prison on account of his public attacks on the policies of Louis Bonaparte. In his conclusion, Proudhon stated that the revolutionary scheme of the future must not be direct legislation, direct government, or simplified government, but must consist in having no government
at all.

> Ni monarchie, ni aristocratie, ni même démocratie, en tant que ce
> troisième terme impliquerait un gouvernement quelconque, agissant
> au nom de peuple, et se disant peuple. Point d'autorité, point de gou-
> vernement, même populaire: la Révolution est là. [45]

His rejection of government also included what he designated as "democracy", since the term implied a certain kind of government. His phrase
"ni même démocratie" seems to indicate that he preferred democracy to
monarchy and aristocracy, but nevertheless rejected them all as being
governmental systems.

This use of "democracy" to describe something which he held to be a
hindrance to the social revolution of the future was probably a somewhat
derogatory use of the term, although we must add that the degree of deroga-
tion is much smaller here than during the spring of 1848.

A rather unconditional derogatory usage is present in this work, however, when he said that "démocratie" was "dernier terme de l'évolution
gouvernementale", just after having declared, "l'histoire des gouvernements
est le martyrologe du prolétariat. " [46] Proudhon also put forward as a kind
of historical law:

> A une démocratie inextricable succédera, sans autre transition, l'empire,
> avec au sans Napoléon. [47]

It is evident that the main reason for his return to a negative attitude
towards what he designated as "democracy" in 1851 was the fact that democracy was considered a form of government. A property such as being a
form of government, however, was not absent in the signification attributed
to this term during the period of honorific application. It is, for example,

most probable that democracy was conceptually regarded as being a form of government when Proudhon held imperative mandates to be necessary properties of democracy, and also when he declared "democracy" to be synonymous with "republic". This change in attitude towards what he designated as "democracy" may therefore be explained as a difference in political opinion and not a difference concerning the signification attributed to "democracy". It may be inserted that in <u>Les confessions d'un révolutionnaire</u> of 1849, unqualified "democracy" was possibly used with a signification which excluded a property such as being a form of government. In that case a change in political outlook would have been connected with a change in the signification of "democracy", but with the retention of an honorific application. Such a use, which would have made honorific application of "democracy" compatible with a principle dislike of all kinds of governments, is not to be found in 1851, however.

A difference of quite another kind appears the following year. In <u>La Révolution sociale</u> Proudhon declared:

> Dans une démocratie, il n'y a lieu, en dernière analyse, ni à constitution ni à gouvernement.

He continued by describing democratic policy:

> La politique se reduit à un simple contrat de garantie mutuelle, de citoyen à citoyen, de commune à commune, de province à province, de peuple à peuple, variable dans ses articles suivant la matière... [48]

This obviously contradicts statements made the previous year, and the use of the term is once more honorific. Especially is his statement that policy was to be reduced to a simple contract of mutual trust very central to all his later ideological works, and his adherents took rather a long time to adopt the term "mutuellistes" in self-denomination.

Another and rather similar use of "pure democracy" is found in this work. Concerning the different kinds of organizations of the Church, Proudhon declared the earliest to have been "la fraternité inorganique, ou démocratie pure". [49] "Pure democracy" here seems to be used synonymously with "inorganic fraternity", and this fraternity is here opposed to what he described as the later governmental systems of the clergy or elders, episcopal federation, and papal monarchy.

This way of using "democracy" and "pure democracy" naturally tends once more towards honorific application. As a typical instance of "democracy" used to label something to which he considered he himself belonged, I quote:

> ... parce que démocratie a combattu la candidature de Louis Bonaparte au 10 décembre, j'y étais; parce qu'elle l'a fait reculer le 29 janvier, j'y étais; parce qu'elle s'est insurgée contre lui le 13 juin, sans prison j'y aurais été ... [50]

When compared with his anti-governmental attitude in his previous work it is not possible to say that these honorific statements contradict an anti-governmental ideology; on the contrary we have found "democracy" used appreciatively to connote something in which, in the last analysis, there was room for neither constitution nor government. The difference between the Proudhon of 1851 and Proudhon of 1852 can thus, on this point, hardly be said to be a difference of political opinion, but seems to have been exclusively a difference relating to mutually incompatible kinds of significations attributed to the term during these two years.

This terminological turning point may appear somewhat unintelligible if only these two works are considered. A few occurrences from a work which appeared at the end of 1851, however, may possibly explain some of the new trends in his terminology as well as in his ideology. In this work, Philosophie du progrès, Proudhon asserted:

> La démocratie, telle que la formulèrent les actes de 1793 et de 1848, a succombé sous la logique de son application. [51]

and he also spoke of "la démocratie française, réfutée par son propre principe. "[52] Here he most probably meant that democracy had been destroyed in France by the masses who voted for Bonaparte. Universal suffrage was then held to be a proper principle of democracy. In these statements we see at least in part a continuation from his derogatory usage of the same year, when "democracy" signified a governmental system.

Proudhon did not, however, identify everything he designated as "democracy" with these phenomena. He admitted that up to that time democracy had been imitating the monarchical philosophy, but he added:

> C'est pour cela que la démocratie n'a jamais été qu'une fiction incapable de se constituer.

He continued saying,

> ...il est temps qu'elle apprenne à penser par elle-même; qu'elle pose le principe qui lui est propre, et qu'en s'affirment d'une manière positive, elle porte au complet le système des idées sociales. [53]

According to this it looks as if Proudhon operated with two concepts, 'actual democracy', or 'fictive democracy', and 'proper principle of democracy', where the former, being a governmental system, had little or nothing in common with the latter.

What was meant more concretely by the second concept is not very clear, but Proudhon presumably had a socialist property in mind. Proper principle, in any case, is here different from what he recently considered as the proper principle of democracy. It is obvious that he greatly approved of this latter concept, which implies a certain kind of conditioned honorific application of "democracy", even if it must be added that Proudhon was not in favour of properties which were generally attributed the existing significations of "democracy", but only approved of those which he thought ought to be attributed to the proper signification of this term. Such a relationship naturally makes the kind of application somewhat complicated. But this way of using the term marks an adequate starting point for the unreserved honorific application of La révolution sociale, 1852, where the term was used to signify something in which, in the last analysis, there was no room for either constitution or government. This latter trend is the last in the very varied and interesting terminology employed by Proudhon as the result of the events of the February Revolution. This revolution was without doubt the cause of various important changes in political language, but it will be very difficult, if not impossible, to find any other area in contemporary political language which was so marked by varying and incompatible trends.

b. After the February Revolution

Like most other political thinkers, Proudhon used "democracy" rather
seldom during the eighteen-fifties, and no frequency similar to his usage
during the February Revolution is to be found until the last years of his
life. [54]

In 1858 Proudhon asserted that in spite of his disdain for popular ballots,

> ...j'appartions à la démocratie; je ne me sépare point d'elle, et nul n'a
> le droit de m'en exclure. [55]

"Democracy" is here regarded as something with which he wished to associate. What he meant by "democracy", however, is not clear, He presumably spoke about it as inter alia the great popular movement in favour of
universal suffrage and voting by ballot.

Proudhon then asked:

> Suis-je donc traître ou scissionaire parce que je dis que la démocratie est
> infectée, et que, plus que personne, elle a servi la contrerévolution? [56]

This is put in the form of a question, but Proudhon certainly considered it
his duty to state in what way democracy was infected and why it had served
the counterrevolution. This is probably best explained by the assertion:

> La démocratie, depuis qu'elle est devenue une puissance, une mode, a
> épousé successivement toutes les idées les plus contraires à sa nature.[57]

According to Proudhon these ideas included the various religious trends as
well as communism, feudalism, monopolism, and free enterprise in the
field of economics, and dictatorial, imperial, absolutist, and chauvinistic
systems in the field of politics. He concluded:

> Elle [la démocratie] a pris tous les systèmes, toutes les utopies, toutes
> les charlataneries, n'ayant rien su découvrir dans la pensée qui l'avait
> produite. [58]

These statements indicate an application of "democracy" fairly similar
to that seen in Philosophie du progrès, On the one hand, very negative
properties are attached to what Proudhon would probably have designated as
"contemporary democracy" or "actual democracy". On the other hand, it
is evident that he held all the dictatorial and chauvinistic systems mentioned
to be contrary to the nature of democracy and also contrary to the idea which
had produced democracy. This probably implies an honorific application of
expressions like "original democracy" and "democracy per se" and also of
unqualified "democracy" when used with a signification which Proudhon held
to be the proper one.

Such a differentiated application, and in particular the way in which he
considers negative properties to be contrary to the nature of democracy,
may lead one to expect Proudhon to tend towards a positive evaluation of
what received the label "democracy". This is not the case, however. On
the next occasion, this differentiated attitude disappears completely, and
there seems to be only a very derogatory use of "democracy" in Du principe
fédératif, of 1863. This work contains the essence of his permanent

dislike of any kind of centralized power, and this dislike is expressed on a theoretical level.

In Proudhon's opinion federal systems and decentralization were the only possible escape from authoritarian government. Referring to Lamartine, he said:

La démocratie se donne pour libérale, républicaine, socialiste même, dans le bon et vrai sens du mot. [59]

At this time Proudhon heartily disagreed with this, and he continued:

La démocratie s'en impose à elle même. Elle n'a jamais compris le triônom révolutionnaire, Liberté - Égalité - Fraternité. - Sa devise, définitivement adoptée, est à un seul terme, UNITÉ.

The term "unity" in this work signifies a tendency towards strong centralized governmental authority, or even towards despotism, and the strong association Proudhon makes between "unity" and "democracy" in this work is typical of his application of the latter term.

Proudhon further held that democracy had no respect for the principle of free credit, and that it trembled when faced with conscious workers. He even used "democracy" to label the political body that had delegated unrestricted power to General Cavaignac in June 1848 to crush the workers in Paris. As a general maxim, Proudhon asserted that he who desired liberty must work for federation, he who desired a republic must work for federation, and he who desired socialism must work for federation. In contrast to federation,

...la démocratie a pour principe l'unité; sa fin, c'est l'unité; son moyen, l'unité; sa loi, toujours l'unité. L'unité est son alpha et son omega, sa formule suprême, sa raison dernière. [60]

A very similar formulation is:

La démocratie fait bon marché de la liberté individuelle et du respect des lois, incapable de gouverner à d'autres conditions que celles de l'unité, qui n'est autre chose que le despotisme. [61]

This work was partly written during the Italian struggle for unity; a struggle which Proudhon frequently associated with what he here held to be democracy. Proudhon also frequently displayed his contempt for Garibaldi and Mazzini and their political aims. His attitude towards providing French military assistance to aid the cause of Italian unity was negative, and he had nothing but contempt for those among the French, generally in opposition to Napoleon III, who heartily approved of the Emperor's military undertakings against Russia and Austria. It was probably some such factor that lay behind the statement:

La démocratie, en effet, est essentiellement militariste. [62]

Other very derogatory occurrences are frequent in this work. When compared with his terminology of 1858 it is evident that strongly negative properties were not only attributed to actual democracy, while considering these to be contrary to the real nature of democracy, but probably, without reservation he regarded them as essential to what he here designated as "democracy". It is possibly somewhat doubtful whether properties like militaristic character, anti-socialistic character, etc, can be regarded as conceptual characteristics of the concept 'democracy' with which Proudhon operated in this work. From a certain point of view, these properties may more probably be considered to be inevitable consequences, but not conceptual characteristics of what he designated as "democracy". In any case a property like a form of government of an extremely centralized kind is a characteristic of this sort, which implies that democracy, as understood in this work, conceptually was incompatible with any kind of federalism. Since favour of federalism and a hearty dislike of any kind of centralization are consistent characteristics of Proudhon's ideology, this in itself can be regarded as furnishing sufficient proof that Proudhon operated with a concept 'democracy' different from those applied during periods when "democracy" was used honorifically.

With regard to the terminology in Du principe fédératif, however, in spite of Proudhon's frequent and most derogatory use of "democracy", an occurrence of "democratic" is found which is very likely to be honorific. In discussing the political forms of the future, which would replace existing centralized governments, Proudhon emphasized the importance of autonomous groups. He went on to say:

> Ces groupes sont eux-mêmes des petits États, organisés démocratiquement sous la protection fédérale. [63]

It is probable that "democratic" was used here to characterize something of which he approved, and keeping in mind the close association between federalism and what he called "democracy", it is evident that in this statement "democratic" could not have been used to designated properties which in other places he had considered essential to what he designated as "democracy". This use of "democratic" is the only example I have found of a probably honorific application of this term in this work. "Democracy" seems to have been used exclusively to designate something of which he disapproved absolutely.

Proudhon's application of "democracy" in this work, which is as derogatory as that of the spring of 1848, marks the last published usage of the term during his lifetime. There are, however, occurrences in posthumous works.

De la capacité politique des classes ouvrières can possibly be described as his most influential work, and it was regarded for a long time as his political testament. Although it was written only a year after Du principe fédératif, we find once again a certain kind of honorific application of "democracy". Of the increasing political activity of the French workers, Proudhon stated:

> C'est par là que la Démocratie française, au dix-neuvième siècle, se distingue de toutes les démocraties antérieures: Le Socialisme, comme on l'a appelé, n'est pas autre chose. [64]

According to this, Proudhon operated with two concepts: 'French democracy during the nineteenth century' and 'all other democracies'. The former was obviously held to be identical with socialism, and while increasing political activity of the workers was a necessary characteristic of the former, the latter was probably characterized by its absence. It is obvious that Proudhon greatly favoured the former, and it can be seen from the context that he had a decentralized system of workers' co-operation in view. This implies that the expression "French democracy during the nineteenth century" was used with a very different signification from the one attributed to "democracy" the previous year.

It is not clear how Proudhon eventually might have used unqualified "democracy" in this work. But we should not expect an unreserved honorific application if the term was to be used to designate a genus of which the concepts mentioned were species. It can also be seen that Proudhon used "Démocratie travailleuse" and "Démocratie ouvrière" and not "démocratie" as the label of something of which he greatly approved; [65] though it must also be mentioned that unqualified "démocratique" was once used in an obviously honorific way when he pointed out:

L'idée mutuelliste, qui fait aujourd'hui la base de l'émancipation démocratique. [66]

In his posthumous works Proudhon even used the unqualified term "democracy" in an unreservedly honorific way in France et Rhin, an unfinished and somewhat sketchy work. In regard to the English Constitution, Proudhon declared that representative rule and parliamentarism were incompatible with democracy. "Démocratie" here seems to have been used synonymously with "un système de suffrage universel, d'égalité politique complète."[67] Economic equality was said to be the basis of political equality, while parliamentarism and representative rule rested on class privileges. Elsewhere Proudhon considered that economic equality, as well as abolishing all class privileges, would replace free competition by mutual co-operation and free workers' associations. According to Proudhon, this implied:

La constitution politique se trouve la même que la constitution économique. ... Cette identité des deux constitutions est la dogme de la démocratie. [68]

What Proudhon meant by "identité" is not clear. Perhaps he primarily intended to emphasize that political equality was exclusively conditioned by economic equality, and that this viewpoint was essential for what he here regarded as democracy. This indicates a use of "democracy" where the term primarily signified a political idea, or a principle, or, maybe, a political group, but hardly a certain kind of government. Since mutual co-operation and workers' associations were regarded as being necessary for economic equality, we may infer that Proudhon also believed these things to be essential to democracy, or that the favouring of these factors was implicit in the signification attributed to "democracy". This indicates an application of "democracy" which cannot only be regarded as honorific, but may even be said to indicate a usage where Proudhon identifies his own ideals with the connotation of the term. On this point there is some degree of difference between this application and that in De la capacité politique des classes ouvrières, where probably only one species of 'democracy' was said to be marked by mutual co-operation and workers' associations. It must be mentioned that this last use of "democracy" is in harmony with Proudhon's earlier attitude towards "l'idée mutuelliste, qui fait aujourd'hui la base de l'émancipation démocratique". The terminological difference is very great when we compare this use with that employed in Du principe fédératif, where anything characterized by mutual co-operation and workers' associations was most certainly incompatible with the signification he attributed to "democracy" at that time.

The application in France et Rhin appears to represent the final use of "democracy" on the part of Proudhon's very productive pen. The period after 1852 is characterized by a high degree of heterogeneous terminology, while it is difficult to find any changes in political outlook during the same period. Such factors, _inter alia_, make an inquiry into the use of "democracy" by Proudhon very interesting. Generally, Proudhon's political ideas are fairly consistent and stable. There are a few small exceptions, for example, his different attitudes towards possible abstention from the presidential election of 1848, but these are overshadowed by his lasting hatred of all kinds of authoritarian and centralized rule, and by his habit of identifying himself with popular federal self-rule and the mutual co-operation of the workers. This ideological stability constitutes a rather strange background in the light of the very different kinds of significations he attributed to "democracy" and especially of his repeated switches from honorific to derogatory applications, and even from very honorific to very derogatory kinds of usage, and vice versa.

These changes were mainly caused by Proudhon's way of attributing mutually incompatible kinds of connotations to "democracy", and, except for the change in 1851, to a very small degree by his having been conditioned by differences in political outlook. As regards his very honorific and very derogatory applications, a most important aspect was without doubt that different properties attributed to the significations of the word at different times were not of minor importance in relation to his general political outlook, but, on the contrary, they promoted very high degrees of positive or negative value judgements.

Generally speaking, although Proudhon presents an extremely varied use of "democracy", probably one of the most heterogeneous applications ever produced, this part of his terminology cannot be regarded as having an arbitrary or accidental character. In contrast to several other political thinkers, Proudhon used "democracy" fairly seldom with different significations in one and the same writing. There were thus several periods in Proudhon's application of "democracy", in my opinion there were nine periods of application, all of them fairly consistent if regarded as independent or autonomous units. This indicates a kind of temporary terminological homogeneity, although it does not contradict what has been said concerning the extremely heterogeneous picture presented by all these periods taken as a whole.

CHAPTER IX

MARX AND ENGELS

1. Marx and Engels up to 1848

In contemporary communist terminology "democracy" occupies a most central and laudatory position. We have seen earlier, especially in the language of Babeuf and Cabet, a way of using this term to signify a classless society ruled by the proletariat. Such a usage is also partly to be found in the language of Marx, and especially in that of Engels. This trend is by no means exclusive, even in the years up to 1848, and it cannot be regarded as predominant when the whole written production of Marx and Engels is taken into consideration. Thus honorific as well as derogatory applications of "democracy" can be found in the terminology of Marx and Engels, and in certain cases very honorific and very derogatory. The political terminology of the young Marx can hardly be regarded as a trend within communist language. The young Marx was without doubt a social critic, a most severe social critic at that, but not a socialist. Discussions of social and political matters were far from infrequent, but the idealist handling of the problems in connection with the Entfremdung was very different from what was later to mark the essentials of historical materialism.

This inquiry derives benefit from a fairly frequent use of "democracy" in at least one manuscript of the young Marx. Kritik des Hegelschen Staatsrechts was written during the spring and summer of 1843 but was never published during Marx's lifetime. Here, when Marx was twenty-four years old, he severely criticized Hegel's placing the State, the constitution, and the laws above man. Marx said this was typical of nearly all modern political thought which regarded laws, and not human beings, as essentials in social life. This tendency furthermore had made man look upon laws and constitutions as things of a divine origin, and not as things which should serve human needs. In this way, man was alien to political life as such. In the words of the young Marx:

> Das politische Leben im modernen Sinne ist der Scholazismus des Volkslebens. Die Monarchie ist der vollendete Ausdruck dieser Entfremdung.[1]

In sharp contrast to this alienation of monarchy, democracy was marked out as the only form of rule in which the constitution should and did serve man.

> In der Demokratie erscheint die Verfassung selbst nur als eine Bestimmung, und zwar Selbstbestimmung des Volkes. In der Monarchie haben wir das Volk der Verfassung; in der Demokratie die Verfassung des Volks. Die Demokratie ist das aufgelöste Rätsel aller Verfassungen. Hier ist die Verfassung nicht nur an sich, dem Wesen nach, sondern der Existenz, der Wirklichkeit nach in ihren wirklichen Grund, den wirklichen Menschen, das wirkliche Volk, stets zurückgeführt und als sein eigenes Werk gesetzt. Die Verfassung erscheint als das, was sie ist, freies Produkt des Menschen.[2]

Marx went on to say that by destroying the riddle of the constitution, democracy restored man as a free social being, and on this point there was no difference between the formal principle and the factual content. In so far as "politics" was used to mean "constitution", Marx also agreed with the opinion,

... dass in der wahren Demokratie der politishe Staat untergehe. [3]

This statement probably contains Marx's first formulation concerning the withering away of the State, a question which occurs several times in his political thinking. On this point, there is obviously a continuity between the young Marx and the Marx who generally operates in the history of political ideas, even if there are important differences on other points. Marx here used "democracy" in a most honorific way. Used to express a concept according to which destruction of the riddle of the constitution was conceptually attributed to the concept 'democracy', the word "democracy" occupies a key position. Furthermore this reference to law and constitution as something alienated in relation to man marks a central aspect of his general thinking about man's being influenced, or even subdued, by Entfremdung (estrangement or alienation in his social relationship). This problem of Entfremdung occupies a fairly central place in contemporary Western discussion,[4] and it is therefore of importance that it should be intimately connected with the early use of "democracy".

An application of "democracy" very similar to that seen in Kritik des Hegelschen Staatsrechts is provided in a letter from Marx, dated May 1843, to his friend Ruge. Deploring the mental narrowness of the German Philistine, or Spiessbürger, Marx held out human self-confidence, or freedom, as the main remedy for such people.

Das Selbstgefühl des Menschen, die Freiheit, wäre in der Brust dieser Menschen erst wieder zu erwecken. Nur dies Gefühl, welches mit den Griechen aus der Welt und mit dem Christentum in den blauen Dunst des Himmels verschwindet, kann aus der Gesellschaft wieder eine Gemeinschaft der Menschen für ihre höchsten Zwecke, einen demokratischen Staat machen. [5]

"Ein demokratischer Staat" is evidently synonymous with "eine Gemeinschaft der Menschen für ihre höchsten Zwecke. " Marx, without reservation, approves of what he regards as a democratic State. In this case, and especially in connection with this relation of synonymity, Marx may even be said to have used "democratic State" not only in an honorific way but eulogistically, or with a positive value judgement implicit in the expression. Here, too, the democratic principle is contrasted with the monarchical one. Contempt of human beings, furthermore, was regarded as essential to the latter. "Das Prinzip der Monarchie überhaupt ist der verachtete, der verächtliche, der entmenschte Mensch. "

This early use of "democracy" and closely related terms, which touches a central aspect of the political thinking of the young Marx, who clearly used these expressions with a very positive evaluation, may, from a certain point of view, be regarded as a natural starting point for a broad and honorific use during his later years. As indicated above, however, such a view is oversimplified, even if a very honorific application is also to be found later. On the whole, several trends in the early Marx terminology cannot be regarded as typical of his later use. In sharp contrast to later years, Marx at this time, for example, when he was about twenty-five years old, used "idealist" appreciatively, [6] and the few occurrences of "communism" and "communist" are of a fairly derogatory kind. [7]

With regard to "democracy", a trend rather different from what has been seen can already be found in Zur Judenfrage, written in the autumn of 1843 and printed the following year. Here Marx expresses the view that the political State was of a religious kind because man could realize his self only outside and not inside this State. Religion was also said to be "der Ausdruck der Trennung und der Entfernung des Menschen vom Menschen". He went on:

> Christlich ist die politische Demokratie, indem in ihr der Mensch, nicht nur ein Mensch, sondern jeder Mensch, als souveränes, als höchstes Wesen gilt, aber der Mensch, in seiner unkultivierten, unsozialen Erscheinung, der Mensch in seiner zufälligen Existenz, der Mensch wie er geht und steht, der Mensch wie er durch die ganze Organization unserer Gesellschaft verdorben, sich selbst verloren, veräussert, unter die Herrschaft unmenschlicher Verhältnisse und Elemente gegeben ist, mit einem Wort, der Mensch der noch kein wirkliches Gattungswesen ist. [8]

"Political democracy" is here used with a meaning which differs sharply in important respects from the earlier usage of "democracy" and "democratic State". Previously the sovereignty of free man, or real man, had been an essential part, if not the exclusive part, of the signification of "democracy" and "democratic State", while sovereignty of man as an uncultivated and inferior being plays a similar role in the signification of "political democracy" as used here. It is of no importance here that Marx used "political democracy" and not simply "democracy". Unqualified "democracy" is used with a signification identical to that of "political democracy" when Marx continued:

> Phantasiegebild, der Traum, das Postulat des Christentums, die Souveränität des Menschen, aber als eines fremden, von dem wirklichen Menschen unterschiedenen Wesens, ist in der Demokratie unwirkliche Wirklichkeit, Gegenwart, weltliche Maxime.

It can be observed that this change in the signification of "democracy" does not correspond to any principal theoretical change. In Zur Judenfrage the central topic is also man's being really man; and here, too, real man, or der wirkliche Mensch, is contrasted to der entmenschte Mensch. Unlike later such instances, where possible explanations concerning changes in terminology may be at hand, I cannot here suggest the reason behind this new way of using "democracy".

There is fairly little to be added concerning the use of "democracy" in other of Marx's earlier writings. [9] I have found only a few other occurrences in his first articles concerning economics, philosophy, and politics, and also in the works Die heilige Familie, and Die deutsche Ideologie. In Die heilige Familie, "der demokratische Repräsentativ-staat" was probably used synonymously with "der vollendete moderne Staat", [10] but not in such a way as to make it possible to draw any further conclusions. In Die deutsche Ideologie, which Marx also worked out in co-operation with Engels, we are told,

> ... dass in einem demokratischen Repräsentativstaat wie Nordamerika die Klassenkollosionen bereits eine Form erreicht haben, zu der die konstitutionellen Monarchien erst hingedrängt werden. [11]

By this statement he probably means that the struggle between the two classes -- bourgeoisie and proletariat -- had reached a higher and more developed level in what he considered a democratic representative State than in a constitutional monarchy. We see that North America, probably the United States, was regarded as one of the denotata of the expression "democratic representative State". In neither case can we say that "democratic representative State" occupies a central position in his terminology. This use of "democratic" can therefore best be regarded as a somewhat accidental use to which Marx attached fairly little importance.

Turning from Marx to Engels, it must be said initially that while Marx used "democracy" in a fairly theoretical way, or to mark out general problems within human society, Engels' application was much more directly connected with concrete political events. The first occurrences of "democracy" are thus to be found in articles written in England, where he referred to the Chartists as "die radikale Demokratie", [12] or "die demokratische Partei in England. " [13] In a review of Carlyle's Past and Present, Engels heavily opposed Carlyle's favourite idea concerning the need for a new aristocracy. With regard to democracy, Engels stated:

> Die Demokratie ist allerdings nur Durchgangspunkt, aber nicht zu einer neuen, verbesserten Aristokratie, sondern zur wirklichen, menschlichen Freiheit. [14]

Here "democracy" is probably used in an honorific way. It is certain that by "real human freedom" Engels referred to something similar to a communistic or classless society. In saying that democracy was a transitional stage to real freedom, it is somewhat unclear whether Engels used "democracy" to mean the rule of the proletariat or a kind of rule which by universal suffrage and the possibility of political organization made the proletarian victory possible. It is obvious that by "democracy" he did not mean what he considered to be real human freedom.

A somewhat different aspect is evident in an article in The New Moral World. Engels here firstly declared: "The French revolution was the rise of democracy in Europe". He continued, however:

> Democracy is, as I take all forms of government to be, a contradiction in itself, an untruth, nothing but hypocrisy (theology, as we Germans call it), at bottom. [15]

This reveals Engels' temporary dislike of every kind of government, including what he regards as democracy. What he more directly meant by "democracy" in this connection, however, is not clear. We are only told that democracy, like all other forms of government, must fall apart, since hypocrisy could not survive, and that the contradictions hidden in democracy would of necessity erupt. The choice rested therefore between undisguised despotism and regular slavery or real liberty and real equality; the latter were to be found in communism.

Here, too, "democracy" signified a transitional stage, but a transitional stage not only to communism, but possibly also to despotism. This is therefore an important addition to his previous statements about democracy.

A more differentiated and qualified use of the term occurs in his central work Die Lage der arbeitenden Klasse in England (1845). Here Engels stated that the English Chartist was a republican even if he never or seldom used the work "republican". The Chartist nevertheless sympathized with

all republican parties, but preferred "democrat" in self-denomination
("sich lieber einen Demokraten nennt"). He continued:

> Aber er ist mehr als blosser Republikaner; seine Demokratie ist keine
> bloss politische. [16]

This statement can probably be taken to imply that "democracy" generally expressed a purely political concept, but that the term as used by the
Chartists signified something not purely political. This difference is explained some pages later, where Engels asserted that in addition to the six
points in the People's Charter, the English workers were also in favour of
a ten-hour working day, protection of the workers, and the abolition of the
existing poor law; these Engels held to be directly opposed to free enterprise. According to him, these factors separated the proletariat from the
middle-class and Chartism from radicalism. He concluded:

> Darin liegt aber auch der Unterschied der chartistischen Demokratie von
> aller bisherigen, politischen Burgeoisie-Demokratien. Der Chartismus
> ist wesentlich sozialer Natur. [17]

Here Engels apparently operates with two concepts, 'Chartist democracy' and 'political bourgeois democracy', the former representing a new
element in politics and the latter a traditional one. The difference between
them is obviously the social, and perhaps even the socialist, character of
the former. It is difficult to say in what way Engels would have used unqualified "democracy" at that time, but in the light of the previous quotation
he would presumably have used it to designate a wider concept or genus of
which the other two were species.

Important applications of "democracy" and related terms are also to
be found in an article on the English Constitution. Here Engels emphasized
that the struggle of the workers for political and social rights was steadily
increasing. He asserted:

> Die nächste Zukunft Englands wird die der Demokratie sein. ... Aber was
> für eine Demokratie! Nicht die der französischen Revolution, deren
> Gegensatz die Monarchie und der Feudalismus war, sonder die Demo-
> kratie, deren Gegensatz die Mittelklasse und der Besitz ist. Der Kampf
> der Demokratie gegen die Aristokratie in England ist der Kampf
> der Armen gegen die Reichen. Die Demokratie, der England entgegen-
> geht, ist eine soziale Demokratie. [18]

Here unqualified "democracy" is used, apparently with intent, in an ambiguous way. On the one hand, the term was used to signify the contrast to
monarchy and feudalism, and, on the other, the contrast to middle class and
property. Obviously Engels attributed this latter signification to the term
concerning the political and social struggle in England. By introducing the
qualified expression "social democracy" Engels probably wanted to make
use of an expression which he considered to be more precise than "democracy" and which had also been used almost synonymously with "Chartist
democracy" in the previous quotation.

Immediately following this statement, Engels introduced a new qualified
expression:

> Aber die blosse Demokratie ist nicht fähig, soziale Übel zu heilen, der
> Kampf der Armen gegen die Reichen kann nicht auf dem Boden der Demo-
> kratie oder der Politik überhaupt ausgekämpft werden. Auch diese Stufe

ist also nur ein Übergang, das letzte rein politische Mittel, das noch zu
versuchen ist, und aus dem sich zugleich ein neues Element, ein über
alles politische Wesen hinausgehendes Prinzip entwickeln muss. Dies
Prinzip ist das der Sozialismus. [19]

Here what was termed "pure democracy" and "democracy" seem to
have been restricted exclusively to the field of politics, and these expressions are therefore used with a different signification from that of "social
democracy" and from that of one occurrence of "democracy" in the previous
quotations. Pure democracy was contrasted to what he held to be socialism,
but we are not informed about the relationship between socialism and
what he designated as "social democracy" and "democracy" when the latter
term was used in relation to the future of England. It is probable that his
statement that pure democracy was completely political and incapable of
curing social difficulties scarcely conveys anything about what he designated
as "social democracy". Engels himself is far from being clear on this
point, however. This does not imply a conclusion that there was no difference at all, or only a small one, among what Engels here calls "socialism",
"social democracy", and, in part, "democracy". This question is still
open. Perhaps at that time Engels would have favoured three mutually exclusive concepts; 'political democracy', 'social democracy', and 'socialism',
the second concept being placed somewhere between the first and the third.

Up to this time Engels had used the unqualified term "democracy" predominantly to express a political concept. The statements we have just
been considering offer an exception to the rule which does not undermine the
truth of it. A rather different way of using "democracy" is to be found in
the autumn of 1845.

In a description of a great fraternal festival held in London, in September 1845, to celebrate the foundation of the French Republic, Engels
declared:

Die Fraternisierung der Nationen unter der Fahne der modernen Demokratie, ... zeigt, dass die Massen und Ihre Repräsentanten besser wissen
was die Glocke geschlagen hat, als die deutsche Theorie. [20]

He made this reference to the German theory because of its alleged tendency
to speak

... von der Demokratie, von der Demokratie schlechthin, von der Demokratie als solcher, ... die den Durchschnitt der griechischen, römischen,
amerikanischen und französischen Demokratie bildet, kurz vom Begriff
der Demokratie. [21]

According to Engels, abstract reasoning of this kind was pure nonsense for
any member of a political movement. He further contrasted this German
theoretical terminology with that of the English, the French, and the few
German participants at the festival, by declaring that when these men used
terms like "democracy" or "fraternity of nations", they were not thinking
exclusively of political phenomena. This latter application was evidently
accepted by Engels as the correct one.

In der Wirklichkeit haben diese Worte ["Demokratie", "Fraternisierung
der Nationen"] jetzt einen sozialen Sinn, in den die politische Bedeutung
aufgeht.

Engels continued by asserting that the French Revolution, with its slogan "Guerre aux palais, paix aux chaumières", was more than a struggle about this or that form of government, and he concluded:

> Die französische Revolution war von Anfang bis zu Ende eine soziale Bewegung, und nach ihr ist eine rein politische Demokratie vollends ein Unding geworden. [22]

Here we are presented with a very different view from that of November two years earlier, when he had stated that the French Revolution was the rise of democracy in Europe but allowed "democracy" to express a purely political concept. [23] This signifies a change in his view of the French Revolution as well as in the meaning he attributed to "democracy". This use of "democracy" with a social signification occurred at least once in his earlier writings, but his view of purely political democracy as nonsense marks a new trend in his terminology.

Engels continued:

> Die Demokratie, das ist heutzutage der Kommunismus. Eine andere Demokratie kann nur noch in den Köpfen theoretischer Visionäre existieren,.... Die Demokratie ist proletarisches Prinzip, Prinzip der Massen geworden. Die Massen mögen über diese einzig richtige Bedeutung der Demokratie mehr oder wenig klar sein, aber für alle liegt wenigstens das dunkle Gefühl der sozialen gleichen Berechtigung in der Demokratie. Die demokratischen Massen können bei der Berechtigung der kommunistischen Streitkräfte ruhig mitgezählt werden. Und wenn sich die proletarischen Parteien verschiedener Nationen vereinigen, so haben sie ganz recht, das Wort Demokratie auf ihre Fahnen zu schreiben, denn mit ausnahme derjenigen, die nicht zählen, sind im Jahre 1846 alle europäische Demokraten mehr oder weniger klare Kommunisten. [24]

This statement is one of the strongest ever made supporting a relation of synonymity between "democracy" and "communism", and between "democrats" and "communists". Here it is likely that Engels had been influenced to a considerable degree by the terminology he contrasted with what he described as the empty abstractions of German theory; there is evidence in his writings of a tendency in that direction during the greater part of his stay in England. This synonymity or near synonymity between "democracy" and "communism" is not meant to be of a general character, regardless of space and time. His frequent use of expressions like "is today", "... has become a proletarian principle", "... in the year of 1846", makes it rather clear that his intention was probably to point out a relation which existed at that time in Europe only. This kind of limitation concerning time is also evident in the conclusion of this essay. After having described the enormous enthusiasm of this international meeting, Engels asked:

> Habe ich recht, wenn ich sage, dass die Demokratie heutzutage der Kommunismus ist?; [25]

he obviously expected an answer in the affirmative.

Rather similar terminology occurs in an article in The Northern Star concerning political conditions in Germany. Engels stated broadly that between 1815 and 1830 the working-class movement had been made more or less subservient in all countries to the liberal middle-class movement. This was because until the moment the middle class had become exclusively the ruling class, the working class had not been able to

see the total difference between liberalism and democracy -- emancipation of the middle classes and emancipation of the working classes ...
the difference between liberty of <u>money</u> and liberty of <u>man</u>.[26]

"Democracy" is very probably used synonymously with "emancipation of
working classes" as well as with "liberty of <u>man</u>", whereas "liberalism"
was used synonymously, or nearly synonymously, with "emancipation of the
middle classes" and "freedom of money".

It is most likely that by "emancipation of the working classes" Engels
had in mind a communistic policy carried out by the ruling proletariat. Thus
"democracy" was not only to signify a proper means towards the realization
of communism, but was to connote such a policy directly. In other words,
as in his description of the fraternal festival, Engels operated here with a
concept 'democracy' of which a communistic policy was a conceptual characteristic and not only a more or less probable consequence. His belief that
the policy of the working classes had necessarily to be connected with that
of the middle classes as long as the middle classes themselves were progressive and revolutionary marks an important element in Marxist and
Leninist political philosophy. It was repeated several times in the writings
of Engels and Marx, and at times in a terminology very different from that
used in this article.

These later writings of Engels typify his and Marx's intense political
agitation during the two years preceding the February Revolution, an agitation which culminated in their <u>Communist Manifesto.</u>   Hardly anything
similar is found in Marx's writings in the years preceding 1846, however.
His writings during these years were mainly of a philosophical and economic
kind; and as already pointed out, only a few occurrences of "democracy"
are to be found there. These were of a rather abstract and theoretical kind,
especially when compared with the frequent honorific and concrete applications found in the writings of Engels. Engels' period in England and his
contact with the Chartist movement may be considered to be among the
main factors that influenced him.

A similar kind of relationship can be seen from the spring of 1846 up
to 1848. By far the majority of the occurrences appear in Engels' writings.
A few also occur in works which were the result of their direct co-operation
and extremely few originate exclusively from Marx.

Their first use of "democracy" occurs in an address to the English
Chartists and Feargus O'Connor, one of their leaders, conveying congratu-
lations and a declaration of solidarity. This address was written on behalf
of the German Democratic Communists of Brussels and was signed "The
Committee, Engels, Ph. Gigot, Marx."

In this address it was initially pointed out that the ground had been
cleared by the political retreat of the landed aristocracy and that the struggle
between middle class and proletariat, between capital and labour, must
reach a solution.   It was further stated that the contending parties had had
their respective battle-cries forced upon them by their interests and mutual
positions. According to the German Democratic Communists, the slogan of
the middle class was: "Extension of commerce by any means whatsoever,
and a ministry of Lancashire cotton lords to carry it out, " while the proletarians used as their motto:

A democratic reconstruction of the Constitution upon the basis of the
People's Charter. [27]

Feargus O'Connor was personally complimented for his brilliant speech at the Nottingham election, and especially for what the committee considered to be

... the striking delineation given in it of the contrast between working class democracy and middle class liberalism.

Finally, gratitude was expressed to O'Connor for the noble and enlightened manner in which The Northern Star was conducted.

We hesitate not a moment in declaring that the Star is the only English newspaper (save, perhaps, The People's Journal ...), which knows the real state of parties in England; which is really and essentially democratic; which is free from national and religious prejudice, which sympathizes with the democrats and working men (now-a-days the two are almost the same), all over the world; which in all these points speaks the mind of the English working class, and therefore is the only English paper really worth reading for the Continental democrats.[28]

"Democracy" was used in a very honorific way by Marx, Engels, and Gigot. We do not know who originally formulated the text in this address, but it must have been accepted by all three of them. The almost identical nature of the democratic movement and the proletarian struggle was here emphasized, and "democracy" also seems to a large degree to have been reserved as a slogan for the proletariat. There was also almost a relation of identity between those designated as "democrats" and those designated as "working men".

Here we have a use of "democracy" which was presumably accepted by Marx. In what follows, however, we are once more to be left almost exclusively to the writings of Engels. No occurrence has been found in Marx's Misère de la philosophie.[29]

In The Northern Star of March 1847, Engels described the new constitution in Prussia. According to him, this constitution was insignificant in itself, but it marked an epoch for Prussia and would very soon lead to a representative constitution for the middle classes, a free press, and independent judges, and thus to the downfall of absolutism and nobility. Full of revolutionary optimism, and drawing a clear parallel with earlier events in France, Engels asserted that this "marks the repetition of Prussia. " Even if the revolutionary movement which was soon to begin was only of direct interest to the middle class, it was not at all unimportant to the people.

From the moment the power of the middle classes is constituted, from that moment begins the separate and distinct democratic movement. In the struggle against despotism and aristocracy, the people, the democratic party, cannot but play a secondary part; the first place belongs to the middle classes. From the moment, however, the middle class establish their own government, identify themselves with a new despotism and aristocracy against the people, from that moment democracy takes a stand as the only the exclusive movement party.[30]

"Democracy" and "distinct democratic movement" are used here to signify that popular force which was to be a minor ally of the middle class up to their political victory, and afterwards its bitter opponent. This statement is rather similar to what he wrote about Germany in The Northern Star on 4 April 1846. There, too, the democratic movement was said to be the subservient ally of the middle class until this class itself had become the exclusive ruler. In both cases we see the essence of the contemporary revolutionary strategy of Marxism: first a temporary political alliance between bourgoisie and proletariat against the aristocracy, then, after victory, a proletarian front against the bourgeoisie.

It is typical of one trend in Engels' terminology that "democracy" was evidently used in several places to connote the proletarian force. [31] Such an application is not unique in Engels' language during the years before 1848, however. Earlier I quoted examples of a different kind of terminology in which "democracy" was used to signify something which was regarded as a suitable means towards the realization of communism, but where any distinct communistic policy was not included in the signification of the term. A return to this kind of terminology, or a use of "democracy" and "democrat" different from that of 1845-46, when these terms were used as synonyms, or near synonyms, of "communism" and "communist", is evident in October 1847 in an attack on the radical author Karl Heinzen. In the introduction Engels declared:

Sie [die Kommunisten] greifen ihn an, nicht in ihrer Eigenschaft als Kommunisten, sondern in Eigenschaft als Demokraten. Es ist nur zufällig dass gerade die Kommunisten die Polemik gegen ihn veröffnet haben, wenn auch gar keine Kommunisten in der Welt wären, so müssten die Demokraten doch gegen Heinzen auftreten. ... Die Kommunisten, weit entfernt, unter den gegenwärtigen Verhältnissen mit den Demokraten nutzlose Streitigkeiten anzufangen, treten vielmehr für den Augenblick in allen praktischen Parteifragen selbst als Demokraten auf. Die Demokratie hat in allen zivilisierten Ländern die politische Herrschaft des Proletariats zur notwendigen Folge, und die politische Herrschaft des Proletariats ist die erste Voraussetzung aller kommunistischen Massregeln. So lange die Demokratie noch nicht erkämpft ist, so lange kämpfen Kommunisten und Demokraten also zusammen, so lange sind die Interessen der Demokraten zugleich die der Kommunisten. [32]

"Democrats" and "communists" are used here to designate two different but not mutually independent phenomena in political life. On the one hand, communists and democrats are spoken of as two different political groupings with several identical interests and as political allies up to the time when democracy was to be established, but probably no longer. On the other hand, Engels also spoke of the communists as presenting themselves, for the moment, as democrats in all practical questions; and he even declared that the communists attacked Heinzen, not in their capacity as communists, but as democrats. The latter statement can be taken to imply that any person designated by Engels as "communist" at that time was also designated as "democrat", or that anything subsumable under a concept 'communist' was also subsumable under a concept 'democrat'. The latter concept is here without doubt the wider one, since Engels could imagine a world without communists but not without democrats. Any communist was thus, for the present, also a democrat, but not vice versa. This argument is without doubt evidence of an important modification of Engels' earlier statements that any democrat, or almost any democrat, was a communist, and that, at that time, democracy was communism. "Democracy" here signifies something which in civilized countries would certainly lead to the rule of the proletariat, but it was not used directly to connote a rule of that kind. On the contrary, it looks as if the distinctively proletarian struggle was not to start before democracy was established. It is therefore clear that "democracy" was here used to designate a political concept which did not necessarily include any communistic or proletarian property.

As for Engels' reservation that democracy would necessarily result in this kind of rule in civilized countries only, we may assume that democracy in non-civilized countries might be of another kind. A month later Engels declared:

> Es gibt zwei Gegenden in Europe, in denen sich die alte christlich-germanische Barbarei in ihrer ursprünglichen Gestalt, beinahe bis aufs Eichelfressen, erhaltet hat, Norwegen und die Hochalpen, namentlich die Urschweiz. ... Sowohl Norwegen wie die Urschweiz sind demokratisch organisiert. Aber es gibt verschiedenerlei Demokratien, und es ist sehr nötig, dass die Demokraten der zivilizierten Länder endlich die Verantwortlichkeit für die norwegische und urschweizerische Demokratie ablehnen. [33]

Engels thus did not refuse Norway and Switzerland the label "democracies", nor did he hesitate to regard these countries as denotata of "democracy", although they were to a very great extent Christian and Teutonic barbarisms. He added, however, that there were different kinds of democracies and continued:

> Die demokratische Bewegung erstrebt in allen zivilizierten Ländern in letzter Instanz die politische Herrschaft des Proletariats.

According to Engels, this democratic movement was conditioned by the existence of a proletariat, a bourgeoisie, and an industrial system, and these factors were not present in what he described as the famous peasant rule of Norway [34] or among the rude herdsmen of Switzerland. He concluded by saying:

> ... die Demokratie der zivilizierten Länder, die moderne Demokratie, hat also mit der norwegischen und urschweizerischen Demokratie durchaus nichts gemein. [35]

At this point Engels used "democracy" with an extremely wide connotation. The way he characterized one kind of democracy as having nothing whatsoever in common with other kinds makes it difficult even to imagine a concept 'democracy' of which all kinds were species. While "modern democracy" signified something which he considered to be aiming at or leading to the rule of the proletariat, this expression did not connote such a rule directly. And unqualified "democracy" cannot even be said to have signified a proper means in the proletarian struggle; this implies an application of the term that differs from some of the earlier trends in Engels' usage.

A rather different use of "democratic" occurs in the French paper L'Atilier during the same month. Engels commented, with regard to the political attitude and behaviour of the workers in the cotton industry in Lancashire,

> ... vous ne trouverez des hommes plus sincèrement attachés aux principes démocratiques, plus fortement résolus à secouer la joug des capitalistes exploiteurs, sous lequel ils se voient actuellement accablés que ces mêmes ouvriers des fabriques de coton du Lancashire. [36]

Here, "most sincerely attached to the democratic principles" was probably used synonymously with "resolved most steadfastly to shake off the yoke of the capitalist exploiters". Communistic behaviour was probably a conceptual characteristic of 'democratic principles' as understood in this statement. This use of "democratic" has a signification different from that of "democracy" in the last occurrences discussed, and apparently Engels temporarily returned to a similar terminology in describing the fraternal festival in September 1845. On the whole, this alternation between "democracy" and "democratic" with significations including and not including communist policy, and in which "democracy" connoted a proper political road to communism, is distinctly characteristic of Engels' terminology before 1848.

In contrast to the above, Marx, somewhat later, used "communistic" to describe something quite different from what he characterized as "democratic". In a speech on the celebration of the Polish Revolution, Marx attacked those who declared the revolution in Cracow to have been communistic, and he asked:

> Ou bien la révolution cracovienne était-elle communiste pour avoir voulu instituer un gouvernement démocratique? Personne ne taxera les citoyens millionnaires de Berne et de New-York d'avoir des velléités communistes. [37]

The millionaires of Berne and New York were probably regarded by Marx as furnishing sufficient proof that anyone desiring, or having obtained a democratic government, need not necessarily be inclined towards communism. This statement shows, without any doubt, the great difference between the significations Marx there attributed to the terms "democratic" and "communistic". He evidently considered democratic as opposed to feudal; what he called "la Pologne féodale" was thus contrasted with what he called "la Pologne démocratique". He seems further to have agreed completely with the leading Polish revolutionaries that Polish democracy was impossible without the abolition of feudal rights and without the agrarian movement which transformed serfs into free and modern property holders. [38]

Here, as on many other occasions, Marx sympathized greatly with the agrarian revolutionary movement in Poland. It can therefore be said that where events in Poland were concerned, he used the word in an honorific way. However, Marx used the word here to describe a government founded upon private property. This way of using "democratic" need not imply that a kind of capitalist policy was implicit in its signification, even if what he held to be democratic was compatible with capitalism. At different times in his life Marx approved of political movements that differed from communism and socialism, and it is therefore not strange that he used "democratic" here in an honorific way. This honorific usage did not issue from Marx the communist ideologist. On this point there is considerable difference between his terminology and that of Engels.

This speech was made as late as 22 February 1848, when political riots had started in Paris. I include both this speech and the Communist Manifesto in this section, since both were written before the outbreak of revolutionary events in France.

The Communist Manifesto, or Manifest der Kommunistischen Partei, which was the original title, was written during December 1847 and January 1848. It appeared in the press in February 1848, and its main revolutionary expectations were directed towards future political events in Germany, not in France.

The main aim of the communists, like that of all other proletarian
parties, was declared here by Marx and Engels to be the consolidation of
the proletariat as a class, the overthrow of the political domination of the
bourgeoisie, and the conquest of political power through the proletariat.[39]
They were most likely referring to these things later on when they stated:

> Wir sahen schon oben, dass der erste Schritt in der Arbeiter-revolution
> die Erhebung des Proletarists zur herrschenden Klasse, die Erkämpfung
> der Demokratie ist. [40]

In the English versions of their manifesto, "Erkämpfung der Demokratie"
is generally translated "to establish democracy"; and according to this,
we can say that Marx and Engels most probably used "to raise the prole-
tarist to ruling class" synonymously with "to establish democracy", or
"rule of the proletariat" synonymously or almost synonymously with "democracy". Here we have a use of "democracy" different from that of "democratic government" in Marx's speech on Poland, in February of the same
year; and there is also a use of "democracy" in this important ideological
document that differs from that generally found in Engels' writings during
the preceding one and a half years. Whereas in these "democracy" predominantly signified something which was regarded as a proper means to
the rule of the proletariat, here the term is apparently used directly to
connote such a rule itself.

I can offer no explanation of this divergence. There are no other
occurrences of "democracy" to be found in this manifesto, though in the
concluding lines we are told that democratic parties were groupings with
which the communists were co-operating in all countries.

> Die Kommunisten arbeiten endlich überall an der Verbindung und Ver-
> ständigung der demokratischen Parteien aller Länder. [41]

What was meant here by "democratic" is not clear, however. Perhaps a
hint lies in the fact that this statement was made after they had declared
that the communists supported every revolutionary movement directed
against existing political and social conditions. The use of "endlich" before
the mentioned plans for co-operation with all democratic parties may be
taken to indicate that Marx and Engels here regarded what they designated
as "democratic parties" as something slightly different from revolutionary
movements. But this point of view is hypothetical.

This last point, however, may also indicate a kind of ambiguous application of "democracy" and "democratic" in this manifesto. On the whole,
"ambiguous" is without doubt the most accurate way to describe Marx's and
Engels' application of "democracy". Attempts to construct a single connotation will remain impossible if the majority of the occurrences are taken
into consideration. This is not unique, however, and the degree of ambiguity is probably smaller in Marx and Engels than in many other ideologists who used the term somewhat frequently over a period of several years.

With regard to Marx's and Engels' relationship, their use of "democracy" and related terms up to the February Revolution presents the rather
strange fact that Marx alone in his character as communist ideologist never
used "democracy" in an honorific way, although Engels frequently used the
term appreciatively. There are honorific applications in writings of which
Marx was co-author, as in the address to O'Connor and the Manifesto,
where Marx's contribution was most likely the greater, but I have not found

a single occurrence of an honorific usage in writings of which Marx alone was the author.

The reason for this distinct verbal preference on Engels' part is not easy to explain. His rather long stay in England and his contact with the Chartists are scarcely sufficient reasons. On the other hand, we have not been able to discover any ideological difference between Marx and Engels during these four years, the years which were the first of their lifelong friendship and mutual co-operation.

It must also be added, however, that in spite of ambiguities and in spite of the difference between Engels and Marx concerning frequency in application, there is one feature which primarily characterizes their usage of "democracy" prior to 1848: the word is, to a marked extent, used appreciatively or pronounced with a positive evaluation, even with enthusiasm. This rule holds from the earliest of Marx's Philosophische Frühschriften up to the Communist Manifesto, although there were without doubt different degrees of enthusiasm, and also different premises for positive evaluation.

2. Marx and Engels during the February Revolution

All the following occurrences of "democracy" and related terms in the writings of Marx and Engels are to be found in the daily paper Neue Rheinische Zeitung, up to 1849. This paper appeared from 1 June 1848, with Marx as chief editor and Engels as one of the six members of the editorial board, and with Organ der Demokratie as its sub-title.

In general, the political articles of Marx and Engels during this period are to a very large extent linked with concrete and actual events. They are thus of a much less general kind than some of the political and historical essays on proletarian strategy which they had written in previous years. The character of these articles is also reflected in their application of "democracy", which mainly occurs in rather briefly elaborated statements.

In connection with one of his political attacks upon the Prussian Prime Minister, the bourgeois politician Hansemann, Engels referred in June to the editorial staff, and possibly also to his readers as "uns Demokraten."[42] But it is not possible to see what signification he attributed to the term, although it is significant to find "democrats" used in official self-denomination.

A few days later, Engels stated that the people consisted of the workers, and the democratic bourgeoisie, as opposed to the high bourgeoisie. A few lines later he used "democracy" to signify the contrast to the united reactionary parties of the nobility and the high bourgeoisie and also declared that acknowledgement of the Revolution

... das hiess die demokratische Seite der Revolution anerkennen gegenüber der hohen Bourgeoisie. [43]

"Democratic" and "democracy" in the sense of something opposed to the high bourgeoisie are also to be found in a later statement by Marx or Engels. With regard to the Ministry of Camphausen, it was said:

Im Dienst der grossen Bourgeoisie musste es [das Ministerium Camphausen] die Revolution um ihre demokratische Früchte zu prellen suchen, im Kampf mit der Demokratie musste es sich mit der aristokratischen

Partei verbünden und das Werkzeug ihrer kontrerevolutionären Gelüste werden. [44]

What was more directly meant by "democracy" and "democratic" is not clear, however. That the terms signified something opposed to the high bourgeoisie does not imply that they were used here to connote the rule of the proletariat, or something characterized by that rule. Such a usage might have been expected in accordance with the terminology of the Communist Manifesto, but such a use of "democracy" would have made an expression like "democratic bourgeoisie" self-contradictory. It must be emphasized that a particularly proletarian and communistic policy was not carried out by Marx and Engels during this first revolutionary year, although Neue Rheinische Zeitung was the only paper to defend the workers' uprising in Paris in June that year. Marx declared that it was the exclusive right of what he held to be the democratic press to give the laurels to the wounded and hungry proletarians in Paris, men who had been slaughtered by Cavaignac, whose leaders had been deported, and whose wives and children were thrown into boundless misery. [45] Neither Marx nor Engels, however, used "democracy" or "democratic" to characterize this attempted proletarian revolution. According to their revolutionary strategy, they, like Lenin and Trotsky, frequently asserted that every proletarian revolution was to succeed a bourgeois one. According to them, the February Revolution in France as well as the March revolution in Germany were certainly bourgeois or middle-class revolutions. Their attacks on the high bourgeoisie in Germany were caused by the miserable behaviour of this class during the March Revolution, which was, according to Marx and Engels, far from complete. It is most certainly this middle-class revolution which Marx or Engels had in mind when declaring:

Berlin ist nicht und wird nie werden der Sitz der Revolution, die Hauptstadt der Demokratie. [46]

"The seat of the revolution" here seems to be used synonymously with "the capital of democracy"; but as we have mentioned, "revolution" probably did not signify a proletarian or a communist revolution.

As regards the Polish question, and what they held to be Prussian crimes against Poland, Marx and Engels were absolutely in favour of a German revolutionary war against Russia:

Die Herstellung eines demokratischen Polens ist die erste Bedingung eines demokratischen Deutschlands.

The ruling German politicians, however, were not brave enough to claim Polish independence with arms in their hands, and they were also uneasy concerning the consequences of a revolutionary war, because

...der Krieg mit Russland war der vollständige, offne und wirkliche Bruch mit unsrer ganzen schmachvollen Vergangenheit, war die wirkliche Befreiung und Vereinigung Deutschlands, war die Herstellung der Demokratie auf den Trümmern der Feudalität und des kurzen Herrschaftstraums der Bourgeoisie. [47]

This attitude towards democracy as something which was to be built not only on the ruins of feudalism but also on the short bourgeois dream of political power may be taken to indicate that "democracy" was used here to connote a kind of proletarian rule. The last statement in particular about

the short bourgeois dream makes this indication probable. However, unlimited rule by the bourgeoisie was not at all what Marx and Engels had in
mind as the consequences of a middle-class revolution. They wished this
revolution to bring about the foundation of a centralized republic with universal suffrage, civil rights, public education, and some degree of nationalization of the means of communication, but by no means complete socialism.
It is probably the realization of these and similar aims which the authors
had in view when they stated that war against Russia would mean, <u>inter alia</u>,
the foundation of democracy, although we cannot exclude other possibilities.
This use of "democracy", associated with the middle-class revolution, was
probably typified in an occurrence like <u>Organ der Demokratie</u> which, as we
have mentioned, was the sub-title of the daily newspaper <u>Neue Rheinische
Zeitung.</u> This was the most frequent kind of occurrence of "democracy" in
that revolutionary year. What was directly meant by this use of "democracy" was not explained at the time. But the policy of the paper, to defend
consistently the extreme left factions in the middle-class revolution, to
forward the cause of the workers in special cases, but not to adopt a general socialist and communist policy, is quite a good indication.

Many years afterwards, in an article about Marx and <u>Neue Rheinische
Zeitung,</u> Engels stated that the contemporary proletariat in Germany had
been much too weak and politically too immature to form its own mass
party.

> Damit war uns, als wir in Deutschland eine grosse Zeitung begründeten,
> die Fahne von selbst gegeben. Es konnte nur die der Demokratie sein.[48]

This banner was to be that of a democracy which had a proletarian character
in particular questions. He added that the only alternative to this policy had
been to lecture on communism in a small and unimportant paper (<u>Winkel-
blättchen</u>), and to become a utopian sect instead of a political party.

This was written about thirty-five years later, and must therefore be
regarded with reserve from an historical and especially from a terminological point of view. It gives some explanation of the use of the term in
the sub-title of their newspaper, however.

When compared with their verbal application before the February
Revolution, this usage of "democracy" can in certain ways be said to have
a different signification from those attributed earlier to this term. Thus it
is evident that there is a difference between their usage in the newspaper
and in the <u>Communist Manifesto</u>, where "democracy" was directly used to
connote the rule of the proletariat. In several of Engels' statements the
term was used almost synonymously with "communism". On the other hand,
there were also occurrences in Engels' statements very similar to those in
the newspaper; Marx's application should especially be mentioned -- he
never used "democracy" with a signification identical with that of "communism", as, for example, in his speech on Poland in February 1848. Thus
if there were terminological differences in relation to their earlier application, there was also a certain terminological continuity; and February
1848 represented no definite verbal turning-point.

In 1848, however, Marx and Engels did not regard their paper as an
ordinary organ of the parliamentarian left. In their eyes the <u>Neue Rheinische Zeitung</u> was without doubt something extraordinary in German at that
time. Even if "democracy" can generally be said to have been used in an
honorific way and "democrats" in self-denomination, Marx and Engels
never identified themselves with everyone they designated as "democrats".

Wir haben es bei den vielfachen verschiedenen Elementen, aus denen
sich die demokratische Partei in Deutschland gebildet hat, im Gegenteil
für dringend nötig gehalten, niemand schärfer zu überwachen, als gerade
die Demokraten. [49]

Special attention was paid to the democrats, not because of any direct
danger from that camp, but because of the lack of energy, courage, and
political knowledge among democratic leaders, which might be, and even
was, very dangerous in special situations. The use of "democrats" in this
quotation hardly makes it possible that Marx and Engels would have used
"democrats" as a self-denomination at that precise moment. "Democrats"
here seems to designate an out-group in relation to the editorial staff of
Neue Rheinische Zeitung.

There is not much more to be said concerning the use of "democracy"
by Marx and Engels in the Neue Rheinische Zeitung during its period as a
newpaper. "Democracy" and related terms occur up to May 1849, when
this newpaper was suppressed and Marx was expelled from Germany. In
December 1848 Marx was one of the three members of what was termed
"die Rheinische Kreisausschuss der Demokraten", which called upon all
democrats to refuse to pay taxes to the Prussian government. [50]

During the first part of his stay in London, Marx was still of the opinion
that a new revolutionary wave would follow the defeats of 1848 and 1849. For
most of 1850, Marx and Engels were issuing the Neue Rheinische Zeitung
again, but now in the form of a periodical with Politisch-ökonomische Revue
and not Organ der Demokratie as its sub-title.

Occurrences of "democracy" are infrequent in this short-lived periodical. In the second number Marx spoke about the montagne as "der parla-
mentarischen Vorkämpfer der demokratischen Kleinbürgerschaft", and he
also proclaimed that, contrary to the solid class foundation of other parties,

...die Partei des Berges dagegen vertrat eine zwischen der Bourgeoisie
und dem Proletariat schwebende Masse, deren materielle Interessen
demokratische Institutionen verlangten. [51]

The association between "democratic" and "democrats", on the one
hand, and the petty bourgeoisie, on the other, is made much clearer in a
political pamphlet which Marx and Engels sent to different members of the
Kommunistenbund in Germany. Here "Die demokratische Partei" was
used synonymously with "die Partei der Kleinbürgerschaft". [52] A little later
on they stated that the treacherous part played by the German liberal bourgeoisie in 1848 would be taken over in the approaching revolution by the
democratic petty bourgeoisie. They even maintained that the Democratic
Party was much more dangerous to the workers than the earlier Liberal
Party.

Diese Partei, die demokratische, die den Arbeitern weit gefährlicher
ist als die frühere liberale, besteht aus drei Elementen. [53]

These elements were declared to be the progressive section of the higher
bourgeoisie, the democratic-constitutional petty bourgeoisie, and the republican petty bourgeoisie. According to Marx and Engels, the latter was
composed of men who had been members of democratic congresses and
committees, leaders of democratic unions, and editors of democratic news-
papers.

There are several other similar occurrences in this pamphlet. "Demo-

cratic" is used extensively to characterize petty bourgeois elements in
society, and the workers were further advised to form organizations independently of the democrats. In a letter which Marx wrote to Engels on 13
July 1851, this pamphlet was referred to as "au fond nichts als ein Kriegsplan gegen die Demokratie". [54]

When compared with their earlier application of "democracy" during
the February Revolution, there is a striking difference in attitude here
towards what was designated as "democracy". Although Marx and Engels
had used Organ der Demokratie as a sub-title of their paper for nearly one
year and had also used "democrats" extensively in self-denomination, such
an application was almost unthinkable after they had declared the Democratic Party to be an extreme danger for the workers, and especially after
Marx had described their political pamphlet as "nothing but a plan of war
against democracy". This does not in itself necessarily imply that "democracy" was used with a different signification from that of 1848. The term,
for example, in Marx's letter was used with a signification different from
that attributed to it in the Communist Manifesto, since synonymity in these
cases would have implied that Marx had written a pamphlet which he said
was nothing but "ein Kriegsplan gegen die Herrschaft des Proletariats";
this we can regard as an impossibility. This kind of difference, however,
does not imply any difference in signification between 1848 and 1850, since
their daily paper contained an application of "democracy" which in its turn
was also different from that in the Communist Manifesto. Further, Marx's
theory about the treacherous part played by the petty bourgeoisie was not
elaborated before his stay in London. Thus a new kind of revolutionary
strategy is revealed; this might have been sufficient reason for derogatory
use of a term which had been used in self-denomination two years earlier.
But the relevant texts do not furnish the foundation for any definite conclusion on this point. The change from a rather honorific to derogatory use
was mainly caused by a difference in political outlook, but the possibility
remains of a change in the signification of the term. If, for example,
"democrats" had been used in 1850 not only to denote people whose interests
were for the moment identical with those of the petty bourgeoisie but even
directly to connote people who per definitionem were representatives of that
social class, then a difference in the signification of this term would have
been mentioned. But nothing definite can be said at this time.

The pamphlet under discussion was written at a time when Marx and
Engels were convinced that there would very soon be a new revolution on
the Continent. This optimism disappeared during the summer, and in September of that year Marx strongly attacked those communists who were
dogmatic rather than critical, idealistic rather than materialistic, and who,
instead of analyzing the political situation, believed the proletarian will to be
the single revolutionary factor. According to Marx, the workers would
have to live through fifteen, twenty, or fifty years of civil wars, not to
change external conditions, but to change themselves. He concluded:

> Wie von den Demokraten das Wort Volk zu einem heiligen Wesen gemacht
> wird, so von euch das Wort Proletariat. Wie die Demokraten schiebt
> ihr der revolutionären Entwicklung die Phrase der Revolution unter. [55]

"Democrats" is used here, without reservation, to designate people
who subordinated the revolutionary development to the revolutionary phrase
by sanctifying the word "people", which without doubt indicates a derogatory application of "democrats".

Marx's new revolutionary strategy is evident in the last number of the
Neue Rheinische Zeitung. In a famous declaration, Marx asserted in
November 1850 that any revolution was unthinkable in periods of general
prosperity and that a new set of revolutions was possible only in connection
with a new economic crisis in bourgeois society, or when the forces of production collide with the bourgeois mode of production. Here, in short, is
the essence of all later Marxist revolutionary theory. In the same number
Marx also spoke about the concrete political situation. Concerning the
Chartists, Marx emphasized that the masses of really proletarian workers
belonged to revolutionary fractions. He also declared:

> Die Kleinbürger, die sich noch in der Partei befinden, verbunden mit
> der Aristokratie der Arbeiter, bilden eine reindemokratische Fraktion,
> deren Programm sich auf die Volkscharte und einige andere kleinbür-
> gerliche Reformen beschränkt. [56]

"Reindemokratisch" was probably a new term in Marx's vocabulary.
It is difficult to tell whether this term signified something different from the
connotation of unqualified "democratic". It is nevertheless of importance
that he used the term to describe a faction with a petty bourgeois program
and consisting predominantly of petty bourgeois elements. Feargus O'Connor was mentioned by Marx as the leader of this petty bourgeois faction of
the Chartists. Thus we once more find a close association between O'Connor and something characterized by "democratic" or some closely related
word. Although O'Connor, in 1846, had been personally complimented by
Marx and Engels for editing a journal which was declared to be really and
essentially democratic, "purely democratic" was now not connected with
any kind of laudable evaluation. In both cases it can further be seen that
O'Connor's policy was closely attached to the People's Charter; this may
indicate that the difference on this point was mainly a new way of estimating
this political program, and not so much of attributing a new signification to
"democratic".

In conclusion, it is this association between the petty bourgeoisie and
what was designated as "democracy" and related terms that characterizes
the use of this term during 1850. When compared with the earlier application, the nature of the difference may be said to have been of a somewhat
uncertain and complicated kind. In several places we have found the change
from honorific to derogatory use to have been caused more by changes in
political opinion than by change of a terminological kind, which implies that
we have been dealing to a greater degree with differences in conceptions
and not so much with a conceptual change. This does not eliminate terminological differences, however. Compared with the great changes in the
significations attributed to "democracy" by Proudhon and Tocqueville during
this period, these differences are smaller. They are nevertheless far from
unimportant, and they assume greater importance by comparison with some
trends in Engels' language before 1848.

The most marked characteristic in their use of "democracy" during the
years 1848-50 was the change from a clearly honorific to a clearly derogatory application. Of the several aspects in their terminology on this point,
the most general is reflected in the fact that the same men who began in
1848 by editing a journal, Organ der Demokratie, ended by writing a Kriegsplan gegen die Demokratie and by pronouncing reindemokratisch with contempt.

3. Marx and Engels after 1850

The first uses of "democracy" and related terms in the writings of Marx
after 1850 are to be found, like many of his earlier applications, within the
context of the February Revolution and the political events that followed in
France. Der achtzehnte Brumaire des Louis Bonaparte was written at the
beginning of 1852 and appeared first in America in the periodical Die Revolution, edited by Marx's friend Wedemayer. In this book Marx paid much
attention to the social and political functions of the petty bourgeoisie. He
admitted that the petty bourgeoisie was not guided by a fundamental kind of
class egotism, but that it believed instead that the special condition of re-
lease would be a general kind of reconciliation between classes. He continued:

> Man muss sich ebensowenig vorstellen, dass die demokratischen Reprä-
> sentanten nun alle shopkeepers sind oder für dieselben schwärmen. Sie
> können ihrer Bildung und ihrer individuellen Lage nach himmelweit von
> ihnen getrennt sein. Was sie zu Vertretern des Kleinbürgers macht, ist,
> dass sie im Kopfe nicht über die Schranken hinauskommen, worüber jener
> nicht im Leben hinauskommt, dass sie daher zu denselben Aufgaben und
> Lösungen theoretisch getrieben werden, wohin jene das materielle Inter-
> esse und gesellschaftliche Lage praktisch treiben. [57]

"Democratic representatives" here seems to have been used exclusively
to designate persons who were of necessity, and for ideological reasons,
representatives of the petty bourgeoisie. Marx admitted that these representatives might come from other social strata than the petty bourgeoisie, but
his statement that some kind of mental narrowness made them the representatives of that class was made without any reservations.

The signification here attributed to "democratic representatives" is
also attributed a little later on to "democrats". Concerning the lack of class-
consciousness of the democrats, Marx here declared,

> ... der Demokrat, weil er das Kleinbürgertum vertritt, also eine Über-
> gangsklasse, worin die Interessen zweier Klassen sich zugleich abstump-
> fen, dünkt sich über den Klassengegensatz überhaupt erhaben. [58]

Here is an application of "democrats" and "democratic representative"
very similar to that in his writings during 1850. The above quotations may
even be said to be defining statements about what Marx held to be democratic
representatives and democrats. It is probable that here Marx was of the
opinion that representation of the petty bourgeoisie was a factor which necessarily, or even per definitionem, was an essential mark of the connotation
attributed to "democratic representative" and "democrat". Thus in contrast
to 1850, there here seems to be an example of the use of "democrat" with
a signification which must differ from the one attributed to this term when
it was used in self-denomination during 1848.

Other derogatory applications occur frequently in this book. But Marx
did not only use the term "democrats" to designate politicians of whom he

disapproved. The term "Sozialdemokratie" is also used here in a derogatory way. Regarding the common program of socialists and bourgeois republicans in February 1849 and their formation of joint electoral committees,
Marx declared:

> Den sozialen Forderungen des Proletariats ward die revolutionäre Pointe
> abgebrochen und eine demokratische Wendung gegeben, den demokra-
> tischen Ansprücken des Kleinbürgertums die bloss politische Form ab-
> gestreift und ihre sozialistische Pointe herausgekehrt. So entstand die
> Sozialdemokratie.

Marx also used the expression "die neue Montagne" to characterize this
kind of political combination. As a further characterization of this political phenomenon, he stated:

> Der eigentümliche Character der Sozialdemokratie fasst sich dahin zu-
> sammen, dass demokratisch-republikanische Institutionen als Mittel ver-
> langt werden, nicht um zwei Extreme, Kapital und Lohnarbeit, beide auf-
> zuheben, sondern um ihren Gegensatz abzuschwächen und in Harmonie
> zu verwandeln. [59]

This definition of the proper character of social democracy is rather similar
to his definitions of the political function of the petty bourgeoisie. This fact
and especially the alleged reconciliation of class contradictions make it
certain that Marx did not approve of this political combination of proletarians
and petty bourgeoisie, which he named with a term that may be said to be
the counterpart of the English term "social democracy".

This book is Marx's last important work concerning the political events
of the February Revolution. It is also the last with frequent occurrences of
"democrats", "democratic", and related terms. The following decades
were very important years in the lives of Marx and Engels from a theoretical point of view; and after 1864, their important participation in the International Workmen's Association came about. But occurrences of "democracy" and related terms were few during this long period, especially when
compared with the frequency with which they were applied earlier.

The term is to be found in Marx's articles in the New York Tribune. In
regard to what he held to be the aggressive policy of Russia, Marx drew attention in April 1853 to the curved western frontier of that country. According to Marx, the Russian government was of the opinion that this frontier
needed regulation and that the natural frontier of Russia was from Danzig,
or even from Stettin, to Trieste. He drew attention to the relationship
between the revolutionary movements in the West and Russian absolutism:

> Russland ist entschieden eine Eroberernation und war es auch ein ganzes
> Jahrhundert lang, bis ihm die grosse Bewegung von 1789 einen furcht-
> baren Gegner voll lebendiger Tatkraft schuf. Wir meinen die europäische
> Revolution, die Explosivkraft der demokratischen Ideen und den der
> Menschheit eingeborenen Freiheitsdurst. Seit jener Zeit gab es tatsäch-
> lich bloss zwei Mächte auf dem europäischen Kontinent; Russland mit
> seinem Absolutismus, die Revolution mit der Demokratie. [60]

"Democracy" and "democratic ideas" are used here in a way which is
very closely associated with the revolutionary movements in Europe after
1789. What he meant directly by those terms is not quite clear. It is obvious that they are honorific; this is very different from a major part of
his usage of these terms after 1850. "Democracy" and "democratic" did

not signify something exclusively linked up with the socialist revolution, but were probably only associated with European revolution in general; the honorific application is without doubt because of the extremely great contrast between Russian absolutism and what he here held as democracy and democratic.

Almost the same application occurs nine days later, when Marx stated himself to be in favour of the creation of an independent Christian state on the ruins of European Turkey. He continued:

> Schon der nächste revolutionäre Vorstoss vermag den längst sich vorbereitenden Konflikt zwischen russischem Absolutismus und europäischer Demokratie herbeizuführen. [61]

Here, too, "European democracy" is conceived as signifying something opposed to Russian absolutism and associated with the onset of revolution. In these statements we find no association between what he held to be democracy and petty bourgeoisie, an association which had been very distinct a year earlier. In relation to the association between democracy and revolution, in these articles Marx seems to have returned temporarily to the terminology typical of most of his writings during 1848.

An application differing from the one in the New York Tribune occurs in a German newspaper two years later. In describing Palmerston, Marx maintained in 1855:

> Er versteht es, demokratische Phraseologie mit oligarchischen Ansichten zu verzöhnen; die Frieden predigende Bourgeoisie mit der hochfahrenden Sprache von Englands aristokratischer Vergangenheit zu decken. [62]

"Democratic phraseology" can be said to have been used here synonymously with "bourgeoisie preaching the cause of peace". Thus "democratic" was used to characterize something which Marx did not consider to be revolutionary, and it is also most probable that he did not use the term in an honorific way.

More concretely, by "democratic phraseology" Marx probably had in mind the pacifist argumentation rather common among the adherents of free trade. Under the leadership of Cobden and Bright these people did not support the war against Russia. Their attitude was thus diametrically opposed to that of Marx and Engels, who frequently called for a more energetic warfare. Thus "democratic" was used to characterize something contrary to Marx's political views.

Later, "democracy" and related terms become rather scarce in the writings of Marx and Engels. The term is not to be found in the Inaugural Address (1864), for example. There are, however, a few occurrences in letters from Marx to Engels, none of them honorific. On 7 September 1864, Marx wrote on the political situation during the presidental election in America. With regard to the possibility of political stability, he commented:

> Aber diese Wahlzeit ist in dem Musterland des Demokratenschwindels voll von Zufälligkeiten. [63]

Two years later, on 7 July 1866, Marx described the successful workers' demonstration which had been held in London. According to him, this demonstration was the biggest since 1849, and it had been led by an adherent of Marx and Engels. In conclusion Marx said:

Hier zeigt sich der Unterschied, wenn man hinter den Kulissen <u>wirkt</u> und öffentlich verschwindet, von der Demokratenmanier, öffentlich sich wichtig zu machen und <u>Nichts</u> zu tun. [64]

In addition, Marx's rough characterization of the political thinking of Wilhelm Liebknecht should be mentioned. On 10 August 1869, he asserted:

Das Vieh glaubt an den zukünftigen "Staat <u>der</u> Demokratie"! Unter der Hand ist das bald das konstitutionelle England, bald die bürgerliche Vereignigten Staaten, bald die elende Schweiz. Von revolutionärer Politik hat "es" keine Ahnung. [65]

It is difficult to see the significations of "democrats" and "democracy" as they are used in these passages. They have certainly been used to indicate phenomena of which he definitely disapproved; this excludes the possibility that, in these letters at least, Marx might have used "democrat" as a self-denomination, or was in favour of anything designated as "democracy". How far his terminology in these private letters was reflected in his public writings at that time is a question that must be left open, since it has not been possible to find any occurrences in his public writings before his discussion of the Commune in Paris.

In his important political analysis, <u>Der Bürgerkrieg in Frankreich</u>, of 1871, the revolutionary task of the proletariat was not only to conquer the organs of political power in the bourgeois State, but to destroy these organs and build up new ones. In regard to the Commune, Marx stated that this assembly had represented something quite different from ordinary parliamentary bodies. It had been a working instead of a talking assembly because it had not been confined to debates and legislation while leaving the executive power to another organ. By this policy, and by its organized popular defence, Marx maintained:

Die Kommune machte das Stichwort aller Bourgeoisrevolutionen -- Wohlfeile Regierung -- zur Wahrheit, indem sie die beiden grössten Ausgabequellen, die Armee und das Beamtentum, aufhob, ... Sie verschaffte der Republik die Grundlage wirklich demokratischer Einrichtungen. [66]

"Truly democratic institutions" is probably used to signify the kind of government which combined legislative and executive functions and organized a popular police and a popular army, as did the Commune. Marx continued, however:

Aber weder "wohlfeile Regierung", noch die "wahre Republik" war ihr Endziel; beide ergaben sich nebenbei und von selbst.

The final aim of the Commune was the abolition of private ownership of the means of production and thereby of class society. Democratic institutions in Marx's sense were, therefore, not the goal of the Commune but only a proper political means towards that end, even though this also indicates a rather central application of "democratic".

By declaring the political institutions of the Commune to be democratic, Marx used a kind of argument similar to that in his very early criticism of Hegel's political philosophy. Here, too, the State, until then a parasitic growth, was absorbed in the community, and was to be no longer superior to the nation. Political power was to be given to responsible servants of the people. Marx first of all had in mind permanent contact between electors and representatives and recall by the electorate of any representative at any time. In that way, man was no longer alienated from the State (even if the word "Entfremdung" was not used in 1871). Marx also contrasted this form of rule, where the governing body was servant and not master, with the usual form of rule, where the people decided once in three or six years which member of the ruling class in Parliament should represent and also crush the people. Thus "democratic", in spite of its infrequent usage, nevertheless occupies a fairly central position; and it is also important that Marx here used an argument and a terminology almost identical with that which we saw when "democracy" connoted the destruction of the riddle of the State and the restoration of popular rule on a purely human basis.

For the rest, "democracy" and related words are far from frequent in the terminology of the older Marx. No occurrences have been found in Das Kapital, nor did Marx use this term in his speech in Amsterdam in 1872, where he clearly admitted that socialism, in certain countries, might be achieved through peaceful means.

Although "democracy" was used in an honorific way in connection with the Commune, a somewhat different aspect can be seen in Marx's critique of the Gotha Program, in 1875. Here Marx spoke most ironically about the political principles of this program, which he deemed to contain nothing "ausser der alten weltbekannten demokratischen Litanei". Summing up, Marx said that this program on the one hand represented a typical obedient-subject attitude, influenced by Lassalle's followers, and on the other a democratic belief in utopias, both of which were alien to socialism. In his own words:

> Doch das ganze Programm, trotz alles demokratischen Geklingels, ist durch und durch vom Untertanenglauben der Lasalleschen Sekte an den Staat verpestet oder, was nicht besser, vom demokratischen Wunderglauben, oder vielmehr ist ein Kompromiss zwischen diesen zwei Sorten, dem Sozialismus gleich fernen, Wunderglauben. [67]

What exactly was meant by "democratic" is not absolutely clear in this statement, but it is certain that the word was used in a far from honorific way, and it seems first of all to have been written with the intention of creating some degree of indulgent contempt. It may be objected that Marx did not intend this critique to be published, since he sent it in a letter to Wilhelm Bracke and referred to it as "kritische Randglossen". In form, these critical comments resemble more a draft than a completed article. On the other hand, they can definitely not be regarded as accidental remarks, and Bracke was also explicitly told to forward the critique to leading socialists such as Auer, Bebel, and Liebknecht.

Comparing Marx's terminology with that of Engels', we find the somewhat strange phenomenon that while Engels frequently and Marx seldom used "democracy" before 1848, the contrary obtains after the February Revolution. Marx's use of "democracy" was generally sparse after 1852, but there are frequent occurrences in Der achtzehnte Brumaire. Nothing similar is at hand in Engels' writings. And in Engels' later years the term is used infrequently.

In Anti-Düring Engels used "bourgeois democracy" to indicate something which, contrary to what he termed "proletarian democracy", could not create a proletarian will among the toiling masses. [68] Unqualified "democracy", however, does not seem to appear in this extensive work.

In a letter to Bebel, dated 11 December 1884, Engels used "pure democracy" in a way which can be described as very derogatory. He declared that he was of the opinion that pure democracy was of less importance in Germany than in other countries having older industrial development.

Aber das verhindert nicht, dass sie [die reine Demokratie] im Moment der Revolution als äusserste bürgerliche Partei, -- als letzter Rettungsanker der ganzen bürgerlichen und selbst feudalen Wirtschaft momentan Bedeutung bekommen kann. Alles, was reaktionär war, gebärdet sich dann demokratisch. [69]

From other parts of the letter it can be seen that Engels primarily had in mind political developments in Germany between March and September 1848, and that his intention was to demonstrate that universal suffrage, in certain situations, might be the final sheet anchor of reaction against the revolutionary masses. Thus universal suffrage was an essential property of what Engels designated in this context as "pure democracy". He uses this expression in a derogatory way, not because he attributed to "democracy" a different signification from the one he used after 1848, but because he had probably developed a new way of estimating the political consequences of universal suffrage in special situations. The idea is probably a new element in Engels' political thinking. It may also be of some importance to note that Engels used "pure democracy" -- and not the unqualified term. This may perhaps be taken to indicate that he might have used "democracy" with a somewhat different signification, although it can also imply the opposite, in that unqualified "democratic" was used to characterize that kind of behaviour which could be adequate for political reactionists in certain situations.

In Der Ursprung der Familie des Privateigenthums und des Staats, of 1884, Engels' use of "democracy" and related terms is apparently limited to two occurrences of "democratic republic". "Democratic republic" is used on the first occasion to signify the most developed kind of State, in which only the final decisive struggle between the bourgeoisie and proletariat was to take place.

Die höchste Staatsform, die demokratische Republik, ... die Staatsform ist in der der letzte Entscheidungskampf zwischen Proletariat und Bourgeoisie allein ausgekämpft werden kann. [70]

He continued that, officially, the democratic republic was not aware of any differences in wealth. He added, however,

...in ihr [der demokratischen Republik] übt der Reichtum seine Macht indirekt, aber um so sichrer aus. Einerseits in der Form der direkten Beamtenkorruption, wofür Amerika klassisches Muster, andererseits in der Form der Allianz von Regierung und Börse,

and as examples of this form of alliance, Engels referred to France and to Switzerland. Engels admitted that this alliance between exchange and government was not restricted to democratic republics, but was also an important characteristic of countries like England and Germany. Thus the indirect but more secure influence of wealth cannot be regarded as a sufficient criterion of a form of rule being a democratic republic. Contemporary Germany and England are mentioned as examples of countries affected by such an influence, but without having such a form of government. On the other hand, some influence of wealth may be regarded as a necessary condition for a form of rule to be what Engels designated as a "democratic republic". This certainly excludes the possibility of any honorific application in this case and the possibility that the expression, as used here, might describe any kind of socialist rule.

A derogatory use of "democratic republic" also occurs in 1891 in Engels' preface to a new edition of Marx's analysis of the Commune in Paris. Engels referred here to the popular belief that something important and brave had been achieved in abandoning the hereditary monarchy and preferring a democratic republic. He was of another opinion, however:

> In Wirklichkeit aber ist der Staat nichts als eine Maschine zur Unterdrückung einer Klasse durch eine andere, und zwar in der demokratischen Republik nicht minder als in der Monarchie. [71]

Judging by the context, it is probable that he regarded a democratic republic as a machine by which the bourgeoisie suppressed the proletariat and not vice versa. At almost the same point, however, and like Marx twenty years earlier, Engels referred to the policy of the Commune, as

> ...diese Sprengung der bisherige Staatsmacht und ihre Ersetzung durch eine neue, in Wahrheit demokratische. ...[72]

He also stated that the Commune meant the dictatorship of the proletariat.[73] It can thus be seen that "truly democratic" could be used to characterize a State executing the class rule of the proletariat, while "democratic republic", in the same place, was probably used to signify an organ of bourgeois suppression. This indicates an ambiguous use of "democratic".

A related kind of ambiguity occurs in one of Engels' last political writings. In his critique of the socialist program which was later adopted at Erfurt in 1892, Engels drew attention to the fact that no antimonarchical policy was included in it.

> Wenn etwas feststeht, so ist es dies, dass unsere Partei und die Arbeiterklasse nur zur Herrschaft kommen kann unter der Form der demokratischen Republik. Diese ist sogar die spezifike Form für die Diktatur des Proletariats, wie schon die grosse französische Revolution gezeigt hat. [74]

What he held as a democratic republic here seems, at least with regard to its form, to be identical with the dictatorship of the proletariat. This conforms with his opinion of the Commune as truly democratic but contradicts other items of his terminology. In the same text, however, Engels referred to "demokratische Republiken wie Frankreich und Amerika".[75] Apart from this classification of France and America among the denotata of "democratic republics", nothing reveals what he meant by this expression. But since it is most probable that Engels held the dictatorship of the proletariat to be different from the kind of rule which was to be found in America and France, it can be inferred that "democratic republic" was used here with two different significations.

There is a marked difference between the frequency with which this term was applied by Engels up to 1850 and its relative sparseness during his last forty-five years. As a fairly typical example it can be mentioned that "democracy" does not occur in his moderate and even reformist introduction to a new edition of Marx's <u>Die Klassenkämpfe in Frankreich</u>, of 1895. This introduction was his last political writing. With regard to honorific versus derogatory application, varying trends are noted; but in general, Engels after 1850 was very different from the Engels who asserted in 1845: "Die Demokratie das ist heutzutage der Kommunismus. "

Neither Marx nor Engels made frequent use of "democracy" and related terms after Marx had written Der achtzehnte Brumaire des Louis Bonaparte in 1852, and their later application of the term is somewhat arbitrary and peripheral. It is possible that a complete Gesamtausgabe, the non-existence of which all researchers in the history of ideologies deplore, might have provided more evidence. But, even a complete edition of the writings of Marx and Engels would have failed to furnish rich material from the latter half of their lives. By far the greater part of their application of "democracy" is to be found before, during, and shortly after the February Revolution. Here there is a distinct verbal difference between Marx and Engels. Although most occurrences in Engels' language occurred in what he wrote prior to 1848 and were of an honorific kind, a contrary relationship is evident in Marx's terminology. Marx seldom used this word before 1848, but applied it frequently shortly after that time, generally, apart from his use in the Neue Rheinische Zeitung, in a derogatory way. The best example is without doubt the terminology in Der achtzehnte Brumaire, the only one of Marx's printed works to contain frequent application of the term, where it was used to indicate something which he regarded as being dangerous for the struggle of the proletariat.

CHAPTER X

LIBERALISM AND RADICALISM

1. John Stuart Mill

Here, as in several other chapters in this work, difficulties arise of grouping together different political thinkers in one chapter. The political thinkers discussed under this heading present a fairly heterogeneous picture. On the one hand, John Stuart Mill, John Austin, and probably also Sidgwick can be classified as Utilitarians, although their opinions often differ from those of the original Utilitarians; on the other, it is difficult to find much in common between such thinkers as Herbert Spencer, Green, Bagehot, and Masaryk. That they are not discussed in separate chapters is partly due to their generally infrequent use of the term "democracy". And in any case the most important sections of this chapter are without doubt those concerning John Stuart Mill, Austin, and Sidgwick. Among these, John Stuart Mill stands out. His use of "democracy" covers an important section of the use in the nineteenth century taken as a whole. In his terminology, and in his writings, there is a concentrated elaboration of the problems under discussion among the most important liberal ideologists. In his political philosophy as well as in his political language there are, for example, trends similar to those we have seen in persons as different from one another as Bentham and Tocqueville, even though his thinking as well as his terminology are very much his own.

Of the Utilitarians, whereas Bentham used "democracy" almost exclusively in an honorific way and James Mill rejected what he designated as "democracy" because he considered it to be a direct form of rule, the application in John Stuart Mill's terminology is somewhat varied. This application is partly to be found in connection with his criticism of earlier Utilitarian views, and elsewhere reveals key points of his political philosophy.

Chronologically the earliest use of "democracy" in Mill's writings probably occurs in a short untitled essay in London Review of 1835, when Mill was twenty-nine years old. In this essay he maintained that government by a select body, and not by the public collectively, was an essential condition of good government. Political questions should not be decided by appealing to the judgement or the will of the uninstructed masses but by the deliberately formed opinions of the few who were especially educated for the task. He admitted this element of good government had seldom been present in aristocracies, certainly not in the British aristocracy. On the other hand, the aristocracies of Rome, Venice, and Holland could be considered to have been hard-working and experienced. The best form of government, according to Mill, however, was to be found in Prussia, which was governed by a powerful and strongly organized aristocracy of the most highly educated men in the kingdom.

This is a rather strong view in favour of the rule of the enlightened few. Mill stated of democracy:

The idea of a rational democracy is, not that the people themselves govern, but that they have security for good government. [1]

According to Mill, the people were to have security for good government by retaining ultimate control in their own hands. The qualification "rational" is probably used with the intention of distinguishing this kind of democracy, of which he approved, from other kinds of government termed "democracy", of which he did not approve.

Mill further stated that the interest of the people lay in choosing as their rulers the most instructed and able persons that could be found and in allowing them to exercise their knowledge and ability for the good of the people under the control of free discussion. Mill was clearly of the opinion that

... a democracy thus administrated would unite all the good qualities ever possessed by any government. [2]

It can be seen, however, that Mill was not certain whether what he designated as the "constitution of democracy itself" would provide adequate security for its being understood in that spirit. And he feared that the people would not only restrict their power to that of ultimate control but would possibly interfere in the government and make their legislators mere delegates for carrying into execution the preconceived judgement of the majority. According to Mill:

If the people do this, they mistake their interest; and such a government, though better than most aristocracies, is not the kind of democracy which wise men desire. [3]

A few lines later, this form of government is called the "perversion of the true idea of an enlightened democracy".

These statements suggest that Mill was operating with two rather different concepts, "rational democracy" and "enlightened democracy" being conceptual designations of one, and "perversion of the true idea of enlightened democracy" that of the other. These concepts were probably species of a genus 'democracy' with "constitution of democracy itself" and possibly unqualified "democracy" as conceptual designations. It is clear that he approved of the former species and disapproved of the latter, and this probably made his attitude towards the genus somewhat reserved; this is rather evident in his comment that the constitution of democracy itself was probably not a sufficient condition for rational government.

Mill's fear of unlimited popular government and his favouring the rule of the enlightened few were most probably due to his belief that the people were not capable of judging their own interests. From an ideological point of view, there is a rather important difference in relation to the earlier Utilitarian views of Bentham and James Mill.

A year later, Mill declared:

The triumph of democracy, or in other words, of the government of public opinion, does not depend upon any individual or set of individuals that it ought to triumph, but upon the natural laws of the progress of wealth, upon the diffusion of reading, and increase of the facilities of human intercourse. [4]

"Democracy" is certainly used here synonymously with "government of public opinion", and it can be observed that Mill here did not speak about different kinds of democracies. He only stated that the triumph of that kind of government depended on the progress of wealth and the general level of education among the masses. Mill went on to say that for a rational person there were only two positions which it was possible to adopt with regard to the advance of democracy. One should either aid the democratic movement, if it was thought that the masses were prepared for complete political control over their government, or exert one's utmost efforts in contributing to prepare them, if it was thought that the masses were unprepared. Which alternative he himself preferred is not mentioned but I assume that he was in favour of the latter.

Like Tocqueville, Mill seems here to regard the democratic movement as inevitable. This essay is also influenced by Tocqueville's ideas on many points: Mill includes, for example, a quotation from the first part of De la Démocratie en Amérique. But unlike Tocqueville, who generally used "democracy" synonymously with "social equality", Mill seems generally to have restricted this term to signify a certain kind of rule.

The difference between his terminology and that of Tocqueville is possibly best explained in his review of De la Démocratie en Amérique. Here Mill stated that it was necessary to observe that by "democracy" Tocqueville did not in general mean any particular form of government and that he could conceive of a democracy under an absolute monarch. Mill continued:

> By Democracy, M. de Tocqueville understands equality of conditions; the absence of all aristocracy, whether constituted by political privileges, or by superiority in individual importance and social power. It is towards Democracy in this sense, towards equality between man and man, that he conceives society to be irresistibly tending. Towards Democracy in the other, and more common sense, it may or may not be travelling. [5]

Here Mill is not directly contrasting his own use of "democracy" with that of Tocqueville. By referring to what he held as the other, the more common sense of the term, however, he intended to include his own application of "democracy" in that terminological trend.

Somewhat later on in this review, however, Mill used "democracy" other than as the expression of a political concept. Concerning the political future of England, Mill stated that the power which was to succeed that of the aristocracy was not that of the numerical majority, but that of the middle class. He added:

> The middle class in this country is as little in danger of being outstripped by the democracy below, as being kept down by the aristocracy above. [6]

"Democracy" is clearly used here to signify the social strata below the middle class, which contradicts my hypothetical conclusions concerning the implications of his statements about Tocqueville's terminology, and which also differs from his general tendency to let "democracy" connote a political form of rule.

In this same review, however, we find an application of the term which directly contradicts the above signification. Two pages later, Mill repeated that the government of England was progressively changing from the government of the few to the government, not of the many, but of many, or the middle class. He went on to say:

> To most purposes, in the constitution of modern society, the government of a numerous middle class is democracy. Nay, it not merely is democ-

racy, but the only democracy of which there is yet any example; what is called universal suffrage in America arising from the fact that America is all middle class.

Thus, Mill considered democracy to be identical with the government by the middle class. Universal suffrage was not incompatible with granting the label "democracy" to a form of rule, but neither was it a sufficient or a necessary property for a State to be a democracy according to Mill's criteria at this point. It can be added that universal suffrage most certainly was only compatible with a State being a democracy if, or in so far as, the people corresponded with what Mill considered to be the middle class. The initial part of the statement, that democracy "to most purposes" was the government of the middle class, may be taken to indicate some degree of reservation. However, by his going on to say that such a form of government was not only democracy, but the only form of democracy that had ever existed in practice, every reservation seems to have been eliminated.

This application can most probably be regarded as the first according to which "democracy" was used exclusively to connote the political rule of the middle class, and where it hardly mattered whether or not the middle class represented a majority of the population. Compared with Mill's earlier use of the term, this application represents a terminological change. The difference is most evident when this application is compared with the one in this same essay where "democracy" was used to signify the social strata below the middle class. But there is no association and no identification of rule of the middle class with democracy in statements where "democracy" was used to express a purely political concept.

From a general point of view, it can tentatively be said that Mill's early use of "democracy" reveals a somewhat varied picture with regard to the signification he attributed to this term. Ideologically these ways of using the term generally display some degree of fear of the rule of the uneducated masses, a phenomenon which is primarily present in his identification of democracy with the rule of the middle class.

A somewhat different picture is found in Mill's defence of revolutionary rule in France after the February Revolution. Replying to the criticisms of Lord Brougham, Mill stated that he agreed with him that there were no original ideas in the revolutionary constitution. According to Lord Brougham, this was a great fault, whereas Mill held that

... it [the constitution] is, in fact, a digest of the elementary doctrine of representative democracy. ... To those who disapprove of democracy, it is, of course, unacceptable. [7]

Why Mill should have used the term "representative democracy" and not unqualified "democracy" is not clear, since he apparently never used the unqualified term to connote a form of direct popular government. It is most probable that he here used "representative democracy" as well as "democracy" to signify a kind of government based upon universal male suffrage in a country where the greater part of the population did not belong to what Mill held as middle class. Thus we can speak of a difference in the signification of the term when compared with this last application of "democracy".

Mill evidently considered himself to be in favour of what he designated as "democracy" and "representative democracy". A somewhat similar application of "democratic" also occurs in an essay a little later, in which Mill declared that:

It is not among men of talent, sprung from the people and patronized and flattered by the aristocracy, that we look for leaders of a democratic movement. [8]

Here Mill probably regarded himself as belonging to that movement which he described as "democratic". Mill's attitude towards rule based upon universal suffrage seems to have become much more positive during the period of the February Revolution; this probably influenced his use of "democracy", although the material on this point is rather meagre.

Honorific applications of "democracy" and "democratic" are found in a private letter dated 1858. Mill here, inter alia, wrote:

...the representation of minorities seems to me not only a good but highly democratic measure. The ideal of a democracy is not that a mere majority of the people should have all the representation, but that if possible every portion of the constituency should possess an influence in the election proportional to its numbers. [9]

Proportional representation, or a representation of minorities, also, is one of Mill's favourite political tenets. It is evidence of an honorific application that he here associated proportional representation with what he termed "democratic measure" and "ideal of democracy". Proportional representation was implicit in the signification of the "ideal of democracy" as used here.

Honorific application does not occur in his famous work On Liberty, 1859, however, in which I have been able to find only a rare use of "democratic" and none of "democracy".

One of Mill's main ideas in this work was that the individual was not only in need of protection against the tyranny of one or that of the few but that the tyranny of the majority should also be included among the evils against which modern society ought to be on its guard, especially the tyranny of the prevailing opinion and feeling and the tendency of society to impose its own ideas and rules of conduct on those who dissented from them.

Mill admitted that tyrannical government had generally been of an aristocratic or monarchical kind. Probably in criticism of earlier Utilitarians, he went on to say that he could not agree with what he held to be the thought common among the last generation of European liberalists that the nation did not need to be protected against its own will and that there was no danger of its tyrannizing over itself. According to Mill:

In time, however, a democratic republic came to occupy a large portion of the earth's surface, and made itself felt as one of the most powerful members of the community of nations; and elective and responsible government became subject to the observations and criticisms which wait upon a great existing fact. [10]

Here the United States most certainly represents the denotatum of "democratic republic". Mill continued by referring to the fact that it was perceived that such phrases as "self-government" and "the power of the people over themselves" did not express the true state of the case. Mill himself is here fairly reserved in his judgement; for him "democratic republic" did not signify a rule which was necessarily a tyranny of the majority; on the other hand, it is characteristic of his terminology in this work that he did not consider such tyranny to be incompatible with what he labelled with this expression.

Other uses of "democratic" in this work also occur in connection with references to the tyranny of prevailing opinion. Here he drew attention first to the fact that whenever the Puritans had been sufficiently powerful, they had endeavoured to suppress all public and nearly all private amusements, such as music, dancing, and the theatre. Describing another more likely contingency, he declared:

> There is confessedly a strong tendency in the modern world towards a democratic constitution of society, accompanied or not by popular political institutions. It is affirmed that in the country where this tendency is most completely realized -- where both society and government are most democratic -- The United States -- the feeling of the majority, to whom any appearance of a more showy or costly style of living than they can hope to rival is disagreeable, operates as a tolerably effectual sumptuary law, and that in many parts of the Union it is really difficult for a person possessing a very large income, to find any mode of spending it, which will not incur popular disapprobation. [11]

There is here some similarity between Mill's terminology and the greater part of that of Tocqueville. Mill, too, could use "democratic constitution of society" as signifying a kind of society which was not necessarily governed in a popular way, and he probably used that expression to connote society marked by some degree of social equality. Mill further admitted that statements like the one above were doubtless exaggerated, but he also added:

> The state of things they describe is not only conceivable and possible, but a probable result of democratic feeling, combined with the notion that the public has a right to a veto on the manner in which individuals shall spend their incomes. [12]

Since Mill made special mention of the public veto as being combined with democratic feeling, it is rather certain that this public veto is not included in the signification of "democratic feeling" as he used it here. "Democratic feeling" may therefore be taken to signify a feeling in favour of a plain way of life. Even if "democratic feeling" was not used to connote such popular veto, it is fairly certain that what Mill designated as "democratic feeling", "democratic society", and "democratic government" were compatible with such a public veto by the prevailing majority opinion.

These uses of "democratic" seem to be the only occurrences to be found in this central work, and it cannot be said that this term has been used here in an honorific way.

A more frequent use of "democracy" and related terms occurs in Thoughts on Parliamentary Reform of the same year. "Democratic reformers" is used to describe those politicians with whom Mill disagreed on certain political principles. Mill agreed with those reformers in looking forward to universal suffrage as an ultimate aim. But he dissented from them in the matter of the equal individual vote. According to Mill, human beings were far from equal in worth, and he was in favour of a plurality of votes for those who could afford a reasonable presumption of superior knowledge and cultivation. [13] Mill did not say directly whether or not this plurality of votes for certain citizens was compatible with what he held to be democracy. His disagreement with those whom he designated as "democratic reformers" may be taken to indicate that he was in favour of a relationship of incompatibility, and it is likely that Mill would not have used "democratic reformers" as a self-denomination when writing this statement.

Mill later on wrote on the representation of minorities:

> I am inclined to think that the prejudice which undoubtedly exists in the minds of democrats against this principle, arises only from their having not sufficiently considered its mode of operation. It is an eminently democratic principle. The elementary propositions of the democratic creed imply it as an inevitable corollary.[14]

This application of "democratic" is very similar to that occuring in a private letter the previous year.[15] Here the representation of minorities is described, as in one of his earlier statements, as an inevitable implication of even the elementary propositions of what he designated "democratic creed". This implies that, according to Mill, no one could support what he held to be the democratic creed without being in favour of the representation of minorities, at least having considered the mode of operation of this representation sufficiently. This kind of honorific use of "democratic principle" and "democratic creed", however, does not necessarily imply that Mill was in favour of what he held to be the democratic creed and democratic principle. Mill was here in favour of <u>one</u> implication only of what he designated "democratic creed", and he did not say anything about eventual other implications. His rejection of equal suffrage may make a possible favouring of the other implications less likely.

In <u>Considerations on Representative Government</u> of 1861, the work which contains his most frequent use of "democracy", Mill returns to the question of the representation of minorities. Starting with a meta-occurrence, Mill declared:

> Two very different ideas are usually confounded under the name democracy. The pure idea of democracy, according to its definition, is the government of the whole people by the whole people, equally represented. Democracy as commonly conceived and hitherto practiced, is the government of the whole people by a mere majority of the people, exclusively represented.[16]

Here he stated that popular rule by proportional representation was the definition of what was designated the "pure idea of democracy". By contrasting the pure idea of democracy with what he held as the current conception of democracy and of democratical policy and by pointing out that two very different ideas were confounded under the name "democracy", Mill draws an important line of demarcation between his own terminology and what he considered to be the vernacular. Mill also asserted that non-proportional representation was not only contrary to all just government

> ...but above all, contrary to the principle of democracy, which professes equality as its very root and foundation.[17]

What Mill here considered to be the current signification of "democracy" he first stated to be very different from the pure idea of democracy and, secondly, to be contrary to what he held to be the principles of democracy. These statements constitute a good foundation for labelling the general application of the term a "misuse of the term "democracy"." Somewhat later Mill also said proportional representation of minorities represents "the only true type of democracy", while the others were referred to as

... the falsely-called democracies which now prevail, and from which the current idea of democracy is exclusively derived. [18]

The latter kind of government was described as that government "which now usurps the name of democracy", and it was also referred to much later in the work as "that falsely called democracy". [19] These charges of misuse of "democracy" represent an unusual phenomenon in disputes concerning political language in that the predominant use of the term is declared to be a misuse and a terminological usurpation.

Mill even included the American form of government among these "false democracies". He asserted that:

> In the false democracy which, instead of giving representation to all, gives only to the local majorities, the voice of the instructed minority may have no organs at all in the representative body.

In support of this view, Mill went on to say that it was an admitted fact that the highly cultivated members of the community, except those who were willing to become the servile mouthpieces of inferior minds and to sacrifice their own opinions, did not even offer to stand for Congress or the State legislatures in what he described as the "American democracy, which is constructed on this faulty model." [20] A few pages later, and in contrast to the probably moderate character of the future English democracy, Mill said;

> ... in the United States, where the numerical majority have long been in full posession of collective despotism, they would probably be as unwilling to part with it as a single despot, or an aristocracy. [21]

These statements imply that the United States, according to Mill's criteria, had a form of government which was a false democracy, or a form of government which usurped the title of "democracy". This accusation of terminological misuse contradicts other parts of his writings. In On Liberty, for example, he declared that America had a democratic form of government. And even in the work under discussion, after having once more outlined the difference between the true and false types of democracy, Mill referred to America as belonging to the former and not the latter type. [22]

With regard to his attitude towards different kinds of popular rule, Mill's dislike of government by a mere majority of the people is very evident. But he expressed no unreserved positive judgement in favour of popular rule with proportional representation either. This form of government was, according to him, the only true type of democracy as contrasted with the government which usurped the name "democracy". Mill held that, even in a real democracy, absolute power on behalf of the numerical majority was no impossibility. In that case the numerical majority could be exclusively composed of a single class, alike in biases, prepossessions, and general modes of thinking which were very different from those of the most cultivated. He concluded:

> The constitution would therefore still be liable to the characteristic evils of class government. [23]

He admitted, however, that this liability would be much smaller than under the kind of government which usurped the name of "democracy". Absolute power and class government were thus phenomena which, in Mill's view, were not incompatible with what he designated as "the only true type of democracy". On the other hand, he mentioned that democratic institutions had produced a marked superiority of mental development among the lowest class of Americans when compared with the corresponding classes in England and elsewhere. He asserted that political life in America was a most valuable school, but he was also of the opinion that it was a school from which the ablest teachers were excluded, as the first minds in the country were as much kept out of public functions as if they were under formal disqualification. How far he attributed such phenomena to a general concept 'democracy' and not merely to 'American democracy' is not clear, however. But he certainly considered such phenomena to be compatible with what correctly could be designated as "democracy". In contradiction to some earlier statements, here is another clear example of his opinion that the American form of rule belonged to the correct kind of democracy and that it did not usurp the name "democracy".

In this work Mill was also the spokesman for plurality of votes for certain qualified groups in order to counterbalance the power of the majority. [24] He was also in favour of some kind of second chamber composed of all living public men who had held important political office or employment. [25] He described this organ as representing a centre of resistance to the predominant power in a constitution,

> ...and in a democratic constitution, therefore, a nucleus of resistance to democracy. [26]

A second chamber was thus not incompatible with what he designated as a "democratic constitution", even if it was also declared to be "a nucleus of resistance to democracy." By this last expression Mill probably meant something like a checking body, or a moderator of rule by the numerical majority. I can find no direct evidence whether or not a system of plural votes was compatible with what Mill designated as "democracy". However, he introduced this discussion:

> Democracy is not the ideally best form of government, -- unless it is so organized that no class, not even the most numerous, shall be able to reduce all but itself to political insignificance. [27]

It is fairly certain that he regarded plurality of votes as one of the means of preventing such abuse. This may be taken to indicate that, according to Mill, a form of government might be characterized by plurality of votes for certain qualified groups without losing the label "democracy".

Two of his letters include important statements concerning democracy. During the American Civil War, he wrote that he hoped this great trial of American institutions would do the work of a whole age in stimulating thoughts on the most important topics. He continued:

> I have long thought that the real ultimate danger of democracy was intellectual stagnation, and there is a very good side to anything which has made that impossible for at least a generation to come. [28]

It is not clear why Mill had changed his opinion, however. A little more than one and a half years later, Mill stated in another letter that if Tocqueville had lived to see what had become of the States thirty years after he saw them, he would have acknowledged that many of his unfavourable anticipations had not been realized. Mill added:

> Democracy has been no leveller there as to intellect and education, or respect for true personal superiority. Nor has it stereotyped a particular cast of thought. [29]

It must be observed, however, that democracy as conceived in these letters is something whose results were not absolutely incompatible with intellectual stagnation and stereotyped thought. Mill only said that intellectual stagnation as the result of democracy was impossible for at least a generation, and that democracy in America had been no leveller of intellect and education. These points are nevertheless rather important.

Mill had changed his opinion concerning democracy and intellectual stagnation because of similar thoughts. From an ideological point of view it is naturally of the greatest interest to discover that Mill, in 1863, declared that he had long thought intellectual stagnation to be the ultimate danger of democracy. This point is seldom mentioned directly in any of his writings, although the problem was clearly presented in On Liberty. But this different outlook is probably of no great importance concerning the signification attributed to "democracy". When, for example, Mill said that democracy in America had become no leveller as to intellect, education, and personal superiority, or when he spoke about his earlier fear of intellectual stagnation, these statements can most certainly be regarded as synthetic and not as analytic ones. In neither case are we faced with properties which were conceptually attributed to what he designated as "democracy". Thus neither the absence nor the presence of intellectual stagnation was included in the signification of "democracy" as used in these letters, and such an application seems to be fairly typical of a greater part of his application of this term.

In his Autobiography, referring to his political opinion during what he held to be the third period of his mental progress, the years after 1840, Mill stated that private property and inheritance appeared to him as the dernier mot of legislation, although he wished to abolish primogeniture and entails. Concerning the improvement of the condition of the poor, he had hoped that universal education, leading to voluntary restraint on population, might make the situation of the poor more tolerable. Summing up, he said

... in short, I was a democrat, but not the least a socialist. [30]

It is here difficult to discover more concretely what he intended to convey by "democrat". It is evident that he used the term as self-denomination and that the term was used with a signification different from that of "socialist", as the label for a man who, unlike the socialists, wished to cure social ills with a higher degree of education.

"Democrat" is also used in self-denomination where he discusses writing On Liberty and refers to the great part played by Mrs. Taylor in its composition. Mill acknowledged that a great many of the ideas in the book were inspired by her, and he added:

There was a moment in my mental progress when I might easily have fallen into a tendency towards over-government, both social and political; as there was also a moment when, by reaction from a contrary excess, I might have become a less thorough radical and democrat than I am. [31]

The process of becoming a radical and a democrat is here contrasted with a negative attitude towards over-government; or perhaps democracy is contrasted with laissez-faire. This statement naturally does not convey much, except that it probably shows that a democrat was a man in favour of some degree of State intervention. With his other statement in view, we may therefore conclude that Mill here considered a democrat to be different from a socialist as well as from an adherent of laissez-faire.

Of his parliamentary life Mill relates that some conservatives had hoped to find an opponent of democracy in him,

> ... as I had shown in my political writings that I was aware of the weak points in democratic opinions.

If the Tories had really read his writings, however,

> ... they would have known that after giving full weight to all that appeared to me well grounded in the argument against democracy, I unhesitatingly decided in its favour, while recommending that it should be accompanied by such institutions as were consistent with its principle and calculated to ward off its inconveniences. [32]

Mill here mentioned proportional representation and plural voting.

This use of "democracy" is the last one I can find in the writings of Mill. He considered proportional representation and plural voting for certain groups to be perfectly compatible with what was designated as "democracy", but, on the other hand, there is no evidence that Mill regarded any of these properties as necessary for a form of rule to be called a "democracy". From a political point of view, this attitude towards proportional representation is very similar to the views presented in Considerations on Representative Government.

"Democracy" is used here with a somewhat different signification from the one used in the latter work in which proportional representation was regarded as an absolutely necessary condition for a State to be correctly designated as a "democracy".

Mill wished to secure a preponderance of talents and learning by giving as much as ten votes to the most highly educated, while unskilled workers would possess a single vote only. Mill feared rule by the uneducated masses. In Considerations on Representative Government, Mill held such an unequal system to be subsumable under what he designated as "democracy". This can be regarded as a peculiarity in Mill's terminology, since other political thinkers, from different points of view, would probably declare such a system to be definitely incompatible with what was labelled with this term.

Mill greatly favoured a system of democracy which would include proportional representation and plural voting. He even held such kind of government to be the best form of rule. There were other kinds of democracies of which he not was in favour, however, such as democracy without proportional representation. Such a relationship is generally apt to make an honorific use of "democracy" a somewhat conditional one. Mill's attitude towards what he designated as "democracy" in this last quotation is probably somewhat more reserved than can be seen at a first reading.

Mill's somewhat reserved attitude on this point is a fairly consistent trend in his use of the term. This general absence of a clearly honorific application is caused at least in part by the nature of the significations attributed to "democracy" -- significations which are somewhat, but generally not very, different and in which a fairly wide connotation is a general characteristic. More concretely, this absence can be regarded as conditioned by repeated ways of operating with rather broad concepts, or genera, 'democracy' covering several different species, of which some were held to be favourable for the promotion of intellectual liberty and others not. This implies that Mill could not have considered absence of liberty to be a necessary condition for a form of State to be labelled "democracy"; on the other hand, it cannot be concluded that the presence of liberty would necessarily have been included in such a denomination, which would have been necessary for an unreserved honorific application by Mill.

2. Austin

John Austin, another Utilitarian, introduced his <u>Plea for the Constitution</u>, 1859, by saying that in his youth his great admiration for Bentham had naturally led him to accept Bentham's political opinions without sufficient examination. Although his admiration for Bentham's genius had increased in intensity, he now dissented from many of Bentham's views on law and on various related subjects. He was of the opinion, for example, that the bulk of the working class was not yet qualified for political power, and that the lower classes and the middle class ought not to predominate in the House of Commons. He further maintained that the aristocratic elements in the constitution were necessary, although he stressed that he was by no means a worshipper of the great and the rich and their style of living.

In considering whether the British government ought to be classed with aristocracies or democracies, it was necessary first of all, according to Austin, to distinguish between the larger body in which the supreme power ultimately resides, the <u>forma imperii</u>, or the form and nature of sovereignty itself, <u>and</u> the comparatively minute body by which supreme power was exercised, the <u>forma regiminis</u>, or the form of the <u>gestion</u> or management, which gave sovereignty practical effect. In relation to the first of these distinctions, Austin held sovereignty in England to reside in the King, the House of Lords, and the electoral body of the Commons. He went on to say:

> With regard to the form of the sovereignty, the British Government is decidedly more democratical than any other assignable government which has governed a great nation through a long and eventful period. [33]

As proof of his argument, Austin stated that when the population of Attica was compared with that of the United Kingdom, and when the number of the sovereign Athenian people was compared with the popular body which was sovereign in England, one would probably find that the latter body was relatively larger. The condition for a <u>form</u> of sovereignty to be what he characterized as "democratic" seems therefore to be exclusively dependent on the relationship between the number of sovereign people and the number of inhabitants. Austin did not give any concrete information about the conditions for a form of sovereignty to be democratic, but the characterization of the form of sovereignty of the British government of 1859 certainly excludes the possibility that he might have held universal suffrage, or even suffrage for a majority of the male adult population, to be a necessary condition for a form of sovereignty being characterized by "democratic".

Austin admitted, however, that

> ... the federal government of the North American Union, and the separate governments of the several United States, are certainly more democratical than the government of the mother country.

But he added that the solidity of those governments had not been tried by time and, further, that the singular natural advantages, economic and otherwise, with which these States had been favoured had enabled them to live and prosper with a small degree of governing and therefore to bear what Austin, without explanation, called the "evils of extreme democracy". [34] Since he perhaps considered certain evils were necessarily connected with what he designated as "extreme democracy", Austin would not have used the expression in an honorific way. This does not imply, however, that he used unqualified "democracy" derogatorily. It is not a negative value judgement that he considered the form of the British Government to be more democratic than any other government of some age. His statement that the American Government had not been tested by time made it possible for him to admit, without contradicting himself, that the American form of government was more democratic than that of England while maintaining that the form of the British Government was decidedly more democratic than any other which had been tested over a long and eventful period.

Austin continued;

> But if, in respect to its form, the British Government ranks with democracies, it is the most democratical in spirit and effect of all governments past and present. [35]

In support of this view, Austin stated that the interests and opinions of the entire population, and not only of the sovereign body, were habitually consulted by the legislative and executive power. This habit of consulting the interests of the entire population was contrasted with the practice of the American Government of ignoring the interests and feelings of its large slave population. As far as we can see, this consultation is Austin's sole criterion in judging the British Government as the most democratic of all governments in spirit and effect. He made no other comparison except his references to the American Government.

By referring to the spirit and effect of a government, Austin introduces a third variety, different from the form of sovereignty as well as from the form of the management of sovereignty. Spirit and effect seem thus to have been regarded as something different from, and independent of, form of sovereignty in the statement quoted. When, a little later, Austin discussed the form of the gestion, or management of sovereignty, this question, too, seems to be treated independently of the spirit and effect of the government. But why Austin introduced this new distinction, of which he made no mention in his introduction, is not clear.

Describing the forma regiminis, the gestion of sovereignty, or the nature of the body which rules in practice, Austin was of the opinion that the British Government might be considered an aristocracy, especially since Parliament was only a minute fraction of the sovereign body and an even minuter fraction of the entire nation. [36] Thus, according to Austin, any government by elected representatives was to be designated as an "aristocracy" with regard to its form of managing its sovereignty as long as the body of elected representatives was comparatively small when compared with the sovereign body. Practically all kinds of representative rule, even one based upon universal and equal suffrage, would thus, according to this criterion, be of an aristocratic kind. And "democracy" could probably only be used to signify a direct government where the governing body was the whole, or a larger part, of the sovereign nation.

In a footnote to this page, Austin also stated that "aristocracy", besides signifying an elevated and privileged class,

...signifies properly a form of government, that is, any government in which the sovereign body is a comparatively small fraction of the entire nation.

Austin was also of the opinion that

...democracy ... signifies properly a form of government, that is, any government in which the governing body is a comparatively large fraction of the entire nation. [37]

This implies that neither England nor America could be regarded as democracies according to his criterion, although such a conclusion is not directly drawn. This occurrence is among the last to state that any kind of representation was incompatible with a State being a democracy.

Austin here operated with three distinctions in relation to whether a State was a democracy or not. Firstly, the forma imperii, according to which America generally was more democratic than England, but England more democratic than any other country, if only older and more established governing systems were taken into consideration. Secondly, the spirit and effect of the government, according to which England, without reservation, was the most democratic country, both past and present. And thirdly, the forma regiminis, according to which neither England nor America could be regarded as democracies.

Austin did not make an expressed use of these three distinctions in any later use of the term in this pamphlet. Once, for example, he asserted that he did not agree with those who held "popular government" to be synonymous with "free government". He went on to say that the British Government, in relation to that of the United States,

...though the less democratical of the two, is yet the more free or the less mischievously restrictive. [38]

Here Austin probably had only the forma imperii in mind, but he was nevertheless writing as if the American Government generally was more democratic than the British, and without having in mind that, according to him, there were other kinds of distinction which might make the relationship a contrary one. "Popular government" is here probably used synonymously with "democracy" or "democratic government". Austin's main objections to the British Government's becoming more democratic was his fear that government, in that way, would become less free and more restrictive. Here Austin presents a greater difference in relation to the earlier Utilitarians than anything found in the writings of John Stuart Mill.

In general, it can be said that the greater part of Austin's use of "democracy" is most probably contained in this pamphlet. Only one occurrence of "democracy" has been found in his main work, Lectures on Jurisprudence. Here he stated, with regard to classification of forms of government, that if the proportion of the sovereign number to the number of the entire community was extremely small, the supreme government was an oligarchy; if the proportion was small, but not extremely small, it was an aristocracy; and if

...the proportion be deemed large, the supreme government is styled popular, or is styled a democracy. [39]

"Popular government", it seems, is here said to be synonymous with "democracy". This way of using the term accords with his earlier application of "democracy" in relation to the <u>forma imperii</u>. None of the other distinctions discussed above were taken into consideration.

3. Green

As far as we can see, only a few occurrences of "democracy" are to be found in the writings of Thomas Hill Green. In <u>Lectures on the Principles of Political Obligation</u>, Green declared in regard to the Austinian definition of sovereignty:

> Even in the most thorough democracy, where laws are passed in the assembly of the whole people, it is still with determinate persons, viz. a majority of those who meet in the assembly, that this power resides. [40]

Direct and unrestricted popular participation in the making of laws thus seems, according to Green, to be a necessary as well as a sufficient condition for a "most thorough democracy". This does not tell us much about the signification he attributed to the unqualified term "democracy". This seems to have been the sole occurrence of the term in this important political work.

In the "Lecture on Liberal Legislation and Freedom of Contract", Green first referred to the Parliament of 1868 as "the more democratic Parliament of 1868". [41] "More democratic" is probably used to indicate that the Parliament of 1868 was elected on a wider popular franchise than any preceding one. A little later, it can be seen that Green referred to the time "before we had a democratic house of commons"; [42] and according to the context, it seems that he had the Parliament of 1868 in mind. These statements imply that Green held the House of Commons of 1868 to be what he characterized as "democratic". Thus Green cannot be said to have regarded universal suffrage as a necessary property of a national assembly characterized as "democratic".

Referring to his desire to diminish excessive drinking, Green also said:

> This then, along with the effectual liberation of the soil, is the next great conquest which our democracy, on behalf of its own true freedom, has to make. [43]

It is not possible, however, to see exactly what signification he attributed to "democracy" in this statement. When speaking of diminishing excessive drinking and of agrarian reform, Green obviously indicated certain political and social aims of what he held to be democracy, but there is no reason to regard these factors as conceptual characteristics of his concept 'democracy', or as being included in the connotation of "democracy". On the other hand, it looks as if freedom, or even what Green held to be true freedom, was conceptually attributed to the concept 'democracy' with which Green operated in this quotation. This indicates an honorific application of "democracy". This is probably confirmed by "our democracy" used to label something which he very likely considered himself to belong to.

4. Spencer

Herbert Spencer also made infrequent use of "democracy" and related terms.
Although Green's writings disclose a fairly honorific application, Spencer's
extremely few uses are somewhat derogatory. From an ideological point of
view, this diversity may be regarded as fairly symptomatic of the difference
between the idealistic thinking of Green, on the one hand, and the systematic
antagonism to state interference, on the other. Turning directly to the
leading representative of one trend in British liberalism, a few rather unimportant uses occur in Political Institutions. Spencer here maintained
that the power of one, of the few and skilled ones, and of all were the original components of political power among primitive men. He stated further,

> A despotism, an oligarchy, or a democracy, is a type of government in
> which one of the original components has greatly developed at the expence
> of the other two. [44]

Democracy is here, most probably, a kind of government in which the political power of all is developed at the expense of the political power of the few
or the political power of one. What Spencer designated as "despotism",
"oligarchy", and "democracy" were contrasted with different forms of mixed
governments. It is not possible to see which of these different forms Spencer himself favoured. His way of classifying certain kinds of governments
as despotisms, oligarchies, or democracies reminds us of Aristotle's view
that these forms of governments were corruptions of constitutions. [45] Nothing
similar to this negative attitude can be discerned in Spencer, however.

Somewhat later, Spencer declared,

> Up to the time of Solon, democratic government did not exist in Greece.
> The only actual forms were the oligarchic and the despotic. [46]

Neither this quotation nor its context conveys much, except that like the first
statement, they tell us that democratic government is different from despotism and oligarchy and probably was introduced into Greece by Solon.

These two uses of "democracy" and "democratic" are the sole occurrences I have been able to find in this voluminous work. It is even stranger
that, as far as I can see, "democracy" and related terms do not occur at all
in the three large volumes of his Scientific, Political and Speculative Essays,
of which the political essays form a large proportion.

In The Man versus the State, Spencer's only use of "democracy" and
related terms is probably limited to his mention of Hyndman's small political party. According to Spencer, the final result of this group's policy
would be the revival of despotism and grinding tyranny and the creation of a
state that was omnipotent in relation to the individual. Spencer did not make
any special use of "democratic" in this connection, except for describing the
group with "Democratic Federation", which was its official name. [47] The
only conclusion I may draw from this is probably that in not refusing to label
such a group "democratic", he believed that although its policy would result
in tyranny this was not incompatible with calling it "democratic".

Spencer frequently asserted in this work that he was not an adherent of the divine right of the majority, and he concluded by saying,

> The function of Liberalism in the past was that of putting a limit to the powers of kings. The function of true Liberalism in the future will be that of putting a limit to the powers of Parliaments. [48]

Unfortunately, Spencer made no application of "democracy" in connection with these points of view. But if he had, it may be assumed that he would hardly have used "democracy" in an honorific way.

A few uses also occur in his Autobiography. Of his stay in America, 1882, Spencer mentions that in Philadelphia a committee of citizens had been formed for the purpose of putting a check on the economic extravagance of the local authorities, and he also believed that there were similar committees in other American cities. He commented:

> A generation ago it was commonly thought that democracy was, and would be, economical; since nothing could be more obvious than that when the people had power, they would not tolerate the wasteful expenditure of the money which they furnished. But experience is not verifying this a priori conclusion in America, and is not verifying it with us. [49]

This statement does not convey very much concerning the meaning of "democracy", only that democracy was something which Spencer considered to exist in America in 1882 and in England when writing this autobiography, and that democracy was equivalent to the rather vague fact that people had power. Contrary to expectation, democracy could be wasteful; this is a fairly important non-conceptual characteristic, but it is of rather small importance in relation to the signification attributed to "democracy".

As a political leitmotiv, Spencer held that although old kinds of coercive government, like that of the king and the landed classes, were dissolving, new kinds of coercive governments were evolving. Spencer, especially, had rule of the working class in mind. He concluded:

> The old coercive shell having been cast off, a new coercive shell is in the course of development; for in our day, as in past days, there co-exist the readiness to coerce and the readiness to submit to coercion. [50]

"Democracy" is not used here, but this statement is referred to in the index as "democracy: ..., coercive tendency. " [51] However, since this autobiography appeared posthumously, it is improbable that Spencer himself did the index, and this use of "democracy" therefore may not be regarded as an occurrence in his terminology, although it might well have been accepted by Spencer.

5. Bagehot

Although Spencer's view of democracy as having a coercive and anti-liberal nature was somewhat indistinct in his terminology, the same trend is more obvious in the language of Walter Bagehot. Such an application, which would evidently imply that the term was used in a derogatory way, does not occur in an essay Bagehot wrote in early youth, however. In this Bagehot stated that the distinction between democracy and autocracy, or between the rule of the people and rule of the mob, was essential in political life, and he continued:

> Democracy, in its proper sense, is that form by which a wise and en-
> lightened nation govern themselves. [52]

According to this statement, not only popular rule but also that the people
should be wise and enlightened were most probably conceptual characteristics of his concept 'democracy', which most certainly implies that "democracy" was used here in an honorific if not eulogistic way.

In later years, however, in relation to the internal crisis in America in
1861, Bagehot stated with regard to democratic government:

> Its special characteristic is, that it places the entire control over the
> political action of the whole state in the hand of the common labourers,
> who are of all classes the least instructed -- of all the most aggressive --
> of all the most likely to be influenced by local animosity -- of all the most
> likely to exaggerate every momentary sentiment -- of all the least likely
> to be capable of a considerable toleration for the constant oppositions of
> opinion, the not unfrequent differences of interests and the occasional
> unreasonableness of other states. [53]

At this time, rule by the enlightened and the wise was definitely not to
be found among the conceptual characteristics of what he designated as
"democracy" and "democratic government". It even looks as if the democratic form of government was at this time very similar to what he had described earlier as autocracy, and the opposite of democracy.

Perhaps aggressiveness and intolerance cannot be regarded as conceptual characteristics of his concept 'democratic government', and control by
the common labourers can be held as the main, and possibly even the sole,
characteristic of that kind. An uninstructed, aggressive, and intolerant
kind of policy may, however, more probably be regarded as a non-conceptual
characteristic of this concept, although it is not possible to reach a definite
conclusion.

In 1865, along with several other political thinkers, Bagehot classified
imperial rule in France under what he designated as "democracy". In contrast to the feudal and legitimate monarchs who had claimed obedience on
grounds of duty, Bagehot said Louis Napoleon was a Benthamite despot, who
was in favour of achieving the greatest happiness of the greatest number by
way of absolute government. He said further:

> The French Empire is really the best finished democracy which the
> world has ever seen. [54]

He declared that what the many desired was embodied with a readiness and
efficiency which had no parallel, either in past or contemporary experience.

No other factors were mentioned here in support of his classification of
the French imperial rule. Perhaps Bagehot thought that this readiness and
efficiency to do what the many desired was a sufficient as well as necessary
criterion of a democratic government, and that it was not a necessary condition for a democracy to be framed within an absolute imperial rule; on
the other hand, there is no doubt that imperial rule was quite compatible
with a state being designated "democracy" or even "best finished democracy
the world has ever seen. "

It should be added that imperial rule in France was by no means treated
with reverence by Bagehot. This implies that he did not use "democracy" in
an honorific way in this essay, although the negative evaluation was perhaps
less than that attached to the signification of "democratic government" four

years earlier. Terminologically it is rather evident that "democracy" was used here with a different signification from that of "democratic government", since Bagehot most certainly did not favour a relationship of identity between being entirely under the control of the common labourers, on the one hand, and the greatest amount of readiness and efficiency to embody what the many desired, on the other. It is also obvious that Bagehot did not consider the French government to be under the control of the workers.

The signification attributed to "democracy" in the last quotation also clearly differs from that in our first, or from the form of rule by which a wise and enlightened nation governed itself. Thus, "democracy" and "democratic government" were used to designate three different concepts in the language of Bagehot. That he used "democratic government" once and "democracy" twice is of little or no importance, since, as far as I can see, "democracy" was always used to signify some kind of government.

6. Sidgwick

Returning to the utilitarian [55] trend in English political philosophy, we find arguments in Elements of Polititics (1891) by Henry Sidgwick that are related to central trends in the writings of John Stuart Mill and Austin. Although Sidgwick was rather afraid of unrestricted rule by the majority, he was more moderate on this point than Austin, and possibly somewhat more moderate than Mill.

In classifying different forms of government, Sidgwick started by saying that in ordinary political life the term "democracy" was not only used to signify a special kind of government but also represented a widely and enthusiastically accepted political ideal. According to Sidgwick, many people advanced as the principle of democracy that all laws should be framed with a view to the welfare of the people at large. Sidgwick, however, held this to be indistinguishable from the principle of any good government and that this principle was conceded by modern advocates of every form of civilized government. To treat it as the characteristic principle of democracy only would introduce a fundamental confusion in political thought.

Sidgwick went on to describe how the fundamental principle of democracy was to be defined when limited to the consideration of the structure of government. According to him, there were two competing definitions, or rather two distinct principles, which were explicitly or implicitly assumed in arguing in favour of democratic institutions.

> One of these, -- which I myself accept as the principle that the modern State should aim at realizing -- is "that government should rest on the active consent of the citizens", the other is "that any one self-supporting and law-abiding citizen is, on the average, as well qualified as another for the work of government". [56]

Sidgwick added that in the main he rejected this latter proposition, but admitted that there might be a tendency to accept and act upon the second proposition when a democracy, as defined by the first principle, was fully developed.

Sidgwick did not mean that he refused the second proposition the label "democratic", only that he rejected it as a principle towards which modern society ought to aim. In order to define the former proposition more precisely, he stated that by active consent he meant something quite different from passive acquiscence or absence of any conscious desire to change the structure of government; a phenomenon which might exist under a pure monarchy as well as under an oligarchy. According to Sidgwick, active consent implied that the citizens were conscious that they could legitimately alter the structure or the action of their government if a sufficient number of them chose to go through a certain process. He held that the democratic principle excluded any fundamental laws requiring more than a bare majority to alter it and that it might be doubted whether it was consistent with the principle of democracy to require a majority of the citizens, instead of a majority of voters, to approve any change in the constitution. Sidgwick himself, however, did not hold such an opinion.

That a democratic government must be supported by a majority of the citizens did not imply for Sidgwick, however, that such consent was needed for the validity of every governmental decision. Such an implication would, most certainly, make democratic government impossible. Sidgwick argued that it must be taken

> ...as commonly admitted that the democratic principle must be practically limited by confining the authoritative decision of the people at large to certain matters and certain periodically recurring times. [57]

He continued that it was also generally admitted that the great majority of governmental decisions must be committed to bodies or individuals who should have the power of decision without the active consent, and even against the wish, of the majority.

Here Sidgwick did not say anything directly about the application of what he held to be the principle of democracy but was probably referring only to what he held to be generally admitted, although he was probably of a similar opinion himself. The importance of this statement is that "democratic principle" was used to signify something limited and that Sidgwick believed that the great majority of governmental decisions should be committed to certain bodies and individuals. This raises the question as to how far if at all, rule by chosen representatives was compatible with what Sidgwick held to be the democratic principle. Sidgwick said that it was generally accepted by theoretical advocates of democracy in modern times that the part of government's work that was entrusted to particular individuals or elected assemblies should be entrusted to specially qualified persons. So far as this was admitted, however, Sidgwick considered that some degree of aristocracy was implicitly accepted. His definition of aristocracy was that the work of government was a form of skilled labour which should be in the hands of those who possessed the skill. He concluded:

> Hence, I do not consider representative government -- even when the suffrage is universal -- as merely a mode of organizing democracy, but rather as a combination or fusion of democracy and aristocracy. [58]

Thus no rule by elected representatives, according to this statement, would seem to be completely subsumable under a concept 'democracy' with "democracy" as the conceptual designation. Here is one of the later instances of an important and central tradition in political language. And as a matter of interest, this statement was made nearly a hundred years after Robespierre had declared democracy to be a kind of representative rule. It must be observed, however, that unlike several earlier political philosophers, Sidgwick did not regard representative rule, as such, as alien

to what he designated as "democracy". A necessary condition of this relationship between these two political phenomena seems to be that Sidgwick
considered that an aristocratic principle, or governing by the specially
qualified, lay behind the principle of representation. This aristocratic
principle seems to be a necessary property of what he held to be the system
of representative government. If Sidgwick could have conceived of a government that was representative because of its extension of territory or the
number of its inhabitants in the way in which, for example, Bentham justified representation, then he might have regarded such a government as
belonging to the denotata of "democracy" as used by him. No such reflections are to be found in Sidgwick's argument, however.

A possible objection might be that, in speaking about the representative
system as being not "merely a mode of organizing democracy", Sidgwick
used "democracy" in the sense of the second definition: "that any one self-
supporting and law-abiding citizen is, on the average, as well qualified as
another for the work of government. " This would naturally reduce the importance of his statement concerning representation and what he designated
as "democracy". Sidgwick generally seems to have stated which of the two
definitions he was using in his discussions of democracy in Elements of
Politics, and the first definition was the one usually referred to. He made
no comment on this important statement, however, and even opened his
discussion of the representative principle by referring to the second definition. [59] A little later, however, he obviously used "democratic government" in the sense of government based on the active consent of the citizens. [60] It is scarcely possible that Sidgwick had the second definition in
mind when discussing democracy in relation to representation on the following page. This would imply that representative government, which, according to him, was a combination of democracy and aristocracy, was a combination or fusion of the principle "that any one self-supporting and law-abiding
citizen was, on the average, as well qualified as another for the work of
government" with the principle that the work of government was a form of
skilled labour that should be in the hands of qualified persons. This combination is obviously self-contradictory. I am therefore inclined to conclude
that in Sidgwick's opinion democracy, according to the second definition,
was incompatible with any kind of representative rule but that democracy,
according to the first definition, was compatible with, but nevertheless
different from, representation, or that "democracy" might not connote a
representative kind of government when used alone.

Sidgwick's other use of "democracy" seems to be in conformity with
what has been elaborated here. He concluded this classification of governments by saying:

> The representative system naturally combines with democracy an ele-
> ment of aristocracy. [61]

Here "democracy" is obviously used in accordance with the first definition.

Finally, it can be said that he was probably in favour of "democracy"
when the term was used to connote government by consent and when democracy was combined with the representative principle. He was, however, of
the opinion that even the aristocratic principle, which was included in the
representative form of government, would not always furnish a sufficient
means to prevent the masses from forcing through legislation oppressive to
the rich. He himself was of the opinion that this danger could not be completely guarded against, but he hoped that the danger might be reduced if the

legislators were to receive no salary, since they would then be more independent and drawn mainly from the minority of persons of wealth and lei-
sure. In his view, the principle of non-salaried legislators was much to
be preferred to limited suffrage or plural votes for certain qualified
groups. [62]

7. Masaryk

Generally a reserved attitute, in certain cases even a very reserved attitude
towards what was termed "democracy" is a predominant trend among the
political thinkers discussed in this chapter. A very honorific application is
found, however, in the language of Thomas Masaryk. Masaryk also differs
from the other ideologists in this chapter by not letting "democracy" signify
a certain kind of government. In May 1912 Masaryk gave a speech at a
Czeck student conference which was printed in a pamphlet with the French
title of L'idée démocratique et la politique. In relation to the viewpoints of
Ostrogorski, and especially those of Michels, who considered that any multi-
party parliamentarian rule of necessity tended towards oligarchy, Masaryk
stressed that popular administration was the main task of democracy. In
opening his speech Masaryk said:

> La démocratie est vraiment une contradictio in adjecto, si l'on met
> l'accent sur cratie, gouverner; ... [63]

This is probably a meta-occurrence, since it is probably "democracy" and
not 'democracy' to which Masaryk was referring. He continued:

> Démocratie signifie gouvernement du peuple, mais il faut l'entendre non
> dans le sens de gouvernement et de domination, mais dans celui de ges-
> tion, d'administration par le peuple. L'administration, la gestion des
> affaires est la chose capitale pour une démocratie. [64]

In contrast to several other thinkers, especially Austin, Schérer, and
Maine, all of whom declared democracy to be exclusively a form of government, Masaryk here held democracy to be a certain kind of administration.
While "democracy" has been used quite frequently to signify something other
than a form of government -- for example, a political attitude, a political
group, an ideological principle, social and economic equality, etc. -- we
have seldom found this stated explicitly. The usual practice has been to
let "democracy" connote an ideological principle, a way of life, or a theory
of social equality without entering into discussion as to whether democracy
was a form of government. On this point it may be added that Masaryk's
formulation is not as definite as contrary statements favouring democracy
being exclusively a form of government. His somewhat paradoxical way of
declaring democracy to signify government by the people, but not in the
sense of government and domination, may require some degree of modification.

The association, or even identification, of democracy with a certain
kind of administration is made fairly explicit later in his speech. Stating
that aristocracy was the opposite of democracy and that governing was everything for an aristocracy, Masaryk concluded:

Démocratie administrative et gouvernement aristocratique s'opposent l'un à l'autre. [65]

It seems that by Masaryk's criteria the expressions "administrative democracy" and "aristocratical government" may have been pleonastic.
  Masaryk held that aristocracy was alien to work, but

> ...la démocratie est fondée sur le travail: c'est pourquoi les travailleurs s'organisent démocratiquement ... c'est la démocratie dans le vrai sens du mot qui s'organisent là, à côté de ces autres travailleurs, ceux de l'intelligence. [66]

This statement does not directly convey what Masaryk meant by "democracy in the true sense of the word. " He continued, however, by emphasizing that no one ought to think that democracy was natural: on the contrary, it was attainable only through personal struggle and effort. In his opinion, aristrocracy was natural; and since everyone desired to become a master, everyone was also in a certain way an aristocrat. He continued:

> Mais pour arriver à être un démocrate conscient et non seulement un démocrate en paroles, mais dans chacun de nos actes -- nous avons beaucoup à faire et c'est à cela que doit tendre le démocrate 'intellectuel'. [67]

It can probably be inferred from this that any man who is a conscious democrat -- and probably any person really deserving the label of "democrat" -- must permanently suppress his natural wish to become a master and begin to treat all human beings as his equals. He probably had this in mind when using the expression "democracy in the true sense of the word" to designate the kind of organization found among workers and intellectuals. On this point we meet a conceptual characteristic of the concepts 'democrat' and 'democracy' as used by Masaryk, and even the sole conceptual characteristic, since it is probable that Masaryk believed that to treat all other human beings as one's equals was not only a necessary but also a sufficient condition for a real democrat and a true democracy. In this way Masaryk indicates that his version of democracy was an ethical ideal; he may therefore be said to have gone beyond his initial belief that democracy was a certain kind of administration.
  Discussing the relationship between democracy and other political systems, Masaryk held that the democrat regarded liberalism with scepticism because economic competition at that time had become the idea of the conservatives. [68] Masaryk also rejected the marxist ideology as purely economic and not philosophic. He openly declared himself to be a socialist, but added that social questions for a modern democrat were not only of an economic but also of a philosophical kind. [69] He also considered a democrat to be different from an extreme radical because of the latter's alleged lack of a realistic and emperical attitude in the field of politics. [70]
  In an essay printed some months earlier, which was given the title "Les difficultés de la démocratie", we find an application of "democracy" fairly similar to that of the speech discussed. Here, too, Masaryk began:

> La démocratie n'est pas de nos jours, à proprement parler, le gouvernement populaire, mais l'administration populaire -- l'administration est la vraie tâche de la démocratie. [71]

With the exception of the restriction "n'est pas de nos jours", this statement is very similar to the first quoted from Masaryk. In this essay there

is a more explicit change from the view of democracy as a kind of administration to democracy as a form of human behaviour. Masaryk stated that
universal suffrage was far from sufficient to create a democratic spirit and
that a true democrat behaved in a democratic way not only in parliament but
in the circle of his friends and his family as well. He concluded:

> La démocratie est une conception du monde et une règle de vie. La
> démocratie est une conséquence et une exigence politique de la morale
> humaniste moderne. [72]

Since most people, and probably Masaryk as well, would admit to a certain
difference between a kind of administration and a kind of human behaviour,
we find some degree of difference between the significations he attributed to
"democracy" in this passage and our initial quotation. Here, too, it can be
said that although several applications of "democracy" can be found which
are used much as the word is used in this quotation, seldom has it been described as a kind of human behaviour and human attitude with such direct-
ness.

Apart from Masaryk's general attitude towards democracy as a consequence and exigence of modern humanistic morality, he did not elaborate
here on the kind of human behaviour and attitude he had in mind. Perhaps
Masaryk was thinking about the properties given in his speech, although
there is no direct proof here in favour of such a hypothesis. But even if we
do not accept this assumption, we find more concrete aspects a few pages
earlier in this essay. Here Masaryk said of the relationship between democracy and the church:

> La démocratie est, dans son essence une a-théocratie, et pratiquement,
> une anti-théocratie. [73]

His main argument in favour of this point was that monarchism most
frequently found moral support in a privileged church which had a kind of
religious monopoly within the State, but that democracy must be built on a
purely human and secular basis. For the sake of brevity, and to explain
this antithesis between democracy and theocracy, "démocratie" might be
replaced by the term "anthropocratie".

It can be seen that Masaryk's dislike of any kind of privileged church,
and especially the Roman Catholic church, was mainly caused by his negative attitude towards hierarchical institutions. With regard to hierarchy he
said: "Le catolicisme dans son essence est à ce point aristocratique". [74]
This dislike was not limited to social institutions such as hierarchies, however, but was based upon his rejection of any kind of orthodoxy or organized
authority in spiritual life. Evidently as an elaboration of the definition of
democracy as a kind of human behaviour and view of life, Masaryk held that
democracy was founded on science. Science was, inter alia, characterized
by publicity and the possibility of criticism; democracy must therefore be
characterized by the possibility of full public criticism of all sectors in
social and political life. He went on to say that scientific behaviour employed exact methods; democratic policy was therefore inductive and realistic, while an aristocracy generally behaved in a deductive, non-realistic,
arbitrary, and scholastic manner. He concluded:

> L'antithèse de la science et de la théologie est l'antithèse même de la
> démocratie et de l'aristocratie (monarchie). [75]

A few pages later he said:

La théocratie était croyante, la démocratie est critique et scientifique.
La foi et la sciénce sont aussi une forme de l'antithèse de l'aristocratie
et de la démocratie. [76]

The latter statement was made to point out the difference between
modern philosophy and the alleged medieval belief in the authority of the
emperor and the pope. Both quotations indicate an association between
empirical and unorthodox methods in science and what Masaryk labelled
"democracy", and it is probable that a scientific attitude was included in
the signification of "democracy" as used here. A formulation like "democracy is critical and scientific" is likely to be an analytic and not synthetic
statement according to Masaryk. Whether Masaryk held democracy to be
incompatible with any religious belief is not clear. The above formulation
may be taken as an indication of incompatibility, although it should be added
that the statement that democracy was primarily to be found in Protestant
and particularly in Calvinist countries [77] may make a negative relationship
less probable. Although Masaryk definitely believed democracy to be based
upon a non-religious foundation, he probably did not see a strict incompatibility; these two phenomena, based on entirely different philosophical bases,
nevertheless might have a certain kind of coexistence.

As was mentioned previously, there also can be found in this essay
some degree of change from the view that democracy was a kind of administration to that of democracy as a view of life. But while Masaryk in the
speech drew attention primarily, and perhaps even exclusively, to the idea
of treating all men as one's equals, we find in this essay a distinct elaboration of the difference between orthodox theocracy and theology, on one hand,
and the scientific and non-religious essence of democracy, on the other.
And even if we admit that to Masaryk the idea of treating all other human
beings as one's equals was probably related to free and unorthodox methods
in science, we may also assume some degree of difference at this point
between the significations attributed to "democracy".

If Masaryk's use of "democracy" is compared with those of a few other
political thinkers, a very great difference can be seen between this application and those found in the writings of Lamartine, Cabet, Bergson, Maritain,
and Nietzsche, [78] all of whom believed democracy to be essentially Christian.
Probably the greatest difference is that between Masaryk and Brunetière.
The latter declared that analytical and empirical methods in science, available only to the few, were aristocratic, while democracy primarily existed
in such things as the collective faith of the Catholic church and the equalitarian discipline of the army. [79]

Where the general trends in Masaryk's political thinking are concerned,
it is evident that "democracy", as used in the speech and the essay under
discussion, occupies a central as well as lauditory position in his terminology. It may even be said that for Masaryk all the major virtues were
included in the related significations he attributed to "democracy" in these
contexts. [80]

CHAPTER XI

FRENCH CONSERVATISM[1]

A negative, even a very negative, attitude towards what was designated as "democracy" was a clear characteristic of the terminology of French political thinkers like de Maistre, Bonald, and Guizot. Among political thinkers discussed in this chapter, a derogatory usage of "democracy" is also generally to be found. This is partly because democracy was considered to be opposed to social hierarchies, alien to science and intellectual competence, an anti-military attitude, or even a revolutionary force. This derogatory application is not without exception, however. Thus an honorific use of "democracy" is evident in Brunetière's terminology, where this traditionalist thinker identified his Catholic and pro-military ideas with what he designated as "democracy". Typical of differences in political outlook, Renan used "democracy" appreciatively in a few cases when he thought that democracy would make war impossible; and Faguet, who elsewhere used "democracy" derogatorily, in one case altered his view when he declared the army to be the noble and brilliant expression of democracy.

1. Renan

Several statements in Renan's terminology are relevant to the alleged anti-hierarchical nature of democracy. In May 1848, at the age of twenty-five, Renan severely criticized Catholic attempts to reconcile the Catholic tradition with popular representation and universal suffrage. He referred to "des moines transformés en ardents démocrates" [2] as one of the miracles of that year. To the question,

> Quelle a été la forme dont le gouvernement de l'Eglise s'est rapproché de plus en plus?,

Renan answered,

> La forme la moins démocratique, celle où les rangs sont séparés par la barrière la plus infranchissable, je veux dire par un caractère sacré, indélébile. La hiérarchie est la base de tout le système catholique; elle est "de foi", comme disent les théologiens. [3]

Thus he definitely refused the label "democratic" to the Catholic church on the grounds that it was founded upon a hierarchical structure. This implies that democracy, according to his view, was incompatible with any kind of hierarchy and probably that the democratic form of government was of all forms the one most opposed to the hierarchical form.

These occurrences of "democrats" and "democratic" are the only ones found in this essay, and they can probably be regarded as the first in Renan's writings. It is difficult to say more than that "democratic" seemed to characterize an anti-hierarchical form of rule. The context makes it clear that Renan was not in favour of Catholic institutions. This may be taken to indicate that "democratic" was used in an honorific way, although the conclusion is rather uncertain.

Renan did not use "democratic" hypothetically in an honorific manner in his first important work L'avenir de la science -- pensées de 1848. This work was written in the spring of 1849, and, unlike the time when he was writing the article quoted above, he was apt to have been influenced by the workers' uprising in June and the electoral victory of Louis Bonaparte. In L'avenir de la science Renan held the ideal government to be one in which competent men would handle governmental questions like scientific ones, and he further maintained:

> La politique est une science comme une autre, et exige apparemment autant d'études et de connaissances qu'une autre. [4]

Renan contrasted this ideal of a scientific rule with what he termed "democracy" as well as with "aristocracy".

> En appelant démocratie et aristocratie les deux partis qui se disputent le monde, on peut dire que l'un et l'autre sont, dans l'état actuel de l'humanité, également impossibles.

Regarding the character of democracy, Renan continued:

> Car les masses étant aveugles et inintelligentes, n'en appeler qu'à elles, c'est en appeler de la civilisation à la barbarie. [5]

"Democracy" is most probably used here to signify a governmental system whose main characteristic was that it appealed to the masses only; according to Renan, this was an appeal to barbarism from civilization, since he considered the masses, at least in his time, to be blind and unintelligent.

On the other hand, Renan held that an aristocracy would constitute an odious monopoly if it did not have as its main goal the mental improvement of the masses. This seems to indicate that his earlier statement about their alleged blindness and lack of intelligence had a temporary and not a general validity. Probably Renan considered both aristocracies and democracies to be impossible forms of government, he was not of the opinion that aristocracies considered the improvement of the masses to be their main duty.

Renan's personal approbation of the improvement of the masses is given a little later in his work in connection with a somewhat more favourable attitude towards what he designated as "democracy". He refers to Aristotle's view, according to which the unintelligent, or those who were slaves by nature, had to obey the intelligent. Thus a revolt by the unintelligent would be as much a crime as for the body to make itself the master of the soul. Renan also added:

> A ce point de vue, les conquêtes de la démocratie seraient les conquêtes de l'esprit du mal, le triomphe de la chair sur l'esprit.

Renan continued, however:

> Mais c'est ce point de vue même qui est décevant. [6]

He went on to say that progress had banished that aristocratic theory and had placed the weak on the same level as the strong. He also emphasized that any man could possess moral principles. He admitted that it was impossible to love the people in its present condition, but concluded by saying that he personally was convinced that unless everything was done to elevate the masses, culture would soon relapse into barbarism.

Here, too, Renan probably used "democracy" to connote a governmental system whose main characteristic was its appeal for the masses, and he does not seem to have been in favour of it. But this attitude is probably somewhat more favourable here than in the previous quotation. Thus he probably did not associate barbarism with democracy but believed barbarism to be the result of a particular aristocratic policy. Renan also disagreed with the Aristotelian view that the conquests of democracy were conquests by an evil spirit, or the triumph of the flesh over the soul. Renan's main reason for withholding approval from what he termed "democracy" was the lack of education among the masses, but this does not imply that he was an antagonist of democracy as such. What he designated as "democracy" was probably to be approved of in a well-educated society. Nor was Renan an opponent of the principle of universal suffrage; the only necessary condition he made was that

Le suffrage universel ne sera légitime que quand tous auront cette part d'intelligence sans laquelle on ne mérite pas le titre d'homme, [7]

The above quotations are good examples of Renan's political attitude, but they are not of great importance concerning the signification he attributed to "democracy". It is difficult to say whether Renan here used "democracy" to designate a purely political concept whose main characteristic was universal suffrage or whether he also included a social factor such as absence of hierarchies in its signification. Renan may have regarded these two things as mutually dependent and felt no need to differentiate on this point.

A slightly different picture is presented several years later in Renan's famous work Vie de Jesus, 1863. In relation to St. Luke's gospel Renan held that pure ebonism, or the thesis that only the poor were to be saved and that the reign of the poor was to come, had been Jesus' doctrine. He added that this doctrine represented no new phenomenon in human history, since,

... le mouvement démocratique le plus exalté dont l'humanité ait gardé le souvenir (le seul aussi qui ait réussi, car seul il s'est tenu dans le domaine de l'idée pure) agitait depuis longtemps la race juive. La pensée que Dieu est le vengeur du pauvre et du faible contre le riche et le puissant se retrouve à chaque page des écrits de l'Ancien Testament.[8]

That God was considered to an avenger of the poor and weak against the rich Renan probably regarded as a sufficient, perhaps a necessary, proof that what he termed as "the most exalted democratic movement to be found within human memory" was an old and familiar trend for the Jewish race. This means his use of "democratic" has a signification similar to, or even identical with, opposition to the influence and power of the rich. With this signification probably restricted to the social field, and with no reference to forms of government, we may speak about a certain change from his earlier use of "democracy" with a signification predominantly restricted to political or governmental forms.

Perhaps Renan regarded this equalitarian movement with some degree of sympathy. It is certain that "democratic" was not used here in a derogatory way, although we have previously noted this tendency in Renan's works. A return to a derogatory, even an unconditional derogatory, application occurs some years later. In 1869, in proposing the establishment of a

constitutional monarchy in France, Renan said that constitutional monarchy
in England had fostered a much greater degree of personal freedom than
any absolute dogmas about the sovereignty of the people. "Democracy" is
not used in connection with these statements, however. The term is to be
found in a qualified form when Renan declared society to be a hierarchy in
which every individual was noble and sacred. He further stated that every
being, even animals, possessed certain rights; but he also asserted that
all beings were not equals and that all were members of a vast corporation,
or parts of an immense organism which constituted a divine work. Renan
concluded:

> La négation de ce travail divin est l'erreur où verse facilement la
> démocratie française. [9]

Like our first quotation, French democracy is here contrasted with
hierarchical society. Although in the earlier example the absence of any
hierarchies seemed to be included in the signification of "democracy", Renan
here probably did not attribute absence of the alleged divine inequality to
his concept 'French democracy'; and there is good reason to regard this
last statement as being synthetic and not analytic. It is not clear whether in
using "French democracy" and not simply "democracy", Renan intended to
draw some line of demarcation between democracy in general and the French
species.

A few pages later Renan used unqualified "democrat" to label the kind
of man who considered the happy peasants of l'ancien régime to have been
exploited and deceived.

> Le démocrate traite de dupe le paysan d'ancien régime qui travaille
> pour ses nobles, les aime et jouit de haute existence que d'autres mènent
> avec ses sueurs.

We find occurrences of "democracy" and "democratic" very similar to this
use of "democrat" in statements like:

> L'école démocratique ne voit pas que la grande vertu d'une nation est de
> supporter l'inégalité traditionelle, [10]

and when he contrasted what he held as "l'arrogance d'une démocratie" with
earlier times when

> ... tous alors participaient de la vie de tous; le pauvre jouissait de la
> richesse du riche, le moine des joies du mondain, le mondain des prières
> du moine; pour tous, il y avait l'art, la poésie, la religion. [11]

Partly in contrast to his last use of "French democracy", "democracy"
and "democrat" seem here not only to connote a system or a person whose
actual policy was against the alleged happy and harmonious inequality but the
terms may even be said to signify something or someone who per definitinem
opposed this idyllic hierarchy. Although when Renan spoke of French democracy tending towards the negation of divine inequality, he might have
imagined a kind of democracy that was not necessarily of an anti-hierarchical kind, but this is not likely according to the last three quotations. Thus
an anti-hierarchical property may be regarded as implicit in Renan's signification of "democracy", "democrat", and "democratic" as used in the last
statements. In this case there is possibly some difference in relation to the
signification of "French democracy" which occurred a few pages earlier.
The qualification "French" is of little or no importance in this connection,

since Renan also in the last quotations drew attention to French social life.

Renan's evaluation of what was designated as "democracy" and "democrat" in these statements is obviously negative. A very different relationship is to be found, however, during the Franco-German war one year later. Renan, who had been in favour of a cultural and political union between France, England, and Germany, was deeply depressed by the war. He believed that an immense and increasing majority of all nations hated war and that a warlike spirit was only found among the nobility in the north of Germany and in Russia. It is certain that he held democracy to be opposed to war and, possibly, even incompatible with any kind of military policy.

La démocratie ne veut pas, ne comprend pas la guerre.

Of Prussian officers, he stated:

Le progrès de la démocratie sera la fin du règne de ces hommes de fer, survivants d'un autre âge. [12]

Here the central point is without doubt his marked change in attitude towards what he termed "democracy", especially when compared with his attitude a year earlier. It is difficult to say whether an anti-military policy was a conceptual characteristic of his concept 'democracy' or whether he considered that kind of policy to be a fairly certain consequence of such a social and political system. On my part I think the latter alternative is the more probable and that Renan possibly believed the alleged anti-militaristic character of democracy to have been caused, inter alia, by its non-hierarchical character. According to this point of view, there is perhaps no reason to think that Renan used "democracy" with a signification differing from that he attributed to the term the previous year. The difference between a derogatory and an honorific application may therefore be regarded exclusively as a change in attitude, or as a normative and not a terminological change. Renan might well have declared democracy to be anti-militaristic in 1869 as well, but at that time it would probably not have been connected with such a positive evaluation as it received in 1870.

Renan himself was clearly aware that his attitude differed from that of the previous year,

... j'ai des appréhensions contre certaines tendances de la démocratie, et je les ai dites, il y a un an, avec sincérité. [13]

It is difficult to accept that Renan was apprehensive of only certain tendencies of what he designated as "democracy", since he disliked it unreservedly. The honorific way in which he used the term here is rather evident, however. He concluded with a clear hint to the Prussian officers:

Mais certes, si la démocratie se borne à débarrasser l'espèce humaine de ceux qui, pour la satisfaction de leurs vanités et de leurs rancunes, font égorger des millions d'hommes, elle aura mon plein assentiment et ma reconnaissante sympatie. [14]

There is no honorific usage of "democracy", however, in Renan's main political work, La réforme intellectuelle et morale de la France. This work was written in 1872, soon after the French defeat; and in it he seems to have regarded what he designated as "democracy" as probably the main cause of this national disaster. He said, for example:

La démocratie est le plus fort dissolvent de l'organisation militaire.

> L'organisation militaire est fondée sur la discipline; la démocratie est la négation de la discipline. [15]

The German victory was the victory of disciplined over undisciplined men. A very similar use of "democracy" occurs in statements like,

> La démocratie fait notre faiblesse militaire et politique; elle fait notre ignorance, notre sotte vanité, [16]

> La démocratie ne discipline ni ne moralise, [17]

and

> Il y a quelque chose que la démocratie ne fera jamais, c'est la guerre. [18]

As in 1870 this is a very great change in attitude and we have no special reason to think that he was using "democracy" with a signification that differed from that attributed to the term two years earlier. There is more reason for believing that he attributed a non-military character to his concept 'democracy', but such possible differences concerning the signification he attributed to "democracy" are nevertheless of small importance when compared with the very great change in attitude towards professional warfare. Thus, the very differentiated picture of Renan's use of "democracy" during the three years from 1869-72, when he turns from a derogatory to a fairly honorific application and then returns to a very derogatory one, can with rather good reason be regarded as reflecting differences in his attitude towards certain phenomena and not as differences of a terminological kind. This is a rather rare phenomenon, since changes from a derogatory to an honorific application of words are generally accompanied by some kind of terminological change.

The differences in Renan's attitude between 1870 and 1872 hardly imply a complete change. In both cases, a fairly high degree of French patriotism is probably present. One of the main causes of the change from an honorific to a derogatory application is probably that in 1870 Renan had the Prussian army in mind when he praised the non-military character of democracy; on the other hand, he restricted his attention to the French army when he complained of the non-military character of democracy two years afterwards. His change was one of emphasis rather than a purely normative change or a change of principle. This does not refute what has been said concerning a change in attitude versus a change in terminology, however.

With regard to other uses of "democracy" in this work, there is little that might show new uses after 1870. There is clearly a derogatory trend in his work; and as far as can be seen, there are no occurrences to indicate that the term was not used in a derogatory way. Concerning the alleged non-military character of democracy, it has already been noted that Renan mentioned as its main cause the absence of discipline. In addition Renan believed that a lack of recognition of science to be an important cause of this non-military character. In his opinion, the organization of war had become a scientific and administrative problem, and these questions were much too complicated for what he called "democracy".

> La démocratie à la française ne donnera jamais assez d'autorité aux savants pour qu'ils puissent faire prévaloir une direction rationelle. [19]

Why Renan used the phrase "French type of democracy" and not just "democracy" is not clear. Perhaps he wished to make some distinction between French and American democracy. One possible indication in this direction is a later statement to the effect that the French democratic party did not look to the American republic as its political ideal and that, in general, this party was guided by socialist tendencies that were contrary to the American idea of freedom and property. [20] On the other hand, I must add that any qualified use of "democracy" is seldom found in his work, and generally, lack of understanding the importance of science is the characteristic of what he labelled with unqualified "democracy". [21]

As with earlier queries concerning Renan's terminology it is difficult to say whether or not he conceptually attributed absence of an understanding of science to his concept 'democracy'. The quotation above may tend towards a non-conceptual interpretation; although in other cases Renan might have admitted statements like "democracy is alien to science" to be analytic and not synthetic. Finally Renan strongly emphasized his horror of rule by the uneducated. Contrary to some of his earlier statements, he seems here to have regarded the masses as forever uneducated and ignorant. His central idea was that <u>raison générale</u> and not <u>volonté générale</u> should rule the nation, and it seems that reason and knowledge were to be found exclusively among the highly educated few. This idea is important in much of his political thinking, but it is more predominant here than in any earlier work; a factor which is more probably connected with his increasingly derogatory use of "democracy".

2. Schérer

Edmond Schérer used "democracy" in a derogatory way in his main political work <u>La démocratie et la France</u>, 1883. In this he follows the predominant application of Renan, although Schérer tries explicitly to restrict the signification of "democracy" to cover a form of government only. On this point there is a marked similarity between Austin, Maine, and Schérer. On one of the first pages of Schérer's work, he states that he wanted

> ... de montrer que la démocratie ne nous donnera ni l'âge d'or ni le pays de Cocagne, mais qu'elle est tout simplement une forme de gouvernement, semblable aux autres en ce qu'elle a ses inconvénients aussi bien que ses avantages. [22]

With the last part of this statement, Schérer probably intended to place himself in an objective position, apart from those who considered that democracy brought only inconveniences as well from those drawing attention solely to its advantages. This way of contrasting his own version of democracy exclusively with the view that democracy would bring the golden age to humanity shows a onesidedness which increases to a marked degree in this work.

Discussing the properties he attributed to the signification of "democracy", a central statement is to be found when he said:

> La démocratie est le gouvernement exercé par l'ensemble des citoyens, et comme le gros d'une population se compose partout de ce qu'on appelle les classes inférieures, toute démocratie est nécessairement le gouvernement du pays par ceux qui gagnent leur vie au jour le jour. [23]

Although many people, including those who approve of what they designate as "democracy", would agree with Schérer that democracy is government exercised by the whole population, few would accept what he held to be a necessary implication of the first point of view. For Schérer, it was obviously beyond doubt that the greater part of the population consisted of inferior classes, and he also held it as axiomatic that they earned their living from day to day. Thus, Schérer could even define democracy as government by those who earned their living from day to day, and he evidently expected this definition to be accepted by all who agreed with the first part of his statement.

A further link in this chain of persuasive definitions occurs a few lines later:

La démocratie, qui est le règne de l'ouvrier, a les travers de l'ouvrier, celui de ne reconnaître pour vrai travail que le travail manuel, [24]

At this point we not only find a definition of democracy as rule of and by the workers but, because of Schérer's unreserved manner of attributing to the workers the view that only manual work was real work, it can most probably be inferred that he even defined democracy as government by persons hostile to intellectual work. Thus, hostility towards intellectual work may not only be regarded as a fairly certain consequence of what Schérer considered to be democracy but also a conceptual characteristic of his concept 'democracy'.

With such view, it is natural that Schérer held democracy to be necessarily characterized by mediocracy and that he regarded liberty as alien to democracy. Schérer emphasized that liberty was conditioned by inequality, since inequality would always be the result of the free development of natural forces.

L'essence de la démocratie, au contraire, c'est l'égalité et, par concéquent, la dépression de tout ce qui tend à dépasser le niveau. [25]

Introductorily Schérer spoke about democracy as having advantages as well as disadvantages. It is difficult, however, if at all possible, to find an advantage to be gained by what Schérer held to be democracy. The only exception occurs where he said:

La force de la démocratie, c'est de se donner pour but le bien du plus grand nombre. [26]

He added that this aim was not limited to material well-being alone but that it included intellectual advancement. Schérer seems, however, to have had little faith in the possibility that this aim might be achieved and his main objection was that "la démocratie est profondément idéaliste". [27] Such idealism was primarily caused by the fact that democracy was permanently linked to the abstract dogma of equality, while inequality was considered to be an irreducible reality. This reservation naturally reduces the alleged advantage of democracy.

In a review of Popular Government, by Henry Summer Maine, Schérer later held that since the masses instinctively felt themselves to be incompetent in fields where historical learning was necessary, the development of democracy would gradually abolish external relations between governments. Schérer also spoke of the democratic aversion to great power, glory, influence, and aggrandizement and concluded:

C'est que tout cela signifie la guerre, et c'est que les démocraties sont nécessairement pacifiques. [28]

On this last point, as well as on several others, Schérer argues in a way
resembling Renan. And as with Renan's language, it is difficult to say
whether or not a peaceful character was conceptually attributed to his concept 'democracy'. This should probably be regarded as a conceptual characteristic rather than a consequence although Schérer's statement is not clear
on this point. Similar to the predominant tendency in Renan, Schérer, too,
held the pacific character of democracy to be a disadvantage of that political
system, although such an attitude is less obvious in Scherer's writings than
in those of Renan. On the other hand, Schérer did not declare at any time
that the non-military character of democracy was an important advantage.

3. Brunetière

As did various other conservative ideologists in France, the traditionalist
thinker Ferdinand Brunetière also drew attention to the relationship between
the army and what he designated as "democracy". Contrary to the general
trend, however, are found several arguments in his writings in favour of
absolute compatibility and even of a very close and intimate relationship
between the army and what he held to be democracy.

Brunetière asserted that the army, and the army alone, was the centre
of national life in a democracy. In contrast to the civil services, the aristocracy, and the universities, he described the army as being recruited
from all regions of the country and from all classes of the people. It was
evidently primarily these factors that made him say:

> L'armée enfin analogue ou conforme, dans son organisation comme dans
> son esprit, à la démocratie dont elle émane.... L'armée rappelant pour
> ainsi dire, de génération en génération la démocratie à son principe
> essentiel. [29]

Apparently the essential principle of democracy, according to Brunetière, consisted mainly, or even exclusively, of being common to all citizens of a country. It was obviously his opinion that the French army was in
conformity with this egalitarian criterion that made him declare democracy
and the army to be analogous in organization as well as in spirit. This does
not imply that Brunetière held democracy to be in conformity with any kind
of organized military institution. An indispensible claim was evidently that
the army was based upon universal and compulsory service. Thus Brunetière would most probably not have considered the existing British army to
be analogous to, or in conformity with, democracy. On the other hand, he
seems to have been clearly aware of the existence of a hierarchy even in
the French army, and we may therefore infer that he regarded neither hierarchy nor military discipline as incompatible with a democracy.

At this point is a use of "democracy" which, from a certain point of
view, is contrary to what is found in Renan and Schérer, although Renan and
Schérer mainly drew attention to the waging of war, while Brunetière was
occupied with the army as a social institution. According to Brunetière, the
army was la grande niveleuse in French political and social life, this was
brought about because peasants and aristocrats, workers and intellectuals,
were submitted to the same discipline, thus fulfilling the egalitarian claims
of democracy.

With regard to the relationship between religion and democracy, Brunetière said in another speech that he believed there had always been

> ...une convenance intime et profonde entre les vérités de la religion, et
> cette aspiration vers la liberté, vers l'égalité des conditions, vers la
> fraternité qui semble être, en effet, dans l'histoire, le caractère le plus
> permanent de la démocratie. [30]

In support of this profound and intimate relationship between the truth of
religion and the most permanent characteristics of democracy, Brunetière
referred to an earlier speech in which he had declared that democracy could
only find its justification in the Christian religion[31] and went on to say that
liberty, equality, and fraternity had been introduced in the world by Christianity.

By the Christian religion, Brunetière probably had in mind Roman
Catholicism only. The differentiation is not elaborated upon here; but in
another speech made during the same year, he declared that Calvin had
transformed popular and democratic religion into an aristocratic one. [32]
His main argument in favour of this point of view was that Calvin, with his
analytical and scientific approach to religion, had transformed religion
from a social matter into an individual one. According to Brunetière, individualism and analysis, in contrast with collective faith, were exclusively
connected with aristocracies. Unreflecting and collective faith was, on the
contrary, the main feature of something characterized as "democratic".
This use of "democratic" was probably conditioned by his view that religious
faith was available to all, while he regarded the individualistic, analytic
and rational ways of thought in the field of science as accessible only to a
few individuals. Here we are probably faced with a relation of incompatibility between science and what he held to be democracy. On different occasions similar relationships have been presented, but this is probably the
only time when such an alleged incompatibility has been regarded as an
advantage of what was held to be democracy. This is the main reason why
this nationalistic, conservative, and traditionalist thinker used "democracy"
in an honorific way. In his opinion, individualism and rationalism were extremely opposed to the Catholic and military traditions of France, and he
obviously used "democracy" to signify something in high conformity with
those traditions.

This relation of conformity probably does not imply that Brunetière held
militarism and Catholicism necessarily to be properties implicit in the
signification he attributed to "democracy". At this point, Brunetière mainly
drew attention to the egalitarian character of the army and the anti-individu-
alistic character of Catholicism in indicating this alleged conformity. Thus
democracy had essential properties in common with the French army as
well as with the Catholic church; but it is probably not possible to say that
democracy was necessarily of a military and Catholic character, nor is
there reason to believe this alleged conformity to have been restricted to
the army and the Church if other institutions were characterized by uniform
equality or collective faith. These latter phenomena were closely related,
if not identical, to Brunetière. It is thus most likely that he could not conceive of any real equality unless a people shared the same belief. And such
equality is obviously an essential part, if not the whole, of the signification
he attributed to "democracy".

4. Bourget

Contrary to Brunetière's honorific application of "democracy", Paul Bourget
seems to have used the term in a derogatory way in the rather few occurrences found in his writings. A good indication of this is his opinion that
democracy and revolution were the two idols of the masses, or idola fori
according to the philosophy of Bacon.[33] He did not explain why he held
democracy to be an idol, however.

Bourget was of the opinion that democracy and effective military policy
mutually excluded each other. He stated that Gambetta and Bismarck were
both in favour of popular rule in France. According to Bourget, Bismarck
understood realistically enough that this would mean a militarily weak
France. Bourget went on to say:

Il [Bismarck] savait que cette formule: une Démocratie guerrière, est
synonyme de cette autre: un cercle carré.[34]

It is evident that Bourget agreed with Bismarck, that he, too, held an expression like "warlike democracy" to be analogous with "square circle".
Since everyone will obviously admit that circles and squares, per definitionem, are different phenomena, this formulation is a good example of
Bourget's opinion that conceptually democracy had to have an anti-warlike
or anti-military character. Thus, to say that democracy was anti-warlike
would be an analytic, and not a synthetic, statement, and to be anti-warlike
would be included in his signification of "democracy". On this point, there
is a marked difference between Bourget and Brunetière but a fairly high
degree of similarity between Bourget and most of the other ideologists discussed in this chapter.

Turning to another point of view, Bourget held what he regarded as the
democratic doctrine to be not in conformity with biology. In proof of this
argument Bourget maintained:

Qui dit évolution dit en effet le contraire de révolution. ... Qui dit
sélection dit inégalité et inégalité héritée.

He concluded by asking:

De la doctrine démocratique ou de la nôtre, laquelle se conforme à ces
deux maîtresses lois des sciences naturelles?[35]

Obviously he expected an answer in favour of the latter doctrine. Evolution
and selection he considered to be basic scientific laws, and it is evident that
he did not regard what he designated as "democratic doctrine" to be in conformity with these two laws. His declarations that evolution was the contrary of revolution and that natural selection was connected necessarily with
hereditary inequality are therefore good indications that what he held as the
democratic doctrine was equalitarian and probably that it included some kind
of revolutionary policy as well. If this use of "democratic" is in conformity
with Bourget's use of "democracy", then equality as well as some kind of
revolutionary policy would have to be included in the signification of the

term. No occurrences of "democracy" to confirm or deny such an hypothesis are available, however.

Nothing is mentioned here concerning the relationship between this democratic doctrine and democracy having a pacifist character. It may be assumed that Bourget would have rejected the possibility of an egalitarian doctrine with a warlike character; and thus, this use of "democratic" may be said to have been in conformity with the occurrence of "democracy" under discussion. No direct proof of this hypothesis is available, however.

5. Maurras

Like several other French conservative thinkers, Charles Maurras drew attention to the relationship between democracy and military spirit.   In 1909, in Enquête sur la monarchie, Maurras asserted:

Notre démocratie n'avait pas été pure avant la fin du XIXe siècle. [36]

His only criterion for this statement was his argument that earlier the French people had possessed a certain degree of military spirit and the desire for forceful reunion with Alsace-Lorraine. Thus a certain degree of military spirit would be sufficient to deny a country the label "pure democracy", which implies that the absence of such a spirit was necessarily included in the signification of the phrase "pure democracy". Maurras went on to say:

Cet esprit militaire comportait des respects, des enseignements, des vertus que la démocratie exclut ou qu'elle dédaigne.

As in our first quotation, there seems to be an inverse relationship here between democracy and military spirit, although this formulation can indicate that absence of military spirit was regarded by Maurras as being a non-conceptual characteristic of the concept 'democracy'. According to the latter hypothesis, or if Maurras considered absence of military spirit to be a non-conceptual characteristic, the significations attributed to "pure democracy" and unqualified "democracy" as used in these two statements would differ. Such a difference is indicated in the first quotation, in which Maurras could probably conceive of a democracy which was not necessarily characterized by absence of military spirit, but in which such absence was evidently needed in order that a democracy should be pure.

A rather detailed description of his classification of central political concepts is given somewhat later in his work. Initially Maurras declared a republic to be a form of state that excluded the leadership of a single person; and at the same time he held a republic to be compatible with an oligarchy or an aristocracy in the sense of government by the few or government by the best. Maurras was also of the opinion that a republic might be democratic but a democracy was not always republican. He went on to say:

La loi de la démocratie est d'exclure l'hérédité; elle se déclare le gouvernement du plus grand nombre: tantôt, césarienne ou plébiscitaire, elle est le gouvernement du chef unique élu par ce nombre; tantôt, républicaine, elle veut être le gouvernement de tous par tous, et elle est en réalité le gouvernement de plusieurs que le nombre est censé avoir choisis. [37]

Maurras here evidently operated with one broad concept, or the genus 'democracy', of which 'cæsaristic democracy', or 'plebiscitarian democracy', and 'republican democracy' were species. And it further looks as if to exclude heredity and to declare itself to be the government by the greatest number were held by Maurras to be the conceptual characteristic of his genus 'democracy'. They were perhaps the only characteristics common to all kinds of democracies. By drawing attention to the exclusion of heredity, Maurras used an argumentation similar to that of Bonald almost ninety years earlier.[38] By using "declare" in connection with the government of the greatest number, it may be assumed that Maurras intended to say that democracy did not always follow this rule. 'Cæsaristic democracy' or 'plebiscitarian democracy' evidently represented a kind of democracy that was not subsumable under his concept 'republic'. Under this species of democracy the chief of state is indeed elected by the greatest number. According to the context, Maurras considered the imperial rule of Napoleon III and perhaps that of Napoleon I to represent typical examples of this kind of democracy; although the latter eventuality makes his earlier statements about democracy and military spirit sound somewhat strange. It is clear that Maurras did not hold republican democracy to be the government of all by all, as this form of rule, according to him, claimed. Also Maurras did not seem to consider the governing body in a republican democracy to be really elected by the greatest number. His definition of republican democracy as in reality government by several persons who are regarded as being elected by the greatest number may indicate an hypothesis of that kind; although it is not possible to decide which concrete phenomena, such as nomination, parliamentary political practice, influence of professional politicans, etc., Maurras had in mind.

A derogatory application of "democracy" is not the primary characteristic of Maurras' rather detailed definition. According to the general trends in his political thinking, the alleged exclusion of heredity naturally indicates a negative evaluation, even if nothing explicit is said at this point. A derogatory usage is more evident in our first quotations concerning military spirit and democracy and pure democracy. And a derogatory application is also visible when Maurras discussed workers' organizations. He was of the firm opinion that such organizations were absolutely necessary in a modern society. He emphasized, however, that the organizations should not be founded democratically. Every kind of organization is in need of differentiation, classification, and hierarchies; and he went on to say:

La démocratie a pour essence de renier ou de négliger ces lois éternelles. [39]

He appended in a footnote,

On a discuté sur cette essence. Mais elle n'est pas discutable. C'est une folie pure que de changer le sens des mots. Et, politiquement, c'est plus qu'une folie, c'est une faute grave.

According to the first part of this quotation, Maurras may have had a functional and not a conceptual view in mind, or he may be drawing attention to the political consequences of what he held to be democracy. According to the footnote, however, it seems as if he definitely considered the denial or neglect of the absolute need of differentiation, classification, and hierarchies to be implicit in the signification of "democracy". Thus, a somewhat new aspect is added to the signification of the term as described in his detailed classification of the different concepts 'democracy'. It must be mentioned, however, that to Maurras, this denial and neglect of the absolute necessity for hierarchies was evidently intimately connected with factors such as the exclusion of heredity and the declaration that it was government by the greatest number. It is also clear that Maurras admitted that this signification had not been unanimously agreed upon, but if his habit of condemning those who changed the significations of words, and especially political words, is kept in mind, Maurras can reasonably be regarded as having indicated this signification of the term as being the one which was both traditional and established in the vernacular and probably as having held all other use of the term to be terminological misuse. In the light of the last quotation, Maurras' negative evaluation of "democracy" is obvious; although it may be added that while a derogatory application seems most evident, there is probably no reason to think that he used "democracy" dyslogistically or with a negative evaluation implicit in the signification of the word.

Frequent application of "democracy" does not occur in <u>Enquête sur la monarchie</u>, which may be regarded as the most important political work of Maurras' earlier period. The occurrences quoted do reveal central areas of his political thinking, however, and the few other occurrences are similar to those quoted. [40] At one point, for example, he stated that democracy was incompatible with decentralization because the democracy destroyed the superior virtue demanded by the latter. [41] Maurras' use of "democracy" in works other than the one quoted is of minor importance before 1920, since they do not differ from the one discussed. [42] It may be mentioned that the term was applied in an increasingly derogatory manner from the twenties and thirties onwards, although this period is not within the scope of this work.

6. Faguet

Emile Faguet frequently stressed the danger of growing popular power for the political and intellectual capacity. This is a point also discussed by Renan, Schérer, and Maurras. Faguet's liberal outlook, however, differs on many points from the authoritarian attitude of Maurras. This alleged danger receives a great deal of attention in <u>Le culte de l'incompétence</u>, 1910, a work that can probably be regarded as his most important, and which contains his main application of "democracy" and related terms.

In this work Faguet frequently emphasized that the people at large were generally in favour of incompetent rulers. This was not only because the people were unable to judge whether a man was competent or not, but also because of their desire for rulers with thoughts, feelings, and a level of education similar to their own. In his opinion this was an extremely important matter,

> ... car elle touche au fond même à l'essence même de l'esprit démocratique. [43]

Elaborating further, Faguet maintained that when a people were under the influence of what he called the "democratic tarantella", they first wished all men to be equal and, in consequence, to suppress any kind of inequality, the natural as well as artificial. They wished to abolish heriditary nobility as well as hereditary monarchy and hereditary property, since all of them formed the basis of artificial inequality. They were, however, no more in favour of natural inequalities like differences in intelligence, ability, and learning. These kinds of inequality could not be abolished since they were natural ones, but they might be neutralized if competent persons were regarded as being in favour of inequality and therefore too suspect to hold office:

La compétence est encore à ce point de vue en mauvaise posture. [44]

These statements demonstrate a close association between democracy, on the one hand, and, on the other, abolition of differences of wealth and rank as well as the exclusion of competent men from public positions. Faguet's negative attitude is most evident in these statements. It is, however, doubtful whether this elimination of the influence of competence was conceptually attributed to his concept 'democracy'. Perhaps Faguet equated his concept 'democracy' with government by the people at large, and the alleged elimination of competence can be regarded as belonging to a more functional, and not a conceptual, aspect of this concept. In that case these statements would have been of a synthetic, not of an analytic, kind, and rule by incompetence would not have been included in his significations of "democracy". Possibly, however, Faguet considered democracy and rule by competent persons conceptually to exclude each other. The last quotation may be interpreted to favour such a view, and it may also indicate that something more than direct popular power -- for example, the influence of what he held to be a democratic spirit -- was needed to eliminate the competent.

Four pages later, Faguet stated that if one supposed a legislative assembly to be composed exclusively, or predominantly, of men of property, superior learning, and intelligence, "alors la démocratie est simplement supprimée". [45] According to this, even a government with a national assembly elected by the broadest franchise would cease to be a democracy if the legislative assembly consisted of men of property and talent. Thus, the presence of wealth and competence would furnish a sufficient condition to deny that a state was a democracy, this implies that absence of competence was a conceptual characteristic of his concept "democracy", or that he considered absence of competence, or even the cult of incompetence, as implicit in his signification of "democracy".

On this point, however, some reservation seems to have been made on the same page:

On voit bien qu'il est presque impossible à la démocratie, si elle veut être, de tenir compte des compétences et qu'il lui est à peu près impossible de ne pas les écarter.

This statement probably marks some degree of modification in relation to the previous quotation. Here there is no relationship of absolute incompatibility between democracy and rule by competent persons. Even if the degree of reservation is extremely small, it is not absolutely impossible that Faguet might have imagined a democracy that was not necessarily characterized by the absence of competent persons. Because of this, it seems doubtful whether one can regard absence of competence as a conceptual characteristic; although Faguet's formulation and especially the manner of retaining competent persons in government to be almost impossible for a democracy, if it wanted to remain a democracy, may indicate a conceptual and not a functional aspect. On the whole, it is impossible to formulate a definite conclusion at this point, since Faguet seems to have alternated between formulations of more or less conceptual and functional kinds. It is nevertheless of importance that this relationship between democracy and incompetence can not definitely be regarded as non-conceptual. On this point there is a difference between Faguet and other ideologists, Maine, for example, who discussed similar problems, but who probably held absence of competence to belong entirely to the non-conceptual field.

Probably as an example of the alleged absence of competence, Faguet later declared that modern democracy was not governed by laws. He emphasized that a legislative assembly ought to be the soul, not only the image, of a country. With regard to France, he declared that the current national assembly only represented, and was only capable of representing, the passions of the country. This meant

> ... en d'autres termes, la démocratie moderne n'est pas gouvernée par des lois, mais par des décrets. [46]

Faguet's main argument was that decrees were temporary and exclusively inspired by a particular circumstance, but a law was an ancient rule confirmed by long usage. Again, he stated that a law was a kind of spiritual aristocracy, representing the political wisdom and learning of earlier generations by which, and only by which, national continuity could exist. [47] At this point, rule by law and modern democracy seem to exclude each other: this may imply that absence of rule of law was implicit in the signification of "modern democracy". In support of this point of view, Faguet introduced a quotation from Aristotle, the philosopher whom he held to have been most precise concerning this question. But in this statement Aristotle was discussing only one kind of democracy in describing a form of rule in which sovereignty is transferred from law to the passions of the multitude. And it is clear that even in this quotation, Aristotle might have conceived of other kinds of democracies which were governed according to stated laws. [48] Faguet, however, seems to have had no reservations concerning what he designated as "modern democracy". It is not clear why he should have used "modern democracy" and not unqualified "democracy". Perhaps, like Aristotle, he intended to draw attention to different kinds of democracies or wanted to distinguish modern democracy from one or several earlier kinds; this differentiation is not present in any of Faguet's works, however.

On one occasion in his work Faguet declared that democracy, in its desire to eliminate the influence of competent persons, favoured complete nationalization of all social branches. He also held a socialist form of state to be "l'état extrême et -- l'état complet de ce régime."[49] This formulation may indicate that Faguet held "complete democracy" to be synonymous with "socialist form of state".

In the work .... et l'horreur des responsabilités, the confirmation of Le culte de l'incompétence, Faguet stated that France was a pure democracy. He went on to say that when he had drawn attention to the inconveniences and drawbacks of such a form of rule, some people had mentioned the antique democracies and the American democracy in proof of a contrary point of view. In reply Faguet asserted:

> C'est confondre république et démocratie et il n'y a pas de confusion plus forte. [50]

According to Faguet, antique democracies had never existed. On the contrary, the antique republics had been aristocracies, except the Athenian in

which, for a short time, democracy had established itself coincident to the
decline of the nation. He gave no reasons why the antique republics should
have been aristocracies and not democracies, however, but we may assume
that his main argument would have been that antique republics were generally governed by an instructed minority. Faguet continued:

> Quant à la république américaine, elle est une monarchie constitutionelle;
> elle n'est pas autre chose qu'une monarchie constitutionelle. [51]

His main, or even his sole, reason for refusing the label "democracy" to
the United States and declaring it to be nothing more than a constitutional
monarchy was evidently his estimation of the political function of the American president. Faguet held the American president to be a sovereign
because of his great power over foreign as well as domestic policy and his
independence of any parliament. He admitted that the president was a
sovereign pro tempore, but this did not alter his position. Faguet was even
of the opinion that the American president was more of a monarch than the
British king or the German emperor. He provided no argument to support
this point of view, and it may therefore be inferred that for a state to possess
what Faguet held to be a sovereign was sufficient condition for it not to
belong to the denotata of "democracy". Thus, absence of a sovereign was
probably a conceptual characteristic of his concept 'democracy'; and we
may also assume that this alleged absence was related to his general statement about democracy and rule by incompetence.

Faguet probably intended these arguments to silence the critics who
opposed his theory that democracy necessarily, or almost necessarily,
meant rule by incompetents; and as far as can be seen, nothing having
further relevance for the signification of "democracy" appeared in this work.
Statements similar to those made earlier were frequently repeated.

For a broader picture of Faguet's application of "democracy", a few
examples of his usage from earlier, minor writings may be given. Generally these are fairly similar to those in his two central works. He attributed
absence of intellectual superiority to democracy several times, and there
is good reason to believe that on one occasion he held intellectual superiority
to be conceptually incompatible with his concept 'democracy'. [52] On the
other hand, there is a difference in relation to his later terminology when,
in 1901, he wrote: "Les Etats-Unis sont une démocratie politique". [53]

The same year, in reviewing the speeches of Brunetière that we have
discussed, Faguet's argumentation and terminology were almost identical
with those of Brunetière. Faguet, too, considered the army to be a school
in fraternity and equality, since young men from all social classes served
under the same discipline, and in his opinion the army was la grande niveleuse. Concerning its equalitarian character, Faguet even stated:

> Non seulement l'armée est démocratique, mais on peut dire qu'il n'y a
> que dans l'armée que la démocratie existe d'une manière pratique.

And of the egalitarian and the anti-capitalistic character of the army -- the
only place where money was out of question -- Faguet concluded:

> Elle [l'armée] est comme l'expression brilliante et noble de la démo-
> cratie elle-même. [54]

First of all we are struck by Faguet's attitude towards what he labelled
"democracy". Although a derogatory application was most probably a
permanent tendency in his writing before and after this review, the present

use of the term is likely to have been honorific, especially when we re-
member Faguet's positive attitude towards the army. There is without
doubt much similarity between his close identification of what he designated
as "democracy" in an egalitarian institution and his other use of the term,
although absence of competence is definitely not implied in the signification
of "democracy" at this point. Thus it may be concluded that there are some
changes in the signification of "democracy".

Faguet's belief in a intimate relationship between the army and democracy seems to have appeared only in this review of Brunetière's speeches.
In 1899, for example, Faguet held democracy to be "très patriote, mais en
même temps très peu militaire. "[55] And in 1907, in his usual way, Faguet
declared that democracy essentially aimed at making all men equal and
therefore eliminated the most natural inequality without recognizing superiority of any kind. He went on to say that superiority was a military instinct
and that the army needed a hierarchical corps of officers, and he concluded:

> Cet instinct militaire est juste l'opposé de l'instinct égalitaire.[56]

Thus there is the fairly interesting phenomenon of an ideological, and probably also a terminological, trend clearly interrupted by the argumentation
and terminology in the review of Brunetière. It is fairly certain that this
interruption was limited to the confrontation with these speeches.

7. Le Bon

Gustave Le Bon, like Faguet, associated a rather hostile attitude towards
intellectual capacity with what he held to be democracy. In Psychologie des
foules, of 1895, Le Bon deplored that mankind should be entering the era of
the masses; the central concrete point of his argument was:

> Si les démocraties eussent possédé le pouvoir qu'elles ont aujourd'hui à
> l'époque où furent inventés les métiers mécaniques, la vapeur et les
> chemins de fer, la réalisation de ces inventions eût été impossible, ou ne
> l'eût été qu'au prix de révolutions et de massacres répétés. ... Il est
> heureux, pour les progrès de la civilisation, que la puissance des foules
> n'ait commencé à naître que lorsque les grandes découvertes de la
> science et de l'industrie étaient déjà accomplies.[57]

What Le Bon regarded as democracy is clearly connected in this context
with hostility towards technical invention and scientific discoveries. On
this point Le Bon uses arguments similar to those of Maine several years
earlier.[58] And as in Maine's terminology, technical and scientific stagnation was probably not implicit in Le Bon's signification of "democracy".
While there is obviously a clear association between this kind of stagnation
and what he labelled "democracy", it may have been regarded as a social
and cultural consequence of democracy and not as a conceptual characteristic of his concept 'democracy'. In other words, his statements about alleged hostility towards technical and scientific discoveries were probably of
a synthetic and not an analytic kind. It is evident that "democracy" was used
here synonymously with "power of the masses", but there is perhaps no
reason to assume that Le Bon used "democracy" here with a signification
different from that used by those in favour of what they labelled with this
term but who disagreed with Le Bon over intellectual stagnation. Few people

today would agree with Le Bon that great technical inventions and scientific discoveries were accomplished in 1895.

Generally Le Bon's use of "democracy" as synonymous with "power of the masses" seems to have been the predominant application in this work. A different application occurs in connection with his comments on England, however. In a general way Le Bon initially stated:

Les noms ne sont que de vaines étiquettes dont l'historien qui va un peu au fond des choses n'a pas à se préoccuper. [59]

As an example of this semantic point, Le Bon mentioned England as the most democratic country in the world, but nevertheless it had a monarchical form of government. On the other hand, he said, the most severe despotism was to be found in the Latin-American republics, in spite of their republican constitutions. Here Le Bon was making use of political terms which he himself obviously did not hold to be empty labels. It was probably a kind of current verbal application only, "republic" being used to denote the Latin-American republics and "monarchy" to denote the form of rule in England. His sole argument in favour of his statement that England was the most democratic country in the world was a quotation from the American journal Forum:

L'Angleterre est aujourd'hui le pays le plus démocratique de l'univers, celui où les droits de l'individu sont le plus respectés, et celui où les individues possèdent le plus de liberté.

Properties such as the greatest respect for individual rights and the greatest amount of individual liberty do not seem to be regarded by Le Bon as mere consequences of democratic rule but can even be held to be implicit in the signification "most democratic" as used in this quotation. Le Bon himself agreed with the statement; and since the power of the masses cannot be said to be identical with these properties, the signification he attributed to "most democratic" differs from what he generally attributed to "democracy". Le Bon probably considered these properties to be the contrary of what he held to be the power of the masses.

This way of using "democracy" and "democratic" with mutually incompatible significations is never admitted by Le Bon, although he clearly pointed out ambiguous use of political terms in general and especially of "democracy" in the vernacular. In discussing the function of words and formulas, Le Bon opened his argument by stating that in some mysterious way the masses generally became intoxicated by words. He said that it would be easy to build a pyramid higher than that of Cheops with the bones of men who had fallen victims to the force of words and formulas. He added that it was generally the words with vaguely defined significations which possessed the greatest force of action, and he referred to words like "democracy", "socialism", "liberty", and "equality". Le Bon further observed that the words currently employed among the masses were given different significations by different peoples. As an example, he stated:

Chez les Latins le mot démocratie, signifie surtout effacement de la volonté et de l'initiative de l'individu devant celles de la communauté représentées par l'Etat. C'est l'Etat qui est chargé de plus en plus de diriger tout, de centraliser, de monopoliser et de fabriquer tout. ...
Chez l'Anglo-saxon, celui d'Amérique notamment, le même mot démocratie signifie au contraire développement intense de la volonté et de l'individu, effacement aussi complet que possible de l'Etat,... [60]

Thus the same word signified for one people something contrary to the significations attributed to it by another people.

We have here two descriptive definitions of the use of "democracy" within two special fields of application. Le Bon's thesis of the emotive function of words and formulas and their ability to intoxicate men's minds may be generally sound. But his statement concerning the concrete examples is faulty. Le Bon's statements are apparently not based upon empirical research into current political terminology, but are founded upon what he regarded, by impression or intuition, as the two significations of the term. On this point, however, Le Bon is far from alone, and has only used methods similar to those of many others dealing with the same problem. Without empirical research into current verbal usage, Le Bon and others should have made some reservations in connection with their assertions in this complicated field, since it is easy to find examples, particularly in English political language, [61] which directly contradict their assertions. Apart from the writings of Bentham and perhaps those of Godwin, I have found no occurrences to support this version of the alleged English use of "democracy". Compared with his other uses of "democracy" and related terms in this work, Le Bon subscribed to what he held to be the Anglo-Saxon verbal application when he declared that England, with its guarantee of individual rights, was the most democratic country in the world, and he subscribed to what he held to be the Latin application when stating that democracy, by means of repression, was a hindrance to technical invention and scientific discovery.

Little from Le Bon's other writings is relevant to our purpose. In La Psychologie Politique, he said:

> Gouvernement populaire ne signifie nullement gouvernement par le peuple, mais bien par ses meneurs. [62]

It is possible that he might have used "democracy" here synonymously with "popular government", and was thus of the opinion that democracy was not government by the people but by its leaders. But evidence of such a relationship is not strong enough.

CHAPTER XII

BRITISH CONSERVATISM AND CONSERVATIVE LIBERALISM[1]

Although an extensive application of "democracy" is found in the language of earlier British conservative thinkers such as Carlyle, Disraeli, May, Lecky, Acton, and Maine, the term occurs fairly infrequently in the terminology of James F. Stephen.

A clearly honorific application of "democracy" was used by the young Disraeli who declared England, in 1835, to be a "complete democracy". On the other hand, Carlyle generally used this word derogatorily, although in one case even he evidently identified himself with what he termed "democracy" when he said:

> All that Democracy ever meant lies there; the attainment of a truer and truer <u>Aristocracy</u>, or Government again by the Best.

In this chapter, such variation will not be found. On one hand, the extremely derogatory application that was a predominant characteristic of Carlyle's use of "democracy" is difficult to find; yet on the other hand, it is impossible to find occurrences that indicate honorific application. On the whole the variations encountered here are fairly small. There are no important differences among the political authors discussed, nor are there important ambiguities within their use of "democracy". Generally a derogatory application is the central characteristic of their terminology. And this common mark predominates to a degree seldom found in political terminology, where ambiguities and variations occur more frequently than do stable and fairly uniform verbal applications.

1. Stephen

A derogatory use of "democracy" is among the most important characteristics of Stephen's use of the term. The main theme of his central political work, <u>Liberty, Equality, Fraternity</u>, 1873, is that the wise minority are the rightful masters of the foolish majority. Stephen also maintained that it was cowardly to deny the right to coerce out of fear that force might be misapplied against oneself. In one sense, a horse is stronger than a man, but nevertheless a man who held that horses and men ought to be independent of each other for fear of the horse riding the man would be a poor creature. [2]

In conformity with this view favouring the leadership of the wise and few, Stephen held that

> ... the growth of liberty in the sense of democracy tends to diminish, not to increase, originality and individuality. [3]

As his main argument, he said that to make all men equals, as far as laws could make men equals, was to make each hopelessly feeble in the presence of an overwhelming majority. The existence of such a state of society would reduce individuals to impotence, and to tell them to be powerful, original, and independent under such conditions would be mockery, like plucking a bird's feathers in order to put it on a level with the beasts and then telling it to fly.

To Stephen "democracy" here seems to signify a state of society and not a particular form of government, and he seems to consider a high degree of equality to be a necessary, perhaps a sufficient, condition for a society to be labelled "democracy". Although this equalization was most likely implicit in his connotation of "democracy", the same cannot be said of the alleged elimination of originality and independence, since he probably held these factors to be consequences of the equalitarian process and not conceptual characteristics of his concept 'democracy'.

A somewhat similar argument occurs later in his book. Stephen maintained that the terms "liberty" and "freedom" were used in very different ways by enthusiastic people. Of "liberty" he said:

> No way of using the word, however, is so common as when it is used to signify popular government. People who talk of liberty mean, as a general rule, democracy or some kind of government which stands rather nearer to democracy than the one under which they are living. This, generally speaking, is the Continental sense of the word. [4]

Somewhat different from our first quotation, where "democracy" seemed to signify a state of society, the term was used here to signify a form of government. Democracy and governments closer to democracy than to any other form are probably subsumable under his concept 'popular government'. Thus Stephen may have used "popular government" with a somewhat broader signification than that of "democracy", or used "democracy" to connote exclusively a purer form of what he labelled "popular government". In arguing against the alleged trend of using "liberty" in the vernacular and especially in political language on the Continent, Stephen stated:

> Now democracy has, as such, no definite or assignable relation to liberty. [5]

As proof of this view, he went on to say that the degree to which governmental power interferred with individuals depended upon the size of the country, the density of population, the national temper, and the like, although the form of the government had little to do with the matter. Here liberty is evidently regarded by Stephen as a phenomenon in which the degree of governmental interference in individual matters is rather small. Stephen certainly considered democracy to be something that could exist quite independently of liberty, although there is no reason to believe that he here held democracy to be incompatible with liberty. Thus there is an indirect criticism of an alleged use of "liberty", even if there is no direct charge of misuse of the term.

Stephen also stated that all human experience proved that if restraints were minimized, or if the largest possible measure of liberty was accorded to all human beings, the result would not be equality but inequality reproducing itself in a geometrical progression. The liberty to acquire property was the most important of all liberties, and private property was the very essence of inequality. [6] "Democracy" does not occur in these statements; but if Stephen still considered a high degree of equality to be the main characteristic of democracy, then liberty and democracy were not only different phenomena, but could probably be regarded as incompatible. Any such conclusion was not formulated by Stephen, however.

In addition, as a consequence of the equalitarian mark of democracy, Stephen also seems to have attributed a rather revolutionary and even sanguinary character to such a form of rule. He declared democracy to be a system that embodied in its most intense form all the bitterness and resentment which could possibly be stored up in the hearts of the most disappointed, envious, and ferociously vengeful members of the human race. He concluded:

It [democracy] is the poor saying to the rich, "We are masters now, by the establishment of liberty, which means democracy, and as all men are brothers, entitled to share and share alike in the common stock, we will make you disgorge or we will put you to death. " [7]

This use of "democracy" has a signification rather closely associated with, or perhaps even identified with, a violent social revolution by the poor. We noted a similar use of the term during the first half of the century by the otherwise very different ideologists such as Babeuf, Mazzini, and Guizot, but this application is rather rare in the latter half of the century, although it cannot be limited to this occurrence in the language of Stephen.

2. May

In the preface to his great historical work, Democracy in Europe, 1877, Thomas Erskine May declared that Montesquieu had pointed out the various senses in which the term "liberty" has been understood and that he, for his part, would add that "democracy" had acquired at least as many. He opened a rather detailed descriptive survey of the different applications of "democracy" with the statement:

As a form of government it [the term "democracy"] signifies the sovereignty of the whole body of the people. [8]

May added, however, that as there were as many degrees and conditions of democracy as of liberty

... the term also comprehends the political power or, influence, of the people, under all forms of government.

It is this last application which May generally considered to be his own in this work. Thus he declared:

It denotes a principle or force, and not simply an institution, and it is in this sense, that the term is to be generally understood, in this history.

This statement seems to imply that "democracy" was used for the most part to signify popular forces struggling for greater political power and attempting to further the political principle that political power ought to belong to the people at large.

May declared that "democracy" had also been used in other senses which, if not so accurate, had been sanctioned by conventional use. May gave the example:

In default of a more extended vocabulary, it is often spoken of as a revolutionary force, opposed to existing institutions, if not to law and order, ... in view of many popular movements abroad, such a term can scarcely be misapplied.

May also declared that the term "democracy" sometimes referred to the humbler citizens of a State as opposed to the aristocracy, and finally that the term was used to denote a certain State such as the Athenian or the French democracies. He concluded by saying that the sense in which the word was used could in any case only be judged from the context. [9]

May gives a rather detailed survey of what he held to be the different applications of "democracy" at that time. In his use of the term, many occurrences, among several hundred, are in conformity with what he held to be current in the political terminology. A few of the more typical applications which are found in connection with central political thoughts in his work are quoted.

In comparison with the political experiences which could be noted from the February Revolution, May declared that in England the time-honoured home of freedom, the government enjoyed the hearty confidence of the people. He further asserted that only those governments were secure which rested upon the broad basis of public opinion and national support, and he concluded:

> From this critical year of revolutions the moral may be drawn, that freedom is the surest safeguard against democracy. [10]

"Democracy" probably signifies here "a revolutionary force, opposed to existing institutions, if not to law and order". The use in this quotation seems to be May's personal application of the term and not how he held it to be used in default of a more extended vocabulary.

A similar way of using "democratic" occurs when he declared the execution of Charles I to have been "the most democratic act in the history of Europe. "[11] "Most democratic" is here used to describe an act May considered to have been revolutionary as well as criminal.

At a rather central point in this work, in surveying the main difference between France and England, May stated:

> The history of one, in modern times, is the history of democracy, not of liberty; the history of the other is the history of liberty, not of democracy. [12]

The history of England was the history of popular rights and franchises acquired, maintained, extended, and developed without subverting the ancient constitution of the State, and he added that it was a history of reforms, not of revolutions. Possibly he regarded this to be a condition contrary to what he designated as "democracy"; this also seems to indicate an association between democracy and revolutionary policy. In addition to this non-revolutionary characteristic, May considered the history of England to be the history of liberty because the permanent and gradual development of popular rights and extended franchise did not destroy the ancient constitution. What he called "liberty" is contrasted here with "democracy". It is hardly possible to say, according to this quotation, that May used the terms "liberty" and "democracy" to designate two incompatible phenomena, but it is nevertheless obvious that he felt that these phenomena could exist independently of each other.

A similar relationship between the significations of "democracy" and "liberty" occurs in a short description of the first part of the reign of Queen Victoria, in which he maintained that "liberty rather than democracy advanced. "[13] It is difficult to tell whether "democracy" was used to connote a form of state, a political principle, or the influence of the people, but at least the term was used to signify something very different from what he regarded as the current political constitution or institutions of England -- phenomena which he held to be the freest and best in the world. Here is most probably found the main reason for his derogatory usage of "democracy".

3. Maine

Henry Summer Maine started his essay "The Nature of Democracy", 1866, by referring to the works of Austin and Schérer:

> M. Schérer, so far as my knowledge extends, has been the first French writer to bring into clear light the simple truth stated by Austin, that Democracy means properly a particular form of government. [14]

The context makes it clear that Maine was speaking about the signification of "democracy" and not about the content of 'democracy' of which "democracy" was used as conceptual designation. This statement can be taken to confirm that Maine also regarded "democracy", when correctly used, as connoting exclusively a form of government. In the text of this statement it is probably correct to agree with Maine in his opinion of Schérer as the first French writer to declare democracy to be a form of government only, although Schérer was probably talking about the concept 'democracy' and not directly about the signification of "democracy". Maine was also probably correct in his opinion of Austin, since Austin stated that "democracy" properly signified a form of government and used the term predominantly in this sense. However, Austin once held the British government to be "the most democratical in spirit and effect of all governments past and present".[15] His criterion for this statement was probably that the interests of the whole population, and not only those of the sovereign body, were habitually consulted. Austin himself was in favour of the British government's possessing this special kind of democratic character in spite of his admission that, in its form of sovereignty, the American government was certainly more democratic than the government of the mother country. A State might then, according to Austin, be democratic, or even most democratic, in a way that was independent of its form of government, that is, "democracy", within a certain context, might signify something other than a form of government.
Maine continued, still referring to "democracy",

> There is no word about which a denser mist of vague language, and a larger heap of loose metaphors, has been collected.

This point is elaborated upon a little later when Maine held it to be exceedingly remarkable that "democracy", in current terminology, was used under the various disguises of "freedom", "revolution", "republic", "popular government", and "reign of the people". He continued:

> Every sort of metaphor, signifying irresistible force, and conveying admiration or dread, has been applied to it by its friends or its enemies. [16]

As examples of this use, he mentioned an unnamed English orator who had compared democracy with the grave, taking everything and giving nothing back. On the other hand, he quoted the American historian Bancroft who, inter alia, had declared democracy to be "the change which Divine wisdom ordained, and which no human policy or force could hold back, -- and as certain as the decrees of eternity." As an example of what he held to be still more eulogistic and confused terminology, Maine quoted an unnamed disciple of Walt Whitman who had written, "O glancing eyes! O leaping shining waters! Do I not know that thou, Democracy, dost control and inspire: that thou too hast relations to them, as Niagara has relations to Erie and Ontario."[17] Maine reacted rather heavily against poetic terminology in the field of politics and maintained that if this man were to have been confronted with the dictum that democracy was a form of government, his poetical vein might have been drowned but his mind would have been invigorated by the healthful douche of cold water. It must be observed that although Maine did not favour what he designated as "democracy", he indicated his dislike not only towards those who used "democracy" as a eulogistic metaphor but also towards those who, like the English orator, used it as a dyslogistic one.

Concerning his own application of the term, Maine said:

Although Democracy does signify something indeterminate, there is nothing vague about it. It is simply and solely a form of government. It is the government of the State by the Many, as opposed, according to the old Greek analysis, to its government by the Few, and to its government by One.[18]

In this statement, the occurrence of "democracy" in the first sentence may be regarded as a meta-occurrence, while "it" in the second sentence most probably refers to the concept 'democracy' and not to the term. By "indeterminate" Maine had in mind that the border between government by the few and by the many was necessarily indistinct. But this statement, however, did not imply that democracy nevertheless remained exclusively a form of government.

Thus government by the many can reasonably be held to be the exclusive connotation expressed by "democracy" as used in Maine's central statement. As far as can be seen, there are no occurrences in his terminology that contradict this application.

In several places Maine emphasized that democracy could not be regarded as a progressive kind of government. On this point he said:

The delusion that Democracy, when it has once had all things put under its feet, is a progressive form of government, lies deep in the convictions of a particular political school; but there can be no delusion grosser.[19]

As in one of Le Bon's later statements, Maine emphasized that all that had made England famous and wealthy had been the work of minorities, sometimes very small ones. It seemed to him quite certain that if England had had a widely extended franchise and a large electoral body for four centuries, there would have been no reformation of religion, no change of dynasty, no toleration of dissent, and even no accurate calendar, and that the threshing-machine, the powerloom, the spinning-jenny, and, possibly, the steam-engine would have been prohibited. Maine added that even in his time vaccination was in the utmost danger, and he was also of the opinion that one could generally say that the gradual establishment of the masses in power was the blackest omen for all legislation founded on scientific opinion, which required extension of mind to understand it and self-denial to submit to it. [20] A similar argument occurs in another essay in which he also held universal suffrage to have excluded free trade from the United States. [21] Perhaps Maine's stay in India, where, as he said, he had been struck by what he described as the enormous apathy of the people, was an important reason behind his general scepticism about the ability of the masses to govern themselves.

Maine's dislike of what he designated as "democracy" was based on his view of it as a form of government characterized by political and economic stagnation. Whether Maine would have regarded stagnation as a conceptual characteristic of his concept 'democracy' is doubtful. Maine held government by the many to be a conceptual characteristic and that aversion for technical improvement and scientific discoveries was an inevitable consequence of that form of government, although a non-conceptual characteristic. Thus intellectual and technical stagnation was probably not implicit in his signification of "democracy". It is likely that Maine did not operate with a concept 'democracy' different from those who approved of government by the many, but he certainly disagreed with the latter concerning its non-conceptual characteristics.

Maine also held democracy to be a rather insecure and unstable form of government, since the chief democratic right was the right to censure one's superiors. Since he regarded obedience as the great military virtue, Maine, for similar reasons, held that:

> No two organisations can be more opposed to one another than an army scientifically disciplined and equipped, and a nation democratically governed. [22]

This association of democracy with intellectual, political, and economic stagnation is a broad ideological trend in the latter half of the nineteenth century, especially in French political thought. In England Maine can probably be regarded as the ideologist who most explicitly indicated such an association.

4. Acton

While Maine primarily drew attention to the alleged antiprogressive character of democracy, in the ideological writings of the liberal Catholic Lord Acton are found problems concerning the relationship between democracy and liberty or the possibility of individual independence and the right to dissent. Such a problem is evident in one of his earlier essays, dating from 1861, in which he discussed the political causes of the American Revolution. In introduction he said, "The fate of every democracy, of every government based on the sovereignty of the people, " [23] depended upon the choice made between absolute power, on one hand, and the restraint furnished by legality and authority of tradition, on the other. "Democracy" is probably used here synonymously with "government based on the sovereignty of the people". Acton went on to say that in the choice between rule by will and physical force and rule by law, popularly governed States offered a strict analogy with monarchies, which were also either despotic or constitutional. According to Acton, however, democracy and monarchy gravitated in different directions,

...democracy tends naturally to realize its principle, the sovereignty of the people, and to remove all limits and conditions of its exercise, whilst monarchy tends to surround itself with such conditions.

The resistance of a king is gradually overcome by those who seek to share his power, but a similar process does not take place in what Acton held to be democracies. He concluded:

Hence monarchy grows more free, in obedience to the laws of its existence, whilst democracy becomes more arbitrary. [24]

As well as being used synonymously with "government based on the sovereignty of the people", "democracy" is used here to label a form of government that tends to become more and more arbitrary by removing limits and legal conditions. However, Acton referred to a choice between absolute power and constitutional or legal power, therefore these properties hardly represent what he conceptually attributed to his concept 'democracy'.

A similar problem is discussed later in his essay when Acton maintained that civil equality must be founded on social equality and on national unity and that these things were the strength of the American republic. He went on to say:

Pure democracy is that form of government in which the community is sovereign, in which, therefore, the State is most nearly identified with society.

He added that society existed for the protection of interests but the State existed for the realization of rights, and that the State set up a moral, objective law and pursued an object distinct from the ends and purposes of society.

This is essentially repugnant to democracy, which recognizes only the interests and rights of the community, and is therefore inconsistent with the consolidation of authority which is implied in the notion of the State. It resists the development of the social into the moral community. If, therefore, a democracy includes persons with separate interests or an inferior nature, it tyrannizes over them. There is no mediator between the part and the whole; there is no room, therefore, for differences of class, of wealth, of race, equality is necessary to the liberty which is sought by a pure democracy. [25]

Acton obviously regarded democracy and pure democracy as alien to his conception of the State. The concept 'State', according to him, seems first of all to include a moral and legal authority, authority which was on a higher level than that of society and which was to serve as a mediator among different sections of society and between the different sections and the whole. In contrast to his earlier statement, here democracy is said to tyrannize persons with separate interests, which implies that dissentient opinions would be suppressed. Even if Acton admitted that democracy seeks liberty, it is probable that he would not have regarded liberty as compatible with such a form of government, since liberty, as he understood it, implied that separate interests were not tyrannized and possibly also that there ought to be at least some room for differences of class, race, and wealth. Thus democracy and liberty seem mutually exclusive, although it is difficult to say whether he included absence of liberty in the signification of "democracy" and "pure democracy" as used here. However, the statements about the alleged tyrannizing of separate interests seem synthetic, not analytic, so that absence of liberty would not have been implicit in his signification of "democracy". To return to Acton's text, he commented on the fate of the American republic,

> It is simply the democracy of the French revolution that has destroyed the union, by disintegrating the remnants of English traditions and institutions. [26]

Acton also drew attention to the necessity for national unity in a democracy. His main argument was that aristocracies generally had more sympathy and more intercourse with foreign aristocracies than with the rest of the nation. The bonds of class were stronger than those of nationality, so that "a democracy in abolishing classes, renders national unity imperative. " [27] In another essay Acton maintained that the theory of national unity was a product of democracy; and he added that in contrast to this theory of national unity, the claims of national liberty belonged to the theory of freedom. He went on to say:

> These two views of nationality, corresponding to the French and English systems, are connected in name only, and are in reality the opposite extremes of political thoughts. [28]

Referring to the French system of nationality, or to the theory of national unity, Acton was of the firm opinion that this system represented a perpetual supremacy of the collective will, to which every other influence must defer and which therefore overruled the rights and wishes of the population, absorbed their divergent interests in a fictitious unity and sacrificed their several inclinations to the higher claim of nationality. According to Acton, this theory was incompatible with liberty; and since this theory of national unity was a necessary consequence of the form of rule which he designated "democracy", it may be inferred that on this point he held democracy to be incompatible, or almost incompatible, with liberty. Again it is difficult to see whether absence of liberty was included in his signification of "democracy". From a comparative point of view, it can be observed that Acton used terminology and argumentation similar to, but earlier than, May's, especially in his way of contrasting the alleged democratic tradition of France with the liberal tradition of England.

Several years afterwards, in 1878, when reviewing May's work, Acton stated:

> The effective distinction between liberty and democracy ... cannot be too strongly drawn. [29]

He went on to say, in an historical survey, that slavery had rather frequently been associated with democracy by ancient philosophers as well as Confederate ideologists in the United States: that from the best days of Athens, from the days of Anaxagoras, Protagoras, and Socrates, there had existed a strong affinity between democracy and religious persecution; and that the bloodiest deeds between the wars of religion and the Revolution had been due to the fanatism of men living in the primitive republics of the Rhætian Alps, where only one out of six democratic cantons tolerated Protestants. Acton held that in the Netherlands in 1578 the fifteen Catholic provinces would have joined in the revolt but for the furious bigotry of Ghent, and that the democracy of Friesland was the most intolerant of the States. In America, aristocratic colonies had defended toleration against their democratic neighbours; and Acton finally declared that down to the eighteenth century, religious liberty had been understood more often in monarchies, even in those that were absolute, than in free commonwealths. [30] Religious liberty was acknowledged by Richelieu while he was constructing the despotism of the Bourbons, as it was by the electors of Brandenburg at the time when they made themselves absolute. In England, after Clarendon, the notion of indulgence had been inseparable from the reign of Charles II. [31]

This historical survey was without doubt intended to serve as proof of his statement that the strongest possible distinction must be drawn between democracy and liberty. But how far, or indeed whether, he regarded democracy to be incompatible with liberty is not clear. It is obvious that Acton was of the opinion that these phenomena could exist independently and that democracy in many cases had been characterized by absence of liberty. These things cannot, however, necessarily be said to imply incompatibility. Acton's statement concerning the strong affinity between democracy and religious persecution, which he believed to have existed since the best days of Athens, may be taken to indicate a relationship of incompatibility; although this statement, at least in some interpretations of "affinity", cannot be regarded as sufficient proof of such a relationship. In that case, the relationship between democracy and liberty in this last statement may be related to the one in our first quotation from Acton, in which democracy was said to tend towards arbitrary government, but also in which absence of liberty was probably not a necessary property of "democracy". The question of this relationship is of great importance in an inquiry into the connotation attributed to "democracy" by Acton. On the one hand, there are occurrences which may indicate a relationship of mutual incompatibility between liberty and democracy, although, on the other hand, there is little proof that absence of liberty is a conceptual characteristic of his concept 'democracy'. It is, however, obvious that Acton not only held democracy to be very different from liberty but that he also regarded democracy as something which had been and might be again dangerous to liberty. It is probably this reason first of all that prevented this outstanding advocate of personal independence and individual liberty from ever using "democracy" in an honorific way.

5. Lecky

Like May and Acton, William E. H. Lecky drew attention to the relationship between liberty and democracy. In his central work, Democracy and Liberty, 1896, Lecky maintained:

> A tendency to democracy does not mean a tendency to parliamentary government, or even a tendency towards greater liberty. On the contrary, strong arguments may be adduced, both from history and from the nature of things, to show that democracy may often prove the direct opposition of liberty.

As examples of this view, he continued:

> In ancient Rome the old aristocratic republic was gradually transformed into a democracy, and it then passed speedily into an imperial despotism. In France a corresponding change has more than once taken place.

With regard to this last point, Lecky said:

A despotism resting on a plebescite is quite as natural a form of democracy as a republic, and some of the strongest democratic tendencies are
distinctly adverse to liberty. Equality is the idol of democracy, but, with
the infinitely various capacities and energies of men, this can only be
attained by a constant, systematic, stringent repression of their mutual
development. [32]

These statements can, at least, be said to reveal clearly that Lecky
regarded what he held to be democracy to be extremely different from
liberty. On this point Lecky seems to have been in favour of an even
stronger line of demarcation than Acton. In contrast to other conservative
political thinkers, Lecky regarded democracy as a form of government not
only apt to lead to despotism but even held plebescitarian despotism to be
subsumable under a concept 'democracy', with "democracy" as its conceptual designation. It is likely that Lecky considered the imperial rules of
both Napoleons to be examples of this species of the genus 'democracy'.
This indicates a terminology that, at this point, is similar to those of Maurras and Bagehot.

Lecky shared Stephen's opinion that inequality was certain to ensue
wherever the natural forces had unrestricted play. And he probably thought
a rather high degree of unrestricted play in social life was essential to what
he designated as "liberty".

Whether Lecky held democracy and liberty to be mutually incompatible
phenomena in political life or whether he included the absence of liberty in
the signification of "democracy" are problems similar to those in Acton's
terminology. When, for example, Lecky declares some of the strongest
democratic tendencies to be distinctly adverse to liberty, he may be suggesting a relationship of mutual incompatibility. On the other hand, when he
speaks about constant, stringent, and systematic suppression, he evidently
held this to be a fairly inevitable means of arriving at democracy. But there
is no reason for thinking that these factors are necessarily implicit in the
signification of "democracy". It is, in any case, certain that he held democracy and liberty to be very different phenomena, although it is not possible
to conclude that there is a relationship of incompatibility. However, the
degree of probability of such a relationship is somewhat greater in Lecky's
statements than in Acton's arguments.

Concerning his use of "democracy" and related terms, there is little
that may help to solve these problems of definition, in spite of a rather frequent application of these terms in his work. As an example of a rather
symptomatic application of "democratic", Lecky declared the Church and the
guild to have been "the two most democratic institutions in the Middle Ages".[33]
He considered the Church to have taught the essential spiritual equality of
mankind and, further, to have placed men from the servile classes on a
pedestal before which kings and nobles were compelled to bow. At the same
time the Church had also been the most tremendous instrument of spiritual
tyranny the world had ever seen. The guild had organized industry on a self-
governing and representative basis, at the same time restricting and regu-
lating it in all its details with the most stringent despotism. These statements reveal Lecky's belief that it was definitely compatible for institutions
to be both democratic and tyrannical, even despotic.

Lecky considered one of the greatest divisions in existing politics to be
whether, in the last resort, the world should be governed by its ignorance or
by its intelligence. According to one party, the party to which Lecky him-

self undoubtably belonged, the preponderant power should be with education and property; according to the other, the ultimate source of power belonged legitimately to the majority of the nation, or,

> In other words, to the poorest, the most ignorant, the most incapable, who are necessarily the most numerous.[34]

"Democracy" or related terms do not directly occur in this text, but "The democratic theory" is used as the title of the page; and it is evidently this theory only that Lecky had in mind here.

It was mentioned initially that a derogatory application of "democracy" is a common mark of the political theorists discussed in this chapter. Stephen, May, Maine, Acton, and Lecky present a uniform picture on this point, something seldom found in political language when several authors are considered collectively. There is among these men probably not that degree of negative evaluation apparent when, for example, Burke said a perfect democracy to be the most shameless thing in the world. More significantly, however, is surely that there is not to be found any influence from Disraeli's early honorific application. On this aspect there is also a difference between these authors and most other groups of conservative ideologists; for example, we have seen occurrences in Hegel's terminology which probably can be regarded as honorific uses of "democracy", and among French contemporary conservatives is clearly seen an honorific usage by Brunetière and, in a few cases, even by Renan and Faguet.

The consistently negative evaluation of "democracy" cannot be said, however, to have been founded upon identical premises. To a large extent, democracy was without doubt conceived as an egalitarian system by all the authors in question; but Stephen and May to a certain degree regarded democracy as a revolutionary force, while Maine held democracy to be alien to science and intellectual progress because of its alleged slowness and stability. Furthermore, the negative attitudes of May, Lecky, and especially Acton were primarily caused by their viewing democracy as a potential, or even real, danger to tolerance and freedom of speech. This last attitude, which was an important tendency in political thought in the nineteenth century, characterizes a greater part of Tocqueville's political thinking, and can also be seen in John Stuart Mill's writings. However, no author drew so sharp a distinction between liberty and democracy as Acton.

CHAPTER XIII

GERMAN CONSERVATISM

Renan, Faguet, and Maurras among French political thinkers and especially Maine, Acton, and Lecky among the British present a somewhat homogeneous picture. In this chapter the picture is more heterogenous. There is not, for example, much in common between Nietzsche and the political historian Treitschke, nor is there much common ground between Thomas Mann and Meinecke. Difficulties will probably always arise when literary authors are discussed in connection with political theorists. In this case, however, to drop Nietzshe and Thomas Mann would be a serious omission, since each presents a usage of "democracy" that contains several interesting aspects.

In regard to their attitudes towards what they designated "democracy", Treitschke's use like that of Fichte, Schleiermacher, and Stahl is fairly, but not extremely, derogatory. Hegel's use was rather neutral. Nietzsche used "democracy" derogatorily, in certain cases probably even dyslogistically. Thomas Mann, in one of the most fascinating works written during World War I, used "democracy" on the whole very derogatorily; but it is possible, however, to find occurrences of the term in his work that are clearly honorific.

1. Nietzsche

In general, "democracy" is used infrequently in Nietzsche's works. This quantitative absence does not imply, however, that central areas in his political thought are not revealed in his application of this and closely related terms. Properties of which he greatly disapproved were attributed to, or associated with, what he designated as "democracy". In spite of Nietzsche's literary manner his various applications of the term present a straightforward picture, since generally he took the negative character of democracy for granted.

This derogatory way of using "democracy" is not exclusive to his verbal usage. A somewhat differentiated picture may be discerned in <u>Menschliches, Allzumenschliches</u> (1878). Writing on political power, Nietzsche stated that in earlier times every State had been founded upon a religious or divine basis. He contrasted the traditional with the democratic State, asking:

> Wie aber, wenn jene ganz verschiedene Auffassung des Begriffes der Regierung, wie sie in demokratischen Staaten gelehrt wird, durchzudringen anfängt. Wenn man in ihr Nichts als das Werkzeug des Volkswillens sieht, kein Oben im Vergleich zu einem Unten, sondern lediglich eine Function des alleinigen Souverains, des Volkes. [1]

To which his answer was:

> Die Missachtung, der Verfall und der Tod des Staates, die Entfesselung

der Privatpersonen... ist die Consequenz des demokratischen Staats-
begriffs, hier liegt seine Mission. [2]

According to these statements, Nietzsche's opinion of the concept
'democratic government' tallied with the general view in democratic countries; a government which was nothing but an instrument of the popular will.
He was obviously of the opinion that, if it were generally accepted, this
form of rule would bring about the disgrace as well as the decline and death
of the State and the emancipation of men as private individuals. He was also
of the opinion that the founding of political power on a purely human basis
was a quite new chapter in the history of mankind. Thus he was not very
optimistic concerning this new form of government, but he also admitted
that it might possibly bring with it some good, without explaining what he
had in mind. It is of importance that "democratic" was not used here to
characterize a kind of government of which Nietzsche definitely disapproved.

Concerning the aim and means of what he termed "democracy", Nietzsche
stated in the second part of this work:

Die Demokratie will möglichst Vielen Unabhängigkeit schaffen und ver-
bürgen, Unabhängigkeit der Meinungen, der Lebensart und des Erwerbs.[3]

To achieve these kinds of independence, the rich as well as those without
property would have to be deprived of their suffrage, since he considered
these classes, as well as political parties, to be the great enemies of independence. He added:

Ich rede von der Demokratie als von etwas Kommendem. Das, was schon
jetzt so heisst, underscheidet sich von den älteren Regierungsformen
allein dadurch, dass es mit neuen Pferden fährt: die Strassen sind noch
die alten, und die Räder sind auch noch die alten. [4]

This seems to imply that Nietzsche preferred to use "democracy" to connote
some future kind of government only, and that he therefore regarded all use
of this term, when applied to contemporary forms of government, to be incorrect. On this point it must be objected that Nietzsche himself, in the first
part of this work, had probably used "democratic States" to designate new,
but nevertheless contemporary, phenomena.

It is not possible to say how far this future rule affected Nietzsche's
likes and dislikes, since he says too little to warrant any conclusion. I found
one more application which, at least, cannot be said to be obviously derogatory. By way of contrast a very derogatory use of "democratic movement"
occurs in Jenseits von Gut und Böse (1886), in which Nietzsche bitterly
attacked the Christian religion, and asserted:

Die demokratische Bewegung macht die Erbschaft der christlichen. [5]

According to him, both movements were characterized by flattery of the
vulgar morality of the herd. He was primarily referring to himself, when
he stated:

Wir denen die demokratische Bewegung nicht bloss als eine Verfallsform
der politischen Organisation, sondern als Verfalls-, nämlich Verkleiner-
ungsform des Menschen gilt, als seine Vermittelmässigung und Werth-
Erniedrigung. [6]

Here we are struck by his negative attitude towards what he designated "democratic movement", especially when compared with his fairly neutral attitude

towards what he had labelled "democratic States" and "democracy" eight years earlier. This change cannot be explained by suggesting that Nietzsche was using "democratic" with a signification identical with the one attributed to this word earlier on or that he evaluated "democratic" in a more hostile way than before while the signification of "democratic" remained unchanged. It seems that human decline and human diminution, and making men mediocrities and degrading their values, were properties conceptually attributed to what here received the label "democratic movement". In that case, a rather high degree of <u>Werth-Erniedrigung</u> was implicit in the signification of "democratic", which implies that this is a dyslogistic and not merely a derogatory application of the word. It is thus fairly reasonable to assume that a statement like "the democratic movement is a bad movement" was an analytic and not a synthetic statement in Nietzsche's text. Since no dyslogy is present in the earliest occurrences of "democratic" and "democracy", there is a change in his signification of "democratic". From a broader point of view, this change may be regarded as one of the signs of the difference between the tender Nietzsche, the philosopher of culture and the classical philologist, and the severe Nietzsche, the moral prophet with the will-to-power philosophy.

There is little material which answers the question why Nietzsche considered the democratic movement to be degrading to human values. It seems as if his only argument on this point was that the democratic movement was the heir of Christianity and thus carried on what he regarded as the vulgar flattery of the herd. Elsewhere in this work, however, Nietzsche once said that great reverence for women as well as the absence of respect for old people were essential for what he described as "demokratische Hang und Grundgeschmack". Nietzsche also clearly associated the democratic system with the industrial and capitalistic spirit, as opposed to a warlike and aristocratic one. [7] These factors had without doubt a negative value for him. A still more negative aspect is apparent when he speaks about

... die demokratische Idiosynkrasie gegen Alles, was herrscht und herrschen will,

and when this alleged peculiarity is referred to as

... der moderne Misarchismus (um ein schlechtes Wort für eine schlechte Sache zu bilden). [8]

He further declared independence of scientists, or their emancipation from philosophy, to be a special part of "das demokratische Wesen und Unwesen". According to him, this tragic emancipation was the reason for the self-worship prevalent among contemporary scientists and for their becoming narrow-minded specialists and colour-blind Utilitarians who could see nothing in philosophy but a long chain of disproved systems. [9] These factors cannot be regarded as the only reasons Nietzsche condemned the democratic movement or why he probably used "democratic" dyslogistically, but it seems reasonable to include them among the key factors causing this application of "democratic".

In rather high conformity with these uses of "democratic", a very derogatory, if not dyslogistic, application of "democrat" occurs in <u>Götzen-Dämmerung</u>, of 1888. In explaining what he meant by liberty, Nietzsche emphasized:

> Freiheit bedeutet, dass die männlichen, die kriegs- und siegesfrohen
> Instinkte die Herrschaft haben über andre Instinkte, zum Beispiel über
> die des "Glücks".

After this ironical remark on Utilitarian happiness and pleasure, he went on
to point out that the really free man trampled under foot the despicable de-
lights dreamt of by certain inferior beings.

> Der freigewordene Mensch, um wie viel mehr der freigewordene Geist,
> tritt mit Füssen auf die verächtliche Art von Wohlbefinden, von dem
> Krämer, Christen, Kühe, Weiber, Engländer und andre Demokraten
> träumen. [10]

Shopkeepers, Christians, cows, women, and Englishmen represented the
denotata of "democrats"; this is in itself evidence of a negative evaluation
of those persons. It may even look as if this dreaming of mean delight and
vulgar pleasure was the only characteristic common to these different kinds
of democrats. Thus, a person would be a democrat if, and only if, he had
these despicable dreams, and these dreams would therefore be a necessary
as well as a sufficient characteristic of a democrat according to Nietzsche's
definition. This use of "democrat" has a dyslogistic signification, or a
negative value-judgement implicit in the signification of the word.

There is little to add concerning Nietzsche's later use of these terms.
In Götzen-Dämmerung he referred to his earlier statements in Menschliches,
Allzumenschliches, according to which democracy marked the decline of the
State. At this point he also referred to the imperial German Reich as a
semi-democracy. [11] This last statement can probably be taken to reveal that
some of the negative properties Nietzsche attributed to democracy were also
ascribed to contemporary Germany. Finally, from among the rare applications of these terms in Der Wille zur Macht, I quote:

> Die Demokratie repräsentirt den Unglauben an grosse Menschen und an
> Elite-Gesellschaft: "Jeder ist Jedem gleich". "Im Grunde sind wir alle-
> sammt eigennütziges Vieh und Pöbel. "[12]

And a few lines earlier he stated:

> "Der Wille zur Macht" wird in demokratischen Zeitaltern dermaassen
> gehasst, dass deren ganze Psychologie auf seine Verkleinerung und Ver-
> leumdung gerichtet scheint.[13]

Nietzsche thus fairly consistently used "democracy" and "democratic"
to connote and characterize phenomena which were contrary, or almost
contrary, to what he thought essential for an ethical revival. This process
is clearly discernible after his writing of Menschliches, Allzumenschliches.
In this sense only did these terms occupy a central position in his terminology. As in earlier occurrences, we are struck by Nietzsche's attitude
towards what he termed "democracy" and "democratic", and it is difficult to
see what factual significations he attributed to these terms here. From a
certain point of view it might be said that Nietzsche used "democracy" here
to signify rule of the many and that he estimated such a rule very negatively.
If this is so, Nietzsche operated with a concept 'democracy' identical to that
of his political adversaries, and disagreement was therefore limited to non-
conceptual characteristics. Such a relationship can be found at several
places in political terminology, and there is evidence of it, for example, in
Maine's use of "democracy". [14] As in other occurrences, the negative

characteristics which Nietzsche attributed to democracy seem to be conceptual rather than non-conceptual. Thus by considering a characteristic like "all men are selfish beasts and belong to the mob" as conceptually belonging to his concept 'democracy', a fairly high degree of Werth-Erniedrigung may also be regarded here as implicit in Nietzsche's signification of "democracy".

2. Treitschke

During the first half of the eighteen-nineties, the historian Heinrich von Treitschke gave several political lectures at the University of Berlin. These lectures were published posthumously in 1898 under the label Politik. This is probably Treitschke's main political work and the writing most central to political conservatism in Germany during the last decades of the nineteenth century.

Treitschke's estimation of what he designated as "democracy", like that of Nietzsche, was negative, although there is a marked difference between them in degree and intensity and Treitschke's political argumentation differs clearly from Nietzsche's, which was mainly ethical. Where Treitschke's general political outlook was concerned, he held it to be an axiom that nature had made all organisms unequal. In his opinion both monarchy and aristocracy were founded upon a kind of inequality given by nature herself. In contrast to these political systems, he maintained:

> Alle Demokratie ausgeht von dem Widerspruch gegen das natürliche. Die Demokratie setzt eine allgemeine Gleichheit voraus, die in der Wirklichkeit nirgends vorhanden ist. [15]

This assessment of equality as a conditio sine qua non for democracy, yet non-existent in real life, may suggest that Treitschke considered that democracy was a political and social impossibility. But Treitschke spoke of democracy on several occasions as something which did exist in contemporary life, thus implying that this statement cannot be interpreted strictly. It seems that Treitschke primarily intended to emphasize the difficulty of establishing a democracy rather than the impossibility of it, even if the text may be interpreted in favour of the latter alternative.

In Treitschke's statements on Russia occurs a close association, if not identification, of equality with what he regarded as a country with a democratic character. When referring to the upper classes in Russia, he stated that a true nobility did not exist in that country. By true nobility, Treitschke obviously had in mind a social class which derived its high status from birth and not by grace of the monarch. He went on to say:

> Petersburg hat einen demokratischen Charakter, nirgends gilt die Geburt so wenig wie dort; aber es herrscht nicht die gleiche Freiheit, sondern die gleiche Knechtschaft. Über allen Untertanen steht unbeschränkt die Macht des Zaren. [16]

By St. Petersburg, Treitschke probably had the whole Russian Empire in mind and considered the capital as representative of the form of rule in the rest of the country -- a kind of argument which sometimes occurs in political and historical writings, especially in relation to centralized forms of rule. With regard to Treitschke's arguments, it seems fairly certain that the fact that birth played a smaller role in Russia than anywhere else was, for him, a sufficient condition for a form of government to have a democratic character. It is certain that he did not regard liberty, or even some degree of liberty, to be a necessary condition for something to have a democratic character. He seems to have held equality in servitude, to the same degree as equality in freedom, to be a sufficient condition of democratic character. According to this quotation it is probable that Treitschke meant that Russia was a democracy or that contemporary imperial Russia could be reckoned among the denotata of "democracy" as used by him. But any discussion of Russia in relation to democracy is exclusively limited to this statement, whereas he several times declared that countries like Switzerland and United States were democracies.

Concerning his way of classifying central political concepts, Treitschke held 'aristrocracy' and 'democracy' to be species of the broader concept or genus 'republic' [17] and 'immediate democracy' and 'representative democracy' to be species of the genus 'democracy'. Referring to small Swiss cantons like Uri and Appenzell-Innerrhoden, he said:

Hier wird die unmittelbare Demokratie am besten verwirklicht sein.

Regarding more extensive and populous societies, he went on to say:

Feiner, komplizierter, aber auch weniger demokratisch ist die mittelbare, repräsentative Demokratie, denn in jeder Form der Wahl liegt ein aristokratisches Element. [18]

He thus regarded immediate democracy as more democratic than representative democracy, and like Sidgwick, he stated that election included an aristocratic element. But, possibly in contrast to Sidgwick and a few other political theorists, Treitschke did not refuse to give the label "democracy" in some qualified form to the latter kind of government.

Among other central properties which Treitschke attributed to, or associated with, what he held to be democracy, he considered envy to be rather intimately connected with that form of rule;

...eine furchtbar dämonische, niederträchtige Leidenschaft der Demokratie: der Neid. [19]

He evidently regarded this alleged relationship between democracy and envy as a consequence of the equalitarian character of the former. He discussed a related problem a few pages later when he stated that little could be done in democracies for the promotion of art and science since the masses would never understand or recognize what was excellent in these fields. In proof of this he mentioned Switzerland, where he considered primary schools and hospitals to be of a very high standard, but where the same could not be said about the universities. He concluded:

Auf Universitäten erwirbt man sich eben eine aristokratische Bildung; die natürliche Neigung der Demokratie aber wünscht ein Mittelmass der Bildung wie des Wohlstandes auf möglichst weite Kreise verbreitet, über dies Mass hinaus will sie nicht gehen. [20]

On this point it is somewhat difficult to say whether he attributed envy and intellectual mediocrity conceptually to his concept 'democracy' or whether he was mainly drawing attention to a merely functional aspect of this form of rule. On the basis of the above quotation, I prefer the latter alternative. A different relationship seems to occur a few pages later, however. With regard to cultural and intellectual life in America, Treitschke said:

> Es herrscht da drüben eine Dünne der geistigen Luft, die nicht bloss mit der jungen kolonialen Kultur sondern auch mit der demokratischen Staatsform zusammenhängt. Hier sollen Talente über eine gewisse Höhe nicht steigen, das ist undemokratisch. [21]

According to this statement, intellectual mediocrity could not only be regarded as a certain consequence of a democratic form of rule but was even conceptually attributed to his concept 'democratic form of State'. In particular his formulation "das ist undemokratisch", regarding free growth of talents, may be taken as a fairly good indication of Treitschke's way of considering a statement like "democracy means mediocrity in intellectual life" to be analytic and not synthetic. Thus, a certain amount of intellectual mediocrity would be implicit in the signification of "democracy".

Turning to another problem, Treitschke maintained that a certain kind of hero-worship was widespread in democracies. In sharp contrast to envy, people in democracies often idolized certain leaders in such a way that these leaders could easily obtain absolute power. Here Treitschke referred in a general way to the rules of Pericles, Andrew Jackson, and Lincoln, and he drew special attention to the dictatorships of the two Napoleons. [22] He also held dictatorship to represent a permanent danger to democracy. Here we probably find a functional and not a conceptual aspect of his version of democracy. Thus the alleged idolatry of certain leaders would mark a rather important political phenomenon but, even so, cannot be regarded as implicit in Treitschke's signification of "democracy". With regard to the dictatorships of the two Napoleons, it is also important to note that while Treitschke regarded these dictatorships as being more than accidental consequences of a democratic development, there is little reason to believe that he held cæsarism to represent a kind of democracy or that such a form of rule was subsumable under his concept 'democracy'. This would imply that a country ceased to be a democracy when a popular leader obtained absolute power by becoming emperor. On this point there may therefore be some difference between Treitschke and ideologists such as Lecky, Bagehot, and Maurras; the latter considered that the rules of the two Napoleons represented a kind of democracy.

In the writing quoted, Treitschke's use of "democracy" is negative or derogatory; but in contrast to Nietzsche's terminology, a dyslogistic use of the term cannot be seen. In contrast to these negative aspects, however, Treitschke also said that democracies might, to a considerable degree, promote patriotism within certain nations. Here he was primarily referring to Switzerland. It is likely that promotion of patriotism was a factor which Treitschke greatly favoured. But Treitschke went on to declare that this kind of patriotism was frequently accompanied by a kind of idolatry of national institutions -- institutions which nobody therefore dared to attack. As a concrete example, Treitschke stated that he doubted whether any Swiss author would dare to speak about the drawbacks of democracy in the same frank manner as several German authors spoke about the drawbacks of monarchy in their country. In contrast to his opinion of patriotism in general, this idolatry and alleged lack of courage civile among Swiss authors were judged negatively. [23]

Treitschke's statements about patriotism are most likely of a synthetic kind and do not, therefore, say much directly about the signification of "democracy" as he used it. But it is of interest to observe some divergence from his generally derogatory application, although the divergence is rather small and occurs infrequently.[24] Some degree of difference exists on this point between Treitschke and other conservative ideologists like Schérer, Bourget, May, Acton, and Lecky. The latter probably used "democracy" exclusively in a derogatory way.

3. Thomas Mann and a few other German conservatives

During World War I, and especially after the United States joined the belligerents, the word "democracy" occupied a central position in Allied propaganda, finding its most symptomatic expression in Wilson's slogan "To make the world safe for democracy". With the intention of counteracting Wilson's attempts to set the German people apart from their alleged autocratic and militaristic leadership, five German thinkers and scientists, von Harnack, Meinecke, Sering, Troeltsch, and Hintze addressed the Prussian Diet. These lectures were soon afterwards printed under the title Die deutsche Freiheit. In this work, which is propaganda of a remarkably high level for times of war, we find a tendency to use "democracy" and "democratic world" as labels of Germany's enemies. Meinecke, for instance, maintained:

> Die heutige demokratische Welt fordert von uns, dass wir demokratisch werden. ... Man will uns demokratisieren, um uns zu desorganisieren.[25]

According to this statement, Allied opinion that Germany, in contrast to themselves, was not a democracy could not be contested; this probably limited "democracy" exclusively to the Allies in Meinecke's terminology.

Meinecke's application is not alone to this work, however. Troeltsch considered the tendency towards democracy to be universal within all modern States, not excluding Germany, and he concluded:

> Der ganze demokratische Feldzug ist demgegenüber Lüge, Unwissenheit und Dünkel, ein unverschämtes Rattenfängerlied.[26]

There was hardly any ideolgical difference between Troeltsch and Meinecke, which indicates that they differed in their use of "democratic". Further, Troeltsch's refusal to acknowledge the Allied claim that their war was a democratic one did not prevent him from using "Western democracies" to designate Germany's enemies, and the formulation "Ansturm der westlichen Demokratie" was even used as the title of his address.[27] Thus, unqualified "democracy" and "Western democracy" were evidently used with different significations.

In spite of its fairly high ideological level, this work, with its rather sparse application of "democracy", is not the main German source for our inquiry. A far more interesting picture is given in the vivid and varied Betrachtungen eines Unpolitischen of Thomas Mann. From a literary point of view, and possibly also from an ideological one, this is one of the most important books written during World War I. It may also be regarded as the key work in favour of official German policy. It was published in 1919, but was written partly at the beginning of the war and partly during the winter of 1917-18.

In the Introduction Mann declared:

Wenn in den folgenden Abhandlung die Identität der Begriffe "Politik" und "Demokratie" verfochten oder als selbstverständlich behandelt wird, so geschiet es mit einem ungewöhnlich klar erkannten Recht.

His sole argument in favour of this relation of identity was:

Man ist nicht ein "demokratischer" oder etwa ein "konservativer" Politiker. Man ist Politiker oder man ist es nicht. Und ist man es, ist man Demokrat. Die politische Geisteseinstellung ist die demokratische; der Glaube an die Politik der an die Demokratie, den <u>contrat social</u>. [28]

He further stated that more than hundred and fifty years ago, Rousseau had been the father of democracy by virtue of the fact that he had been father of the political spirit itself.

Since Mann was here asserting a relation of identity between the concepts 'democracy' and 'politics' and as he was using the terms "democracy" and "politics" as conceptual designations, this may be taken to imply that he also intended to use "democracy" synonymously with "politics" and "democratic" with "political". Such a relation of synonymity would have implied that he could have used "Betrachtungen eines Nicht-Demokraten" as the title of his work and that an expression like "political democracy" would have been a pleonasm and "undemocratic politics" a self-contradiction in his terminology. It can also be said that Mann seems to have been largely in favour of such a relation of synonymity. In the introduction he also emphasized

... dass Demokratie, dass Politik selbst dem Deutschen Wesen fremd und giftig ist. [29]

"Democracy" is probably used here synonymously with "politics itself", and an almost identical terminological relationship probably occurs when, with horror, he spoke of

... Deutschlands seelische Bekehrung zur Politik, zur Demokratie. [30]

A somewhat different relationship is present, however, in his statement:

Die deutsche Demokratie ist nicht echte Demokratie, denn sie ist nicht Politik, nicht Revolution. [31]

Politics and revolution are here very clearly associated with what Mann termed "pure democracy", although he used "German democracy" at the same time to connote something which was not characterized by these properties. He thus used a qualified form of "democracy" to signify something which was not characterized by politics; this may indicate that at this point Mann would not unreservedly have declared unqualified "democracy" to be synonymous with "politics". But a strictly logical and consistent terminology is by no means the main characteristic of the writings of one of the most eminent authors of this century. Mann did nevertheless identify what he termed "pure democracy" with politics and revolution. A similar relationship is fairly evident in his statement that the essence of German democracy would never be politics

... solange sie eben deutsche Demokratie, d. h. mehr "deutsch" als "Demokratie" sein wird. [32]

In the main text, which was probably written in the autumn of 1914, "democracy" and related terms were also used largely to signify politics or something almost identical with what he understood by politics. For example

Mann quoted an earlier answer made to a reporter in which he had asserted:

> Politisierung und Demokratisierung, das ist doch ein und dasselbe. [33]

The context makes it clear that he definitely accepted the terminology of this earlier statement. A similar statement is: "Die Demokratisierung, d. h. die Politisierung der Nation. " [34] A little later Mann stated that "national" and "conservative" meant one and the same thing, as did "democratic" and "international". With regard to the cosmopolitan character of German humanism, Mann considered this humanism to be quite different from internationalism, and he also asserted:

> Der deutsche Weltbürger ist kein politischer Bürger, er ist nicht politisch, -- während die Demokratie nicht nur politisch, sondern die Politik selber ist. [35]

He also stated that politics and democracy were un-German and even anti-German. Still later he asserted:

> Demokratie, das bedeutet Herrschaft der Politik; Politik das bedeutet ein Minimum von Sachlichkeit. Der Fachmann aber ist sachlich, das heisst unpolitisch, das heist undemokratisch. Fort mit ihm! [36]

In these occurrences "democracy" or some related term is used synonymously with "politics" or some related expression like "to make something political". It is evident that the term was used here in a very derogatory way. As a further example of a derogatory application of "democracy", in a reference to one of Wagner's statements Mann did not think it impossible that music might disappear completely as the result of democracy and civilization. He even spoke of finis musicae as the vision of democracy. [37] Elsewhere, Mann held that vulgar avarice and the rule of money, even hoarding of food in times of war, were evidence of democracy.[38] There are similar occurrences where he used the term in a very derogatory way.

It is doubtful whether the disappearance of music and vulgar avarice can be regarded as conceptual characteristics of his concept 'democracy'. These can more reasonably be regarded as consequences and not as conceptual characteristics. It is certain, however, that to be entirely of a political nature, or even to be identical with politics, was conceptually attributed to what he designated as "democracy" in these statements. While Mann's great dislike of what he labelled with this term is evident, it is doubtful whether the fact that it was a bad system can be regarded as implicit in the signification he attributed to "democracy". Mann's negative statements should probably be regarded as synthetic and not analytic. Thus, "democracy" would have been used derogatorily, but not dyslogistically. No definite conclusion is possible, however.

An extremely different way of using this term is found in the latter part of this work, however. In a discussion of the Franco-Russian alliance, Mann maintained that democracy was quite compatible with absolutism, and he continued:

> Nur der Politiker, nämlich jemand, der die Bedeutung staatlicher Verfassungsformen bis zur Absurdität überschätzt und verkennt, kann Demokratie und Autokratie für menschliche Gegensätze halten, nur er weisst nicht, dass wahre d. h. menschliche Demokratie eine Sache des Herzens und nicht der Politik, dass sie Brüderlichkeit und nicht Freiheit "und" Gleichheit ist. [39]

In this passage "true democracy" and "human democracy" were used to designate a concept which was probably exclusively limited to matters of the heart, and it even looks as if politics was conceptually debarred from this concept 'true democracy'. This marks a use of "true democracy" with a signification which not only differs from, but even absolutely contradicts, the predominant trend in this work. In further elaboration of what he held to be true democracy and of his opinion that Russia was a true democracy, Mann said:

> Russland war in tiefster Seele immer demokratisch, ja christlich kommu-
> nistisch, d. h. brüderlich gesonnen, und Dostojewskij schien zu finden,
> dass für diesen Demokratismus das patriarchalisch-theokratische Selbst-
> herrschertum eine angemessenere Staatsform darstelle, als die soziale
> und atheistische Republik.

"True democracy", "human democracy", "democratic", and "democraticism" are without doubt used here in honorific ways; and with the emphasis on fraternity, as contrasted to politics, it is certain that Mann must have considered the Russian way of life to be part of what _he_ held as culture, in contrast to civilization and politics. Mann's great hope was a future alliance between Russia and Germany, because German as well as Scandinavian authors, and especially Nietzsche and Hamsun, had been considerably influenced by Dostoievsky, while French and English authors remained unaffected. In this connection, Mann also declared the Franco-Russian military partnership to be a misalliance:

> ... denn die Demokratie des Herzens ist der Demokratie des Prinzips und
> der humanitären Rhetorik menschlich tief überlegen. [40]

Here Mann introduces two different concepts 'democracy of hearts' and 'democracy of principle and humanitarian rhetoric', and it is evident that the former was identical with what he designated here as "true democracy" and the latter was identical with what he generally labelled as "democracy" in this book. He does not elaborate on the possible properties common to these two concepts, but it would hardly have been possible for him to mark out any characteristic common to these extremely different concepts, one of which had its prototype in the fraternity of the plain and pious Russian way of life and the other in French politics. It would at least be very difficult to construct a genus of which these two concepts were species. In using "democracy of principle and humanitarian rhetoric" to designate one of these concepts, Mann continues his established way of letting "democracy" signify something identical with politics. Thus, we cannot speak of a complete terminological change in relation to his discussion of Russia. But the mere fact that "true democracy" was used to signify something that had nothing to do with politics marks a terminological anomaly of great importance, which affects the central topic of this extensive work.

This anomaly might have been caused at least in part by the interval of about three years that elapsed between his writing of the first and the last parts of the work. Yet Mann used "democratic" in a non-political sense at least once rather early in the work, and in a way fairly similar to his usage in his discussion of Russia. Referring to his novel Königliche Hoheit, Mann said that an Austrian reviewer had once spoken of it as a banner of the new democracy, and Mann seems largely to be in agreement. He stated that the novel was very individualistic, but added,

...dass ein tiefes Zögern jene Wendung zum Demokratischen, zur Ge-
meinsamkeit und Menschlichkeit begleitet. [41]

"Democratic" seems to be used here substantively, and was probably synonymous with what can perhaps be translated as "fellowship and humanity". It
was also thus used to signify something contrasting with individualism; something which was consistently attributed to politics. Thus there is at least
one occurrence of "democratic" in the first part of this book where the use
of the term is in conformity with Mann's subsequent statements to the effect
that Russia represented true democracy.

Following on his statements about Dostoievsky and true democracy,
Mann used "democrat" and "democracy" in senses very near to politicians
and politics. He even did so in connection with later statements about Russia
and Dostoievsky. In contrasting Tolstoy and Dostoievsky, Mann declared
that the former had made a religion out of social life; and this religion was
merely an ideology of social welfare and plain happiness. He concluded:
"Aber damit ist Tolstoi Demokrat, ist er Politiker." [42] He went on to say
that, without directly being a Westerner but as the representative of Russian
democracy, Tolstoy nevertheless justified the strange West-East military
alliance. This Dostoievsky never did.

Related occurrences of "democracy", when used to signify something
near to or even identical with politics, occur at several places in the last
part of this book. [43] The terminological anomaly in connection with Mann's
statements on Dostoievsky and Russian inward life cannot therefore be said
to represent a difference between the terminology used in the earlier and
later parts of the work. One can hardly criticize Thomas Mann for this inconsistent usage, since, with regard to the use of "democracy", inconsistent
terminology is a widespread phenomenon in the language of ideologists who
used the term frequently. But it is a little strange to hear Mann, after
having criticized the Franco-Russian alliance, speak ironically about the
men of letters who were defending that unnatural union, and

...der zu diesem Behufe mit Worte spielt: mit dem Worte "demokratisch"
zum Beispiel, das er nach Bedürfnis und Gefallen in religiös-menschlicher
oder in rational-politischer Bedeutung gebraucht. [44]

In his later political writings, and especially in his speeches "Von
deutscher Republik", "Vom kommenden Sieg der Demokratie", and "Das
Problem der Freiheit", Mann's uses of "democracy" were rather different
from those observed in Betrachtungen eines Unpolitischen, and they were
exclusively honorific. These speeches, however, are outside the scope of
our research.

CHAPTER XIV

LATER SOCIALISM

An unambiguous application of "democracy" is not to be found in earlier socialist thought. Not only have there been important differences between Proudhon's and Marx's terminology, for example, but there have also been very different and sometimes clearly incompatible trends in the uses of "democracy" by Marx or Proudhon individually. In this chapter ambiguities of such extent will not be found, though this does not imply that ambiguities of different kinds will not be encountered. With regard to the significations attributed to "democracy", one might anticipate a tendency to regard revolution and democracy as contrary elements in political life. To a fairly large extent such a relationship is to be found in the use of "democracy" by Kautsky and Bernstein and also by the Fabians. On this point there is a certain continuity from Marx and Engels after the February Revolution, when they, too, several times held democracy and revolution to be contrary factors. This trend is not the only one. In Rosa Luxemburg's use of "democracy" there is a tendency to regard the working class as the only democratic factor, a feature in common with much in Marx and Engels before 1848. Other questions arise as to whether democracy is only a means towards socialism or whether socialism is a part of democracy, as claimed by some of the Fabians at this later period; and there is a question of democracy and self-rule in the workshop, a problem several times entered upon by Proudhon, and here taken up by Cole.

1. Bernstein

Among later socialist theoreticians, an important position is occupied by Eduard Bernstein. In his attempts to get the German socialists to adopt an evolutionary policy, Bernstein placed himself in the centre of ideological debate among socialist thinkers. On a fairly high theoretical level he attempted to show that some, but not all, Marxist axioms were out of date. These ideological controversies are revealed by the application of "democracy" by various socialist thinkers who took part in this theoretical struggle. In his empirical attempt at a revision of Marxism, Bernstein's work Die Voraussetzungen des Socialismus und die Aufgaben der Sozialdemokratie, of 1899, is of great significance. This work also contains the most frequent as well as the most important occurrences of "democracy" in his verbal usage.
    Bernstein absolutely disagreed with those socialists who held that the trade unions would eventually become the exclusive managers of industry in a socialist society. According to Bernstein, the trade unions would have to share this power with the State or with municipal bodies. His main argument against this kind of exclusiveness consisted in pointing out the dangers of trade unions becoming closed corporations with all the drawbacks of monopoly.

He further held this kind of exclusiveness to be a contradiction with socialism as well as with democracy. This problem therefore gave rise to
another:

> Was ist Demokratie? ... Die Antwort hierauf scheint sehr einfach, auf den
> ersten Blick möchte man sie mit der Uebersetzung: "Volkherrschaft" für
> abgethan halten. [1]

He pointed out, however, that even short reflection would make it clear that
this definition was a purely formal one. Referring to the current use of the
term, he maintained:

> Fast alle, die heute das Wort Demokratie gebrauchen, darunter mehr wie
> eine blosse Herrschaftsform verstehen.

Evidently with the intention of defining the signification of "democracy", he
continued:

> Viel näher werden wir die Sache kommen, wenn wir uns negativ aus-
> drücken und Demokratie mit Abwesenheit von Klassenherrschaft über-
> setzen, als Bezeichnung eines Gesellschaftszustandes, wo keiner Klasse
> ein politisches Privilegium gegenüber der Gesamtheit zusteht.

Here "democracy" is directly said to be synonymous with "absence of class
rule", which implied that this term, when correctly applied, was to be used
exclusively to designate a state of society where no classes were in possession of exclusive political privileges. Bernstein further held that herein lay
the explanation why monopoly for a corporation was anti-democratic in principle.

According to these statements, "democracy" seems first of all to signify a state of society and not a particular form of government alone. On
the whole, such an application is fairly typical of Bernstein's use of "democracy", although some modification may be discerned a little later in this
work. From the quotation it is evident that Bernstein did not hold "democracy" to be synonymous with "popular rule" or "Volksherrschaft". The
relationship between the significations of these two expressions is also
touched on when Bernstein went on to say that the definition of democracy as
the absence of class rule had the advantage that democracy might then, in
contrast to popular rule, be associated to a much smaller degree with suppression of the minority by the majority. Bernstein probably held such
suppression not to be compatible with what he designated as "democracy",
and on this point he also referred to a general tendency of the time:

> Wir finden heute die Unterdrückung der Minderheit durch die Mehrheit
> "undemokratisch", obwohl sie ursprünglich mit der Volksherrschaft durch-
> aus vereinbar gehalten wurde. ... In dem Begriff Demokratie liegt eben
> für die heutige Auffassung eine Rechtsvorstellung eingeschlossen: die
> Gleichberechtigung aller Angehörigen des Gemeinwesens, und an ihr findet
> die Herrschaft der Mehrheit worauf in jeden konkreten Fall die Volks-
> herrschaft hinausläuft, ihre Grenze. [2]

Equal rights for all citizens, as well as majority rule, he most likely considered to be conceptual characteristics of the concept 'democracy' presented
in this quotation. It also looks as if majority rule was a conceptual characteristic shared by 'democracy' and 'popular rule' whereas equality of rights
belonged exclusively to the former concept. Thus, there was a marked
difference between what Bernstein held to be democracy and popular rule.

Bernstein also drew attention to the great difference between democracy and the earlier French view on popular sovereignty with its unrestricted power of the majority in accordance with the theory of <u>contrat social</u>. It is possible that Bernstein considered equal rights for all citizens and rule by the majority to be not only necessary but also, when taken together, sufficient conditions for a society to be a democracy; or a society was a democracy if, and only if, it was in possession of both these characteristics. The fact that rule by the majority was held as a necessary condition of democracy may be said to modify, in some small degree, his initial statement that "democracy" might well be synonymous with "absence of class rule".

Although Bernstein most probably considered that suppression of the minority was incompatible with democracy as he understood it, his statement that democracy might be associated to a smaller degree than popular rule with suppression of the individual might be taken to reveal that he considered some degree of suppression of the individual to be compatible with democracy. On this point he also admitted:

Gewiss, die Demokratie ist keine absolute Schutzwehr gegen Gesetze, die von Einzelnen als tyrannisch empfunden werden. [3]

He added, however, that the tyranny of the majority in times of civil war was quite different from the rule of majority in modern democracies and that experience had proved that suppression and passion in internal struggles steadily decreased the longer a State was in possession of democratic institutions.

Bernstein held that for people who could not imagine that socialism could be brought about without violence, democracy would certainly be regarded as a disadvantage. For other people, however -- and here Bernstein certainly included himself -- who were not supporters of the utopian theory that modern nations were moving towards revolutionary catastrophe in which society would be split into independent groups, democracy was something more than a political means which gained approval only as far as it made possible the exploitation of capital. For Bernstein, democracy was a means as well as an end.

Die Demokratie ist Mittel und Zweck zugleich. Sie ist das Mittel der Erkämpfung des Socialismus, und sie ist die Form der Verwirklichung des Socialismus. [4]

Bernstein almost certainly held democracy to be the only means to socialism and the only form under which socialism could be realized. What he considered to be democracy was thus indispensable to socialism, but not vice versa. Bernstein could clearly conceive of a State being a democracy whose form of rule could not be regarded as a means to socialism, for at least several years. He also admitted that democracy could not work miracles; it could not give political leadership to the proletariat in countries like Switzerland, where the proletariat constituted a minority of the population.

What Bernstein held to be democracy was an alternative to violent revolution. Since he probably considered democracy to be the only form under which socialism could be brought about, he thought socialism an impossibility in all countries in which the proletariat was in the minority, and he also believed any kind of dictatorship, whether vested in the majority or the minority, was incompatible with socialism as he understood it.

There is little to be added concerning the use of the term in Bernstein's other works. "Democracy" is there, too, probably without reservations, used in an honorific way, [5] and democracy is also spoken of as having given the class-struggle a non-violent character. [6] A similar use occurs in an essay concerning democracy in the socialist movement, in which Bernstein even quoted several of the statements discussed in this section. Referring to these quotations, and, in particular, to his comment that "democracy" could be translated by "absence of class-rule", Bernstein stated:

> Das ist nur freilich noch sehr relativistisch ausgedrückt, aber weiter als zu einer relativen Demokratie hat es die Welt überhaupt noch nicht gebracht. [7]

This statement may show, on the one hand, that Bernstein probably still favoured his earlier use of "democracy", but, on the other, it may indicate that he might possibly use the term differently under other circumstances, e. g. , when dealing with a democracy which was not relative.

2. Kautsky

The above work by Bernstein was attacked that same year by Karl Kautsky in Bernstein und das sozialdemokratische Programm. Theoretical polemics had previously been exchanged by these two ideologists, but these two works encompass the main ideological controversy within the socialist camp during the twenty years which preceded World War I. Kautsky's criticism was directed against inter alia Bernstein's views concerning the relationship between the democracy and the realization of socialism. There is also criticism of Bernstein's use of "democracy". Quoting Bernstein's statement that "democracy" could be synonymous with "absence of class-rule" or used to designate a state of society where no classes were in possession of political privileges, Kautsky declared that this definition was one-sided because equality of rights was only one of the characteristics of democracy, not the characteristic. Such an argument indicates that Kautsky agreed with Bernstein that absence of class-rule or equality of rights was a necessary condition for a democracy but disagreed that absence of class-rule was a sufficient condition. Kautsky maintained that equality of political rights, or the fact that no class was in possession of political privileges to the detriment of others, existed even during the Roman empire when no class had political rights. He further stated that an anarchical state of society was also conditioned by the absence of these privileges. The anarchist would nevertheless not accept democracy, which Kautsky held to be correct from the anarchical point of view:

> Eben deswegen, weil sie [die Demokratie] eine Herrschaftsform ist. Sie ist die Form der Herrschaft der Majorität. [8]

Bernstein also seems to have held that the rule of the majority was a necessary property of democracy as he understood it. But the quotation from Bernstein may be interpreted in a way which makes equality of political rights not only a necessary but a sufficient condition for a form of rule to be a democracy. Bernstein's other statements can probably not be taken to confirm this view, however. It can further be noted that Kautsky initially also considered equality of rights to be a necessary condition for a democracy. Thus their definitions of democracy are fairly similar on this point, in spite of differing formulations. Bernstein emphasized equality of rights and Kautsky the rule of the majority, but each placed a secondary emphasis in what was primarily emphasized by his opponent in his definition of democracy.

Concerning the question as to whether democracy was compatible with the suppression of minorities, Kautsky quoted Bernstein's statements that such suppression was undemocratic and in practice had steadily decreased the longer a State had democratic institutions. On this point Kautsky was of a different opinion. He inquired ironically where this political practice was to be found. He admitted that political life was rather silent for the moment in a country like England but maintained that the masses of England had in modern times been in favour of a cruel policy against Ireland and that current policy in the colonies, especially in South Africa and India, clearly showed that Englishmen were not unconditionally opposed to the suppression of minorities and the weak. "Democracy" or related terms were not used in his comments on England, but they were clearly formulated with the intention of proving that the people of a country characterized by democratic institutions might nevertheless favour the suppression of minorities. He went on to say:

> Und das demokratische Amerika? Nie lynchte es seine Neger mit grösserer Wollust als jetzt, nie wurden Streikende leichtfertiger niedergeschossen als jetzt, nie zeigten sich die Amerikaner blutdürstiger und tyrannischer gegenüber den Minderheiten.

With regard to France, he emphasized:

> Oder zeigt uns das demokratische Frankreich, dass die Parteikämpfe an Gehässigkeit verlieren, das Individuum höher geschätzt wird und die politische Entwicklung immer mildere Formen annimmt?[9]

Kautsky's answer would without doubt have been in the negative, and "democratic" is thus used to describe two countries, one of which was characterized inter alia by the lynching of negroes, the shooting of strikers, and the tyrannical and sanguinary suppression of minorities, while the other was characterized neither by a decrease of passion in its internal political struggles nor by greater protection of the individual. It can therefore be inferred that Kautsky, unlike Bernstein, did not regard the protection of minorities to be implicit in the signification of "democratic" or of "democracy".

Is this use of "democratic" in conformity with his earlier assertion that equality of rights was one of the characteristics of democracy? A little later Kautsky spoke about

> ...die Demokratie mit ihren Freiheiten und ihrer klaren Einsicht in die Machtverhältnisse der verschiedenen Parteien und Klassen.[10]

What he meant by these liberties is not elaborated upon. But we can assume that he regarded them as making possible a clear insight into the relationship of the power of different parties and classes. According to this hypothesis, democracy must be characterized by the liberty to form political parties and by the liberty of different classes to express legally their political desires and aims. Thus, this statement seems to a certain extent to contradict his earlier ones concerning the American and French democracies, although he was possibly of the opinion that democracy generally was marked by freedom of expression and freedom of forming parties but that this did not imply that democracies could not cruelly suppress certain minorities such as negroes

or strikers. Only an hypothesis such as the above prevents these two statements from contradicting each other.

Speaking of the relationship between democracy and the realization of
socialism, Kautsky held democracy to be a necessary condition for the conquest of political power by the proletariat. [11] What he meant by "democracy"
was not explained in this connection, but perhaps he believed that the establishment of the rule of the proletariat was conditioned by, inter alia, a rule
by the majority characterized by some degree of freedom for different kinds
of political argumentation. But Kautsky, unlike Bernstein, was of the opinion
that democratic forms were probably not sufficient, or not the only adequate
ones, for bringing about this kind of class rule. He admitted that the dictatorship of the proletariat might not be regarded as the sole possibility. But
in general he seems to have regarded democratic forms as insufficient.
Kautsky is not very clear on this point, however, and he was of the opinion
that the best way of treating questions concerning the dictatorship of the
proletariat was to leave them to the future. Such statements may reveal
Kautsky's somewhat vague attitude towards the seizure of political power by
the proletariat, whether it was to be achieved by forceful or non-violent
means, through revolution or evolution -- even if a revolutionary, or a semi-
revolutionary outlook at that time was probably predominant. However,
questions concerning democracy and the realization of socialism seem to
be most relevant to the non-conceptual characteristics of his concept 'democracy' presented in this work, and they are therefore of minor importance
with regard to the signification he attributed to this term. Nevertheless
these statements are good indicators of his attitude towards what he labelled
"democracy".

Nothing in Kautsky's other pre-war writings appears to contradict the
use of the term in the work under discussion. While analytic statements
are rare, the term is used predominantly to name something which was of
high importance to the organization of socialist parties but by which the
class differences in capitalist societies were not to be eliminated, and through
which a social revolution was not to be avoided. The following statements
are typical:

> Die Demokratie ist also unentbehrlich als Mittel, das Proletariat für die
> soziale Revolution reif zu machen. Aber sie ist nicht im Stande, diese
> Revolution zu verhindern. [12] ... Die Demokratie kann die Klassengegen-
> sätze der kapitalistischen Gesellschaft nicht beseitigen, und deren notwen-
> diges Endergebnis, den Umsturz dieser Gesellschaft, nicht aufhalten. [13]

A different political outlook and a different terminology appears in his
later works on the Bolshevik Revolution. These matters will be discussed
in a later chapter.

3. Rosa Luxemburg

As with Kautsky, the main occurrences of the term in Luxemburg's earlier
writings are related to her attacks on Bernstein's revisionist views. But in
contrast to Kautsky, Luxemburg did not directly criticize Bernstein's use of
"democracy", even though indirect criticism is indicated. In her work
Sozialreform oder Revolution?, 1900, one of the points made in her disagreement with Bernstein was her denial that the trend towards democracy
was inevitable in modern civilization. Such a view she declared to be ex-

tremely superficial. First she held that democracy might be found in most different forms of society, such as primitive communism, antique slave societies, medieval city-states, and modern capitalism. She continued:

Zwischen der kapitalischen Entwicklung und der Demokratie lässt sich kein allgemeiner absoluter Zusammenhang konstruiren. [14]

Democracy was thus, from a broader point of view, neither incompatible with nor dependent on a capitalist form of society. She went on to say that with growing militarism and increasing tensions between classes, the bourgeoisie had abandoned their earlier liberal political aims and made alliances with reactionaries, militarists, and imperialists. In this way,

... die sozialistische Arbeiterbewegung eben heute die einzige Stütze der Demokratie ist und sein kann.

She also held that democracy would only become a living phenomenon if, and in so far as, the socialist movement succeeded in its struggle against the policies of reaction. She concluded:

Wer die Stärkung der Demokratie wünscht, auch Stärkung und nicht Schwächung der sozialistischen Bestrebungen wünschen muss, und dass mit dem Aufgeben der sozialistischen Bestrebungen ebenso die Arbeiterbewegung wie die Demokratie aufgegeben wird. [15]

These statements make it fairly clear that, for her, the fate of democracy was intimately connected with the socialist movement, a position partly similar to that of Marx and Engels before 1848. Politically this is of central importance, but it does not convey much concerning the signification she attributed to "democracy", since there is no reason to believe that the socialist movement was conceptually connected with what she held to be democracy. More factual information is given when she emphasized

... die rein demokratischen Ingredienzen (Zutaten) des Staatswesens, das allgemeine Wahlrecht, die republikanische Staatsform, ... [16]

By declaring universal suffrage and a republican form of government to be purely democratic ingredients, she seemed to class these factors as being necessary for a form of rule to have the label "pure democracy", and perhaps, also, the label "democracy", although it is hardly clear whether she regarded these factors sufficient for such a denomination.

In relation to the problems concerning democracy and the seizure of political power by the proletariat, Luxemburg once more held that democracy had become something unnecessary and even unfavourable for the bourgeoisie. She went on to say:

So ist sie [die Demokratie] für die Arbeiterklasse dafür notwendig und unentbehrlich. Sie ist erstens notwendig, weil sie politische Formen (Selbstverwaltung, Wahlrecht u. dergl.) schafft, die als Ansätze und Stützpunkte für das Proletariat bei seiner Umgestaltung der bürgerlichen Gesellschaft dienen werden. Sie ist aber zweitens unentbehrlich, weil nur in ihr, in dem Kampfe um die Demokratie, in der Ausübung ihrer Rechte das Proletariat zum Bewusstsein seiner Klasseninteressen und seiner geschichtlichen Aufgaben kommen kann. [17]

Similar to the first quotation, democracy is here closely connected with the class struggle of the proletariat; but this struggle was not conceptually included in what she held to be democracy. Thus, "democracy" seems ex-

clusively to signify a political means which would make possible the seizure
of political power by the proletariat, but there is probably no reason to think
that the rule of the proletariat was included in this signification. On this
point, there is a marked difference between this use of "democracy" and
that of earlier revolutionary socialists like Babeuf and Engels prior to 1848,
where this term was used at least partially with a signification that was almost identical with the rule of the proletariat. Concrete properties such as
suffrage, probably universal suffrage, and self-management were included
in Luxemburg's signification of "democracy". It looks as if she had others
in mind, but unfortunately for this research, they were not mentioned.

Not much can be added concerning Luxemburg's use of "democracy" and
related terms in her pre-war writings. However, in criticizing the secrecy
of the socialist group meetings in the German Imperial Diet, she once maintained that the relationship between electors and representatives must become much closer in a really democratic party;

> ... in einer von Grund aus demokratishen Partei. [18]

She also referred to existing practices as contrary to the democratic character of the party. "Democratic" is here used with a signification which
seemed to include absence of secrecy as well as the presence of a fairly
close contact between electors and representatives. Such properties, even
if they not are explicitly mentioned, were probably also included in the
signification of occurrences of "democracy" which have been quoted. This
view, which stresses the influence of the rank and file in relation to that of
the political leadership, is a permanent and central trend in Luxemburg's
political thinking. On this point there is a marked difference not only
between Luxemburg and the centralistic and reformist outlook of Bernstein
and the Fabians but also between her revolutionary ideology and the principal theory of Lenin, who asserted that the small group of professional politicians were the guardians of the proletarian class. This aspect came to
play a key role in her use of "democracy" in criticizing Bolshevism in 1918.

4. The Fabians

Turning from the leading German socialist thinkers to the main contributors
to a socialist ideology in England, it can be seen that Sidney Webb, in Fabian
Essays in Socialism (1889), described the irresistible progress of democracy during the last hundred years as having been the main stream which
bore European society towards socialism. Concerning the historical basis
of socialism, Webb held Tocqueville to have hammered this truth into the
reluctant ears of the world two generations before, but he was also of the
opinion that Tocqueville's main work, which was becoming a classic, was a
book which everybody quoted and nobody read. Webb admitted, however,
that the progress of democracy was often imagined to be merely the substitu-
tion of one kind of political machinery for another; and on this point he referred to Sir Henry Maine. He also held that purely political radicals could
not understand why social or economic matters should be mixed with politics,
and he ironically declared them to be historical fossils to whom

> ... mostly through the lack of economics, the progress of Democracy is
> nothing more than the destruction of old political privileges; ... they are

in social matters the empiricist survivals from a prescientific age. [19]

According to these statements, it seems reasonable to infer that for Webb the progress of democracy meant more than the destruction of old privileges. Therefore "democracy", when correctly used, should not designate a concept which was exclusively political; but a social property, perhaps even a socialist property, ought to be included in the signification of the term.

A somewhat different application occurs a little later. Webb here held that the Socialists and a greater part of the Radicals were near each other in political life,

Advocates of social reconstruction had learnt the lesson of democracy, and know that it is through the slow and gradual turning of the popular mind to new principles that social reorganization bit by bit comes.

He also held that all students of society who were abreast of their time realized that important organic changes would only be

...democratic and thus acceptable to a majority of the people, and prepared for in the minds of all. [20]

As used here, "democracy" and "democratic" seem to signify that all important social changes must be gradual and acceptable to the majority, and this implies that any kind of violent revolution would be incompatible with what he designated as "democracy". But by using "democracy" to signify something which had been accepted by the socialists, or by the advocates of social reconstruction, and which probably was relevant only to the methods and means by which social and economic changes were to be achieved, he was designating a concept which was almost exclusively political. Thus, a social property was probably not included in the signification of the term; this implies that "democracy" was used here with a different signification from the one attributed to it in the previous quotation.

Webb returns, or partly returns, to his earlier application a few lines later, however. He stated that many radicals, too, had realized that mere political levelling was insufficient and that both sections had been driven to recognize that the root of the social difficulty was economic.

There is every day a wider concensus that the inevitable outcome of Democracy is the control of the people themselves, not only of their own political organization, but through that, also of the main instruments of wealth production. ... The economic side of the democratic ideal is, in fact, Socialism itself. [21]

According to the former quotation, control of the main instruments of production may probably be regarded as a non-conceptual rather than a conceptual characteristic of his concept 'democracy'; but when he declared socialism to be the economic side of the democratic ideal, Webb seems to have considered socialism to be a conceptual characteristic of his concept 'democratic ideal' or that socialism was included in the signification of "democratic ideal". Further, if "democracy" was to be used in high conformity with this use of "democratic ideal", socialism also ought to have been implicit in the signification of "democracy". According to such an hypothesis, "socialist democracy" would have been a pleonasm and "non-socialist democracy" a self-contradiction. This hypothesis would have been in conformity with his initial assertion that those who could see nothing more in the progress of democracy than the mere destruction of political privileges were "historical fossils".

This somewhat ambiguous application of "democracy" by Webb reveals, on the one hand, his preference for "democracy" to be used with a signification which was not purely political and for a property like socialist economy to be implicit in this signification; and, on the other hand, it reveals the difficulty in practice of doing so in his own concrete terminology, where remnants of the verbal application which he wished to eliminate are in evidence.

With regard to the signification attributed to "democracy" by other Fabian socialists, a use of this term which differs from that of Webb occurs in Bernard Shaw's essay on the transition to socialism. Here Shaw claimed that by making the executives of State departments pass an adequate examination and then making them responsible to governments and governments in their turn responsible to the people, State departments would be guaranteed integrity and efficiency. Thus, the old bugbear of State imbecility did not terrify the socialist; it only made him a democrat. Shaw went on to say:

> But to call himself so simply, would have the effect of classing him with the ordinary destructive politician who is a democrat without ulterior views for the sake of formal Democracy -- one whose notion of Radicalism is the putting up of aristocratic institutions by the roots ... Consequently, we have the distinct term Social Democrat, indicating the man or woman who desires through democracy to gather the whole people into the State, so that the State may be trusted with the rent of the country, and finally with the land, the capital, and the organization of the national industry.[22]

Unqualified "democrat" is used here with a signification very similar to that which Webb attributed to "purely political radical", and at this point Shaw also referred to the vernacular. Unqualified "democracy" does not appear in the first of these statements; but even if "formal democracy" was used to designate a purely political concept, there is no reason to think that unqualified "democracy" was used with a signification differing from that attributed to the qualified expression. In the last statement, unqualified "democracy" seems exclusively to signify a political means, or something through which certain social and economic goals were to be achieved. Thus a social, or socialist, property cannot be regarded as implicit in the signification of the term, and neither here nor elsewhere can I find evidence of any desire for the signification of the term to include such a property. On this point, there is a difference between Webb and Shaw, in spite of the near identity of their political opinions.

A way of using "democracy" which was very similar to that of Shaw is present in the general outlook of Hubert Bland on the transition to socialism. In discussing land policy, Bland held that those radicals who were in favour of free sale and peasant ownership were a less potent revolutionary force than even the Tories themselves. He went on to say:

> From such dangers as these the progress of democracy, by itself, is powerless to save us; for although always and everywhere democracy holds Socialism in its womb, the birth may be indefinitely delayed by stupidity on one side, and acuteness on the other. [23]

"Democracy" is used here to name something that, from a broad point of view, would lead to socialism. The causal relationships are not directly elaborated upon, but we can assume that even if socialism were to be formed in the womb of democracy, a secondary factor would be needed to bring it to birth. Thus, leading to socialism was most probably a non-conceptual characteristic of his concept 'democracy'; this was confirmed by his statement that democracy in itself was powerless to influence certain central social questions.

This use of "democracy", with a signification restricted to the field of politics and lacking a social or socialist property, can be regarded as the predominant trend among the Fabians. In one of the Fabian Tracts, which appeared as a collective work on the general policy of the Fabian Society, it was, for example, said:

> Democracy, as understood by the Fabian Society, means simply the control of the administration by the freely elected representatives of the people. [24]

In addition it was asserted that the Fabians energetically repudiated all conceptions of democracy as a system by which the technical work of government administration and the appointment of public officials should be carried on by referendum or by any other form of direct popular decision. Such an arrangement was perhaps practical in village communities but not in complicated industrial civilizations. Finally, democracy, as understood by the Fabians, made no political distinction between men and women.

This makes it fairly clear that for the Fabians, or at least for the authors of this pamphlet, "democracy" could not be used to connote any kind of direct or non-representative form of government and that female suffrage as well as other political rights for women were necessary properties for a state to be a democracy. It further looks as if socialism, or even a social property, was not included in the signification of "democracy" as used here.

The political language of the Webbs does not share this terminological trend. In Industrial Democracy, of 1902, Beatrice and Sidney Webb stated:

> The persistence of Trade Unionism, and its growing power in the state, indicates, to begin with, that the very conception of democracy will have to be widened, so as to include economic as well as political relations. [25]

This use of "democracy" is reminiscent of a predominant trend in Sidney Webb's essay thirteen years earlier. But whereas at that time democracy was declared to include at least partially social as well as political properties, here we are told only that democracy would include economic as well as political properties. It is evident that the Webbs considered that using "democracy" with a purely political signification was almost universal at that time. They were in favour of a change on this point, a change which they considered a likely one. They did not describe as historical fossils, however, those who used "democracy" in a purely political way, although, as in Sidney Webb's earlier arguments, ironic references are made to those liberals who could see

> ...no more inconsistency between democracy and unrestrained capitalist enterprise, than Washington or Jefferson did between democracy and slave-owning.

5. Jaurès

As in the political language of the Fabians, there are two rather differing trends in the signification of "democracy" in Jaurès's terminology. According to one trend, this leading French reformist socialist seems to have regarded the existence of social classes, or at least the relationship between social classes in contemporary France, to be incompatible with what he designated as "democracy". With regard to the increasing influence of the republican bourgeoisie, Jaurès said in 1895:

... par l'effet de l'existence des classes sociales, le règne de la démocratie n'est qu'apparent: et ce bien d'elle qu'on peut dire qu'elle règne et ne gouverne pas. [26]

Since Jaurès was probably of the opinion that social classes, and especially the republican bourgeoisie, were a result of private ownership of the means of production, he seems to have believed that such private ownership, in other words, capitalism, hindered democracy from becoming more than a formal phenomenon. Such an argument indicates a use of "democracy" in which the absence of capitalism is implicit in its signification, especially since Jaurès did not regard abolition of social classes as something democracy would bring about once established; on the contrary, their abolition was a necessary condition of democracy's existence, or at least of democracy's being more than a formal or illusory kind of rule.

He used "democracy" in a similar way the next year when he emphasized:

C'est qu'il y a contradiction absolue entre la démocratie et une organisation sociale qui livre le pouvoir et les joies de la vie à une oligarchie bourgeoisie. Et il faudra ou que la constitution sociale oligarchie supprime la démocratie, ou que la démocratie suscite une forme sociale nouvelle qui lui soit plus adéquate. [27]

Considering his other statements, by "a new social form" Jaurès not only had in mind a certain reform within the capitalist system but expected the system itself to be replaced by a socialist one. It is also fairly certain that he believed that the power of a bourgeois oligarchy was an inevitable consequence of the capitalist system. Thus, there is probably a contradiction here between democracy and capitalism, a contradiction that seems to have been of a conceptual kind. The absence of capitalism would therefore be implicit in his signification of "democracy", which naturally implies that the term was honorific.

There are several other occurrences of "democracy" in which the term signified a political form which probably could not coexist with capitalism.[28] This trend is not exclusive in this terminology, however. Jaurès attributed a dissimilar signification to the term when he treated the revisionist outlook of Bernstein four years later. Then he said:

La démocratie, comme telle, a sa loi; elle tend évidemment autant qu'elle n'est point contrariée par les forces économiques adverses, à introduire la plus grande somme possible d'égalité entre les hommes, dans la mesure

où cette égalité laisse subsister le privilège fondamental de la propriété. 29

Here he states that a trend towards a rather high degree of social equality
is a consequence of what he here held to be democracy. But this equality
was no necessary consequence of democracy in this case. His reference to
the condition that democracy would promote equality only if it was not faced
with opposing economic forces marks an important reservation on this point.
These things are of no great importance as regards the signification he attributed to "democracy", however, since these characteristics are obviously
not of a conceptual kind. The most important thing is that Jaurès believed
the fundamental privileges of property to be necessarily untouched by democracy as such. This can be taken to imply that he not only regarded democracy as compatible with the existence of these fundamental privileges,
privileges which he held to be essential to capitalism, but that he even held
the existence of these privileges to be an inevitable characteristic of democracy, or that a form of rule would not be a democracy if it attempted to
abolish or succeeded in abolishing these privileges. Thus, the presence of
capitalism is probably one of the conceptual characteristics of his concept
'democracy' as he used it in this statement. This reveals a use of "democracy" with a signification extremely different from, and on certain points
even contrary to, what he attributed to the term in the previous quotations.
This way of introducing a concept 'democracy' extremely different from his
earlier practice may have been at least partly conditioned by his desire to
minimize the influence of Bernstein's thesis that democracy, as a form of
rule, was the only road to socialism; for this Jaurès's earlier use of "democracy" would have been inadequate.
    More broadly, in spite of his rather frequent application of "democracy",
it is often difficult to see in what sense he intended to use this term. Jaurès's
statements on democracy were much more vague, or less ideologically developed, than similar statements by other reformist socialists like Bernstein
and the Fabians. Jaurès's manner of using "democracy" to signify a political system incompatible with, or almost incompatible with, capitalism appears to be a predominant trend in his language, even if there is an example
of a contrary tendency. On at least one occasion he even used "extreme
democracy" to denote the radical bourgeois politicians whom he explicitly
stated must not be confused with persons in favour of collective socialism. 30

6. Cole

Under the partial influence of syndicalist trends, G. D. H. Cole held mere
political means to be far from sufficient for the realization of full freedom
for the working class. Universal suffrage, voting by ballot, and parliamentary rule were to him necessary but not sufficient factors for the establishment of popular self-rule, a phenomenon which was first to be framed
within the workshop itself. These ideological trends are reflected in his use
of "democracy" and related terms and especially in his terminology in The
World of Labour, of 1913, a work which can probably be regarded as the
main treatise on Guild Socialism.
    In conformity with the main trend in his political thinking, Cole said that
the democratic problem was not merely worked through the vexed questions

of parliamentary institutions but arose with equal insistence within the trade
unions. He further held that this sphere was peculiarly instructive,

> ...because, here at least the democracy is being given some chance to
> solve its problems for itself and in its own way.

He went on to say that, with the exception of the Co-operative movement,

> Trade Unionism is the first instance of a democracy really governing it-
> self and dictating its own methods of government. For the first time,
> the three powers, legislative, executive and judicial, are effectively
> united in the same hands. [31]

The division of powers seems thus to have been held to be incompatible with
what he designated as "democracy"; and from the context it can be seen
that he believed democracy had been given this chance in the trade unions
because of the current struggles between officialdom and the rank and file
and between various branches or crafts and their unions. This point is not
further elaborated upon here, but Cole presumably held that democracy was
in fact to be found only in the trade unions and the Co-operative Movement.
His statement about "the first instance of democracy really governing itself"
supports such an hypothesis.

Cole concluded the first chapter of his book by declaring responsibility
to be the best teacher in self-reliance. He also maintained that self-government in the trade unions had done wonders for the workers. He added:

> In controlling industry, democracy will learn the hard lesson of self-
> control and the harder lesson of controlling its rulers, and in so doing,
> it will become actual instead of nominal.

Control of industry seems here to have been regarded as a necessary as
well as a sufficient condition for democracy learning self-control and control of its rulers, two factors which further seem to have been held as indispensable to the label "actual democracy" as opposed to "nominal democracy". Control of rulers and self-control, however, do not seem to have
been necessary properties of what he designated as unqualified "democracy",
since he spoke of these properties as something which democracy would
learn. Thus, Cole probably used "actual democracy" with a signification
differing slightly from that of "democracy", and presumably he used "democracy" to designate a genus 'democracy' of which 'actual democracy' and
'nominal democracy' were species.

He probably used "political democracy" with a signification almost identical with that of "nominal democracy" in the last statement or to signify a
political system with universal suffrage and parliamentary rule, phenomena
which, according to Cole, were far from sufficient for the realization of
freedom for the working classes. A little later, he said:

> Everywhere is found political democracy realized or well on the way to
> realization; and everywhere this democracy is illusory because it is
> accompanied by a tyrannical economic feudalism, which leaves the voter,
> for all his hard-won democratic liberty, still a wage-slave and a member
> of the great class of the disinherited. [32]

His attitude towards political "democracy" as illusory may indicate that he
would deny unqualified "democracy" as a designation of that form of rule,
although he possibly regarded 'non-illusory democracy', on the one hand,
and 'illusory democracy' or 'political democracy', on the other, to be species

of a broader concept with unqualified "democracy" as the conceptual designation. His use of unqualified "democratic" to characterize that kind of
liberty which was compatible with capitalism may be taken as an indication
in that direction. According to this last hypothesis, unqualified "democracy"
would not be used by him with a signification which necessarily included his
favourite plans for self-government in industry.

Much later in this work, "real democratic government" signified a kind
of rule based upon self-governing and fairly independent industrial units
based on the guild socialist scheme. In discussing industrial life in that
future society, Cole said:

> Instead of autocracy checked by insurgence, it will then be possible to
> set up real democratic government; instead of the official, manager, and
> foreman appointed from above, industry will be governed by rulers ap-
> pointed from below. [33]

Real democratic government is here contrasted with autocracy checked by
insurgence, by which he probably meant ordinary parliamentary rule. The
fact that the rulers of industry were to be appointed and controlled by the
workers themselves is regarded by Cole as an indispensable property for
the signification of that expression, probably to the same degree as the ap-
pointments of managers from a central authority would be held incompatible
with labelling a form of rule "real democratic government".

With regard to the future form of political life, Cole also maintained
that the State would not continue to be the bureaucratic mechanism it was at
present:

> New methods of democratic government will be evolved, and, instead of
> the abstract democracy of the ballot-box, there will be a real democracy
> aiming not at increasing continually the absoluteness of its control, but
> at delegating functions to self-governing bodies within itself, and at the
> same time harmonizing their activities with the good of the whole. [34]

"Abstract democracy" is evidently used here with a signification almost
identical with that of "political democracy" or "nominal democracy" earlier
in this work. It is further likely that a fairly high degree of delegation of
functions from the central authority to self-governing bodies was regarded
as a necessary factor for what Cole designated as "real democracy". Cole
must have had self-governing, independent industrial units in mind, and here
is the most important difference between Cole's ideological outlook and the
State-socialist and fairly centralist outlook of the Fabians. This delegation
of power together with workers' control and workers' appointment of managers make up the central points in his form of socialist ideology, and it is
significant that expressions like "actual democracy" and "real democracy"
signified social and political phenomena which were primarily characterized
by those properties. This, without doubt, provides evidence of a central
and honorific application of these somewhat qualified occurrences of "democracy" in his political terminology. Some degree of qualification was probably needed if "democracy" was to obtain this central position, although
Cole's use of qualifications like "actual" and "real" makes this a minor
modification.

CHAPTER XV

ANARCHISM AND SYNDICALISM

1. Bakunin

In the language of the anarchist thinkers "democracy" was characterized by a definitely honorific usage by Godwin while Proudhon presented an extremely varied picture. We now turn to the political language of Bakunin. In the introduction to the French edition of his work it is stated that emphasis was laid upon the presentation of his works in their original form. However, none of his early writings are included in this edition, although this is of no great importance for this research, since occurrences of "democracy" seem to have been rare in the articles and in his interesting human document Confessions from the Peter-Paul Fortress.

The first occurrences of the term, as far as can be seen, are to be found in an open letter to the Central Committee of the Ligue de la Paix et de la Liberté in Geneva in 1867, a letter which has the title Féderalisme, Socialisme et Antithéologisme. Here Bakunin quoted a statement from the Central Committee in which it was desired to

... fonder la paix sur la démocratie et sur la liberté,

and he went on to say that this implied that all members of the League were to be democrats. He continued:

Donc en sont exclus tous les aristocrats, tous les partisans de quelque privilège, de quelque monopole ou de quelque exclusion politiques que ce soit, ce mot de démocratie ne voulant dire autre chose que le gouvernement du peuple par le peuple et pour le peuple, en comprenant sous cette dernière dénomination toute la masse des citoyens.

Bakunin added that today the female citizens were also to be included, and concluded: "Dans ce sens nous sommes certainement tous démocrates. "[1] These statements may be interpreted to mean that aristocrats and advocates of monopolies are necessarily excluded from an organization of democrats and that government for, by, and of the people represents one signification of the term "democracy". His assertion that the members of the League could be democrats only in accordance with this signification of "democracy" may indicate that he believed other significations of this term made it impossible for him to regard himself as a democrat. Bakunin went on to assert that "democracy" was not a satisfactory term to describe the character of the League because it could be used ambiguously. Here he was referring to the tendency of the slave-owners in the southern United States to use "democrat" as a self-denomination and to the reigns of the two Napoleons; he also held that modern cæsarism had proclaimed itself to be democratic and recalled that the military Russian empire had crushed Poland in the name of "democracy". He continued:

Il est évident que la démocratie sans liberté ne peut nous servir de drapeau. [2]

As used here, "democracy" certainly signifies something which did not include liberty as a necessary property, since he did not regard the application of "democracy" by slave-owners and imperial rulers to be a misuse of
the term. An alliance between democracy and liberty was only to be found
in a republic, "donc notre Ligue doit être démocratique et républicaine en
même temps. " He thus regarded "republican" as a necessary modifier of
"democratic" to adequately denominate the League. However, he did not
seem to have regarded "république démocratique" as a political form capable of defending the liberty of the citizens. A little later, he stated:

> ...à deux reprises différentes, La France a perdu sa liberté et a vu sa
> république démocratique se transformer en dictature et en démocratie
> militaires. [3]

Bakunin here put the blame not upon the character of the French people but
upon French political centralization. This might lead one to expect that
"decentralized" or "federal" need be added to "republican" and "democratic"
to make this characterization adequate for Bakunin, but no such tendency is
to be found in this work.

From a more general point of view, it can be added that the use of
"democracy" quoted above to signify government of, by, and for the people
is one of the rare honorific occurrences of the term in Bakunin's writings,
and it is the only time that he approved of something he labelled "government". Later, "government" is used consistently as the label of something
that Bakunin regarded as constituting the essence of any State. [4] And the
State, together with religion, was considered by Bakunin to be one of the
worst organs of human suppression.

Elsewhere, the State, as opposed to society, was declared to have been
born out of violence, war, conquest, and the theological fantasy of nations.
At the same point he also held that a privileged minority and suppression of
the majority were to be found regularly "dans les pays même les plus démocratiques commes Les Etats-Unis de l'Amérique et la Suisse. "[5] Switzerland and the United States are mentioned rather frequently by Bakunin as
being the most democratic countries; and although he considered the forms
of government in those two countries to be somewhat preferable to the
aristocracies and monarchies, it is nevertheless evident that he held democratic countries to suffer from the main drawbacks of any form of State and
to be vastly inferior to a free association of socialist individuals.

As in the first statement quoted, Bakunin referred in 1870 to "démocratie, c'est-à-dire le gouvernement du pays par le peuple. "[6] This time,
however, this term can hardly be said to have been used in an honorific way.
A little later he maintained that the freedom and political rights for the
workers were nothing but fictions in those countries that were politically the
most democratic and most free, and in addition to Switzerland and the United
States, he included England and Belgium among the denotata of "democratic
states". His use of the qualification "politically" in connection with "most
democratic and most free" -- "les pays politiquement les plus démocratiques,
les plus libres" -- may tempt us to believe that in addition to a country being politically democratic, a country may also be democratic non-politically;
however, his later statements make such an hypothesis improbable. Thus
he dropped the qualification "politically" when he went on to state that the
workers were the slaves of their patrons and that they had neither the education nor the necessary independence to exercise their political rights in

a democracy. He reminds us of a famous dictum of Rousseau, when he says about the workers:

> Ils ont, dans les pays les plus démocratiques et qui sont gouvernés par les élus du suffrage universel, un jour de règne ou plutôt un jour de saturnales: c'est celui des élections. [7]

On this day the bourgeoisie spoke about fraternity and equality and addressed the proletariat as the sovereign people. When the election was over, however, all talk about fraternity and equality faded away, the bourgeoisie instated itself in the position of suppressors and exploitors and the proletariat remained slaves. Evidently what Bakunin here held to be democracy and the most democratic countries were primarily characterized by a form of government ruled by persons elected by universal suffrage. It may be assumed that this was the sole conceptual characteristic of his concept 'democracy' as used in this statement. It is obvious that he did not consider this form to be an adequate means for the emancipation of the people at large; on the contrary, he regarded it as being illusory as well as fictive for the great task of liberating humanity. This derogatory application can be regarded as predominant in his terminology. A special cause of this application lay in his attitude towards Marx and Mazzini, his main ideological opponents, whom he believed to be democrats and in favour of democracy. [8] It should be pointed out, however, that neither Mazzini nor Marx applied the term in an particularly honorific fashion, rather the reverse.

In spite of this derogatory application, there are at least two occurrences where "democratic" and "democracy" are used in honorific ways. In his comment on the authoritarian policy of the Workmen's International Association, he said:

> Le Comité Central, après avoir été une institution purement populaire et démocratique, est devenu peu à peu une institution gouvernementale, genevoise, et aristocratique. [9]

Together with "popular", "democratic" is used here to describe an institution opposed to, or perhaps even contrary to, a "governmental, aristocratic, and Genevan one". It is obvious that Bakunin deplored the alleged change in the character of the Central Committee, which may be taken to imply some degree of honorific application of "democratic". Elsewhere he asserted:

> Dans le camp de la démocratie, nous ne connaissons ni révélateurs, ni initiateurs, ni dictateurs, ni tuteurs, ni maîtres. Nous croyens sincèrement à l'instinct morale de chacun, nous cherchons à le deviner, à y puiser nos inspirations et à les formuler. [10]

"The democratic camp" is used here to designate something to which Bakunin considered both he and his adherents belonged. This distinctly in-group attitude towards the democratic camp was perpetuated in the above statement, which is central to his anarchist philosophy. The absence of tutors, masters, dictators, and prophets and the presence of belief in the moral instincts of the individual are certainly among the conceptual characteristics of 'democracy' as presented here. These characteristics would imply a relationship of incompatibility between democracy and any kind of government, which points to a signification of "democracy" that differs from all his earlier applications. Since there is no reason to think that Bakunin's political view here differed from his central political principles, this change

from a derogatory use, or at least a predominantly derogatory use, to a
clearly honorific one must be regarded, not as a change in his political
outlook, but as a change in the connotations attributed to "democracy".

2. Kropotkin

Since no occurrences of "democracy" and only a few related terms have
been found in the writings of Peter Kropotkin, little can be said about the
significations attributed to these terms by this central anarchist philosopher.
In Paroles d'un Révolté, Kropotkin spoke contemptuously of parliamentary
and representative rule and was of the firm opinion that the manipulation of
the popular will was an indispensable property of such rule. To him parliamentary elections were mere comedies:

> Dans la bourgeoise Angleterre et dans la démocratique Suisse, en France
> comme aux Etats-Unis, en Allemagne comme dans la République Argen-
> tine, cette triste comédie n'est-elle pas partout la même? [11]

This comment gives no foundation for research, however. All that can be
said is that "democratic" is used here to describe Switzerland, a country
which, inter alia, was characterized by a political system of which he did
not approve; this can probably be said to mark a derogatory use of the term.
Whether "democratic" was restricted exclusively to Switzerland or whether
the term could also be used of the United States or France is not clear. But
a later statement implies that the term could also be used of the United
States.
   A little later in this work Kropotkin greatly deplored the influence of
capital among members of parliaments and especially the purchase of important posts in the civil service. He went on to say that in contrast to this
political practice,

> ...là où les mœurs sont eminemment démocratiques, comme aux Etats-
> Unis, là où les comités se constituent facilement et contrebalancent
> l'influence de la fortune, on nommera le plus mauvais de tous, le politi-
> cien de profession. [12]

"Eminently democratic" is used here to characterize the customs which,
inter alia, were to be found in a country like the United States. These
customs were remarkable for the ease with which committees were formed
to counterbalance the influence of capital. This was a factor which Kropotkin most certainly approved of, but it is also evident that he regarded the
distribution of posts to professional politicians, for whom he held an exceedingly negative opinion, to be characteristic of these customs. This
probably more than outweighed the positive way in which capital could be
counterbalanced.
   There is little to be added concerning the other works of Kropotkin. In
Anarchist Communism he held that even at that time,

> ...when the Socialists all over Europe are becoming political parties,
> and profess the democratic faith, there remains among most impartial
> men a well-founded fear of the Volkstaat or 'popular State' being as great
> a danger for liberty as any form of autocracy. [13]

"Democratic" here characterizes a faith, or ideology, in a certain kind of State; according to the socialist scheme, this took form in the Volkstaat. Since it is certain that Kropotkin included himself among the impartial men who feared this State to be the equivalent of autocracy, it can be said that here, too, "democratic" is used in a derogatory way. Later in this pamphlet, Kropotkin stated:

As to Anarchy, it is obviously as incompatible with plutocracy as with any other kind of cracy. [14]

Kropotkin would most probably have included what he designated as "democracy" among the phenomena which were incompatible with anarchy.

In The Conquest of Bread Kropotkin once more maintained parliamentary rule and representative government were in complete opposition to the interests of the workers. In this context he used "democrats" to label persons who were generally in favour of parliamentary rule, but who also, in order to eliminate the drawbacks of parliamentarism, hoped to introduce practices like referendum, proportional representation, and the representation of minorities. [15] According to Kropotkin, these reforms were completely illusory, and it is clear that he considered democrats to be in favour of a utopian policy and that he did not include either himself or his adherents among them.

Considering Kropotkin's use of "democratic" and "democrats", it is highly probable that the terms, if used, would not have been applied honorifically, and that they probably would have signified a State governed in the illusory manner of popular representation.

3. Sorel

"Democracy" and "democratic" were generally used in the writings of Bakunin and Kropotkin to describe a political system of which they did not approve, but which they nevertheless did not regard as the worst of existing political systems; but an extremely derogatory use of these terms is found in Sorel's writings. There is good reason to believe that Sorel considered democracy to be the political institution that contrasted most greatly with his syndicalist principles, that represented the greatest danger for what he believed to be the mission of the proletariat.

In his famous work, Réflexions sur la violence, 1906, Sorel asserted several times that the historical effort of the bourgeoisie was the attempt to govern the masses in a way profitable to capitalism by regarding society as a kind of unitary organism. He went on to say:

Tout l'effort révolutionnaire tend à créer des hommes libres; mais les gouvernants démocratiques se donnent pour mission de réaliser l'unité morale de la France. [16]

Revolutionary efforts, that is, revolutionary efforts of a proletarian kind, are here contrasted with the alleged mission of democratic rulers: revolutionary efforts are said to create free men, the alleged mission of democratic rulers was identical with what Sorel held as the main character of the political strategy of capitalism. This indicates without doubt a negative attitude on Sorel's part towards those he called "democratic rulers"; although it may be added that an indication of the policy of these democratic

rulers does not tell us very much about the signification attributed to
"democratic".

At the same place Sorel stated:

On peut encore dire que le grand danger qui menace le syndicalisme
serait toute tentative d'imiter la démocratie.

He went on to say that he greatly preferred organizations to remain weak
and chaotic for some time,

que de tomber sous la domination de syndicats qui copieraient des formes
politiques de la bourgeoisie.

It is fairly evident that the imitation of democracy is held to be the equivalent of copying the political institutions of the bourgeoisie. This may imply
a relationship of identity between political institutions of the bourgeoisie
and democracy. In that case, he not only held a bourgeois or capitalistic
rule to be a consequence of democracy, but he even included it in his signification of the word "democracy". This would imply that an expression
like "capitalist democracy" was a pleonasm and "socialist democracy", a
contradictio in adjecto in Sorel's terminology. According to the evidence
of other occurrences in his terminology, this is a reasonable hypothesis.

These two statements about democracy and democratic rulers touch on
a central point in Sorel's political philosophy. For him syndicalism was to
be based exclusively upon the revolutionary class-consciousness of the
proletariat; and, partly in contrast to the political view of Marx and especially in contrast to that of Lenin, this revolutionary ideology was not to
be framed by intellectual leaders but was primarily the spontaneous reflex
of the instincts of the proletariat, or rather of the class-conscious section
of the proletariat, that minority group which he held to represent the only
sane element in a decadent society. It is evident that any parliamentary
compromise with the bourgeoisie or any parliamentary activity was incompatible with such an ideology.

Sorel was also of the opinion that the old claim for moral unity within
the French nation was the greatest obstacle to the growth of real proletarian
class-consciousness among the workers. By emphasizing the unitary needs
of democracy, this part of Sorel's argument is rather similar to the views
of Robespierre and Saint-Just. The latter had also frequently emphasized
the need for unanimity in a democracy; the only difference being that Robespierre and Saint-Just were highly in favour of such a moral climate, while
the contrary attitude is evident in Sorel's writings.

Other uses of "democracy" in this work by Sorel conform with that discussed above. Somewhat later he stated:

L'experiénce montre que dans tous les pays où la démocratie peut
développer librement sa nature, s'étale la corruption la plus scandaleuse,
sans que personne juge utile de dissimuler ses coquineries: le Tammany-
Hall de New York a toujours été cité comme le type le plus parfait de la
vie démocratique. [17]

He went on to say that in the majority of French cities there were politicians
whose main wish was to follow the lead of their American confederates.
Corruption, however scandalous, was an inevitable characteristic of all
countries in which democracy developed according to its nature. The great
similarity between what he designated as "democracy" and the worst aspects
of capitalism is further emphasized when he stated:

La démocratie électorale ressemble beaucoup au monde de la Bourse;
dans un cas comme dans l'autre, il faut opérer sur la naïveté des
masses, acheter le concours de la grande presse, et aider le hasard
par une infinité de ruses. [18]

Here it may be objected that Sorel uses "electoral democracy" and not unqualified "democracy" to describe a political phenomenon that, in making
use of the naïvety of the masses, buying of the press, etc. , bore a strong
resemblance to the stock exchange and that "democracy" without qualification might therefore have been used in a somewhat different way. Other
occurrences make such an hypothesis unlikely, however. Some kind of
election seems to have been a necessary property of everything he designated "democracy"; "electoral democracy" can therefore probably be regarded as a pleonasm in Sorel's terminology. Sorel also used unqualified
"democrat" to label the politician whose methods were similar to the worst
methods of the businessman. He concluded:

La démocratie est le pays de Cocagne rêvé par les financiers sans
scrupules. [19]

Another derogatory use of "democracy" occurs in Les illusions du
progrès of 1908. Here, too, Sorel drew attention to the unitary character
of democracy[20] and said, most certainly as a consequence of this character,

La démocratie ayant pour objectif la disparition des sentiments de
classe.... . [21]

Sorel commented on a laudatory application of "democracy" by Alfred
Fouillée, in which the latter held that the progress of democracy was the
progress of human dignity, liberty, autonomy, and morality. After stating
that democracy was given compliments it did not deserve, Sorel went on
to say:

Il suffit de regarder autour de nous pour reconnaître que la démocratie
est une école de servilité, de délation et de démoralisation. [22]

He does not directly explain why democracy should have been a "school in
servility, denunciation, and demoralization", but he probably had the close
association between democracy and capitalism in mind. As with other
occurrences, the term is obviously used to describe something that Sorel
evaluated very negatively. Although Sorel refers elsewhere to evil phenomena as a consequence of democracy, here there is good reason to believe that demoralization and servility were conceptually attributed to his
concept 'democracy'. This would probably imply that "democracy" in this
statement was used not only derogatorily but even dyslogistically, or with
a negative evaluation implicit in its signification. Thus a statement like
"democracy is a bad system" would be a tautology or an analytic statement
to Sorel.

A related use of "democracy" to describe something which he greatly
disliked is found among the rare occurrences of this term in Sorel's other
writings. [23] It can therefore be concluded that, in spite of infrequent use,
"democracy" occupies a significant position in Sorel's terminology since he
consistently employed the word to describe the greatest obstacle to the
realization of what he thought essential to human dignity and human progress.
On this point, and in his attributing a mean and vulgar morality to what he
designated as "democracy", there is at least some degree of similarity
between Sorel and Nietzsche.

Within socialist thought, Sorel's use of "democracy" marks the most negative evaluation of "democracy". There is an enormous difference between Sorel's use and that of Babeuf, for example, where the latter uses the term both centrally and honorifically in his revolutionary socialist ideology. And a great difference is also apparent when Sorel is compared with Marx and Engels prior to 1848, when "democracy" was generally used by these two in a way well suited to their revolutionary policy. Needless to say, Sorel also differs clearly from such reformist contemporaries as Bernstein, Jaurès, and the Fabians. Among socialists, a derogatory evaluation of "democracy" was used by Marx and Engels after 1849 and by Proudhon. To Marx and Engels, democracy was in certain cases regarded as the most dangerous phenomenon of a successful revolutionary policy; and during certain periods of his life, Proudhon conceived of democracy to be the greatest opposition to his personal ideal of free human development within a system marked by a high degree of decentralization. These trends were by no means exclusive ones, however. For Proudhon, democracy was not always a centralistic, militaristic, and anti-socialist system; and as with Marx and Engels, a clearly honorific application is several times to be found in his terminology. On this point Sorel is almost unique. His derogatory, if not dyslogistic, use of "democracy" can never be thrown into relief against a neutral or honorific application. Sorel stands out as the only socialist who consistently evaluated negatively what he designated as "democracy". As will be demonstrated later, the use of "democracy" by leading Bolsheviks does not disprove this view, although a negative application can clearly be seen in Bolshevik terminology after 1917. Even in relation to the use of "democracy" by conservatives, Sorel's usage stands out as the most consistently negative; although a derogatory, and in certain cases a very derogatory, application is frequently seen in the terminology of Faguet, Treitschke, and Maurras, for example, there are nevertheless a few occurrences which cannot be classed as derogatory. This cannot be said about Sorel, whose every use of "democracy" seems to have been accompanied by a certain moral contempt which was symptomatic of the mental purity of this great thinker.

4. Lagardelle

In relation to Sorel, Hubert Lagardelle occupies a position of minor importance in political thought. There are, however, some interesting aspects in his use of "democracy" and especially in the relationship between his form of socialism and democracy. In contrast to the rare application of "democracy" in Sorel's writings, Lagardelle made fairly frequent use of the term in his main work Le socialism ouvrier, 1911. This syndicalist ideologist also used the term in a derogatory way, although without the vehemence of Sorel. The first chapter of his work is headed "Socialisme ou démocratie", a formulation which can be taken to indicate that he held "socialism" and "democracy" to signify radically different phenomena in political life. Lagardelle severely attacked the reformist programme adopted by the French Socialist Party at its congress at Tours in 1902. He drew attention to the danger of transforming "le mouvement socialiste en un simple mouvement démocratique"[24] and severely attacked the idea that

Le socialism n'est que l'aboutissant logique de la démocratie. [25]

To the question "Que faut-il entendre par démocratie?", Lagardelle answered:

> C'est à la fois un principe et une forme de gouvernement: un principe, en tant qu'elle proclame l'égalité des droits de tous les citoyens; une forme de gouvernement, en tant qu'elle met l'Etat au service et sous le contrôle de la masse, en tant qu'elle est le gouvernement du peuple par le peuple. [26]

Here there is no evidence of dislike of the political principle or form of state which represented the two connotations of "democracy". He went on to maintain, however, that although democracy aimed at securing equal rights and liberty for all, it could do nothing but support those differences which economic life had drawn between classes. He held that democracy was trying to place itself above the class struggle and that the essential character of democracy lay not only in refusing to admit the class struggle but in suppressing it in the interest of national unity, harmony, and reconciliation between classes. After referring to various statements by Marx and Sorel, he concluded:

> La conception de la lutte de classe, qui est à la base du socialisme est donc contradictoire à la démocratie. [27]

It is not clear whether Lagardelle here held democracy to be a political principle or a form of rule contrary to the class struggle between the bourgeoisie and the proletariat; it may be conjectured that he had both in mind. It is also difficult to see whether the rejection or suppression of the class struggle was conceptually attributed to his concept 'democracy' or whether he intended to discuss a universal political consequence of that system or principle. He probably based his discussion on the first conception, since socialism and class struggle as understood by Lagardelle generally seem to have been per definitionem regarded as incompatible with democracy. An expression like "socialist democracy" would most likely be self-contradictory according to his theories. In any case this presumed contradiction between democracy and socialism is naturally apt to be followed by a derogatory application of "democracy". To a large degree such derogatory use is typical of his application, although this statement is made with reservations. Lagardelle was of the opinion, for example, that the working class needed the freedom of association to be found in a democracy, and he also stated:

> Sur le terrain des libertés politiques et des institutions liberales, démocrates et socialistes, ont-ils des intérêts identiques! [28]

This statement reveals that "democracy" and "democrat" might, from a certain point of view, be used to label something of which he approved. But this relationship was limited to the political field, of which he went on to say:

> Les points communs de la démocratie et du socialisme s'arrêtent la. Les contradictions s'affirment sur le terrain économique.

Here Lagardelle was repeating various of his earlier statements on the incompetence of democracy to solve economic questions and the contradictions between democracy and socialism. To Lagardelle the organization of the proletariat for revolutionary activity belonged to the economic and not to the political fields. He probably saw only a possibility of organizing the proletariat in the field of politics. This factor, which indicates that he believed certain interests to be common to socialists and democrats, may be assumed to undermine the relationship of incompatibility between social- ism and democracy. Although in his opinion democracy offered certain political advantages to socialists, the relationship of mutual incompatibility is not necessarily contradicted. For example, democratic forms of rule might offer certain political advantages for persons in favour of nazism, but nevertheless there is a relationship of mutual incompatibility between nazism and democracy. Lagardelle concluded the first chapter of Le socialisme ouvrier by asserting:

> La démocratie, dominant les conflits des classes, espère les concilier à l'intérieur du regime capitaliste. Le socialisme, se plaçant au cœur des luttes des classes, les pousse à l'extrême et attend de leur solution la fin du monde bourgeoise. La démocratie est conservatrice, le socialisme est révolutionnaire. [29]

According to this statement, Lagardelle was writing primarily about the political aims of democracy in the context of the social-class struggle and not about democracy itself or about that concept he designated as "democ- racy". Social conciliation would not be a part of the signification of "democ- racy" as used here, which may imply that "democracy" had a different con- notation from that in our first quotations where social conciliation may have been implicit in the signification of the term. Such a variation in Lagar- delle's terminology is of minor interest, however, although it touches a fairly important problem. It is obvious that by contrasting democracy and socialism in the struggle of the proletariat, "democracy" was used to label something of which he did not approve. It must be observed, however, that this derogatory application was in relation to the field of economics only. To him, the field of economics was by far the most important, but nevertheless there is some degree of differentiation on this point that cannot be observed in Sorel's writings.

Many other occurrences of "democracy" and related terms are present in this work, but they do not seem to add to those already quoted.

CHAPTER XVI

BOLSHEVISM

1. Lenin

a. Before 1917

Within the camp of revolutionary socialism, different trends in the use of "democracy" have already been observed. Sorel used "democracy" in a derogatory, if not dyslogistic, way, and a contrary application was evident in Babeuf's terminology. As for Marx and Engels, for example, Engels gave his view in 1845: "Die Demokratie das ist heutzutage der Kommunismus." And six years afterwards, Marx characterized one of his revolutionary pamphlets as nothing but "ein Kriegsplan gegen die Demokratie".

Similarly, very different trends can generally be seen within the use of "democracy" by leading Bolsheviks. Anyone who desires to prove either that Lenin was a true and profound democrat or that leading Bolsheviks were definitely not democrats can find accommodating evidence by a biased selection of the terminology used during the Revolution. However, inconsistency is not a characteristic of Lenin's use of "democracy" prior to 1917.

One of Lenin's first uses of "democracy" and related terms occurs in The Tasks of the Russian Social-Democrats, of 1897. In this pamphlet Lenin began by discussing both the economic demands of the proletariat and propaganda in favour of Marxist socialism. Turning to concrete political tasks in contemporary Russia, he emphasized how intimately political work must be connected with socialist propaganda. On this point he maintained that, in addition to disseminating propaganda in favour of socialism,

> Russian Social-Democrats consider it to be their task to carry on propaganda among the masses of the workers in favour of democratic ideas, to spread an understanding of what absolutism means in all its manifestations, its class content, the necessity of overthrowing it. ... [1]

Agitation against absolute rule in Russia and even propaganda in favour of the necessity of overthrowing it are probably considered by Lenin to be necessary properties of the ideas he labelled as "democratic". Although Lenin held democratic, socialist, and economic activities and propaganda to be inseparable, this does not imply that he did not draw a sharp line of demarcation between the activity described as "socialist" and that described as "democratic". According to Lenin, an important difference lay in the fact that in the socialist and economic struggle, the proletariat stood quite alone against the landed nobility and the bourgeoisie, while

> ... in the democratic, the political struggle, however, the Russian working class does not stand alone. [2]

He went on to refer to the oppositional elements from different strata and classes of the population, such as parts of the bourgeoisie and the educated

classes, the petty bourgeoisie, and the nationalities and the religious sects
hostile to absolutism. Unlike "socialist", "democratic" was used exclusively to characterize the political struggle against czarism, which seems
to imply that at this point Lenin used "democratic" with a signification almost purely political.

Lenin's statement about the proletariat not standing alone in the struggle
against absolutism does not imply that the proletariat was an opponent only
of czarism or that the proletariat would fight against czarism only to the
same degree as did the liberal bourgeoisie, for example. On the contrary,
Lenin frequently asserted that the proletariat was also to be in the vanguard
of that struggle. He doubted whether the hostility of all other classes
towards autocracy was absolute, and affirmed:

> The proletariat alone can be ... consistently democratic, the determined
> enemy of absolutism, incapable of making any concessions, or of entering
> into any compromises. [3]

"Consistently democratic" is probably used here with a signification of "unreservedly hostile towards absolutism", a characteristic which he attributed
to the proletariat only. As a causal explanation of this relationship, Lenin
stated first that the proletariat was most affected by the existing political
tyranny in Russia and secondly that

> ... the proletariat is capable of bringing about the complete democrati-
> zation of the political and social system, because such democratization
> would place the system in the hands of the workers. [4]

Why and how this complete democratization would place the political and
social system in the hands of the workers is not elaborated upon.

In his famous work What Is to Be Done?, 1902, Lenin repeats several
of his statements concerning the proletariat as the vanguard not only of the
economic struggle for socialism but also of the more immediate political
struggle against czarism. "Democrats" was apparently used here, too, as
the designation of persons in sharp opposition to the existing absolutistic
rule. It is clear that he included himself as well as his socialist adherents
under this label, but it is also obvious that persons not socialists were included in this group. [5] Every socialist, or social-democrat, was a democrat, but not vice versa, which implies that "democrat" was used with a
wider signification than that of "socialist" or "social democrat", the latter
terms being synonymous or nearly synonymous in Lenin's terminology at
that time.

Lenin also repudiated the criticism voiced in Rabocheye Dyela concerning the alleged anti-democratic tendencies of Lenin and other contributors to Iskra. Lenin first said: "It would be absurd to speak about democracy without publicity," and secondly, he mentioned the principle of election.[6]
According to these criteria, Lenin held the German Socialist Party to be a
democratic organization. This he certainly approved of, but he also emphasized that it was impossible to organize a socialist party in contemporary
Russia according to these criteria. In Russia, any revolutionary organization must be secret and characterized by the strict selection of members and
the training of professional revolutionaries. Lenin admitted that the Russian
socialists' political organization was not in accordance with what he designated as "democracy", but this was because of contemporary conditions in
Russia and not because of any general dislike of such political organization.
Later practice reveals that Lenin did not consider the strict form of a cadre

party to be conditioned by social and political circumstances in a particular country but that it was more likely to represent the way of communist political organization regardless of time and space.

Concerning another aspect of the signification Lenin attributed to "democracy", in referring to statements made by the Webbs and Kautsky on direct rule and the absence of representatives and salaried officials, he declared: "How absurd such a conception of democracy was. "[7] This can be taken to imply that Lenin not only disapproved of such a primitive organization but that he would also refuse it the label "democracy". His statement touches upon an essential point in his political thinking; there is a distinct emphasis on the importance of political leadership. Lenin required an elite of professional revolutionaries, very different from the trade unions which were to be open to any worker. Also, only the Party could impose upon the workers a socialist consciousness; left to themselves they would remain in trade unionism. Socialism was to be engrafted upon the working class by intellectuals outside that class. It is significant that Lenin refers here to the Webbs and Kautsky. At this time Lenin was fairly alone among revolutionary socialists in emphasizing the importance of leadership and not the role of the working class, and the strange phenomenon occurred that viewpoints very similar to Lenin's were adhered to by reformist or semi-reformist socialists like the Fabians and Kautsky, while quite different opinions were held by profound revolutionaries like Trotsky and Rosa Luxemburg. The latter absolutely refused to regard a selected party as the guardian of the whole working class. This aspect is to play a considerable role in Luxemburg's use of "democracy" and especially in her later criticism of revolutionary rule by the Bolsheviks.

Lenin's use of "democracy" and "democrat" in Two Tactics of Social-Democracy in the Democratic Revolution, which was written during the first part of the Revolution of 1905, is similar to his earlier one. Here, too, he repeated that the proletariat was the vanguard in the struggle for democracy and put great emphasis on the difference between a democratic and a socialist revolution. Lenin frequently declared that Russia was not yet ripe for a socialist revolution or a revolution that would eliminate private property and the means of production. He repeatedly maintained that the current revolution in Russia, which he described as "democratic", was a bourgeois revolution which would strengthen, not weaken, the social and economic domination of the bourgeoisie and would not undermine the system of capitalism. [8] To regard the proletariat as forming the vanguard in such a revolution may be considered somewhat paradoxical. It must be observed, however, that Lenin was of the firm opinion that the workers in Russia suffered not so much from capitalism as from the lack of capitalistic development, and he considered everything except the further development of capitalism to be reactionary. [9] He concluded by asserting that the decisive victory over czarism would be "the revolutionary-democratic dictatorship of the proletariat and the peasantry, "[10] an expression which was for several years the main Bolshevik slogan. A dictatorship implied that revolutionary rule should rely on the armed masses and, further, on an uprising, and not on institutions established by legal or peaceful means; this Lenin held to be indispensable if attempts at counter-revolution were to be repulsed. By describing a dictatorship as "democratic", Lenin did not hold what he designated as "democracy" to be incompatible with dictatorship; a relationship emphasized in the postscript to this work. [11] As in earlier statements Lenin also maintained that this dictatorship would not be a socialist one or opposed to capitalism. At the best it might bring about a radical redistribution of land to the advantage of the peasantry, lay the foundation of a thorough improvement of the position of the workers, and carry revolutionary conflagration into Europe.

Little can be added here to what has been said about Lenin's use of "democratic" and "democracy" during the period prior to 1917. In October 1914, while stating that the war in all advanced countries had brought the slogan of the socialist revolution to the fore, Lenin declared that in Russia, the task of the social-democrats was, as heretofore, "to achieve the three fundamental conditions for consistent democratic reform. "[12] These three conditions were: a republic with complete political equality and self-determination for all nationalities, the confiscation of the property of the landlords, and an eight-hour day. Consistent democratic reform thus included somewhat more radical measures that those attributed to democratic dictatorship, but there is a great degree of similarity between these two phenomena, and here, too, Lenin regarded consistent democratic reform as being very different from socialist measures. Thus, it can be inferred that in Lenin's pre-revolutionary terminology there is hardly any tendency towards using "democracy" and related terms to signify a socialist rule. At this point there is a considerable difference between his terminology and that of other socialist ideologists, such as Babeuf, Cabet, and, to a certain extent, Jaurès and the Webbs, and Engels primarily before 1848 in certain writings.

b. During and after the Revolution

Lenin's first use of "democracy" and related terms after the overthrow of the czarist government is probably to be found in the pamphlet The Tasks of the Proletariat in Our Revolution, April 1917. Here Lenin asserted that for the moment there was a dual power in Russia because of the existence of two governments: the Provisional Government, which for the time being was the actual and official government, and the Petrograd Soviet of Workers' and Soldiers' Deputies. In relation to this dual power Lenin considered the Revolution to have approached the revolutionary-democratic dictatorship of the proletariat and peasantry, although this stage had not yet been reached.[13] He regarded soviets like that in Petrograd to represent precisely such a dictatorship.

A little later in the pamphlet Lenin wrote:

The most perfect and advanced type of bourgeois State is the parliamentary democratic republic,

and he went on to say:

But since the end of the nineteenth century, revolutionary epochs have been producing a superior type of democratic State. [14]

Quoting Engels, Lenin somewhat paradoxically declared that this State, in certain aspects, ceased to be a State or was "no longer a state in the proper sense of the word." This new political form was stated to be of the same type as the Paris Commune; and as examples of it, Lenin called attention to the soviets which the Russian Revolution began to create in the years 1905 and 1917. Lenin also held that a republic of soviets united in an All-

Russian Constituent Assembly of the people's representatives, or in a
Council of Soviets, was being realized in Russia at the juncture; this was
identical with the fact that millions of people, "of their own accord, are
creating a democracy in their own way, "[15] "Superior democratic State"
and "democracy in their own way" are probably used here with a signification identical, or nearly so, with that of "revolutionary-democratic dictatorship of the proletariat and peasantry"; and the criteria of the cessation of
such a State were evidently that the standing army and the police were replaced by the armed populace itself. For the rest it is clear that in certain
other respects this State did not cease to be a State or, according to Marxism, a means of suppression in the class struggle. Here Lenin was emphasizing the necessity of a State in a period of revolution in general and in the
period of transition from capitalism to socialism in particular, and he also
emphasized that what was needed was not the customary bourgeois republic
but a State like the Paris Commune. [16] This view can probably be taken to
imply that a superior democratic State, or a democratic dictatorship of the
above-mentioned kind, was adequate for the overthrow of capitalism. Thus,
Lenin attributed to this kind of democratic dictatorship a function new in
relation to his earlier ideology. [17]

In spite of using "superior democratic State" to label the revolutionary
rule which was needed during the transition from capitalism to socialism,
Lenin refused to accept "democrats" as a designation of the Bolsheviks.
Although he rejected the label "social-democrats" in general, wishing to
replace it with the label "Communist", Lenin also held:

> The second part of the name of our Party (Social-Democrats) is also
> scientifically incorrect. Democracy is but one form of the state, whereas
> we as Marxists are opposed to all and every kind of state. [18]

His rejection of the term as a designation of the party is still more evident
when he stated:

> The term democracy is not only scientifically incorrect when applied to
> a Communist Party, it has now, since March 1917, simply become a
> blinker covering the eyes of the revolutionary people and preventing them
> from boldly and freely, on their own initiative, building up the new. [19]

And he declared that the new rule was the political power of the soviets. His
description of this term as a blinker preventing revolutionaries from building up the power of the soviets can, from a terminological point of view, be
said to contradict his use of "superior democratic State" to characterize the
same kind of power. However, Lenin's, as well as Engels', way of discussing the government which was to cease to be a State is apt to be paradoxical, or even self-contradictory. A parallel relationship can be found in his
statement that

> ...we must look forward to a new democracy which is in process of be-
> ing born, and which is already ceasing to be a democracy, [20]

which may make charges of terminological contradiction a little inconvenient.

In The State and Revolution, which was written in September 1917,
"democracy" is frequently, but not consistently, used to signify a form of
State that will disappear when the State withers away. [21] The clearest evidence that Lenin considered democracy to be a kind of State is probably to
be found in his answer to the question whether the principle of the subordi-
nation of the minority to the majority was not to be respected when the State,

and thus democracy, began to wither away. As he was definitely in favour
of this principle, Lenin answered:

> No, democracy is not identical with the subordination of the minority to
> the majority. Democracy is a State which recognizes the subordination
> of the minority to the majority, i. e., an organization for systematic use
> of violence by one class against the other, by one section of the population
> against another. [22]

He went on to say that the communists had as their ultimate aim the abolition of the State, which, according to him, meant the abolition of all use of
violence against man in general.

    This interpretation of democracy as identical with an organization for
the systematic use of violence by one class against another is, however,
contradicted a few pages later. Here Lenin emphasized that there could be
no development towards communism except through the dictatorship of the
proletariat. And he continued:

> But the dictatorship of the proletariat, i. e., the organization of the
> vanguard of the oppressed as the ruling class for the purpose of crushing
> the oppressors, cannot result merely in an expansion of democracy.

He admitted that this rule would involve an immense expansion of democracy,
which for the first time would become democracy for the poor and not democracy for the rich, but it would at the same time impose a series of restric-
tions on the freedom of the oppressors, the exploiters, the capitalists. He
concluded:

> We must crush them [the capitalists] in order to free humanity from
> wage-slavery; their resistance must be broken by force; it is clear that
> where there is suppression there is also violence, there is no freedom,
> no democracy. [23]

His interpretation of democracy here seems to have included the non-existence of suppression and violence, a signification of "democracy" that is on
important points diametrically opposed to the statement six pages earlier.
This use of the term made it inadequate as a designation for any form of
State, and the expansion of democracy within one section of the population
was probably not a sufficient condition for designating something "democracy."
It is also obvious that the dictatorship of the proletariat would be different
from what Lenin here labelled with "democracy".

    A similar heterogeneous terminology concerning the withering away of
the State occurs in the following pages. Here, too, Lenin initially used
"democracy", or rather "democracy without any exceptions", with a signification that excluded the use of violence and suppression. Referring to and
quoting from a letter from Engels to Bebel, dated March 1875, Lenin declared that only in a communist society, when the resistance of the capitalists had disappeared, when there were no classes, only then did "the
State cease to exist" and it "becomes possible to speak of freedom".[24] Lenin
went on to say:

> Only then will really complete democracy, democracy without any ex-
> ceptions, be possible and be realized. [25]

This seems to confirm that democracy, or complete democracy, was incompatible with violence and suppression, and that it would only be realized in
the classless communistic society. According to his earlier statements

concerning the State, and in accordance with his correlation between the cessation of the State and the existence of complete democracy, "really complete democracy" could not be the designation of any form of State. Lenin's attitude was nevertheless somewhat unclear on this point. He continued: "Only then will democracy itself begin to wither away, "[26] and referred to the people who, when freed from capitalistic slavery, would gradually become accustomed to observing the rules of social life without the apparatus for compulsion called "the State". In this last quotation, "democracy itself" is used to designate a kind of State, and it is strange that this State should begin withering away when the State had ceased to exist. It is not clear whether or not Lenin intended to use "really complete democracy" with a signification different from that of "democracy itself". There are situations in which paradoxical expressions may be the most adequate, such as for example, a statement like "a democracy which is no longer a democracy", but Lenin here seems to exceed a reasonable paradox.

Earlier a self-contradictory use of "democracy" and related terms was noted in relation to the rule of the soviets. His reference at the same place to the future abolition of the State seems to be the main cause of the self-contradictory character of his terminology. However, self-contradictions directly connected with the abolition of the State are otherwise rare in his terminology. The predominant trend in Lenin's terminology is to allow "democracy" to connote a kind of State; and apart from the occurrences already discussed, only once among several hundred times has "democracy", or a qualified form of the term, been found to be used to signify something incompatible with the existence of any kind of State. In March 1919, Lenin stated:

> The abolition of the State is the main aim pursued by all Socialists, including, and particularly, Marx. Until this aim has been achieved, true democracy, i. e. equality and liberty, will be impossible. [27]

Aside from the questions concerning democracy and the abolition of the State, the more general trend in Lenin's terminology, his view that rule by the soviets presented a higher kind of democracy, is predominant in his use of "democracy". In his "Theses on the Constituent Assembly", for example, he declared such an assembly to be the highest form of democracy in a bourgeois republic. He continued, however:

> A republic of Soviets is a higher form of democracy than the ordinary bourgeois republic with a Constituent Assembly. [28]

Thus, he did not refuse the label "democracy" to a bourgeois republic, but it is noteworthy that shortly after the November Revolution Lenin declared the republic of soviets to be a higher form of democracy. This would seem to be an application of the term that cannot be said to be derogatory and which conforms with one earlier trend in his terminology.

This honorific use of the term was partly caused because he did not associate democracy with absence of violence during the time of the uprising. Lenin frequently emphasized the right to decide serious political questions, not by vote, but by force; and he was even of the opinion that the solution of central problems could not be effected by means of the ballot but by forceful class struggle only. [29] These statements are not connected with derogatory uses of "democracy", however; and on this point there is a considerable difference between Lenin's language and that of other leading Bolsheviks.

A rather different application occurs in his vigorous polemics against Kautsky, however. In his work <u>Die Diktatur des Proletariats</u>, Kautsky, like various other western ideologists, accused the rule of the Bolsheviks and especially the dissolution of the Constituent Assembly to be contrary to democracy. Replying to this view, Lenin declared on several occasions that the tendency to speak of pure democracy and democracy in general and of democracy as something above class was mockery of the fundamental tenet of socialism. According to Lenin, there was a bourgeois, or capitalistic, democracy and a proletarian democracy, but there was no country in which democracy in general was to be found.[30] Here the non-existence of democracy in general cannot be taken to imply that such an expression could not be used, for example, to designate a genus of which the concrete concepts 'proletarian democracy' and 'capitalist democracy' were species.

A new aspect of his use of "democracy" appears when Lenin opposed Kautsky's view that the protection of minorities was essential to a democracy. He asserted that socialists who were faithful to their international convictions were frequently strangulated in capitalist countries, and he concluded by emphasizing that

> <u>The more highly developed democracy is, the more imminent is the</u> <u>danger of progroms or civil war in connection with any profound political</u> <u>divergence which is dangerous for the bourgeoisie.</u> [31]

"Democracy" in this quotation is synonymous with "bourgeois democracy" or "capitalist democracy" as used by Lenin, and it is certain that the term is used here in a derogatory way. A similar application is found in his statement:

> The <u>more</u> highly democracy is developed, the <u>more</u> the bourgeois parliaments fall under the control of the Stock Exchange and the bankers. [32]

According to this, "democracy" could be used to designate exclusively a capitalist kind of rule. It is thus probable that Lenin regarded political control by the Stock Exchange and the bankers not only as a probable consequence of democracy, but even as a conceptual characteristic of his concept 'democracy'. A related derogatory application occurs on the next page in a comment on foreign policy:

> In all democratic countries -- France, Switzerland, America, or England -- the masses are deceived on an incomparably wider scale and in more subtle manner than in other countries. [33]

At this point he contrasted the open policy of the Soviet government with the secrecy of "all democratic countries", which can certainly be taken to reveal that at this point Bolshevik Russia was not included among the denotata of the expression.

When someone charges a political system with not being a democracy, one way to neutralize or annihilate the propaganda effect of the accusation is to attribute a signification to the antagonist's central term which is negatively evaluated by the antagonist himself. This is evidently what Lenin was doing in these three statements. While he admitted or even agreed with Kautsky that Soviet Russia was no democracy, he attempted to neutralize this statement ideologically by attributing to "democracy" a signification obviously held in low esteem by Kautsky and all other rightwing socialists. For the latter a government not to be controlled by the bankers would certainly not be considered a negative aspect. This attempt at counteracting

Kautsky's propaganda is by no means the only one in this work, however. In contrast to the use of "democracy" already discussed and especially in contrast to his practice of allowing "all democratic countries" to denote countries very different from Soviet Russia, Lenin returns, two pages later, to one of his earlier terminological trends by declaring:

> Proletarian democracy is a million times more democratic than any bourgeois democracy; Soviet government is a million times more democratic than the most democratic bourgeois republic. [34]

Lenin here referred to the fact that the soviets were directly organized by the toiling and exploited masses themselves, and unqualified "democratic" is obviously used with a signification very different from "democracy" and "democratic" in the preceding three quotations. In using "a million times more democratic" to characterize the difference between proletarian democracy and bourgeois democracy, Lenin referred to a kind of democracy that differed from them both. It is hardly possible that Lenin might have said, "Proletarian democracy is a million times more bourgeois democratic than bourgeois democracy" or "proletarian democracy is a million times more proletarian democratic than. ..." This may indicate that here, in contrast to his earlier statements, Lenin was operating with a concept 'democracy in general' or some closely related concept.

There is little to be added concerning Lenin's use of "democracy" and related terms. These terms are frequently used in his writings, and his assertion that the rule of the Bolsheviks represented a higher form of democracy can probably be regarded as the predominant theme, although this trend is far from consistent. Lenin's later application of "democracy" presents a mixed picture. Similar to trends evident in the use of "democracy" by Tocqueville, Proudhon, Thomas Mann, and others, there are factors which Lenin held to be of the highest political importance included in his different significations of the term. In his discussion of the abolition of the State, "democracy" may connote a form of government as well as a political system without government and state. And in Lenin's polemics with Kautsky, "democracy" signifies something necessarily marked by the interests of the bourgeoisie and the influence of the bankers, which did not hinder him from declaring frequently and even in the same work that the Soviet government represented a higher kind of democracy.

In the political writings of Lenin, there are yet many other aspects which deserve the attention of political scientists, although Lenin's use of "democracy" can be said to reveal important central aspects of his political thinking. But without exaggerating the importance of inquiry into his terminology, it is astonishing that this varied usage has not, as far as can be seen, caught the attention of scientists studying the ideology of Bolshevism.

2. Trotsky

Trotsky's main application of "democracy" and related terms occurs in his extremely vigorous polemics against Kautsky. Lenin attacked Kautsky's Die Diktatur des Proletariats, and Trotsky, in Terrorismus und Kommunismus, banished Kautsky's identically titled work, the only difference being that Trotsky used "Anti-Kautsky" as the subtitle of his work, somewhat in the style of Engels.

In general Trotsky uses "democracy" in an extremely derogatory way in this work. With Kautsky, Trotsky also held the Russian revolutionary dictatorship of the proletariat to be very different from democracy. In an historical survey he spoke contemptuously of the petty bourgeois ideologists of the school of Proudhon and denied absolutely the existence of any similarity between them and the Bolsheviks. In his view Proudhon's adherents wanted to mix some kind of democracy with the principle of federation,

... während wir die Demokratie im Namen der konzentrierten Macht des Proletariats ablehnen.

Trotsky also praised the adherents of Blanqui,

... die die Bedeutung der revolutionären Macht begriffen und die Eroberung dieser Macht nicht abergläubisch in Abhängigkeit von formalen Markmalen der Demokratie stellten. [35]

These statements indicate a very derogatory use of "democracy" as something to be rejected by the Russian revolutionaries. At this point Trotsky did not say that formal democracy was not to be taken earnestly by real revolutionaries, but attributed the formal characteristics to what he termed unqualified "democracy".

In a chapter headed "Die Metaphysik der Demokratie", Trotsky declared popular sovereignty, universal suffrage, and different kinds of freedom to be the principles of democracy. He further held:

Als Doktrin der formalen Demokratie erscheint nicht der wissenschaftliche Sozialismus, sondern die Theorie des sog. Naturrechts. [36]

He stated that so-called natural right was characterized by the acknowledgement of eternal and invariable legal norms concerning human rights and that these norms were the ideological superstructure of the class interests of the third estate in its earlier struggles against the privileges and despotism of feudalism. These theoretical principles contrasted sharply with the main trends in dialectical materialism. That Trotsky at this point uses "formal democracy" and not unqualified "democracy" may show that he did not without qualification regard the theory of natural right as a doctrine of "democracy". However, his terminology in the following passage, in which he declared the allegedly metaphysical natural right to be the teaching, the doctrine, or the principle of what he then designated as unqualified "democracy" [37] makes such an hypothesis improbable.

Trotsky admitted that democracy had been progressive in the struggle against feudalism; later, however, the reactionary trends of this metaphysi-

cal natural right became more predominant. His main reason here was that
the theory of democracy, just like Christian spiritualism, legalized slavery
and distress by drawing attention to the formal equality only.

Die mystische Gleichheit des Christentums ist vom Himmel gestiegen in
Form der naturrechtlichen Gleichheit der Demokratie. [38]

He held this kind of equality to be no more useful for the toiler than eternal
happiness.

Trotsky also admitted that in a certain period the proletarian movement
might have made some use of ordinary parliaments. He continued, however,
by holding,

... das bedeutet jedoch keineswegs, dass sie die metaphysische Theorie
der Demokratie prinzipiell anerkannte, die auf den Grundlagen des über-
historischen, über den Klassen stehenden Rechts beruhte. Die prole-
tarische Doktrin betrachtete die Demokratie als Hilfsinstrument der
bürgerlichen Gesellschaft, welches den Aufgaben und Bedürfnissen der
herrschenden Klassen voll und ganz angepasst war. [39]

Trotsky further declared the main political idea of the proletariat to be
"die Demokratie beiseite zu werfen und sie durch einen Arbeitsmechanismus
des Proletariats ... zu ersetzen. "[40] With regard to the ideology of persons he held to be traitors of socialism, he said,

... das theoretische Renegatentum Kautskys besteht eben darin, dass er,
das Prinzip der Demokratie als absolut und unwandelbar anerkennend,
von der materialistischen Dialektik zu dem Naturrecht zurückging.

and concluded:

Die gegenrevolutionäre Ausartung des Parlamentarismus fand ihren
vollendetsten Ausdruck in der Vergötterung der Demokratie durch die
Verfallstheoretiker der II. Internationale. [41]

In these crucial political statements his derogatory way of using "democracy" is striking. According to these statements, Trotsky seems to have
agreed with Kautsky that the revolutionary rule of the Bolsheviks could not
be labelled "democracy", the difference being that Kautsky used "democracy"
in an honorific way, rejecting and accusing the revolutionary rule, and
Trotsky identified himself with that rule and rejected what he designated as
"democracy". This derogatory application is of importance, but it is difficult to see the signification with which Trotsky used "democracy". On the
whole, his negative attitude is so predominant that little is left from which
to deduce a factual connotation. At one point, however, Trotsky briefly
mentioned

... die Prinzipien der Demokratie -- die Volkssouveränitet, das allgemeine und gleiche Wahlrecht, die Freiheiten -- [42]

Unfortunately he did not mention which liberties, but he probably had freedom of the press and freedom to organize political parties in mind. Thus
Trotsky may be said to have operated with a concept 'democracy' in which
popular sovereignty, equal and universal suffrage, and the above-mentioned
liberties were conceptual characteristics. It is, perhaps, less probable
that the theory of natural right can be included among those characteristics;
since according to some of his statements, only the view that democracy was

absolute was attributed to that doctrine. His opinion that democracy was adequate for bourgeois society adjusted to the needs of the ruling classes may be regarded as a particular way of estimating democracy, not as a signification of the term, although these conclusions are somewhat hypothetical.

According to some of his statements, Trotsky held democracy and the dictatorship of the proletariat to be mutually incompatible phenomena. Such a view is hardly confirmed by a somewhat later statement, however. Concerning the Constituent Assembly, Trotsky held:

Unsere Partei weigerte sich nicht, der Diktatur des Proletariats den Weg durch die Pforte der Demokratie zu öffnen,

and he referred to the calling together of this elected assembly. He went on to say, however, that the Russian peasant was politically confused when faced with the half dozen political parties. It seems that by this confusion Trotsky primarily had in mind the backing of the non-Bolsheviks by a large majority of the voters. He concluded:

Die Konstituirende Versammlung stand der revolutionären Bewegung im Wege und wurde hinweggefegt. [43]

In the first quotation, Trotsky seems to have admitted that a proletarian dictatorship, in special situations, might be achieved through a democracy. This implies that there could not, in principle, be a relationship of mutual incompatibility between democracy and the dictatorship of the proletariat, even if these phenomena could exist quite independently of each other. It is obvious that he intimately connected the existence of democracy in contemporary Russia with the Constituent Assembly and that by referring to the break up of that political organ, he clearly admitted that their dictatorship of the proletariat was not framed in democratic forms or that democracy was something which had been tried but soon rejected by the Bolsheviks.

It would be easy to quote many occurrences of a derogatory kind from this work, and occurrences in which the term was used to describe something which did not exist in Soviet Russia. [44] In sharp contrast to this terminological trend, however, there is in this work one occurrence of "democracy" which seems to have been honorific. Trotsky said that because the proletariat had entered the road of revolutionary dictatorship the present policy of the working class was not the struggle for the votes of the peasants but the creation of a real union between the peasants and the proletariat to administer the country in accordance with the interests of the toiling masses. He went on to say:

Diese Demokratie ist etwas tiefer als der Parlamentarismus. [45]

This statement reveals rather clearly that the existing form of proletarian government in Russia was considered by Trotsky to be subsumable under "democracy". It is fairly obvious that Trotsky was of the opinion that there were different kinds of democracy, such as, for example, proletarian rule in Russia and the usual parliamentarism in capitalistic countries; but it is also obvious that he held the Russian proletarian rule to be a more profound democracy than the latter.

Since at this point Trotsky did not indicate an opinion of the nature of the revolutionary rule in Russia which differed from what can be seen in other parts of this work, it can be inferred that he used "democracy" with a signification different from that in the other occurrences. As a background for this use of the term, Lenin rather frequently declared the rule of the soviets to represent a higher form of democracy than ordinary parliamentarism. This occurrence is most likely the only one in this as well as in other works of Trotsky in which he contradicts his view that the proletarian rule in Russia was not a democracy. On this point there is an important terminological difference between Trotsky and Lenin.

There is little to be added here concerning the use of "democracy" and related terms in other works of Trotsky written during the revolution. In History of the Russian Revolution to Brest-Litovsk, the English version of which is cited, Trotsky introductorily declared:

As Marxists, we have never been worshippers of formal democracy. [46]

His statement can be taken to reveal that Trotsky might have been of the opinion that the Bolsheviks were in favour of informal democracy, but his later statements make such a hypothesis uncertain. "Democratic institutions" is used frequently and without qualification to describe a political system which, in times of peace, only lent the class interests a highly imperfect form of expression and, in times of revolution, generally could not keep pace with the rapid progress of the political experience of the masses[47]. This argument was also used in discussing the Constituent Assembly, of which he said:

The material class-content of the Revolution came into an irreconcilable conflict with its democratic forms. [48]

Here he held this conflict to be the reason for the dissolution of the Assembly. He admitted that if might pay the proletariat to wage its class struggle and even to exercise its dictatorship within the frame of democratic institutions, but this was a rule not without exceptions; and he evidently regarded events in Russia as an exception. It was probably this relationship that Trotsky had in mind when he spoke disparagingly of political pedants who could not see the revolutionary logic of the relations of classes and who

... preach for the proletariat banal truths concerning the advantage of democracy for waging class war. [49]

"Democratic" and "democracy" thus seem to have been used to describe political institutions different from and, from a practical point of view, incompatible with those of the proletarian dictatorship in Russia. Compared with the terminology in Terrorismus und Kommunismus, his derogatory use of these terms is somewhat less intense in this work than in his polemics against Kautsky. A relationship of incompatibility between the dictatorship of the proletariat and what he designated as "democracy" is not necessarily implied, but contemporary rule in Russia was clearly not considered to be a democracy in his sense of the term.

Trotsky's use of "democratic" to characterize phenomena opposed to those of a proletarian and revolutionary kind also occurs in somewhat later writings. In his famous work on the lessons of the October Revolution, Trotsky asserted that after the April conference in 1917 there were two mutually hostile points of view within the Bolshevik party, only one of which was consistently revolutionary, or truly Bolshevik.

Theoretisch und politisch ergaben sich zwei feindliche Anschauungen: die demokratische, welche von sozialistischen Schlagworten bemäntelt wurde und die sozial-revolutionäre oder die eigentlich bolschewistische, die Lenin'sche. [50]

A similar application of "democratic", or an application in which the term was used to characterize phenomena contrary to the socialist revolutionary trend in Bolshevism, occurs in several places in this work. [51] There is no tendency here to regard rule in Soviet Russia as a kind of democracy, and none to present to it as a kind of democracy more profound than ordinary parliamentarism.

Little can be said about the terminology in Trotsky's pre-revolutionary writings for lack of available material. From an ideological point of view, attention should be drawn to Trotsky's earlier rejection of Lenin's theory of the Party, or its small but well-disciplined group of professional politicians, as the vanguard and the guardian of the whole working class. In agreement with Plekhanov and Rosa Luxemburg, Trotsky described Lenin's theory in 1904 as a dictatorship over the proletariat, and he predicted a situation in which

> ... the party is replaced by the organization of the party, the organization by the central committee, and finally the central committee by the dictator. [52]

But the use of "democracy" was not linked with these important statements, and further discussion has no place here.

As background to the different trends in Bolshevik terminology from 1917 onwards, the diverging methods of analyzing and predicting future revolutionary movements are of much greater importance than this disagreement concerning the status and organization of the Party. Although the Mensheviks as well as the Bolsheviks held that the future revolution in Russia would be of a bourgeois kind, the Mensheviks inferred that the revolution against czarism must therefore be led by the middle class. On the other hand, Lenin emphasized that the proletariat, as the only revolutionary class, should play the leading role in the struggle against czarism. Trotsky agreed with Lenin on this last point. He differed, however, from Lenin and the Bolsheviks on the nature of the government to be set up by the revolutionary forces. Lenin frequently referred to this revolutionary government as the democratic dictatorship of the proletariat and peasantry and used "democratic" to mark this kind of dictatorship as different from a socialistic or anti-capitalistic one; Trotsky emphasized on several occasions that it was utopianism of the worst kind to expect the armed proletariat, once in power, to make way for the bourgeoisie or to refrain from turning the democratic revolution into a socialistic one. This theory, which contains the essence of Trotsky's famous doctrine on the Permanent Revolution, was elaborated soon after 1905, [53] and can be regarded as his personal contribution to Marxist revolutionary strategy. Events in 1917 were to confirm this prognosis of Trotsky. According to Trotsky, the Bolsheviks under the leadership of Lenin undertook an ideological readjustment (not without an internal struggle) during the spring of 1917.

These differing ideological outlooks seem to have influenced Trotsky's and Lenin's use of "democracy" and related terms during and after the Revolution. Although questions of this kind are apt to be hypothetical, it seems that Trotsky's derogatory use of "democracy" was to a certain extent caused by his opinion that future revolutionary rule in Russia would not have a democratic character as he understood it. Thus it was no new thing for Trotsky to declare that Soviet rule was definitely not a democracy. For similar reasons Lenin's varied application of the term may have been

affected by the fact that he did not abandon the theory of the democratic
dictatorship of the proletariat and peasantry before the spring of 1917.
Because of this, Lenin had to confront and to lead the revolutionary uprising
from a theoretical platform that represented a radically new orientation for
him, [54] a factor that could easily lead to some degree of terminological
instability.

3. Radek, Bukharin, and Kuusinen

In the political terminology of an other leading Bolshevik, Radek, like
Trotsky, seems to have regarded the proletarian dictatorship very different
from, if not opposed to, what he designated as "democracy". His Prole-
tarische Diktatur und Terrorismus was also directed against Kautsky's
Terrorismus und Kommunismus. Speaking of the political development in
Germany during 1919, Radek stated:

> In der Zeit vom Januar bis März verflog der Glaube der Arbeiter an die
> Wunderkraft der Demokratie und der Nationalversammlung, stürmisch
> sprachen sie sich für die Diktatur, für die Räteherrschaft aus. [55]

Democracy and a kind of parliamentarian assembly were here contrasted to
a proletarian dictatorship; and in the same pamphlet Radek declared that
democratic forms of government would necessarily be destroyed in the
revolutionary struggles that take place before the conquest of political power
by the proletariat. [56] The latter statement can be taken to reveal that the
class rule of the proletariat was never to be framed in what he designated
as "democratic forms". This statement may have been at least partly caused
by his belief that it was doubtful whether the class-conscious proletariat
would be backed by a majority of the population at any time before it seized
political power. Radek's main argument in favour of this point of view was
that the workers, under the reign of capitalism, were not only influenced by
the bourgeois press and the bourgeois schools but also by their own impression of the power of the bourgeoisie. [57] According to this hypothesis, Radek
rejected democracy and democratic forms of rule because of his distrust of
the political capacity of the majority in the proletarian class-struggle. This
makes for a close association, if not identification, between democracy and
majority rule.

A related but somewhat different way of using "democracy" and "democratic" is at hand in a pamphlet with a title inspired by Engels, Die Entwicklung des Sozialismus von der Wissenschaft zur Tat. In a chapter headed
"Demokratie oder die Herrschaft der Arbeiterklasse", a formulation which
can be taken to indicate that he held democracy and rule by the working
class to be mutually different phenomena in political life, Radek declared:

> Demokratie ist, konkret genommen, die Herrschaft des Kapitals, die so
> stark und so wohl in dem Bewusstsein der Volksmassen verankert ist,
> dass sie sich den Luxus bewilligen kann, ihnen die Freiheit von Staats-
> angehörigkeiten zu sprechen zu erlauben. [58]

Here he regarded rule by capital as well as freedom to speak about political
matters not only as consequences of a democratic form of rule but even as
conceptual characteristics of the concept 'democracy' as he presented it
here. This implies that any democracy, at least in Radek's view, must

necessarily be rule by capital, but not vice versa. When Radek declared
democracy to be a rule by capital, he probably had in mind his earlier statement that it was doubtful whether the class-conscious proletariat would be
supported by a majority of the population at any time before its conquest of
power. This again indicates an association of majority rule and democracy.
However, the significations of "democracy" in these two writings are not
necessarily identical. In the first pamphlet, rule by capital would probably
be held an inevitable consequence of democracy but would not be attributed
conceptually to 'democracy'. In these two pamphlets is seen the rather
interesting process of a non-conceptual characteristic becoming a conceptual
one.

In addition attention should be drawn to Radek's emphasis of "sprechen".
This may be taken to indicate that he used the term with a narrow signification, or that he wanted to stress that in a democracy people were allowed
to talk about political matters but not to agitate against the existing state
of affairs.

His use of "democracy" with a signification that necessarily included
rule by capital as a property, makes it certain that Radek would not have
used this, or some closely related term, to denote proletarian rule in Russia.
And indeed, a few pages later, he stated:

Die Räterregierung ist keine demokratische Regierungsform. [59]

Apparently there are no occurrences in Radek's writings to contradict
the terminological tendency noted in these quotations, and Lenin's view that
the dictatorship of the proletariat represented a higher form of democracy
does not seem to have moulded Radek's political language at all. Possibly
without exception Radek used "democracy" in a derogatory way and with
significations which excluded the possibility that a revolutionary proletarian
dictatorship might be a denotatum of the term.

There is little to be added here concerning the use of "democracy" and
related terms by other Russian Bolsheviks. According to the French version
of a pamphlet concerning the Communist programme, Bukharin stated:

Comme consequence inévitable du fait que nous considérons la dictature
comme indispensable, s'explique notre lutte contre la forme désuète de
la République parlamentaire bourgeoisie (que l'on appelle parfois "démocratique"). [60]

Rule by the soviets was further contrasted with this outdated rule. Here is
a meta-occurrence of "democratic", or a reference to what Bukharin probably held to be a current application of the term. That he did not make the
smallest objection to this terminology can be taken to indicate that he considered it correct and that he probably included himself among those who
sometimes used "democratic" to characterize the kind of outdated republic
that was incompatible with any kind of dictatorship and which was, therefore,
the object of Bolshevik attacks.

On the other hand, Bukharin and Preobazhensky in their ABC of Communism held that the Soviet rule realized a new and complete kind of democracy, proletarian democracy. The essence of this proletarian democracy
consisted of crushing the power of the bourgeoisie and placing the means of
production in the hands of the workers. [61] To the authors, revolutionary
rule by the proletariat, or proletarian democracy, was probably a species
of a genus 'democracy'. This bears similarity to a trend in Lenin's terminology, and probably excludes the possibility that unqualified "democratic"

might be used to characterize a kind of republic adverse to the rule of proletariat.

Apart from these statements, little of interest is to be found in Bukharin's writings. This is also true of the writings of Zinoviev and Kamenev. Possibly the only important occurrences are to be found in Otto Kuusinen's political self-criticism after the Communist defeat in Finland. In a chapter headed "Der Wahn demokratischer Illusionen," Kuusinen stated that during the Revolution winter of 1918, the Finnish socialists had not contemplated abandoning the universal system of popular representation. "Im Gegenteil", Kuusinen declared,

> ...sie [die finnische Sozialdemokratie] strebte gerade nach einem möglichst noch allgemeineren Volksvertretungssystem, nach einer möglichst demokratischen Regierungsform. [62]

In this statement "democratic form of government" is seemingly used synonymously with "universal system of popular representation". With regard to Kuusinen's ideological retrospect, he considered the political attitude of the socialists in Finland to have been a very dangerous illusion and one of the main causes of the proletarian defeat.

According to Kuusinen, the Finnish socialists had been of the opinion that democracy was the proper road to socialism, and he shortly declared "Weg des Demokratismus" to be synonymous with "Weg des friedlichen Klassenkampfs". [63] Contrary to the earlier socialist view, Kuusinen asserted that violent struggle was indispensable and that the dictatorship of the proletariat was an historical necessity in the period between capitalism and socialism. He further recalled that when the Finnish bourgeoisie commanded the White Guards to crush the organizations of workers in January 1918, the proletarian slogan was: "Wache auf! Die Demokratie ist in Todesgefahr"; [64] and that it was a great political mistake that the revolutionary workers, when taking up arms against the White Guards, had made use of a democratic and not a proletarian slogan. According to Kuusinen, by taking up arms the Finnish proletariat had thrown away any democraticism, just as the Finnish bourgeoisie had. As he used it, "democraticism" was evidently not only incompatible with violent means in general but also with violent means when used as defence in a civil war. He thus emphasized that if the Finnish proletariat had submitted to the bourgeoisie and had quietly let themselves be shot down or put in prison,

> ...in diesem Falle wäre das Programm der demokratischen Schutz- und Rechtsforderungen am Platze gewesen. [65]

These sentences indicate a use of "democraticism" and "democratic" in which a complete pacifism was evidently implicit.

Kuusinen admitted that revolutionaries had rather frequently made use of slogans which did not express the historical aims of the struggle. As an example, he mentioned the adherents of Hus in Bohemia, who were engaged in a true class war; they had nevertheless regarded questions concerning the Lord's Supper as the objects in their struggle. Of the slogan of the Finnish socialists he stated:

> Das demokratische Programm der finnischen Sozialdemokratie stellte in der finnischen Revolution von Winter 1917-1918 eben ein solches "Abenmahls"-Programm dar. [66]

This he declared to have been an important ideological drawback.

These statements reveal rather clearly that in this pamphlet Kuusinen used "democracy", "democratic", and "democraticism" in a way which, from the proletarian and revolutionary points of view, can certainly be said to have been derogatory. And there seems to be no exception to this rule in the language of this pamphlet. On this point there is a high degree of similarity between Kuusinen's terminology and that of Radek, and their use of "democracy" was much closer to Trotsky's application than to Lenin's. However, there is some difference between Kuusinen and Radek, since the former would hardly have stated that, from a concrete point of view, democracy was rule by capital. On the contrary, Kuusinen seems, at least generally, to have regarded democracy as a kind of utopian dream which would be realized neither by the capitalists nor by the socialists.

The application of "democracy" by the leading Bolsheviks illustrate different trends. On the one hand, it is easy to find occurrences, especially in Lenin's writings, according to which Soviet rule was the highest form of democracy; on the other hand, it is even easier to find occurrences in all the Bolshevik ideologists discussed in this chapter according to which any socialist or proletarian rule never could be a democracy.

The difference between the frequent, but by no means exclusively, honorific use of "democracy" by Lenin and the almost exclusively derogatory application by Trotsky and Radek cannot be said to indicate any ideological differences during the time of the Revolution. Trotsky and Radek, as well as Kuusinen, would have used "democracy" in an honorific way if they had employed the term with a signification identical to Lenin's. It is also quite clear that Lenin would without reservation have rejected "democracy" if he had attributed to this term significations identical with those found in the terminology of Trotsky and Radek.

Therefore a terminological difference within the inner circle of leading Bolsheviks cannot be regarded as dependent upon any differences in their political outlook. It must be mentioned that this ideological unanimity can only be dated as far back as the spring 1917; before then there were, for example, rather important differences between Lenin and Trotsky in their attitudes towards the possibility of a proletarian socialist revolution in Russia. But this does not affect what has been said about terminological differences and ideological unanimity during the Revolution. On the whole it looks as if the leading Bolsheviks, who tried to co-ordinate their politics and their political argumentation, gave very little, if any, attention to the question of co-ordinating their use of "democracy".

Turning to the use of "democracy" by the Bolshevik press, significant information is available in Symbols of Democracy by Ithiel de Sola Pool. Here one is told that while "democracy" in the editorials of Izvestia was used occasionally up to 1935, its frequency increased immediately after that year. "Democracy" was used in 12 per cent of the editorials, never favourably, during the two first years after the Revolution. 86 per cent of these instances were antagonistic and the rest neutral. From 1920 tc 1924 the term was used in 8 per cent of the editorials, and of these 63 per cent were antagonistic and the rest neutral. [67] Thus Lenin's habit of using "democracy" in an honorific way, for example, his frequent assertion that Soviet rule represented "a new and higher kind of democracy", did not influence Izvestia's editorials at all. On this point, Izvestia was more in agreement with Trotsky, Radek, and Kuusinen. How far Izvestia's editorials can be considered as representative of the vernacular in contemporary Russia cannot be answered here; but Pool's diligent inquiry into Izvestia's editorials nevertheless supports the view that chiefly a negative application of "democracy" was used by leading Bolsheviks during and shortly after the Revolution. There is a significant difference here between the Russian revolutionaries and Robespierre and his adherents; and there is also an important difference between the Bolsheviks and Marx and Engels up to 1849.

The absence of an honorific use of "democracy" in Izvestia's editorials is also remarkable when compared with the honorific and intense application during the years 1935-1938, when the Soviet Union was "the only true democracy in the world". According to Pool, "democracy" appeared in one-third of Izvestia's editorials during the People's Front period, more than twice as much as in any other country. This canonization of "democracy" did not become a stable part of Soviet Russian terminology, however. Use of "democracy" fell by half during the Stalin-Hitler pact, but nevertheless the term appeared more frequently in Izvestia than in any other important Western paper except Le Temps. With participation in the war, however, "democracy" almost disappeared; only 3 per cent of the editorials used it from 1941 to 1944.

The war that had originally been prepared for as a war of DEMOCRACY against fascism had now become the FATHERLAND WAR. [69]

In contrast to the period prior to 1935, the years 1941 to 1944 were characterized by absence or near absence of "democracy". Thus there is a varied picture of the use of "democracy" in Soviet Russian terminology in general, although later application was much more positive than among leading Bolsheviks during and shortly after the Revolution.

In Trotsky a later use of "democracy" occurs in his famous work La révolution trahie ("The Revolution Betrayed"), 1936; here he used "Soviet democracy" and unqualified "democracy" to signify what would replace Stalin's totalitarian bureaucracy. [69] It is evident that Trotsky used "democracy" appreciatively here. On this point there is a significant difference between the Trotsky of 1936 and the Trotsky of the victorious Red Revolution who pronounced "democracy" with almost unlimited contempt. This honorific application was not a general characteristic of Trotsky's terminology during his exile, however. In 1929, for example, he stated:

Democracy has lost all meaning.... Democracy stands and falls with capitalism.

At the end of 1932, in an open letter to Vandervelde, Trotsky declared with pride that in the October Revolution "we smashed democracy in order to finish with capitalism." [70]

CHAPTER XVII

CENTRAL CRITICS OF BOLSHEVISM

A general characteristic of opponents of the Bolshevik Revolution is their
honorific and central use of "democracy". The Bolsheviks, on the other
hand, are accused of having founded a kind of rule definitely not subsumable
under what their opponents designated as "democracy". This is a fairly
common feature of all later criticism of the Soviet Union, and was probably
encouraged by several important negative trends among the Bolsheviks
themselves. Unlike their successors none of the early critics seems to
have referred to the problem that honorific use of "democracy" was also to
be found among the Bolsheviks, notably Lenin. There is thus no tendency
to criticize any misuse of "democracy", a common feature of later ideological debates. Generally, an honorific and central use of "democracy" in this
context does not imply that every ideologist under discussion in this chapter
used "democracy" as a key term in criticizing the revolutionary rule in
Soviet Russia; on this point Bertrand Russell is a clear exception. Needless to say, although several persons use the same term, they do not use
identical concepts. There are, for example, important differences among
the concepts of 'democracy' made use of by Kautsky, Kelsen, and Rosa
Luxemburg, although all of them deplored the absence of democracy in
Soviet Russia.

1. Kautsky

Among the principle antagonists of the Bolshevik Revolution, Kautsky occupies a central position, as is revealed by the intense polemics by Lenin
and Trotsky against two of his works. In the first of these, <u>Die Diktatur
des Proletariats,</u> Kautsky declared that the democratic and the dictatorial
trends in socialism were essentially different in political method. He went
on to state that his decision in favour of democracy had already been made
by the mere fact of entering upon a discussion of this topic. Dictatorship
was marked by the violent suppression of any dissentient opinion and was
thus incompatible with free discussion.

> So stehen sich die beiden Methoden der Demokratie und der Diktatur
> schon unversöhnlich gegenüber, ehe die Diskussion begonnen hat. Die
> eine vordert, die andere verbietet sie. [1]

According to this statement, free discussion was a property necessary for
democracy, and it was in relation to free discussion that Kautsky here
saw the essential and irreconcilable difference between dictatorship and
democracy.
A similar use of "democracy" is found later in this work:

Die Demokratie bedeutet Herrschaft der Majorität. Sie bedeutet aber nicht minder Schutz der Minderheit. [2]

In accordance with the latter condition, but possibly with the former also, Kautsky did not consider the rule of the Bolsheviks to be a democracy. He probably referred to the vernacular in his attempt to refuse Lenin the right to consider the rule of the soviets to represent a kind of democracy. After saying:

Unter der Demokratie versteht man bisher die Gleichheit der politischen Rechte aller Staatsbürger ... ,

Kautsky went on to refer to the alleged absence of such rights for certain groups in contemporary Russia and to political privileges for other groups. He concluded:

Aber das bezeichnet man nicht als Demokratie. [3]

No accusation of Lenin's misusing "democracy" was put forth by Kautsky, however.

When compared with his pre-war terminology, it can be seen that some difference exists with regard to the signification he attributed to "democracy". Before as well as after the Russian Revolution, Kautsky apparently regarded the rule of the majority as a necessary condition for a democracy. But while at this time he most certainly held the protection of minorities to be a conditio sine qua non for a democracy, in his polemics against Bernstein in 1899 he was much more reserved on this point. For example, Kautsky did not consider the tyrannical and sanguinary suppression of certain minorities, such as the shooting of strikers and lynching of negroes, to be incompatible with a democracy in 1899, [4] whereas in 1918 such things were probably conceptually debarred from his concept 'democracy'. It is difficult to say exactly why Kautsky used "democracy" in his polemics against Lenin with a signification different from the one in his polemics against Bernstein twenty years earlier. The change was presumably caused by a desire to place a popular catchword in a central position in his criticism of Bolshevism, which would have been difficult had he retained the earlier signification. This difference was probably also a consequence of Kautsky's turning in a revisionistic direction; having adopted the majority of Bernstein's ideological views, he had also acquired his way of using "democracy".

A similar terminology is again to be found in Terrorismus und Kommunismus, a work which is an even more violent attack upon the politics and ideology of the Bolsheviks, and which, as we have seen, gave rise to the polemics of Trotsky and Radek. In this work there seem to be hardly any occurrences of "democracy" where the signification differs from his post-revolutionary use of the term. [5] Kautsky here held coercion of the minority by the majority to be compatible with democracy, for example, in relation to a capitalist minority and a proletarian majority, [6] but this probably does not contradict what he said elsewhere about democracy and the protection of minorities. Coercion thus seems to imply that the minority was to submit to the political will of the majority but that this did not include suppression or abolition of the right to free discussion as long as the minority behaved in a non-violent manner. It was only in cases where minorities really intended to take up arms against the majority that Kautsky held violent suppression to be compatible with democracy.

2. Rosa Luxemburg

Like Kautsky, Rosa Luxemburg used "democracy" as a central term in her criticism of Bolshevism. But unlike the right-wing criticism of Kautsky's writings, Luxemburg can probably be said to represent the first revolutionary socialist critic of the political system in the Soviet Union. In September 1918, while in jail in Breslau for antimilitaristic propaganda, Luxemburg wrote her last manuscript of importance, which was published in 1922 by Paul Levi after his exclusion from the Comintern. [7] In this work, Die russische Revolution, Luxemburg attacked right-wing socialists such as Kautsky as well as the Bolsheviks. She herself was an ardent adherent of what she held to be the dictatorship of the proletariat and one of her main arguments was that Lenin and Trotsky, like Kautsky, were falsely contrasting dictatorship with democracy.

> Der Grundfehler der Lenin-Trotzkischen Theorie ist eben der, dass sie die Diktatur, genau wie Kautsky, der Demokratie entgegenstellen. "Diktatur oder Demokratie" heisst die Fragestellung sowohl bei den Bolschewiki, wie bei Kautsky. [8]

This statement indicates that she considered that Kautsky, on the one hand, as well as Lenin and Trotsky, on the other, regarded what they designated as "dictatorship" and "democracy" to be contrary phenomena in political life, and that she, for her part, was of the opinion that this political view and terminology were misguided. Kautsky and usually Trotsky certainly held what they designated as "democracy" to be contrary to dictatorship, but Lenin's terminology is much too heterogeneous on this point to be couched in a single formula.

Criticizing the Bolsheviks' contrast of democracy with dictatorship, Luxemburg, as mentioned, was an ardent adherent of the dictatorship of the proletariat. She was, however, of the opinion that the rule of the Bolsheviks in Russia could not be regarded as a dictatorship of that kind. Her main arguments on this point were that liberty for one party only was not liberty; in her opinion liberty was always and exclusively liberty for those who think differently. [9] Where Bolshevik Russia was concerned, she maintained that without general elections, an absolute freedom of the press, and the right of public meetings, all political life would wither away and the bureaucracy would become the only vital element in public life. She held this to be an inevitable social law and believed that with regard to future political life in Russia, a dozen political leaders would decide everything and only a selection of the working class would sometimes be called together to hear and to applaud the speeches of their leaders and unanimously to agree upon drafted resolutions. Such a rule was not a dictatorship of the proletariat but a dictatorship of politicians in the name of the proletariat, or a dictatorship of a bourgeois or a Jacobin kind. [10] Concerning what she herself regarded as the dictatorship of the proletariat, she initially said:

Es ist die historische Aufgabe des Proletariats, wenn es zur Macht

gelangt, anstelle der bürgerlichen Demokratie sozialistische Demokratie
zu schaffen, nicht jegliche Demokratie abzuschaffen.

With regard to socialist democracy, she held:

> Sie ist nichts anderes als Diktatur des Proletariats. ... Jawohl: Diktatur!
> Aber diese Diktatur besteht in der <u>Art der Verwendung der Demokratie</u>,
> nicht in ihrer Abschaffung, [11]

and she concluded by asserting that this dictatorship must be the active
work of the class and not a dictatorship of a few politicians in the name of
the class.

Thus Luxemburg most certainly held 'socialist democracy' to be identical with 'dictatorship of the proletariat' and "socialist democracy" to be
synonymous with "dictatorship of the proletariat". She here operated with
two concepts, 'socialist democracy' and 'bourgeois democracy', and she
probably held these concepts to be species of a broader concept 'democracy'.
What she regarded as common properties of these two concepts is not
directly clear, but presumably in accusing the Bolsheviks of having abolished
any democracy ("jegliche Demokratie"), she had in mind the properties
which were regarded as common to these two species; or more concretely,
that general elections, a free press, and the right to hold public meetings
were necessary conditions for a political system to be subsumable under the
genus 'democracy' with unqualified "democracy" as the conceptual designation. These factors probably explain why Luxemburg could not accept any
contradiction between democracy and what <u>she</u> held to be dictatorship of the
proletariat. But this relationship is restricted to the proletarian species of
the broader concept 'dictatorship' and does not include dictatorship in
general, as it is certain that she held the Jacobin species of the same concept to be neither compatible with nor subsumable under 'democracy'.

Broadly, Luxemburg's view that the rule of the proletariat was necessarily the rule of the whole class and not the rule of a single party only is
an essential characteristic in her political thought. Earlier she had frequently criticized the centralized models of political organization of moderate socialists like Bernstein and the Fabians. Like Cole, she also stated
that a very close contact between electors and representatives was a necessary characteristic of a democratic party. [12] As early as 1904, Luxemburg
had criticized in <u>Neue Zeit</u> Lenin's organization of Russian socialists into
a <u>cadre party</u>, [13] and especially his view of the small, well-disciplined
party of professional politicians as the guardian of the proletarian class.
But she probably did not make any special use of "democracy" or related
terms in relation to this topic at that time.

To return to the terminology in the pamphlet under discussion, unqualified "democracy" was not only used to designate this broader concept.
In discussing the reformist ideology of Kautsky, she declared it to be
treason for any socialist to renounce a socialist upheaval after the grabbing
of power by drawing attention to the immaturity of the country, "... und sich
nur der Demokratie widmen". [14] In this statement, unqualified "democracy"
is probably used to signify something different from socialism or to designate a concept of which dictatorship of the proletariat, or socialist democracy, was not an example. The signification attributed to the term in this
occurrence may therefore be said to gainsay her general statement to the
effect that there was no contradiction between democracy and the dictatorship of the proletariat.

In spite of her severe criticism of the Bolsheviks, Luxemburg admired Lenin and Trotsky for having given the proletariat in all countries an out-standing example of a revolutionary and anti-imperialist policy. They had in any case been the first to do so. She also admitted that the difficulties had been enormous, especially because of the war and the opportunistic policy of the majority of the German socialists in relation to German military imperialism. As regards this situation, she stated:

> Es hiesse, von Lenin und Genossen Übermenschliches verlangen, wollte man ihnen auch noch zumuten, unter solchen Umständen die schönste Demokratie, die vorbildlichste Diktatur des Proletariats und eine blühende sozialistische Wirtschaft hervorzuzaubern. [15]

It is difficult to find the signification of "most beautiful democracy" as used in this statement. It was presumably something which, for the moment at least, did not exist in Russia; and there is also some degree of association between the connotation of that expression and that of "the finest prototype of dictatorship of the proletariat", even if there is no indication of synonymity between these two expressions.

A use of "democracy" which differs from her predominant application of the term in this pamphlet, and differs widely from its signification as a non-socialist kind of rule, is evident in what was probably her last use of the term. On 14 December 1918, in the paper Die rote Fahne, Luxemburg emphasized that the proletarians must prepare for a civil war in order to win political power. She went on to say:

> Eine solche Ausrüstung der kompakten arbeitenden Volksmasse mit der ganzen politischen Macht für die Aufgabe der Revolution, das ist die Diktatur des Proletariats und deshalb die wahre Demokratie.

In addition she maintained that it was not where proletarians and capitalists were debating in a parliamentarian way, but,

> ... wo die millionenköpfige Proletariermasse die ganze Staatsgewalt mit ihrer schwieligen Faust ergreift, um sie, wie der Gott Thor seinen Hammer, den herrschenden Klasse aufs Haupt zu schmettern, dort allein ist die Demokratie, die kein Volksbetrug ist. [16]

These statements indicate that at that time Luxemburg intended to restrict the signification of "true democracy" and even of unqualified "democracy" to cover exclusively a revolutionary assumption of political power by the armed proletariat. This also implies that, in contrast to different statements made in Die russische Revolution, she then would not have considered any kind of bourgeois rule as subsumable under the genus 'democracy' with "democracy" as a conceptual designation, and that she probably would also have considered all use of "democracy" with a signification different from that of revolutionary rule of the armed proletariat to be a misuse of the term.

Thus during autumn 1918 Luxemburg operated with three different concepts 'democracy'. The first was a rather broad concept which included 'bourgeois democracy' as well as 'socialist democracy', and the latter was identical with what she held to be dictatorship of the proletariat. The function of this concept was primarily to show that a dictatorship of the working class must be drawn up in a democratic way if it were not to degenerate into a dictatorship of a single party only, and this concept therefore occupies a central position in her criticism of the Bolsheviks. A second concept can be observed in her criticism of Kautsky, where absence of socialist undertakings was most probably among the conceptual characteristics and identical with what she designated elsewhere as "bourgeois democracy". Finally, there is a third concept which was evidently limited to the violent seizure of power by the armed proletariat. In all three cases "democracy" was used as conceptual designation, which implies that the term was used with three different significations.

When comparing these applications with her terminology prior to 1914, I find no example in Luxemburg's earlier use of "democracy" to directly connote a revolutionary rule of the armed proletariat. This use can therefore be regarded as a new element in her terminology. On the other hand, some degree of continuity can clearly be seen between her view that a close contact between electors and representatives was a necessary characteristic of a democratic party and her predominant application as presented in this section. I have not observed a differentiated way of operating with species such as 'bourgeois democracy' and 'proletarian democracy' in earlier writings, however.

3. Max Adler

Max Adler, the ideological leader of that socialist trend generally known as Austro-Marxism, occupies a political position somewhat similar to Rosa Luxemburg. He, too, turned against the reformist socialism of Kautsky as well as the politics of the Bolsheviks, and he, too, was in favour of what he held to be the dictatorship of the proletariat but denied that such a dictatorship existed in contemporary Russia.

Adler used "democracy" and related terms in a different way from Luxemburg, however. Not very much is directly said concerning the relationship between democracy and Soviet Russia. In his main work, Die Staatsauffassung des Marxismus, 1922, Adler stated:

> Demokratie bedeutet wörtlich und dem Sinne nach Volksherrschaft, Selbstbestimmung des Volkes. Eine solche ist nur in den Klassengesellschaft auch bei noch so "demokratischer" Verfassung nicht möglich, weil im kapitalistischen Staate die Grundvoraussetzung einer Volksherrschaft fehlt, nämlich das einheitliche Volk. [17]

Popular unity thus seems to have been held as an absolutely necessary condition of what Adler held as democracy; and in using "democratic" within quotation marks, Adler perhaps wished to indicate ironically a terminological application which he himself did not accept. He further declared popular unity to be an impossibility in all societies in which there were different classes with antagonistic interests. This implies that democracy, according to Adler, was to be found exclusively in classless societies; and since he could not have indicated any classless society in the past or present, he must have regarded "democracy" as a future form of human society.

With their emphasis on popular unity, these statements remind us of the political philosophy of Rousseau with its theory of the volonté générale. Adler quotes a passage from one of his earlier pamphlets, Demokratie und Rätesystem, in which he stated that the vital principle of democracy was not the will of the majority but the common will, or the general will, as Rousseau put it. This view that an absolute collective solidarity was the main principle of democracy can probably explain why Adler, when quoting statements by Kautsky and especially by Kelsen, could not agree with their opinion that protection of minorities was essential to democracy. According to him, the protection of minorities was an element of liberal individualism, not of democracy. He went on to say that to consider the protection of minorities as essential to democracy was a fairly common example of the confusion of democracy with liberalism, phenomena between which, Adler believed, there existed profound differences of principle.

> Die Freiheit, und zwar die individuelle, ist der Leitstern des Liberalismus, die Gleichheit dagegen jener der Demokratie. [19]

His view of liberty, or at least of individual liberty, as being part of something which was essentially different from "democracy" can perhaps be taken to indicate that "democracy" for Adler signified a totalitarian form of rule in which every dissentient opinion was to be suppressed. Such a view can scarcely be attributed to Adler, even if his statements seem to point in that direction and even if the consequences of such a political view may be described as totalitarian. Adler's belief, however, in the harmony of the interests of all people in the future classless collectivity was so unreserved that he thought ideological minorities would disappear completely. He probably regarded the protection of minorities and individual freedom as unnecessary factors in what he designated as "democracy".

In addition to the signification which Adler attributed to "democracy" in these statements, however, as regards the vernacular, he proposed a somewhat more qualified kind of terminology. He first declared that the term "democracy" was used ambiguously; and since a clearer terminology was needed, he made the following propositions:

> Da der Begriff der Demokratie sich erst in einer klassenlosen Gesellschaft realisiert, so wollen wir diese volle Demokratie, die soziale Demokratie nennen, während wir alle anderen Formen, die sonst auch als Demokratie bezeichnet werden, die politische Demokratie nennen. [20]

By adopting the term "social democracy" to signify what he had labelled earlier as unqualified "democracy" and by adopting "political democracy" to signify something to which he had refused the label "democracy", Adler made some concessions to what he held to be the vernacular. These concessions were not far-reaching. He believed that what he termed the "concept democracy" would be realized in a classless society only. A similarity to his earlier habit of restricting "democracy" to signify something which could be realized only in a classless society is probably still more marked when he paradoxically said:

> Wo von Demokratie innerhalb einer Klassengesellschaft die Rede ist, damit nur die politische Demokratie gemeint ist, das heisst die Demokratie, die eigentlich keine Demokratie ist und daher überwunden werden muss, wenn man Demokratie will. [21]

In addition, Adler held different kinds of class rule, such as bourgeois parliamentarism and dictatorship of the proletariat, to be species of a broader concept, with "political democracy" as the conceptual designation. These points were not elaborated upon in a detailed way. Adler, like Rosa Luxemburg, did not consider contemporary rule in Russia to be a dictatorship of the proletariat. To him, the rule of the Bolsheviks was merely the dictatorship of a party, not of a class, and thus not in conformity with Marx-

ist philosophy.[22] Such a view most probably implies that he did not hold
Bolshevik rule to be subsumable under what he designated "political democracy", and definitely not under what he designated "social democracy",
"complete democracy", or unqualified "democracy". Compared with
Kautsky, Kelsen, and Luxemburg, Adler has little to say about the relationship between Soviet Russia and what he labelled "democracy" and qualified
occurrences of that term.

4. Kelsen

In his small, but well-known treatise, <u>Vom Wesen und Wert der Demo-
kratie</u>, 1920, Hans Kelsen said that an open confession in favour of autocracy was not to be found during the last decades among important politicians
or among famous man of letters. He went on to say:

> <u>Demokratie</u> ist das die Geister im 19. und 20. Jahrhundert fast allgemein
> beherrschende Schlagwort.[23]

If Kelsen intended to mean that the term "democracy" had been almost
universally used in an honorific way during the nineteenth as well as during
the twentieth century, his statement is an exaggeration. On the contrary,
in both centuries there have been many important ideologists who, in different ways, could not accept "democracy" as a positive slogan. Nor can I
accept absence or near absence of champions of autocracy to imply a positive use of "democracy". Such champions have been somewhat rare during
these decades, but this fact has by no means furnished a sufficient condition
for using "democracy" in an honorific way. The regular appearance of the
term of "democracy" was probably on the increase during the years which
preceded the writing of Kelsen's pamphlet, but this does not imply an almost
universal honorific application.

Kelsen continued by asserting that, therefore, the term, like all slogans,
had lost its fixed signification, and that it was used ambiguously. He added,
however, that faced with the political theory of Bolshevism, democracy had
once more become a problem, as in earlier times when it had been confronted by monarchical autocracy.[24] The latter factor can possibly be taken
to indicate that Kelsen meant that "democracy" would acquire a less ambiguous connotation because of the new ideological debates in relation to Bolshevism or, more concretely, that this term would become less ambiguous
through the existence of a new political system which could not be reckoned
among the denotata of the term.

Kelsen initially considered the synthesis of liberty and equality to be the
characteristics of democracy.[25] Later he declared the system of representation to be a falsification of the democratic idea, and he also said pure
democracy was the direct rule where sovereignty of the people was not
realized through a parliament.[26] This statement does not seem to imply
that Kelsen generally held the system of representation to be incompatible
with what he designated as "democracy", as one might have expected. But
it is clear that he held direct rule to be more purely democratic than representative rule and a fairly permanent contact between voters and representatives to be essential for a democracy. Kelsen referred to parts of the Soviet
system, especially short terms of office, the possibility for the people to
recall their representatives at any time, and a permanent contact between

people and representatives, as belonging to what he designated as "the most true democracy" ("echteste Demokratie").[27]

Kelsen did not, however, include the current form of government in Soviet Russia among those which he regarded as democracies; this plainly implies that he did not hold the above-mentioned phenomena to be sufficient for a form of government to deserve the label "democracy". Referring to the groups of people deprived of political rights, Kelsen held this to be suppression of anything differing from the socialist dogma. He stated that the dictatorship of the proletariat had thereby become the dictatorship of a single political belief founded upon the alleged validity of a certain political ideal.[28] Of this dictatorship Kelsen said:

> Gerade gegenüber solcher Diktatur enthüllt die Demokratie ihr tiefstes Wesen, zeight sie ihren höchsten Wert. Weil sie [die Demokratie] den politischen Willens jedermanns gleich einschätzt, muss sie auch jeden politischen Glauben, jede politische Meinung, deren Ausdruch ja nur der politische Wille ist, gleichermachen achten.[29]

According to Kelsen, this implied the negation of belief in any absolute values. Declaring relativism to be an ideology which was a necessary condition for democratic thought, he concluded:

> Die für die Demokratie so charakteristische Herrschaft der Majorität unterscheidet sich von jeder anderen Herrschaft dadurch, dass sie eine Opposition -- die Minorität -- ihrem innersten Wesen nach nicht nur begrifflich voraussetzt, sondern auch politisch anerkennt und in den Grund- und Freiheitsrechten, im Prinzipe der Proportionalität schützt.[30]

These statements indicate a distinct emphasis on freedom of opinion and the protection of minorities as indispensable properties in the signification of "democracy" according to Kelsen's terminology. On this point, his terminology is very similar to the later trend in Kautsky's use of "democracy". And this definition of democracy can probably be regarded as the main, or perhaps even the exclusive, reason that neither of them could regard Communistic rule in Soviet Russia as a democracy in their sense of the word. Similar points of view have been, and still are, frequent in different Western ideologies.

By holding plurality and freedom of opinions to be conditioned by the absence of belief in any absolute values, and by declaring relativism to be necessary for a democratic ideology, Kelsen used an argumentation somewhat similar to that of Masaryk. For both, democracy was evidently of a purely temporal character, opposed to all kinds of dogmatism, theological as well as political, and intimately connected with empirical and sceptical ways of thinking; this both of them held to be essential for science. Thus these two political thinkers, unlike several others, held democracy and science to be closely related phenomena.

Related political problems were also discussed by Kelsen in his work Sozialismus und Staat. The use of "democracy" and related terms in this work[31] seems to be no different from relevant terminology in the treatise under discussion here.

5. Bertrand Russell

With Luxemburg, Kautsky, and Kelsen, Bertrand Russell joined the few
political thinkers who, very early, worked out a criticism of the principles
of Bolshevism. In 1920 Russell published The Practice and Theory of
Bolshevism, which he stated was the outcome of a visit to Russia supple-
mented by much reading. While he admired the heroic attempts of the
Bolsheviks to create a fundamentally new economic and industrial order,
Russell could not agree with central parts of Bolshevik political theory.
Unfortunately, unlike Kautsky, Luxemburg, and Kelsen, Russell did not use
"democracy" as a central term in his criticism.

The main reason that Russell could not accept the Bolshevik theory was
probably his view that Bolshevism should be reckoned as a religion and not
an ordinary political movement. According to him science was tentative
and piecemeal, believing what it found evidence of and no more, while religion, which went beyond or contrary to evidence, was emotional, dogmatic,
and authoritarian. He concluded:

> Almost all the progress in the world from the earliest times was attribut-
> able to science and scientific temper, almost all the major ills were
> attributable to religion. [32]

Thus Russell can be said to have held Bolshevism to be anti-scientific, which
certainly indicates a negative attitude on this point. In contrast to the statements of Masaryk and Kelsen, however, there is no association in this work
between science and what Russell designated as "democracy", nor any application of this term in connection with statements of theoretical principle.
This eliminates further treatment of this topic.

But there are a few uses of the term in relation to the concrete state of
affairs in Russia. Russell maintained, for example, that it was primarily
as the alleged allies of Western socialism that the Bolsheviks were open to
grave criticism. The question would have been quite different if the Bolsheviks had presented themselves as a national government, or, stripped of
their camouflage, as the successors of Peter the Great. With regard to
democracy, Russell held:

> From what I saw of the Russian character and of the opposition parties,
> I became persuaded that Russia is not ready for any form of democracy,
> and needs a strong government. [33]

According to this statement, "democracy" can be said to have been used to
signify (1) something contrary to a strong government and (2) something
which Russell believed not to exist in Russia and which he did not expect to
see established in that country in the immediate future. With regard to the
function of "democracy" in Russell's vocabulary, the last factor in particular
may explain why he did not use "democracy" to signify something he charged
the Russian revolutionaries with not having established and why he did not
attach more importance to this term in his criticism of the Bolsheviks.

An application of "democratic" similar to his use of "democracy" occurs a few pages earlier in this work. In regard to the threatened famine, Russell stated:

> If Russia were governed democratically, according to the will of the majority, the inhabitants of Moscow and Petrograd would die of starvation. [34]

As it was, these big towns just managed to live by having the whole machinery of the State devoted to their needs. "Governed democratically" is evidently used synonymously with "governed according to the will of the majority"; and in conformity with the occurrence of "democracy" which we have discussed, "democratically" is used here to characterize a kind of government which did not exist in Russia, and which probably even Russell did not hope to see realized in that country, at least during the existent state of affairs.

Absence of any honorific use of "democracy" by Russell in relation to revolutionary Russia does not necessarily imply the absence of any honorific application of this term in relation to the discussion of more general political problems. With regard to the question concerning the means of introducing communism into Western countries, Russell said that it was necessary to have a great body of opinion favourable to communism before a really successful communist State could be introduced. He also attached great importance to self-government in industry. Concerning self-government in general, he admitted that the idea of democracy had become discredited as the result, first of syndicalism, and then of Bolshevism. He went on to say:

> But there are two different things that may be meant by democracy: we may mean the system of Parliamentary government, or we may mean the participation of the people in affairs. [35]

According to Russell, the discredit of the former was largely deserved, but he emphasized that it would be a great misfortune if men should come to think that because parliaments were imperfect, there should be no self-government. Russell's grounds for advocating self-government were primarily that no benevolent despot could be trusted to recognise the interests of his subjects; secondly, that the practice of self-government was the only effective method of political education; and thirdly that it tended to promote order and stable government. Russell himself was certainly in favour of such a political system, at least when faced with general problems in politics; although at that time, he was not in favour either of parliamentary rule or self-government in contemporary Russia. Being generally in favour of one of the two systems which he held as subsumable under what he designated as "democracy", Russell may be said to have used the term in an honorific way in this work, even if his way of identifying his political ideals with what he designated as "democracy" must definitely be said to have been a conditional one.

Finally, a somewhat frequent and also rather honorific application occurs in his Political Ideals, 1917. Like Tocqueville and John Stuart Mill, Russell drew attention to the danger of tyrannical behaviour on the part of the majority. Unlike Mill, however, Russell held that the freedom of different minorities was an indispensable property of "democracy". He once stated:

It is essential to democracy that any group of citizens whose interests or desires separate them at all widely from the rest of the community should be free to decide their internal affairs for themselves. [36]

Other statements of a similar kind occur at several places in this book, [37] and it can be said that "democracy" when thus used occupies a central and laudatory position in his terminology.

This use of the term is not exclusive in this work, however. Earlier Russell had declared democracy to be a device -- the best so far invented -- for diminishing as much as possible the interference of government with liberty. He went on to say:

But democracy is not at all an adequate device unless it is accompanied by a very great amount of devolution. [38]

Russell primarily had in mind the fact that love of uniformity or dislike of differing tastes and temperaments might lead the majority to an unfair control of the minority, which made necessary the devolution of political power to different subordinate groups. As used here, freedom for minorities is hardly implicit in the connotation he attributed to "democracy"; thus the term is used here with a signification different from that in the previous quotation, and also different from "democratic", when Russell said of this unfair control by the majority:

Such a state of affairs is the negation of all democratic principles. [39]

As with his criticism of Bolshevism, "democracy" was therefore used in this work to signify two different phenomena in political life. These phenomena are related to what he held to be parliamentary rule and self-government three years later. Thus, there is hardly any terminological change on this point, though Russell admitted his tendency to let "democracy" connote different things in 1920, nothing in Political Ideals suggests that he himself thought he was using the word ambiguously.

Russell's predominant way of using "democracy" in Political Ideals was certainly that according to which a high degree of freedom for minorities was a necessary, even an essential, property of its signification. Russell can, therefore, with reservation, be said to have generally identified his political ideals with what he designated in this work as "democracy". Three years later these examples of honorific applications greatly decreased but did not disappear in his discussion of revolutionary Russia.

This difference was not caused by any general change in political attitude or terminology. On the contrary the difference seems mainly to have come about because, when Russell was discussing revolutionary Russia, he did not play the role of an ideologist charging the political leaders of that country with failure to adopt the political system which he generally thought ideal; he was more occupied with empirical questions, such as: which concrete forms of rule might be regarded as representing real political possibilities, given the existing state of affairs in Russia.

PART B

SYSTEMATIC APPROACH

Mephistopheles:
Im ganzen -- haltet Euch an Worte!
Dann geht Ihr durch die sichre Pforte
Zum Tempel der Gewissheit ein.

Schüler:
Doch ein Begriff muss bei dem Worte sein.

Mephistopheles:
Schon gut! Nur muss man sich nicht allzu
ängstlich quälen;
Denn eben wo Begriffe fehlen,
Da stellt ein Wort zur rechten Zeit sich ein.

Goethe, Faust 1990-96.

Introduction

The discussion in this part was originally planned as a chapter entitled "Classificatory survey of properties attributed to the meaning of "democracy"". It was soon apparent, however, that some systematization of the material brought forward in this work would require too much space to be included in a single chapter; in addition there was the desire to throw light upon some problems not directly subsumable under properties attributed to the meaning of the word, such as countries explicitly mentioned as democracies, or frequency of "democracy" in political thought. This part of the work is therefore a more independent unit, and the modes of elaboration here clearly differ from those used in Part A.

As was mentioned in the general introduction there are several reasons why the disposition used here should have applied to the work as a whole. As a concession to this point of view I give this part some length, and include a few fairly central quotations. In general, however, I have preferred to refer to statements quoted in the Historical Approach instead of repeating them. Thus the following pages do not stand as an independent part, but must be seen in connection with the Historical Approach.

1. Democracy a form of government, or democracy a social system, or a political or ethical idea

While repeated and intense discussions concerning democracy as a political form of rule, or even exclusively a form of rule, or democracy as a social system, are very frequent in contemporary political debate, discussions of this kind are fairly rare among ideologists treated in this work. The tendency to use "democracy" to signify a certain kind of rule, or a certain kind of government, may be generally regarded as a predominant trend. But few seem to feel any special need to justify such a kind of application in principle. Notable exceptions to this rule are Maine (p. 208), Scherer (p. 189), and Kautsky (p. 230), who explicitly stated that democracy is nothing but a form of government. It may be added, however, that here we do not see any meta-occurrences of "democracy", for example, statements such as: "The word "democracy" connotes exclusively a form of rule. " On the other hand, while the use of "democracy" to signify something different from a form of rule is also a wide-spread phenomenon, few authors are explicit on this point. Chief exceptions are Guizot (p. 76), who declares that democracy was the revolutionary banner of the poor in their struggle with the rich, and who marked out his own (correct) definition of democracy in contrast to the scientific (but uncorrect) way of defining democracy as government by the people at large; and Engels, who, in describing the French Revolution as the rise of democracy in Europe, also stated:

Die französische Revolution war von Anfang bis zu Ende eine soziale

> Bewegung, und nach ihr ist eine rein politische Demokratie vollends ein
> Unding geworden. (p. 137)

But Engels, unlike Guizot, was not absolutely consistent on this point.

Within the same area Masaryk said democracy was not popular government, but popular administration (p.179); and he even considered democracy to be a moral ideal. Max Adler declared that social democracy was
the only true democracy, while political democracy was really no democracy at all (p.277).

In relation to democracy as a form of government or not, Proudhon
once said that in the last analysis, there was no room in a democracy for
either government or constitution (p.124). Similar fairly anarchistic points
of view were also formulated by Lenin when he said that true democracy
would be impossible until the socialist aim of abolishing the State had been
achieved (p. 257). With regard to the signification attributed to "democracy",
Lenin and Proudhon are far from consistent on this point, and Lenin's predominant tendency was without doubt to let "democracy" connote something
of which a form of government was a conceptual characteristic.

Few of the political thinkers under discussion are consistent on this
point. And a great many of them, possibly the majority, alternated between
using "democracy" signifying a form of rule and "democracy" signifying a
social system. Tocqueville, for example, frequently used "democracy" as
signifying social and economic equality, while there are also occurrences
where this word exclusively connoted a kind of rule. In a somewhat similar way, by "democracy" Babeuf generally meant a system of complete
communistic equality; but he once used this term as signifying that kind of
strict and merciless emergency rule by which, and only by which, this
equality was to be achieved (p. 17).

Before 1848, "democracy" to Engels signified partly a socialist system,
and also partly that kind of rule by the proletariat by which this system was
to be established. Engels also used this word in ways different from these
two kinds of application. Even John Stuart Mill, who nearly always used
"democracy" signifying a form of rule, and contrasted his own terminology
with that of Tocqueville, once used "democracy" to denote a special social
stratum of the population.

> The middle class in this country is as little in danger of being outstripped
> from the democracy below, as being kept down by the aristocracy above.

This was stated in Mill's review of Tocqueville's main work, where Mill
said fairly explicitly that his terminology differed from that of Tocqueville.
(p. 160). The practice of alternating between the use of "democracy" to
signify a form of rule and "democracy" to signify a social system is also
evident in the language of Sidney Webb (p. 235).

Thomas Mann frequently and explicitly said that democracy was identical with politics. On one occasion, however, he stated that true democracy
had nothing whatever in common with politics, and that it was primarily to
be found in the pious thoughts of the Russian peasant (pp. 224-26).

Here it is very difficult to distinguish any clear correlation between
political points of view and different uses of "democracy". When, for example, Maine, Schérer, and Kautsky explicitly stated that democracy was
nothing but a form of government, it was by no means because of any intention to reserve "democracy" as their slogan -- an inference which may seem
reasonable. Maine as well as Schérer used "democracy" negatively, and

Kautsky was almost neutral when he held democracy to be nothing but a form of government.

Nor is it possible to find anything in common between Engels and Guizot when the former rejected democracy as a purely political form in contemporary time, and the latter held to be incorrect the usual scientific way of defining democracy as government by the people at large. To Engels democracy as a social and also as a revolutionary factor was warmly appreciated; a contrary attitude is very evident in Guizot. Something like a trend can be observed in the use of "democracy" with a connotation which includes social properties by several socialists, such as Engels, Sidney Webb, and Max Adler. But this trend is by no means a common characteristic of most socialists, and cannot be limited to different groups of socialists.

2. Direct rule versus rule by elected representatives

In a discussion whether "democracy" signifies a form of rule directly carried out by the citizens, or a form of rule by elected representatives, the period of the French Revolution occupies a central position. Previously, "democracy" seems exclusively to have signified direct rule, or a form of government incompatible with any kind of elected representatives. Lucid statements taken from authors outside this framework can be found in the terminology of Hobbes, Spinoza, Montesquieu, and the Federalists (p. 8 and notes 3, 4, 5 to Chapter I.). A possible exception to this rule is Alexander Hamilton, who, in May 1777, used the expression "representative democracy" to signify a form of government in which the legislative, executive, and judicial authorities were vested in select persons, chosen by the people (cf. Christophersen, "An historical outlook on the different usages of the term "democracy"", in Democracy, Ideology and Objectivity, p. 101.). Hamilton did not, however, use unqualified "democracy" to signify a rule of the kind mentioned. Robespierre's speech in February 1794 marks with fair certainty the first distinct use of "democracy" to signify not the direct rule of the people, but a form of State in which the sovereign people do themselves what they are capable of doing and choose delegates or representatives to carry out what they cannot handle themselves (p. 9). Here it must be added, however, that some degree of differentiated language is evident in Thomas Paine's Rights of Man, 1792 (p. 23), in Godwin's Political Justice, 1793 (p. 27), and in de Maistre, 1795 (p. 34). The latter especially seem to have held democracy and rule by representatives to be compatible phenomena.

Among political thinkers who have declared democracy to be nothing but the rule of representatives elected by the people, Bentham occupies the most important position. In one case he emphasized that representative democracy was "the only practicable democracy" and "the only democracy worth the name". He also said that

> ... whatever else has been called democracy has had nothing of democracy but the name. (pp. 95-96)

Even Bentham, however, once used unqualified "democracy" in a way which indicates that he regarded direct rule as subsumable under what he designated "democracy" (p. 97); and his best friend and collaborator, James Mill, used "democracy" in a very different way from Bentham. Somewhat

similarly, Proudhon stated in 1848 that a democracy, in contrast to a republic, was exclusively ruled by elected representatives, and that the political function of the people was definitely limited to the election of representatives (p. 119). While persons who were otherwise different, Robespierre
and Bentham, were both absolutely in favour of representation, to Proudhon, this kind of rule was the ruin and even the negation of popular sovereignty. But Proudhon was far from consistent in attributing this signification to "democracy". Shortly afterwards he said that imperative mandates
were indispensable to what he designated as "democracy" (p. 122).

A most negative attitude towards representation and election was taken
by Bakunin. He seems to have regarded "democracy" as well as "most
democratic country" as signifying a kind of rule which was necessarily
founded upon representation. Echoing Rousseau's famous statement, Bakunin
said that the workers, even in the most democratic countries, had one day
when they were sovereign: election day. When the election was over, all
talk about fraternity and equality would fade away, the capitalists would
resume their position as suppressors and exploiters, and the workers would
remain slaves (p. 244).

In the latter half of the nineteenth century, and later, Robespierre's
and Bentham's manner of explicitly declaring democracy to be a representative form of rule was regarded by many as fairly self-evident, needing no
special justification. There are, in any case, few statements in favour of
such justification, even among people definitely in favour of representative
rule. The Fabians are exceptions to that rule. Democracy, as understood
by them, was the control of the administration of the freely elected representatives of the people. They repudiated all conceptions of democracy as
a system in which government administration should be carried out by referendum or by any other form of direct popular decision (p. 237). Lenin's
comment on primitive forms of direct rule, and the absence of representatives as well as the absence of salaried officials was: "How absurd such a
conception of democracy was" (p. 254). These statements by persons otherwise as different as the Fabians and Lenin may reflect the importance both
parties attributed to political leadership, partly at the expense of the influence of the rank and file.

A more differentiated terminology is to be found in some statements of
John Stuart Mill. Mill did not regard unqualified "democracy" as signifying
a purely representative form of rule, but he introduced a more complex
designation, "rational democracy", signifying a kind of rule in which the role
of the people was exclusively limited to choosing as their rulers the most
educated and able persons. He contrasted this kind of democracy with that
in which the people might directly interfere in the matters of government
and make their legislators mere delegates for carrying into execution the
preconceived judgement of the majority. A somewhat different kind of differentiated terminology is found in the use of "democracy" by John Austin.
According to Austin, it was necessary to distinguish between the forma
imperii and the forma regiminis. According to the former criterion, the
form and nature of sovereignty itself, the question of whether a State was or
was not a democracy depended upon the size of the electoral body. According to the latter criterion, the management which gave to sovereignty its
practical effect, the question depended upon the relationship between the
number of sovereign people and the comparatively small number by which
supreme power was exercised. According to the latter criterion, but not
the former, any State ruled by elected representatives could hardly ever be

a democracy. And Austin also stated that the British Government should be considered an aristocracy, especially since Parliament was only a minor fraction of the entire nation (p. 171).

Among political thinkers who continued the tradition of letting "democracy" signify exclusively a direct kind of popular rule, explicit statements are at hand in the writings of Kant (p. 50), and Schleiermacher (p. 42). All of them evidently regarded any kind of representation as incompatible with what they designated "democracy". Similar points of view are also seen in the argument of Benjamin Constant (p. 52). A more ambiguous use of "democracy" is found in the language of Fichte, who once said that democracy and democratic government, "in the real sense of the word" and even "most real sense of the word", were incompatible with any kind of representation. In the same work, however, Fichte spoke about democracy "in the more narrow sense of the word" as being founded upon some kind of representation, and therefore becoming a legal kind of rule, in contrast to the former (p. 40).

Among other ideologists who continued the tradition established prior to the French Revolution (when "democracy" exclusively signified direct rule) James Mill occupies a key position (p. 99). Here, as we have noted, Mill differs greatly from Bentham. A related kind of terminology, although in a modified form and in relation to somewhat different problems, can be found in the language of Sidgwick as late as 1891. According to Sidgwick, some degree of aristocracy was implicitly accepted in all kinds of representation, and he could therefore not consider representative government, even when suffrage was universal, as merely a method of organizing democracy, but rather as a combination or fusion of democracy and aristocracy (p. 177). This alleged aristocratic character of any kind of election was also mentioned by Treitschke: "Denn in jeder Form der Wahl liegt ein aristokratisches Element" (p. 220). It can be added that none of those who considered democracy to be a direct form of rule adhered to what they designated as "democracy".

In addition to those who held that democracy had to be either a direct or a representative kind, there are also political thinkers who used "democracy" with a fairly wide signification, or who operated with a fairly broad concept or genus 'democracy' of which 'direct democracy' as well as 'representative democracy' are species or sub-concepts. Such a trend is fairly evident in the language of John Stuart Mill, although he used an expression like "rational democracy" to signify the purely representative kind of rule. Related ways of using "democracy" with a fairly wide signification can also be seen in the terminology of Sismondi (p. 72) and Stahl (p. 68).

While questions concerning democracy as a direct or representative kind of rule are not among the most central ones in recent and contemporary political debate, questions concerning the relationship between electors and representatives are among those considered important. John Stuart Mill used an expression like "rational democracy" to signify a rule by independent representatives who definitely were not to carry out the preconceived judgement of their electors, whereas Proudhon once said imperative mandates were essential to what he designated "democracy". Using an argument similar to that of Proudhon, Marx said the Paris Commune had worked out truly democratic institutions. By "democratic institutions", Marx first of all had in mind the direct control of the people over the governing body. According to Marx, the rulers were therefore the servants of the people, not its masters, and he especially drew attention to the fact that any representative might at any time be recalled by the electorate concerned. A use of unqualified "democracy" which on this point was fairly similar to the use of "rational democracy" by John Stuart Mill also occurs in Lenin's language and that of the Fabians. But Rosa Luxemburg -- like Marx -- declared that a very close relationship between electors and representatives was essential "in einer von Grund aus demokratischen Partei" (p. 234). Points of view similar to that of Luxemburg are also central in the political thinking of Kelsen (p. 278) and Cole. The latter consistently maintained that control of the rulers is essential for what he designated "real democracy" and "actual democracy", in contrast to what received the label "formal democracy" (p. 240).

From a more general point of view, in relation to central problems within political thought, it can be added that in socialist ideologies there is hardly any correlation between questions concerning revolutionary versus reformist politics, on one hand, and questions concerning strong leadership versus control by the masses, on the other. On account of Lenin's theory, many people, adherents as well as enemies, have a tendency to associate a revolutionary outlook with centralism and strong leadership. Such a view is oversimplified. Extreme revolutionary socialists such as Lenin, on one hand, and Luxemburg and Trotsky, on the other, represent opposite points of view in relation to questions concerning political leadership and control by the masses. A similar comment can also be made about typically reformist socialists such as the Fabians and Cole. In relation to organization and leadership by an elite, the Fabians adhere to opinions which resemble those of Lenin, while there is a distinct similarity between Cole and Luxemburg in their emphasis of the need for permanent influence and control by the rank and file.

With regard to the character of representation, John Stuart Mill stated several times that proportional representation, which implied the representation of political minorities, was essential to what he designated "democracy". He also held that proportional representation is "the only true type of democracy" in contrast to "the falsely-called democracies which now prevail" (p. 165). Mill was in favour of plural votes for certain qualified citizens; he probably did not regard this as incompatible with what he held to be democracy (p. 168), although there are also formulations which may indicate a relationship of mutual incompatibility (p. 163).

Concerning a quite different problem, whereas some kind of election seems to have been generally regarded as a condition of representation, a different point of view is taken by Disraeli. According to him, an assembly might very well be representative without being elected. As a concrete proof he maintained that the Church of England was not only virtually, but absolutely, faithfully, and efficiently, represented in the House of Lords by the bishops, in spite of the fact that these Lords were not elected by their clergy. Probably for similar reasons Disraeli also said, "There is not a more democratic institution in the country than the Church" (p. 57). As regards general problems in political theory, this view on representation touches a central topic, especially in relation to virtual versus actual representation and also in relation to corporate representation.

3. "Democracy" signifying the rule of the people at large, or "democracy" signifying the rule of a more or less clearly restricted part of the population

While it is easy to find statements in which "democracy" more or less vaguely signifies the rule of the people at large, the rule of the whole people etc., there are also formulations which explicitly define democracy as rule by a fairly restricted part of the population. Apart from authors discussed in this work, Aristotle occupies a key position by virtue of his assertion that democracy was the rule of the poor and oligarchy the rule of the rich, and that it was conceptually irrelevant whether the poor (or the rich) were in the majority or in the minority. According to Aristotle, even if the poor were in the minority, rule by this minority would be a democracy (Politics 1280a, cf. Christophersen in Democracy, Ideology, and Objectivity, pp. 85-86).

Among political thinkers treated in this work there are statements in the terminology of Babeuf and Buonarroti which indicate that to them, "democracy", at least in part, did not signify rule by the people at large, but on the contrary, a kind of revolutionary emergency rule exclusively led by convinced and faithful revolutionaries (p. 17 and p. 20). Benjamin Constant mentioned that even in what he designated as "more absolute democracy" there were certain groups not in possession of political rights: those below a certain age and strangers. A much more important kind of limitation is found in Disraeli's statement in 1835, where he maintained that "the state of our society is that of a complete democracy" -- in spite of his admission that the executive and legislative functions in Britain were performed by two privileged classes of society (p. 58). A somewhat related formulation is also present in the arguments of Carlyle: "All that Democracy ever meant lies there; the attainment of a truer and truer Aristocracy, or Government again by the Best" (p. 66). Carlyle was otherwise far from consistent in attributing such a signification to "democracy".

John Stuart Mill said in 1840 that the government of England would progressively change from government of the few to government of, not the many, but many; he went on:

> To most purposes, in the constitution of modern society, the government of a numerous middle class is democracy.

Of universal suffrage in America, he said,

> What is called universal suffrage in America arising from the fact that America is all middle class. (pp. 160-61)

This way of identifying, or almost identifying, democracy with rule of the middle class, does not occur elsewhere in his writings, although the manner of arguing which is typical of the background to these statements represents a main trend in Mill's political thinking. A distinct negation of democracy as being government by the lower classes is explicit in the thinking of Considérant. Considérant admitted that "democracy" was ambiguously used in the vernacular, and he also held that the honorific application of "democracy" in revolutionary circles represented a great danger. Of himself and his adherents he said that the term "democracy" did not mean government by the lower classes, but signified government of the society in the interest of all by the hierarchic rule of a group of citizens, and that the number of this group must increase with social development (p. 114).

Apart from Babeuf and Buonarroti, the arguments of all authors in this section reflect a fear of the power of the masses, and an attempt to attribute to "democracy" significations which would make it possible to use that term in an honorific way without favouring rule by the masses. Similar statements may be made about Babeuf and Buanarroti, although it is difficult to class these two profound revolutionaries, who feared absence of revolutionary spirit among the masses, with those more or less right-wing or moderate ideologists who feared the contrary.

The identification of democracy with the rule of a certain social class can be noted on several occasions in the political thinking of Marx and Engels. Before 1848 Engels several times used "democracy" as signifying rule by the proletariat. He alternates, however, between using "democracy" as signifying (1) a rule by the proletariat, (2) a political means which will result in such a rule, (3) a socialist or a communist system, and sometimes (4) the socialist movement. In the Communist Manifesto, "democracy" is most probably used synonymously with "rule of the proletariat" (p. 143). Shortly after 1848 there is also a tendency by Marx to identify, or at least to associate, what received the label "democracy" with the rule of a certain social group, but now not the proletariat, but the petty bourgeoisie -- a very important difference (p. 147). In a way somewhat similar to one trend of Marx and Engels before 1848, Lenin also sometimes used "democracy" as a designation of what had been established by the Russian revolutionaries, "a democracy of a new and higher kind" (pp. 255-60). This trend is far from being exclusive in Lenin's language, however.

The identification of democracy with the rule of a certain social class can be seen in the writings of Sorel and Radek, who both used "democracy" as signifying rule by the capitalists or by capital (p. 247 and p. 266).

A related, but nevertheless different way of using "democracy" can be found among a few ideologists who initially defined democracy as the rule of the whole people, but who continued by arguing that since the majority of the people consists of a certain class, and since this class is necessarily in favour of certain points of view, then democracy is also necessarily rule by people of such (vulgar) points of view. A typical example of this kind of persuasive arguing is that of Edmond Schérer. At the outset he says democracy is the government of all citizens, and since the workers are in a clear majority, and since this inferior class regards manual work as the only real work and is hostile to intellectual work, democracy is necessarily the rule of those who earned their living from day to day; the essence of democracy is consequently "la dépression de tout ce qui tend à dépasser le niveau" (p. 190). Bagehot has an argument very similar to that of Schérer (p. 175), and Faguet identifies, or almost identifies, democracy with rule by incompetent persons (p. 197).

Concerning women's rights, extremely few writers, not even John Stuart Mill, make any explicit mention of political rights for women in statements containing "democracy". Bakunin and the Fabians are exceptions. The latter said that democracy, as understood by them, made no political

distinction between men and women (p. 237). Nietzsche said reverence for
women was characteristic of democracy as he understood it.

4. Democracy and self-government in fairly autonomous units

The question of self-government in fairly autonomous units is not a main
topic in this work. It has been touched on to a certain extent in relation to
the problems concerning representation. And it is, perhaps, somewhat
typical that Robespierre, when stating that democracy was not the direct
rule of the people, said that it was still less a State in which a hundred
thousand factions of the people, by contradictory, hasty, isolated measures,
decided the fate of society as a whole (p. 8). In sharp contrast to Robespierre's outlook Proudhon several times declared in different ways that
local autonomy was essential to what he named "democracy" (p. 124). This
autonomy was to be founded on mutual confidence and co-operation and marks
a permanent trend in his thinking. But elsewhere Proudhon held federalism
and democracy to be representative of absolute opposites in political life
(p. 127). Similarly Masaryk and, generally, Bertrand Russell held local
autonomy to be essential to what they regarded as democracy (p. 180 and
p. 282). This is a central point in the guild socialism of Cole, who consistently said that self-rule on the local level, and especially in the trade unions
and workshop, was indispensable for true democracy, rather than nominal
democracy (p. 240).
Concerning federalism, Charles Maurras evidently held democracy and
federalism to represent mutually incompatible factors. His main argument
was that democracy destroyed that kind of quality which decentralization and
federalism needed (p. 196). Lamartine once said that federalism and democracy were different factors in political life (p. 106). The only difference
between these two was that Maurras greatly favoured federalism and decentralization, while Lamartine evidently did not.

5. Democracy, capitalism, and socialism

a. "Democracy" signifying a socialist or a communist system

In Babeuf's political language there are several statements in which "democracy" does not connote any form of rule, but is used to signify a classless
society characterized by a consistent social and economic equality (pp. 15-
17). In one place, however, Babeuf departs from this trend by using "democracy" to signify that strict and revolutionary emergency rule by which,
and only by which, this equalitarian system was to be achieved. Cabet also
used "democracy" almost synonymously with "communism". Cabet said,
for example, that true democrats were communists without knowing it,
and he held it to be a suicide for any democrat to condemn a communist. He
also declared that the use of "democracy" as self-denomination in certain
bourgeois circles represented a blatant misuse of the word (pp. 116-17). Some
degree of terminological differentiation is found, however, when Cabet introduces more qualified designations such as démocratie populaire and démocratie bourgeoise.

The identification of democracy with socialism, or rather with what he held as socialism, is also one of the trends in the language of Proudhon. In one case, he explicitly said that "democracy", "republic", and "socialism" were synonymous terms (p. 122). Several other statements also indicate a relationship of identity or near identity between socialism and what he labelled "democracy"(pp. 121,128), although there are other statements where "democracy" and "socialism" signify contrary phenomena in the field of politics. In Engels' terminology several trends can be traced, especially before 1848. According to one of them, "democracy" directly signified communism.

> Die Demokratie, das ist heutzutage der Kommunismus. Eine andere Demokratie kann nur noch in den Köpfen theoretischer Visionäre existieren. (p. 137)

Similar formulations occur on p. 138 and p. 141.

Tocqueville generally uses "democracy" to signify social and economic equality, especially before 1848. There are, however, no grounds for concluding that he generally identified democracy with socialism. To him, democracy first of all implied equality among individual property owners. In 1848 Tocqueville said that democracy and socialism were not only different, but contrary factors (p. 87). But there are a very few statements in Tocqueville's terminology which indicate a relationship of synonymity between "democracy" and "socialism"; these statements are perhaps of a somewhat accidental kind (p. 88).

This tendency to identify democracy with a communist or socialist system is mainly to be found before 1848, but there are later statements which clearly tend the same way.

In Renan's terminology, "democracy" seems frequently, if not generally, to signify, not a certain kind of rule, but an equalitarian social system, marked by an absolute absence of hierarchies, and in sharp contrast to the influence of the rich. Renan said that the equalitarian doctrine of Jesus was not new in history, because for a long time the Jewish people had been very familiar with "le mouvement démocratique le plus exalté dont l'humanité ait gardé le souvenir". This was because

> ...la pensée que Dieu est le vengeur du pauvre et du faible contre le riche et le puissant se retrouve à chaque page des écrits de l'Ancien Testament. (p. 185)

Among socialists, Sidney Webb said in 1889 that

> ...the economic side of the democratic ideal is, in fact, Socialism itself. (p. 235)

Jaurès, in some cases, maintained that democracy and capitalism represented incompatible factors; this implies that, according to him, democracy was necessarily a socialist system (p. 238). This trend is not exclusive in Jaurès' use of "democracy", however. One trend in his terminology is similar to Faguet's probable belief that "complete democracy" was synonymous with "socialist form of State" (p. 198), the only difference being that while Webb and Jaurès greatly favoured such a social system, Faguet held a contrary attitude. This naturally does not affect the factual signification attributed to "democracy", however. In addition, Max Adler said that social democracy was the only true democracy, in contrast to political democracy, which in reality was no democracy at all. This social democracy was ex-

clusively to be realized in a classless society. It seems, however, that
Adler did not directly use "democracy" to signify a society where all class
differences had been abolished, but more as a kind of rule of which the
absence of any kind of class differences and class rule was a condition.

In sections in Part B, the persons mentioned by no means form a homogeneous assembly. Among those who in certain cases use "democracy" to
connote a socialist or a communist system there are, on the one hand, convinced socialists like Cabet, Engels, Sidney Webb, and to certain extent
Max Adler; on the other hand, there are also profound anti-socialists like
Tocqueville, Faguet, and Renan. The tendency towards such a use of
"democracy" seems to have been more predominant among socialists than
among anti-socialists, but it is nevertheless impossible to distinguish any
correlation between political outlook in general and a certain usage of
"democracy".

b. "Democracy" signifying the rule of the proletariat

As was mentioned in section 3, there are statements in the language of
Babeuf and Buonarroti which indicate that to them "democracy" signified a
kind of revolutionary emergency rule, by which, and only by which, social
equality and a classless society were to be achieved. I make a reservation,
however, that this kind of rule cannot be regarded as rule by the proletariat,
but rather as a dictatorship pretending to act on behalf of the propertyless
masses. Marx and Engels probably used "democracy" synonymously with
"rule of the proletariat" in the Communist Manifesto (p. 143) and related
formulations by Schérer and Bagehot also occur (p. 190 and p. 175). The
only difference being that Schérer and Bagehot greatly disliked such a form
of rule. Lenin, too, declared that revolutionary rule in Soviet Russia
represented "a superior democratic State". Although the reservation made
regarding Babeuf and Buonarroti can be mentioned in connection with Bolshevik revolutionary rule. Lenin's statement, however, is probably only proof
that revolutionary rule in Russia was subsumable under what Lenin designated the "superior democratic State" and it probably does not imply that
Lenin used this expression as necessarily signifying rule by the proletariat.
Other prominent revolutionaries like Trotsky, Radek, and Kuusinen said
that Bolshevik rule was definitely not what they designated as "democracy"
(pp. 261-68).

Rosa Luxemburg, while definitely in favour of what she held to be dictatorship of the proletariat, absolutely denied that such a dictatorship existed in Bolshevik Russia. According to her, Lenin and Trotsky were in
favour of the dictatorship of a single party, not of a dictatorship of the whole
working class. She stated that this latter dictatorship was necessarily of a
democratic kind, in contrast to the dictatorship of a few politicians acting
in the name of the workers. This implies that for her, dictatorship of the
proletariat was subsumable under what she designated "democracy", but does
not imply that "democracy" necessarily signifies such a rule (pp. 273-74).

c. Democracy and revolution

c. 1. Democracy and revolution almost identical phenomena

Among ideologists who declare democracy and revolution to be identical or almost identical phenomena in political life, Mazzini occupies a most central position. On one occasion he said:

> There is a note of strife in the word democracy, it is the cry of Spartacus, the expression of a people in its first attempt to rise. (p. 108)

Similarly, Guizot said that democracy was **not** government by the people, which he declared was the scientific definition, but on the contrary, democracy was a war cry, the banner of the poor and the many in their struggle with the rich and the few (p. 76). In both cases we can probably say that "democracy" was not used as signifying something which was to be achieved by revolutionary means, or as something associated with revolution, but that it directly connotes violent revolution.

Like persons as different as Mazzini and Guizot, Carlyle also to a certain extent used "democracy" as synonymous with "regulated method of rebellion and abrogation" and also as synonymous with "this universal revolt of European Populations" (p. 62 and p. 63). Tocqueville clearly allowed "democracy" to signify a most revolutionary social movement when he asked:

> Pense-t-on qu'après avoir detruit la féodalité et vaincu les rois, la démocratie reculera devant les bourgeois et les riches. S'arrêtera-t-elle maintenant qu'elle est devenue si forte et ses adversaires si faibles? (p. 80)

As regards the years prior to the February Revolution, it can also be seen that Considérant severely deplored the intense and honorific use of "democracy" by revolutionary persons.

> Les parties révolutionnaires font aujourd'hui du mot de "Démocratie" un drapeau de révolution et de guerre, une arme redoutable, les uns contre l'ordre politique et le gouvernement, les autres contre la propriété et la base de l'ordre sociale. (p. 114)

In some cases, but far from all, Marx identified, or strongly associated, revolution with what he held to be democracy. During the February Revolution he once used "der Sitz der Revolution" synonymously with "die Hauptstadt der Demokratie" (p. 145), although by "revolution" Marx very likely here had a middle-class revolution and not a proletarian one in mind. A strong association between democracy and revolution occurred a few years later when Marx pointed out that after the French Revolution,

> ... gab es tatsächlich bloss zwei Mächte auf dem europeischen Kontinent; Russland mit seinem Absolutismus, die Revolution mit der Demokratie. (p. 151)

Similarly Proudhon once used "organization of democracy" synonymously with "social revolution" (p. 122), although it must be kept in mind that Proudhon, by social revolution, probably had something peaceful in mind.

An association between revolutionary policy and what was held to be democracy was also expressed by Charles Maurras. He considered socialism to be revolutionary and anarchic, not because it was socialist, but on account of "le poison démocratique qui s'y mêle toujours" (note 39, ch. XI). Favouring of revolutionary activity was most likely characteristic of persons whom Madame de Staël (p. 54), Bourget (p. 193), and Stephen (p. 205) considered to be democrats. Among fairly conservative ideologists, May maintained, when indicating different ways of using "democracy", that in addition to the sovereignty of the whole body of the people, this term was also used in some other sense; for example:

> In default of a more extended vocabulary, it is often spoken of as a revolutionary force, opposed to existing institutions, if not to law and order. ... In view of many popular movements abroad, such a term can scarcely be misapplied. (p. 206)

As proof, May himself said of the February Revolution that only those governments were secure which rested upon public opinion and support. He added:

> From this critical year of revolutions the moral may be drawn that freedom is the surest safeguard against democracy.

A most explicit way of letting "democracy" exclusively signify the conquering of political power by the armed proletariat is evident in one of the last proclamations of Rosa Luxemburg, in which she emphasized that not in parliamentary debates between the proletariat and the capitalist, but

> ... wo die millionenköpfige Proletariermasse die ganze Staatsgewalt mit ihrer schwieligen Faust ergreift, um sie, wie der Gott Thor seinen Hammer, den herrschenden Klasse aufs Haupt zu schmettern, dort allein ist Demokratie, die kein Volksbetrug ist. (p. 275)

Whereas outstanding revolutionaries, such as Robespierre, Saint-Just, Babeuf, and Buonarroti, used "democracy" in an honorific way, there are, as far as we can see, no occurrences in their terminology where this word was used directly to connote revolutionary upheaval, although the word was certainly used to connote revolutionary rule.

The majority of those who regard democracy to be revolutionary in form, or even as violent revolution, are anti-revolutionary. The alleged revolutionary character of democracy was dreaded by Guizot, Tocqueville, Carlyle, Considérant, Maurras, and May, and it is negatively evaluated by Madame de Staël, Bourget, and Stephen, and strangely enough also by Mazzini. Of course, quite a contrary evaluation is evident in Marx and especially in Rosa Luxemburg. The greater part of the instances where democracy was regarded as revolutionary occurs in the years before and during the February Revolution, as for example in Guizot, Carlyle, Tocqueville, Considérant, Mazzini, and Marx, though much later, examples can be seen in Stephen, May, and Bourget, and in Maurras as late as in 1909 and in Luxemburg in 1918.

c. 2. Democracy and revolution contrary phenomena in political life

While it is sometimes quite easy to find occurrences where "democracy" directly signifies a revolutionary upheaval, or a violent revolutionary policy, the contrary tendency is less explicit. It is not easy, for example, to find statements where "democracy" signifies directly, as well as explicitly, something contrary to revolution. There are nevertheless several cases where "democracy" was used in this way, or at least to express incompatibility with revolution, especially when the context is taken into consideration. For example, in 1851 Marx, in sharp contrast to some of his earlier formulations, described in a letter to Engels one of his most central and revolutionary instructions as being "au fond nichts als ein Kriegsplan gegen die Demokratie" (p. 148). Tocqueville, in a somewhat similar way, referred to the new experience of the February Revolution. According to him, democracy had become a most proper means in the struggle against the revolutionary workers; or in his own words,

... vaincre ainsi la démagogie par la démocratie. (p. 88)

Both statements contain very important points of view with regard to the theoretical new orientation brought out by the events in 1848.

This attitude towards revolution and what received the label "democracy" as representing contrary factors in political life is a widespread tendency in later socialist thought, and can be found in the argument of persons as different as Bernstein, Kautsky, the Fabians, Sorel, and Lagardelle, but not in the writings of Rosa Luxemburg. This contrast between revolutionary conquest of political power on the one hand and what was named "democracy" on the other probably reaches its highest point in Trotsky's work Terrorismus und Kommunismus (p. 261). If a negative attitude of this kind can be regarded as a criterion of an anti-democratic book, Terrorismus und Kommunismus is probably the most anti-democratic book ever written. I have not found so negative an attitude elsewhere, even in fascism and nazism. A use of "democracy" similar to that of Trotsky can also be found in writings of Radek (p. 266) and Kuusinen (p. 268); and to a much smaller extent in Lenin's language.

d. "Democracy" signifying a capitalist system, or rule by the capitalists

While there are few statements in which "democracy" has been used explicitly to signify the rule of the capitalists, there are some occurrences where "democracy" connotes a form of rule extremely favourable to the capitalists or which necessarily was limited to capitalist countries. Here, Sorel is the most explicit. Inter alia, he declared democracy to be the paradise dreamt about by unscrupulous capitalists, and he probably also used "democracy" synonymously with "political forms of the bourgeoisie" (p. 247). An explicit statement is also found in Radek's argument that democracy, from a concrete point of view, was rule by capital, which was so firmly rooted in the consciousness of the masses that it could afford the luxury of allowing the people to discuss political matters (p. 266). Whereas

Trotsky's and Kuusinen's very negative attitudes towards what they called "democracy" were most central in their writings, Radek's opinion that democracy was necessarily capitalist was probably not shared by them. But Lenin once used "democracy" to signify a kind of rule necessarily controlled by the bankers (p. 259).

John Stuart Mill may, from a certain point of view, be classed among those who considered democracy to be rule by the capitalists on the strength of his remark that democracy was the government of a numerous middle class (p. 160). But by middle class, Mill probably had in mind people with some education and with a certain way of public behaviour, and not the capitalists as such.

From another trend in European though there is also a clear association, and to a certain degree, even identification, of capitalism with democracy in the works of central authors such as Carlyle and Nietzsche. Carlyle especially associated several times what he held as democracy with what he regarded as the central characteristics of commercial capitalism. To him, the growth of democracy was equivalent with the tragic fact that "the age of Chivalry is gone, and that of Bankruptcy is come". In one case he also defined democracy as "the consummation of No-government and Laissez-faire" (p. 62). As for Carlyle, laissez-faire was essentially the vulgar and selfish ethics of utilitarianism, worship of wealth, which had made cash payment the only bond between human beings, and had eliminated such noble ideals as reverence, responsibility, obedience, and fidelity. Nietzsche too associated democracy with capitalism. In one place, he clearly associated democracy with the capitalist and industrial spirit, as opposed to the warlike and aristocratic (p. 217). Elsewhere he referred to shopkeepers, Christians, cows, women, and Englishmen as typical representatives of what he held to be democrats (p. 218). A related kind of association between capitalism and democracy was also expressed by Thomas Mann when he said that avarice, the rule of money, and even food hoarding in times of war were the qualifications of democracy (p. 224).

While there are different attitudes towards what was called "democracy" when the word signified rule by the proletariat or rule by the working class, there is, apart from John Stuart Mill, an exclusively derogatory application of this term when it signifies rule of capital, rule by capitalists, or related forms of government.

6. Democracy and freedom

6. a. Freedom essential for anything being a democracy

In this section, the terms "freedom" and "liberty" are used generally to connote freedom of expression. Other kinds of liberty, such as social freedom, which may mean freedom for private enterprise as well as the reduction or elimination of class differences, are not discussed, unless mentioned specifically. I am quite aware that a phrase such as "freedom of expression" may well require a precise definition which can only be touched upon here.

Among formulations which stress freedom of expression as sine qua non for anything to receive the labels "democracy" and "democratic government", Tocqueville's can be regarded as probably the most explicit. He considered the signification of the words "democracy" and "democratic government" to be intimately connected with the idea of political liberty:

> Appeler démocratique un governement où la liberté politique ne se trouve pas, c'est dire une absurdité palpable, suivant le véritable sens du mot. (p. 91)

However, this use of "democracy" is not the only one in Tocqueville's terminology. And Tocqueville's predominant use of "democracy" without doubt expressed a concept of which neither the presence nor the absence of liberty were conceptual characteristics but which from a non-conceptual point of view was frequently regarded as a potential danger to liberty (pp. 81-86).

Hegel, too, declared democracy to be the purest freedom which had existed any time:

> Sie [die Demokratie] ist die schönste Verfassung, die reinste Freiheit, die je existiert hat. (p. 47)

It is difficult, however, to see whether Hegel had freedom of expression in mind. It may be appended that Hegel also stated that the most beautiful was not the most profound and truest form of the concept of the spirit.

Otherwise in sharp contrast to trends in contemporary ideological debate, explicit statements in which "democracy" was used to connote something of which the presence of freedom was an essential characteristic were far from frequent in the nineteenth century, although questions concerning freedom of expression and the protection of minorities were often discussed, possibly on a higher level and in a more differentiated way than in the twentieth century. However, in the terminology of John Stuart Mill, Lord Acton, and generally Tocqueville, there is almost no tendency to identify freedom of speech with "democracy", although "democracy" is certainly used in questions concerning freedom of speech and tolerance.

This does not imply that freedom of speech, tolerance, and the protection of minorities cannot be seen in the signification attributed to "democracy". A high degree of spiritual independence and mutual tolerance seems necessarily to have been included, at least implicitly, in the signification of "democracy" as used by Godwin (p. 26). To a certain degree, this also applies to Bentham (p. 96); yet in his voluminous production, Bentham hardly ever treated the questions of freedom and tolerance systematically, at least not when compared with John Stuart Mill and Tocqueville.

Liberty, as well as equality, seems further to have been identified with what Lamartine and Brunetière held to be democracy, but in a vague manner that makes it difficult to draw any significant conclusions (p. 105 and p. 192). Especially in relation to protection of minorities, a most interesting statement was made by Bernstein in 1899 where he declared suppression of the minority to be undemocratic, even if such suppression was compatible with popular rule:

> Wir finden heute die Unterdrückung der Minderheit durch die Mehrheit "undemokratisch", obwohl sie ursprünglich mit der Volksherrschaft durchaus vereinbar gehalten wurde. (p. 228)

The trend evident in this statement was to a large degree to mould political language after the Russian Revolution. Kelsen, for example, said explicitly that the protection of an opposition, or a minority, was the essential, or even conceptual, characteristic of democracy (p. 279). Kautsky, in 1918, also held freedom of discussion and protection of the minority to be the es-

sential character of "democracy" (p. 271). On this point there is a difference with regard to the earlier signification attributed to "democracy" by
Kautsky in his polemics with Bernstein nineteen years previously (p. 231).
In her criticism of Lenin and Trotsky, 1918, Rosa Luxemburg evidently held
freedom for those who think differently, not only for the adherents of the government, to be indispensable for any form of democratic government (p. 274).
A related use of "democracy" appears in the terminology of Bertrand Russell
in his comment that it was essential to democracy that any group of citizens
whose interests or desires separated them widely from the rest should be
free to decide their internal affairs for themselves (p. 282). Russell was,
however, not entirely consistent in attributing this signification to "democracy".

This attribution to "democracy" of a signification of which freedom of
speech and freedom for minorities was an essential property is a predominant trend among political thinkers who criticized, from different premises,
the revolutionary rule in Russia. This trend is, however, not limited to the
critics. Among persons on the other side of the fence, Lenin once said that
the abolition of the state was the main aim pursued by all socialists. He
continued:

> Until this aim has been achieved, true democracy, i. e. equality and
> liberty, will be impossible. (p. 258)

b. Democracy, a potential danger to freedom

In the history of political ideas, the problem of democracy as a potential
danger to freedom of speech and tolerance ranks among the most important
in nineteenth-century debate. In a study of political semantics, however,
this problem is of lesser importance, although it definitely deserves attention. When someone says, for example, that democracy leads to less liberty
or that a consequence of democracy may be to reduce freedom of speech and
to enforce a higher degree of conformity, we are most probably faced with
non-conceptual characteristics of the concept 'democracy'. The case is
simpler and plainer when the presence (or absence) of freedom of speech is
of necessity included in the signification of "democracy". It is interesting
from a semantic point of view, and especially for political semantics, that
the presence of liberty in many cases was not included in the signification of
"democracy".

As indicated earlier, the view of democracy as more or less a danger to
liberty holds a significant position in the political thinking of Tocqueville,
John Stuart Mill, and Lord Acton. This tendency is a kind of leitmotiv within
the somewhat different thinking of these three men. It is of importance that
this trend is connected with perhaps the most profound elaborations in the
nineteenth century of the questions of freedom of speech and tolerance.

In Tocqueville, there are a few occurrences in which he uses "democracy" to signify something of which freedom is a necessary property (p. 87
and p. 91), and there are also a few in which freedom and what he called
"democracy" seem mutually exclusive (p. 81 and p. 84). By far the predominant tendency, however, was his use of "democracy" as a label of something that might be a danger to freedom and tolerance. Different aspects of
this topic were touched upon and the question of liberty and democracy was
discussed repeatedly but nearly always in a way that deepened the problem.

It is to the advantage of Tocqueville's political thinking that he did not give categoric answers.

John Stuart Mill also discussed the question of liberty and democracy over and over again. As with Tocqueville, there are no definite answers, although Mill was more optimistic than Tocqueville concerning the possibility of combining democracy and liberty. This absence of categoric answers adds to the high level on which Mill treated political questions. Mill sometimes explicitly operated with different kinds of democracy, for example, rational democracy and enlightened democracy in contrast to other kinds of democracy; some of these were more and some were less favourable to the conservation as well as for the realization of freedom and tolerance (p. 159 and p. 166). Within these rather wide limits, Mill is fairly consistent. Unlike Tocqueville, there are probably no occurrences of "democracy" in Mill's terminology in which the presence (or absence) of freedom was explicitly included in the signification of the word.

Acton took a much more negative attitude than Mill towards the possibility of connecting democracy and liberty. This question is a central one for him, and several times he made use of broad historical surveys to show that there had existed for a long time an affinity between democracy and religious persecution and to prove that "the effective distinction between liberty and democracy ... cannot be too strongly drawn" (p. 211). In Acton's argument there are even occurrences which indicate a relationship of mutual incompatibility between freedom and democracy.

An application of "democracy" similar to that of Acton's can be seen in the terminology of other British ideologists, such as Bagehot (p. 175), Herbert Spencer (p. 174), Stephen (p. 204), May (p. 206), Maine (p. 208), and Lecky (p. 213). The latter said, for example, in 1896 that

> Strong arguments may be adduced both from history and from the nature of things that democracy may often prove the direct opposite of liberty.

Lecky also declared that

> A despotism resting on a plebescite is quite as natural a form of democracy as a republic, and some of the strongest democratic tendencies are distinctly adverse to liberty.

Among earlier formulations, in 1859 Disraeli referred to democracy as something which would make liberty insecure and which would culminate in a reaction to despotism. There is a marked contrast between this argument and what he had said twenty years earlier (p. 60).

Among the French ideologists, views similar to those of Acton and Lecky were expressed by Scherer (p. 190), Faguet (p. 197), and Le Bon (p. 200). And among German ideologists, Treitschke held democracy to be compatible with absence of liberty. He said, for example, that St. Petersburg had a democratic character, and he pointed out that Russia was marked by equality in servitude, not by equality in liberty -- every man was subjected to the unlimited power of the Czar (p. 219). Thomas Mann also once said, pure democracy, echte Demokratie, was compatible with absolute rule. He also said, "Russland war in tiefster Seele immer demokratisch" (p. 225). In contrast to all other ideologists from Acton onwards, Mann was in favour of what he here regarded as echte Demokratie,

6. c. Democracy and freedom, incompatible phenomena

Among thinkers who explicitly state that democracy and liberty represent mutually incompatible phenomena or who use "democracy" with a signifi- cation in which absence of freedom is an essential property, Kant occupies a central position. According to him, democracy was necessarily despotism:

> Unter den drei Staatsformen ist die der Demokratie im eigentlichen Ver- stande des Worts notwendig ein Despotism. (p. 49)

His main argument was that there was no separation between legislative and executive power, no representation, and that the majority behaved as if their standpoints had been unanimously agreed upon. This last aspect was touched upon by Schleiermacher (p. 41), as it had been earlier by Hobbes and Spinoza (pp. 50-51). In discussing Kant's political philosophy, Fichte made use of a similar argument and terminology (p. 39). Nevertheless, Fichte used "democracy in the most real sense of the word" as a designation of this political concept, and not "democracy in the more narrow sense of the word" which signified something quite different.

Kant held that democracy was necessarily despotism, not that despotism was necessarily democracy; but Bonald suggested a relation of identity. According to Bonald, democracy and despotism were identical forms of governments (p. 35 and p. 38), and "despotism" was obviously used with a signification that excluded any degree of liberty. This relationship of identity was not expressed in a manner precluding objections, however. A clear association between democracy and despotism, or, more concretely, a declaration that democracy always governs in despotic ways, can also be found in Proudhon. Pointing out the centralized character of democracy, Proudhon said,

> La démocratie ... incapable de gouverner à d'autres conditions que celles de l'unité, qui n'est autre chose que le despotism. (p. 127)

Statements indicating mutual incompatibility between freedom and democ- racy are found in the argument of Sismondi (pp. 71-73). Although this question was probably not explicitly mentioned by Guizot, there is extremely good evidence for thinking that he held freedom of speech and tolerance to be quite incompatible with democracy (pp. 75-78). Nietzsche, too, seems to have regarded freedom and democracy as contrary factors (p. 218), al- though it is difficult to understand precisely what Nietzsche meant by "free- dom".

A related but nevertheless somewhat different problem can be discovered among some ideologists who favoured what they held to be democracy. In the terminology of Buonarroti, "democracy" seems to signify a form of rule marked by a restricted freedom to discuss political matters (p. 19). This restriction of freedom was justified as salus revolutiae. Max Adler severely rounded on those who said liberty was a characteristic of democ- racy. According to him, such an argument mingled democracy and liberal- ism. Liberty and the right to dissent were the characteristics of liberalism, but equality was the essential mark of democracy. He also posited the unan- imous people, das einheitliche Volk, as the prime condition for democracy (p. 276).

6. d. Democracy and dictatorship

Strictly speaking the question of democracy and dictatorship lies outside the topic of this section, but because it is related to questions of liberty and democracy and because it is of interest to contemporary debate, a few comments have been included.

In the form of emergency rule proposed by Babeuf and Buonarroti democracy represented a dictatorial regime. The most explicit occurrence is Babeuf's statement that the terms "democracy" and "Robespierrism" were identical, and the latter term signified a revolutionary dictatorship, or a strict and merciless emergency rule, which was to crush anything that barred the victory of revolution (p. 17). In Babeuf's language, an expression like "leur dictateur" occurs in connection with this view and signifies the rule of Robespierre and the Committee for Public Safety.

In Marx's terminology, however, there is probably no connection between "democracy" and "dictatorship" the few times it occurs. An expression like "Die Diktator des Proletariats" was used only three times in his voluminous writings (Die Klassenkämpfe in Frankreich, 1850; letter to Wedemeyer, 1852; and Kritik des Gothaerprogramms, 1875). Lenin, on the other hand, frequently used the expression "dictatorship of the proletariat" in connection with "democracy". As early as 1905, Lenin denied that there was any incompatibility between dictatorship and democracy. At the same time he also asserted that the decisive victory over czarism was to be "the revolutionary-democratic dictatorship of the proletariat and the peasantry" (p. 254).

In contrast to Lenin, Kelsen and Kautsky said that democracy and dictatorship were contrary phenomena in political life (p. 271). This view occurs in Kautsky only after the Bolshevik Revolution. Rosa Luxemburg differed from both Lenin and Kautsky. She operated with different kinds of dictatorship. According to her, dictatorship of the proletariat was identical with proletarian democracy, and this dictatorship, founded upon the masses, differed greatly from other kinds of dictatorship, for example, bourgeois dictatorship like Jacobin dictatorship or the dictatorship of a single party, ruling in the name of the working class (p. 274). This point of view is central in the thinking of Luxemburg and is also touched upon by Adler (p. 277).

7. Democracy and religion

The relationship between democracy and religion or, more correctly, the relationship between religious faith and religious life and "democracy" is again not a central topic in this work, although it is not without importance. Lamartine occupies a central position among ideologists in favour of a strong association, and possibly even an identification, between democracy and the Cristian faith (p. 104). Cabet also stated,

C'est Jesus, c'est un Dieu qui prescrit ainsi la DÉMOCRATIE parmi tous les Chrétiens et dans l'Humanité tout entière. (p. 117)

In both cases "democracy" was probably used to signify something necessarily marked by Christianity. Renan said that the equalitarian doctrine of
the Jews, as well as the teachings of Jesus, represented

> ... le mouvement démocratique le plus exalté dont l'humanité ait gardé
> le souvenir. (p. 185)

But this statement on the equalitarian character of democracy cannot be
taken to mean that democracy was necessarily Christian.

   Nietzsche's "democracy" also was related to Christianity (p. 217), and
Christians were derogatorily described by him as democrats. However, it
would be going too far to say that "democracy" and "democrats" were used
with a signification of which Christianity was a necessary property, although
there is, without doubt, a strong association (p. 218). Brunetière, too,
said that the Christian religion and democracy were intimately related
phenomena. By the Christian religion, Brunetière evidently had only Catholicism in mind. According to him, Calvinism was aristocratic and analytic,
but Catholicism was collective and democratic (p. 192).

   Among ideologists who considered the Christian religion and democracy
to be very different, if not incompatible, factors, Bonald can be mentioned:

> De religion? la démocratie n'en veut pas, elle a proclamé la loi athée.
> (p. 37)

Similarly Carlyle referred to the close ties between atheism and democracy:

> Thou too, mein Lieber, seest how close it [democracy] is of kin to
> Atheism, and other Isms: he who discovers no God whatever, how shall
> he discover Heroes, the visible Temples of God? (p. 62)

Although Stahl used "democracy" in a way which probably made it compatible
with the Christian religion, "pure democracy", or "reine Demokratie", signifies a rule founded upon a purely human basis, without any religious norms
(p. 69).   Mazzini explicitly rejected "democracy" as a political catchword
when he observed that he and his adherents had fallen as a political party
and must rise as a religious movement (p. 107).   Thomas Mann considered
there to be the greatest possible difference between politics and democracy,
on the one hand, and religion, art, and music, on the other.

   Masaryk is probably the most significant ideologist who favoured what
he designated as "democracy" and who also regarded democracy and religion
as very different phenomena. Although he mainly referred to democracy as
antitheological, not directly antireligious, some formulations may indicate
mutual incompatibility between democracy and religion. For example, he
stated that theocracy demanded belief, but democracy was scientific and
critical; and he also asserted that faith and science were antitheses parallel
to aristocracy and democracy (p. 181). A related view was suggested by
Kelsen, who said that relativism, or belief in the absence of absolute values,
was essential to democratic thought (p. 279), but he did not directly discuss
the relationship between democracy and religion.

   As can be seen, there is by no means a homogenous view of the relationship between religion and democracy. Furthermore, there is no homogeneity
of attitude among those who regard democracy as Christian nor among those
of contrary opinion. In Cabet, Lamartine, and Brunetière the alleged pro-
religious character of democracy was evaluated most positively, but just the

contrary evaluation is apparent in Nietzsche. Bonald, Carlyle, and Stahl pointed to the alleged antireligious character of democracy as a menace, but Masaryk adhered to quite a different view.

8. Democracy, militarism, and pacifism

As with the relationships between democracy and religion and democracy and dictatorship, the question as to whether democracy is militaristic or pacifistic is not central to this work. The question is far from unimportant, however, and probably receives more attention than the question concerning democracy and religion. Lamartine is an important figure among ideologists who declared democracy to be a pacifistic or fairly pacifistic system. In June 1848, he attacked those who desired a revolutionary war to liberate other European peoples. In this connection he used "la République populaire, morale et pacifique" synonymously with "la République démocratique dans le grand et bon sens du mot" (p. 106). In related manner, Charles Maurras used "pure democracy", but hardly unqualified "democracy", to signify a rule necessarily marked by the absence of military spirit (p. 194). On one occasion Marx most probably used "die Frieden predigende Bourgeoisie" synonymously with "demokratische Phraseologie" (p. 152). In these cases a fairly high degree of pacifism is probably included in the significations of "pure democracy", "democratic republic in the great and good sense of the word", etc.

It should be remembered that these views of the pacifistic nature of democracy were by no means accompanied by identical attitudes. For Lamartine, the alleged pacifistic character of democracy was an important advantage, while a contrary attitude was evident in Marx and Maurras. Marx, for example, formulated his statement during the Crimean War when he consistently condemned any attempt at reconciliation with Russia. For Maurras pure democracy primarily meant the impossibility to take revanche for the humiliating defeat of 1871.

Pacifism seems to have been included in the signification in the quoted statements; however, the examples in which democracy is described as unfit for the rational pursuit of war, for example, because of lack of discipline, are more problematic. This aspect is fairly conspicuous in the arguments of Renan (p. 187), Faguet (p. 200), Maine (p. 209), and, to a certain degree, Meinecke (p. 222). Renan in particular returns to this problem. For him the non-military character of democracy was a great advantage when he wrote about Prussian militarism but a great disadvantage when he described the French defeat. In Renan's signification of "democracy", apparently this non-military character was not included in the signification of the word, that is, the non-military character was regarded as a non-conceptual characteristic of the concept 'democracy' although no definite conclusions are possible. A different aspect can be seen in Paul Bourget's terminology, when he said,

Une Démocratie guerrière, est synonyme de cette autre: un cercle carré. (p. 193)

In this case it is evident that democracy was per definitionem necessarily non-military, something Bourget evaluated negatively.

Nietzsche probably regarded war and democracy as contrary phenomena; but it cannot be taken for granted that, by "war", Nietzsche had exclusively military war in mind. It should also be mentioned that Kuusinen obviously held complete non-violence, even accepting one's own death without protest, to be a necessary implication of a democratic programme in contrast to a socialist and revolutionary one (p. 268).

In support of democracy as a militaristic system, Bonald found an identity between democracy and despotism, and held despotism as well as democracy to be violent, cruel, and warlike (p. 38). In one case Proudhon said, "La démocratie, en effet, est essentiellement militariste" (p. 127). Like the conservative Bonald, the radical Quinet stated that the military system of Napoleon, or what Quinet hailed as the military glory of the emperor, represented democracy, even universal democracy (p. 103). Marx also once said,

> Der Krieg mit Russland war der vollständige, offne und wirkliche Befreiung und Vereinigung Deutschlands, war die Herstellung der Demokratie auf den Trümmern der Feudalität und dem kurzen Herrschaftstraum der Bourgeoisie. (p. 145)

In the two latter cases a warlike spirit or militarism is probably not necessarily implicit in the signification of "democracy", even if democracy was held to be highly compatible with such a phenomena.

Of the army as an institution, Brunetière said,

> L'armée enfin analogue ou conforme, dans son organisation comme dans son esprit, à la démocratie dont elle émane. (p. 191)

According to Brunetière, this was because the army was the sole institution in the country to put all social groups under the same discipline, and thus fulfilled the equalitarian aims of democracy. This point was also mentioned once by Faguet, who otherwise held democracy to be unfit for war. Here, too, the army was la grande niveleuse, the only place where money was out of the question, and therefore it was the brilliant and noble expression of democracy (p. 199).

With regard to aggressive versus defensive wars, Godwin said that democracy was unfitted for aggressive wars, but at the same time internal virtues and justice might make democrats into loyal defenders (p. 26). Similarly, Bentham believed that unnecessary wars would not exist in a representative democracy. By unnecessary wars, he evidently had aggressive ones in mind (p. 97). On this point, it can be appended that Robespierre said democracy was the only kind of rule in which every citizen could be counted as a defender. This point was also made by Hegel, who said the right to take part in governmental affairs, as well as the duty to die for the State, was essential to any citizen in a democracy. He made no distinction between aggressive or defensive wars, however. (Cf. footnote 39, chapter III.)

Finally, in relation to violence, Mazzini and Rosa Luxemburg in some cases use "democracy" with a signification which is not only compatible with the use of revolutionary violence but in which such violence was directly included in the signification of the word (p. 108 and p. 275).

Similar to most discussions in this section of my study, the relationship between militarism or pacifism and democracy is characterized by very different views and attitudes. In several cases democracy is regarded as warlike, a view that is evaluated positively as well as negatively; different evaluations are also at hand when democracy is considered as pacifistic. And these different views do not seem to be evenly spaced chronologically. The majority of contexts within which democracy is regarded as warlike are to be found during the first half of the nineteenth century, as, for example in Bonald, Quinet, Marx, when he deemed the establishment of democracy as equivalent to war with Russia, and to a certain degree in Robespierre and Hegel. On the other hand, the view that democracy is pacifistic is to be found mainly after the February Revolution, for example, in Renan, Nietzsche, Maurras, Bourget, Maine, and in Marx's equivalating bourgeois pacifistic talk with democratic phrases.

9. Democracy, science, and intellectual levelling

Few ideologists treated in this work point to any positive connection between science and "democracy". An important exception to this rule is Masaryk, who explicitly said that democracy and science were closely related phenomena, and who also defined the antithesis between faith and science as an antithesis between aristocracy and democracy (p. 181). Kelsen uses a similar argument. Implicitly he probably considered democracy and science to be related, if not almost identical, phenomena (p. 279). The same argument can possibly be found in Bentham and in Godwin.

Although positive statements concerning democracy and science are few, negative ones, which emphasize a great difference, if not incompatibility, between science and democracy, are frequent. In certain cases, probably most typically in Maine and Le Bon, democracy is regarded as something alien, as well as hostile, towards science, technical progress, and rational politics. Maine, for example, emphasized that if for four centuries England had been governed democratically, there would have been no religious reformation, no change of dynasty, no toleration of dissent, and even no accurate calendar; further, the threshing-machine, the power-loom, the spinning-jenny, and possibly also the steam-engine would have been prohibited. Similar arguments occur in Renan, Faguet, Acton, Schérer, Bagehot, and Treitschke, and, to a lesser degree, it is an important trend in the writings of Tocqueville and John Stuart Mill. In most cases it seems reasonable to regard hostility towards science and intellectual levelling as a functional aspect of what was called "democracy" and not directly included in the signification of the term; in other words, hostility towards intellectual competence was a non-conceptual characteristic of the concept 'democracy', with "democracy" as the conceptual designation. Such usage is fairly typical in Maine's use of "democracy", for example. On the other hand, Schérer (p. 190), Faguet (p. 197), and Treitschke (p. 221) used "democracy" in a way that probably included intellectual stagnation, or the cult of incompetence, in the signification of this word.

According to Paul Bourget's somewhat different point of view, the theory of democracy was not in conformity with science, and especially not with biology. He held that evolution, in contrast to revolution, and selection, which implied hereditary inequality, furnished sufficient bases for the falseness of the democratic theory (p. 193). The traditionalist French ideologist Brunetière implied that democracy was very different from science when he declared that Calvin had transformed popular and democratic religion into an aristocratic one. His main argument was that individualism and analysis were aristocratic but collective faith, as found in Catholicism, was available to all and therefore democratic (p. 192). Although other ideologists who held democracy to be alien to science regarded this as an important disadvantage, Brunetière evidently held the contrary opinion.

10. Value judgements implicit in the signification of "democracy"

Eulogistic and dyslogistic use of the term

Although it is often rather easy to see whether a political thinker uses "democracy" to express something he likes or dislikes (when the context or the general attitude is taken into consideration), few statements per se include negative or positive value judgements. When, for example, Engels said, "Die Demokratie das ist heutzutage der Kommunismus," most people will say that Engels here uses "democracy" appreciatively or in an honorific way. This conclusion is only possible, however, when Engels' general political ideology is taken into account. To people who know nothing about Engels, a derogatory application might look to be just as reasonable, since there is little in the signification of "democracy" in the statement as such to reveal approval or disapproval. A quite different relationship is evident, for example, in Lipset's statement:

> A basic premise of this book is that democracy is not only or even primarily a means through which different groups can attain their ends or seek the good society; it is the good society itself in operation. (Lipset, Political Man, the Social Basis of Politics, 1960, p. 403)

In this case, the qualification "good" is directly included in the signification of "democracy", so that "democracy" is not only used in honorific way but is a eulogism, good by its conceptual characteristics, or good per definitionem. Similarly, "democracy" is most obviously a dyslogism, bad per definitionem, when Thomas Aquinas includes the qualification "unjust rule", or "iniquum regimen", in the signification of "democracy":

> Si vero iniquum regimen exerceatur per multos, democratia nuncupatur. (Aquinas, De regimene principum, Liber primus, Selected Political Writings, Oxford 1948, p. 6)

In this study occurrences of "democracy" which can be classified as either obviously dyslogistic or obviously eulogistic are rather few, and even occurrences that are probably dyslogistic or eulogistic are far from frequent. Concerning dyslogistic application, "democracy" can probably be regarded as a dyslogism in Bonald's statements that democracy and despotism were identical forms of rule (p. 35), and also when Kant declared that democracy was necessarily despotism (p. 49). In Kant's as well as in Bonald's language, "despotism" evidently signifies something which is per se bad or unjust; this seems to be a universal trend in later political terminology, although it does not apply to the Greek original of the English word "despotism". It is probably also a dyslogism when Fichte says that democracy, in the real sense of the word, is an illegal constitution, "eine rechtswidrige Verfassung" (p. 39), although other uses of "democracy" by Fichte are hardly in conformity with this trend.

Dyslogistic application of "democracy" was further at hand when Sismondi, inter alia, marked out the activity of demagogues as a necessary characteristic of democracy (p. 71), and when Sorel said democracy was a school of servility, delation, and demoralization (p. 248). Nietzsche, too, in certain cases seems to include a Werth-Ernidriegung in his signification of "democracy" (p. 217), and "democracy" is certainly a dyslogism when Schérer, by some persuasive method, declared democracy to be "la dépression de tout ce qui tend a dépasser le niveau" (p. 190).

Further examples of dyslogistic application are Burke's "a perfect democracy [is] the most shameless thing in the world" (p. 29), and Faguet's possible use of "démocratie" synonymously with "culte de l'incompétance" (p. 197). Bagehot asserted that placing the entire control of the political action of the State in the hands of the common labourers was the special characteristic of democracy, and that this class was the most aggressive, the least reasonable, and the least tolerant one (p. 175).

For eulogistic application of "democracy", still fewer occurrences can be found. The young Marx can probably be classified here for his use of "Ein demokratischer Staat" synonymously with "eine Gemeinschaft der Menschen für ihre höchsten Zwecke" (p. 132). Similarly, "democracy" was probably a eulogism in Michelet's "La démocratie, c'est l'amour dans la Cité, et l'initiation" (p. 100), and also in the very high-pitched formulations, if not revelations, of Quinet (p. 102). Some indications of a eulogistic use of "democracy" can be seen in Masaryk's terminology, although clear examples cannot be found (p. 182). And a similar indication occurs in the argument of the young Bagehot when he says,

Democracy in its proper sense, is that form by which a wise and enlightened nation govern themselves. (p. 175)

On this point there is a marked difference in relation to later statements by Bagehot. Finally Maine gave several references to the dyslogistic, as well as eulogistic, use of "democracy" in contemporary political language and, according to him, such language represented confused thinking (p. 208).

11. Charges of misuse of "democracy"

In several cases a political thinker uses "democracy" in a way which he says differs from other uses of the term; for example, Guizot stated that science defined democracy as government of the people, while he himself declared that democracy was a war cry or the banner of the poor in their struggle with the rich (p. 76). In this case, Guizot evidently regarded his definition as the correct one; however, he does not allege that others misuse the word, at least not explicitly. This is a common trend in contemporary political debate, where the tendency to feel as if one were the legitimate owner of a word is rather widespread, especially in relation to words which are used in an honorific way by onesself.

In the work Democracy in a World of Tensions, 1951 (pp. 462-66), there is substantial material concerning charges of misuse of "democracy" in political debates after 1945. Yet explicit charges of misuse were more frequent and also more intense among contributions not included in the volume. Of the alleged misuse of another central political term, Milton Friedman states that "liberalism" was the proper and rightful label for the political and economic viewpoints elaborated in his book. He added, however, referring to a quotation from Schumpeter, that as a supreme, if unintended, com-

pliment the enemies of private enterprise had thought it advantageous to
adopt this label

> ... so that liberalism has, in the United States, come to have a very
> different meaning than it did in the nineteenth century or does today over
> much of the Continent of Europe. (<u>Capitalism and Freedom</u>, 1962, p. 5)

Friedman also maintains that in the name of welfare and equality, the
twentieth-century liberal favoured a revival of the very policies of State
intervention and paternalism against which classical liberalism fought. An
explicit charge of misuse of "liberalism" was not directly formulated, however, although he underlined the striking change in the meaning attached to
this term and contrasted classical liberalism with what he considered "the
corruption of the term liberalism". Thus we may speak of an implicit
charge of misuse of this word.

Generally speaking, direct allegations of misuse are not common during
the period for this inquiry, even among people who favoured what they named
"democracy". There are, however, a few charges of misuse. When Robespierre asserted that "republic" and "democracy" were synonymous, he
added that this was the case in spite of vulgar misuse (p. 7). Here Robespierre was thinking primarily of the misuse of "republic" and not so much
of "democracy". A much clearer case can be found in Bentham's attack on
those who used "democracy" and "anarchy" synonymously. To him, this
kind of terminology was typical of certain ministerial and absolutist periodicals, and he described it as "twaddle and anility" (p. 98).

A clear charge of misuse of "democracy" occurred in Cabet. While
saying himself that communism was the realization of democracy, he continued that if the bourgeoisie were to keep the people in serfdom and poverty
forever, the title "democracy" which it intended to use was nothing but a
lie (p. 117). Tocqueville once emphasized that the terms "democracy" and
"democratic government" could have only one meaning according to the real
sense of these words: a form of rule under which the people participated
more or less in the governmental affairs. This sense was intimately connected with political freedom. To call a government "democratic" under
which political freedom was not found was, therefore, a palpable absurdity.
In his own words:,

> Appeler démocratique un gouvernement où la liberté politique ne se trouve
> pas, c'est dire une absurdité palpable, suivant le véritable sens du mot.
> (p. 91)

John Stuart Mill pointed out two trends in political terminology; according
to him,

> two very different ideas are usually confounded under the name democ-
> racy. The pure idea of a democracy, according to its definition, is the
> government of the whole people, equally represented. Democracy as
> commonly conceived and hitherto practiced, is the government of the
> whole people by a mere majority of the people, exclusively represented.

Proportional representation represented "the only true type of democracy",
while the other kinds were referred to as "the falsely-called democracies
which now prevail, and from which the current idea of democracy is exclusively derived. " This latter was also mentioned as that form of government
"which now usurps the name of democracy". As a example, Mill pointed
out the "American democracy, which is constructed on this faulty model"

(p.165). These charges are made interesting by the fact that the trend, which was clearly admitted to be the predominant one, was presented as a terminological usurpation. This charge seldom occurs in disputes concerning political terminology; generally, an allegedly predominant trend is used to serve as a justification for accusing others of misuse.

These charges of misuse, made by Robespierre, Bentham, Cabet, Tocqueville, and John Stuart Mill, were all formulated by men who tried to reserve "democracy" for something which they themselves evaluated positively. A quite different attitude can be seen in Charles Maurras' attacks on those who used "democracy" with a signification different from his own. According to Maurras, every kind of organization needed differentiations and hierarchies, and he defined the essence of democracy as the denial or neglect of this eternal law. He appended:

> On a discuté sur cette essence. Mais elle n'est pas discutable. C'est une folie pure que de changer le sens des mots. Et politiquement, c'est plus qu'une folie, c'est une faute grave. (p.195)

In addition to these explicit charges of misuse, there are several statements which implicitly charge misuse of "democracy" among people who use the word differently from the writer. Proudhon, for instance, wrote of an alleged relation of synonymity between "socialism", "republic", and "democracy" and added that anyone who rejected such a relationship of synonymity was neither democrat, socialist, nor republican (p.122). One may also find an implicit charge of misuse in Engels' statement that contemporary democracy was communism, when he added:

> Eine andere Demokratie kann nur noch in den Köpfen theoretischer Visionäre existieren. (p. 137)

A similar accusation occurs in Luxemburg's statement that democracy was not found where capitalists and workers were engaged in parliamentary debate, but where the workers violently crushed the rule of the capitalists, "nur dort ist Demokratie die kein Volksbetrug ist" (p. 122).

Max Adler emphasized that social democracy was the only true democracy; paradoxically he said political democracy was no democracy at all,

> ...die politische Demokratie, ...die eigentlich keine Demokratie ist und daher überwinden werden muss, wenn man Demokratie will. (p. 277)

In this connection Lenin once rejected an expression like "democracy in general" because in political life concrete forms such as bourgeois democracy and proletarian democracy were frequently to be found but democracy in general never was (p. 259). Sidney Webb spoke ironically about people who used "democracy" to connote a political form of rule only, and he even declared them to be empirical fossils from a prescientific age. Webb also maintained that he differed greatly from people who could see no more inconsistency between democracy and unrestrained capitalist enterprise than Washington and Jefferson did between democracy and slave-owning (pp. 234-37).

The criteria for charging other people of misuse of a certain political term are seldom presented by the ideologists discussed in this work. In most cases the correctness of one's own terminology and the incorrectness of clearly different trends seem to be regarded as self-evident; like, for example, references to the "true sense of the word", but with few concrete arguments to support the use of "true". Contrary to contemporary debates, there are here few attempts to mark out an historical trend, or an alleged

historical trend, to justify a special terminology. An exception to this rule
is Sidney Webb who pointed out Tocqueville to prove that the progress of
democracy was something more than merely substituting one kind of political machinery for another.

12. Central examples of ambiguous application of "democracy"

As has been observed, few, if any, of the political thinkers treated in this
work are absolutely consistent in their use of "democracy". (At least, if
by "consistent" we mean attribution of only one connotation to the term
"democracy" over a period of years.) In this section is discussed, not a
list of different kinds of change within the significations of "democracy",
but ambiguities central to the thinking of the various ideologists.

Among the earliest cases, a relatively clear ambiguity occurs in
Fichte's terminology when, in the same work, he uses the expression
"democracy in the most real sense of the term" in a different way from
"democracy in the more narrow sense of the term" (p. 40). More ambiguities occur in Tocqueville's terminology, and especially in his use of
"democracy" to signify: (1) a potential danger to liberty; (2) something
directly alien to liberty; and (3) something of which liberty was the essential property (p. 85 , p. 84 , and p. 91). Typical ambiguities can also be
seen when Tocqueville used "democracy" to signify something contrary to
socialism (p. 87), and in a few other cases to indicate a relationship of
synonymity between "democracy" and "socialism" (p. 88). Similarly, a
central ambiguity occurs in Carlyle's language. Generally he used "democracy" to signify absence of hero worship, or absence of true leadership, but
on one occasion he stated that

> ... all that Democracy ever meant lies there; the attainment of a truer
> and truer Aristocracy or Government again by the Best. (p. 66)

"Democracy" with different significations occurred several times in the
language of Marx and Engels, where "democracy" was sometimes used to
connote the rule of the proletariat (p. 143), sometimes a proper means to
such a rule (p. 140), sometimes communism itself (p. 137), but at other
times something quite different from communism and socialism (p. 146).
In some cases "democracy" signified something almost identical with revolution (p. 145), and in other cases something that was regarded as a great
danger for any kind of revolutionary activity (p. 148). The works of Proudhon probably contain the most ambiguous use of "democracy" ever produced.
During certain periods of his life he believed "democracy" synonymous with
"socialism" (p. 122), and in other periods it connoted something extremely
different from socialism (p. 127). In certain cases it meant sovereignty of
the people (p. 122), which included imperative mandates; in others, quite
the contrary (p. 119). And similar statements apply to democracy being or
not being a State (p. 124), democracy being centralistic and militaristic,
and democracy being federalistic and built upon self-ruling units (p. 129).

In spite of a fairly high degree of consistency, some ambiguity can also
be seen in John Stuart Mill's use of "democracy". In one case, for example,
he referred to "the democracy below the middle class", and in the same essay said that democracy was identical, or almost identical, with rule of the
middle class (p. 160). Very early in Bagehot, democracy, in its proper
sense, was said to be that form by which a wise and enlightened nation governed themselves, but his later use definitely departed from such an appli-

cation (p. 175). A still more obvious ambiguity is found in Thomas Mann's Betrachtungen eines Unpolitischen, in which democracy was explicitly and frequently said to be identical with politics, and politics was said to be the contrary of culture, religion, and art. This did not, however, prevent Mann from declaring that true democracy, wahre Demokratie, was primarily to be found in the pious life of the Russian peasant or from emphasizing that this was absolutely distinct from any kind of politics (p. 225).

Within socialist thought, Jaurès alternated between using "democracy" to signify (1) something which was no real phenomenon as long as the capitalist mode of production existed, and (2) something which could coexist only with capitalism (p. 238). Lenin several times alternated between the following statements: (1) democracy was a form of State; and (2) democracy was no form of State (pp. 256-58). He also stated that democracy was of necessity a form of rule influenced by the capitalists, yet that revolutionary socialist rule in Russia represented a higher kind of democracy (pp. 259-60). An ambiguous application can also be seen in Rosa Luxemburg's later use of "democracy", in certain cases, to signify the violent conquest of political power by the armed proletariat but in other cases to express quite different phenomena (p. 275).

Other examples could be mentioned; and if lesser degrees of ambiguity were to be included, references to nearly the whole of this work would have to be made.

It is much more important, however, to point out that such ambiguous use of "democracy" is of the highest importance in the study of the authors examined here. It may be expected that when a political thinker uses a central word with mutually different significations, the properties which constitute these differences are generally apt to be of minor importance in relation to his general political outlook; but in this work has been found a contrary trend. Some of the most central concepts are in question; for example, liberty and human dignity for Tocqueville; the rule of the proletariat for Marx and Engels; a new aristocracy and a real leadership for Carlyle; centralization versus self-government for Proudhon; politics versus culture, art, and religion for Thomas Mann; capitalism versus rule by the proletariat for Lenin; and the revolutionary conquest of political power for Luxemburg. That ambiguities are most frequently found in connection with the most central topics can hardly be regarded as unique, however, or especially limited to use of "democracy". To mention a few examples, central terms like "reason" and "passion" for David Hume and "war" for Hobbes and Nietzsche were used by these thinkers with different significations, although they are frequently quoted as if they attributed only one connotation to these terms.

Ambiguities and inconsistent terminology are very often given negative evaluation, as something which ought to be avoided. There are without doubt fields in which consistent terminology is of a high importance. Schoolboys and scientists generally ought to avoid ambiguities, but this does not apply to literature and especially not to poetry. Although in parts of this work I may have been tempted to play the pedantic, I cannot wish to see all ambiguity eliminated. Politics and political thinking are not absolutely logical (to make a brief statement about a wide problem), and many fascinating aspects of ideologies would disappear if all terms were used consistently. In political thinking in general, much harm has sometimes been done by overly logical system-makers who try to force political thinking into a waterproof system which is easy to understand and easy to grasp. Most symptomatic

is perhaps the fate of Marx's thinking. His very vivid, manifold, and sometimes contradictory thoughts were presented to humanity via two typical
system-makers, Kautsky and Plekhanov; both of them without doubt very
learned, but neither with the mental surplus that <u>inter alia</u> characterized
Marx. The new creed, flat-footed and dogmatic, presented as Marxism had
in many respects little to do with the original thought; but many people
prefer dogma, they like to feel as if they are resting on a firm basis of
principles, and most socialists generally preferred Kautsky's version to the
original.

13. Countries mentioned as democracies

In discussing which countries have been mentioned as democracies, or, to
speak more technically, countries which have been referred to as belonging
to the denotata of "democracy", I limit myself to explicit statements as to
whether a country is or is not a democracy, and not which countries the
respective thinkers would have classed among democracies according to
their own criteria if they had been asked such a direct question. Since explicit statements can hardly be held as equivalent with which countries they
regarded as democracies, this survey will therefore, in a certain sense,
not be complete. However, the alternative method of treating the problem
would give rise to questions of an extremely hypothetical nature.

a. America

America, or more concretely, the United States of America was most frequently referred to as a democracy. America was classed as a democracy
by Thomas Paine as early as 1792. "It is representation ingrafted upon
democracy. -- What Athens was in miniature, America will be in magnitude"
(p. 23). Whereas Paine referred to America as a democracy only once,
Bentham, the first European political thinker to do so, frequently referred
to America as a democracy and even as the only democracy in the world
(pp. 94, 98). A short reference to America as a democracy was also put
forth by Macaulay (p. 74), and Carlyle said several times that America was
a democracy (p. 65). The most frequent and consistent assertions that
America was a democracy were obviously made by Tocqueville (pp. 79-87).
On one occasion in 1848, Marx referred to the millionaires in New York in
order to prove that anyone in favour of democracy was not therefore necessarily in favour of communism (p. 142), and he later described America as
"das Musterland des Demokratenschwindels" (p. 152). Engels, too, mentioned that America was a democratic republic (p. 155). John Stuart Mill
said several times that America was a democracy, although he also stated
the contrary (pp. 162-65); and John Austin believed that America was certainly a democracy according to the <u>forma imperii</u>, or the form and nature
of sovereignty (p. 169).
    Others who were of the opinion that America was a democracy are Her-
bert Spencer (p. 174), Maine (p. 209), Acton (p. 211), Treitschke (p. 221),
Sorel (p. 247), and Lenin (p. 259). Needless to say, their evaluations differ.
    With regard to the contrary, that America was no democracy, a short
remark from the young Marx may be mentioned:

Sie[die vollständige Demokratie]besteht vorläufig in Amerika noch nicht,
da seine Bürger meist Eigentümer sind . (footnote 9, chapter IX)

Although Guizot clearly held America to be a republic, he denied it the label
"democratic republic"; and according to him, the Americans had never
thought of calling their republic "democratic". Guizot found this to be quite
correct, since the attainment of independence, as well as the foundation of
the republican form of rule, had been the common task of all classes under
the guidance of the richest, the most elevated, and the most educated. It
was obviously these last factors that Guizot considered incompatible with a
democratic form of rule (p. 78). Because of non-proportional representation, or no representation of minorities, John Stuart Mill occasionally
classed America under that form of rule "which now usurps the name democracy" (p. 165). The most distinct statement was probably formulated by
Faguet, who most explicitly said that America was not a democracy but a
constitutional monarchy, and nothing but a constitutional monarchy, because
of the independent and strong position of the president (p. 199). However,
even Faguet once referred to America as a political democracy (p. 199).

b. England

Whereas America was frequently referred to as a democracy, almost the
contrary was true where England (or Great Britain) was concerned. The
young Disraeli alone frequently declared that England was a democracy, and
a "democracy of the noblest character" (p. 58). John Austin also said in
1859 that England should be classed among democracies, according to the
forma imperii, but not according to the forma regiminis; and we have seen
his similar classification of the American form of government. Austin admitted that America was more democratic than England, but he added that
the British Government was decidedly more democratic than any other which
had governed a great nation through a long and eventful period (p. 169).
Austin also introduced another criterion in describing the British Government as, in spirit and effect, the most democratic of all governments past
and present, giving as his reason that the interests and opinions of the entire
population, not only the sovereign body, were habitually consulted by the
legislative and executive power. A hint that Green described England as a
democracy is found in his reference of 1868 to the time "before we had a
democratic House of Commons" (p. 172). Later, Le Bon said that England
was the most democratic country in the world (p. 201), and Nietzsche said
contemptuously that the Englishman was a democrat (p. 218).

c. France

France is the European country which has been described most frequently as
a democracy. But there are few general statements, i. e. , those which are
not limited to one or several of the many constitutional periods in French
political life; for example, Tocqueville in 1856 referred to a certain social
phenomenon in France "après soixante ans de démocratie" (p. 90). May
said that the history of England in modern times was the history of liberty,
not of democracy, while the history of France was "the history of democracy, not of liberty" (p. 206). Guizot referred to two works in which
French society generally was said to be a democratic one (p. 75), but

otherwise, there are very few general statements in relation to France as such. It is most fruitful, therefore, to discuss different periods separately.

c 1. Revolutionary France   The most distinct reference to revolutionary France as a democracy was made by Robespierre, February 1794, when he described the French as the first people on earth who had established true democracy (p. 10). Saint-Just also spoke of democracy as established in revolutionary France (p. 13); and Buonarroti said that democracy had existed during the tides of the revolutionary events, but had later been lost. The identity between democracy and the rule of Robespierre was pointed out by Babeuf, who even said that "Robespierrism" and "democracy" were perfectly identical words (p. 17).

Among persons of quite a different political outlook, Burke seems to have refused France the label "democracy". In 1790 he said,

It [France] affects to be a pure democracy, though I think it in direct train of becoming shortly a mischievous and ignoble oligarchy. (p. 30)

On the other hand, de Maistre probably thought democracy to exist in revolutionary France (p. 35), and Bonald explicitly described revolutionary France as a democracy, which he held as identical with despotism (p. 35). In contrast, Hegel said that revolutionary rule in France had never been a democracy.

In der französischen Revolution ist ... niemals die republikanische Verfassung als eine Demokratie zustande gekommen. (p. 46)

Later, the French Revolution in particular, rather than the revolutionary rule, was referred to as a democracy by different persons such as Michelet (p. 101), Quinet (p. 102), Lamartine (p. 104), Mazzini (p. 107), and Carlyle (p. 62). Engels twice described the French Revolution as the rise of democracy in Europe. In 1843 he probably regarded this revolution as an exclusively political event, or as a struggle concerning forms of government (p. 134), although he emphasized the purely social character of the revolution two years later.

Die französische Revolution war von Anfang bis zu Ende eine soziale Bewegung, und nach ihr ist eine rein politische Demokratie vollends ein Unding geworden. (p. 137)

c 2. The First Empire.   There is not much evidence for the classification of different French forms of rule after Robespierre and up to the First Empire. The only exceptions are probably Babeuf and Buonarroti, who did not consider France as a democracy after the summer of 1794. Nor is there much concerning the First Empire. Of Napoleon's contemporaries, Bonald is probably the only one who thought that Napoleon's rule was a democracy (p. 38). Later, Quinet said that democracy had never triumphed more openly than in Bonaparte's proclamation. Quinet also held that in his earlier victories, Bonaparte had represented the future of French democracy, and that the Emperor, in his military victories, had even been the harbinger of universal democracy (p. 103). Essential points for Quinet were evidently the equalitarian character of the French imperial army which had made la carrière ouverte aux talents and the Emperor's ability to make the French

nation feel and act as a unanimous people. There is fairly strong evidence
that Charles Maurras (p. 195) and Lecky (p. 213) considered the First Empire to be subsumable under what they labelled "democracy". Lecky, for
example, said:

> A despotism resting on a plebiscite is quite as natural a form of democ-
> racy as a republic.

c 3. The Second Republic. There is little pertinent material concerning
the two monarchies after 1815, although several persons discuss the new
regime of February, 1848. Lamartine said that France had changed from
an oligarchy into a complete democracy (p. 106). Among contemporary
French ideologists, Tocqueville (p. 88), as well as Guizot (p. 77), Proudhon (p. 119), and probably Renan (p. 184), said that France had become a
democracy in 1848. Persons otherwise as different as Guizot and Proudhon
evaluated this negatively: Guizot, because he identified democracy with
violent social revolution, and Proudhon, because at that time democracy was
regarded as an alienation of popular sovereignty by rule of elected representatives. Outside France, John Stuart Mill, in polemics with Lord Brough-
ham, hailed the Constitution of 1848 as the digest of the elementary doctrine
of representative democracy (p. 161). Several other ideologists such as
Carlyle, Marx, and Engels frequently used "democracy" in connection with
revolutionary events, 1848, but not especially in relation to the republican
constitution of France.

c 4. The Second Empire. Lecky (p. 213) and Charles Maurras (p. 195)
considered the Second Empire to be a democracy. As mentioned earlier,
Lecky said, "A despotism resting on a plebescite is quite as natural a form
of democracy as a republic, " and on this point he obviously had the Second
Empire in mind. Maurras, too, is fairly clear on this point, especially
when he described the plebiscitarian or cæsaristic form of government as
representing one form of democracy. The clearest statement, however,
was probably formulated by Bagehot, who declared Louis Napoleon to be a
Benthamite despot and said: "The French Empire is really the best finished
democracy which the world has ever seen" (p. 175).
    A somewhat ambiguous trend can be seen in Tocqueville's use of "democ-
racy" in relation to the Second Empire. On the one hand, Tocqueville once
charged those who used the terms "democracy" and "democratic government"
to designate forms of rule in which political liberty was not found of misuse
of these terms (p. 91), and on this point he most probably had the propagandists of the Empire in mind. On the other hand, however, in 1856 he
used "democracy" to describe something which had existed in France from
the Revolution up to that time (p. 90), and in one case he also used an expression like "democratic despotism" (p. 90), probably as a bold criticism
of contemporary imperial rule. In several cases he also referred to contemporary French society as a democratic society. It can be added that
Renan also probably spoke of democracy as something which had existed in
France before 1870 (p. 188).

c 5. The Commune. Marx was the only political thinker in this study to define the Commune as democratic. As early as 1871, Marx stated, "Sie [die Kommune] verschaffte der Republik die Grundlage wirklich demokratischer Einrichtungen" (p. 153). By truly democratic institutions Marx first of all had in mind the fact that governing power was given to the servants of the people. The state was no longer superior to the people, and the standing army and the police were replaced by the armed people itself. Direct control of the people over the rulers, and especially the fact that every representative might at any time be recalled by the electorate, was contrasted by Marx with usual parliamentary rule, in which the people were said to decide once in three or six years which member of the ruling class should represent and crush the people in Parliament.

c 6. The Third Republic. Several authors, such as Renan (p. 188), Bourget (p. 193), Le Bon (p. 200), Sorel (p. 248), Thomas Mann (p. 225), Lenin (p. 259), speak about democracy in France in the time of the Third Republic. Engels, too, referred to France as a democratic republic (p.156). Few of these statements are, however, sufficiently elaborated to warrant further comments. Their political interest lies mainly in the consequences they attributed to the fact that France was a democracy and in their evaluations of this fact, and not whether or not France was a democracy. One exception is Jaurès, who on some occasions said democracy in France would not become a reality as long as class differences prevailed (p. 238). On other occasions, Jaurès used "democracy" with a different signification, however. Some degree of differentiation can also be seen in Maurras' thinking. According to him, France was probably a democracy during the Second Empire and the Third Republic. This republic was not, however, what he considered a pure democracy before the end of the nineteenth century, since a certain military spirit and a desire for forceful reunion with Alsace-Lorraine had been the previous characteristics. Evidently he held that an absence of military spirit was a necessary criterion for France to be, not merely a democracy, but a pure democracy (p. 194).

d. Germany

In our material, Germany, or the German states, are seldom referred to as democracies. The military despotism of Brandenburg and Hessen was quoted by Bonald as proof of an alleged affinity between democracy and military despotism (p. 36), but there is no absolute proof that Bonald directly held Brandenburg and Hessen to be democracies. Later, Nietzsche referred to the German Reich as a semi-democracy (p. 218). On the other hand, outstanding German personalities such as Meinecke and Thomas Mann said that Germany was not a democracy during the First World War. Meinecke, for example, used "democratic world" to designate Germany's enemies; and Thomas Mann frequently said that democracy was un-German (p. 223). Once Mann used the expression "German democracy", however, but he added:

Die deutsche Demokratie ist nicht echte Demokratie, denn sie ist nicht Politik, nicht Revolution.

e. Greece

References to Greece as a democracy are apparently limited to Greek political life in antiquity. Hegel asserted that democracy was the essential
characteristic of political life in classical Greece (p. 45). A shorter reference was formulated by Paine: "What Athens was in miniature, America will
be in magnitude" (p. 23). Burke probably had Greece in mind when he said,

> Until now we have seen no examples of considerable democracies. The
> ancients were better acquainted with them. (p. 30)

Treitschke later referred to Pericles as a democratic ruler (p. 221). Acton
described the democracy in Athens, and especially during the time of Anoxa-
goras, Protagoras, and Socrates, to support his thesis of a long affinity
between democracy and religious persecution and also to underline his view
that the distinction between liberty and democracy could not be too strongly
drawn (p. 211).

Among authors who were more or less skeptical about democracy in
Greece, Bentham referred to representative democracy as the only true
democracy, and told people not to look to Greece and Italy;

> Whatever else has been called democracy, has had nothing of democracy
> but the name.(p. 95)

For different reasons, Lamartine also seems to have denied the term "democracies" to the ancient republics. According to him, these republics were
numerous aristocracies, quite different from the Christian genius of the
democratic republic (p. 105).

Carlyle seems to have refused to give the label "democracy" to Athens
as well as to Rome, since the work there was done, "not by loud voting and
debating of many, but by wise insight and ordering of the few" (p. 61). In
a similar way Faguet said that the antique city-states were not democracies
because they were ruled by powerful and enlightened aristocracies. The
only exception was Athens, where democracy had established itself for a
short time, but this he held to have coincided with the decline of the nation
(p. 198).

In a somewhat different reference to the Greek use of "democracy",
Stahl pointed to an alleged difference between the contemporary and the
classical Greek usages of "democracy". According to Stahl, "democracy"
to the Greeks signified rule by the poorer class (p. 68). Although Aristotle
used "democracy" in this way, such a statement is rather oversimplified,
since the Greek usage contained more aspects than this. (Cf. Christopher-sen,
op. cit. , pp. 78-83.)   Burke (p. 30) and Faguet (p. 198) drew attention to
Aristotle's use of "democracy". The former did so in order to show that
democracy had many striking points of resemblance with tyranny; the latter,
to prove that democracy was not governed by laws.

f. Norway

In spite of having occasionally been painted as a stable and traditional democracy, Norway appears only once in the authors studied, and this mention
was far from flattering. In November, 1847, Engels asserted that Norway
and Switzerland were democracies. He added, however, that the old Christian and Teutonic barbarism were to be found in these two countries espe-

cially. He emphasized that modern democracy, in civilized countries, had nothing whatever in common with this primitive peasant-democracy (p. 141).

g. Russia

g 1. Czarist Russia. Czarist Russia was probably mentioned as a democracy twice. Treitschke held that St. Petersburg had a democratic character because of its equalitarian tendency, even if this was equality in serfdom (p. 219). Thomas Mann said that Russia had always been democratic -- "Russland war in tiefster Seele immer demokratisch" -- and that only a narrowminded Western politician could consider Russian democracy and czarist autocracy to be contrary phenomena (p. 225). On the other hand, several persons pointed to Russia as the contrary of democracy. Macaulay, for example, mentioned Russian autocracy and American democracy as the extreme counterparts on the political spectrum (p. 74). Marx maintained that European democracy and Russian absolutism were eternal enemies (p. 145 and p. 152).

g 2. Bolshevik Russia. Although Lenin said several times that the Bolsheviks had established a democracy of a new and higher kind in revolutionary Russia (p. 258), the contrary view, that this rule was definitely not a democracy, can be seen among prominent Bolsheviks such as Trotsky (p. 261), Radek (p. 267), Kuusinen (p. 268), and to a certain degree, Bukharin (p. 267). Several of Lenin's statements can be reasonably interpreted to imply that revolutionary rule in Russia was definitely not a democracy (p. 259). All of the critics of Bolshevism said that this revolutionary rule was not a democracy. In different ways and from different premises such a view was adhered to by Kautsky (p. 272), Luxemburg (p. 273), Max Adler (p. 277), Kelsen (p. 279), and Bertrand Russell (p. 281). Generally this was evaluated negatively; revolutionary rule in Russia was attacked because it was not democratic. The only exception was Bertrand Russell. Although admitting that Bolshevik Russia was not a democracy, in 1920, he was almost alone in asking the question of what was politically possible, given the existing state of affairs in Russia. It is evident that Russell, at that time, did not even hope that democracy would be immediately established in Russia.

> If Russia were governed democratically, according to the will of the majority, the inhabitants of Moscow and Petrograd would die of starvation.

h. Switzerland

A short reference to Switzerland as a democracy can be found in Hegel (p. 46). There is a more differentiated discussion in Sismondi, who marked out some cantons, but not all, as democracies (p. 71). As mentioned earlier, Engels said that Switzerland, or, more correctly, die Urschweiz, represented a barbaric democracy (p. 141). Marx also once referred to the millionaires in Berne as standing for democracy (p. 142). Finally, Treitschke held certain Swiss cantons to have an immediate democracy, different from representative democracy, and it seems quite certain that he held Switzerland as such to be a democracy (p. 220).

14. Frequency of "democracy" in political thought

Strictly speaking, questions concerning the frequency with which a certain word occurs in texts can only be answered by making use of quantitative methods (counting words, tables, columns, etc.) if frequency were the topic of the research. Although factors such as lack of time and insufficient funds have prevented me from undertaking time-consuming research of this nature, a few opinions seem justified, since this vast field will scarcely be covered by quantitative research in the immediate future and since quantitative analysis may be followed by vague and sometimes misleading generalizations.

As has already been indicated, the French Revolution brought the word "democracy" out of the study and into actual politics. The material studied shows a certain degree of use of the word, although it is not frequently found. Except for a very few unimportant occurrences, "democracy" figures in only one of Robespierre's speeches; it appears more often in the political terminology of Babeuf and Buonarroti. From a qualitative point of view, however, "democracy" occupies a central position, since it seems to have been used when the speaker or writer intended to say something important. A similar statement, qualitatively important but quantitatively infrequent, can be made about Godwin, and also about Paine, whose use of this word was limited to a few occurrences.

Nor was frequent use of "democracy" typical of contemporaries such as Burke, de Maistre, Bonald, Kant, and Fichte, whose attitudes towards the French Revolution were negative. While occurrences are obvious, some even of central importance, no one seems to have felt that he was obliged permanently to repeat this derogatory use of "democracy" in order to be regarded as a faithful anti-Jacobin.

In general, a decline in frequency set in after the Revolution in France. Constant, de Staël, and Châteaubriand seldom used "democracy", nor did Bentham, until 1809. At that time, however, a sudden change took place in Bentham's terminology, "democracy", from Plan of Parliamentary Reform and onwards, became a key term in his language. Frequent use of "democracy" was not found in the terminology of Bentham's friend James Mill, however. During the 1820's, some degree of frequency can be seen in Hegel's terminology, although a broad application is not to be found until the middle of the 1830's, when Tocqueville in particular raised "democracy" to a central position in political language.

The years preceding the February Revolution give evidence to an important increase in application of the word. In addition to Tocqueville, Engels, for example, used "democracy" increasingly during the years before 1848. Considérant used "democracy" very seldom in earlier years, but suddenly applied it extensively after 1843. That year Considérant emphasized:

Le mot de Démocratie est le mot à-la-fois le plus profond, le plus général et le plus puissant qui reste aujourd'hui dans le courant de l'actualité, le seul qui ait un avenir de forte vie dans la publicité active. (p. 114)

During the February Revolution itself, occurrences of "democracy" swell like a large wave. A distinct increase in application can be noted in the period prior to 1848; and during the year 1848-49, "democracy" can be regarded as a key term for persons as different as Marx and Engels, Carlyle, Tocqueville, Guizot, and Proudhon. The February Revolution seems to represent the zenith in the application of "democracy", if the years after 1945 are omitted. During no other time has such a collective eagerness to reserve the label "democracy" for a writer's own political ideas been found; naturally this led to sudden changes in the signification of the word. It was probably no exaggeration when Guizot in 1849 stated that every group used "democracy" as their slogan and he even referred to the empire of the word "democracy" (p. 77).

The years after 1849 mark a decline in frequency of occurrence. Among those discussed before, during, and after the February Revolution, this tendency is relatively small in Proudhon's and John Stuart Mill's terminology, where frequent use of "democracy" generally stabilizes itself. On the other hand, there is a marked decline in Carlyle's works and especially in the writings of Marx and Engels, where frequent application is not found after Der achtzehnte Brumaire. Application remained at a fairly stable level during the time up to 1917. It is not possible to see either an important increase or important decline. There was, without doubt, more frequent application than there generally was before 1848, but less frequent application than during the years 1848-49.

Wilson's message and the Bolshevik Revolution brought about an increased application. But the word was probably less frequently used during the years 1918-22 than during the February Revolution. On this point, I cannot agree with Pool, who says that the heyday of "democracy" was fairly short: little application before 1870 and an increased application from 1917 onwards. (Cf. Related Works, p. 333). Without doubt, "democracy" played an important part as an Allied slogan against Germany, but there were not many attempts on the German side to use "democracy" as their slogan (cf. p. 222). The intense ideological controversies in connection with the Bolshevik Revolution in Russia were probably more important. A most significant trend was to accuse the Russian revolutionaries of having established a rule that was very different from "democracy". However, the Bolshevik leaders, who otherwise definitely co-ordinated their politics, attached very small importance, if any, to the question of co-ordinating their use of "democracy". There are important differences between Lenin, on the one hand, and Trotsky, Radek, and Kuusinen, on the other. The latter, for example, hardly ever tried to refute the view that Soviet rule was no democracy. (As indicated by Pool, Lenin's appreciative use of "democracy" did not mould the editorials of Izvestia, where favourable use of this term cannot be found from 1918-24.)

That important groups in the respective controversies did not, or did very little to, refute their adversaries' accusation that they did not represent democracy presents a picture that differs from that of the February Revolution. It cannot be said that the frequency among those ideologists who used "democracy" in an honorific way about 1920 was as high as in 1848. A good illustration is to compare the application of the term by Marx, Tocqueville, and Proudhon with the terminology of Kelsen, Kautsky, and Russell about 1920. A situation similar to that of 1848, when different groups used "democracy" as their slogan and when "democracy" was the catchword of nearly all the important parties, did not occur until the years after 1945; but then, with a higher intensity and wider extension than ever before. However, this sample among political theorists does not necessarily represent trends within the vernacular, although its usage by political ideologists during the February Revolution was probably typical of contemporary use.

RELATED WORKS

Little has been written previously concerning the topic of this dissertation, nor have inquiries into the meaning and application of "democracy" been frequent in contemporary research. Among authors discussed in this work, some elaboration of the use of "democracy" has been found in the writings of Guizot (p. 75), Considérant (p. 114), May (p. 205), Maine (p. 207), and Le Bon (p. 201), as well as a few others. My comments on these writers will not be repeated here. With regard to research carried out by political scientists and historians, I have not limited myself to works where use of this term occupies an exclusive or major part. The scarcity of material forces me to discuss works where this aspect is only touched on briefly.

1. James Bryce

James Bryce's <u>Modern Democracies</u> (London, 1921), is one of the most central works designating "democracy" as its object. In contrast to several other political scientists who write about democracy as an historical and contemporary phenomenon, but without any mention of the application of the word "democracy", Bryce at least touches on the use of this term. Chapter III, "The Definition of Democracy", opens as follows:

> The word Democracy has been used ever since the time of Herodotus to denote that form of government in which the ruling power of a State is legally vested, not in any particular class or classes, but in the members of the community as a whole. This means, in communities which act by voting, that rule belongs to the majority, as no other method has been found for determining peaceably and legally what is to be deemed the will of a community which is not unanimous. Usage has made this the accepted sense of the term, and usage is the safest guide in the employment of words.

Bryce adds that for the Greeks democracy was opposed to monarchy, the rule of one, and to oligarchy, the rule of a few, which meant a class privileged by either birth or property.

> Thus it (Democracy) came to be taken as denoting in practice that form of government in which the poorer class, always the more numerous, did in fact rule.

Bryce also says;

> Modern times also use it [Democracy] thus to describe what we call "the masses" in contradistinction to "the classes". But it is better to employ the word as meaning neither more nor less than the Rule of the Majority, the "classes and masses" of the whole people being taken together. ...
> So far there is little disagreement as to the sense of the word.

For Bryce it is evident that it is primarily in relation to the application of this definition to concrete cases that disagreement arises (Vol. I, pp. 23-24).

I cannot agree with his statement that, "So far there is little disagreement, " etc. nor can I accept his initial formulation that "the word Democracy has been used ever since the time of Herodotus to denote" etc. If we take only the Greek use of "democracy", Aristotle emphasized that democracy was government by the poor and oligarchy government of the rich, whether or not either side was in a majority or a minority (cf. Politics, 1280 a, and Christophersen, in Democracy, Ideology and Objectivity, pp. 85-86). Therefore, I cannot accept the idea that "democracy" came to denote in practice only that form of government in which the poor class ruled. Here it may be objected that his initial statement can hardly be interpreted very strictly; for example, he probably did not mean,

> ... the word Democracy has been used ever since the time of Herodotus to express one and only one concept, 'government vested in the members of the community as a whole'.

Even if we admit a fairly liberal interpretation, for example, "the word democracy has since the time of Herodotus predominantly been used to denote ..., " it is a little difficult to agree completely. Here it is sufficient to refer to the first two sections of "Systematic Approach", where firstly "democracy" has been used in many occurrences to connote something different from a form of government; and secondly, "democracy" has been used to connote rule by a more or less clearly restricted part of the population.

For the rest, it seems that no empirical research was carried out by Bryce to answer typical empirical questions as to how a term has been used. Perhaps the reason can be found in his concluding remark:

> It is better to employ the word as meaning neither more nor less than the Rule of the Majority.

This normative statement concerning how a word ought to be used, however, is entirely different from a descriptive statement concerning how a term is used, although there are many cases where normative preferences are apt to influence descriptions.

2. Edward Hallet Carr

In contrast to James Bryce, Carr's references to earlier use of "democracy" are all post French Revolution. In his interesting booklet, The Soviet Impact on the Western World (1946), Carr points out in his introduction that Western tradition admits two widely different conceptions of democracy, deriving from the English and the French revolutions respectively. According to him, both the English Civil War and the French Revolution were revolts by the nascent bourgeoisie against a legitimate monarchy and an established church. Both made use of revolutionary dictatorships, those of Cromwell and Robespierre, to bring a new kind of rule to birth. While, however, the philosophy of the English Revolution, as developed by Locke, was based on the rights of the individual against the State, implying tolerance and and the protection of minorities, the philosophy of the French Revolution, as developed by Rousseau, expressed the victory, not of political toleration, but of a particular view of the authority of the State. By accepting the social contract, Rousseau treated it as the final surrender by the individual of his rights against the State. Far from making the State a ring-fence to protect minorities, Rousseau identified society with the State and postulated an all-powerful <u>volonté générale</u> from which it was treason and crime to dissent. So far, with regard to <u>conception</u> of forms of rule, there will be no further elaboration here.

Concerning the use of "democracy", Carr states:

What I have called the English conception of democracy had little influence in Europe in the half century after the French revolution; for few
people would at this time have called Great Britain a democracy.
Throughout this period the word democracy was used throughout Europe
by friend or foe alike in the sense consecrated by the revolution, and
retained its revolutionary connotation unchallenged till after 1848. "Gegen
Demokraten helfen nur Soldaten" was an aphorism attributed to Friedrich
Wilhelm I of Prussia. Marx and Engels in the forties called themselves
"democratic communists", and in the Communist Manifesto the phrases
"to establish democracy" and "to raise the proletariat to the position of
the ruling class" are equivalents. (<u>Soviet Impact</u>. p. 8)

Carr also states that before 1848 nobody had doubted that political democracy (one man, one vote) carried with it social democracy (or the levelling of classes).

I agree with Carr in general, but it is difficult to accept his categorical formulations. It is true, no doubt, that before 1848 "democracy" was often used in a way which Carr vaguely declared as "the sense consecrated by the revolution" or "its revolutionary connotation". Many statements can undoubtedly be quoted to support such a viewpoint; for example, from Babeuf, Buonarroti, Guizot, Mazzini, Marx, Engels, and Tocqueville (cf. the sections "Democracy" signifying a socialist or a communist system (5a); "Democracy" signifying the rule of the proletariat (5b); Democracy and revolution (5c); and Democracy and dictatorship (6d)). On the other hand, typical conservatives like Hegel (pp. 45-47) and especially Disraeli (pp. 57-59) used "democracy" fairly positively as early as the 1820s and 1830s. The young Disraeli almost identified his own political ideals with what he called "democracy".

On different premises it is difficult to agree with Carr that before 1848 nobody doubted that political democracy (one man, one vote) carried with it social democracy (the levelling of classes). In several cases "democracy" was used to mean social equality, revolution by the poor, etc. This was not because of any belief that social equality was to be achieved via universal suffrage, but the word was directly used to connote social equality, revolution by the poor, etc. Guizot's argument was probably the most explicit. Guizot's own definition, democracy as violent revolution of the poor, was contrasted to the scientific, but uncorrect, way of defining democracy as government by the whole people (cf. above, p. 76). On the other hand, Bentham was absolutely in favour of one man and one vote. Yet in his systematic elaboration of the consequences of universal suffrage, there is nothing which indicates that he ever thought it would bring with it social equality or the levelling of classes.

Carr further says that the February Revolution was a turning point in the use of "democracy", since the middle class, having attained its primary

political object, and being frightened by the ulterior revolutionary aspirations of the masses, ceased to be revolutionary.

> From 1848 onwards therefore political democracy ("liberal democracy")
> and social democracy ("socialism" or "communism") were to be found
> throughout Europe on opposite sides of the barricades. It was not that
> after 1848 "socialism" or "communism" became revolutionary (they al-
> ways had been), but that "democracy" ceased to be revolutionary and
> tended more and more to be associated with conservatism.

Carr adds:

> In England, where there had been no 1848, the same developments
> followed later. The word democracy long remained in bad odour with
> the English ruling classes. ... But by the turn of the century these in-
> hibitions had been overcome; and since that time democracy has been
> continually invoked by conservatives, in England as elsewhere, as a
> bulwark of defence against the revolutionary onslaughts of socialism and
> communism.

On this point I agree with Carr, but here, too, it is difficult to accept
his categorical formulations. The February Revolution without doubt led
to very important differences concerning ways of using "democracy".
Tocqueville's use was probably most typical. In 1848 he suddenly identified
what he designated as "democracy" with individual liberty, and asserted
that democracy and socialism were not only different, but even contrary
phenomena. Still, there was no complete and consequent change even in
this case (cf. above, pp. 86-90). A similar comment can be made about
the different set of applications of "democracy" in the terminology of Marx
and Engels during and shortly after 1848 (cf. above, pp. 144-50).

I also agree with Carr that the word "democracy" remained in bad
odour with the English ruling class for a long time, but according to my
material, it is difficult to see any great differences between English and
French use on this point (cf. Chapters XI-XII).

I also accept that in several cases a radical kind of socialism was contrasted with what was designated "democracy"; Sorel was probably most
typical on this point. But while a positive use of "democracy" seems to
have been a most usual trend among reformists and moderate socialists
like Bernstein, the Fabians, Cole, and usually Jaurès, positive use was
not limited to reformist socialists in this period. A fairly honorific application of "democracy" can also be seen in the earlier writings of typical
revolutionary socialists such as Rosa Luxemburg and Lenin before 1917,
although "democracy" in these latter cases scarcely ever connoted the
revolutionary conquering of political power by the proletariat. According
to our material, it is difficult to support Carr's view that since the turn of
the century, democracy was continually invoked by conservatives as a bul-
wark of defence against socialism and communism. Undoubtedly, "democracy" generally was a central term used by very different critics of Bolshevik revolutionary rule, but this is relevant only to the period after 1917.
Luxemburg, 1918, directly let "democracy" connote armed conquest of
political power by the proletariat. It is a drawback that, apart from one
quotation from Lenin, Carr does not mention the use of this term by Bolshevik leaders, but goes on to consider Stalin's application of "democracy".
As mentioned earlier, use of this word by the central revolutionary leaders
is evidence of very different trends. On the whole, we must therefore con-

clude that the picture presented by Carr has been a little oversimplified, although it must be emphasized that few, if any, political scientists would be able to treat a complicated problem in such a stimulating way.

3. Arne Næss

As a special example of related works, I draw attention to Arne Næss, Interpretation and Preciseness (Oslo 1953), where pages 300-37 are devoted to an illustration of a connotational occurrence analysis. Næss's main objective is to find out what the Soviet author Zaslavski means by the words "democracy", "democratic", "democrats", etc., according to the application of these words in Zaslavski's booklet La démocratie soviétique, officially translated into French by J. Hepner in 1946. Næss here presents a list of the 192 occurrences of "democracy" in this booklet and works out a list consisting of sentences assumed to have a meaning for the author of the text analysed. This is followed by inferences which are sentences expressing to the analyst and his readers the same meaning that the implications hold for the author; and finally, there are two sections concerning precization.

This analysis represents something unique in the fields of inquiry into word meaning. I know of no other work where inquiry into the meaning of a word has been worked out in such a penetrating and systematic way. Yet objections can be raised on account of the character of the material used as the object of research. From the viewpoint of political theory, not much of interest can be found in this booklet by Zaslavski, a pamphlet which represents typical Stalinist propaganda, and of very small, if any, theoretical value. The whole analysis may therefore be regarded as wasting fine tools on bad material. The question would have been quite different if a central word in an important work had been made the object of an analysis of this kind, for example, "passion" and "reason" as used by David Hume in his Treatise of Human Nature. In my opinion, the usefulness of this analytic method is also dependent on a somewhat limited number of occurrences. To use it directly in relation to Tocqueville, for example, would require too much space.

Explaining his reason for using this text, Næss says:

His [Zaslavski's] book is preferred to the works of Lenin and Stalin as an object of analysis because in the latter works, the term "democracy" occurs relatively seldom, whereas in Zaslavski's text of 107 small pages it occurs 192 times. (Interpretation p. 301)

Apart from the question of the advisability of attempting to equate Zaslavski with Lenin and Stalin, Næss's explanation is partly incorrect. Stalin was indeed sparing in his use of "democracy". But few ideologists have used the word so frequently as Lenin.

4. R. R. Palmer

Palmer's inquiry into the application of "democracy" refers mainly to his article "Notes on the Use of the Word "Democracy", 1789-1799", Political Science Quarterly, vol. LXVII no. 2 (1953), of which central parts were reproduced in his work, The Age of the Democratic Revolution, 1959. As indicated, the research presented here is restricted to ten years, but ten very important years in relation to the use of "democracy". With regard to research limited to a certain period his article represents probably the most thorough inquiry ever written. The material reveals diligent study of French, English, American, Belgian, Dutch, German, and Italian sources. In certain cases, however, too much importance is attached to the occurrence of a word in a certain text and not enough to how the word was actually used, i. e., with what connotation.

Palmer's direct interpretation of special texts is generally sound. Robespierre tried to define democracy in a new way, to disengage it from the old sense of direct rule which was inapplicable in modern conditions. But Palmer should not equate Robespierre with Thomas Paine in this connection ("Use of the Word, "Democracy"", p. 212). Paine was fairly vague on this point and thus can hardly be regarded as having held democracy to be a purely representative form of rule (cf. above, pp. 22-24).

In relation to the material, there is some neglect in drawing attention to the use of "democracy" by political thinkers. It is far from unimportant to find statements from a political club in Amsterdam, a burgomaster in Aachen, or an Italian bishop, especially when trying to find a trend in the vernacular; but several important political thinkers are not mentioned at all. Fichte and Burke are treated, but Burke in a somewhat fragmentary way, and Kant, de Maistre, and Bonald are not mentioned at all. It is also strange that Godwin receives no attention, especially since in Political Justice, 1793, he used "democracy" in a very honorific way (cf. above, p. 26), and honorific use seems to be of central importance to Palmer. A more serious neglect, however, is that Babeuf is not included among persons using "democracy" and "democrats" in an honorific manner. Babeuf used these terms in a way which is central to his political thinking, and he was also the leader of a certain political group. He used "democracy" with a somewhat special signification: social equality and revolutionary emergency rule. These oversights possibly do not represent very considerable omissions. Any scientist is probably always quick to note shortcomings within his own field but Palmer does not pretend to present an inquiry into the application of the term within principal political thought. It is a little difficult, though, to agree with him when he concludes a section of his book with these words:

> It is therefore no anachronism to apply the word "democratic" to the eighteenth-century revolution. It was the last decade of the century that brought the word out of the study and into actual politics. (The Age of the Democratic Revolution, p. 20)

I agree with the last statement concerning the actual use of the word. But it is one thing to discover a certain terminology among special persons and another to consider the same word eo ipso a legitimate description of these same groups one hundred and seventy years later. It cannot be taken for granted that "democratic" was used at that time with a connotation identical with what contemporary and probably Western readers attribute to this term now. So many different things have been designated as "democracy" and "democratic" that a large number of them would be regarded as quite anachronistic by many people today.

5. Ithiel de Sola Pool

Among the contributors to Democracy in a World of Tensions, a Symposium Prepared by UNESCO (1951), Pool was among the very few to bring an historical approach to bear on the different uses of "democracy", and the only author to give a comprehensive and interesting survey. An inquiry into the application of "democracy" was also made by Pool in Symbols of Democracy (1952, with the collaboration of Harold D. Lasswell, Daniel Lerner, et al.). In the former, Pool indicates three different kinds of application: (1) the classical use dating from the time when "democracy" was coined in ancient Greece until the ninteenth century; (2) Western use, representative government with extensive civil liberties; and (3) Eastern use, government by an elite on behalf of the many, or poor. With regard to classical use, Pool states that "democracy" had a fairly uniform meaning up to the middle of the nineteenth century, and this meaning ranged between the related concepts, 'government of the many', and 'government of the poor'. He mentions Aristotle as belonging to the minority using the latter of these concepts.

Concerning the relationship between these three kinds of application, Pool says:

> At first glance it would seem that the Russian conception is closer to historical meaning than is the Western. In a strictly formal sense this is true. The verbal changes involved in getting from the classic to the Russian definition are smaller than those involved in getting to the Western definition. Aristotle would have understood Vyshinsky, but not Thomas E. Dewey.

He adds, however, that in a realistic sense, the contemporary Western use is nearer to the classical definition than is the Russian, since many facts referred to by the Russian definition are incompatible with classical democracy. He states finally:

> Pericles could have operated in London or Paris, but not in Moscow.
> (Democracy in a World of Tensions, p. 331)

Many of Pool's stimulating statements are acceptable. There are important differences between Aristotle's use of "democracy", for example, and contemporary Western use; and democracy which, according to Aristotle, was government by the poor, cannot be held to be identical with contemporary Eastern use if this is interpreted as government by an elite on behalf of the poor. As I mentioned in an earlier work (Chapter 4 in Democracy, Ideology, and Objectivity), however, I cannot follow Pool when he uses an expression like "classical democracy" in the singular. Greek terminology was so differential with regard to "democracy" that it is not possible to press it into one single concept, 'classical democracy'. Not only would it be impossible for Pericles to operate in Moscow today, but it would also have been very difficult for him to have operated in certain States designated as "democracies" by Aristotle (cf. Christophersen, op. cit., p. 91). Nor can I fully agree with Pool when he says:

> Even such anti-democratic writers as Plato and Aristotle knew that in a democracy the city is full of freedom and frankness. (Pool, op. cit., p. 352)

In one case, for example, Aristotle described a form of government where everything was determined by the majority of votes and nothing by law. The people there were sovereign, not as individuals, but in their collective capacity, and he concluded:

> Anyone, therefore, may with great justice blame such a government as being a democracy and not a free State. (Aristotle, Politics, 1291 b.)

I fully agree with most of what Pool says about the use of "democracy" during the nineteenth century. There is well-documented evidence behind his general statements on the Chartist programme, Tocqueville's earlier writings, Marx and Engels, the Paris Commune, etc. Some degree of simplification is probably unavoidable when a vast problem must be treated in relatively few pages, but misleading simplifications occur very rarely. One point must be corrected, nevertheless. Pool says that Marx considered himself a democrat, and he also states that

> he called himself a democrat and talked about democracy all through his lifetime. (Pool, op. cit. p. 333)

With some reservations I can accept the idea that Marx used "democrat" in self-designation up to 1849. But after that time a negative application was a fairly distinct characteristic of his terminology, although this cannot be described as the sole trend.

With regard to the transition to the modern Western application of "democracy", Pool points out correctly that by 1848 Tocqueville used "democracy" in a new sense by identifying it with liberty, although Bentham's use can also be noted in the process of redefining democracy to mean representative government with extensive civil liberties. Concerning the Eastern application of "democracy", it is also true that in the Leninist version of Marxism, a shift was made from the concept of government by the people to government for the people. Pool presents a conclusive inquiry concerning this topic. Since this section is preoccupied with conceptions of forms of rule, however, and very little with actual terminology, any further comments are not of interest in this context.

The second work in question, Symbols of Democracy, is part of a series of studies undertaken by the Hoover Institute, which concerned revolutionary developments in the international scene over the past sixty years (about 1890-1950). For this particular study, the sample consists of newspaper editorials from the prestige papers of five major powers: Great Britain, France, Russia, Germany, and the United States. This newspaper analysis is essentially a word count, where the coders were given a list of a certain number of key terms. Regarding the application of "democracy", this quantitative analysis produces much interesting information; for example, on the increase in the frequency of occurrences: on a word scale, "democracy" occurred in 2% of the editorials in 1914, while it appeared in as much as 12% in 1918 (op. cit. p. 6). Concerning Soviet application, whereas use of "democracy" was very moderate up to 1935, it increased immediately after that year. During 1935-38, the People's Front Period, "democracy" appeared in one-third of Izvestia editorials, or more than twice as much as in any other country. (It was also pointed out that the Soviet editorials were four or five times as rich in ideological symbols in general as New York Times or The Times.) During the Hitler-Stalin pact, use of "democracy" fell by half, but was still used more than in any other paper but Le Temps. With actual participation in the war, however, "democracy almost disappeared. Only 3 % of the editorials used it from 1941 through 1944.

> The war that had originally been prepared for as a war of DEMOCRACY against fascism had now become the FATHERLAND WAR. (op. cit. pp. 10-11)

Other important information is given on most pages of this booklet, but since most of it falls outside the period ot this research, I must deal only with topics of more direct relevance. In his fairly brief introduction, Pool states that the heyday of the symbol "democracy" has been a short one. According to him, a century ago "democracy" was a favoured symbol for small extremist plebeian groups only.

> But since 1870 this term, once so disturbing and revolutionary in flavor, has become respectable and comfortable. (op. cit. p. 1)

Arthur Rosenberg is referred to as support for this point of view. Rosenberg will be discussed later, but we consider the change to be slight in 1870. The February Revolution, as indicated by Carr and others, can more justifiably be quoted as representing a kind of reinterpretation of "democracy". Nor can we accept "democracy's" heyday as a short one, dating from about 1918. There was no permanent, stable, and comprehensive honorific use of "democracy" during the whole of the nineteenth century. Although I have not made a quantitative analysis, it is evident that honorific use was most intense during the February Revolution. As mentioned above, the years around 1848 mark a kind of zenith in positive application of "democracy", probably even when compared to 1918. That this trend partly tended to fade away is quite another matter.

With regard to earlier Soviet use, it is of great interest to hear that "democracy" was not used honorifically during the first years after the October Revolution or during the Leninist era.

> In the first two years of the Revolution the term was used in 12% of the editorials, never favorably: 86% of these instances were antagonistic and the rest neutral. From 1920 to 1924 the term was used in 8% of the editorials and of these, 63% were antagonistic and again, the rest neutral. (op. cit. p. 14)

This absence of honorific use is remarkable when compared with the honorific and intense application during the years 1935-38, when Stalin's personal dictatorship was complete. There are also some differences between this early application and the period 1925-34, when this dictatorship consolidated itself. During that time, "democracy" was used in 6% of the editorials, and among these, we are told, favourable and unfavourable uses of the term were evenly distributed.

It is strange that Lenin's habit of partly, or even predominantly, using "democracy" in an honorific way did not mould the terminology in Izvestia editorials -- Lenin's assertion, for example, that Soviet rule represented "a new and higher kind of democracy". On this point, therefore, Izvestia was much more in agreement with Trotsky, Radek, and Kuusinen than with Lenin. This ambivalence is also touched on by Pool. I cannot, however, agree with Pool when he says, "Throughout his life Lenin called himself a "consistent democrat". " Nor can I accept that "the dictatorship of the proletariat was described as the "democratic dictatorship of workers and peasants. "" (op. cit. p. 15).

In relation to the former statement, it can be mentioned that Lenin also used "democracy" and "democrats" in a derogatory way (cf. above, p. 259). In relation to the latter, Lenin's slogan was the "revolutionary democratic dictatorship of the workers and peasants, " and not merely "democratic dictatorship", etc. Lenin definitely did not say that such a dictatorship was a dictatorship of the proletariat. When he coined this slogan in 1905, it was in relation to what he then thought essential for Russian revolutionary activity at that time. By this slogan Lenin primarily intended to place the workers in the vanguard of the struggle against czarism. But the dictatorship in question would not undermine the capitalist system, since Russia was not yet regarded as ripe for a socialist revolution. It was on this point that Trotsky put forth his idea concerning dictatorship of the proletariat and the Permanent Revolution against Lenin's "merely democratic" dictatorship (cf. note 53, chapter XVI).

6. Arthur Rosenberg

From many points of view, Rosenberg's work, Demokratie und Sozialismus (Amsterdam, 1938), deserves attention. It is still one of the central dissertations within the political history of the last hundred and fifty years. I shall touch on one small part of his work only: his comment concerning the use of the term "democracy". But even in this field, Rosenberg's work is most unusual, in that it is introduced by six pages on how "democracy" has been used in various historical contexts, and in that this was done as early as 1938, a time when almost nothing had been written on this topic.

Rosenberg opens with a reference to Babeuf. According to Rosenberg, Babeuf consistently designated himself a "democrat", and held Robespierre, the man of terror, as representative of the prototype of democracy. He also quotes Babeuf's famous dictum:

Robespierrism is democracy, and these two words are perfectly identical.

I accept this, and I also agree with Rosenberg when he points to the great difference between this dictum in 1796 and the views prevalent in 1938, a time when probably few, if any, considered Robespierre to be the incarnation of democracy (Demokratie und Sozialismus, p. 9). Rosenberg proceeds to quote from the Communist Manifesto, according to which raising the proletariat to the position of ruling was equivalent to establishing democracy; and Rosenberg states with regard to the vernacular:

Marx und Engels konnten damals so schreiben, ohne dass sie befürchten mussten, unter den Volksmassen irgendein Missverständnis oder irgendeine Verwirrung zu erregen. (Ibid. p. 10)

Rosenberg also quotes from an article by Engels in <u>Deutsche Brüsseler Zeitung</u> (October 1847), in which Engels said that democracy, in all civilized countries, must lead to rule of the proletariat (cf. p. 140). Rosenberg makes no distinction, however, between democracy which is directly the rule of the proletariat and democracy leading to such a rule, but limits his survey to pointing out the near relationship and similarity between the proletarian and communist movement and what was designated as "democracy". Rosenberg then quotes from a speech from quite a different camp -- that made by Bismarck, November 1849, in the Prussian Diet, in which he used "democrat" to designate the red agitators of the agrarian revolution who called upon their countrymen to deliver up not only the estates of nobility, but also the soil of the farmers.

When changes in signification of the term are concerned, Rosenberg unfortunately makes no reference to Tocqueville's terminology during the February Revolution. It is strange that Rosenberg makes no mention of the important differences in the attitudes of Marx and Engels at that time towards what they called "democracy". For example, on the one hand, an honorific application of this word is found in the <u>Communist Manifesto</u>, to which we have already referred, and on the other, a very derogatory application is evident when Marx said in 1851 that one of his central revolutionary instructions was nothing but "ein Kriegsplan gegen die Demokratie" (cf. above, p. 148). Though obviously very well informed with regard to Marx's and Engels' writings, Rosenberg's first reference to a change in the use of "democracy" is a letter from Engels, December 1884. Here, "pure democracy" was used to label something which might serve as the only chance for the bourgeois, and even for the feudal social system during a revolutionary crisis (cf. above, p. 155).

As later proofs, Rosenberg selected prominent anti-communists like Wilson and Rathenau as prototypes of democracy in about 1920. He effectively contrasts these prototypes with earlier ones, finally quoting Urbahns, a prominent German communist, who after the revolutionary disaster in Hamburg in 1923, declared to the court:

> Die Massen werden mit uns sagen: Lieber im Feuer der Revolution verbrennen, als auf dem Misthaufen der Demokratie verrecken. (op. cit. p. 14).

In relation to this quotation, Rosenberg emphasizes the vast difference between Babeuf and Urbahns, concluding:

> Man sieht, dass im Laufe der letzten 140 Jahre der Begriff der Demokratie sich gründlich gewandelt hat, und dass die Wendung irgendwie in der Periode zwischen 1850 und 1880 liegen muss.

Central points have been indicated by Rosenberg, although these quotations are far too few to warrant any firm conclusions. In relation to the most negative use of "democracy" by a revolutionary communist like Urbahns. it might be objected, for example, that an honorific use of "democracy" can be found in 1918, in one of the last proclamations of Rosa Luxemburg, where "democracy" was even used to connote the revolutionary conquest of political power by the armed proletariat (cf. above, p. 275). It is more important that this single letter from Engels is no proof that the change in question took place somewhere between 1850 and 1880. As mentioned in connection with Pool, there is much more reason to regard the February Revolution as representing a kind of turning point, although this period cannot be seen as an absolute change. Many of the simple and fairly clear rules worked out at earlier dates need to be modified in relation to later research. Although this section from Rosenberg's work must be regarded as a mere sketch, it is none the less a pioneering work in which this eminent historian has drawn attention to central aspects.

7. J. L. Talmon

In The Origins of Totalitarian Democracy (1952), Talmon maintains that the ideas behind the Jacobins and the Babeuvist conspiracy -- which were inspired by Rousseau -- represented a totalitarian trend in political thought. Since this is not a history of political ideas, I must refrain from a broad treatment of this theme. However, a small section of this inquiry is entitled "The Definition of Democracy" (pp. 201-3). Unfortunately this section is short (a little more than two pages, with about one page appended in the notes, p. 325), and these few pages are limited exclusively to the use of "democracy" by Babeuf and Buonarroti, with nothing said about Robespierre and Saint-Just. On this point there is a difference between Talmon and Rosenberg. Talmon's statements in relation to Babeuf and Buonarroti are basically sound. The equalitarian character of their kind of democracy is clearly pointed out, as well as the idea of the enlightened vanguard and revolutionary emergency rule. At this point we miss Babeuf's central statement concerning the identity between "democracy" and "Robespierrism", especially since this statement links his thinking to the political practice of Robespierre. It is, however, quoted at length a little later on (p. 220).

As to Talmon's main thesis, I accept several of his points of view on the use of "democracy". There is undoubtedly a vast difference between "democracy" as used by these French revolutionaries who introduced this word as a slogan in modern political terminology and later Western application of the same term, where civil liberties are emphasized. On this point I have disagreed with Palmer, who in turn seems to disagree absolutely with Talmon. But something different from Western does not necessarily mean Eastern. The political spectrum has more than two colours, and the French Revolution does not quite fall within the framework of contemporary problems from the cold war. As far as we can see, democracy for these leading French revolutionaries was a kind of emergency rule, even a sanguinary emergency rule to a certain extent, if necessary. There is nevertheless an important difference between emergency rule, which is of temporary character, and a totalitarian régime, under which suppression of dissentient opinions is a permanent and central characteristic of a fairly stable society. It is difficult to see, for example, any particularly totalitarian trends in the various kinds of emergency rule worked out by Marx, Lenin, and Trotsky, while on the other hand, there are generally no direct references to "clear and present danger" in what was said by Stalinists in justification of the one-party system, absence of any rights for political minorities, etc., in a society of fairly stable and permanent structure.

To mention another example, the Nazi extermination of the Jews was never justified, yet was carried out as being a kind of emergency measure, conditioned by exceptional circumstances; it is much more natural to regard it as an inherent part of the régime itself.

In the ideology of the French revolutionaries, however, totalitarian symptoms can be seen in parts of Rousseau's political theory, and also in Saint-Just's <u>Institutions Républicaines</u>. This naturally makes the picture more complicated, even if it does not undermine what has been said concerning the difference between a <u>totalitarian</u> regime and an <u>authoritarian</u> one, where the latter differs from the former in the things that either (1) involve severe discipline, suppression of minorities, etc., which are limited to certain sectors of the society, such as the military, where a certain degree of authoritarianism is unavoidable; or (2) are planned or justified in connection with a transitional stage only. Many of the severe measures carried out or planned by the Jacobins and Babeuf may to a greater degree be classed as temporary authoritarian emergencies, rather than permanent totalitarian trends. A definite conclusion is scarcely possible. To a certain extent, this criticism of some of Talmon's views is also a criticism of points of view suggested earlier by myself (cf. Christophersen, in <u>Democracy</u> ..., pp. 109-12).

A second work by Talmon is <u>Political Messianism, the Romantic Phase</u>, 1960. This work is learned, stimulating, and, to a certain extent, provocative. Since it contains no section concerning the actual use of "democracy" by the ideologists in question, however, it will not be discussed here.

NOTES

CHAPTER I

REVOLUTIONARY IDEOLOGIES

1. "Rapport sur les principes de morale politique qui doivent guider la convention", 18 pluviôse year II, in Discours et rapports de Robespierre, ed. Charles Vellay (Paris 1908), pp. 326-27.

2. This translation seems to be rather widespread in English textbooks. Cf. e.g., a quotation in R. R. Palmer, "Notes on the Use of the Word "democracy" 1789-1799", Political Science Quarterly, vol. LXVIII, No. 2 (June 1953), p. 214.

3. Cf. Hobbes, Leviathan, 1651, in The Moral and Political Works of Thomas Hobbes (1750), p. 177. Spinoza, Tractatus Politicus, 1657, in Opera (1925), vol. III, p. 323, and Montesquieu, De l'esprit des lois (1748), bk. XI, chap. 4. A more detailed inquiry into this topic will be found in Christophersen, "An historical outlook on the different usages of the term "democracy"", in Democracy, Ideology and Objectivity, by Arne Næss and associates, Jens A. Christophersen and Kjell Kvalø, (Oslo 1956), pp. 97-104.

4. Cf. his statement, "Aristocraticum imperium illud esse diximus, quod non unus, sed quidam ex multitudine selecti tenent. Dico expresse, quod quidam selecti tenent. Nam præcipua est differentia inter hoc, & Democraticum imperium, quod scilicet in imperio Aristocratico gubernandi jus a sola electione pendeat; in Democratico autem maximine a jure quodam innato, vel fortuna adepto. " -- Spinoza, op. cit. p. 323.

5. Cf. the following statement of Madison in The Federalist, "The two great points of difference between a democracy and a republic are: firstly, the delegation of government, in the latter, to a small number of citizens elected by the rest; secondly, the greater number of citizens, and the greater sphere of country, over which the latter may be extended". -- Federalist, No. X, November 1787.

6. Cf. Alexander Hamilton and Thomas Jefferson, "American Writers' series", ed. Frederick C. Prescott (1934), p. 11.

7. Robespierre, Discours, p. 262.

8. Ibid. p. 327.

9. Ibid. p. 328.

10. Ibid. p. 332.

11. Loc. cit.

12. Ibid. p. 328.

13. Ibid. p. 327.

14. Ibid. p. 351.

15. "Le Défenseur de la Constitution", April-May 1792, in ibid. p. 182.

16. Ibid. p. 396.

17. On 19 March 1641 the entire body of freemen of Rhode Island "unani-mously agreed upon, that the government, which this body politic doth attend into this island, and the jurisdiction thereof, in favour of our Prince, is a DEMOCRACIE, or popular government; that it is to say it is in the power of the body of freemen orderly assembled, or major part of them, to make or constitute just Lawes, by which they will be regulated, and to depute from among themselves such ministers as shall see them faithfully executed between man and man. " -- George Bancroft, History of the United States (Boston 1862), vol. I, p. 393.

18. Cf. the following statement of Pericles: "It is true that our govern-ment is called a democracy, because its administration is in the hands, not of the few, but of the many. " -- Thucydides, History, bk. II, chap. 37.

19. Cf. Oeuvres complètes de Saint-Just, ed. Charles Valley (Paris 1908), vol. I, pp. 264-71.

20. Ibid. vol. II, p. 258.

21. Ibid. pp. 258-59.

22. Ibid. vol. II, p. 377.

23. Ibid. vol. II, p. 231. A related absence of association between mod-esty and what was called "republic" also occurs in October 1793, "Vous avez à punir non seulement les traitres, mais les indifférentes mêmes; vous avez à punir quiconque est passif dans la République et ne fait rien pour elle: car depuis que le peuple français a manifesté sa volonté, tout ce qui lui est opposé est hors le souverain; tout ce qui est hors le souverain est ennemi. " -- Ibid. vol. II, p. 76.

24. 27 July 1794.

25. Le Tribun du Peuple, 14 vendemaire year III, in Pages choisies de Babeuf, ed. Maurice Dommanget, (Paris 1935), p. 171. Dommanget inserts that it is probably not true that Babeuf had changed his name at the beginning of the Revolution. According to him, Babeuf did not assume the name Camille before 1791.

26. Ibid. p. 166.

27. Le Tribun de Peuple, No. 29, 1 nivôse year III, in ibid. p. 192.

28. Ibid. pp. 246-47.

29. Ibid. p. 256.

30. The best proof of Babeuf's feeling for equality is probably a letter to his son Robert, 14 pluviôse year II, or 2 February 1794, "Plus de riches durs et qui insultent à la misère des malheureux, plus de pauvres qui manquent de tout, et qui, pour soutenir une triste existence, sont obligés de vendre leur services aux riches, de s'en rendre esclaves et d'être en tout soumis à leurs volontés. Mon ami, cette égalité si precieuse, dont la sublimité du principe t'a frappé, c'est ma morale, c'est la religion de ton père, c'est sa constitution, sa loi; c'est l'objet de toutes ses affections .... " -- Ibid. p. 158,

31. Ibid. p. 286.

32. Cf. footnote by Dommanget, ibid. p. 284.

33. Buonarroti, Histoire de la conspiration pour l'égalité, dite de Babeuf, 1828 (Paris 1850), p. 20.

34. Ibid. p. 154.

35. Ibid. p. 85 footnote.

36. Cf., e.g., ibid. pp. 47, 57, 65, 97, 98.

37. Cf., e.g., his view concerning two opinions among the republicans, "ceux qui faisaient souvent céder les principes de la justice à leurs commodités particulières, prirent le nom de patriotes de 1789; les autres qui se distinguaient par leur persévérance à défendre la démocratie, s'appelèrent les égaux. " -- Ibid. p. 39.

38. Rousseau, Du contrat social (1762), bk. III, chap. 4.

CHAPTER II

EARLY RADICALISM

1. Rights of Man, pt. II, 1792, in Complete Writings of Thomas Paine (New York 1945), vol. I, p. 369.

2. Loc. cit.

3. Ibid. p. 371.

4. This is similar to Paine's statement: "The monarchical form, there-fore, could not be a substitute for the democratical, because it has equal inconveniences. " -- Loc. cit.

5. Loc. cit.

6. Ibid. pp. 371-72.

7. Godwin, Inquiry Concerning Political Justice, 1793 (2nd ed. , London 1796), vol. II, p. 110. This work is hereafter referred to as Political Justice,

8. Ibid. p. 503.

9. Godwin was not consistent, however. A few years after the appear-ance of Political Justice, he married Mary Wolstonecraft. But at the time of writing his main work, he was an ardent antagonist of marriage.

10. Ibid. p. 113.

11. Ibid. p. 115.

12. Ibid. pp. 115-16.

13. Cf. ibid. pp. 169-70.

14. Ibid. pp. 170-71.

15. Ibid. p. 173.

16. Loc. cit.

CHAPTER III

EARLY CONSERVATISM

1. Reflections on the Revolution in France, 1790, in The Works of Ed-mund Burke (London 1886), vol. II, p. 365.

2. Ibid. p. 396.

3. Ibid. p. 396.

4. Loc. cit.

5. Loc. cit.

6. Cf. loc. cit. footnote. The quotation from Aristotle is the following one: "The ethical character is the same, both exercise despotism over the better class of citizens; and decrees are in the one what ordinances and arrests are in the other: the demagogue too, and the court favourite, are not unfrequently the same identical men, and always bear a close analogy; and these have the principal power, each in their respective forms of government, favourites with the absolute monarch, and demagogues with a people such as I have described. " -- Politics, 1292 a.

7. Loc. cit.

8. Burke, op. cit. pp. 396-97.

9. A Vindication of Natural Society, 1756, in Works, vol. I, p. 27.

10. An Appeal from the New to the Old Whigs, 1791, in ibid. Vol. III, p. 78.

11. Reflections on the Revolution in France, 1790, in ibid. Vol. II, p. 363.

12. This occurrence is probably the only one which may justify Paine's remark, "Mr. Burke is so little acquainted with constituent principles that he confounds democracy and representation together. " -- Rights of Man, 1792, in Writings, vol. I, p. 369.

13. Cf. Reflections, in Works, vol. II. p. 329, and Thoughts on the French Affairs, 1791, in Works, vol. III, p. 369.

14. Considérations sur la France, 1797, in Oeuvres complètes de Joseph de Maistre (Lyon 1891), vol. I, p. 42.

15. Ibid. p. 131.

16. Étude sur la souveraineté. This manuscript dated 1794, 1795, and 1796, partly printed 1815. In Oeuvres, vol. I, p. 426.

17. Cf. Aristotle, Politics, 1279b.

18. Cf. Rousseau, Du contrat social, bk. III, chap. IV.

19. De Maistre, op. cit. p. 465.

20. Ibid. p. 466.

21. Cf. the following statement, "Mais dire que la souveraineté ne vient pas de Dieu parce qu'il se sert des hommes pour l'établir, c'est dire qu'il n'est pas le créateur de l'homme parce que nous avons tous un père et une mère. " -- Ibid. p. 313.

22. Ibid. p. 423. 22b. Ibid. p. 452.

23. "Fragment sur la France", undated, in Oeuvres, vol. I, p. 205.

24. Théorie du pouvoir politique et religieux, 1796, in Oeuvres complètes de M. de Bonald, ed. l'abbé Migne (Paris 1859), vol. I, p. 351.

25. Ibid. pp. 355-56.

26. Ibid. p. 358.

27. Ibid. p. 637.

28. "De la philosophie morale et politique", 1805, in Oeuvres, vol. III, p. 482.

29. "Quelques notions de droit", undated, in Oeuvres, vol. II, pp. 218-19.

30. "De loi sur l'organisation des corps administratifs", undated, but written after 1815, in Oeuvres, vol II, p. 369.

31. Ibid. pp. 357-58.

32. Grundlage des Naturrechts, pt. 1, 1797, in Fichtes Werke (Leipzig 1908), vol. II, p. 17.

33. Ibid. p. 162.

34. Ibid. p. 163.

35. Grundlage des Naturrechts, pt. 2, 1797, in Werke, vol. II, p. 290.

36. Grundlage, I, p. 166.

37. Schleiermacher, Ueber die Begriffe der verschiedenen Staatsformen, 1814, in Abhandlungen der Königlichen Akademi der Wissenschaften in Berlin 1814-15, Philosophische Klasse, p. 20.

38. Ibid. p. 23.

39. Ibid. p. 31. The text in English is meant to be only an interpretation of Schleiermacher's statement and not a translation.

40. Ibid. p. 35.

41. Brouillon zur Ethik, 1805, in Schleiermachers Werke (Leipzig 1913), vol. II, p. 191.

42. Zur Pädagogik, 1813, in ibid. vol. III, p. 417.

43. Ibid. p. 419.

44. "Die Lehre vom Staat", different lectures 1817-29, in ibid, vol. III, p. 562.

45. Aphorismen über den Staat, No. 40, in ibid. vol. III, p. 618.

46. Hegel, Vorlesungen über die Philosophie der Weltgeschichte, I, in Philosophische Bibliothek, No. 171a, ed. Georg Lasson (Leipzig 1920), p. 118.

47. Ibid. p. 119.

48. Ibid. p. 121.

49. Vorlesungen über die Philosophie der Weltgeschichte, III, in ibid. No. 171c, p. 602.

50. Ibid. p. 604.

51. Various statements of Hegel confirm these points of view. "Wenn die partikulären Zwecke und Leidenschaften eintreten, dann hört der allgemeine Geist auf. Nur weil alle Individuen in diesem objektiven Geiste leben, haben alle auch Berechtigung an dem Staate, das Recht, über ihn zu beratsschlagen, und die Pflicht, für ihn zu sterben. " And consequently, "zu den Forderungen einer demokratischen Verfassung führt der Satz, dass die Beschlüsse über den Staat die Angelegenheit aller Bürger sei. " -- Ibid. p. 605. On this point a related formulation occurs in Robespierre's speech. "Il n'est que la démocratie où l'Etat est véritablement la patrie de tous les individus qui le composent, et peut compter autant de défenseurs intéressés à sa cause qu'il renferme de citoyens. " -- Robespierre, op. cit. p. 328.

52. Hegel, op. cit. p. 607.

53. Ibid. p. 608.

54. Ibid. p. 610.

55. Ibid. p. 612.

56. Ibid. p. 609.

57. Ibid. p. 608.

58. Cf. , e. g. , Hegel, Grundlinien der Philosophie des Rechts, 1821, in ibid. No. 124, pp. 222, 230.

CHAPTER IV

EARLY CONSTITUTIONALISM

1. Zum Ewigen Frieden, 1795, in Kleinen Schriften zur Geschichtsphilosophie, Ethik und Politik, Philosophische Bibliothek, ed. Vorländer (Leipzig 1913), No. 47, vol. I, p. 128.

2. Ibid. pp. 128-29.

3.   Ibid. p. 129.

4.   Loc. cit.

5.   Ibid. p. 160.

6.   De Corpore Politico, 1650, in The Moral and Political Works of Hobbes (London 1750), p. 59.

7.   Tractatus Theologico-politicus, 1670, in Opera (Heidelberg 1925), vol. III, p. 193. In the words of Spinoza: "Talis vero societatis jus Democratia vocatur, quæ proinde definitur cætus universus hominum, qui collegialiter summum jus ad omnia, quæ potest habet. Ex quo sequitur summam potestatem nulla lege teneri, sed omnes ad omnia ei parere debere. "

8.   Cf. Spinoza, Tractatus Politicus, 1677, in ibid. vol. III, p. 323, and Hobbes, Leviathan, 1651, in op. cit. p. 177.

9.   Principes de Politique, 1815, in Constant, Cours de politique constitutionelle (Paris 1861), vol. I, p. 11.

10.   Ibid. p. 12.

11.   Ibid. p. 53.

12.   Réflexions sur les Constitutions et les Garanties, avec une Exquisse de Constitution, 1814, in ibid. vol. I, p. 214.

13.   De l'Esprit de Conquète et de l'Usurpation, 1814, in ibid. vol. II, p. 210.

14.   Madame de Staël, Considération sur la Révolution Françoise, 1817, (2nd. ed. , 1819), vol. II, p. 120.

15.   Ibid. p. 146.

16.   Ibid. p. 146.

17.   Ibid. vol. III, p. 43.

18.   Ibid. p. 255.

19.   Ibid. p. 256.

20.   Réflexions politiques, 1814, in Oeuvres complètes de Châteaubriand, ed. Sainte-Beuve (Paris 1911), vol. VII, pp. 88.

21.   Essais sur les révolutions anciennes et modernes, 1797, in ibid. vol. I, p. 495.

22.   Polemique, July 1824, in ibid. vol. VIII, p. 69.

CHAPTER V

MID-CENTURY CONSERVATISM

1. <u>What Is He</u>?, in <u>Whigs and Whiggism, Political Writings by Benjamin Disraeli</u>, ed. W. Hutcheson (London 1913), p. 17.

2. Ibid. p. 18.

3. Disraeli seems here to neglect the fact that similar methods had been used by the Tories, 1713, to ratify the Treaty of Utrecht.

4. Ibid. p. 19.

5. <u>Morning Post</u>, 5 September 1835. These articles were republished under the title <u>Peers and People</u>, in <u>Political Writings</u>, p. 106.

6. <u>Vindication of the English Constitution</u>, 1835, in ibid. p. 150.

7. Ibid. p. 189.

8. Ibid. p. 216.

9. Ibid. p. 228.

10. <u>Peers and People</u>, 1835, in ibid. p. 64. Similar points of view are found on pp. 63, 96, 109, 185.

11. Ibid. p. 230.

12. Ibid. p. 229.

13. Ibid. p. 229.

14. <u>The Spirit of Whiggism</u>, 1836, in ibid. p. 337.

15. Ibid. p. 340.

16. Ibid. p. 345.

17. <u>Hansards's Parliamentary Debates</u> (London 1859), vol. CLIII, p. 1245.

18. "The Diamond Necklace", 1837, in <u>Carlyle's Works</u> (London 1896-99), vol. XXVIII, p. 337.

19. <u>Chartism</u>, 1839, in ibid. vol. XXIX, p. 158.

20. Ibid. p. 159.

21. Loc. cit.

22. Past and Present, 1843, in ibid vol. X, p. 215.

23. Latter-Day Pamphlets, I, February 1850, in ibid. vol. XX, p. 5.

24. Ibid. pp. 8-9.

25. Ibid. p. 9.

26. Ibid. p. 10.

27. Ibid. p. 11.

28. Ibid. p. 11.

29. Ibid. p. 12.

30. Loc. cit.

31. Ibid. p. 21.

32. Loc. cit.

33. Cf. ibid. p. 22.

34. Ibid. p. 120, Pamphlet III, April 1850.

35. Loc. cit.

36. Cf. "Shooting Niagara: And After?", 1867, in ibid. vol. XXX, pp. 1-2.

37. Early Kings of Norway, in ibid. vol. XXX, p. 308.

38. Stahl, Rechts und Staatslehre auf der Grundlage christlicher Weltanschauung (Heidelberg 1856), vol. II, p. 211. This work constitutes the second part of his work Die Philosophie des Rechts.

39. Ibid. p. 213.

40. Ibid. p. 213 footnote.

41. Cf. Aristotle, Politics, 1280a.

42. Cf. Christophersen, op. cit. pp. 78-79.

43. Ibid. p. 213.

44. Ibid. p. 474.

45. Ibid. p. 486.

46. Ibid. pp. 486-87.

CHAPTER VI

MODERATE LIBERALISM

1. Sismondi, Études sur les constitutions des peuple libres (Paris 1836), pp. 23-24. This work constitutes vol. I of his Études sur les sciences sociales.

2. Ibid. p. 61.

3. Ibid. p. 63.

4. Ibid. p. 63.

5. Ibid. p. 65.

6. Ibid. p. 69.

7. Cf., e.g., ibid. pp. 134-35, 244.

8. Cf., e.g., Tingsten, De konservative idéerna (Stockholm 1939), p. 115.

9. "On Mitford's History of Greece", Knight's Quarterly Magazine, (November 1824), reprinted in The Works of Lord Macaulay (1866), vol. VII, p. 688.

10. Loc. cit.

11. Ibid. p. 689.

12. "Utilitarian Theory of Government", 1829, in ibid. vol. V, p. 311.

13. Edouard Alletz, De la démocratie nouvelle, ou des mœurs et de la puissance des classes moyennes en France (1834), and Auguste Billiard, Essai sur l'organisation démocratique de France (1837).

14. Guizot, "De la démocratie dans les sociétés modernes", Révue Française (1837), p. 194.

15. Ibid. p. 196.

16. Ibid. p. 197.

17. Ibid. p. 202.

18. Guizot, De la Démocratie en France (1849), p. 9.

19. Ibid. p. 10.

20. Ibid. p. 33.

21. Ibid. p. 36.

22. Ibid. pp. 39-40.

23. Cf. Christophersen, op. cit. pp. 106-9, 131-32.

24. Tocqueville, De la Démocratie en Amérique I, 1835, in Oeuvres
     complètes, ed. J. P. Mayer (Paris 1951), vol. I, pt. 1, p. 52. Since
     only the three first volumes of this new edition of Oeuvres complètes
     were available, I was obliged to quote from the earlier edition of 1866
     also.

25. Ibid. p. 45.

26. Ibid. p. 4.

27. Ibid. p. 1.

28. Ibid. p. 4.

29. Regarding Tocqueville's attitude, a most central formulation occurs on
     p. 5: "Instruire la démocratie... régler ses mouvements, substituer
     peu à peu la science des affaires à son inéxpérience, la connaissance
     de ses vrais intérêts à ses aveugles instincts; adapter son gouverne-
     ment aux temps et aux lieux: le modifier suivant les circonstances et
     les hommes, tel est le premier des devoirs imposé de nos jours à
     ceux qui dirigent la société. "

30. Ibid. p. 53.

31. Ibid. p. 257.

32. Ibid. p. 266.

33. Ibid. p. 267.

34. Tocqueville added in relation to these and very similar remarks: "Si
     ces lignes parviennent jamais en Amérique, je suis assuré de deux
     choses: la première, que les lecteurs élèveront tous la voix pour me
     condamner; la seconde, que beaucoup d'entre eux m'absoudront au
     fond de leur conscience. " -- Ibid. p. 269.

35. Ibid. p. 431. This well-known prognosis about Russia and America
     scarcely represents an absolutely original thought. Deutscher, for
     example, speaks about the predictions of Saint-Simon, "predictions
     which are less known but more original than those made by Tocque-
     ville later. " -- The Prophet Unarmed (1959), p. 435.

36. Letter to Eugène Stoffels, 21 February 1835, in Oeuvres Complètes, ed. Madame de Tocqueville (Paris 1866), vol. V, p. 426.

37. "État social et politique de la France avant et depuis 1789", London and Westminster Review (1836), here from the French version, Oeuvres Complètes (1951), vol. II, p. 53.

38. Ibid. p. 62.

39. De la Démocratie en Amérique II, 1840, in ibid. (1951), vol. I, II, p. 7.

40. Ibid. p. 17.

41. Ibid. p. 18.

42. Ibid. p. 19.

43. Cf. ibid. p. 104.

44. Cf. ibid. p. 322.

45. Ibid. p. 328.

46. Cf. ibid. p. 323.

47. Letter to John Stuart Mill, 18 December 1840, in ibid. (1866), vol. VI, pp. 107-8.

48. Letter to John Stuart Mill, 15 November 1839, in ibid. (1866), vol. VI, p. 94.

49. "Discours prononcé à L'Assemblé Constituante sur la question de droit au travail", 12 September 1848, in ibid. (1866), vol. IX, p. 544.

50. Ibid. p. 545.

51. Cf. pp. 81-82.

52. Ibid. pp. 545-46.

53. De la classe moyenne et du peuple, October 1847, in ibid. (1866), vol. IX, p. 517.

54. Ibid. p. 518.

55. Souvenirs d'Alexis de Tocqueville, written 1850 (Paris 1942), p. 110.

56. Ibid. p. 32.

57. Ibid. p. 72.

58. Ibid. p. 83.

59.   Ibid. p. 85.

60.   L'Ancien Régime et la Révolution, 1856, in Oeuvres (1951), vol. II,
      p. 75.

61.   Ibid. p. 148.

62.   Ibid. p. 213.

63.   "Notes et pensées relatives à un ouvrage sur la révolution. " These
      notes are not dated, but were probably written sometime between 1856
      and 1859. In ibid. (1866), vol. VIII, p. 184.

64.   Ibid. p. 185.

65.   Letter to M. Freslon, 11 September 1857, ibid. (1866), vol. VI, pp.
      407-8.

CHAPTER VII

RADICALISM

1.   Cf. A Fragment on Government, 1776, in The Works of Jeremy Ben-
      tham (London 1838-42), pt. I, pp. 276-80.

2.   Defence from particular experience in the case of Ireland, 1777 or
      1778 to 1783, in ibid. pt. X, p. 615.

3.   Emancipate your colonies, 1793, in ibid. pt. IV, p. 409. This
      pamphlet was not published for sale before 1830.

4.   Plan of Parliamentary Reform, 1817, in ibid. pt. X, p. 437.

5.   Ibid. p. 438.

6.   Ibid. p. 447.

7.   Loc. cit.

8.   Ibid. p. 451.

9.   Ibid. p. 447.

10.   Restrictive and Prohibitory Commercial System, 1821, in ibid. pt. IX,
      p. 100.

11.   The Constitutional Code, first volume printed 1827, parts of the second
      one 1830, but not completed until Works, pt. XVII, p. 10.

12.   Cf. ibid. p. 28.

13. Ibid. p. 32.

14. Ibid. p. 47. Bentham also held, for rather similar reasons, that there were to be no rebels in what he called "representative democracy". Cf. ibid. p. 134.

15. On Houses of Peers and Senates, 1830, in ibid. pt. IV, p. 448.

16. Ibid. p. 449.

17. Ibid. p. 449.

18. James Mill, Essay on Government, 1824, here from 1937 ed. , introduction by Ernest Baker (Cambridge), p. 8.

19. Ibid. p. 9.

20. Cf. ibid. pp. 16, 29, 31, 72.

21. For example, "the most perfect representative of militant democracy is Jules Michelet", Soltau, French Political Thought in the Nineteenth Century (London 1931), p. 107. Charles Maurras has a chapter called "Michelet ou la démocratie" in Trois idées politiques (Paris 1898).

22. Michelet, Le Peuple (Paris 1846), p. 5.

23. Ibid. p. 80.

24. Ibid. p. 222.

25. Ibid. p. 276.

26. Ibid. p. 331.

27. Michelet, Histoire de la révolution française, 1847, here from edition of 1868, vol. VI, p. 152.

28. Ibid. p. 148.

29. The ideological attitude of Michelet is probably best explained by his statement: "Toute Histoire de la Révolution jusqu'ici était essentiellement monarchique (Telle pour Louis XVI, telle pour Robespierre). Celle-ci est la première républicaine, celle qui a brisé les idoles et les dieux. De la première page à la dernière elle n'a en qu'un héros: le peuple. " -- Ibid. vol. VII, p. 495.

30. Ibid. vol. VI, p. 149.

31. Le Christianisme et la Révolution française, 1845, in Oeuvres complètes de Edgar Quinet (Paris 1865), vol. III, p. 262.

32. Ibid. p. 263.

- 353 -

33. Ibid. p. 263.

34. Ibid. p. 264.

35. Michelet, for example, once declared: "Saintes baïonettes de France, cette lueur qui plane sur vous, que nul œil ne peut soutenir, gardez que rien ne l'obscurcisse. " -- Le Peuple, p. 145.

36. Quinet, op. cit. pp. 249-50.

37. Loc. cit.

38. Ibid. pp. 251-52.

39. Lamartine, Histoire des Girondins I, 1847, here from 1851 ed. , vol. I, p. 15.

40. Cf. Bergson, Le deux sources de la morale et de la religion (1932), p. 304, and Maritain, Christianisme et démocratie (1945), p. 25.

41. Lamartine, op. cit. p. 44.

42. Ibid. vol. II, p. 286.

43. Ibid. vol. II, p. 288.

44. I have here in mind La France parlementaire, La Politique rationelle, and Memoires politiques, none of which are available in Norway.

45. Lamartine here used the term "réforme" in relation to the political events of 1789.

46. Speech in Chamber of Deputies, 10 January 1839. In Les grands orateurs républicains, vol. VII, Lamartine, ed. André Toledano (Monaco 1949-50), p. 91.

47. Speech in the National Assembly, 18 June 1848, ibid. p. 186.

48. Ibid. p. 195.

49. Speech in National Assembly, 6 September 1848, ibid. p. 200.

50. The use of the expressions "first chamber" and "second chamber" are somewhat arbitrary in political language. "Second chamber" may, as in Sweden, refer to the directly elected one, and "first chamber", the more federal one. In relation to Bentham and Lamartine I have used the contrary terminology, in accordance with the usage of these authors.

51. Speech in National Assembly, 27 September 1848, ibid. p. 213.

52. Cf. Henri Michel, L'Idée de l'État (Paris 1898), pp. 327-31. Of Lamartine, Michel asserts: "Nul n'avait plus activement travaillé à

populariser la notion de l'État démocratique; nul ne s'en était formé une image plus haute, plus noble et plus juste. "

53. "Faith and Future", 1835, originally written in French, quotation here from <u>Duties of Man and Other Essays by Joseph Mazzini</u> (London 1907), p. 170.

54. Ibid. p. 192.

55. Ibid. p. 193.

56. Ibid. p. 173.

57. Ibid. p. 174.

58. "Europe: Its Condition and Progress", <u>Westminster Review</u> (April 2, 1852), in Mazzini, <u>Essays</u> (Newcastle 1887), p. 277.

59. "To the Italian Working Class", 1860, in <u>Duties of Man</u>, p. 1.

60. "From the Council to God", <u>Fortnightly Review</u> (June 1870), in ibid. p. 289.

61. "To the Italians", 1871, in ibid. p. 238.

62. "M. Renan and France", 1872, in <u>Essays</u> (1887), p. 322.

63. Ibid. p. 323.

CHAPTER VIII

EARLIER SOCIALISM

1. <u>Traité de l'Association domestique-agricole II</u>, 1822, in Fourier, <u>Oeuvres</u> (Paris 1840), vol. III, p. 387.

2. Ibid. III, in <u>Oeuvres</u>, vol. IV, p. 583.

3. Considérant, <u>Destinée sociale</u>, 1834 (Paris, 2nd ed. 1848), vol. I, p. 128.

4. Ibid. vol. II, p. 307.

5. Considérant, <u>De la politique générale et du rôle de la France en Europe</u> (Paris 1840), p. 126.

6. Loc. cit.

7. <u>Destinée sociale</u>, vol. II, p. 318.

8. Ibid. vol. I, p. ix.

9. Considérant, <u>Principes du Socialisme, Manifeste de la Démocratie au xixe siècle</u> (Paris 1847), p. 60. First published 1843.

10. Cf. p. 77.

11. Ibid. p. 61.

12. Ibid. p. 53.

13. Cf. ibid. p. 73.

14. Owen, <u>The New Existence of Man upon Earth</u> (1854), pt. I. p. 6. I have in vain tried to find occurrences in <u>Millenium Gazette, A New View of Society</u> (1818), and <u>The Book of the New Moral World</u> (1836).

15. Ibid. pt. IV, p. 15. Similar views are also expressed in "Address of Robert Owen to the advanced minds of those who desire to change governments to become republics on the individual principle of society", <u>Millennial Gazette</u> (1 August 1857).

16. Cabet, <u>La catalysme sociale</u> (Paris 1845), p. 20.

17. Loc. cit.

18. Cabet, <u>Salut par l'union ou Ruine par la division</u> (Paris 1845), p. 49.

19. Loc. cit.

20. Cabet, <u>Le vraie Christianisme</u> (Paris 1848), pp. 160-61.

21. Cabet, <u>Voyage en Icarie</u> (Paris 1848), p. 442.

22. <u>Qu'est-ce que la propriété</u>, 1840, in <u>Oeuvres Complètes de P. J. Proudhon</u> (Paris 1873), vol. I, p. 212.

23. <u>De la création de l'ordre dans l'humanité</u>, 1843, in ibid. vol. III, p. 294.

24. Ibid. p. 337.

25. Ibid. p. 339.

26. <u>Solution du Problème social</u>, 1848, this chapter dated March 26, in ibid. vol. VI, p. 39.

27. Ibid. p. 49.

28. Ibid. p. 50.

29. Ibid. p. 49.

30.   Ibid. p. 55.

31.   Ibid. p. 57.

32.   Ibid. p. 68.

33.   Cf. p. 77.

34.   Cf. e. g. , ibid. vol. XVII, pp. 30, 71, 103.

35.   "Toast à la révolution", Le Peuple, 17 October 1848, in ibid. vol. XVII, p. 142.

36.   Cf. "La presidence", Le Peuple, in ibid. vol. XVII, p. 171. This article is not dated, but appears after that of October.

37.   "Manifeste électorale du Peuple", 8-15 November 1848, in ibid. vol. XVII, p. 181.

38.   Ibid. p. 182.

39.   Ibid. p. 190.

40.   "Un dernier mot sur la Banque du Peuple", Le Peuple, 17 April 1849, in ibid. vol. XVIII, p. 110.

41.   "La République et la coalition", Le Peuple, 19 April 1849, in ibid. vol. XVIII, p. 126.

42.   Les confessions d'un Révolutionnaire, 1849, in ibid. vol. IX, p. 11.

43.   Ibid. p. 74.

44.   Ibid. p. 286.

45.   Idée générale de la révolution au XXe siècle, 1851, in ibid. vol. X, p. 130.

46.   Ibid. p. 111.

47.   Ibid. p. 113.

48.   La révolution sociale, 1852, in ibid. vol. VII, p. 35.

49.   Ibid. p. 69.

50.   Ibid. p. 161.

51.   Philosophie du progrès, November 1851, in ibid. vol. XX, pp. 6-7.

52.   Ibid. p. 80.

53.   Ibid. p. 13.

54. Proudhon died in 1865.

55. De la justice dans la révolution et dans l'église, 1858, in ibid. vol. XXI, p. 75.

56. Loc. cit.

57. Ibid. p. 76.

58. Loc. cit.

59. Du principe fédératif, 1863, in ibid. vol. VIII, p. 98.

60. Ibid. p. 100.

61. Ibid. p. 99.

62. Ibid. p. 94.

63. Ibid. p. 238.

64. De la capacité politique des classes ouvrières, written 1864, in Oeuvres posthumes (1873), p. 47.

65. Cf. ibid. pp. 341-43.

66. Ibid. p. 231.

67. Cf. France et Rhin, in Oeuvres posthumes de P. J. Proudhon (1868), p. 230.

68. Ibid. p. 231.

69. At this point a section dealing with Lassalle's use of "democracy" was originally included. Although the term occurs frequently, I have found it reasonable to drop this section. This is mainly because the references in question reveal very little or nothing concerning the connotation attributed to this term. Lassalle's use seems generally to be limited to rhetoric trivialities such as: "Bei der Demokratie allein ist alles Recht", or "Es lebe die demokratische soziale Agitation". Cf. Lassalles Reden und Schriften, ed. Bernstein (Berlin 1892), vol. I, pp. 303, 550; and vol. II, pp. 411, 577, 578, 587, 666, 731, 898, 904.

CHAPTER IX

MARX AND ENGELS

1. "Aus der Kritik der Hegelschen Rechtsphilosophie", March-August 1843, in Marx-Engels, Historisch-kritische Gesamtausgabe, ed.

Rjazanov and Adoratsky (Moscow 1929-35), pt. 1, vol. I, first half-volume, p. 436 (later referred to as MEGA).

2. Ibid. p. 434.

3. Ibid. p. 435.

4. Cf., for example, Erich Thier, Das Menschenbild des jungen Marx, (Göttingen 1957). Also Lars Roar Langslet, Karl Marx og menneskets "fremmedgjørelse" (Oslo 1963).

5. Letter to Ruge, May 1843, MEGA 1, vol. I, I, p. 561.

6. In this letter to Ruge, Marx, inter alia, said, "Die Idealisten, welche die Unverschämtheit haben, den Menschen zum Menschen machen zu wollen, ergriffen das Wort und während der König altdeutsch phantasierte, meinten sie, neudeutsch philosophieren zu dürfen." -- Ibid. p. 564.

7. 16 October 1842, Marx stated on behalf of the editorial staff in Rheinische Zeitung, "Die 'Rheinische Zeitung', die den kommunistischen Ideen in ihrer jetzigen Gestalt nicht einmal theoretische Wirklichkeit zugestehen, also noch weniger ihre praktische Verwirklichung wünschen oder auch für möglich halten kann, wird diese Ideen einer gründlichen Kritik unterwerfen." -- MEGA 1, vol. I, I, p. 263.
    In a letter to Ruge, September 1843, Marx said with regard to the principle nature of Deutsch-Französische Jahrbücher, "Ich bin daher nicht dafür, dass wir eine dogmatische Fahne aufpflanzen, im Gegenteil. Wir müssen den Dogmatikern nachzuhelfen suchen, dass sie ihre Sätze sich klar machen. So ist namentlich der Kommunismus eine dogmatische Abstraktion, ..." -- MEGA 1, vol. I, I, p. 573.

8. Zur Judenfrage, 1844, in ibid. vol. III, p. 298.

9. An occurrence of some importance, however, is given in the form of a notice in Thomas Hamilton's Men and Manners in America (1833), in German translation. In addition to a great many experts, and in conformity with the author's point of view, Marx wrote, "sie [die vollständige Demokratie] besteht vorläufig in America noch nicht, da seine Bürger meist Eigentümer sind." -- Excerpte 1840-43, in ibid. vol. I, II, p. 136.

10. Cf. Die heilige Familie, in ibid. vol III, p. 298.

11. Die deutsche Ideologie, written 1845-46, in ibid. vol. V, p. 326.

12. "Stellung der politischen Partei", Rheinische Zeitung, 24 December 1842, in ibid. vol. II, p. 358.

13. "Briefe aus London I", in ibid. vol. II, p. 365.

14. "Die Lage Englands", 1843, Deutsch-Französische Jahrbücher, in ibid. vol. II, p. 429.

15. "Progress of Social Reform on the Continent", The New Moral World, 4 November 1843, in ibid. vol. II, p. 436.

16. Die Lage der arbeitenden Klasse in England, 1845, in ibid. vol. IV, p. 217.

17. Ibid. p. 223.

18. "Die Lage Englands: Die englische Konstitution", Vorwärts, 19 October 1844, in ibid. vol. IV, p. 333.

19. Ibid. pp. 333-34

20. "Das Fest der Nationen in London", November-December 1845, printed in Rheinische Jahrbücher, 1846, in ibid. vol. IV, p. 457.

21. Ibid. pp. 457-58.

22. Ibid. p. 458.

23. Cf. p. 134.

24. Ibid. pp. 458-59.

25. Ibid. p. 471.

26. "The State of Germany", The Northern Star, 4 April 1846, in ibid. vol. IV, p. 493.

27. Address of the German Democratic Communists of Brussels to Feargus O'Connor, The Northern Star, 25 July 1846, in ibid. vol. VI, p. 25.

28. Ibid. p. 26.

29. This work, directed against Proudhon's La philosophie de la misère, was written in French. It was much later translated into German by Kautsky and Bernstein.

30. "The Prussian Constitution", The Northern Star, 6 March 1847, in ibid. vol. VI, pp. 257-58.

31. The quotation in question also is a very important statement concerning revolutionary strategy. I must add that by saying, "in the struggle against despotism and aristocracy, the people, the democratic party, cannot but play secondary part, the first place belongs to the middle classes", Engels presents a very different political view from one of the main theories of Lenin's What is to be done? As far as I know, this Menschevik statement of Engels has never been commented on by any historians of communistic theory such as Rosenberg, Schlesinger, Carr, et al.

32. "Die Kommunisten und Karl Heinzen", <u>Deutsche Brüsseler Zeitung</u>, 7 October 1847, in ibid. vol. VI, p. 289.

33. "Der Schweizer Bürgerkrieg", <u>Deutsche Brüsseler Zeitung</u>, 14 November 1847, in ibid. vol. VI, p. 342.

34. Engels here used the Norwegian term "bonde-regimente".

35. Ibid. p. 343.

36. "Les maîtres et les ouvriers en Angleterre", <u>L'Atelier</u>, November 1847, in ibid. vol. VI, p. 331.

37. "Discours de M. Karl Marx", 22 February 1848, in ibid. vol. VI, p. 410.

38. Cf. ibid. p. 411.

39. Cf. <u>Manifest der Kommunistischen Partei</u>, 1848, in ibid. vol. VI, p. 538. 538.

40. Ibid. p. 545.

41. Ibid. p. 557.

42. "Berliner Vereinbarungsdebatten", <u>Neue Rheinische Zeitung</u>, 7 June 1848, in ibid. vol. VII, p. 34. This newspaper is later referred to as <u>NRhZ</u>.

43. "Die berliner Debatte über die Revolution", <u>NRhZ</u>, 7 June 1848, in ibid. vol. VII, p. 51.

44. "Sturz des Ministeriums Camphausen", <u>NRhZ</u>, 23 June 1848, in ibid. vol. VII, p. 83. It is sometimes impossible to know whether the author of special articles was Marx or Engels, since almost no articles in <u>NRhZ</u> were signed. The Marx-Engels-Lenin Institute has undertaken diligent research to include the writings of Marx and Engels only in this volume of the <u>Gesamtausgabe.</u> It has, however, not always been possible to identify the author as either Marx or Engels.

45. Cf. "Die Junirevolution", <u>NRhZ</u>, 29 June 1848, in ibid. vol. VII, p. 118.

46. "Die "Zeitungshalle" über die Rheinprovinz", <u>NRhZ</u>, 27 August 1848, vol. VII, p. 322.

47. "Die Polendebatte in Frankfurt", <u>NRhZ</u>, 20 August 1848, in ibid. vol. VII, pp. 303-4.

48. "Marx und die <u>Neue Rheinische Zeitung</u>, 1848", 1884, here from ibid. vol. VII, Einleitung, p. xi.

49.　"Die Polendebatte in Frankfurt", <u>NRhZ</u>, 3 August 1848, in ibid. vol. VII, p. 324.

50.　Cf. Ibid. p. 446.

51.　This article was reprinted in <u>Klassenkämpfe in Frankreich</u>, ed. Engels (1895), this quotation is from the 1911 ed., p. 69. Since the <u>Gesamtausgabe</u> of the Marx-Engels-Lenin Institute unfortunately only covers the political writings of Marx and Engels up to December 1848, I have been obliged to use different sources for their later production. After this chapter was written, a new edition of Marx and Engels' works was published by Dietz Verlag, East Berlin: <u>Karl Marx -- Friedrich Engels Werke</u>. This edition began to be published in 1961 and is not completed (29 volumes have been published). In spite of diligent editorial work, it is generally not on the same scholarly level as the <u>MEGA</u>; for example, all texts are in German, even where Marx and Engels originally wrote in French or in English. On several points I have tried to find in this edition new material for this research, but save for a few items nothing has been found that is not already available in other sources.

52.　Cf. <u>Ansprache der Zentralbehörde an den Bund vom März,</u> 1850, printed as appendix to <u>Enthüllungen über den Kommunistenprosess zu Köln</u> (1852). Here quoted from the edition of 1940, Moscow, p. 108.

53.　Ibid. p. 110.

54.　<u>MEGA</u> 3, vol. I, p. 214.

55.　Marx in <u>Londoner Zentralbehörde des Kommunistenbunds</u>, 15 September 1850, quoted from Engels' introduction to <u>Enthüllungen</u>, p. 32.

56.　<u>Neue Rheinische Zeitung</u>, November 1850, <u>Aus dem literärischen Nachlass von Marx, Engels und Lassalle</u>, ed. Mehring (1902), vol. III, p. 468.

57.　<u>Der achtzehnte Brumaire des Louis Bonaparte</u>, 1852 (Berlin 1914), p. 37.

58.　Ibid. p. 40.

59.　Ibid. p. 37.

60.　"Der wirkliche Streitpunkt in der Türkei", <u>New York Tribune</u>, 12 April 1853, in <u>Gesammelte Schriften von Karl Marx und Friedrich Engels, 1852 bis 1863</u>, ed. Rjazanov, vol. I, p. 159. These articles were originally written in English; it has, however, been possible to find only the German version.

61.　"Was soll aus den Europäischen Türkei werden?", <u>New York Tribune</u>, 21 April 1853, in ibid. p. 170.

62.　"Palmerston", <u>Neue Oder-Zeitung</u>, 16 February 1855, in ibid. vol. II, p. 466.

63.   <u>MEGA</u> 3, vol. III, p. 191.

64.   <u>MEGA</u> 3, vol. III, p. 343.

65.   <u>MEGA</u> 3, vol. IV, p. 219.

66.   <u>Der Bürgerkrieg in Frankreich</u>, 1871 (Berlin 1920), p. 93.

67.   "Kritik des Gothaer Programms", <u>Neue Zeit</u>, No. 18 (1890-91) p. 574.

68.   Cf. <u>Herr Eugen Dührings Umwälzung der Wissenschaft</u>, (<u>Anti-Dühring</u>) 1878, in <u>Sonderausgabe</u>, <u>MEGA</u>, p. 174.

69.   Engels to Bebel, 11 December 1884. Engels' part of the correspondence unfortunately was not available, so I quoted from Rosenberg, <u>Demokratie und Sozialismus</u> (Amsterdam 1938), p. 12.

70.   <u>Der Ursprung der Familie, des Privateigenthums und des Staats</u>, 1884 (Stuttgart 1900), p. 181.

71.   This preface from 1891, ibid. pp. 133-34.

72.   Ibid. p. 133.

73.   "Der deutsche Philister ist neuerdings wieder in heilsamen Schrecken geraten bei dem Wort: Diktatur des Proletariats. Nun gut, ihr Herren, wollt ihr wissen, wie diese Diktatur aussieht? Seht euch die Pariser Kommune an. Das war die Diktatur des Proletariats. " -- Ibid. p. 134.
      This view of the Commune was not the only one in the thinking of Marx and Engels, however. Although Marx also spoke several times about the Commune as a proletarian victory, by 1881, he evidently looked upon it in a different way. In a letter that year, he stated that the Commune merely represented the rising of a town under exceptional conditions, and with the majority of the rebels of non-socialist conviction. Cf. <u>Selected Correspondence</u>, <u>1846-95</u> (New York 1942), p. 387.

74.   "Zur Kritik des Socialdemokratischen Programmentwurfs", <u>Die Neue Zeit</u>, vol. XX (1902), p. 11.

75.   Ibid. p. 10.

CHAPTER X

LIBERALISM AND RADICALISM

1.   <u>London Review</u> (July-October 1835), in John Stuart Mill, <u>Dissertations and Discussions</u> (2nd ed., London 1867), vol. I, p. 470.

2. Ibid. p. 472.

3. Ibid. p. 473.

4. "Civilization", London and Westminster Review (April 1836), in ibid. vol. I, p. 173.

5. "M. de Tocqueville on Democracy in America", Edinburgh Review, (October 1840), in ibid. vol. II, pp. 7-8.

6. Ibid. p. 19.

7. "Vindication of the French Revolution of February 1848", Westminster Review (April 1849), in ibid. vol. II, p. 401.

8. "Enfranchisment of Women", Westminster Review (July 1851), in ibid. vol. II, p. 447.

9. Letter to Judge Chapman, 8 July 1858, in The Letters of John Stuart Mill, ed. Hugh Elliot (London 1910), vol. I, p. 210.

10. On Liberty (London 1859), pp. 11-12.

11. Ibid. pp. 156-57.

12. Ibid. p. 157.

13. Cf. Thoughts on Parliamentary Reform, 1859, in Dissertations, vol. III, pp. 18-21.

14. Ibid. p. 28.

15. Cf. p. 162.

16. Considerations on Representative Government (London 1861), p. 132.

17. Ibid. p. 133.

18. Ibid. p. 162.

19. Ibid. p. 237.

20. Ibid. p. 146.

21. Ibid. p. 152.

22. Ibid. pp. 162-64.

23. Ibid. p. 162.

24. Cf. ibid. pp. 172, 180.

25. Cf. ibid. p. 244.

26. Ibid. p. 241.

27. Ibid. p. 163.

28. Letter to Judge Appleton, 24 September 1863, in <u>Letters</u>, vol. I, p. 302.

29. Letter to Edwin Godkin, 24 May 1865, in <u>Letters</u>, vol. II, p. 35.

30. <u>Autobiography</u> (London 1877), p. 231. This part written previous to, or during, 1860.

31. Ibid. p. 252. This part written 1870.

32. Ibid. p. 309 (1870).

33. Austin, <u>A Plea for the Constitution</u> (London 1859), p. 9.

34. Ibid. p. 10.

35. Loc. cit.

36. Loc. cit.

37. Ibid. p. 10, footnote.

38. Ibid. p. 14.

39. Austin, <u>Lectures on Jurisprudence</u> (3rd ed. 1863), vol. I, p. 245.

40. Green, <u>Lectures on the Principles of Political Obligation</u>, delivered 1879-80 (London 1895), p. 97.

41. "Liberal Legislation and Freedom of Contract", 1881, <u>Works of Thomas Hill Green</u>, ed. Nettleship (London 1911), vol. III, p. 368.

42. Ibid. p. 369.

43. Ibid. p. 386.

44. Herbert Spencer, <u>Political Institutions</u>, pt. V of <u>Principles of Sociology</u> (London 1882), p. 317.

45. Cf. Aristotle, <u>Politics</u>, 1279.

46. Spencer, op. cit. p. 391.

47. Cf. Spencer, <u>The Man versus the State</u>, 1884 (1950), pp. 46-51.

48. Ibid. p. 130.

49. Spencer, <u>An Autobiography</u> (London 1904), vol. II, pp. 401-2.

50. Ibid. p. 466.

51. Ibid. p. 517.

52. "Thoughts on Democracy", undated, in Works and Life of Walter Bagehot, ed. Mrs. Russell Barrington (London 1915), vol. VIII, p. 240.

53. "The American constitution at the present crisis", National Review (1861), in ibid. vol. III, p. 367.

54. "Cæsarism as it existed in 1865", in ibid. vol. IV, p. 314.

55. Sidgwick can fairly reasonably be classed among the utilitarian thinkers, in spite of several intuitive elements in his ethics where he tried to reconcile John Stuart Mill's utilitarianism with the philosophy of conscience and moral imperative of Kant.

56. Sidgwick, The Elements of Politics (London 1891), p. 584.

57. Ibid. p. 586.

58. Ibid. p. 590.

59. Cf. Ibid. p. 587.

60. Cf. ibid. p. 589.

61. Ibid p. 596.

62. Cf. ibid. pp. 591-92.

63. L'idée démocratique et la politique, in Masaryk, Les problèmes de la démocratie, ed. G. Winter and R. Telstik (Paris 1924), p. 31.

64. Loc. cit.

65. Ibid. p. 32.

66. Ibid. p. 34.

67. Ibid. p. 35.

68. Cf. ibid. p. 44.

69. Cf. ibid. pp. 46-47.

70. Cf. ibid. pp. 47-48.

71. "Les difficultés de la démocratie", first published in Frankfurter Zeitung, 24 December 1911, reprinted in ibid. p. 62.

72. Ibid. p. 64.

73. Ibid. p. 56.

74. Ibid. p. 57.

75. Ibid. p. 56.

76. Ibid. p. 59.

77. Cf. ibid. p. 57.

78. Cf. pp. 304-05.

79. Cf. p. 192.

80. On this point there is some degree of similarity between Masaryk and Seymour Martin Lipset. The latter concludes his main work by saying: "A basic premise of this book is that democracy is not only or even primarily a means through which different groups can attain their ends or seek the good society; it is the good society itself in operation. " -- Political Man, The Social Basis of Politics (New York 1960), p. 403.

CHAPTER XI

FRENCH CONSERVATISM

1. I must admit that the classification of such different ideologists as Renan, Faguet, Brunetière, Maurras, et al. represents a somewhat difficult task, and that probably no classification can be definitive. In the thinking of Renan, Faguet, Schérer, and Le Bon, liberal trends are easily discovered, although similar trends are relatively few in the authoritarian thinking of Maurras as well as in the traditionalist ideology of Brunetière. I have, therefore, chosen to use the somewhat vague term "conservatism" as the heading of this chapter, even if I do not claim absolute validity for the classification.

2. "Du liberalisme clerical", May 1848, in Renan, Questions contemporaines (2nd ed. , Paris 1868), p. 420.

3. Ibid. p. 436.

4. Renan, L'avenir de la science, 1849 (11th ed. , 1900), p. 350.

5. Ibid. p. 337.

6. Ibid. p. 339.

7. Ibid. p. 340.

8. Renan, Vie de Jesus, 1863 (18th ed. 1883), p. 187.

9. "La monarchie constitutionelle en France", <u>Revue de Deux Mondes</u>, November 1869, in Renan, <u>La réforme intellectuelle et morale</u> (3rd. ed. , Paris 1872), p. 242.

10. Ibid. p. 249.

11. Ibid. p. 246.

12. "La guerre entre la France et l'Allemagne", <u>Revue des Deux Mondes</u>, 15 September 1870, in ibid. p. 162.

13. Ibid. pp. 163-64. Renan here referred to the treated essay.

14. Ibid. p. 164.

15. <u>La réforme intellectuelle et morale de la France</u>, 1872, in ibid. p. 54.

16. Ibid. p. 64.

17. Ibid. p. 65-66.

18. Ibid. p. 66.

19. Ibid. p. 66.

20. Ibid. pp. 114-15.

21. Cf. ibid. pp. 45, 103.

22. Schérer, <u>La démocratie et la France</u> (Paris 1883), p. 3.

23. Ibid. pp. 46-47.

24. Ibid. p. 47.

25. Ibid. p. 52.

26. Ibid. p. 64.

27. Ibid. p. 65.

28. "Du gouvernement démocratique", in Scherer, <u>Études sur la littéra-ture contemporaire</u> (Paris 1889), vol. IX, p. 264.

29. "La nation et l'armée", speech in Paris, 26 April 1899, in Brunetière, <u>Discours de Combats</u> (Paris 1902), pp. 230-31.

30. "L'action catholique," speech in Tours, 23 February 1901, in <u>Dis-cours de Combat</u> (1903), p. 113.

31. Cf. ibid. p. 47.

32. Cf. "L'œuvre de Calvin", speech in Geneva, 24 December 1901, in ibid. pp. 141, 144.

33. Cf. "Coup d'œil sur l'histoire de France", in Bourget, Pages de critique et de doctrine (Paris 1912), vol. II, p. 6.

34. "Les mémoires d'une patriote", ibid. p. 47.

35. "La renaissance du traditionalisme en politique", speech June 1904, in ibid. p. 142.

36. Maurras, Enquête sur la monarchie, 1909 (1924), p. xvi.

37. Ibid. p. lxxxv.

38. Cf. p. 35.

39. Ibid. p. 333. At this point Maurras also stated: "Ce qui rend le socialisme anarchique et révolutionnaire, ce n'est point ce qu'il a de socialiste, c'est le poison démocratique qui s'y mêle toujours. "

40. Cf. ibid. pp. 230, 231.

41. Cf. ibid. p. 230.

42. Concerning our research, very little is, for example, to be found in Trois idées politiques; Châteaubriand, Michelet, Saint-Beuve (1898). On this point it must be added that occurrences from L'Action française ought to have been included in this chapter; this periodical was, however, unfortunately not available in Norway.

43. Faguet, Le culte de l'incompétence, 1910 (Paris 1914), p. 25.

44. Ibid. p. 27.

45. Ibid. p. 31.

46. Ibid. p. 78.

47. Ibid. p. 84.

48. Cf. Aristotle, Politics, 1292a, "Dans les gouvernements démocratiques où la loi règne, il n'y a pas des démagogues; ce sont les citoyens les plus recommandables qui ont la prééminence; mais une fois que la loi a perdu la souveraineté, il s'élève une foule des démagogues. "

49. Faguet, op. cit. p. 54.

50. Faguet, ... et l'horreur des responsabilités, 1911 (1914), p. 160.

51. Ibid. pp. 160-61.

52.	Cf. , e. g. , "La démocratie, c'est-à-dire un état social où les peuples ne sont plus gouvernés, mais se gouvernent eux-mêmes, dans un esprit de conservation pacifique, d'économie, de <u>statu quo</u> et de timidité, avec une grande défiance à l'égard de toute supériorité intellectuelle. " "Que sera le XXe siècle?" -- <u>Questions Politiques</u> (Paris 1899), p. 253. A similar formulation occurs in his work <u>Le socialisme en 1907</u> (Paris 1907), p. 108.

53.	Faguet, <u>Problèmes politiques du temps présent</u> (Paris 1901), p. xiv.

54.	"Armée et démocratie", ibid. pp. 128-31.

55.	"Que sera la XXe siècle?", <u>Questions Politiques</u>, p. 307.

56.	Faguet, <u>Le Socialisme en 1907</u>, p. 109.

57.	Le Bon, <u>Psychologie des foules</u>, 1895 (Paris 1911), p. 44.

58.	Cf. p. 208.

59.	Ibid. p. 76.

60.	Ibid. p. 96.

61.	Cf. , for example, the use of "democracy" by May, Spencer, Maine, Acton, Lecky, etc. From a certain point of view, this version of Le Bon may be taken as refuting his opinion that "les noms ne sont que de vaines étiquettes dont l'historien que va un peu au fond des choses n'a pas à se préoccuper. " -- Ibid. p. 76.

62.	Le Bon, <u>La Psychologie politique</u> (Paris 1910), p. 124.

CHAPTER XII

BRITISH CONSERVATISM AND CONSERVATIVE LIBERALISM

1.	In this classification Bernard Bosanquet ought to have been included among the political thinkers treated in this section. I have found, however, that "democracy" and related terms were so rarely and so accidentally used by him that any discussion was pointless. Cf. Bosanquet, <u>The Philosophical Theory of the State</u>, 1899 (1951), pp. 69, 92, 164.

2.	Cf. Stephen, <u>Liberty, Equality, Fraternity</u>, 1873 (2nd ed. , London 1874), p. xvii.

3.	Ibid. p. 46.

4.	Ibid. p. 186.

5.   Ibid. p. 186.

6.   Cf. ibid. p. 198.

7.   Ibid. p. 199.

8.   May, Democracy in Europe (London 1877), vol. I, pp. vi-vii.

9.   Cf. ibid. p. vii.

10.   Ibid. vol. II, p. 279.

11.   Ibid. vol. II, p. 413.

12.   Ibid. vol. II, p. 334.

13.   Ibid. vol. II, p. 476.

14.   "The Nature of Democracy", in Maine, Popular Government (London 1886), p. 59.

15.   Cf. p. 170.

16.   Ibid. p. 68.

17.   Cf. ibid. pp. 69-70.

18.   Ibid. p. 59.

19.   Ibid. p. 97.

20.   Cf. ibid. p. 98.

21.   Cf. "Prospects of Popular Government", in ibid. p. 36.

22.   Ibid. p. 22.

23.   "Political causes of the American revolution", The Rambler (May 1861), in Acton, Essays on Church and State (London 1952), p. 291.

24.   Ibid. p. 292.

25.   Ibid. p. 336.

26.   Ibid. p. 338.

27.   Ibid. p. 337.

28.   "Nationality", Home and Foreign Review (July 1862), in Acton, History of Freedom and Other Essays (London 1909), p. 288.

29.   "May's Democracy in Europe", The Quarterly Review (January 1878), in ibid. p. 63.

30. Acton here used the expression "free commonwealths" to describe states in which there had generally been a smaller degree of religious liberty than in absolute monarchies.

31. Cf. ibid. p. 64.

32. Lecky, Democracy and Liberty, 1896 (London 1899), vol. I, p. 256.

33. Cf. ibid. vol. I, p. 257.

34. Ibid. vol. I, pp. 25-26.

CHAPTER XIII

GERMAN CONSERVATISM

1. Menschliches, Allzumenschliches I, 1878, Aphorism No. 472, in Nietzsche, Werke (Leipzig 1900), vol. II, p. 345.

2. Ibid. p. 348.

3. Ibid. II, Aphorism No. 292, in ibid. vol. III, p. 352.

4. Loc. cit.

5. Jenseits von Gut und Böse, 1886, Aphorism No. 202, in ibid. vol. VII, p. 136.

6. Ibid. Aphorism No. 203, p. 137.

7. Cf. ibid. Aphorism No. 239, p. 197.

8. Ibid. pt. II, Aphorism No. 12, p. 371.

9. Cf. ibid. pt. I, Aphorism No. 204, pp. 143-44.

10. Götzen-Dämmerung, 1888, in ibid. vol. VIII, p. 149-50.

11. Cf. ibid. p. 151.

12. Der Wille zur Macht, Aphorism No. 752, in ibid. vol. XVI, p. 195.

13. Ibid. Aphorism No. 751, p. 194.

14. Cf. p. 209.

15. Treitschke, Politik, 1898 (3rd ed., Berlin 1913), vol. I, p. 62.

16. Ibid. p. 314.

17. Cf. ibid. vol. II, p. 208.

18. Ibid. vol. II, p. 257.

19. Ibid. vol. II, p. 260.

20. Ibid. vol. II, p. 263.

21. Ibid. vol. II, p. 271.

22. Cf. ibid. vol. II, p. 262.

23. Cf. Ibid. vol. II, p. 253.

24. Some degree of honorific application probably also occurs when Treitschke held democracy, as well as monarchy, in contrast to aristocracy, to favour the well-being of the common man. Cf. ibid. vol. II, p. 208.

25. Die deutsche Freiheit (Gotha 1917), p. 30.

26. Ibid. p. 110.

27. Cf. ibid. p. 79.

28. Thomas Mann, Betrachtungen eines Unpolitischen (Berlin 1919), p. xxxi.

29. Ibid. p. xxxii.

30. Ibid. p. xxxvii.

31. Ibid. p. xxxx.

32. Loc. cit.

33. Ibid. p. 217.

34. Ibid. p. 229.

35. Ibid. p. 247.

36. Ibid. p. 291.

37. Cf. ibid. p. xxxxii.

38. Cf. ibid. p. 224.

39. Ibid. p. 441.

40. Ibid. p. 442.

41. Ibid. p. 63.

42. Ibid. p. 548.

43. Cf. ibid. pp. 518, 521, 550.

44. Ibid. p. 442.

CHAPTER XIV

LATER SOCIALISM

1. Bernstein, Die Voraussetzungen des Sozialismus und die Aufgaben der Sozialdemokratie (Stuttgart 1899), p. 122.

2. Ibid. p. 123.

3. Ibid. p. 124.

4. Ibid. p. 124.

5. Cf., e.g., Bernstein, Der Revisionismus in der Sozialdemokratie (1909), p. 49.

6. Cf. Bernstein, Zur Geschichte und Theorie des Sozialismus (1901), p. 334, and Die heutige Sozialdemokratie in Theorie und Praxis (1906), p. 38.

7. Bernstein, "Die Demokratie in der Sozialdemokratie", Sozialistische Monatshefte (1908), p. 1106.

8. Kautsky, Bernstein und das sozialdemokratische Programm (1899), p. 170.

9. Ibid. p. 171.

10. Ibid. p. 172.

11. Ibid. p. 171.

12. Kautsky, Die soziale Revolution (1902), p. 45.

13. Kautsky, Der Weg zur Macht (1910), p. 52. (This quotation from an essay of Kautsky from 1893.)

14. Sozialreform oder Revolution?, 1900, in Luxemburg, Gesammelte Werke (Berlin 1928), vol. III, p. 80.

15. Ibid. p. 84.

16. Ibid. p. 82.

17. Ibid. p. 89.

18. "Militz und Militarismus", <u>Leipziger Volkzeitung</u>, February 1898, in
     ibid. vol. III, p. 143. Cf. her statement: "In einer von Grund aus
     demokratischen Partei kann das Verhältnis zwischen Wählern und Ab-
     geordneten unter keinen Umständen durch den Wahlakt und die mehr
     äusserlich-formelle, summarische Berichterstattung auf den Partei-
     tagen als erledigt erachtet werden. "

19. "The Basis of Socialism. Historic", <u>Fabian Essays in Socialism</u>
     (London 1889), p. 34.

20. Ibid. pp. 34-35.

21. Ibid. p. 35.

22. "The Transition to Social Democracy. Transition", ibid. p. 182.

23. "The Transition to Social Democracy. The Outlook", ibid. p. 214.

24. <u>Report on Fabian Policy,</u> Fabian Tract No. 70 (1896), p. 5.

25. Sidney and Beatrice Webb, <u>Industrial Democracy</u> (London & New York
     1902), pp. 840-41.

26. "Organisation socialiste", <u>La Revue Socialiste</u> (April 1895), in <u>Oeuvres
     de Jean Jaurès</u> (Paris 1931), vol. III, p. 321.

27. "Vers la justice", <u>La Dépêche de Toulouse</u>, 26 November 1896, in
     ibid. vol. III, p. 416.

28. Cf. e. g. , ibid. vol. VI, pp. 151, 363.

29. "Bernstein et l'évolution", speech in Paris, 10 February 1900, in
     ibid. vol. VI, p. 126.

30. Cf. ibid. vol. VI, p. 183.

31. Cole, <u>The World of Labour</u> (London 1913), p. 24.

32. Ibid. p. 44.

33. Ibid. p. 383.

34. Ibid. p. 421.

CHAPTER XV

ANARCHISM AND SYNDICALISM

1. Féderalisme, Socialisme et Antithéologisme, 1867, in Œuvres de Bakounine (Paris 1907), vol. I, p. 8.

2. Ibid. p. 9.

3. Ibid. p. 11.

4. Cf. Dieu et l'Etat, 1870, in ibid. vol. I, p. 324.

5. Ibid. p. 287.

6. Ibid. vol. IV, p. 179. Untitled manuscript.

7. Ibid. p. 191.

8. Cf. ibid. vol. IV, pp. 440-45, 471.

9. Protestation de l'Alliance, 1871, in ibid. vol. VI, p. 27.

10. Réponse à l'Unita Italiana, 1871, in ibid. vol. VI, p. 294.

11. Kropotkin, Paroles d'un Révolté (Paris 1885), p. 190.

12. Ibid. p. 196.

13. Kropotkin, Anarchist Communism, 1887 (London 1920), p. 6.

14. Ibid. p. 29.

15. Kropotkin, The Conquest of Bread (London 1906), p. 214.

16. Sorel, Réflexions sur la violence, 1906 (Paris 1925), p. 268.

17. Ibid. p. 340.

18. Ibid. p. 341.

19. Ibid. p. 342.

20. Cf. Sorel, Les illusions du progrès, 1908 (Paris 1925), p. 9.

21. Ibid. p. 122.

22. Ibid. p. 273.

23. Cf. Sorel, <u>La décomposition du marxisme</u>, 1907 (Paris 1910), p. 64-66, and <u>Materiaux d'une théorie du proletariat</u>, 1905 (Paris 1929), pp. 53, 191, 383, and 394.

24. Lagardelle, <u>Le socialisme ouvrier</u> (Paris 1911), p. 9.

25. Ibid. p. 41.

26. Ibid. p. 42.

27. Ibid. p. 44.

28. Ibid. p. 49.

29. Ibid. p. 51.

CHAPTER XVI

BOLSHEVISM

1. <u>The Tasks of the Russian Social-Democrats</u>, 1897, in Lenin, <u>Selected Works in Twelve Volumes</u> (New York not dated), vol. I, p. 500. For people familiar with the terminology during and after the Revolution only, it can be mentioned that Lenin and his adherents used "social-democrats" as a self-denomination up to 1917. On several points the Russian original texts have been consulted to avoid possible misunderstandings arising from translations. In this work Dr. John Sanness has been very helpful. As regards Trotsky's <u>Terrorismus und Kommunismus</u>, no Russian edition has been available; but in this case we cannot exclude the possibility that the German edition was in fact the original one, since this work was evidently written primarily for foreign, and especially for German, readers, and not so much for Russians. It can in any case be taken for granted that Trotsky himself sanctioned this German edition in Petrograd, 1920.

2. Ibid. p. 501.

3. Ibid. p. 504. At this point Lenin contradicts rather central statements of Engels, cf. note 31, chap. IX.

4. Loc. cit.

5. Cf. <u>What Is to Be Done?</u>, 1902, in ibid. vol. II, pp. 102-3.

6. Cf. ibid. pp. 152-53.

7. Ibid. p. 156.

8. Cf. , e. g. , <u>Two Tactics of the Social-Democracy in the Democratic Revolution</u>, April 1905, in ibid. vol. III, pp. 52, 73.

9. Cf. ibid. p. 75.

10. Ibid. p. 82.

11. Cf. ibid. p. 125.

12. "The War and the Russian Social-Democracy", October 1914, in ibid. vol. V, p. 129.

13. Cf. The Tasks of the Proletariat in our Revolution, April 1917, in ibid. vol. VI, pp. 48-49.

14. Ibid. p. 55-56.

15. Ibid. p. 56.

16. Cf. ibid. p. 56.

17. From an ideological point of view this new theory may be said to mark Lenin's acceptance of Trotsky's theory of the Permanent Revolution according to which the democratic revolution was to be immediately followed by a socialist one.

18. Ibid. p. 73.

19. Ibid. p. 74.

20. Loc. cit.

21. Cf., e.g., The State and Revolution, 1917, in ibid. vol. VII, p. 18-19.

22. Ibid. p. 75.

23. Ibid. pp. 80-81.

24. Lenin is quoting from Engels' letter.

25. Ibid. p. 81.

26. Loc. cit.

27. "Theses and report on bourgeois democracy and the dictatorship of the proletariat," March 1919, in ibid. vol. VII, p. 232.

28. "Theses on the Constituent Assembly", 24 December 1917, in ibid. vol. VI, p. 447.

29. Cf. ibid. vol. VI, pp. 335, 447-83.

30. Cf. The Proletarian Revolution and the Renegade Kautsky, November 1918, and "Theses and report on bourgeois democracy and the dictatorship of the proletariat", March 1919, in ibid. vol. VII, pp. 129, 223.

31.   The Proletarian Revolution, p. 132.

32.   Loc. cit.

33.   Ibid. p. 133.

34.   Ibid. p. 135.

35.   Trotsky, Terrorismus und Kommunismus, Anti-Kautsky (Petrograd 1920), pp. 18-19.

36.   Ibid. p. 25.

37.   Cf. ibid. pp. 25-29.

38.   Ibid. p. 27.

39.   Ibid. p. 27.

40.   Ibid. p. 28.

41.   Ibid. p. 29.

42.   Ibid. p. 24.

43.   Ibid. p. 30.

44.   With regard to his derogatory use of the term, the clearest evidence is probably to be found in the preface to this work where he held: "Die Demokratie, die sich selbst überlebt hat, entscheidet nicht eine Frage, hindert nicht einen Gegensatz, heilt nicht eine Wunde, verhindert weder die Aufstände von rechts noch von links -- sie ist kraftlos, unbedeutend, verlogen und dient nur dazu, die rückständigen Schichten des Volkes, besonders des Kleinbürgertums, in Verwirrung zu bringen. " -- Ibid. p. vii.

45.   Ibid. p. 32.

46.   Trotsky, History of the Russian Revolution to Brest-Litovsk (London 1919), p. 118.

47.   Cf. ibid. p. 118-23.

48.   Cf. ibid. p. 122.

49.   Loc. cit.

50.   Trotsky, 1917, Die Lehren der Revolution (1925), p. 37.

51.   Cf. ibid. pp. 19-24, 31.

52. Trotsky, <u>Nashi Politicheskie Zadachi</u> ("Our Political Tasks") (Geneva 1904). Quotation from E. H. Carr, <u>The Bolshevik Revolution</u> (London 1950), vol. I, p. 33.

53. This theory of the Permanent Revolution was first systematically presented in Trotsky's <u>Results and Prospects</u> (1906). In a later essay in 1909, Trotsky described the points where the Bolsheviks and Mensheviks respectively departed from his own view. "If the Mensheviks, starting from the abstraction, 'our revolution is bourgeois', arrive at the idea of adapting the whole tactics of the proletariat to the behaviour of the liberal bourgeoisie before its conquest of state power, the Bolsheviks, proceeding from an equally barren abstraction, 'a democratic, not a socialist, dictatorship' arrive at the idea of a bourgeois-democratic self-limitation of the proletariat in whose hands state power rests. It is true, there is a very significant difference between them in this respect: while the anti-revolutionary sides of Menshevism are already displayed in full force now, the anti-revolutionary traits of Bolshevism threaten enormous danger only in the event of a revolutionary victory. " This essay printed as appendix to Trotsky, <u>1905</u> (2nd ed. , 1922), p. 285. Concerning the alleged anti-revolutionary traits of Bolshevism, Trotsky added in a footnote in 1922 that this did not happen because, "Bolshevism under the leadership of Lenin undertook its ideological re-equipment (not without an internal struggle) in the Spring of 1917. "

54. This alleged theoretical new orientation is a somewhat disputed event in political history. On the one hand, Trotsky speaks about the ideological re-equipment undertaken by the Bolsheviks in the spring of 1917. On the other, such an outstanding historian as Arthur Rosenberg declared with regard to Lenin in November, 1917: "Lenin wollte damals keine Abschaffung des Privateigentums in Russland, keine Enteignung des Mittelstandes . ... Lenin ist noch in die Oktober-Revolution mit dem festen Willen hineingegangen, in Russland nur die bürgerliche Revolution zu vollenden, aber diese radikal und konsequent. " -- <u>Geschichte des Bolschevismus</u> (Berlin 1932), p. 105. A more moderate view is taken by E. H. Carr who says: "The October revolution had triumphed with the Bolsheviks still divided on the scope of the revolution, and uncertain whether to regard it as bourgeois-democratic or as proletarian-socialistic. " -- <u>The Bolshevik Revolution</u> (London 1950), vol. I, p. 105.

55. Radek, <u>Proletarische Diktatur und Kommunismus</u> (1919), p. 35.

56. Cf. ibid. p. 36.

57. Loc. cit.

58. As no foreign version of this pamphlet was available, the quotation has been translated from the Norwegian version, <u>Socialismens utvikling fra vitenskap til handling</u> (Kristiania undated), p. 26. I have chosen to translate into German, since a direct translation from Norwegian to German may be the most adequate, and since the terminology in this version is rather clearly influenced by its having been translated from German.

59. Ibid. p. 29. As proof of a much later derogatory application I may mention that, before the trials in Moscow, 1937, Radek used "democracy" and "broad democracy" to designate a phenomenon of importance for people with dissentient views only; Radek very certainly had in mind people, like himself, who had wrongly had no faith in the Stalinist policy. "Menschen streiten um Demokratie nur dann, wenn sie in den grundlegenden Fragen nicht einverstanden sind, wenn sie dagegen einverstanden sind empfinden sie nicht das Bedürfnis nach einer breiten Demokratie. " -- Prozessbericht über die Strafsache des sowjet-feindlichen trotzkistischen Zentrums (Moscow 1937), p. 93.

60. Bukharin, Le Programme des Communistes (1919), p. 19.

61. Cf. Das ABC des Kommunismus (Petrograd 1920), p. 158.

62. Kuusinen, Die Revolution in Finnland, Selbstkritik (Petrograd 1919), p. 23.

63. Cf. ibid. p. 27.

64. Ibid. p. 29.

65. Ibid. p. 32.

66. Ibid. p. 33.

67. Cf. Pool et al, Symbols of Democracy (1952), p. 14.

68. Ibid. pp. 10-11.

69. Cf. Trotsky, La révolution trahie (Paris 1936), p. 325.

70. Cf. Arthur Spencer, "Strange Interlude", Survey, No. 49 (October 1963), p. 121.

CHAPTER XVII

CENTRAL CRITICS OF BOLSHEVISM

1. Kautsky, Die Diktatur des Proletariats (Vienna 1918), p. 4.

2. Ibid. p. 15.

3. Ibid. p. 33.

4. Cf. p. 231.

5. Cf. Kautsky, Terrorismus und Kommunismus (Berlin 1919), pp. 118, 152.

6. Cf. ibid. p. 124.

7. I must here insert that this manuscript was not regarded by Luxemburg herself as definitely completed, and that she probably would have made some additions and alterations if she herself had been able to publish it. Later research has discovered a few rather small differences between the original text of her manuscript and that of the printed pamphlet, Die russische Revolution. Cf. Felix Weil, "Rosa Luxemburg über die russische Revolution", Archiv für die Geschichte des Socialismus und der Arbeiterbewegung, vol. XIII (1928), p. 286. None of these differences has any importance for our inquiry, however.

8. Luxemburg, Die russische Revolution (Frankfurt am Main 1922), pp. 114-15.

9. Cf. ibid. p. 109.

10. Cf. ibid. p. 113.

11. Ibid. p. 116.

12. Cf. p. 240.

13. Cf. "Organisationsfragen der russischen Sozialdemokratie", Neue Zeit, No. 42 (1904), pp. 484 et seq., also printed in Iskra. Points very similar to those of Luxemburg were expressed the same year by Trotsky; cf. his warning that if the socialist party was to be organized in accordance with the principles of Lenin, a situation would arise in which "the party is replaced by the organization of the party, the organization of the party by the central committee, and the central committee by the dictator. " -- Quoted from Carr, The Bolshevik Revolution (London 1950), vol. I, p. 33.

14. Ibid. p. 115.

15. Ibid. p. 118.

16. Quoted from Paul Frölich, Rosa Luxemburg, Gedanke und Tat (Paris 1939), p. 263.

17. Max Adler, Die Staatsauffassung des Marxismus (Vienna 1922), p. 122.

18. Cf. ibid. p. 123.

19. Ibid. p. 140.

20. Ibid. p. 126.

21. Loc. cit.

22. Cf. ibid. pp. 188-89.

23. Kelsen, <u>Vom Wesen und Wert der Demokratie</u> (Tübingen 1920), p. 3.

24. Cf. ibid. p. 4.

25. Cf. ibid. p. 5.

26. Cf. ibid. p. 14.

27. Cf. ibid. p. 16.

28. Cf. ibid. p. 34.

29. Ibid. p. 36.

30. Loc. cit.

31. Cf. Kelsen, <u>Sozialismus und Staat</u> (Stuttgart 1923), pp. 66, 188, 193.

32. Bertrand Russell, <u>The Practice and Theory of Bolshevism</u> (London 1920), p. 113.

33. Ibid. p. 107.

34. Ibid. p. 104.

35. Ibid. pp. 183-84.

36. Bertrand Russell, <u>Political Ideals</u> (New York 1917), pp. 79-80.

37. Cf. ibid. , e.g. , pp. 85, 86, 91, 92.

38. Ibid. p. 31.

39. Ibid. pp. 91-92.

INDEX OF PROPER NAMES